SolidWorks 2013 Tutorial

David C. Planchard & Marie P. Planchard CSWP

ISBN: 978-1-58503-779-7

Publications

Schroff Development Corporation

www.SDCpublications.com

Schroff Development Corporation

P.O. Box 1334

Mission KS 66222

(913) 262-2664

www.SDCpublications.com

Publisher: Stephen Schroff

Trademarks and Disclaimer

DS SolidWorks® Corp. is a Dassault Systèmes S.A. (Nasdaq: DASTY) company that develops and markets software for design, analysis, and product data management applications. Microsoft® Windows, Microsoft Office® and its family of products are registered trademarks of the Microsoft Corporation. Other software applications and parts described in this book are trademarks or registered trademarks of their respective owners.

Dimensions of parts are modified for illustration purposes. Every effort is made to provide an accurate text. The authors and the manufacturers shall not be held liable for any parts or drawings developed or designed with this book or any responsibility for inaccuracies that appear in the book. Web and company information was valid at the time of the printing.

Examination Copies

Teacher evaluation copies for 2013, 2012, 2011, 2010, 2009, 2008 and 2007 SolidWorks books are available with classroom support materials (PowerPoint presentations, labs, avi files, Term Projects, quizzes and more) with all initial and final SolidWorks models. Books received as examination copies are for review purposes only. Examination copies *are not intended for student* use. Resale of examination copies or student use is prohibited.

All assemblies and components for the final ROBOT assembly displayed on the cover are located on the enclosed DVD under the Chapter 5 models folder. SolidWorks 2013 Tutorial with Video Instruction is target toward a technical school, two year college or four year university instructor/student or industry professional that is a beginner or intermediate user.

Electronic Files

Any electronic files associated with this book or DVD are licensed to the original user only. These files may not be transferred to any other party without the written consent of the publisher Schroff Development Corporation or D&M Education LLC.

INTRODUCTION

SolidWorks 2013 Tutorial with Video Instruction is target towards a technical school, two year college, four year university or industry professional that is a beginner or intermediate CAD user. The text provides a student who is looking for a step-by-step project based approach to learning SolidWorks with an enclosed 1.5 hour video instruction DVD, SolidWorks model files, and preparation for the CSWA exam.

The book is divided into two sections. Chapters 1 - 7 explore the SolidWorks User Interface and CommandManager, Document and System properties, simple machine parts, simple and complex assemblies, design tables, configurations, multi-sheet, multi-view drawings, BOMs, Revision tables using basic and advanced features along with Intelligent Modeling Techniques, SustainabilityXpress, SimulationXpress and DFMXpress.

Chapters 8 - 11 prepare you for the new Certified SolidWorks Associate Exam (CSWA). The CSWA certification indicates a foundation in and apprentice knowledge of 3D CAD and engineering practices and principles.

Follow the step-by-step instructions and develop multiple assemblies that combine over 100 extruded machined parts and components. Formulate the skills to create, modify and edit sketches and solid features.

Learn the techniques to reuse features, parts and assemblies through symmetry, patterns, copied components, design tables and configurations. Learn by doing, not just by reading!

Desired outcomes and usage competencies are listed for each chapter. Know your objective up front. Follow the steps in each chapter to achieve your design goals. Work between multiple documents, features, commands, custom properties and document properties that represent how engineers and designers utilize SolidWorks in industry.

LINKAGE Assembly
Courtesy of Gears Educational
Systems

About the Cover

Create the final ROBOT assembly illustrated on the cover. The physical components and corresponding Science, Technology, Engineering, and Math (STEM) curriculum are available from Gears Educational Systems. All assemblies and components for the final ROBOT assembly are located on the DVD under the Chapter 5 model folder.

Pneumatic Components Diagram
Courtesy of Gears Educational Systems

About the Authors

David Planchard is the founder of D&M Education LLC. Before starting D&M Education, he spent over 27 years in industry and academia holding various engineering, marketing, and teaching positions and degrees. He holds five U.S. patents and one international patent. He has published and authored numerous papers on Machine Design, Product Design, Mechanics of Materials, and Solid Modeling. He is an active member of the SolidWorks Users Group and the American Society of Engineering Education (ASEE). David holds a BSME, MSM with the following Professional Certifications: CCAI, CCNA, CCNP, CSWA, CSWP, CSDA, CSWSA-FEA. David is a SolidWorks Solution Partner, an Adjunct Faculty member and the SAE advisor at Worcester Polytechnic Institute in the Mechanical Engineering department.

Marie Planchard is the Director of World Education Markets at DS SolidWorks Corp. Before she joined SolidWorks, Marie spent over 10 years as an engineering professor at Mass Bay College in Wellesley Hills, MA. She has 14 plus years of industry software experience and held a variety of management and engineering positions. Marie holds a BSME, MSME and CSWP, CSDA, CSWSA-FEA. She is an active member of the American Society of Mechanical Engineers (ASME) and the American Society for Engineering Education (ASEE).

David and Marie Planchard are co-authors of the following books:

- **A Commands Guide for SolidWorks® 2013**, 2012, 2011, 2010, 2009 and 2008

- **A Commands Guide Reference Tutorial for SolidWorks® 2007**

- **Assembly Modeling with SolidWorks® 2012,** 2010, 2008, 2006, 2005-2004, 2003 and 2001Plus

- **Drawing and Detailing with SolidWorks® 2012,** 2010, 2009, 2008, 2007, 2006, 2005, 2004, 2003, 2002 and 2001/2001Plus

- **Engineering Design with SolidWorks® and Video Instruction 2013**, 2012, 2011, 2010, 2009, 2008, 2007, 2006, 2005, 2004, 2003, 2001Plus, 2001 and 1999

- **Engineering Graphics with SolidWorks and Video Instruction 2013**, 2012, 2011, 2010

- **SolidWorks® The Basics with Multimedia CD** 2009, 2008, 2007, 2006, 2005, 2004 and 2003

- **SolidWorks® Tutorial with Video Instruction 2013**, 2012, 2011, 2010, 2009, 2008, 2007, 2006, 2005, 2004, 2003 and 2001/2001Plus

- **The Fundamentals of SolidWorks®: Featuring the VEXplorer robot, 2008** and 2007

- **Official Certified SolidWorks® Associate Examination Guide, Version 4, 2012, 2011, 2010,** Version 3; 2011, 2010, 2009, Version 2; 2010, 2009, 2008, Version 1; 2007

- **Official Certified SolidWorks® Professional (CSWP) Certification Guide with Multimedia DVD, 2011, 2010**

- **Official Guide to Certified SolidWorks Associate Exams: CSWA, CSDA, and CSWSA-FEA, Version 1; 2013, 2012**

- **Applications in Sheet Metal Using Pro/SHEETMETAL & Pro/ENGINEER**

Acknowledgments

Writing this book was a substantial effort that would not have been possible without the help and support of my loving family and of my professional colleagues. I would like to thank Professor John Sullivan and Robert Norton and the community of scholars at Worcester Polytechnic Institute who have enhanced my life, my knowledge, and helped to shape the approach and content to this book.

The author is greatly indebted to my colleagues from Dassault Systèmes SolidWorks Corporation for their help and continuous support: Jeremy Luchini, Avelino Rochino, and Mike Puckett.

Thanks also to Professor Richard L. Roberts of Wentworth Institute of Technology, Professor Dennis Hance of Wright State University, and Professor Jason Durfess of Eastern Washington University who provided insight and invaluable suggestions.

Finally to my wife, who is infinitely patient for her support and encouragement and to our loving daughter Stephanie who supported me during this intense and lengthy project.

Contact the Authors

This is the 10th edition of this book. We realize that keeping software application books current is imperative to our customers. We value the hundreds of professors, students, designers, and engineers that have provided us input to enhance our book. We value your suggestions and comments. Please visit our website at **www.dmeducation.net** or contact us directly with any comments, questions or suggestions on this book or any of our other SolidWorks books at dplanchard@msn.com or planchard@wpi.edu.

Note to Instructors

SolidWorks 2013 Tutorial with Video Instruction is target towards a technical school, two year college, four year university or industry professional that is a beginner or intermediate CAD user. The text provides a student who is looking for a step-by-step project based approach to learning SolidWorks with an enclosed 1.5 hour video instruction DVD, SolidWorks model files, and preparation for the CSWA exam.

The physical components and corresponding Science, Technology, Engineering, and Math (STEM) curriculum are available from Gears Educational Systems. Additional information (four chapters) on the SolidWorks Certified Associate CSWA exam is provided at the end of the book, to assist the user to take and pass the CSWA exam (a recognized industry CAD standard).

Please contact the publisher **www.schroff.com** for additional classroom support materials: PowerPoint presentations, Adobe files along with avi files, term projects, quizzes with initial and final SolidWorks models and tips that support the usage of this text in a classroom environment.

Trademarks, Disclaimer and Copyrighted Material

DS SolidWorks Corp. is a Dassault Systèmes S.A. (Nasdaq: DASTY) company that develops and markets SolidWorks® software for design, analysis and product data management applications. Microsoft Windows®, Microsoft Office® and its family of products are registered trademarks of the Microsoft Corporation. Other software applications and parts described in this book are trademarks or registered trademarks of their respective owners.

The publisher and the authors make no representations or warranties with respect to the accuracy or completeness of the contents of this work and specifically disclaim all warranties, including without limitation warranties of fitness for a particular purpose. No warranty may be created or extended by sales or promotional materials. Dimensions of parts are modified for illustration purposes. Every effort is made to provide an accurate text.

The authors and the manufacturers shall not be held liable for any parts, components, assemblies or drawings developed or designed with this book or any responsibility for inaccuracies that appear in the book. Web and company information was valid at the time of this printing.

The Y14 ASME Engineering Drawing and Related Documentation Publications utilized in this text are as follows: ASME Y14.1 1995, ASME Y14.2M-1992 (R1998), ASME Y14.3M-1994 (R1999), ASME Y14.41-2003, ASME Y14.5-1982, ASME Y14.5M-1994, and ASME B4.2. Note: By permission of The American Society of Mechanical Engineers, Codes and Standards, New York, NY, USA. All rights reserved.

Additional information references the American Welding Society, AWS 2.4:1997 Standard Symbols for Welding, Braising, and Non-Destructive Examinations, Miami, Florida, USA.

References

- SolidWorks Users Guide, SolidWorks Corporation, 2013
- ASME Y14 Engineering Drawing and Related Documentation Practices
- Beers & Johnson, Vector Mechanics for Engineers, 6th ed. McGraw Hill, Boston, MA

- Betoline, Wiebe, Miller, <u>Fundamentals of Graphics Communication</u>, Irwin, 1995

- Hibbler, R.C, <u>Engineering Mechanics Statics and Dynamics</u>, 8th ed, Prentice Hall, Saddle River, NJ

- Hoelscher, Springer, Dobrovolny, <u>Graphics for Engineers</u>, John Wiley, 1968

- Jensen, Cecil, <u>Interpreting Engineering Drawings</u>, Glencoe, 2002

- Planchard & Planchard, <u>Drawing and Detailing with SolidWorks</u>, SDC Pub., Mission, KS 2012

- Walker, James, <u>Machining Fundamentals</u>, Goodheart Wilcox, 1999

- 80/20 Product Manual, 80/20, Inc., Columbia City, IN, 2009

- Reid Tool Supply Product Manual, Reid Tool Supply Co., Muskegon, MI, 2007

- Simpson Strong Tie Product Manual, Simpson Strong Tie, CA, 2009

- Ticona Designing with Plastics - The Fundamentals, Summit, NJ, 2008

- SMC Corporation of America, Product Manuals, Indiana, 2011

- Emhart - A Black and Decker Company, On-line catalog, Hartford, CT, 2009

Every license of SolidWorks contains a copy of SolidWorks SustainabilityXpress. SustainabilityXpress calculates environmental impact on a model in four key areas: *Carbon Footprint, Energy Consumption, Air Acidification and Water Eutrophication.* Material and Manufacturing process region and Transportation Usage region are used as input variables.

During the initial SolidWorks installation, you are requested to select either the ISO or ANSI drafting standard. ISO is typically a European drafting standard and uses First Angle Projection. The book is written using the ANSI (US) overall drafting standard and Third Angle Projection for drawings.

All templates, logos, and needed models for this book are included on the enclosed DVD.

Copy the model folders from the DVD to your local hard drive. Work from your local hard drive. View the 1.5 hour video instruction DVD for additional help.

Screen shots in the book were made using SolidWorks 2013 SP0 running Windows® 7.

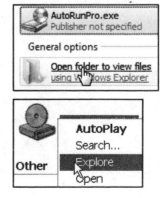

Additional projects are included in the exercise section of Chapter 5. Copy the components from the Chapter 5 Homework folder located on the DVD. View all components. Create an ANSI assembly document.

Insert and create all needed components and mates to assemble the assembly and to simulate proper movement per the provided avi file located on the DVD.

Chapter 5 Homework
Name
Bench Vice Assembly Project
Butterfly Valve Assembly Project
Drill Guide Assembly Project
Kant Twist Clamp Assembly Project
Pipe Vice Assembly Project
Pulley Assembly Project
Quick Acting Clamp Assembly Project
Radial Engine Assembly Project
Shock Assembly Project
Welder Arm Assemlby Project

TABLE OF CONTENTS

The Instructors DVD contains PowerPoint presentations, Adobe files along with avi files, Term Projects, quizzes with initial and final SolidWorks models.

Avi Folder
Project Folder
3D Modeling Features and Strategy
Alphabet of lines and Precedent of Line Types
Annotations in Drawings
Assemblies and Mates in General
Basic Sketching
Boolean Operation
Calipers - General
Design Intent
Drafting and Dimensioning Standards
Drawing Dimension Alignment tool - Dimension Palette
Fasteners in General
Fundamental ASME Y14.5 Dimensioning Rules
Gears using SolidWorks
General GDT information
General Tolerancing and Fits
Hidden vs. Suppress in an Assembly
History of Engineering Graphics
Layout Assembly Design
Materials in General
Measurement and Scale
Non-Standard Drawing View Types
Open a Drawing Document 2012
Open an Assembly Document 2012
Part and Drawing Dimensioning
Planes, Measurement tool, Equations, Design Tables and Configurations
Simplifying Large Assemblies
SolidWorks Basic Concepts
SolidWorks Drawing Documents in General
SolidWorks Simulation FEA Overview
SolidWorks Toolbox
Split Line tool for a Static load analysis using SimulationXpress
Surface Finish
Sustainbility_Presentation
Tolerance, Weld and Texture Symbols
Types of Fits

What is SolidWorks?

SolidWorks® is a mechanical design automation software package used to build parts, assemblies and drawings that takes advantage of the familiar Microsoft® Windows graphical user interface.

SolidWorks is an easy to learn design and analysis tool, (SolidWorks SimulationXpress, SolidWorks Motion, SolidWorks Flow Simulation, etc.) which makes it possible for designers to quickly sketch 2D and 3D concepts, create 3D parts and assemblies and detail 2D drawings.

In SolidWorks, you create 2D and 3D sketches, 3D parts, 3D assemblies and 2D drawings. The part, assembly and drawing documents are related. Additional information on SolidWorks and its family of products can be obtained at their URL, www.SolidWorks.com.

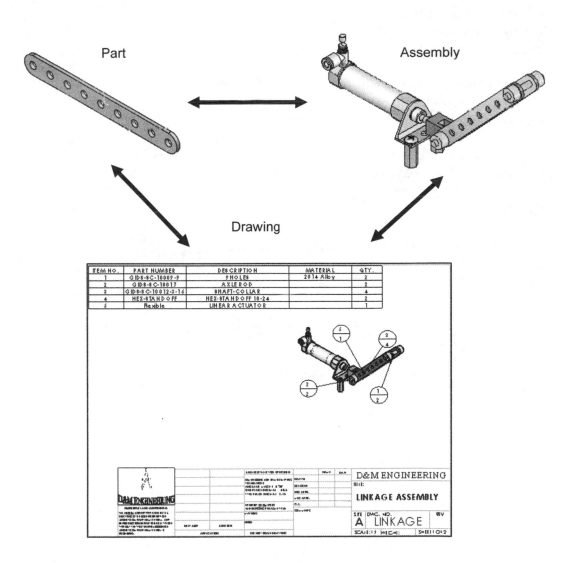

Features are the building blocks of parts. Use features to create parts, such as: Extruded Boss/Base and Extruded Cut. Extruded features begin with a 2D sketch created on a Sketch plane.

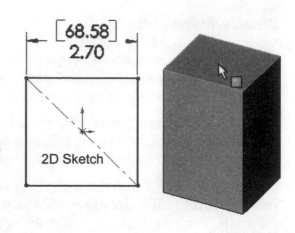

The 2D sketch is a profile or cross section. Sketch tools such as: lines, arcs and circles are used to create the 2D sketch. Sketch the general shape of the profile. Add Geometric relationships and dimensions to control the exact size of the geometry.

Create features by selecting edges or faces of existing features, such as a Fillet. The Fillet feature rounds sharp corners.

Dimensions drive features. Change a dimension, and you change the size of the part.

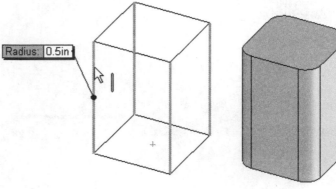

Apply Geometric relationships: Vertical, Horizontal, Parallel, etc. to maintain Design intent.

Create a hole that penetrates through a part. SolidWorks maintains relationships through the change.

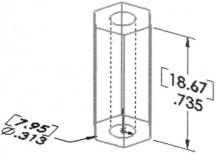

The step-by-step approach used in this text allows you to create parts, assemblies and drawings by doing, not just by reading.

The book provides the knowledge to modify all parts and components in a document. Change is an integral part of design.

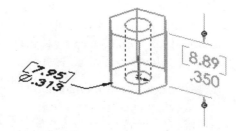

Design Intent

What is design intent? All designs are created for a purpose. Design intent is the intellectual arrangements of features and dimensions of a design. Design intent governs the relationship between sketches in a feature, features in a part and parts in an assembly.

The SolidWorks definition of design intent is the process in which the model is developed to accept future modifications. Models behave differently when design changes occur.

Design for change! Utilize geometry for symmetry, reuse common features, and reuse common parts. Build change into the following areas that you create:

- **Sketch**

- **Feature**

- **Part**

- **Assembly**

- **Drawing**

When editing or repairing geometric relations, it is considered best practice to edit the relation vs. deleting it.

Design Intent in a sketch

Build design intent in a sketch as the profile is created. A profile is determined from the Sketch Entities. Example: Rectangle, Circle, Arc, Point, Slot etc. Apply symmetry into a profile through a sketch centerline, mirror entity and position about the reference planes and Origin. Always know the location of the Origin in the sketch.

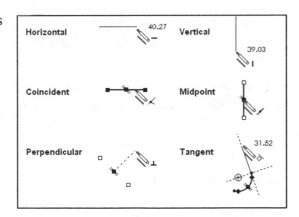

Build design intent as you sketch with automatic Geometric relations. Document the decisions made during the up-front design process. This is very valuable when you modify the design later.

A rectangle (Center Rectangle Sketch tool) contains Horizontal, Vertical and Perpendicular automatic Geometric relations.

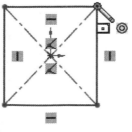

Apply design intent using added Geometric relations if needed. Example: Horizontal, Vertical, Collinear, Perpendicular, Parallel, Equal etc.

Example A: Apply design intent to create a square profile. Sketch a rectangle. Apply the Center Rectangle Sketch tool. Note: No construction reference centerline or Midpoint relation is required with the Center Rectangle tool. Insert dimensions to fully define the sketch.

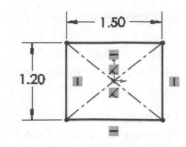

Example B: If you have a hole in a part that must always be 16.5mm≤ from an edge, dimension to the edge rather than to another point on the sketch. As the part size is modified, the hole location remains 16.5mm≤ from the edge as illustrated.

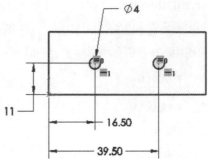

Design intent in a feature

Build design intent into a feature by addressing End Conditions (Blind, Through All, UpToVertex, etc.) symmetry, feature selection, and the order of feature creation.

Example A: The Extruded Base feature remains symmetric about the Front Plane. Utilize the Mid Plane End Condition option in Direction 1. Modify the depth, and the feature remains symmetric about the Front Plane.

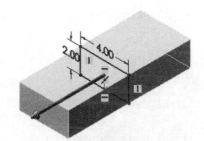

Example B: Create 34 teeth in the model. Do you create each tooth separate using the Extruded Cut feature? No.

Create a single tooth and then apply the Circular Pattern feature. Modify the Circular Pattern from 32 to 24 teeth.

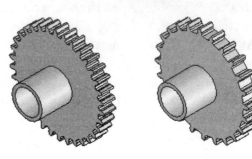

Design intent in a part

Utilize symmetry, feature order and reusing common features to build design intent into a part. Example A: Feature order. Is the entire part symmetric? Feature order affects the part.

Apply the Shell feature before the Fillet feature and the inside corners remain perpendicular.

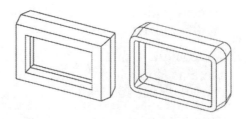

Design intent in an assembly

Utilizing symmetry, reusing common parts and using the Mate relation between parts builds the design intent into an assembly.

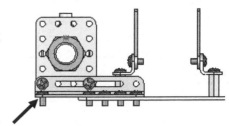

Example A: Reuse geometry in an assembly. The assembly contains a linear pattern of holes. Insert one screw into the first hole. Utilize the Component Pattern feature to copy the machine screw to the other holes.

Design intent in a drawing

Utilize dimensions, tolerance and notes in parts and assemblies to build the design intent into a drawing.

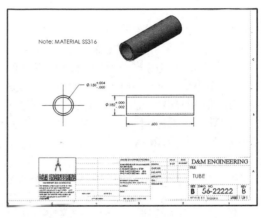

Example A: Tolerance and material in the drawing. Insert an outside diameter tolerance +.000/-.002 into the TUBE part. The tolerance propagates to the drawing.

Define the Custom Property Material in the Part. The Material Custom Property propagates to your drawing.

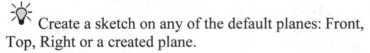 Create a sketch on any of the default planes: Front, Top, Right or a created plane.

Additional information on design process and design intent is available in SolidWorks Help.

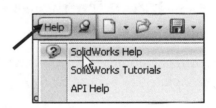

The book is design to expose the new user to many tools, techniques and procedures. It may not always use the most direct tool or process.

Every license of SolidWorks contains a copy of SolidWorks SustainabilityXpress. SustainabilityXpress calculates environmental impact on a model in four key areas: *Carbon Footprint, Energy Consumption, Air Acidification and Water Eutrophication*. Material and Manufacturing process region and Transportation Usage region are used as input variables.

Overview of Chapters

Chapter 1: Linkage Assembly

Chapter 1 introduces the basic concepts behind SolidWorks and the SolidWorks 2013 User Interface.

Create a file folder to manage projects. Create three parts: AXLE, SHAFT-COLLAR, and FLATBAR. Utilize the following features: Extruded Boss/Base, Extruded Cut and Linear Pattern.

Create the LINKAGE assembly. The LINKAGE assembly utilizes the SMC AirCylinder component located on the enclosed DVD in the book. Note: Copy all SolidWorks files from the DVD to your hard drive. Work from your hard drive.

Chapter 2: Front Support Assembly

Chapter 2 introduces various Sketch planes to create parts. The Front, Top and Right Planes each contain the Extruded Boss/Base feature for the TRIANGLE, HEX-STANDOFF and ANGLE-13HOLE parts.

Utilize Geometric relationships in your sketch.

Create the SCREW part using the following features: Revolved Base, Extruded Cut, Fillet and Circular Pattern.

Create the FRONT-SUPPORT assembly. Utilize additional parts from the Web or the enclosed DVD to create the RESERVOIR SUPPORT assembly in the Chapter exercises.

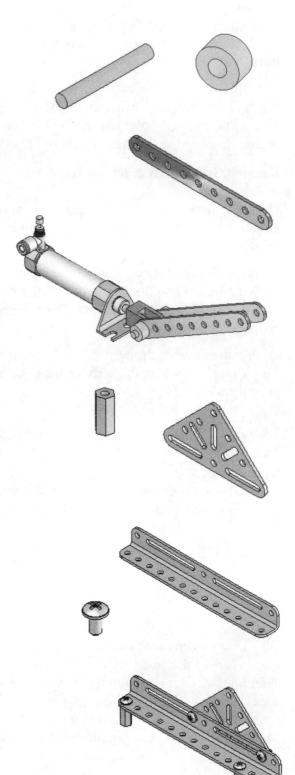

Chapter 3: Fundamentals of Drawing

Chapter 3 covers the development of a customized Sheet format and Drawing template.

Review the differences between the Sheet and the Sheet format. Develop a company logo from a bitmap or picture file.

Create a FLATBAR drawing. Insert dimensions created from the part features. Create the LINKAGE assembly drawing with multiple views and assemblies.

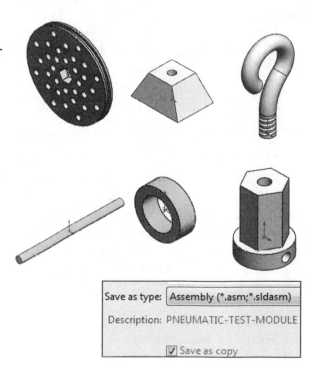

ITEM NO.	PART NUMBER	DESCRIPTION	MATERIAL	QTY.
1	Flexible	LINEAR ACTUATOR		1
2	GIDS-SC-10017	AXLE ROD		2
3	GIDS-SC-10009-9	9HOLES	2014 Alloy	2
4	GIDS-SC-10012-3-16	SHAFT-COLLAR		4
5	HEX-STANDOFF	HEX-STANDOFF		2

D&M ENGINEERING
TITLE:
LINKAGE ASSEMBLY
SIZE DWG. NO.   REV
A   LINKAGE
SCALE: 1:1 WEIGHT: SHEET 1 OF 2

Develop and incorporate a Bill of Materials into the drawing Custom Properties in the parts and assemblies. Add information to the Bill of Materials in the drawing. Insert a Design Table to create multiple configurations of parts and assemblies.

Chapter 4: Advanced Features

Chapter 4 focuses on creating six parts for the PNEUMATIC-TEST-MODULE Assembly: WEIGHT, HOOK, WHEEL, HEX-ADAPTER, AXLE-3000 and SHAFTCOLLAR-500.

Apply the following Advanced model features: Plane, Lofted Base, Extruded Cut, Swept Base, Dome, Helix and Spiral, Swept Cut, Extruded Boss/Base, Revolved Cut, Extruded Cut, Circular Pattern, Axis and Hole Wizard.

Reuse existing geometry and modify existing parts to create new parts with the Save as copy command.

Save as type: Assembly (*.asm;*.sldasm)

Description: PNEUMATIC-TEST-MODULE

☑ Save as copy

Chapter 5: PNEUMATIC-TEST-MODULE Assembly and Final ROBOT Assembly

Chapter 5 focuses on the PNEUMATIC-TEST-MODULE Assembly and the final ROBOT Assembly.

Create the WHEEL-AND-AXLE assembly. First, create the 3HOLE-SHAFTCOLLAR assembly and the 5HOLE-SHAFTCOLLAR assembly.

Insert the WHEEL part, AXLE 3000 part, HEX-ADAPTER part and SHAFTCOLLAR-500 part.

Insert the FLAT-PLATE part that was create in the Chapter 2 exercises. Insert the LINKAGE assembly and add components: HEX-STANDOFF, AXLE and SHAFT-COLLAR.

Insert the AIR-RESERVOIR-SUPPORT assembly. Insert the SCREW part. Utilize the Feature Driven Component Pattern tool and the Linear Component Pattern tool.

Insert the FRONT-SUPPORT assembly and apply the Mirror Components tool to complete the Pneumatic Test Module Assembly.

Create the final ROBOT Assembly as illustrated with the Robot-platform sub-assembly, PNEUMATIC-TEST-MODULE sub-assembly, basic_integration sub-assembly and the HEX-ADAPTER component. Add additional components in the Chapter exercises.

Learn the process to work with multiple documents between parts and assemblies and to apply the following Assembly tools: Insert Component, Standard Mates: Concentric, Coincident, and Parallel, Linear Component Pattern, Feature Driven Component Pattern, Circular Component Pattern, Mirror Components and Replace Components.

Note: All assemblies and components for the final ROBOT assembly are located on the DVD under the Chapter 5 models folder.

Additional projects are included in the exercise section of this chapter. Copy the components from the Chapter 5 Homework folder located on the DVD. View all components.

Create an ANSI assembly document. Insert and create all needed components and mates to assemble the assembly and to simulate proper movement per the avi file located on the DVD.

Chapter 5 Homework

Name

- Welder Arm Assemlby Project
- Radial Engine Assembly Project
- Quick Acting Clamp Assembly Project
- Kant Twist Clamp Assembly Project
- Pulley Assembly Project
- Drill Guide Assembly Project
- Butterfly Valve Assembly Project
- Pipe Vice Assembly Project new
- Bench Vice Assembly Project
- Shock Assembly Project

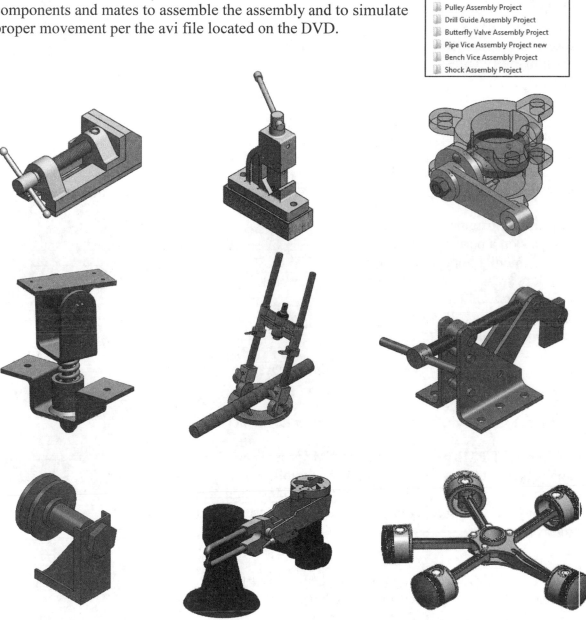

Chapter 6: **SolidWorks SimulationXpress, Sustainability, and DFMXpress**

Chapter 6 introduces three general SolidWorks analysis tools: SimulationXpress, SustainabilityXpress and DFMXpress.

Execute a SolidWorks SimulationXpress analysis on a part. Determine if the part can support an applied load under a static load condition.

Perform a SustainabilityXpress analysis on a part. View the environmental impact calculated in four key areas: *Carbon Footprint, Energy Consumption, Air Acidification and Water Eutrophication*.

Material, Manufacturing process region and Usage region are used as input variables.

Compare similar materials and environmental impacts.

Implement DFMXpress on a part. DFMXpress is an analysis tool that validates the manufacturability of SolidWorks parts. Use DFMXpress to identify design areas that may cause problems in fabrication or increase the costs of production.

The book is designed to expose the new user to many different tools, techniques and procedures. It may not always use the most direct tool or process.

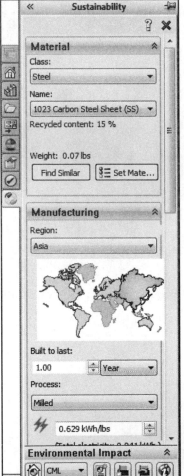

Chapters 8 - 11: Introduction to the Certified SolidWorks Associate Exam

DS SolidWorks Corp. offers various stages of certification representing increasing levels of expertise in 3D CAD design as it applies to engineering: *Certified SolidWorks Associate CSWA, Certified SolidWorks Professional CSWP and Certified SolidWorks Expert CSWE* along with specialty fields in Simulation, Sheet Metal, and Surfacing.

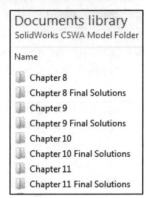

The CSWA Certification indicates a foundation in and apprentice knowledge of 3D CAD design and engineering practices and principles. The main requirement for obtaining the CSWA certification is to take and pass the on-line proctored 180 minute exam (minimum of 165 out of 240 points). The new CSWA exam consists of fourteen questions in the following categories and subject areas:

- *Drafting Competencies*: (Three questions - multiple choice - 5 points each).

- *Basic Part Creation and Modification*: (Two questions - one multiple choice / one single answer - 15 points each).

- *Intermediate Part Creation and Modification*: (Two questions - one multiple choice / one single answer - 15 points each).

- *Advanced Part Creation and Modification:* (Three questions - one multiple choice / two single answers - 15 points each).

- *Assembly Creation and Modification*: (Two different assemblies - four questions - two multiple choice / two single answers - 30 points each).

Note: Download the needed components during the exam for create the assembly.

A total score of 165 out of 240 or better is required to obtain your CSWA Certification.

For additional detail exam information see The **Official Guide to Certified SolidWorks Associate Exams: CSWA, CSDA, and CSWSA-FEA** book. This book is written to assist the SolidWorks user to pass the associate level exams. Information is provided to aid a person to pass the Certified SolidWorks Associate (CSWA), Certified Sustainable Design Associate (CSDA) and the Certified SolidWorks Simulation Associate Finite Element Analysis (CSWSA FEA) exams. The primary goal of this book is not only to help you pass the exams, but also to ensure that you understand and comprehend the concepts and implementation details of the process.

About the Book

You will find a wealth of information in this book. The book is a project based - step-by step text written for new and intermediate users. The following conventions are used throughout this book:

- The term document refers to a SolidWorks part, drawing or assembly file.

- The list of items across the top of the SolidWorks interface is the Menu bar menu or the Menu bar toolbar. Each item in the Menu bar has a pull-down menu. When you need to select a series of commands from these menus, the following format is used: Click **Insert**, **Reference Geometry**, **Plane** from the Menu bar. The Plane PropertyManager is displayed.

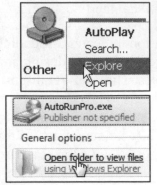
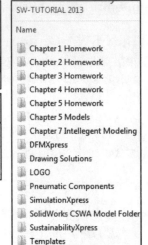

- The book is organized into chapters. Each chapter is focused on a specific subject or feature. Use the enclosed DVD to obtain parts and models that are used in this book and to view the features created in each Chapter.

- The ANSI overall drafting standard and Third Angle projection is used as the default setting in this text. IPS (inch, pound, second) and MMGS (millimeter, gram, second) unit systems are used.

- Copy all folders and files from the DVD to your hard drive. Work from the hard drive. All assemblies and components for the final ROBOT assembly are located on the DVD in the Chapter 5 Models folder.

The following command syntax is used throughout the text. Commands that require you to perform an action are displayed in **Bold** text.

Format:	Convention:	Example:
Bold	<ul><li>All commands actions.</li><li>Selected icon button.</li><li>Selected icon button.</li><li>Selected geometry: line, circle.</li><li>Value entries.</li></ul>	<ul><li>Click **Options** from the Menu bar toolbar.</li><li>Click **Corner Rectangle** ▢ from the Sketch toolbar.</li><li>Click **Sketch** ✏ from the Context toolbar.</li><li>Select the **centerpoint**.</li><li>Enter **3.0** for Radius.</li></ul>
Capitalized	<ul><li>Filenames.</li><li>First letter in a feature name.</li></ul>	<ul><li>Save the **FLATBAR** assembly.</li><li>Click the **Fillet** feature.</li></ul>

Windows Terminology in SolidWorks

The mouse buttons provide an integral role in executing SolidWorks commands. The mouse buttons execute commands, select geometry, display Shortcut menus and provide information feedback.

A summary of mouse button terminology is displayed below:

Item:	Description:
Click	Press and release the left mouse button.
Double-click	Double press and release the left mouse button.
Click inside	Press the left mouse button. Wait a second, and then press the left mouse button inside the text box. Use this technique to modify Feature names in the FeatureManager design tree.
Drag	Point to an object, press and hold the left mouse button down. Move the mouse pointer to a new location. Release the left mouse button.
Right-click	Press and release the right mouse button. A Shortcut menu is displayed. Use the left mouse button to select a menu command.
ToolTip	Position the mouse pointer over an Icon (button). The tool name is displayed below the mouse pointer.
Large ToolTip	Position the mouse pointer over an Icon (button). The tool name and a description of its functionality are displayed below the mouse pointer.
Mouse pointer feedback	Position the mouse pointer over various areas of the sketch, part, assembly or drawing. The cursor provides feedback depending on the geometry.

A mouse with a center wheel provides additional functionality in SolidWorks. Roll the center wheel downward to enlarge the model in the Graphics window. Hold the center wheel down. Drag the mouse in the Graphics window to rotate the model.

Visit SolidWorks website: http://www.solidworks.com/sw/support/hardware.html to view their supported operating systems and hardware requirements.

SolidWorks					
Operating Systems	**SolidWorks 2009**	**SolidWorks 2010**	**SolidWorks 2011**	**SolidWorks 2012**	**(SolidWorks 2013)**
Windows 7	✘	✔*	✔	✔	✔
Windows Vista	✔	✔	✔	✔	✔
Windows XP	✔	✔	✔	✔	✘
Minimum Hardware	Configuring a SolidWorks Workstation				
RAM	2 GB or more				
Disk Space	5 GB or more				
Video Card	Certified cards and drivers				
Processor	Intel or AMD with SSE2 support. 64-bit operating system recommended				
Install Media	DVD Drive or Broadband Internet Connection				

The Instructors DVD contains PowerPoint presentations, Adobe files along with avi files, Term Projects, quizzes with the initial and final SolidWorks models.

The book is design to expose the new user to numerous tools and procedures. It may not always use the simplest and most direct process.

The book does not cover starting a SolidWorks session in detail for the first time. A default SolidWorks installation presents you with several options. For additional information for an Education Edition, visit the following sites: http://www.solidworks.com/goedu and http://www.solidworks.com/sw/education/6443_ENU_HTML.htm.

SW-TUTORIAL 2013

Name

- Chapter 1 Homework
- Chapter 2 Homework
- Chapter 3 Homework
- Chapter 4 Homework
- Chapter 5 Homework
- Chapter 5 Models
- Chapter 7 Intellegent Modeling
- DFMXpress
- Drawing Solutions
- LOGO
- Pneumatic Components
- SimulationXpress
- SolidWorks CSWA Model Folder
- SustainabilityXpress
- Templates

- Avi Folder
- Project Folder
- 3D Modeling Features and Strategy
- Alphabet of lines and Precedent of Line Types
- Annotations in Drawings
- Assemblies and Mates in General
- Basic Sketching
- Boolean Operation
- Calipers - General
- Design Intent
- Drafting and Dimensioning Standards
- Drawing Dimension Alignment tool - Dimension Palette
- Fastners in General
- Fundamental ASME Y14.5 Dimensioning Rules
- Gears using SolidWorks
- General GDT information
- General Tolerancing and Fits
- Hidden vs. Suppress in an Assembly
- History of Engineering Graphics
- Layout Assembly Design
- Materials in General
- Measurement and Scale
- Non-Standard Drawing View Types
- Open a Drawing Document 2012
- Open an Assembly Document 2012
- Part and Drawing Dimensioning
- Planes, Measurement tool, Equations, Design Tables and Configurations
- Simplifying Large Assemblies
- SolidWorks Basic Concepts
- SolidWorks Drawing Documents in General
- SolidWorks Simulation FEA Overview
- SolidWorks Toolbox
- Split Line tool for a Static load analysis using SimulationXpress
- Surface Finish
- Sustainbility_Presentation
- Tolerance, Weld and Texture Symbols
- Types of Fits

goEDU

Installation Instructions

Education User License Agreement (EULA)

System Requirements

Product Description

Instructions to Access Instructors' Curriculum

Workgroup PDM Installation Instructions

Workgroup PDM Video Tutorials

Chapter 1

LINKAGE Assembly

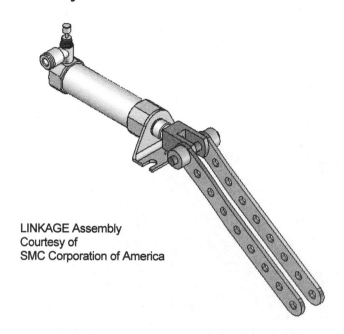

LINKAGE Assembly
Courtesy of
SMC Corporation of America

Below are the desired outcomes and usage competencies based on the completion of Chapter 1.

Desired Outcomes:	Usage Competencies:

• Create three parts:
 	
  o AXLE
 	
  o SHAFT-COLLAR
 	
  o FLATBAR
	• Understand the SolidWorks default User Interface. Establish a SolidWorks session.
	
	• Create 2D sketch profiles on the correct Sketch plane.
	
	• Apply the following 3D features: Extruded Boss/Base, Extruded Cut and Linear Pattern.

• Create an assembly: o LINKAGE assembly	• Understand the Assembly toolbar. • Insert components into an assembly. • Apply the following Standard mates: Concentric, Coincident and Parallel.

Notes:

Chapter 1 - LINKAGE Assembly

Chapter Objective

SolidWorks is a design software application used to model and create 2D and 3D sketches, 3D parts, 3D assemblies and 2D drawings. The chapter objective is to provide a comprehensive understanding of the SolidWorks default User Interface and CommandManager: *Menu bar toolbar, Menu bar menu, Drop-down menu, Context toolbar / menus, Fly-out FeatureManager, System feedback, Confirmation Corner, Heads-up View toolbar and an understanding of Document Properties.*

Obtain the working familiarity of the following SolidWorks sketch and feature tools: *Line, Circle, Centerpoint Straight Slot, Smart Dimension, Extruded Boss/Base, Extruded Cut and Linear Pattern.*

Create three individual parts: AXLE, SHAFT-COLLAR and FLATBAR.

Create the assembly, LINKAGE using the three created parts and the downloaded subassembly - AirCylinder from the DVD in the book.

On the completion of this chapter, you will be able to:

- Start a SolidWorks session and navigate through the SolidWorks (UI) and CommandManager.

- Set units and dimensioning standards for a SolidWorks document.

- Generate a 2D sketch and identify the correct Sketch plane.

- Add and modify sketch dimensions.

- Create a 3D model.

- Understand and apply the following SolidWorks features:

  o Extruded Boss/Base, Extruded Cut and Linear Pattern

- Insert the following Geometric relations: Vertical, Horizontal, Coincident, MidPoint, Parallel and Equal.

- Download an assembly into SolidWorks and create an assembly.

- Understand the Assembly toolbar.

- Apply the following Standard mates: Coincident, Concentric and Parallel.

Chapter Overview

SolidWorks is a 3D solid modeling CAD software package used to produce and model parts, assemblies, and drawings.

SolidWorks provides design software to create 3D models and 2D drawings.

Create three parts in this chapter:

- AXLE

- SHAFT-COLLAR

- FLATBAR

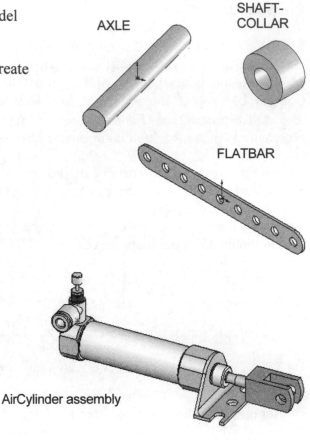

Download the AirCylinder assembly from the enclosed DVD.

The AirCylinder assembly is also available from the internet.

Combine the created parts and the downloaded AirCylinder assembly to create the LINKAGE assembly.

AirCylinder assembly

Illustrations in the book display the default SolidWorks user interface for 2013 SP0.

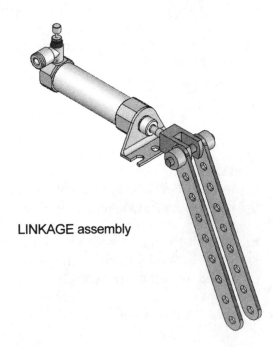

Every license of SolidWorks contains a copy of SolidWorks SustainabilityXpress. SolidWorks SustainabilityXpress calculates environmental impact on a model in four key areas: *Carbon Footprint, Energy Consumption, Air Acidification and Water Eutrophication*. Material and Manufacturing process region and Transportation Use region are use as input variables.

LINKAGE assembly

AXLE Part

The AXLE is a cylindrical rod. The AXLE supports the two FLATBAR parts.

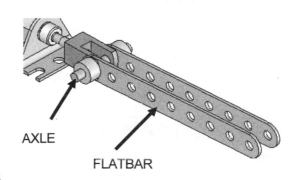

Tangent edges and origins are displayed for educational purposes in this book.

AXLE

FLATBAR

The AXLE rotates about its axis. The dimensions for the AXLE are determined from other components in the LINKAGE assembly.

Start a new SolidWorks session. Create the AXLE part.

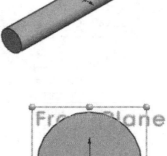

AXLE

Apply the feature to create the part. Features are the building blocks that add or remove material.

Utilize the Extruded Boss/Base 🔲 tool from the Features toolbar to create a Boss-Exturde1 feature. The Extruded Boss/Base feature adds material. The Base feature (Boss-Extrude1) is the first feature of the part. The Base feature is the foundation of the part. Keep the Base feature underline.

The Base feature geometry for the AXLE is a simple extrusion. How do you create a solid Extruded Boss/Base feature for the AXLE?

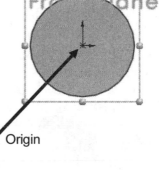

- Select the Front Plane as the Sketch plane.

- Sketch a circular 2D profile on the Front Plane, centered at the Origin as illustrated.

Origin

- Apply the Extruded Boss/Base Feature. Extend the profile perpendicular (⊥) to the Front Plane.

Utilize symmetry. Extrude the sketch with the Mid Plane End Condition in Direction 1. The Extruded Boss/Base feature is centered on both sides of the Front Plane.

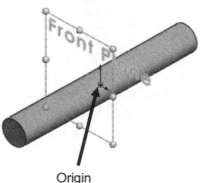

Start a SolidWorks session. The SolidWorks application is located in the Programs folder.

Origin

SolidWorks displays the Tip of the Day box. Read the Tip of the Day to obtain additional knowledge on SolidWorks.

Create a new part. Select File, New from the Menu bar toolbar or click New □ from the Menu bar menu. There are two options for new documents: *Novice* and *Advanced*. Select the Advanced option. Select the default Part document.

Activity: Start a SolidWorks Session

Start a SolidWorks 2013 session.

1)   Click **Start** from the Windows Taskbar.

2)   Click **All Programs** All Programs ▶.

3)   Click the **SolidWorks 2013** folder.

4)   Click the **SolidWorks 2013** application. The SolidWorks program window opens. Note: Do not open a document at this time.

5)   If you do not see the below screen, click the SolidWorks **Resources** 🏠 tab on the right side of the Graphics window location in the Task Pane as illustrated.

6)   **Hover** the mouse pointer over the SolidWorks icon as illustrated.

7)   **Pin** the Menu Bar toolbar. View your options.

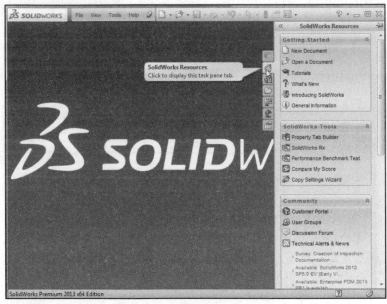

🔆 If available, double-click the SolidWorks 2013 icon on the Windows Desktop to start a SolidWorks session.

🔆 The book is written using Microsoft Office 2010 on Windows® 7 utilizing SolidWorks 2013 SP0.

Activity: Understand the SolidWorks User Interface and CommandManager

---

Menu bar toolbar

SolidWorks 2013 (UI) is design to make maximum use of the Graphics window area. The default Menu bar toolbar contains a set of the most frequently used tool buttons from the Standard toolbar. The available tools are:

- **New** 🗋 - Creates a new document

- **Open** 🗁 - Opens an existing document

- **Save** 💾 - Saves an active document

- **Print** 🖨 - Prints an active document

- **Undo** ↺ - Reverses the last action

- **Select** ▨ - Selects Sketch entities, components and more

- **Rebuild** 🛢 - Rebuilds the active part, assembly or drawing

- **File Properties** 🗐 - Shows the summary information on the active document

- **Options** 📧 - Changes system options and Add-Ins for SolidWorks.

💡 The Search *Knowledge Base* and *Community Forum* option from the Menu Bar toolbar requires Internet access.

Menu bar menu

Click SolidWorks in the Menu bar toolbar to display the Menu bar menu. SolidWorks provides a Context-sensitive menu structure. The menu titles remain the same for

all three types of documents, but the menu items change depending on which type of document is active.

Example: The Insert menu includes features in part documents, mates in assembly documents, and drawing views in drawing documents. The display of the menu is also dependent on the workflow customization that you have selected. The default menu items for an active document are: *File, Edit, View, Insert, Tools, Window, Help, Pin.*

The Pin option displays the Menu bar toolbar and the Menu bar menu as illustrated. Throughout the book, the Menu bar menu and the Menu bar toolbar is referred as the Menu bar.

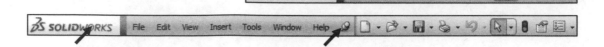

Until a file is converted to the current version of SolidWorks and saved, a warning icon is displayed on the Save tool as illustrated.

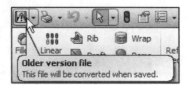

Drop-down menu

SolidWorks takes advantage of the familiar Microsoft® Windows® user interface. Communicate with SolidWorks either through the; *Drop-down menu, Pop-up menu, Shortcut toolbar, Fly-out toolbar* or the *CommandManager.*

A command is an instruction that informs SolidWorks to perform a task. To close a SolidWorks drop-down menu, press the Esc key. You can also click any other part of the SolidWorks Graphics window, or click another drop-down menu.

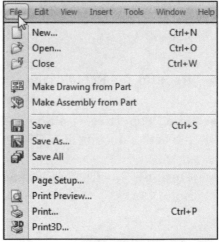

Right-click

Right-click in the: *Graphics window, FeatureManager,* or *Sketch* to display a Context-sensitive toolbar. If you are in the middle of a command, this toolbar displays a list of options specifically related to that command.

Press the **s** key to view/access previous command tools in the Graphics window.

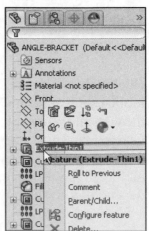

Consolidated toolbar

Similar commands are grouped in the CommandManager.
Example: Variations of the Rectangle sketch tool are grouped in a
single fly-out button as illustrated.

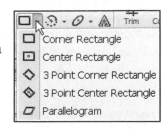

If you select the Consolidated toolbar button without expanding:

- For some commands such as Sketch, the most commonly
used command is performed. This command is the first listed and
the command shown on the button.

- For commands such as rectangle, where you may want to
repeatedly create the same variant of the rectangle, the last used
command is performed. This is the highlighted command when
the Consolidated toolbar is expanded.

System feedback

SolidWorks provides system feedback by attaching
a symbol to the mouse pointer cursor. The system
feedback symbol indicates what you are selecting or
what the system is expecting you to select.

As you move the mouse pointer across
your model, system feedback is provided to
you in the form of symbols, riding next to
the cursor arrow as illustrated.

Confirmation Corner

When numerous SolidWorks commands are active, a symbol or a set of
symbols are displayed in the upper right hand corner of the Graphics
window. This area is called the Confirmation Corner.

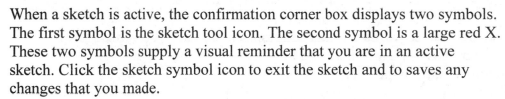

When a sketch is active, the confirmation corner box displays two symbols.
The first symbol is the sketch tool icon. The second symbol is a large red X.
These two symbols supply a visual reminder that you are in an active
sketch. Click the sketch symbol icon to exit the sketch and to saves any
changes that you made.

When other commands are active, the confirmation corner box provides a
green check mark and a large red X. Use the green check mark to execute
the current command. Use the large red X to cancel the command.

Heads-up View toolbar

SolidWorks provides the user with
numerous view options from the
Standard Views, View and Heads-up
View toolbar.

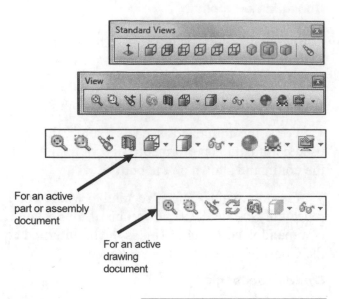

The Heads-up View toolbar is a
transparent toolbar that is displayed
in the Graphics window when a
document is active.

You can hide, move or modify the
Heads-up View toolbar. To modify
the Heads-up View toolbar: right-
click on a tool and select or deselect
the tools that you want to display.

The following views are available:
Note: *The available views are
document dependent.*

- *Zoom to Fit* 🔍 : Zooms the
  model to fit the Graphics window.

- *Zoom to Area* 🔍 : Zooms to the
  areas you select with a bounding box.

- *Previous View* ✎ : Displays the previous view.

- *Section View* ▥ : Displays a cutaway of a part or assembly,
  using one or more cross section planes.

🔆 The Orientation dialog has a new option to display a view
cube (in-context View Selector) with a live model preview. This
helps the user to understand how each standard view orientates the
model. With the view cube, you can access additional standard
views. The views are easy to understand and they can be accessed
simply by selecting a face on the cube.

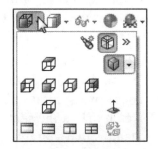

To activate the Orientation dialog box, press the spacebar or
click the View Orientation 📷 ˙icon from the Heads up View
toolbar. The active model is displayed in the View Selector in
an Isometric orientation (default view).

As you hover over the buttons in the Orientation dialog box,
the corresponding faces dynamical highlight in the View
Selector. Select a view in the View Selector or click the view
from the Orientation dialog box. The Orientation dialog box
closes and the model rotates to the selected view.

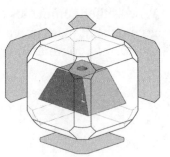

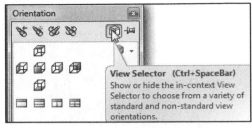

☀ Click the View Selector icon in the Orientation dialog box to show or hide the in-context View Selector.

☀ Press **Ctrl + spacebar** to activate the View Selector.

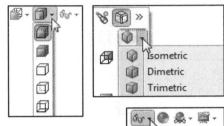

☀ Press the **spacebar** to activate the Orientation dialog box.

- *View Orientation box* 📄 ˅: Provides the ability to select a view orientation or the number of viewports. The available options are: *Top, Left, Front, Right, Back, Bottom, Single view, Two view - Horizontal, Two view - Vertical, Four view*. Click the drop-down arrow 📦 ˅ to access Axonometric views: Isometric, Dimetric and Trimetric.

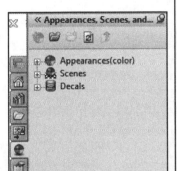

- *Display Style* 📄 ˅: Provides the ability to display the style for the active view: The available options are: *Wireframe, Hidden Lines Visible, Hidden Lines Removed, Shaded, Shaded With Edges*.

- *Hide/Show Items* 👓 ˅: Provides the ability to select items to hide or show in the Graphics window. The available items are document dependent. Note the View Center of Mass ✛ icon.

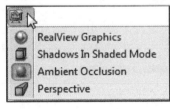

- *Edit Appearance* 🔵: Provides the ability to edit the appearance of entities of the model.

- *Apply Scene* 🎨 ˅: Provides the ability to apply a scene to an active part or assembly document. View the available options.

- *View Setting* 🖥 ˅: Provides the ability to select the following settings: *RealView Graphics, Shadows In Shaded Mode, Ambient Occlusion* and *Perspective*.

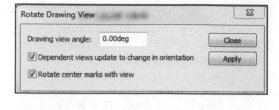

- *Rotate view* ⟳ : Provides the ability to rotate a drawing view. Input Drawing view angle and select the ability to update and rotate center marks with view.

- *3D Drawing View* 🔄 : Provides the ability to dynamically manipulate the drawing view in 3D to make a selection.

 The default part and document setting displays the grid. To deactivate the grid, click Options 📋, Document Properties tab. Click Grid/Snaps; uncheck the Display grid box.

Add a custom view to the Heads-up View toolbar. Press the space key. The Orientation dialog box is display. Click the New

View 🔧 tool. The Name View dialog box is displayed. Enter a new named view. Click OK.

The book does not cover starting a SolidWorks session in detail for the first time. A default SolidWorks installation presents you with several options. For additional information, visit the following sites: http://www.solidworks.com/goedu and http://www.solidworks.com/sw/education/6443_ENU_HTML.htm.

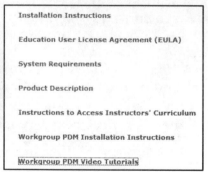

SolidWorks Help and Tutorials

The SolidWorks Help Topics contains step-by-step instructions for various commands.

The Help ❓ icon is displayed in the dialog box or in the PropertyManager for each feature. Display the SolidWorks Help Home Page. Use SolidWorks Help to locate information on What's New, sketches, features, assemblies and more.

- Click **Help** from the Menu bar.

- Click **SolidWorks Help**. The SolidWorks Help Home Page is displayed by default. View your options.

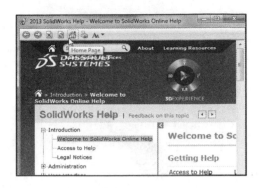

🔅 SolidWorks Web Help is active by default under Help in the Main menu.

Close Help. Return to the SolidWorks Graphics window.

- Click the **Home Page** 🏠 icon to return to the Home Page.

- **Close** ⊠ the SolidWorks Home Page dialog box.

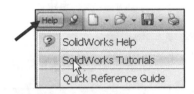

Display and explore the SolidWorks tutorials.

- Click **Help** from the Menu bar.

- Click **SolidWorks Tutorials**. The SolidWorks Tutorials are displayed. The SolidWorks Tutorials are presented by category.

- Click the **Getting Started** category. The Getting Started category provides 30-minute lessons on parts, assemblies, and drawings. This section also provides information for new users who are switching from AutoCAD to SolidWorks. The tutorials provide links to the CSWP and CSWA certification programs and a new What's New Tutorials for 2013.

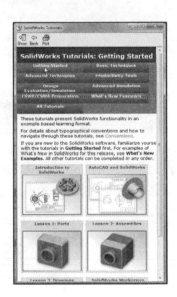

🔅 SolidWorks Corporation offers various levels of certification representing increasing levels of expertise in 3D CAD design as it applies to engineering.

The *Certified SolidWorks Associate* CSWA certification indicates a foundation in and apprentice knowledge of 3D CAD design and engineering practices and principles.

The main requirement for obtaining the CSWA certification is to take and pass the three hour, seven question on-line proctored exam at a Certified SolidWorks CSWA Provider; "university, college, technical, vocational or secondary educational institution" and to sign the SolidWorks Confidentiality Agreement.

Passing this exam provides students the chance to prove their working knowledge and expertise and to be part of a worldwide industry certification standard.

- **Close** the ⊠ Online Tutorial dialog box. Return to the SolidWorks Graphics window.

SolidWorks CommandManager

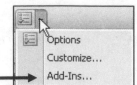

The SolidWorks CommandManager is a *Context-sensitive toolbar* that automatically updates based on the toolbar you want to access. By default, it has toolbars embedded in it based on your active document type. When you click a tab below the CommandManager, it updates to display that toolbar. Example, if you click the Sketch tab, the Sketch toolbar is displayed. The default Part tabs are: *Features, Sketch, Evaluate, DimXpert* and Office *Products*.

Below is an illustrated CommandManager for a default Part document.

If you have SolidWorks, SolidWorks Professional, or SolidWorks Premium, the Office Products tab appears on the CommandManager as illustrated.

Select the Add-Ins directly from the Office Products tab.

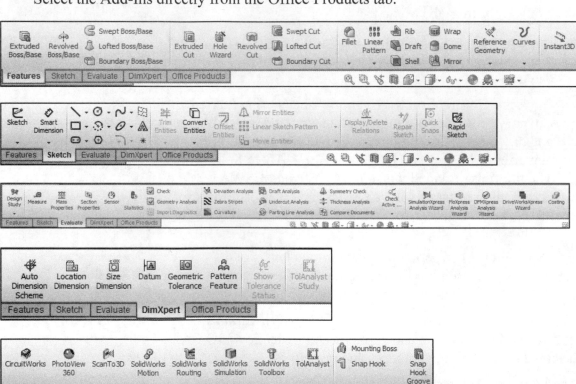

To customize the CommandManager, right-click on a tab and select Customize CommandManager.

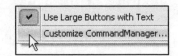

Below is an illustrated CommandManager for the default Drawing document. The default Drawing tabs are: *View Layout, Annotation, Sketch, Evaluate* and *Office Products*.

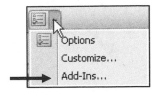

 Double-clicking the CommandManager when it is docked will make it float. Double-clicking the CommandManager when it is floating will return it to its last position in the Graphics window.

Select the Add-Ins directly from the Office Products tab.

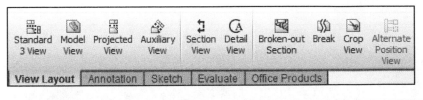

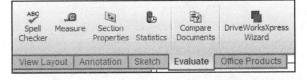

To add a custom tab to your CommandManager, right-click on a tab and click Customize CommandManager from the drop-down menu. The Customize dialog box is displayed.

You can also select to add a blank tab and populate it with custom tools from the Customize dialog box.

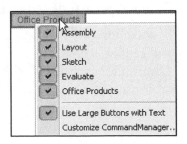

Below is an illustrated CommandManager for the default Assembly document. The default Assembly tabs are: *Assembly, Layout, Sketch, Evaluate* and *Office Products*.

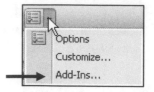

If you have SolidWorks, SolidWorks Professional, or SolidWorks Premium, the Office Products tab appears on the CommandManager

 Select the Add-Ins directly from the Office Products tab.

 Instant3D and Rapid Sketch tool is active by default.

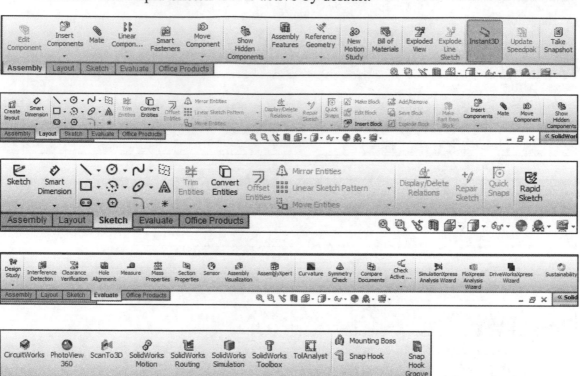

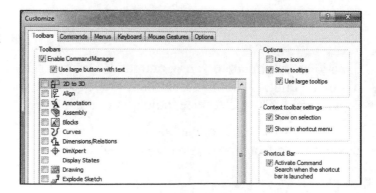

By default, the illustrated options are selected in the Customize box for the CommandManager.

Right-click on an existing tabs, and click Customize CommandManager to view your options.

Drag or double-click the CommandManager and it becomes a separate floating window. Once it is floating, you can drag the CommandManager anywhere on or outside the SolidWorks window.

To dock the CommandManager when it is floating, perform one of the following actions:

- While dragging the CommandManager in the SolidWorks window, move the pointer over a docking icon - ⬛Dock above, ⬛Dock left, ⬛Dock right and click the needed command.

- Double-click the floating CommandManager to revert the CommandManager to the last docking position.

Screen shots in the book were made using SolidWorks 2013 SP0 running Windows® 7 Ultimate.

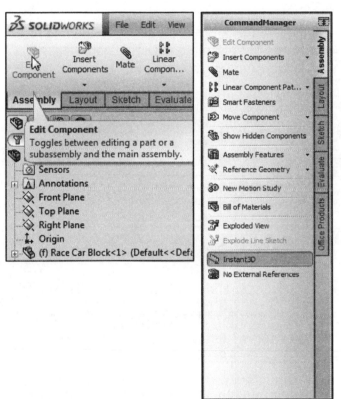

To save space in the CommandManager, right-click in the CommandManager and uncheck the Use Large Buttons with Text box. This eliminates the text associated with the tool.

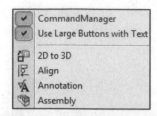

FeatureManager Design Tree

The FeatureManager design tree is located on the left side of the SolidWorks Graphics window. The FeatureManager provides a summarize view of the active part, assembly, or drawing document. The tree displays the details on how the part, assembly or drawing document was created.

Understand the FeatureManager design tree to troubleshoot your model. The FeatureManager is used extensively throughout this book.

The FeatureManager consist of five default tabs:

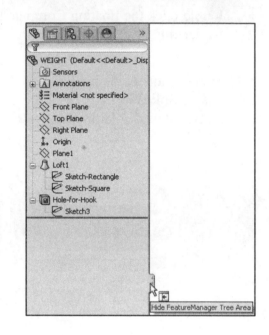

- *FeatureManager design tree* tab

- *PropertyManager* tab

- *ConfigurationManager* tab

- *DimXpertManager* tab

- *DisplayManager* tab

Select the Hide FeatureManager Tree Area

arrows as illustrated to enlarge the Graphics window for modeling.

DimXpert provides the ability to graphically check if the model is fully dimensioned and tolerance. DimXpert automatically recognize manufacturing features. Manufacturing features are *not SolidWorks features*. Manufacturing features are defined in 1.1.12 of the ASME Y14.5M-1994 Dimensioning and Tolerancing standard. See SolidWorks Help for additional information.

When you create a new part or assembly, the three default Planes (Front, Right and Top) are align with specific views. The Plane you select for the Base sketch determines the orientation of the part.

Various commands provide the ability to control what is displayed in the FeatureManager design tree. They are:

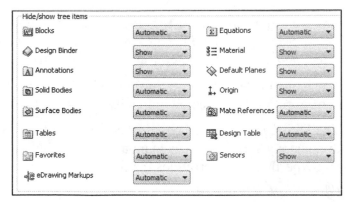

1. Show or Hide FeatureManager items.

☼ Click **Options** ⊞ from the Menu bar. Click **FeatureManager** from the System Options tab. **Customize** your FeatureManager from the Hide/Show Tree Items dialog box.

2. Filter the FeatureManager design tree. Enter information in the filter field. You can filter by: *Type of features, Feature names, Sketches, Folders, Mates, User-defined tags* and *Custom properties*.

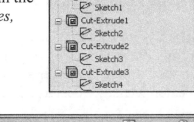

☼ Tags are keywords you can add to a SolidWorks document to make them easier to filter and to search. The Tags ✎ icon is located in the bottom right corner of the Graphics window.

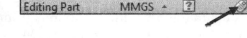

☼ To collapse all items in the FeatureManager, **right-click** and select **Collapse items**, or press the **Shift +C** keys.

The FeatureManager design tree and the Graphics window are dynamically linked. Select sketches, features, drawing views, and construction geometry in either pane.

Split the FeatureManager design tree and either display two FeatureManager instances, or combine the FeatureManager design tree with the ConfigurationManager or PropertyManager.

Move between the FeatureManager design tree, PropertyManager, ConfigurationManager, and DimXpertManager by selecting the tabs at the top of the menu.

☼ Right-click and drag in the Graphics area to display the Mouse Gesture wheel. You can customize the default commands for a sketch, part, assembly or drawing.

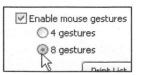

The ConfigurationManager is located to the right of the
FeatureManager. Use the ConfigurationManager to create,
select and view multiple configurations of parts and assemblies.

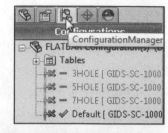

The icons in the ConfigurationManager denote whether the
configuration was created manually or with a design table.

The DimXpertManager tab provides the ability to insert
dimensions and tolerances manually or automatically. The
DimXpertManager provides the following selections: *Auto
Dimension Scheme* , *Show Tolerance Status* , *Copy
Scheme* and *TolAnalyst Study* .

 TolAnalyst is available in SolidWorks Premium.

Fly-out FeatureManager

The fly-out FeatureManager design tree
provides the ability to view and select items
in the PropertyManager and the
FeatureManager design tree at the same time.

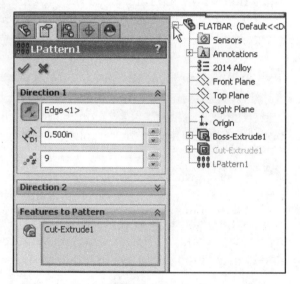

Throughout the book, you will select
commands and command options from the
drop-down menu, fly-out FeatureManager,
Context toolbar or from a SolidWorks
toolbar.

Another method for accessing a
command is to use the accelerator key.
Accelerator keys are special key strokes
which activate the drop-down menu options.
Some commands in the menu bar and items
in the drop-down menus have an underlined
character.

Press the Alt key followed by the corresponding key to the
underlined character activates that command or option.

Press the **s** key to view the Shortcut toolbar. Shortcut
menus provide convenient access to previous applied tools
and commands.

Illustrations may vary depending on your SolidWorks
version and operating system.

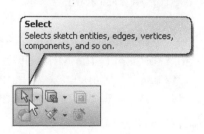

Task Pane

The Task Pane is displayed when a SolidWorks session starts. The Task Pane can be displayed in the following states: *visible or hidden, expanded or collapsed, pinned or unpinned, docked or floating.*

The Task Pane contains the following default tabs:

- *SolidWorks Forum* 🗨 tab

- *SolidWorks Resources* 🏠 tab

- *Design Library* 📚 tab

- *File Explorer* 📁 tab

- *View Palette* 🖼 tab

- *Appearances, Scenes, and Decals* ⚫ tab

- *Custom Properties* 📝 tab

SolidWorks Forum

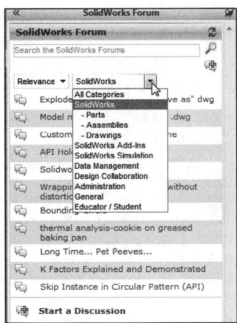

Click the SolidWorks Forum 🗨 tab to search directly within the Task Pane. An internet connection is required. You are required to register and to login for postings and discussions.

🔆 Additional tabs are displayed with Add-Ins. The SolidWorks Forum is an Add-in.

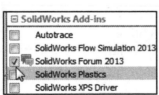

SolidWorks Resources

The basic SolidWorks Resources  menu displays the following default selections: *Getting Started, SolidWorks Tools, Community, Online Resources* and *Tip of the Day*.

Other user interfaces are available during the initial software installation selection: *Machine Design, Mold Design* or *Consumer Products Design*.

Design Library

The Design Library 🏛 contains reusable parts, assemblies, and other elements including library features.

The Design Library tab contains four default selections. Each default selection contains additional sub categories.

The default selections are:

- *Design Library*

- *Toolbox (Add-in)*

- *3D ContentCentral (Internet access required)*

- *SolidWorks Content (Internet access required)*

🔅 Activate the SolidWorks Toolbox. Click Tools, Add-Ins.., from the Main menu, check the SolidWorks Toolbox box and SolidWorks Toolbox Browser box from the Add-ins dialog box.

To access the Design Library folders in a non-network environment, click Add File Location

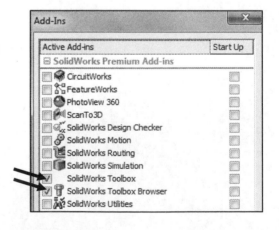

🏛 and browse to the needed path. Paths may vary depending on your SolidWorks version and window setup. In a network environment, contact your IT department for system details.

🔅 Access the SolidWorks Toolbox directly from the Office Products tab.

File Explorer

File Explorer 🗁 duplicates Windows Explorer from your local computer and displays:

- *Resent Documents*

- *Directories*

- *Open in SolidWorks and Desktop* folders

Search

The SolidWorks Search box is displayed in the upper right corner of the SolidWorks Graphics window (Menu Bar toolbar). Enter the text or key words to search.

New search modes have been added to SolidWorks Search. You can search the *Knowledge Base*, *Community Forum*, *Commands*, and *Files and Models*. Internet access is required for the Community Forum and Knowledge Base.

View Palette

The View Palette 🖳 tool located in the Task Pane provides the ability to insert drawing views of an active document, or click the Browse button to locate the desired document.

Click and drag the view from the View Palette into an active drawing sheet to create a drawing view.

🔆 The selected model is 3LINKS in the illustration.

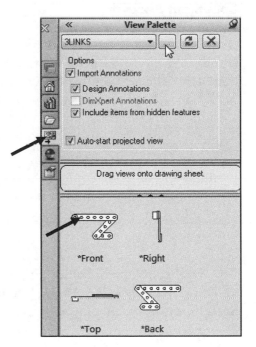

Appearances, Scenes, and Decals

Appearances, Scenes, and Decals 🌑 provide a simplified way to display models in a photo-realistic setting using a library of Appearances, Scenes, and Decals.

An appearance defines the visual properties of a model, including color and texture. Appearances do not affect physical properties, which are defined by materials.

Scenes provide a visual backdrop behind a model. In SolidWorks, they provide reflections on the model. PhotoView 360 is an Add-in. Drag and drop a selected appearance, scene or decal on a feature, surface, part or assembly.

Custom Properties

The Custom Properties 📑 tool provides the ability to enter custom and configuration specific properties directly into SolidWorks files.

Document Recovery

If auto recovery is initiated in the System Options section and the system terminates unexpectedly with an active document, the saved information files are available on the Task Pane Document Recovery tab the next time you start a SolidWorks session.

🔅 Run DFMXpress from the Evaluate tab or from Tools ➤ DFMXpress in the Menu bar menu. The DFMXpress icon is displayed in the Task Pane.

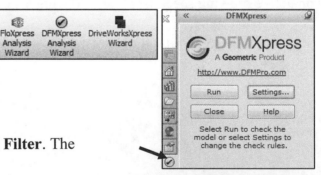

🔅 To display the Selection Filter toolbar, click **View**, **Toolbars**, **Selection Filter**. The Selection Filter is displayed.

🔅 To clear a Filter icon ⬚▽, click **Clear All Filters** from the Selection Filter toolbar.

Motion Study tab

Motion Studies are graphical simulations of motion for an assembly. Access MotionManager from the Motion Study tab. The Motion Study tab is located in the bottom left corner of the Graphics window.

Incorporate visual properties such as lighting and camera perspective. Click the Motion Study tab to view the MotionManager. Click the Model tab to return to the FeatureManager design tree.

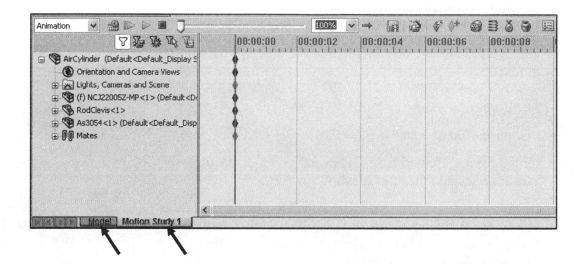

The MotionManager display a timeline-based interface, and provide the following selections from the drop-down menu as illustrated:

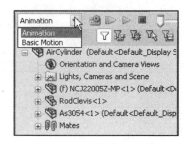

- *Animation:* Apply Animation to animate the motion of an assembly. Add a motor and insert positions of assembly components at various times using set key points. Use the Animation option to create animations for motion that do **not** require accounting for mass or gravity.

- *Basic Motion:* Apply Basic Motion for approximating the effects of motors, springs, collisions and gravity on assemblies. Basic Motion takes mass into account in calculating motion. Basic Motion computation is relatively fast, so you can use this for creating presentation animations using physics-based simulations. Use the Basic Motion option to create simulations of motion that account for mass, collisions or gravity.

If the Motion Study tab is not displayed in the Graphics window, click **View, MotionManager** from the Menu bar.

For older assemblies created before 2008, the Animation1 tab maybe displayed. View the Assembly Chapter for additional information.

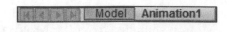

To create a new Motion Study, click **Insert, New Motion Study** from the Menu bar.

If the Motion Study tab is not displayed in the Graphics window, click **View, MotionManager** from the Menu bar.

Activity: Create a New Part

A part is a 3D model, which consist of features. What are features?

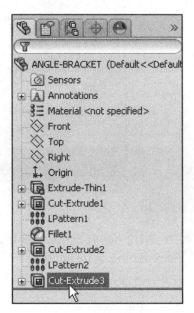

- Features are geometry building blocks.

- Features add or remove material.

- Features are created from 2D or 3D sketched profiles or from edges and faces of existing geometry.

- Features are an individual shape that combined with other features, makes up a part or assembly. Some features, such as bosses and cuts, originate as sketches. Other features, such as shells and fillets, modify a feature's geometry.

- Features are displayed in the FeatureManager as illustrated (Extrude-Thin1, Cut-Extrude1, LPattern1, Fillet1, Cut-Extrude2, Lpatern2, and Cut-Extrude3).

You can suppress a feature. A suppress feature is display in light gray.

The first sketch of a part is called the Base Sketch. The Base sketch is the foundation for the 3D model. The book focuses on 2D sketches and 3D features.

During the initial SolidWorks installation, you were requested to select either the ISO or ANSI drafting standard. ISO is typically; a European drafting standard and uses First Angle Projection. The book is written using the ANSI (US) overall drafting standard and Third Angle Projection for drawings.

There are two modes in the New SolidWorks Document dialog box: *Novice* and *Advanced*. The *Novice* option is the default option with three templates. The *Advanced* mode contains access to additional templates and tabs that you create in system options. Use the *Advanced* mode in this book.

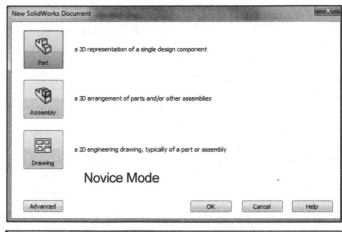

Create a New part.

8)   Click **New** ☐ from the Menu bar. The New SolidWorks Document dialog box is displayed.

Select Advanced Mode.

9)   Click the **Advanced** button to display the New SolidWorks Document dialog box in Advance mode.

10)   The Templates tab is the default tab. Part is the default template from the New SolidWorks Document dialog box. Click **OK**.

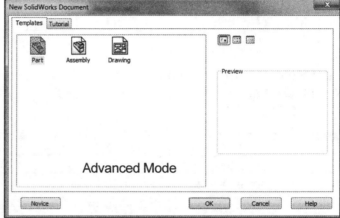

☀ SolidWorks Web Help is active by default under Help in the Main menu bar.

The *Advanced* mode remains selected for all new documents in the current SolidWorks session. When you exit SolidWorks, the *Advanced* mode setting is saved.

The default SolidWorks installation contains two tabs in the New SolidWorks Document dialog box: *Templates* and *Tutorial*. The *Templates* tab corresponds to the default SolidWorks templates. The *Tutorial* tab corresponds to the templates utilized in the SolidWorks Tutorials.

☀ During the initial SolidWorks installation, you are request to select either the ISO or ANSI drafting standard. ISO is typically a European drafting standard and uses First Angle Projection. The book is written using the ANSI (US) overall drafting standard and Third Angle Projection for all drawing documents.

Part1 is displayed in the FeatureManager and is the name of the document. Part1 is the default part window name. The Menu bar, CommandManager, FeatureManager, Heads-up View toolbar, SolidWorks Resources, SolidWorks Search, Task Pane, and the Origin are displayed in the Graphics window.

The Origin 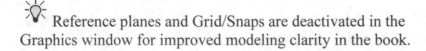 is displayed in blue in the center of the Graphics window. The Origin represents the intersection of the three default reference planes: *Front Plane*, *Top Plane* and *Right Plane*. The positive X-axis is horizontal and points to the right of the Origin in the Front view. The positive Y-axis is vertical and point upward in the Front view. The FeatureManager contains a list of features, reference geometry, and settings utilized in the part.

Click **View**, **Origins** from the Menu bar menu to display the Origin in the Graphics window.

Edit document units directly from the Graphics window as illustrated.

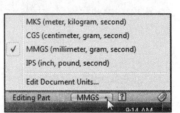

Reference planes and Grid/Snaps are deactivated in the Graphics window for improved modeling clarity in the book.

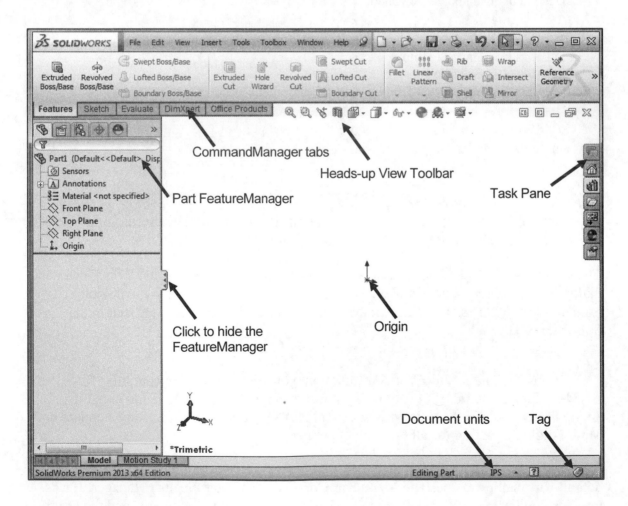

The CommandManager is document dependent. The tabs are located on the bottom left side of the CommandManager and display the available toolbars and features for each corresponding tab. The default tabs for a Part are: *Features*, *Sketch*, *Evaluate*, *DimXpert* and *Office Products*.

The Features icon and Features toolbar should be selected by default in Part mode.

The CommandManager is utilized in this text. Control the CommandManager display.

Right-click in the gray area to the right of the Options 🔲 ⁻ icon in the Menu bar toolbar. A complete list of toolbars is displayed. Check CommandManager if required.

🔆 Another way to display a toolbar, click **View, Toolbars** from the Menu bar menu. Select the required toolbar.

Select individual toolbars from the View, Toolbars list to display in the Graphics window. Reposition toolbars by clicking and dragging.

🔆 Click **View, Origins** from the Menu bar menu to display the Origin in the Graphics window.

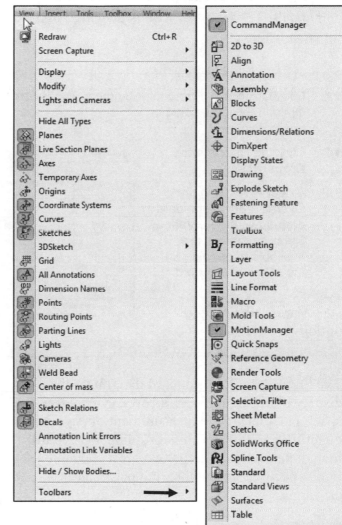

Activity: Create the AXLE Part

Set the Menu bar toolbar and Menu bar menu.

11) Click **SolidWorks** to expand the Menu bar menu.

12) Pin  the Menu bar as illustrated. Use both the Menu bar menu and the Menu bar toolbar in this book.

🔅 The SolidWorks Help Topics contains step-by-step instructions for various commands. The Help ⍰ icon is displayed in the dialog box or in the PropertyManager for each feature.

Set the Document Properties.

13) Click **Options** 🗒 from the Menu bar. The System Options General dialog box is displayed

14) Click the **Document Properties** tab.

15) Select **ANSI** from the Overall drafting standard drop-down menu. Various Detailing options are available depending on the selected standard.

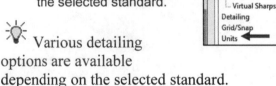

🔅 Various detailing options are available depending on the selected standard.

The Overall drafting standard determines the display of dimension text, arrows, symbols, and spacing. Units are the measurement of physical quantities. Millimeter dimensioning and decimal inch dimensioning are the two most common unit types specified for engineering parts and drawings.

The primary units in this book are provided in IPS, (inch, pound, second). The optional secondary units are provided in MMGS, (millimeters, grams, second) and are indicated in brackets [ ].

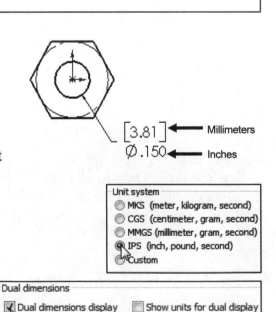

Most illustrations are provided in both inches and millimeters.

Set the document units.

16) Click **Units**.

17) Click **IPS** (inch, pound, second) [**MMGS**] for Unit system.

18) Select **.123, [.12]** (three decimal places) for Length basic units.

19) Select **None** for Angle decimal places.

20) Click **OK** from the Document Properties - Units dialog box. The Part FeatureManager is displayed.

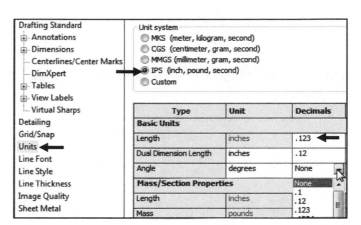

Activity: AXLE Part-Extruded Base Feature

Insert a new sketch for the Extruded Base feature.

21) Right-click **Front Plane** from the FeatureManager. This is your Sketch plane. The Context toolbar is displayed.

22) Click **Sketch** ⌐ from the Context toolbar as illustrated.

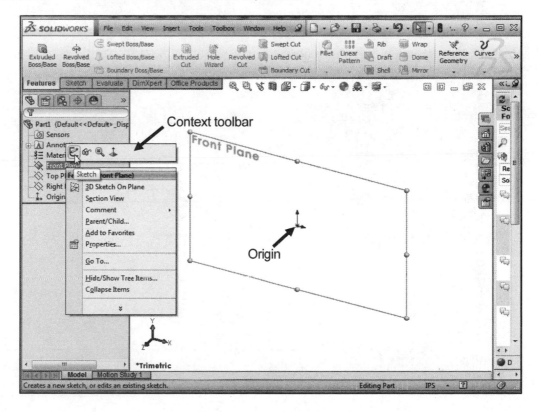

The Sketch toolbar is displayed. Front Plane is your Sketch plane. Note: the grid is deactivated for picture clarity.

You can also click the Front Plane from the FeatureManager and click the Sketch tab from the CommandManager.

23)   Click the **Circle** ⊘ tool from the Sketch toolbar. The Circle PropertyManager is displayed.

The Circle-based tool uses a Consolidated Circle PropertyManager. The SolidWorks application defaults to the last used tool type.

24)   Drag the **mouse pointer** into the Graphics window. The cursor displays the Circle icon symbol ⊘ .

25)   Click the **Origin** ⤙ of the circle. The cursor displays the Coincident to point feedback symbol.

26)   Drag the **mouse pointer** to the right of the Origin to create the circle as illustrated. The center point of the circle is positioned at the Origin.

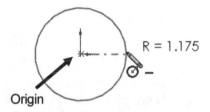

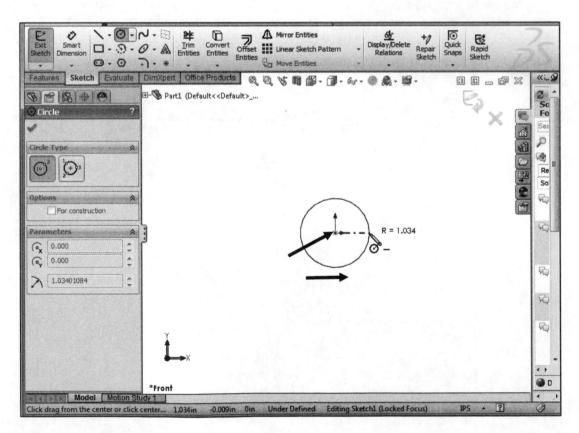

27) Click a **position** to create the circle. The activated circle is displayed in blue.

Add a dimension.

28) Click **Smart Dimension** ✎ from the Sketch toolbar. The cursor displays the Smart Dimension icon ⟋⟍.

29) Click the **circumference** of the circle.

30) Click a **position** diagonally above the circle in the Graphics window.

31) Enter **.188**in, **[4.78]** in the Modify dialog box. Note The Dimension Modify dialog box provides the ability to select a unit drop-down menu to directly modify units in a sketch or feature from the document properties.

32) Click the **Green Check mark** ✔ in the Modify dialog box. The diameter of the circle is .188 inches.

If required, click the blue arrow head dots to toggle the direction of the dimension arrow. The circular sketch is centered at the Origin. The dimension indicates the diameter of the circle.

🔆 Press the f key to fit the part document to the Graphics window.

🔆 Add relations, then dimensions. This keeps the user from having too many unnecessary dimensions. This also helps to show the design intent of the model. Dimension what geometry you intent to modify or adjust.

🔆 The Dimension Modify dialog box provides the ability to create an equation driven dimension relative to a function or File Property. See SolidWorks Help for additional detail information.

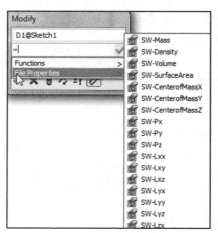

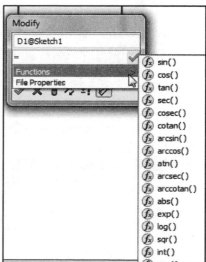

Extrude the sketch to create the Base
Feature.

33) Click the **Features** tab from the
CommandManager.

34) Click the **Extruded Boss/Base**
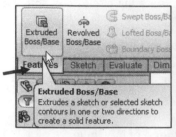 Features tool. The Boss-
Extrude PropertyManager is
displayed. Blind is the default End
Condition in Direction 1.

35) Select **Mid Plane** for End
Condition in Direction 1.

36) Enter **1.375**in, [**34.93**] for Depth in
Direction 1. Accept the default
conditions.

37) Click **OK** ✔ from the Boss-
Extrude PropertyManager. Boss-
Extrude1 is displayed in the
FeatureManager.

Fit the model to the Graphics window.

38) Press the **f** key. Note the location
of the Origin in the model.

💡 Use Symmetry. When possible
and if it makes sense, model objects
symmetrically about the origin.

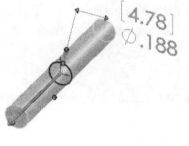

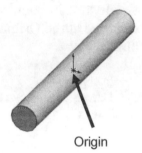

Origin

💡 Rename a feature or sketch.
Slowly click the feature or sketch name twice and enter the new
name when the old one is highlighted.

💡 Right-click anywhere on an extruded feature to set or modify
the end condition from the shortcut menu. Click in empty space, on
geometry, or on the handle. The shortcut
menu provides options for Direction 1 and
Direction 2. Note: Options are document
dependent.

💡 Display an Isometric view of the
model. Press the **space bar** to display the
Orientation dialog box. Click the
Isometric view 🔲 icon.

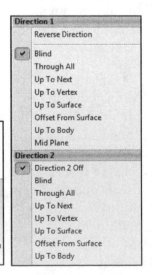

The Boss-Extrude PropertyManager displays the parameters utilized to define the feature. The Mid Plane End Condition in the Direction 1 box extrudes the sketch equally on both sides of the Sketch plane. The depth defines the extrude distance.

The Boss-Extrude1 feature name is displayed in the FeatureManager. The FeatureManager lists the features, planes, and other geometry that construct the part. Extrude features add material. Extrude features require the following: *Sketch Plane*, *Sketch* and *depth*.

The Sketch plane is the Front Plane. The Sketch is a circle with the diameter of .188in, [4.76]. The Depth is 1.375in, [34.93].

For many features; (Extruded Boss/ Base, Extruded Cut, Simple Hole, Revolved Boss/Base, Revolved Cut, Fillet, Chamfer, Scale, Shell, Rib, Circular Pattern, Linear Pattern, Curve Driven Pattern, Revolved Surface, Extruded Surface, Fillet Surface, Edge Flange and Base Flange) you can enter and modify equations directly in the PropertyManager fields that allow numerical inputs. You can create equations with global variables, functions, and file properties without accessing the Equations, Global Variables and Dimensions dialog box.

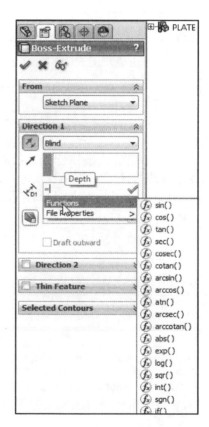

For example, in the PropertyManager for the Extruded Boss/Base feature, you can enter equations in:

- Depth fields for Direction 1 and Direction 2

- Draft fields for Direction 1 and Direction 2

- Thickness fields for a Thin Feature with two direction types

- Offset Distance field

To create an equation in a numeric input field, start by entering = (equal sign). A drop-down list displays options for global variables, functions, and file properties. Numeric input fields that contain equations can display either the equation itself or its evaluated value. You can toggle between the equation and the value by clicking the Equations or Global Variable button that appears at the beginning of the field.

Activity: AXLE Part-Save

Save the part.

39) Click **Save As** from the Drop-down Menu bar.

40) Click the **DOCUMENTS** file folder. Note: The procedure will be different depending on your Operating System.

41) Click **New Folder**.

42) Enter **SW-TUTORIAL-2013** for the file folder name. Note: In this book all models, assemblies and templates are saved to the SW-TUTORIAL-2013 folder.

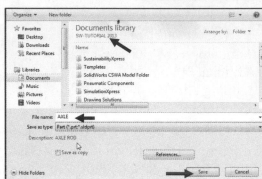

43) Double-click the **SW-TUTORIAL-2013** file folder. SW-TUTORIAL-2013 is the Save in file folder name.

44) Enter **AXLE** for the File name.

45) Enter **AXLE ROD** for the Description.

46) Click **Save**. The AXLE FeatureManager is displayed.

🔅 Organize parts into file folders. The file folder for this chapter is named: SW-TUTORIAL-2013. All documents for this book are saved in the SW-TUTORIAL-2013 file folder.

🔅 Copy all files from the DVD in the book to the created SW-TUTORIAL-2013 folder on your system.

Activity: AXLE Part - Edit Appearance

Modify the color of the part.

47) Right-click the **AXLE** 🍊 AXLE icon at the top of the FeatureManager.

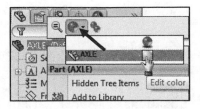

48) Click the **Appearances** drop-down arrow.

49) Click the **Edit color** box as illustrated. The Color PropertyManager is displayed. AXLE is displayed in the Selection box.

50) Select a **light blue** color from the Color box. View your options.

51) Click **OK** ✔ from the Color PropertyManager. View the AXLE in the Graphics window.

Use the Appearances PropertyManager to apply colors, material appearances, and transparency to parts and assembly components. For sketches or curves only, use the Sketch/Curve Color PropertyManager to apply colors.

🔆 The Advanced tab includes the Illumination and Surface Finish tabs, and additional options in the Color/Image and Mapping tabs. To display the simplified Color/Image or Mapping interfaces, click the Basic tab.

Sketching in SolidWorks is the basis for creating features. Features are the basis for creating parts, which can be put together into assemblies.

The sketch status appears in the window status bar and in the FeatureManager. Colors indicate the state of individual sketch entities. Sketches are generally in one of the following states:

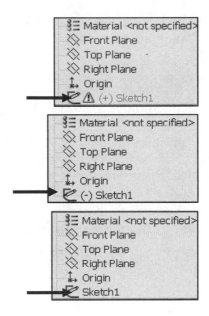

1.) *(+) Over defined.* The sketch is displayed in red.

2.) *(-) Under defined.* The sketch is displayed in blue.

3.) *No prefix.* The sketch is fully defined. This is the ideal sketch state. A fully defined sketch has complete information (manufacturing and inspection) and is displayed in black.

The SketchXpert PropertyManager provides the ability to diagnose an over defined sketch to create a fully defined sketch. If you have an over defined sketch, click Over Defined at the bottom of the Graphics window toolbar. The SketchXpert PropertyManager is displayed. Click the Diagnose button.

Select the desired solution and click the Accept button from the Results box.

Activity: AXLE Part-View Modes

Orthographic projection is the process of projecting views onto Parallel planes with $\perp$ projectors.

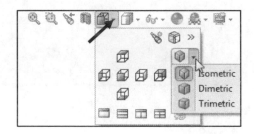

The default reference planes are the Front, Top and Right Planes.

The Isometric view displays the part in 3D with two equal projection angles.

The Heads-up View toolbar illustration may vary depending on your SolidWorks release version.

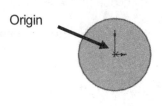

Origin

Click **View**, **Origins** from the Menu bar menu to display the Origin in the Graphics window.

Display the various view modes using the Heads-up View toolbar.

52)   Click **Front view** 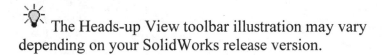 from the Heads-up View toolbar.

53)   Click **Top view** from the Heads-up View toolbar.

54)   Click **Right view** from the Heads-up View toolbar.

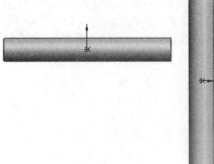

55)   Click **Isometric view** 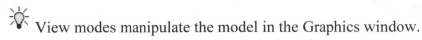 from the Heads-up View toolbar.

🔆 View modes manipulate the model in the Graphics window.

Display the various View modes.
56)   Press the lower case **z** key to zoom out.

57)   Press the upper case **Z** key to zoom in.

58)   Click **Zoom to Fit** 🔍 to display the full size of the part in the current window.

59)   **Right-click** in the Graphics window. View the available view tools.

60)   Click **inside** the Graphics window.

Rotate the model.
61)   Click the **middle mouse** button and move your mouse. The model rotates. The Rotate icon ⟳ is displayed.

62)   Press the **up arrow** on your key board. The arrow keys rotate the model in 15 degree increments.

🔆 View modes remain active until deactivated from the View toolbar or unchecked from the pop-up menu.

🔆 Utilize the center wheel of the mouse to Zoom In/Zoom Out and Rotate the model in the Graphics window.

View the various Display Styles.
63)   Click **Isometric view** 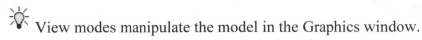 from the Heads-up View toolbar.

64)   Click the **drop-down arrow** from the Display Styles box from the Heads-up Views toolbar as illustrated. SolidWorks provides five key Display Styles:

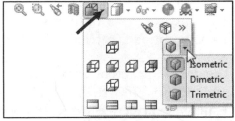

- *Shaded* ▢. Displays a shaded view of the model with no edges.

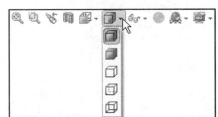

- *Shaded With Edges* ▢. Displays a shaded view of the model, with edges.

- *Hidden Lines Removed* 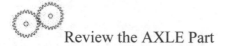. Displays only those model edges that can be seen from the current view orientation.

- *Hidden Lines Visible* ⬛. Displays all edges of the model. Edges that are hidden from the current view are displayed in a different color or font.

- *Wireframe* ⬛. Displays all edges of the model.

Save the AXLE part.

65)   Click **Save** 💾. The AXLE part is complete.

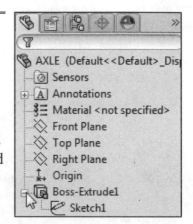

Review the AXLE Part

The AXLE part utilized the Extruded Boss/Base feature. The Extruded Boss/Base feature adds material. The Extruded feature required a Sketch Plane, sketch and depth. The AXLE Sketch plane was the Front Plane. The 2D circle was sketched centered at the Origin. A dimension defined the overall size of the sketch based on the dimensions of mating parts in the LINKAGE assembly.

The default name of the Base feature is Boss-Extrude1. Boss-Extrude1 utilized the Mid Plane End Condition. The Boss-Extrude1 feature is symmetrical about the Front Plane.

The Edit Color option modified the part color. Select the Part icon in the FeatureManager to modify the color of the part. Color and a prefix define the sketch status. A blue sketch is under defined. A black sketch is fully defined. A red sketch is over defined.

The default Reference planes are the Front, Top, and Right Planes. Utilize the Heads-up View toolbar to display the principle views of a part. The View Orientation and Display Style tools manipulate the model in the Graphics windows.

Instant3D provides the ability to click and drag geometry and dimension manipulator points to resize features in the Graphics window, and to use on-screen rulers to measure modifications. In this book, you will primarily use the PropertyManager and dialog boxes to create and modify model dimensions. Explore Instant3D as an exercise.

SHAFT-COLLAR Part

The SHAFT-COLLAR part is a hardened steel ring fastened to the AXLE part.

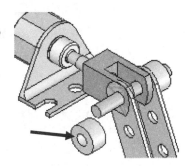

Two SHAFT-COLLAR parts are used to position the two FLATBAR parts on the AXLE.

Create the SHAFT-COLLAR part.

Utilize the Extruded Boss/Base 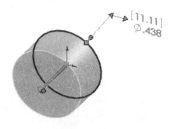 feature. The Extruded Boss/Base feature requires a 2D circular profile.

Utilize symmetry. Sketch a circle on the Front Plane centered at the Origin.

Extrude the sketch with the Mid Plane End Condition. The Extruded Boss/Base feature (Boss-Extrude1) is centered on both sides of the Front Plane.

SHAFT-COLLAR

The Extruded Cut  feature removes material. Utilize an Extruded Cut feature to create a hole. The Extruded Cut feature requires a 2D circular profile. Sketch a circle on the front face centered at the Origin.

The Through All End Condition extends the Extruded Cut feature from the front face through all existing geometry.

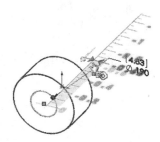

🔆 At this time, apply the Extruded Cut feature for a Through All hole vs. using the Hole Wizard. The book is design to expose the new user to various tools and design intents.

🔆 You can also apply the Instant3D tool to create a Through All hole.

Activity: SHAFT-COLLAR Part-Extruded Boss/Base Feature

Create a New part.

66) Click **New** 🗋 from the Menu bar. The New SolidWorks Document dialog box is displayed. The Templates tab is the default tab. Part is the default template from the New SolidWorks Document dialog box.

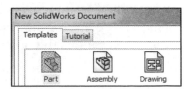

67) Double-click **Part**. The Part FeatureManager is displayed.

Save the part.

68) Click **Save As** from the drop-down Menu bar.

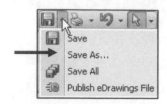

69) Enter **SHAFT-COLLAR** for File name in the SW-TUTORIAL-2013 folder.

70) Enter **SHAFT-COLLAR** for Description.

71) Click **Save**. The SHAFT-COLLAR FeatureManager is displayed.

Set the Dimension standard and part units.

72) Click **Options** 📋 , **Document Properties** tab from the Menu bar.

73) Select **ANSI** from the Overall drafting standard drop-down menu.

74) Click **Units**.

75) Click **IPS** (inch, pound, second), [**MMGS**] for Unit system.

76) Select **.123**, [**.12**] (three decimal places) for Length units Decimal places.

77) Select **None** for Angular units Decimal places.

78) Click **OK** from the Document Properties - Units dialog box.

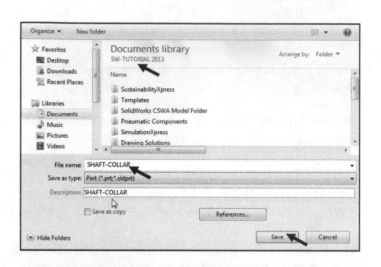

🔅 To view the Origin, click **View**, **Origins** from the Menu bar menu.

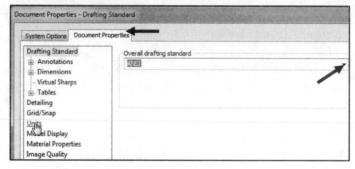

🔅 When you create a new part or assembly, the three default Planes (Front, Right and Top) are align with specific views. The Plane you select for the Base sketch determines the orientation of the part.

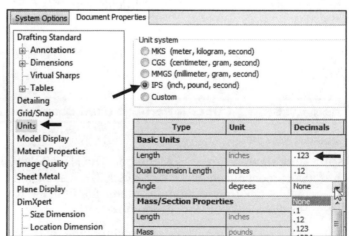

Insert a new sketch for the Extruded Base feature.

79) Right-click **Front Plane** from the FeatureManager. This is the Sketch plane. The Context toolbar is displayed.

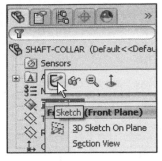

80) Click **Sketch** ⎿ from the Context toolbar as illustrated. The Sketch toolbar is displayed.

81) Click the **Circle** ⊘ tool from the Sketch toolbar. The Circle PropertyManager is displayed. The cursor displays the Circle

icon symbol ⊘ .

82) Click the **Origin** ⌊⸱. The cursor displays the Coincident to point feedback symbol.

83) Drag the **mouse pointer** to the right of the Origin as illustrated.

84) Click a **position** to create the circle.

Add a dimension.

85) Click **Smart Dimension** ⬦ from the Sketch toolbar.

86) Click the **circumference** of the circle. The cursor displays the diameter feedback symbol.

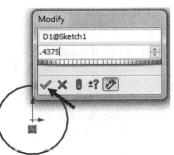

87) Click a **position** diagonally above the circle in the Graphics window.

88) Enter **.4375**in, **[11.11]** in the Modify dialog box.

89) Click the **Green Check mark** ✅ in the Modify dialog box. The black sketch is fully defined.

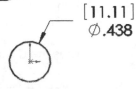

$[11.11]$
$\varnothing.438$

Note: Three decimal places are displayed. The diameter value .4375 rounds to .438.

Extrude the sketch to create the Base feature.

90) Click the **Features** tab from the CommandManager.

91) Click the **Extruded Boss/Base** 🗔 features tool. The Boss-Extrude PropertyManager is displayed.

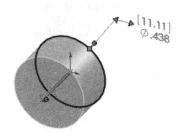

92) Select **Mid Plane** for End Condition in Direction 1.

93) Enter **.250**in, **[6.35]** for Depth. Accept the default conditions. Note the location of the Origin.

94) Click **OK** ✅ from the Boss-Extrude PropertyManager. Boss-Extrude1 is displayed in the FeatureManager.

Fit the model to the Graphics window.
95)   Press the **f** key.

96)   Click **Trimetric** from the Heads-Up View toolbar.

Save the model.

97)   Click **Save** .

Activity: SHAFT-COLLAR Part-Extruded Cut Feature

Insert a new sketch for the Extruded Cut feature.

98)   Right-click the **front circular face** of the Boss-Extrude1 feature for the Sketch plane. The mouse pointer displays the face

feedback icon.

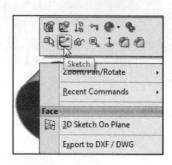

View the mouse pointer feedback icon for the correct geometry: line, face, point or vertex.

99)   Click **Sketch** from the Context toolbar as illustrated. The Sketch toolbar is displayed. This is your Sketch plane!

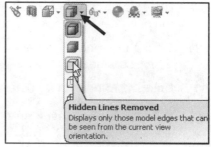

100) Click **Hidden Lines Removed** from the Heads-up View toolbar.

101) Click the **Circle** tool from the Sketch toolbar. The Circle PropertyManager is displayed. The cursor

displays the Circle icon symbol .

102) Click the red **Origin** . The cursor displays the Coincident to point feedback symbol.

103) Drag the **mouse pointer** to the right of the Origin.

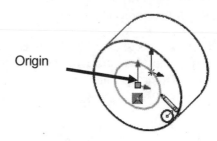

Origin

104) Click a **position** to create the circle as illustrated.

Add a dimension.

105) Click the **Smart Dimension** Sketch tool.

106) Click the **circumference** of the circle.

107) Click a **position** diagonally above the circle in the Graphics window.

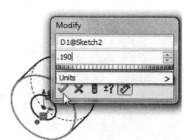

108) Enter **.190**in, [**4.83**] in the Modify dialog box.

109) Click the **Green Check mark** in the Modify dialog box.

Insert an Extruded Cut feature.

110) Click the **Features** tab from the
CommandManager.

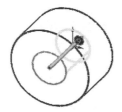

111) Click **Extruded Cut** 🔳 from the Features
toolbar. The Cut-Extrude PropertyManager
is displayed.

112) Select **Through All** for End Condition in
Direction 1. The direction arrow points to the
back. If needed, click the Reverse Direction
button. Accept the default conditions.

113) Click **OK** ✔ from the Cut-Extrude
PropertyManager. Cut-Extrude1 is displayed in the
FeatureManager.

🔆 The Extruded Cut feature is named Cut-Extrude1. The
Through All End Condition removes material from the Front
Plane through the Boss-Extrude1 geometry.

🔆 Model about the origin; this provides a point of reference.

🔆 Press the **spacebar** to activate the Orientation dialog box.

Activity: SHAFT-COLLAR-Modify Dimensions and Edit Color

Modify the dimensions.

114) Click **Trimetric view** 🔲 from the Heads-up View toolbar.

115) Click the **z** key a few times to Zoom in.

116) Double-click the **outside cylindrical face** of the
SHAFT-COLLAR. The Boss-Extrude1 dimensions are
displayed. Sketch dimensions are displayed in black. The
Extrude depth dimensions are displayed in blue.

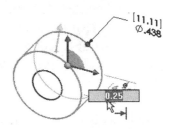

117) Double-click the **.250**in, [**6.35**] depth dimension.

118) Enter **.500**in, [**12.70**].

119) Click **Rebuild** 🔴 from the Menu bar.

The Boss-Extrude1 feature and
Cut-Extrude1 feature are modified.

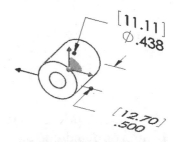

Return to the original dimensions.

120) Click the **Undo** ↩ tool from the Menu bar.

121) Click **Shaded With Edges** 🔲 from the
Heads-up View toolbar.

Modify the part color.

122) Right-click the **SHAFT-COLLAR Part** 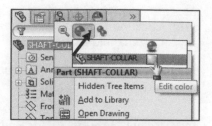 SHAFT-COLLAR icon at the top of the FeatureManager.

123) Click the **Appearances** drop-down arrow.

124) Click the **Edit color** box as illustrated. The Color PropertyManager is displayed. SHAFT-COLLAR is displayed in the Selection box.

125) Select a **light green** color from the Color box.

126) Click **OK** ✅ from the Color PropertyManager. View the SHAFT-COLLAR in the Graphics window.

Save the SHAFT-COLLAR part.

127) Click **Save** 🖫. The SHAFT-COLLAR part is complete. Note: all sketches are and should be fully defined.

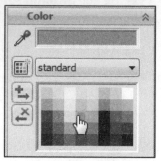

Review the SHAFT-COLLAR Part

The SHAFT-COLLAR utilized an Extruded Boss/Base 🖻 feature. The Extruded Boss/Base feature adds material. An Extruded feature required a Sketch Plane, sketch and depth.

The Sketch plane was the Front Plane. The 2D circle was sketched centered at the Origin. A dimension fully defined the overall size of the sketch. The default name of the feature was Boss-Extrude1. Boss-Extrude1 utilized the Mid Plane End Condition. The Boss-Extrude1 feature was symmetric about the Front Plane.

The Extruded Cut 🖻 feature removed material to create the hole. The Extruded Cut feature default named was Cut-Extrude1. The Through All End Condition option created the Cut-Extrude1 feature. Feature dimensions were modified. The Edit Color option was utilized to modify the part color.

🔅 Click **Options**, **Document Properties** tab, **Dimension** and click the **Smart** box to have the dimension leader arrow head point inwards for ANSI.

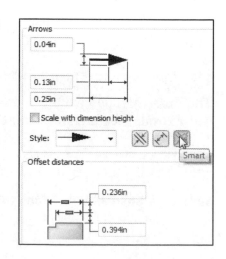

FLATBAR Part

The FLATBAR part fastens to the AXLE. The FLATBAR contains nine, ∅.190in holes spaced 0.5in apart.

The FLATBAR part is manufactured from .090inch 6061 alloy.

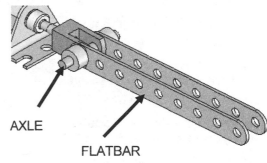

AXLE

FLATBAR

Create the FLATBAR part. Utilize the new Straight Slot Sketch ⬭ tool with an Extruded Boss/Base 🔲 feature. The Extruded feature requires a 2D profile sketched on the Front Plane.

The Straight Slot Sketch tool automatically applies design symmetry, (Midpoint and Equal geometric relations). Create the 2D profile centered about the Origin. Relations control the size and position of entities with constraints.

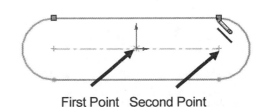

First Point   Second Point

[4.83]
∅.190

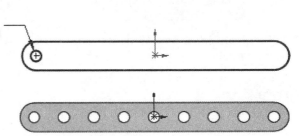

Utilize an Extruded Cut 🔲 feature to create the first hole. This is the seed feature for the Linear Pattern.

Utilize a Linear Pattern ⠿ feature to create the remaining holes. A Linear Pattern creates an array of features in a specified direction.

💡 Add relations, then dimensions. This keeps the user from having too many unnecessary dimensions. This also helps to show the design intent of the model. Dimension what geometry you intent to modify or adjust.

Activity: FLATBAR Part-Extruded Base Feature

Create a New part.

128) Click **New** ⬚ from the Menu bar. The New SolidWorks Document dialog box is displayed. The Templates tab is the default tab. Part is the default template from the New SolidWorks Document dialog box.

129) Double-click **Part**. The Part FeatureManager is displayed.

Save the part.
130) Click **Save As** from the drop-down Menu bar.

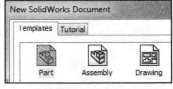

131) Enter **FLATBAR** for File name in the SW-TUTORIAL-2013 folder

132) Enter **FLAT BAR 9 HOLES** for Description.

133) Click **Save**. The FLATBAR FeatureManager is displayed.

Set the Dimension standard and part units.

134) Click **Options** 📋 , **Document Properties** tab from the Menu bar.

135) Select **ANSI** from the Overall drafting standard drop-down menu.

136) Click **Units**.

137) Click **IPS**, [**MMGS**] for Unit system.

138) Select **.123**, [**.12**] for Length units Decimal places.

139) Select **None** for Angular units Decimal places.

140) Click **OK** to set the document units.

Insert a new sketch for the Extruded Base feature.

141) Right-click **Front Plane** from the FeatureManager. This is the Sketch plane.

142) Click **Sketch** 🖉 from the Context toolbar as illustrated. The Sketch toolbar is displayed.

Utilize the Consolidated Slot Sketch toolbar. Apply the Centerpoint Straight Slot Sketch tool. The Straight Slot Sketch tool provides the ability to sketch a straight slot from a center point. In this example, use the origin as your center point.

143) Click the **Centerpoint Straight Slot** 🔲 tool from the Sketch toolbar. The Slot PropertyManager is displayed.

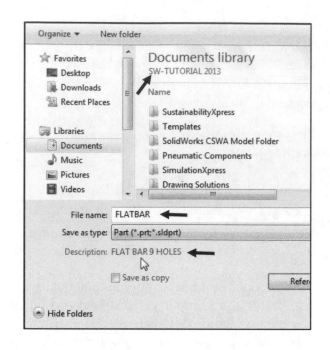

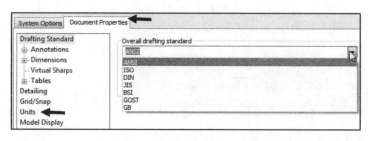

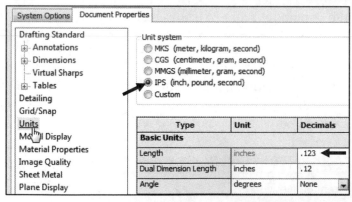

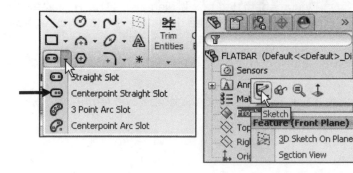

Create the Straight Slot with three points.
144) Click the **Origin**. This is your first point.

145) Click a **point** directly to the right of the Origin. This is your second point.

146) Click a **point** directly above the second point. This is your third point. The Straight Slot is displayed.

147) Click **OK** ✔ from the Slot PropertyManager

View the Sketch relations.
148) Click **View**, **Sketch Relations** from the Menu bar menu. View the sketch relations in the Graphics window.

Deactivate the Sketch relations.
149) Click **View**; uncheck **Sketch Relations** from the Menu bar. The Straight Slot Sketch tool provides a midpoint relation with the Origin and Equal relations between the other sketch entities.

Add a dimension.
150) Click the **Smart Dimension** ✐ tool from the Sketch toolbar.

151) Click the **horizontal centerline**.

152) Click a **position** above the top horizontal line in the Graphics window.

153) Enter **4.000**in, [**101.6**] in the Modify dialog box.

154) Click the **Green Check mark** ✔ in the Modify dialog box.

155) Click the **right arc** of the FLATBAR.

156) Click a **position** diagonally to the right in the Graphics window.

157) Enter **.250**in, [**6.35**] in the Modify dialog box.

158) Click the **Green Check mark** ✔ in the Modify dialog box. The black sketch is fully defined.

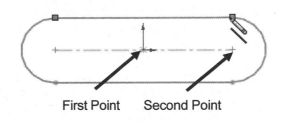

First Point   Second Point

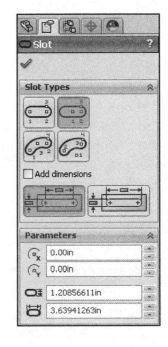

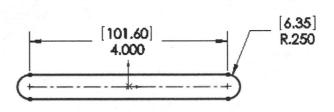

💡 Model about the Origin: This provides a point of reference for your dimensions to fully define the sketch.

💡 It's considered best practice to fully define all sketches in the model. However; there are times when this is not practical. Generally when using the Spline tool to create a freeform shape.

Extrude the sketch to create the Base (Boss-Extrude1) feature.

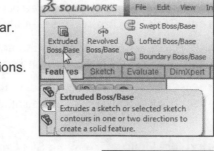

159) Click **Extruded Boss/Base** from the Features toolbar. The Boss-Extrude PropertyManager is displayed.

160) Enter .090in, [**2.29**] for Depth. Accept the default conditions.

161) Click **OK** from the Boss-Extrude PropertyManager. Boss-Extrude1 is displayed in the FeatureManager.

Fit the model to the Graphics window.
162) Press the **f** key.

Save the FLATBAR part.

163) Click **Save** .

Click **View, Origins** from the Menu bar menu to display the Origin in the Graphics window.

Activity: FLATBAR Part-Extruded Cut Feature

Insert a new sketch for the Extruded Cut Feature.
164) Right-click the **front face** of the Boss-Extrude1 feature in the Graphics window. This is the Sketch plane. Boss-Extrude1 is highlighted in the FeatureManager.

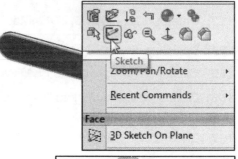

165) Click **Sketch** from the Context toolbar as illustrated. The Sketch toolbar is displayed.

Display the Front view.

166) Click **Front view** from the Heads-up View toolbar.

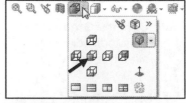

167) Click **Hidden Lines Removed** from the Heads-up View toolbar.

The process of placing the mouse pointer over an existing arc to locate its center point is called "wake up".

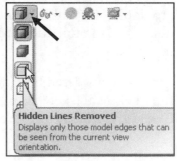

Rename a feature or sketch for clarity. Slowly click the feature or sketch name twice and enter the new name when the old one is highlighted.

Wake up the Center point.

168) Click the **Circle** ⊘ Sketch tool from the Sketch toolbar. The Circle PropertyManager is displayed.

Center point of the arc

169) Place the **mouse pointer** on the left arc. Do not click. The center point of the slot arc is displayed.

170) Click the **center point** of the arc.

171) Click a **position** to the right of the center point to create the circle as illustrated.

Add a dimension.

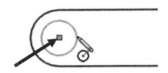

172) Click the **Smart Dimension** ⊘ Sketch tool.

173) Click the **circumference** of the circle.

174) Click a **position** diagonally above and to the left of the circle in the Graphics window.

175) Enter **.190**in, **[4.83]** in the Modify box.

[4.83]
⌀.190

176) Click the **Green Check mark** ✔ in the Modify dialog box.

177) Click **Isometric view** 🔲 from the Heads-up View toolbar.

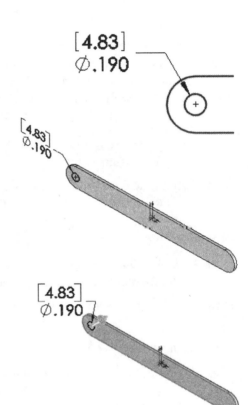

178) Click **Shaded With Edges** 🔲 from the Heads-up View toolbar.

Insert an Extruded Cut feature.

179) Click the **Features** tab from the CommandManager.

180) Click **Extruded Cut** 🔲 from the Features toolbar. The Cut- Extrude PropertyManager is displayed.

181) Select **Through All** for End Condition in Direction 1. The direction arrow points to the back. Accept the default conditions.

182) Click **OK** ✔ from the Cut-Extrude PropertyManager. The Cut-Extrude1 feature is displayed in the FeatureManager.

Save the FLATBAR part.

183) Click **Save** 💾.

💡 Think design intent. When do you use various End Conditions? What are you trying to do with the design? How does the component fit into an Assembly?

The blue Cut-Extrude1 icon indicates that the feature is selected.

Select features by clicking their icons in the FeatureManager or by selecting their geometry in the Graphics window.

When you create a new part or assembly, the three default Planes (Front, Right and Top) are align with specific views. The Plane you select for the Base sketch determines the orientation of the part.

Activity: FLATBAR Part-Linear Pattern Feature

Create a Linear Pattern feature.

184) Click the **Linear Pattern** ⣿ tool from the Features toolbar. The Linear Pattern PropertyManager is displayed. Cut-Extrude1 is displayed in the Features to Pattern box. Note: If Cut-Extrude1 is not displayed, click inside the Features to Pattern box. Click Cut-Extrude1 from the fly-out FeatureManager.

185) Click the **top edge** of the Boss-Extrude1 feature for Direction1 in the Graphics window. Edge<1> is displayed in the Pattern Direction box.

186) Enter **0.5**in, [**12.70**] for Spacing.

187) Enter **9** for Number of Instances. Instances are the number of occurrences of a feature.

188) The Direction arrow points to the right. Click the **Reverse Direction** ⤵ button if required.

189) Check **Geometry Pattern** from the Options box.

190) Click **OK** ✓ from the Linear Pattern PropertyManager. The LPattern1 feature is displayed in the FeatureManager.

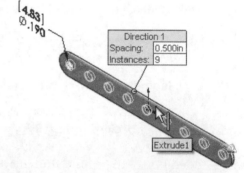

Design Intent is how your part reacts as parameters are modified. Example: If you have a hole in a part that must always be .125≤ from an edge, you would dimension to the edge rather than to another point on the sketch. As the part size is modified, the hole location remains .125≤ from the edge.

Save the FLATBAR part.

191) Click **Save** 🖫 . The FLATBAR part is complete.

Close all documents.
192) Click **Windows, Close All** from the Menu bar.

To remove Tangent edges, click **Display/Selections** from the Options menu, check the **Removed** box.

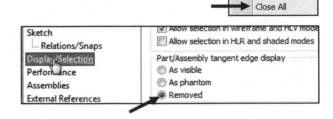

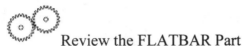

Review the FLATBAR Part

The FLATBAR part utilized an Extruded Boss/Base 🖻 feature as the first feature. The Sketch plane was the Front Plane. The 2D sketch utilized the Straight Slot Sketch tool to create the slot profile.

You added linear and radial dimensions to define your sketch. You applied the Extruded Boss/Base feature with a Blind End Condition in Direction 1. Boss-Extrude1 was created.

You created a circle sketch for the Extruded Cut feature on the front face of Boss-Extrude1. The front face was your Sketch plane for the Extruded Cut feature. The Extruded Cut 🖻 feature removed material to create the hole. The Extruded Cut feature default name was Cut-Extrude1. The Through All End Condition option in Direction 1 created the Cut-Extrude1 feature. The Cut-Extrude1 feature is the seed feature for the Linear Pattern of holes.

The Linear Pattern 🃏 feature created an array of 9 holes, equally spaced along the length of the FLATBAR part.

LINKAGE Assembly

An assembly is a document that contains two or more parts. An assembly inserted into another assembly is called a sub-assembly. A part or sub-assembly inserted into an assembly is called a component. The LINKAGE assembly consists of the following components: AXLE, SHAFT-COLLAR, FLATBAR and AirCylinder sub-assembly.

Establishing the correct component relationship in an assembly requires forethought on component interaction. Mates are geometric relationships that align and fit components in an assembly. Mates remove degrees of freedom from a component.

Mate Types

Mates reflect the physical behavior of a component in an assembly. The components in the LINKAGE assembly utilize Standard mate types. Review *Standard*, *Advanced* and *Mechanical* mate types.

Standard Mates:

Components are assembled with various mate types. The Standard mate types are:

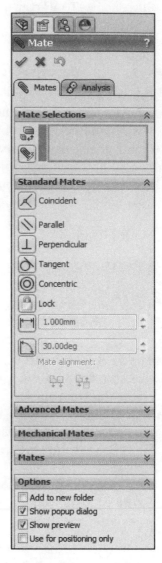

Coincident Mate: Locates the selected faces, edges, or planes so they use the same infinite line. A Coincident mate positions two vertices for contact

Parallel Mate: Locates the selected items to lie in the same direction and to remain a constant distance apart.

Perpendicular Mate: Locates the selected items at a 90 degree angle to each other.

Tangent Mate: Locates the selected items in a tangent mate. At least one selected item must be either a conical, cylindrical, spherical face.

Concentric Mate: Locates the selected items so they can share the same center point.

Lock Mate: Maintains the position and orientation between two components.

Distance Mate: Locates the selected items with a specified distance between them. Use the drop-down arrow box or enter the distance value directly.

Angle Mate: Locates the selected items at the specified angle to each other. Use the drop-down arrow box or enter the angle value directly.

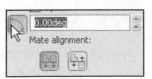

There are two Mate Alignment options. The Aligned option positions the components so that the normal vectors from the selected faces point in the same direction. The Anti-Aligned option positions the components so that the normal vectors from the selected faces point in opposite directions.

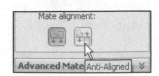

Mates define the allowable degrees of freedom in an assembly. There are six degrees of freedom: 3 translational and 3 rotational.

Advanced Mates:

The Advanced mate types are:

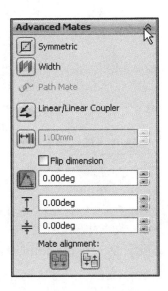

Symmetric Mate: Positions two selected entities to be symmetric about a plane or planar face. A Symmetric Mate does not create a Mirrored Component.

Width Mate: Centers a tab within the width of a groove.

Path Mate: Constrains a selected point on a component to a path.

Linear/Linear Coupler Mate: Establishes a relationship between the translation of one component and the translation of another component.

Distance Mate: Locates the selected items with a specified distance between them. Use the drop-down arrow box or enter the distance value directly.

Angle Mate: Locates the selected items at the specified angle to each other. Use the drop-down arrow box or enter the angle value directly.

Mechanical Mates:

The Mechanical mate types are:

Cam Mate: Forces a plane, cylinder, or point to be tangent or coincident to a series of tangent extruded faces.

Hinge Mate: Limits the movement between two components to one rotational degree of freedom.

Gear Mate: Forces two components to rotate relative to one another around selected axes.

Rack Pinion Mate: Provides the ability to have Linear translation of a part, rack causes circular rotation in another part, pinion, and vice versa.

Screw Mate: Constrains two components to be concentric, and adds a pitch relationship between the rotation of one component and the translation of the other.

Universal Joint Mate: The rotation of one component (the output shaft) about its axis is driven by the rotation of another component (the input shaft) about its axis.

Example: Utilize a Concentric mate between the AXLE cylindrical face and the FLATBAR Extruded Cut feature, (hole). Utilize a Coincident mate between the SHAFT-COLLAR back face and the FLATBAR front flat face.

The LINKAGE assembly requires the AirCylinder assembly. The AirCylinder assembly is located on the SolidWorks Tutorial DVD in the Pneumatic Components folder.

Activity: AirCylinder Assembly-Open and Save As option

Copy the folders and files from the DVD in the book.

193) Minimize the SolidWorks Graphics window.

194) Insert the DVD from the book into your computer. If required, **exit** out of AutoPlay for the Video Instruction.

195) Click **Open folder to view files**. View the available folders.

196) Copy the folders and files from the DVD to your SW-TUTORIAL-2013 folder on the hard drive. If needed create the SW-TUTORIAL-2013 folder on your hard drive.

Return to SolidWorks. Create a new assembly.

197) Maximize the SolidWorks Graphics window.

198) Click **New** ☐ from the Menu bar. The New SolidWorks Document dialog box is displayed. The Templates tab is the default tab.

199) Double-click **Assembly** from the New SolidWorks Document dialog box. The Begin Assembly PropertyManager is displayed.

200) Click the **Browse** button. Browse to the **SW-TUTORIAL-2013/Pneumatic Components** folder. Note: Open models are displayed in the Open documents box.

201) Click the **Filter Assemblies (*.asm;*sldasm)** button in the Open dialog box to view assembly documents.

202) Double-click the **AirCylinder** assembly from the SW-TUTORIAL-2013/Pneumatic Components folder. This is an assembly that you copied from the DVD in the book. The AirCylinder assembly is displayed in the Graphics window.

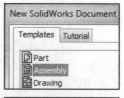

Mate to the first component added to the assembly. If you mate to the first component or base component of the assembly and decide to change its orientation later, all the components will move with it.

Determine the static and dynamic behavior of mates in each sub-assembly before creating the top level assembly.

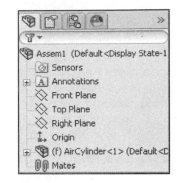

Resolve an Assembly. Right-click the **assembly name** or **component name** from the FeatureManager. Click **Set Lightweight to Resolved**.

203) Click **OK** ✔ from the Begin Assembly PropertyManager to fix the AirCylinder assembly in the Graphics window. The (f) symbol is placed in front of the AirCylinder name in the FeatureManager.

204) If required, click **Yes** to Rebuild.

205) Click **Save As** from the Menu bar.

206) Select **SW-TUTORIAL-2013** for Save in folder.

207) Enter **LINKAGE** for file name.

208) Click the **References** button. An assembly and drawing document has part/component references. You must save the assembly document and all of the reference components to the same folder.

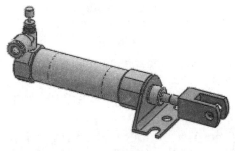

209) Click the **Browse** button from the Specify folder for selected items.

210) Select the **SW-TUTORIAL-2013** folder.

211) Click **OK** from the Browse For Folder dialog box.

212) Click **Save All**. The LINKAGE assembly FeatureManager is displayed.

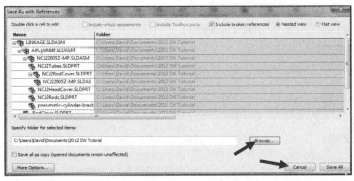

You can also use the Pack and Go option to save an assembly or drawing with references. The Pack and Go tool saves either to a folder or creates a zip file to e-mail. View SolidWorks help for additional information.

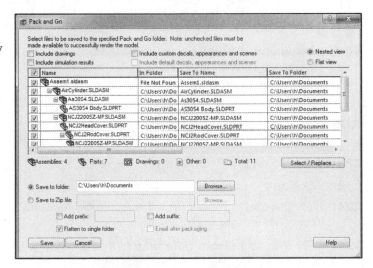

The AirCylinder assembly and its references are copied to the
SW-TUTORIAL-2013 folder. Assemble the AXLE to the
holes in the RodClevis.

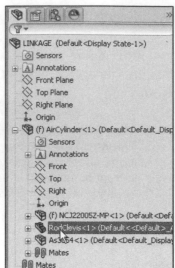

Display the RodClevis component
in the FeatureManager.

213) **Expand** the AirCylinder
assembly in the
FeatureManager.

214) Click **RodClevis<1>** from
the FeatureManager.
Note: The RodClevis is
displayed in blue in the
Graphics window.

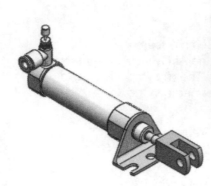

If required hide the Origins.

215) Click **View**; uncheck
Origins from the Menu
bar.

The AirCylinder is the first component in the LINKAGE
assembly and is fixed (f) to the LINKAGE assembly Origin.

Display an Isometric view.

216) Click **Isometric view** 🔲 from the Heads-up View toolbar.

Insert the AXLE part.

217) Click the **Assembly** tab in the CommandManager.

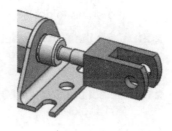

218) Click the **Insert Components** 🔧 Assembly tool. The Insert
Component PropertyManager is displayed.

219) Click the **Browse** button. Browse to the **SW-TUTORIAL-2013**
folder. Note: If AXLE is active, double-click AXLE from the Open
documents box. Skip the next few steps.

220) Click the **Filter Parts (*.prt;*sldprt)**
button in the Open dialog box to view
part documents.

221) Double-click **AXLE** from the SW-
TUTORIAL-2013 folder. Click a
position to the front of the AirCylinder assembly as illustrated.

Move the AXLE component.

222) Click a **position** in front of the RODCLEVIS.

Enlarge the view.

223) **Zoom in** on the RodClevis and the AXLE.

Insert a Concentric mate.

224) Click the **Mate** 📎 tool from the Assembly toolbar. The Mate
PropertyManager is displayed.

225) Click the inside **front hole face** of the RodClevis. The
cursor displays the face feedback symbol.

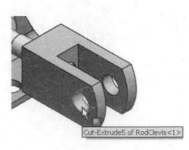

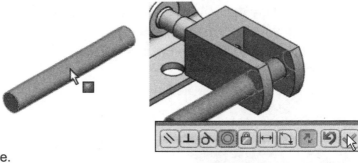

226) Click the **long cylindrical face** of the AXLE. The cursor displays the face feedback symbol. The selected faces are displayed in the Mate Selections box. Concentric mate is selected by default. The AXLE is positioned concentric to the RodClevis hole.

227) Click the **Green Check mark** ✔ as illustrated.

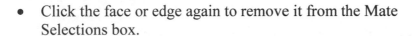

Move the AXLE.

228) Click and drag the **AXLE** left to right. The AXLE translates in and out of the RodClevis holes.

The Mate Pop-up toolbar is displayed after selecting the two cylindrical faces. The Mate Pop-up toolbar minimizes the time required to create a mate.

Lock   Flip Mate Alignment

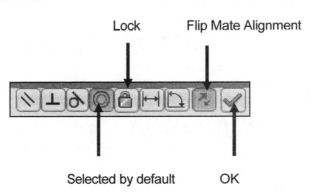

Selected by default   OK

💡 Position the mouse pointer in the middle of the face to select the entire face. Do not position the mouse pointer near the edge of the face. If the wrong face or edge is selected, perform one of the following actions:

- Click the face or edge again to remove it from the Mate Selections box.

- Right-click in the Graphics window. Click Clear Selections to remove all geometry from the Items Selected text box.

- Right-click in the Mate Selections box to either select Clear Selections or to delete a single selection.

- Utilize the Undo button to begin the Mate command again.

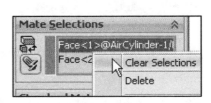

Display the Top view.

229) Click **Top view** ⬜ from the Heads-up View toolbar.

Expand the LINKAGE assembly and components in the fly-out FeatureManager.

230) Expand the LINKAGE assembly from the fly-out FeatureManager.

231) Expand the AirCylinder assembly from the fly-out FeatureManager.

232) Expand the AXLE part from the fly-out FeatureManager.

Clear all sections from the Mate Selections box.

233) If needed, right-click **Clear Selections** inside the Mate Selections box.

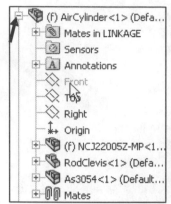
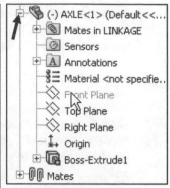

Insert a Coincident mate.

234) Click the **Front Plane** of the AirCylinder assembly from the fly-out FeatureManager.

235) Click the **Front Plane** of the AXLE part from the fly-out FeatureManager. The selected planes are displayed in the Mate Selections box. Coincident mate is selected by default.

236) Click the **Green Check mark** .

237) Click **OK** from the Mate PropertyManager.

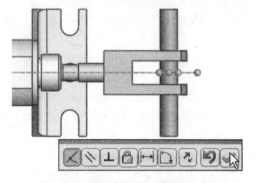

The AirCylinder Front Plane and the AXLE Front Plane are Coincident. The AXLE is centered in the RodClevis.

Display the Mates in the FeatureManager to check that the components and the mate types correspond to the design intent. Note: If you delete a mate and then recreate it, the mate numbers will be in a different order.

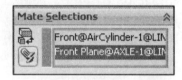

Display an Isometric view.

238) Click **Isometric view** .

Display the Mates in the folder.

239) Expand the Mates folder in the FeatureManager. View the created mates.

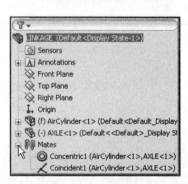

Activity: LINKAGE Assembly-Insert FLATBAR Part

Insert the FLATBAR part.

240) Click the **Insert Components** Assembly tool. The Insert Component PropertyManager is displayed.

241) Click the **Browse** button.

242) Browse to the **SW-TUTORIAL-2013** folder.

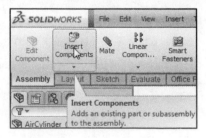

243) Click the **Filter Parts (*.prt;*sldprt)** button in the Open dialog box to view part documents.

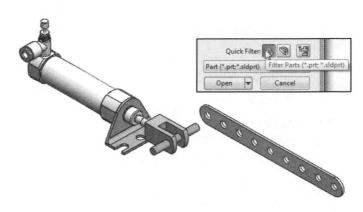

244) Double-click **FLATBAR**.

Place the component in the assembly.

245) Click a **position** in the Graphics window as illustrated. Note: Use the z key to Zoom out if required.

Enlarge the view.

246) Zoom in on the AXLE and the left side of the FLATBAR to enlarge the view.

Insert a Concentric mate.

247) Click the **Mate** ✎ tool from the Assembly toolbar. The Mate PropertyManager is displayed. If required, right-click **Clear Selections** inside the Mate Selections box.

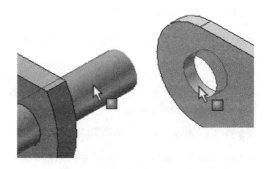

248) Click the inside **left hole face** of the FLATBAR.

249) Click the **long cylindrical face** of the AXLE. The selected faces are displayed in the Mate Selections box. Concentric is selected by default.

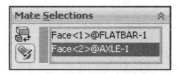

250) Click the **Green Check mark** ✔.

Fit the model to the Graphics window.

251) Press the **f** key.

Move the FLATBAR.

252) Click and drag the **FLATBAR**. The FLATBAR translates and rotates along the AXLE.

Insert a Coincident mate.

253) Click the **front face** of the FLATBAR.

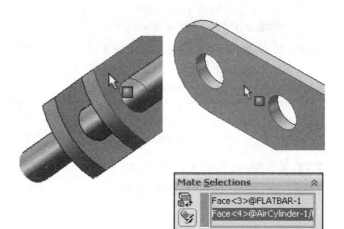

254) Rotate the model view the back face of the RodClevis.

255) Click the **back face** of the RodClevis as illustrated. The selected faces are displayed in the Mate Selections box. Coincident is selected by default.

256) Click the **Green Check mark** ✔ .

257) Click **OK** ✔ from the Mate
PropertyManager.

Display the Isometric view.

258) Click **Isometric view** ⬛ from the
Heads-up View toolbar.

Insert the second FLATBAR component.

259) Click the **Insert Components** 🐾
Assembly tool. The Insert Component
PropertyManager is displayed.

260) Click the **Browse** button.

261) Browse to the **SW-TUTORIAL-2013**
folder.

262) Click the **Filter Parts (*.prt;*sldprt)**
button in the Open dialog box to view
part documents.

263) Double-click **FLATBAR**.

264) Click a **position** to the front of the
AirCylinder in the Graphics window as
illustrated.

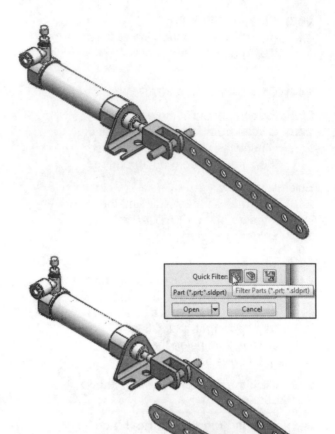

Enlarge the view.
265) **Zoom in** on the second FLATBAR
and the AXLE.

Insert a Concentric mate.

266) Click the **Mate** 🖇 tool from the
Assembly tool. The Mate
PropertyManager is displayed.

267) Click the **left inside hole face** of the
second FLATBAR.

268) Click the **long cylindrical face** of the
AXLE. The selected faces are
displayed in the Mate Selections box.
Concentric is selected by default.

269) Click the **Green Check mark** ✔ .

270) Click and drag the **second
FLATBAR** to the front.

Fit the model to the Graphics window.
271) Press the **f** key.

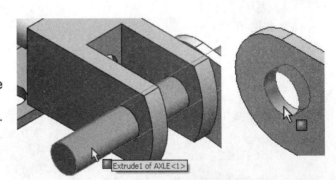

Insert a Coincident mate.

272) Press the **left arrow key** approximately 5 times to rotate the model to view the back face of the second FLATBAR.

273) Click the **back face** of the second FLATBAR.

274) Press the **right arrow key** approximately 5 times to rotate the model to view the front face of the RodClevis.

275) Click the **front face** of the RodClevis. The selected faces are displayed in the Mate Selections box. Coincident is selected by default.

276) Click the **Green Check mark** ✓ .

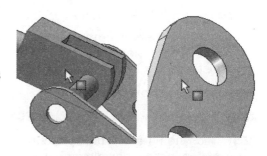

Insert a Parallel mate.

277) Press the **Shift-z** keys to Zoom in on the model.

278) Click the **top narrow face** of the first FLATBAR.

279) Click the **top narrow face** of the second FLATBAR. The selected faces are displayed in the Mate Selections box.

280) Click **Parallel** ⟍ .

281) Click the **Green Check mark** ✓ .

282) Click **OK** ✓ from the Mate PropertyManager.

283) Click **Isometric view** 🔲 from the Heads-up View toolbar.

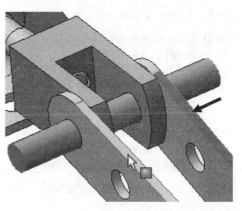

Move the two FLATBAR parts.

284) Click and drag the **second FLATBAR**. Both FLATBAR parts move together.

View the Mates folder.

285) **Expand** the Mates folder from the FeatureManager. View the created mates.

 Determine the static and dynamic behavior of mates in each sub-assembly before creating the top level assembly.

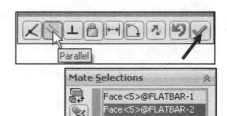

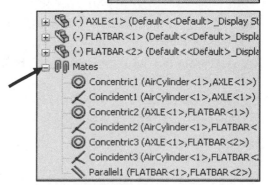

Activity: LINKAGE Assembly-Insert SHAFT-COLLAR Part

Insert the first SHAFT-COLLAR.

286) Click the **Insert Components** Assembly tool. The Insert Component PropertyManager is displayed.

287) Click the **Browse** button.

288) Browse to the **SW-TUTORIAL-2013** folder.

289) Click the **Filter Parts (*.prt;*sldprt)** button in the Open dialog box to view part documents.

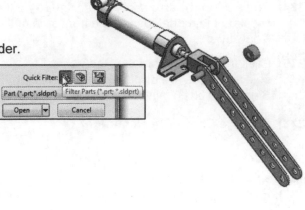

290) Double-click **SHAFT-COLLAR**.

291) Click a **position** to the back of the AXLE as illustrated.

Enlarge the view.

292) Click the **Zoom to Area** tool.

293) **Zoom-in** on the SHAFT-COLLAR and the AXLE component.

Deactivate the tool.

294) Click the **Zoom to Area** tool.

Insert a Concentric mate.

295) Click the **Mate** tool from the Assembly toolbar. The Mate PropertyManager is displayed.

296) Click the **inside hole face** of the SHAFT-COLLAR.

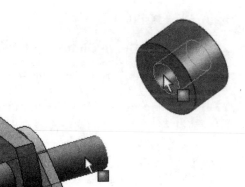

297) Click the **long cylindrical face** of the AXLE. The selected faces are displayed in the Mate Selections box. Concentric is selected by default.

298) Click the **Green Check mark** .

Insert a Coincident mate.

299) Press the **Shift-z** keys to Zoom in on the model.

300) Click the **front face** of the SHAFT-COLLAR as illustrated.

301) **Rotate** the model to view the back face of the first FLATBAR.

302) Click the **back face** of the first FLATBAR. The selected faces are displayed in the Mate Selections box. Coincident is selected by default.

303) Click the **Green Check mark** ✅.

304) Click **OK** ✅ from the Mate PropertyManager.

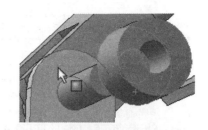

Display the Isometric view.

305) Click **Isometric view** 🧊 from the Heads-up View toolbar.

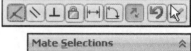

Insert the second SHAFT-COLLAR.

306) Click the **Insert Components** 🖾 Assembly tool. The Insert Component PropertyManager is displayed.

307) Click the **Browse** button.

308) Browse to the **SW-TUTORIAL-2013** folder.

309) Click the **Filter Parts (*.prt;*sldprt)** button in the Open dialog box to view part documents.

310) Double-click **SHAFT-COLLAR**.

311) Click a **position** near the AXLE as illustrated.

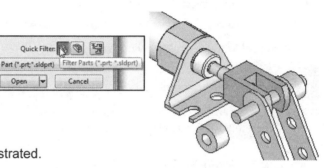

Enlarge the view.

312) Click the **Zoom to Area** 🔍 tool.

313) **Zoom-in** on the second SHAFT-COLLAR and the AXLE to enlarge the view.

314) Click the **Zoom to Area** 🔍 tool to deactivate the tool.

Insert a Concentric mate.

315) Click **Mate** 🖉 from the Assembly toolbar. The Mate PropertyManager is displayed.

316) Click the **inside hole face** of the second SHAFT-COLLAR.

317) Click the **long cylindrical face** of the AXLE. Concentric is selected by default. The selected faces are displayed in the Mate Selections box.

318) Click the **Green Check mark** ✅.

Insert a Coincident mate.

319) Click the **back face** of the second SHAFT-COLLAR.

320) Click the **front face** of the second FLATBAR. The selected faces are displayed in the Mate Selections box. Coincident is selected by default.

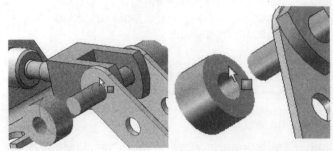

321) Click the **Green Check mark** .

322) Click **OK** ✔ from the Mate PropertyManager.

323) **Expand** the Mates folder. View the created mates.

Display an Isometric view.

324) Click **Isometric view** 📦 from the Heads-up View toolbar.

Fit the model to the Graphics window.

325) Press the **f** key.

Save the LINKAGE assembly.

326) Click **Save** 💾. Click **Rebuild and Save** the document. The LINKAGE assembly is complete.

💡 Use the Pack and Go option to save an assembly or drawing with references. The Pack and Go tool saves either to a folder or creates a zip file to e-mail. View SolidWorks help for additional information.

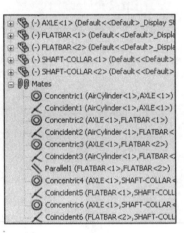

 Review the LINKAGE Assembly

An assembly is a document that contains two or more parts. A part or sub-assembly inserted into an assembly is called a component. You created the LINKAGE assembly. The AirCylinder sub-assembly was the first component inserted into the LINKAGE assembly. The AirCylinder assembly was obtained from the DVD in the book and copied to the SW-TUTORIAL-2013 folder.

The AirCylinder assembly was fixed to the Origin. The Concentric and Coincident mates added Geometric relationships between the inserted components in the LINKAGE assembly.

To remove the fixed state, Right-click a component name in the FeatureManager. Click Float. The component is free to move.

The AXLE part was the second component inserted into the LINKAGE assembly. The AXLE required a Concentric mate between the two cylindrical faces and a Coincident mate between two the Front Planes.

The FLATBAR part was the third component inserted into the LINKAGE assembly. The FLATBAR required a Concentric mate between the two cylindrical faces and a Coincident mate between the two flat faces.

A second FLATBAR was inserted into the LINKAGE assembly. A Parallel mate was added between the two FLATBARs.

Two SHAFT-COLLAR parts were inserted into the LINKAGE assembly. Each SHAFT-COLLAR required a Concentric mate between the two cylindrical faces and a Coincident mate between the two flat faces.

Motion Study - Basic Motion Tool

Motion Studies are graphical simulations of motion for assembly models. You can incorporate visual properties such as lighting and camera perspective into a motion study. Motion studies do not change an assembly model or its properties. They simulate and animate the motion you prescribe for your model. Use SolidWorks mates to restrict the motion of components in an assembly when you model motion.

Create a Motion Study. Select the Basic Motion option from the MotionManager. The Basic Motion option provides the ability to approximate the effects of motors, springs, collisions and gravity on your assembly. Basic Motion takes mass into account in calculating motion. Note: The Animation option does not!

Activity: LINKAGE Assembly-Basic Motion

Insert a Rotary Motor using the Motion Study tab.

327) Click the **Motion Study 1** tab located in the bottom left corner of the Graphics window. The MotionManager is displayed.

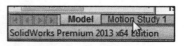

328) Select **Basic Motion** for Type of study from the MotionManager drop-down menu as illustrated.

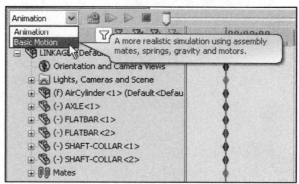

329) Click **Motor** 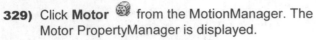 from the MotionManager. The Motor PropertyManager is displayed.

330) Click the **Rotary Motor** box.

331) Click the **FLATBAR front face** as illustrated. A red Rotary Motor icon is displayed. The red direction arrow points counterclockwise.

332) Enter **150 RPM** for speed in the Motion box.

333) Click **OK** ✔ from the Motor PropertyManager.

Record the Simulation.

334) Click **Calculate** . The FLATBAR rotates in a counterclockwise direction for a set period of time.

335) Click **Play** ▷. View the simulation.

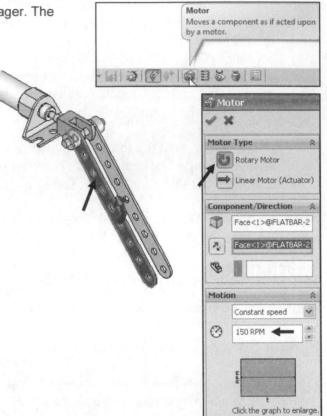

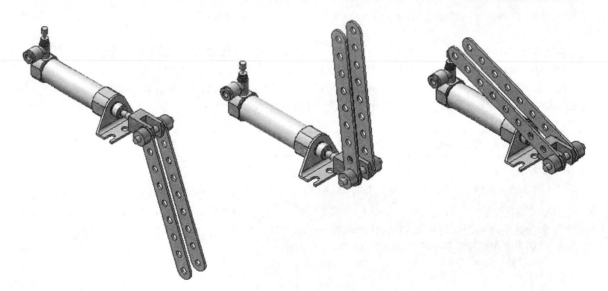

LINKAGE Assembly Basic Simulation

Save the simulation in an AVI file to the SW-TUTORIAL-2013 folder.

336) Click **Save Animation**.

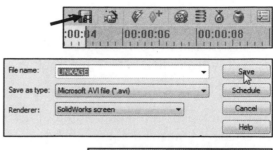

337) Click **Save** from the Save Animation to File dialog box. View your options.

338) Click **OK** from the Video Compression box.

Close the Motion Study and return to SolidWorks.

339) Click the **Model** tab location in the bottom left corner of the Graphics window.

Fit the assembly to the Graphics window.

340) Press the **f** key.

Save the LINKAGE assembly.

341) Click **Save** 💾.

Exit SolidWorks.

342) Click **Windows**, **Close All** from the Menu bar.

The LINKAGE assembly chapter is complete.

🔆 Rename a feature or sketch for clarity. Slowly click the feature or sketch name twice and enter the new name when the old one is highlighted.

🔆 Use the Pack and Go option to save an assembly or drawing with references. The Pack and Go tool saves either to a folder or creates a zip file to e-mail. View SolidWorks help for additional information.

Review the Motion Study

The Rotary Motor Basic Motion tool combined Mates and Physical Dynamics to rotate the FLATBAR components in the LINKAGE assembly. The Rotary Motor was applied to the front face of the FLATBAR. You utilized the Calculate option to play the simulation. You saved the simulation in an .AVI file.

🔍 Additional details on Motion Study, Assembly, mates, and Simulation are available in SolidWorks help. Keywords: Motion Study and Basic Motion.

Chapter Summary

In this chapter, you created three parts (AXLE, SHAFT-COLLAR and FLATBAR), copied the AirCylinder assembly from the DVD in the book and created the LINKAGE assembly.

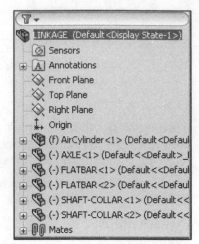

You developed an understanding of the SolidWorks User Interface: Menus, Toolbars, Task Pane, CommandManager, FeatureManager, System feedback icons, Document Properties, Parts and Assemblies.

You created 2D sketches and addressed the three key states of a sketch: *Fully Defined*, *Over Defined* and *Under Defined*. Note: Always review your FeatureManager for the proper sketch state.

You obtained the knowledge of the following SolidWorks features: Extruded Boss/Base, Extruded Cut, and Linear Pattern. Features are the building blocks of parts. The Extruded Boss/Base feature required a Sketch plane, sketch, and depth.

The Extruded Boss/Base feature added material to a part. The Boss-Extruded1 feature was utilized in the AXLE, SHAFT-COLLAR and FLATBAR parts.

The Extruded Cut feature removed material from the part. The Extruded Cut feature was utilized to create a hole in the SHAFT-COLLAR and FLATBAR parts. Note: Both were Through All holes. We will address the Hole Wizard later in the book.

The Linear Pattern feature was utilized to create an array of holes in the FLATBAR part.

When parts are inserted into an assembly, they are called components. You created the LINKAGE assembly by inserting the AirCylinder assembly, AXLE, SHAFT-COLLAR and FLATBAR parts.

Mates are geometric relationships that align and fit components in an assembly. Concentric, Coincident and Parallel mates were utilized to assemble the components.

You created a Motion Study. The Rotary Motor Basic Motion tool combined Mates and Physical Dynamics to rotate the FLATBAR components in the LINKAGE assembly.

During the initial SolidWorks installation, you are requested to select either the ISO or ANSI drafting standard. ISO is typically an European drafting standard and uses First Angle Projection. The book is written using the ANSI (US) overall drafting standard and Third Angle Projection for drawings.

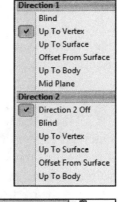

You can right-click anywhere on an extruded feature and change the end condition from a shortcut menu. You can click in empty space, on geometry, or on the handle. The shortcut menu provides options for Direction 1 and Direction 2. Note: Options are document dependent.

For many features; (Extruded Boss/ Base, Extruded Cut, Simple Hole, Revolved Boss/Base, Revolved Cut, Fillet, Chamfer, Scale, Shell, Rib, Circular Pattern, Linear Pattern, Curve Driven Pattern, Revolved Surface, Extruded Surface, Fillet Surface, Edge Flange and Base Flange) you can enter and modify equations directly in the PropertyManager fields that allow numerical inputs.

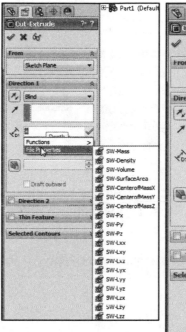
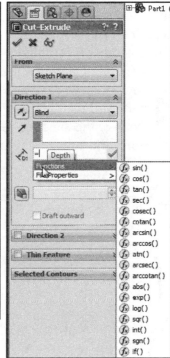

Create equations with global variables, functions, and file properties without accessing the Equations, Global Variables and Dimensions dialog box.

For example, in the Extruded Cut PropertyManager you can enter equations in:

- Depth fields for Direction 1 and Direction 2

- Draft fields for Direction 1 and Direction 2

- Thickness fields for a Thin Feature with two direction types

- Offset Distance field

To create an equation in a numeric input field, start by entering = (equal sign). A drop-down list displays options for global variables, functions, and file properties. Numeric input fields that contain equations can display either the equation itself or its evaluated value.

Click the What's new ![icon] icon in the PropertyManager to learn what's new about a feature or option.

Design Intent is how your part reacts as parameters are modified. Example: If you have a hole in a part that must always be .125≤ from an edge, you would dimension to the edge rather than to another point on the sketch. As the part size is modified, the hole location remains .125≤ from the edge.

The Instance to Vary option in the Linear Pattern PropertyManager allows you to vary the dimensions and locations of instances in a feature pattern *after it is created*. You can vary the dimensions of a series of instances, so that each instance is larger or smaller than the previous one. You can also change the dimensions of a single instance in a pattern and change the position of that instance relative to the seed feature of the pattern. For linear patterns, you can change the spacing between the columns and rows in the pattern.

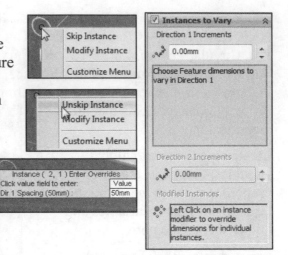

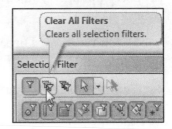

To display the Selection Filter toolbar, click **View**, **Toolbars**, **Selection Filter**. The Selection Filter is displayed.

To clear a Filter icon , click **Clear All Filters** from the Selection Filter toolbar.

Chapter Terminology

Utilize SolidWorks Help for additional information on the terms utilized in this chapter.

Assembly: An assembly is a document which contains parts, features, and other sub-assemblies. When a part is inserted into an assembly it is called a component. Components are mated together. The filename extension for a SolidWorks assembly file name is .SLDASM.

Component: A part or sub-assembly within an assembly.

Cursor Feedback: Feedback is provided by a symbol attached to the cursor arrow indicating your selection. As the cursor floats across the model, feedback is provided in the form of symbols, riding next to the cursor.

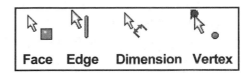

Dimension: A value indicating the size of feature geometry.

Drafting Standard: A set of drawing and detailing options developed by national and international organizations. The Dimensioning standard options are: ANSI, ISO, DIN, JIS, BSI, GOST and GB.

Features: Features are geometry building blocks. Features add or remove material. Features are created from sketched profiles or from edges and faces of existing geometry.

Instance Number: The instance number increments every time you insert the same component or mate. If you delete a component or mate and then reinsert the component or mate in the same SolidWorks session, the instance number increments by one.

Mates: A mate is a geometric relationship between components in an assembly.

Mouse Buttons: The left and right mouse buttons have distinct meanings in SolidWorks. Left mouse button is utilized to select geometry. Right-mouse button is utilized to invoke commands.

Part: A part is a single 3D object made up of features. The filename extension for a SolidWorks part file name is .SLDPRT.

Plane: To create a sketch, select a plane. Planes are flat and infinite. They are represented on the screen with visible edges. The reference plane for this project is the Front Plane.

Relation: A relation is a geometric constraint between sketch entities or between a sketch entity and a plane, axis, edge, or vertex.

Sketch: The name to describe a 2D profile is called a sketch. 2D Sketches are created on flat faces and planes within the model. Typical geometry types are lines, arcs, rectangles, circles, polygons and ellipses.

Status of a Sketch: Three states are utilized in this chapter: *Fully Defined*: Has complete information (dimensions and geometric relations) displayed in black, *Over Defined*: Has duplicate (dimensions or geometric relations) displayed in Red/Yellow or *Under Defined*: There is inadequate definition (dimensions or geometric relations) displayed in Blue and black.

Toolbars: The toolbar menus provide shortcuts enabling you to quickly access the most frequently used commands.

Trim Entities: Deletes selected sketched geometry. Extends a sketch segment unit it is coincident with another entity.

Units: Used in the measurement of physical quantities. Millimeter dimensioning and decimal inch dimensioning are the two types of common units specified for engineering parts and drawings.

Questions

1. Explain the steps in starting a SolidWorks session.

2. Describe the procedure to begin a new 2D sketch.

3. Explain the steps required to modify units in a part document from inches to millimeters.

4. Describe the procedure to create a simple 3D part with an Extruded Boss/Base (Boss-Extrude1) feature.

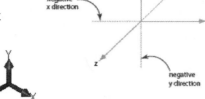

5. Identify the three default Reference planes in SolidWorks.

6. Describe a Base feature? Provide two examples from this chapter.

7. Describe the differences between an Extruded Boss/Base feature and an Extruded Cut feature.

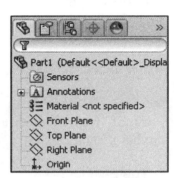

8. The sketch color black indicates a sketch is _____ defined.

9. The sketch color blue indicates a sketch is _____ defined.

10. The sketch color red indicates a sketch is _____ defined.

11. Describe the procedure to "wake up" a center point in a sketch.

12. Define a Geometric relation. Provide three examples.

13. Describe the procedure to create a Linear Pattern feature.

14. Describe an assembly or sub-assembly.

15. What are mates and why are they important in assembling components?

16. In an assembly, each component has_____ # degrees of freedom? Name them.

17. True or False. A fixed component cannot move in an assembly.

18. Review the Design Intent section in the book. Identify how you incorporated design intent into a part or assembly document.

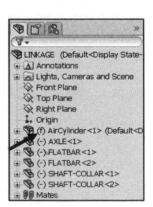

Exercises

Exercise 1.1: Identify the Sketch plane for the Boss-Extrude1 (Base) feature as illustrated. Simplify the number of features!

A: Top Plane

B: Front Plane

C: Right Plane

D: Left Plane

Correct answer _____.

Create the part. Dimensions are arbitrary.

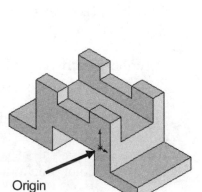

Exercise 1.2: Identify the Sketch plane for the Boss-Extrude1 (Base) feature as illustrated. Simplify the number of features!

A: Top Plane

B: Front Plane

C: Right Plane

D: Left Plane

Correct answer _____.

Create the part. Dimensions are arbitrary.

Exercise 1.3: Identify the Sketch plane for the Boss-Extrude1 (Base) feature as illustrated. Simplify the number of features!

A: Top Plane

B: Front Plane

C: Right Plane

D: Left Plane

Correct answer _____.

Create the part. Dimensions are arbitrary.

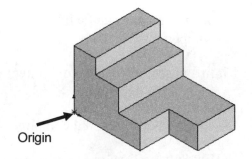

Exercise 1.4: FLATBAR - 3HOLE Part

Create an ANSI, IPS FLATBAR - 3HOLE part document.

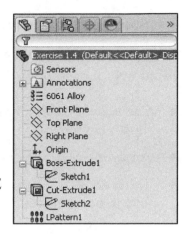

- Utilize the Front Plane for the Sketch plane. Insert an Extruded Base (Boss-Extrude1) feature. No Tangent Edges displayed.

- Create an Extruded Cut feature. This is your seed feature. Apply the Linear Pattern feature. The FLATBAR - 3HOLE part is manufactured from 0.06in., [1.5mm] 6061 Alloy.

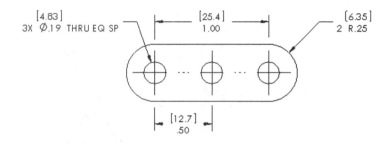

Exercise 1.5: FLATBAR - 5HOLE Part

Create an ANSI, IPS, FLATBAR - 5HOLE part as illustrated.

- Utilize the Front Plane for the Sketch plane. Insert an Extruded Base (Boss-Extrude1) feature.

- Create an Extruded Cut feature. This is your seed feature. Apply the Linear Pattern feature. The FLATBAR - 5HOLE part is manufactured from 0.06in, [1.5mm] 6061 Alloy.

- Calculate the required dimensions for the FLATBAR - 5HOLE part. Use the following information: Holes are .500in. on center, Radius is .250in., and Hole diameter is .190in.

- No Tangent edges displayed.

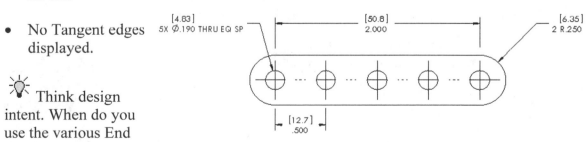

⚡ Think design intent. When do you use the various End Conditions and Geometric sketch relations? What are you trying to do with the design? How does the component fit into an Assembly?

Exercise 1.6: Simple Block Part

Create the illustrated ANSI part. Note the location of the Origin in the illustration.

- Calculate the overall mass of the illustrated model.

- Apply the Mass Properties tool.

- Think about the steps that you would take to build the model.

- Review the provided information carefully.

- Units are represented in the IPS, (inch, pound, second) system.

- A = 3.50in, B = .70in

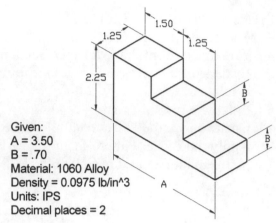

Given:
A = 3.50
B = .70
Material: 1060 Alloy
Density = 0.0975 lb/in^3
Units: IPS
Decimal places = 2

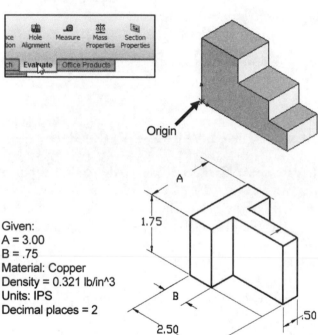

Origin

Exercise 1.7: Simple Block Part

Create the illustrated ANSI part. Note the location of the Origin in the illustration.

Create the sketch symmetric about the Front Plane. The Front Plane in this problem is **not** your Sketch Plane. Utilize the Blind End Condition in Direction 1.

Given:
A = 3.00
B = .75
Material: Copper
Density = 0.321 lb/in^3
Units: IPS
Decimal places = 2

- Calculate the overall mass of the illustrated model.

- Apply the Mass Properties tool.

- Think about the steps that you would take to build the model.

- Review the provided information carefully. Units are represented in the IPS, (inch, pound, second) system.

- A = 3.00in, B = .75in

Note: Sketch1 is symmetrical.

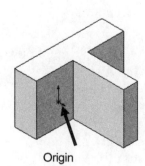

Origin

Exercise 1.8: Simple Block Part

Create an ANSI part from the illustrated model. Note the location of the Origin in the illustration.

- Calculate the volume of the part and locate the Center of mass with the provided information.

- Apply the Mass Properties tool.

- Think about the steps that you would take to build the model.

- Review the provided information carefully.

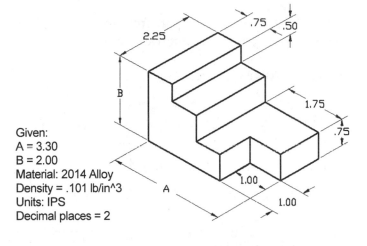

Given:
A = 3.30
B = 2.00
Material: 2014 Alloy
Density = .101 lb/in^3
Units: IPS
Decimal places = 2

Exercise 1.9: Simple Block Part

Create an ANSI, MMGS part from the illustrated drawing: Front, Top, Right and Isometric views.

Note: The location of the Origin in the illustration. The drawing views are displayed in Third Angle Projection.

- Apply 1060 Alloy for material.

- Calculate the Volume of the part.

- Locate the Center of mass.

Think about the steps that you would take to build the model. The part is symmetric about the Front Plane.

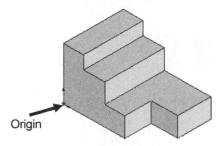

Origin

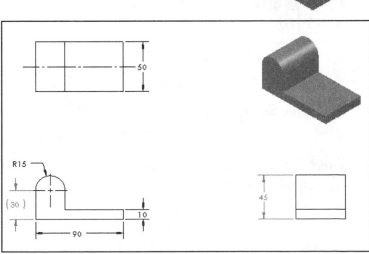

Origin

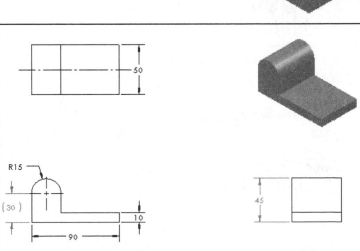

Exercise 1.10: Simple Block Part

Create the ANSI, MMGS part from the illustrated drawing: Front, Top, Right and Isometric views.

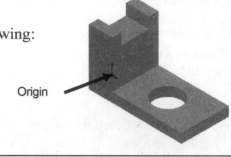

Origin

- Apply 1060 Alloy for material.

- The part is symmetric about the Front Plane.

- Calculate the Volume of the part and locate the Center of mass.

Think about the steps that you would take to build the model.

The drawing views are displayed in Third Angle Projection.

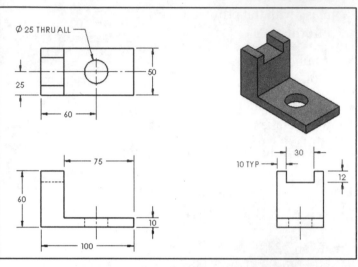

Exercise 1.11: LINKAGE-2 Assembly

Create the LINKAGE-2 assembly.

- Open the LINKAGE assembly from the Chapter 1 homework folder on the DVD in the book. If required, set the LINKAGE assembly to (**Lightweight to Resolved**).

- Select Save As from the drop-down Menu bar.

- Check the Save as copy check box.

- Enter LINKAGE-2 for file name. LINKAGE-2 ASSEMBLY for description.

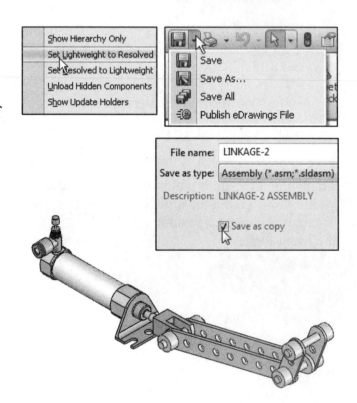

The FLATBAR-3HOLE part was created in
Exercise 1.4. Utilize two AXLE parts, four SHAFT
COLLAR parts, and two FLATBAR-3HOLE parts
to create the LINKAGE-2 assembly as illustrated.

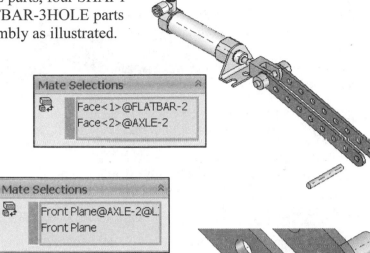

- Insert the first AXLE part.

- Insert a Concentric mate.

Insert a Coincident mate.

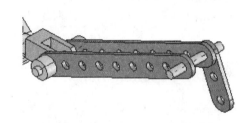

- Insert the first
  FLATBAR-3HOLE
  part.

- Insert a Concentric mate.

- Insert a Coincident mate.

- Perform the same procedure for the second
  FLATBAR-3HOLE part.

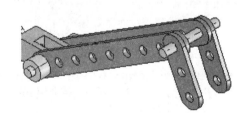

- Insert a Parallel mate between the 2 FLATBAR-
  3HOLE parts. Note: The 2 FLATBAR-3HOLE
  parts move together.

🔆 When a component is in the Lightweight
state, only a subset of its model data is loaded in
memory. The remaining model data is loaded on an
as-needed basis.

🔆 When a component is *fully resolved*, all its
model data is loaded in memory.

- Insert the
  second AXLE
  part.

- Insert a
  Concentric
  mate.

- Insert a
  Coincident mate.

- Insert the first SHAFT-COLLAR part.

- Insert a Concentric mate.

- Insert a Coincident mate.

- Perform the same tasks to
  insert the other three
  required SHAFT-
  COLLAR parts as
  illustrated.

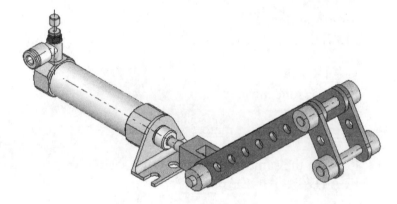

Exercise 1.12: LINKAGE-2 Assembly Motion Study

Create a Motion Study using
the LINKAGE-2 Assembly that was
created in the previous exercise.

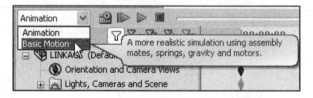

- Create a Basic Motion Study.

- Apply a Rotary Motor to the front
  FLATBAR-3HOLE as illustrated.

- Play and Save the Simulation.

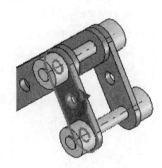

Exercise 1.13: ROCKER Assembly

Create a ROCKER assembly. The ROCKER assembly consists of two AXLE parts, two FLATBAR-5HOLE parts, and two FLATBAR-3HOLE parts.

The FLATBAR-3HOLE parts are linked together with the FLATBAR-5HOLE.

The three parts rotate clockwise and counterclockwise, above the Top Plane. Create the ROCKER assembly.

- Insert the first FLATBAR-5HOLE part. The FLATBAR-5HOLE is fixed to the Origin of the ROCKER assembly.

- Insert the first AXLE part.

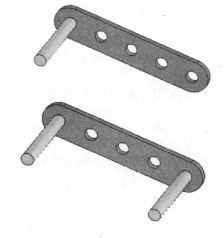

- Insert a Concentric mate.

- Insert a Coincident mate.

- Insert the second AXLE part.

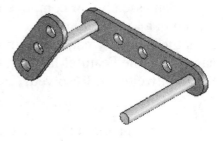

- Insert a Concentric mate.

- Insert a Coincident mate.

- Insert the first FLATBAR-3HOLE part.

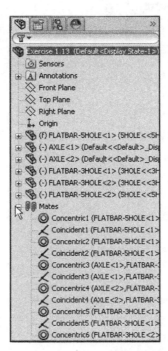

- Insert a Concentric mate.

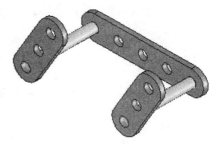

- Insert a Coincident mate.

- Insert the second FLATBAR-3HOLE part.

- Insert a Concentric mate.

- Insert a Coincident mate.

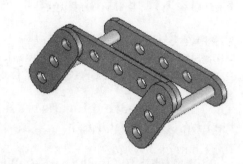

- Insert the second FLATBAR-5HOLE part.

- Insert the required mates.

Note: The end holes of the second FLATBAR-5HOLE are concentric with the end holes of the FLATBAR-3HOLE parts.

Note: In mechanical design, the ROCKER assembly is classified as a mechanism. A Four-Bar Linkage is a common mechanism comprised of four links.

Link1 is called the Frame.

The AXLE part is Link1.

Link2 and Link4 are called the Cranks.

The FLATBAR-3HOLE parts are Link2 and Link4. Link3 is called the Coupler. The FLATBAR-5HOLE part is Link3.

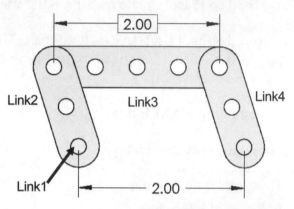

If an assembly or component is loaded in a Lightweight state, right-click the assembly name or component name from the FeatureManager. Click Set Lightweight to Resolved.

Determine the static and dynamic behavior of mates in each sub-assembly before creating the top level assembly.

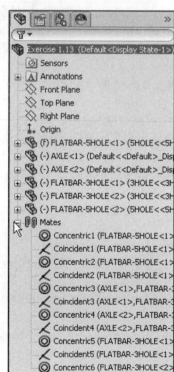

Exercise 1.14: 4 Bar linkage

Create the 4 bar linkage assembly as illustrated. Create the five components as illustrated. Assume dimensions. You are the designer.

View the avi file for required movement in the Chapter 1 homework folder on the DVD in the book.

In an assembly, fix (f) the first component to the origin or fully define it to three reference planes.

Insert all needed mates to simulate the movement of the 4 bar linkage assembly.

Read the section on Coincident, Concentric and Distance mates in SolidWorks help and in the SolidWorks 2013 Tutorial book.

Create a base with text for extra credit.

Below are sample models from my Freshman Engineering class.

Note the different designs to maintain the proper movement of the 4 bar linkage using a base.

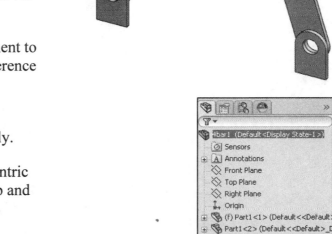

Notes:

Chapter 2

FRONT-SUPPORT Assembly

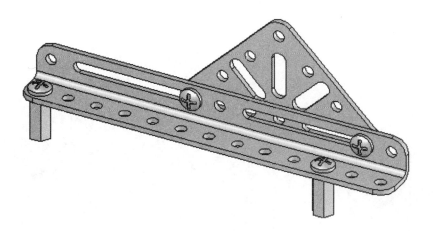

Below are the desired outcomes and usage competencies based on the completion of Chapter 2.

Desired Outcomes:	**Usage Competencies**:

• Create four parts:
 	
   o HEX-STANDOFF
 	
   o ANGLE-13HOLE
 	
   o TRIANGLE
 	
   o SCREW
	• Apply the following model features: Extruded Boss/Base, Extruded Thin, Extruded Cut, Revolved Boss/Base, Hole Wizard, Linear Pattern, Circular Pattern, Mirror, Fillet and Chamfer.
	
	• Apply sketch techniques with various sketch tools and Construction geometry.

• Create an assembly: o FRONT-SUPPORT assembly	• Comprehend the assembly process and insert the following Standard mate types: Concentric, Coincident, Parallel and Distance.

Notes:

Chapter 2 - FRONT-SUPPORT Assembly

Chapter Objective

Create four new parts utilizing the Top, Front and Right Planes. Determine the Sketch plane for each feature. Obtain the knowledge of the following SolidWorks features: *Extruded Boss/Base, Extruded Thin, Extruded Cut, Revolved Boss/Base, Hole Wizard, Linear Pattern, Circular Pattern, Fillet and Chamfer.*

Apply sketch techniques with various Sketch tools: *Line, Circle, Corner Rectangle, Centerline, Dynamic Mirror, Straight Slot, Trim Entities, Polygon, Tangent Arc, Sketch Fillet, Offset Entities and Convert Entities.*

Utilize centerlines as construction geometry to reference dimensions and relationships.

Create four new parts:

1. HEX-STANDOFF
2. ANGLE-13HOLE
3. TRIANGLE
4. SCREW

Create the FRONT-SUPPORT assembly.

On the completion of this chapter, you will be able to:

- Select the correct Sketch plane.
- Generate a 2D sketch.
- Insert the required dimensions and Geometric relations.
- Apply the following SolidWorks features:
  - Extruded Boss/Base
  - Extruded Cut
  - Extruded Thin
  - Revolved Base
  - Linear and Circular Pattern
  - Mirror
  - Fillet
  - Hole Wizard
  - Chamfer

Chapter Overview

The FRONT-SUPPORT assembly supports various pneumatic components and is incorporated into the PNEUMATIC-TEST-MODULE.

Create four new parts in this chapter:

1. HEX-STANDOFF

2. ANGLE-13HOLE

3. TRIANGLE

4. SCREW

Create the FRONT-SUPPORT assembly using the four new created parts.

The FRONT-SUPPORT assembly is used in the exercises at the end of this chapter and in later chapters of the book.

HEX-STANDOFF

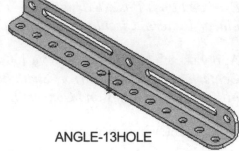

ANGLE-13HOLE

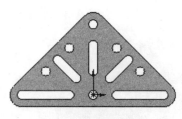

TRIANGLE

SCREW

To display the Origin, click **View**, **Origins** from the Menu bar menu.

Think design intent. When do you use the various End Conditions and Geometric sketch relations? What are you trying to do with the design? How does the component fit into an assembly?

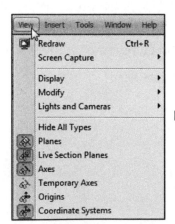

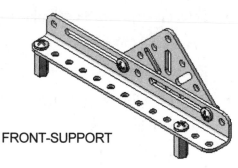

FRONT-SUPPORT

Reference Planes and Orthographic Projection

The three default ⊥ Reference planes represent infinite 2D planes in 3D space:

- Front
- Top
- Right

Planes have no thickness or mass.

Orthographic projection is the process of projecting views onto parallel planes with ⊥ projectors.

The default ⊥ datum planes are:

- Primary
- Secondary
- Tertiary

These are the planes used in manufacturing:

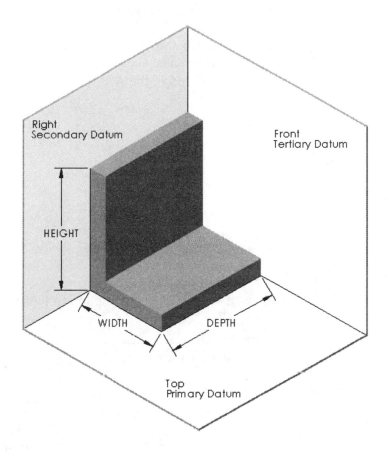

- Primary datum plane contacts the part at a minimum of three points.
- Secondary datum plane contacts the part at a minimum of two points.
- Tertiary datum plane contacts the part at a minimum of one point.

The part view orientation depends on the Base feature Sketch plane.

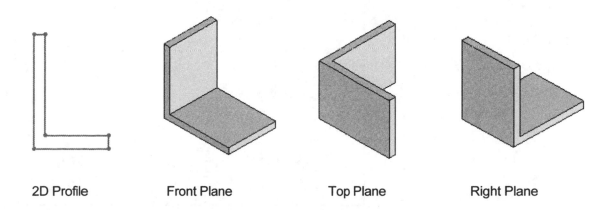

2D Profile   Front Plane   Top Plane   Right Plane

The part view orientation is dependent on the Base feature Sketch plane. Compare the available default Sketch planes in the FeatureManager: *Front, Top and Right Plane*.

Each Boss-Extrude1 feature above was created with an L-shaped 2D Sketch profile. The six principle views of Orthographic projection listed in the ASME Y14.3M standard are:

- Top
- Front
- Right side
- Bottom
- Rear
- Left side

SolidWorks Standard view names correspond to these Orthographic projection view names.

ASME Y14.3M Principle View Name:	SolidWorks Standard View:
Front	Front
Top	Top
Right side	Right
Bottom	Bottom
Rear	Back
Left side	Left

The standard drawing views in Third Angle Orthographic projection are:

- Front
- Top
- Right
- Isometric

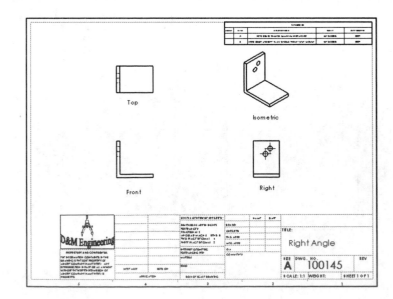

There are two Orthographic projection drawing systems. The first Orthographic projection system is called the Third Angle projection. The second Orthographic projection system is called the First Angle projection. The systems are derived from positioning a 3D object in the third or first quadrant.

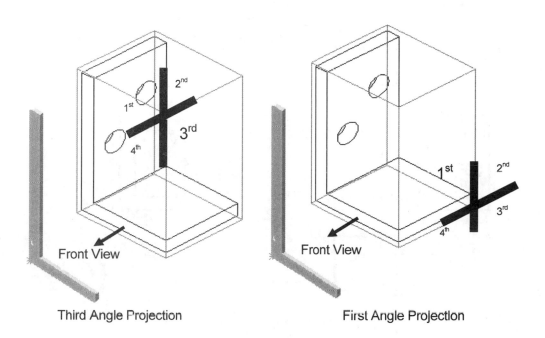

Third Angle Projection   First Angle Projection

Third Angle Projection

The part is positioned in the third quadrant in third angle projection. The 2D projection planes are located between the viewer and the part. The projected views are placed on a drawing.

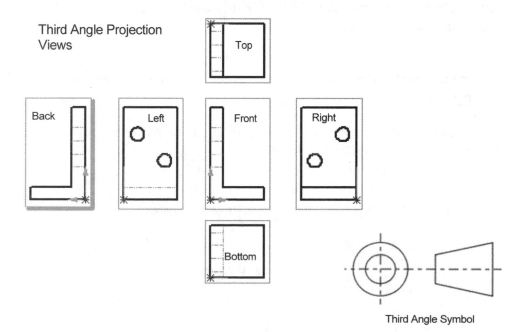

First Angle Projection

The part is positioned in the first quadrant in First Angle projection. Views are projected onto the planes located behind the part. The projected views are placed on a drawing. First Angle projection is primarily used in Europe and Asia.

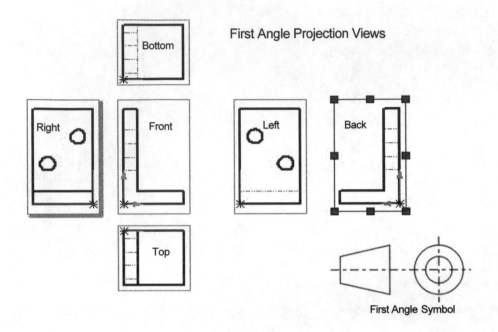

First Angle Projection Views

First Angle Symbol

Third Angle projection is primarily used in the U.S. & Canada and is based on the ASME Y14.3M Multi and Sectional View Drawings standard. Designers should have knowledge and understanding of both systems.

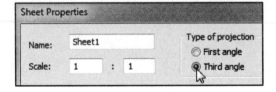

There are numerous multi-national companies.
Example: A part is designed in the U.S., manufactured in Japan and destined for a European market.

Third Angle projection is used in this text. A truncated cone symbol appears on the drawing to indicate the Projection System:

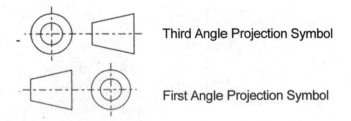

Third Angle Projection Symbol

First Angle Projection Symbol

Select the Sketch plane based on symmetry and orientation of the part in the FRONT-SUPPORT assembly. Utilize the standard views: *Front, Back, Right, Left, Top, Bottom* and *Isometric* to orient the part. Create the 2D drawings for the parts in Chapter 3.

HEX-STANDOFF Part

The HEX-STANDOFF part is a hexagonal shaped part utilized to elevate components in the FRONT-SUPPORT assembly. Machine screws are utilized to fasten components to the HEX-STANDOFF.

Create the HEX-STANDOFF part with the Extruded Boss/Base ▣ feature. The Sketch plane for the HEX-STANDOFF Boss-Extrude1 feature is the Top Plane.

Create the HEX-STANDOFF in the orientation utilized by the FRONT-SUPPORT assembly.

Origin

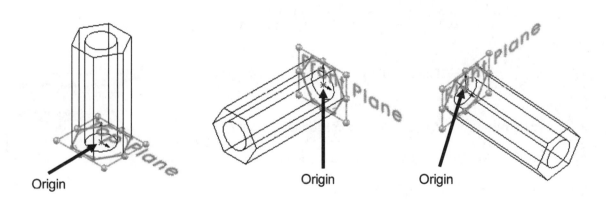

Origin   Origin   Origin

Note the location of the origin in the model.

☼ All sketches should be fully defined in the FeatureManager.

☼ Insert Geometric relations first and then dimensions in a sketch to maintain design intent.

The Boss-Extrude1 feature sketch consists of two profiles. The first sketch is a circle centered at the Origin on the Top Plane.

The second sketch is a polygon with 6 sides centered at the Origin. The polygon utilizes an inscribed circle to construct the geometry.

Geometric relations are constraints that control the size and position of the sketch entities. Apply a Horizontal relation in the polygon sketch.

Origin

Extrude the sketch perpendicular to the Top Plane. Utilize the Edit Sketch tool to modify the sketch.

The Hole Wizard feature creates complex and simple Hole features. Utilize the Hole Wizard feature to create a Tapped Hole.

The Tapped Hole depth and diameter are based on drill size and screw type parameters. Apply a Coincident relation to position the Tapped Hole aligned with the Origin.

Activity: HEX-STANDOFF Part-Extruded Boss/Base Feature

Create a New part.

1) Click **New** ⬚ from the Menu bar. The Templates tab is the default tab. Part is the default template from the New SolidWorks Document dialog box.

2) Double-click **Part**. The Part FeatureManager is displayed.

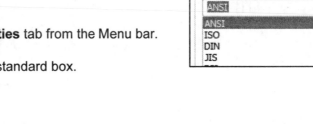

Set the dimensioning standard and part units.

3) Click **Options** 📋, **Document Properties** tab from the Menu bar.

4) Select **ANSI** from the Overall drafting standard box.

Set document units and decimal places.
5) Click **Units**.

6) Select **IPS**, [**MMGS**] for Unit system.

7) Select **.123**, [**.12**] for Length units Decimal places.

8) Select **None** for Angular units Decimal places.

9) Click **OK**. The Part FeatureManager is displayed.

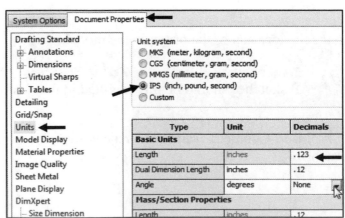

The primary units are provided in IPS, (inch, pound, seconds). The optional secondary units are provided in MMGS, (millimeter, gram, second) and are indicated in brackets [ ]. Illustrations are provided in inches and millimeters.

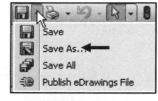

Save the part.
10)　Click **Save As** from the drop-down Menu bar.

11)　Select the **SW-TUTORIAL-2013** folder.

12)　Enter **HEX-STANDOFF** for File name.

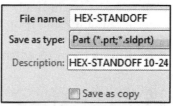

13)　Enter **HEX-STANDOFF 10-24** for Description.

14)　Click **Save**. The HEX-STANDOFF FeatureManager is displayed.

Select the Sketch plane.
15)　Right-click **Top Plane** from the FeatureManager. This is the Sketch plane.

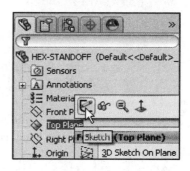

Insert a Boss-Extrude1 feature (Base feature) sketched on the Top Plane. Note: A plane is an infinite 2D area. The blue boundary is for visual reference.

Insert a new sketch.
16)　Click **Sketch** from the Context toolbar. The Sketch toolbar is displayed.

17)　Click the **Circle** Sketch tool. The Circle PropertyManager is displayed.

18)　Drag the **mouse pointer** into the Graphics window. The cursor displays the Circle icon .

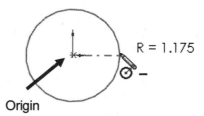

Origin

R = 1.175

19)　Click the **Origin** .

20)　Drag the **mouse pointer** to the right of the Origin.

21)　Click a **position** to create the circle as illustrated.

Insert a Polygon.
22)　Click the **Polygon** Sketch tool. The Polygon PropertyManager is displayed. The cursor displays the Polygon icon .

23)　Click the **Origin** as illustrated.

24) Drag the **mouse pointer** horizontally to the right.

25) Click a **position** to the right of the circle to create the hexagon as illustrated.

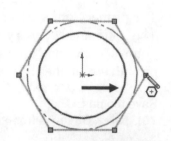

Add a dimension.

26) Click the **Smart Dimension** ✧ Sketch tool.

27) Click the **circumference** of the first circle.

28) Click a **position** diagonally above the hexagon to locate the dimension.

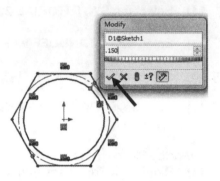

29) Enter **.150**in, [**3.81**] in the Modify box.

30) Click the **Green Check mark** ✔ in the Modify dialog box.

31) Click the **circumference** of the inscribed circle.

32) Click a **position** diagonally below the hexagon to locate the dimension. Enter **.313**in, [**7.95**] in the Modify box.

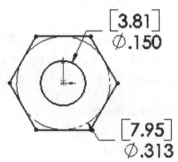

33) Click the **Green Check mark** ✔ in the Modify dialog box. The black sketch is fully defined.

34) Press the **f** key to fit the model to the Graphics window.

💡 If required, click the arrow head dot to toggle the direction of the dimension arrow.

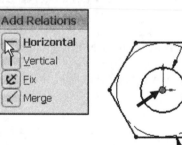

35) Click **OK** ✔ from the Dimension PropertyManager.

Add a Horizontal relation.

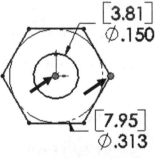

36) Click the **Origin** ⊥. Hold the **Ctrl** key down.

37) Click the right most **point** of the hexagon as illustrated. The Properties PropertyManager is displayed.

38) Release the **Ctrl** key. Click **Horizontal** ▬ from the Add Relations box. Click **OK** ✔ from the Properties PropertyManager.

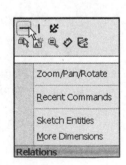

💡 You can also right-click and click **Make Horizontal** from the Context toolbar.

Extrude the sketch.
39) Click the **Features** tab in the CommandManager.

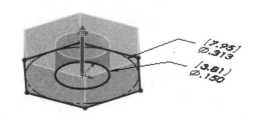

40) Click **Extruded Boss/Base** 🗔 from the Features toolbar. The Boss-Extrude PropertyManager is displayed. Blind is the default End Condition in Direction1. The direction arrow points upward.

41) Enter **.735**in, [**18.67**] for Depth.

42) Click **OK** ✔ from the Boss-Extrude PropertyManager. Boss-Extrude1 is displayed in the FeatureManager.

Fit the model to the Graphics window.
43) Press the **f** key.

The Boss-Extrude1 feature (Base feature) was sketched on the Top Plane. Changes occur in the design process. Edit the sketch of Boss-Extrude1. Delete the circle and close the sketch. Apply the Hole Wizard feature to create a Tapped Hole.

Edit Sketch1
44) **Expand** Boss-Extrude1 in the FeatureManager.

45) Right-click **Sketch1** in the FeatureManager.

46) Click **Edit Sketch** 🖼 from the Context toolbar.

Delete the inside circle.
47) Click the **circumference** of the inside circle as illustrated. The Circle PropertyManager is displayed.

48) Press the **Delete** key.

49) Click **Yes** to the Sketcher Confirm Delete message. Both the circle geometry and its dimension are deleted.

Save and close the sketch.
50) Click **Save** 💾 .

51) Click **OK** to Rebuild. The Boss-Extrude1 feature is updated. Note: Sketch1 is fully defined.

Fit the model to the Graphics window.
52) Press the **f** key.

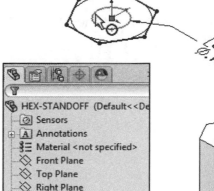

Activity: HEX-STANDOFF Part-Hole Wizard Feature

Insert a Tapped Hole with the Hole Wizard feature tool. Create a 2D Sketch.

53) Click **Hidden Lines Visible** ⬜ from the Heads-up View toolbar.

54) Click **Hole Wizard** 📷 from the Features toolbar. The Hole Specification PropertyManager is displayed.

Note: For metric, utilize ANSI Metric and M5x0.8 for size.

55) Click **Straight Tap** for Hole Specification.

56) Select **Ansi Inch**, [**Ansi Metric**] for Standard.

57) Select **Bottoming Tapped Hole** for Type.

58) Select **#10-24**, [**Ø5**] for Size.

59) Select **Through All** for End Condition.

60) Click the **Cosmetic thread** box. Accept the default conditions.

61) Click the **Positions** tab.

62) Click the **top face** of Boss-Extrude1 to the right of the origin. Do not select the center of the part.

63) Click the **center of the part** to locate the center point of the hole as illustrated. The Tapped Hole is displayed in yellow. Yellow is a preview color.

The Point ✳ Sketch tool is automatically selected. No other holes are required. You created a Coincident relation to the center point of the Tapped Hole in the Top view.

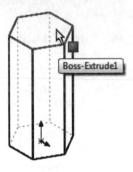

64) Right-click **Select** to deselect the Point Sketch tool.

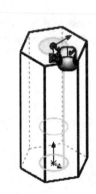

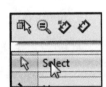

65) Click **OK** ✔ from the Hole Position PropertyManager.

The #10-24 Tapped Hole1 feature is displayed in the
FeatureManager. Sketch3 determines the center point location of
the Tapped Hole. Sketch2 is the profile of the
Tapped Hole.

Save the HEX-STANDOFF part.

66) Click **Shaded With Edges** 🔲 from the
Heads-up View toolbar.

67) Click **inside** the Graphics window.

68) Click **Save** 💾. The HEX-STANDOFF is
complete. View the Threads.

🔅 To view the thread, right-click the Annotations folder, click
Details. Check the Cosmetic thread box and the Shaded cosmetic
threads box. Click OK.

 Review the HEX-STANDOFF Part

The HEX-STANDOFF part utilized the Extruded Boss/Base feature. The
Boss-Extrude1 feature required a sketch on the Top Plane. The first profile
was a circle centered at the Origin on the Top Plane. The second profile
used the Polygon Sketch tool. You utilized the Edit Sketch tool to modify
the Sketch profile and to delete the circle.

The Hole Wizard feature created a Tapped Hole. The Hole Wizard feature
required the Boss-Extrude1 top face as the Sketch plane.

A Coincident relation located the center point of the Tapped Hole aligned
with respect to the Origin.

ANGLE-13HOLE Part

The ANGLE-13HOLE part is an L-shaped support
bracket. The ANGLE-13HOLE part is manufactured
from 0.090in, [2.3] aluminum.

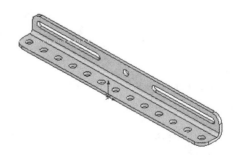

There ANGLE-13HOLE part contains fillets, holes,
and slot cuts.

Simplify the overall design into seven features.
Utilize symmetry and Linear Patterns.

The open L-Shaped profile is sketched on the
Right Plane.

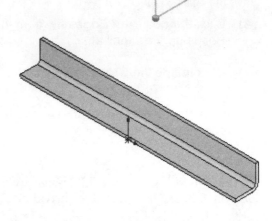

Utilize an Extruded Thin 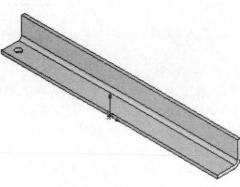 feature with the
Mid Plane option to locate the part symmetrical
to the Right Plane.

Insert the first Extruded Cut 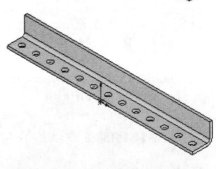 feature for the
first hole. This is the seed feature for the Linear
Pattern. The hole sketch is located on the top face
of the Extruded Thin feature.

Insert a Linear Pattern feature to create an array
of 13 holes along the bottom horizontal edge.

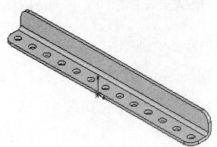

Insert a Fillet feature to round the four corners.

Model about the origin, this is great because it
provides a point of reference.

Insert the second Extruded Cut 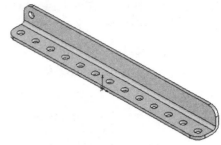 feature on the front face of the Extruded Thin feature. This is the seed feature for the second Linear Pattern.

Insert a Linear Pattern 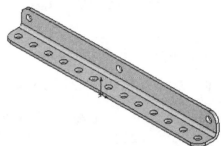 feature to create an array of 3 holes along the top horizontal edge.

Utilize the Sketch Mirror tool to create the slot profile. Use the Slot Sketch tool.

Insert the third Extruded Cut 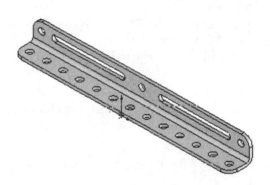 feature to create the two slots.

Select the Sketch plane for the Base feature that corresponds to the parts orientation in the assembly.

Activity: ANGLE-13HOLE Part-Documents Properties

Create a New part.

69) Click **New** ⬜ from the Menu bar. Part is the default template from the New SolidWorks Document dialog box.

70) Double-click **Part**. The Part FeatureManager is displayed.

Set the dimensioning standard and part units.

71) Click **Options** 🔲, **Document Properties** tab from the Menu bar.

72) Select **ANSI** from the Overall drafting standard drop-down menu.

73) Click **Units**.

74) Select **IPS, [MMGS]** for Unit system.

75) Select **.123**, [**.12**] for Length units Decimal places.

76) Select **None** for Angular units Decimal places. Click **OK**.

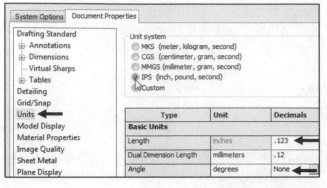

Save the part.

77) Click **Save As** from the Menu bar.

78) Select the **SW-TUTORIAL-2013** file folder.

79) Enter **ANGLE-13 HOLE** for File name.

80) Enter **ANGLE BRACKET-13 HOLE** for Description.

81) Click **Save**. The ANGLE-13 Hole FeatureManager is displayed.

Activity: ANGLE-13HOLE Part-Extruded Thin Feature

Insert an Extruded Thin feature sketched on the Right Plane.
Select the Sketch plane.

82) Right-click **Right Plane** from the FeatureManager.

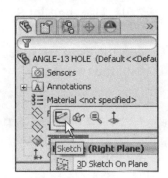

Sketch a horizontal line.

83) Click **Sketch** ⊑ from the Context toolbar. The Sketch toolbar is displayed.

84) Click the **Line** ＼ Sketch tool from the Sketch toolbar.

85) Click the **Origin** ⊬ as illustrated.

86) Click a **position** to the right of the Origin.

Sketch a vertical line.

87) Click a **position** directly above the right end point.

De-select the Line Sketch tool.

88) Right-click **Select** in the Graphics window.

Origin

Add an Equal relation.

89) Click the **vertical** line. Hold the **Ctrl** key down.

90) Click the **horizontal line**.

91) Release the **Ctrl** key.

92) Right-click **Make Equal** ＝ from the Context toolbar.

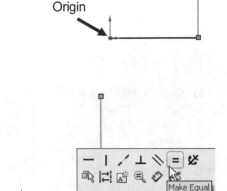

93) Click **OK** ✔ from the Properties PropertyManager.

Add a dimension.

94) Click the **Smart Dimension** ✎ Sketch tool.

95) Click the **horizontal** line.

96) Click a **position** below the profile.

97) Enter **.700**in, [**17.78**] in the Modify box.

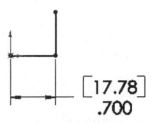

98) Click the **Green Check mark** ✓. The black sketch is fully defined.

☀ Save rebuild time. Add relations and dimensions to fully define a sketch. Fully defined sketches are displayed in black.

Extrude the sketch.

99) Click **Extruded Boss/Base** ▣ from the Features toolbar. The Boss-Extrude PropertyManager is displayed.

100) Select **Mid Plane** for End Condition in Direction 1.

101) Enter **7.000**in, [**177.8**] for Depth. Note: Thin Feature is checked.

102) If need, click the **Reverse Direction Arrow** button for One-Direction. Material thickness is created above the Origin.

103) Enter **.090**in, [**2.3**] for Thickness.

104) Check the **Auto-fillet corners** box.

105) Enter **.090**in, [**2.3**] for Fillet Radius.

Origin

106) Click **OK** ✓ from the Boss-Extrude PropertyManager. Extrude-Thin1 is displayed in the FeatureManager. Sketch1 is fully defined.

Fit the model to the Graphics window.
107) Press the **f** key.

☀ Think design intent. When do you use the various End Conditions and Geometric sketch relations? What are you trying to do with the design? How does the component fit into an Assembly?

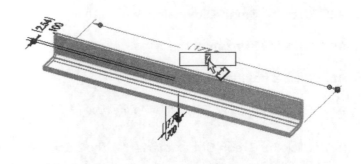

☀ Clarify the Extrude-Thin1 feature direction and thickness options. Utilize multiple view orientations and Zoom In before selecting OK ✔ from the Boss-Extrude PropertyManager.

Modify feature dimensions.

108) Click **Extrude-Thin1** in the FeatureManager.

109) Click the **7.000**in, [**177.80**] dimension in the Graphics window.

110) Enter **6.500**in, [**165.10**].

111) Click **inside** the Graphics window.

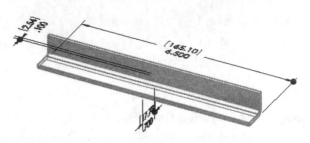

Save the model.

112) Click **Save** 🖫.

Activity: ANGLE-13HOLE Part-Extruded Cut Feature

Insert a new sketch for the Extruded Cut feature.

113) Right-click the **top face** of Extrude-Thin1 as illustrated. This is the Sketch plane.

114) Click **Sketch** ✏ from the Context toolbar. The Sketch toolbar is displayed.

115) Click **Top view** 🔲 from the Heads-up View toolbar.

116) Click the **Circle** ⊙ Sketch tool.

117) Sketch a **circle** on the left side of the Origin as illustrated.

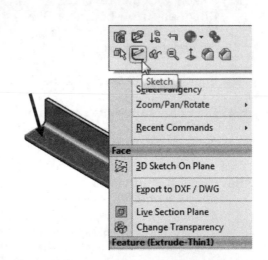

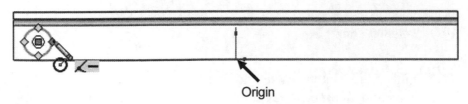

Origin

Add dimensions.

118) Click the **Smart Dimension** ✧ Sketch tool.

119) Click the **Origin** .

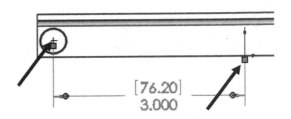

120) Click the **center point** of the circle.

121) Click a **position** below the horizontal profile line.

122) Enter **3.000**in, [**76.2**].

123) Click the **Green Check mark** ✔.

124) Click the **bottom horizontal line**.

125) Click the **center point** of the circle.

126) Click a **position** to the left of the profile.

127) Enter **.250**in, [**6.35**].

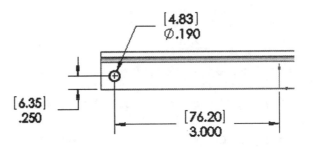

128) Click the **Green Check mark** ✔.

129) Create a diameter dimension. Click the **circumference** of the circle.

130) Click a **position** diagonally above the profile.

131) Enter **.190**in, [**4.83**].

132) Click the **Green Check mark** ✔.

Insert an Extruded Cut Feature.

133) Click **Extruded Cut** 🔲 from the Features toolbar. The Cut-Extrude PropertyManager is displayed.

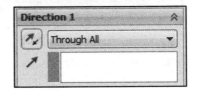

134) Select **Through All** for End Condition in Direction 1. Accept the default conditions.

135) Click **OK** ✔ from the Cut-Extrude PropertyManager. Cut-Extrude1 is displayed in the FeatureManager. Cut-Extrude1 is the seed feature for the Linear Pattern feature of holes.

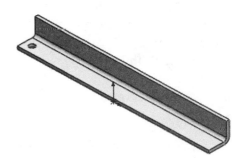

136) Click **Isometric view** 🔳 from the Heads-up View toolbar.

Save the model.

137) Click **Save** 💾.

Activity: ANGLE-13HOLE Part-Linear Pattern Feature

Insert a Linear Pattern feature.

138) Click **Top View** ⊞ from the Heads-up View toolbar.

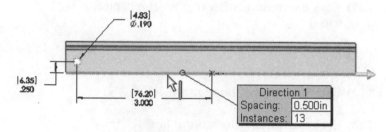

139) Click **Linear Pattern** ⣿ from the Features toolbar. The Linear Pattern PropertyManager is displayed. Cut-Extrude1 is displayed in the Features to Pattern box.

140) Click the **bottom horizontal edge** of the Extrude-Thin1 feature for Direction1. Edge<1> is displayed in the Pattern Direction box. The direction arrow points to the right. If required, click the Reverse Direction button.

141) Enter **0.5**in, [**12.70**] for Spacing.

142) Enter **13** for Number of Instances.

143) Click **OK** ✔ from the Linear Pattern PropertyManager. LPattern1 is displayed in the FeatureManager.

144) Click **Isometric view** 🧊 from the Heads-up View toolbar.

Save the ANGLE-13HOLE part.

145) Click **Save** 💾. Note: All sketches should be fully defined in the FeatureManager.

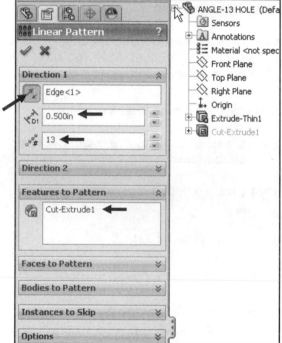

🔅 Use Symmetry. When possible and if it makes sense, model objects symmetrically about the origin. Even if the part is not symmetrical, the way it attaches or is manufactured could have symmetry.

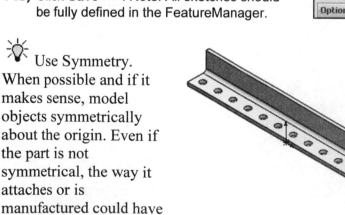

Activity: ANGLE-13HOLE Part - Fillet Feature

Insert a Fillet Feature.
146) Zoom in on the right top edge as illustrated.

147) Click the **right top edge** of the Extrude-Thin1 feature.

148) Click **Fillet** 🔘 from the Features toolbar. The Fillet PropertyManager is displayed.

149) Click the **Manual** tab. Constant radius is the default Fillet Type.

150) Enter **.250** [**6.35**] for Radius.

151) Click the **right bottom edge**. Edge<1> and Edge<2> are displayed in the Items To Fillet box. Note the new fillet pop-up menu.

152) Click **OK** ✔ from the Fillet PropertyManager. Fillet1 is displayed in the FeatureManager.

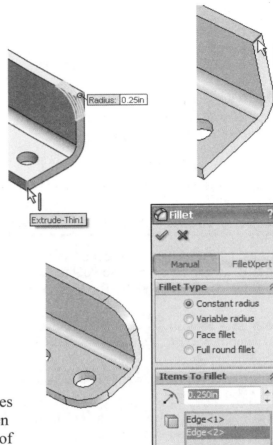

🔅 Two Fillet PropertyManager tabs are available. Use the Manual tab to control features for all Fillet types. Use the FilletXpert tab when you want SolidWorks to manage the structure of the underlying features only for a Constant radius Fillet type. Click the [?] button for additional information.

Fit the model to the Graphics window.
153) Press the **f** key.

Edit the Fillet feature.
154) Zoom in on the left side of the Extrude-Thin1 feature.

155) Right-click **Fillet1** from the FeatureManager.

156) Click **Edit Feature** from the Context toolbar. The Fillet1 PropertyManager is displayed.

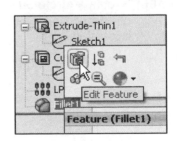

157) Click the **left top edge** and **left bottom edge**. Edge<3> and Edge <4> are added to the Items To Fillet box.

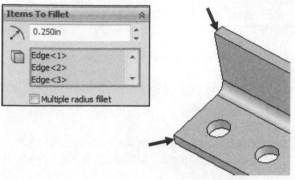

158) Click **OK** ✔ from the Fillet1 PropertyManager. The four edges have a Fillet feature with a .250in radius.

Display the Isometric view.

159) Click **Isometric view** 🔲 from the Heads-up View toolbar.

Save the ANGLE-13HOLE part.

160) Click **Save** 💾.

Activity: ANGLE-13HOLE Part-Second Extruded Cut / Linear Pattern

Insert a new sketch for the second Extruded Cut feature.

161) Right-click the **front face** of the Extrude-Thin1 feature in the Graphics window. The front face is the Sketch plane.

162) Click **Sketch** ✏ from the Context toolbar. The Sketch toolbar is displayed.

163) Click **Front view** 🔲 from the Heads-up View toolbar.

164) Click **Wireframe** 🔲 from the Heads-up View toolbar to display LPattern1.

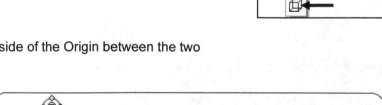

Note: Do not align the center point of the circle with the center point of the LPattern1 feature. Do not align the center point of the circle with the center point of the Fillet radius. Control the center point position with dimensions.

165) Click the **Circle** ⊙ Sketch tool. The cursor displays the Circle icon ⊙.

166) Sketch a **circle** on the left side of the Origin between the two LPattern1 holes as illustrated.

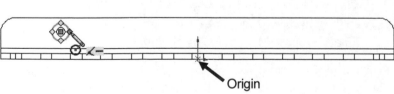

Origin

Add dimensions.

167) Click the **Smart Dimension** ✎ Sketch tool.

168) Click the **Origin** ⊥—.

169) Click the **center point** of the circle.

170) Click a **position** below the horizontal profile line. Enter **3.000**in, [**76.20**].

171) Click the **Green Check mark** ✔ .

172) Click the **top horizontal line**.

173) Click the **center point** of the circle.

174) Click a **position** to the left of the profile.

175) Enter .**250**in, [**6.35**]. Click the **Green Check mark** ✔ .

176) Click the **circumference** of the circle.

177) Click a **position** above the profile.

178) Enter .**190**in, [**4.83**].

179) Click the **Green Check mark** ✔ .

Insert an Extruded Cut Feature.

180) Click **Extruded Cut** 🔲 from the Features toolbar. The Cut-Extrude PropertyManager is displayed

181) Select **Through All** for End Condition in Direction1. Accept the default conditions.

182) Click **OK** ✔ from the Cut-Extrude PropertyManager. Cut-Extrude2 is displayed in the FeatureManager.

Create the second Linear Pattern Feature.

183) Click **Linear Pattern** ⣿ from the Features toolbar. The Linear Pattern FeatureManager is displayed. Cut-Extrude2 is displayed in the Features to Pattern box.

184) Click inside the **Pattern Direction** box.

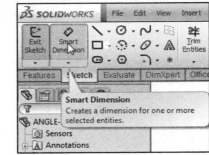

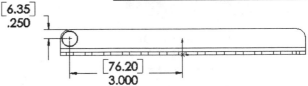

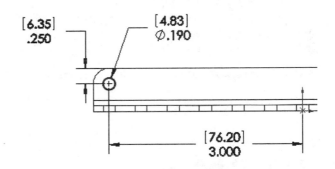

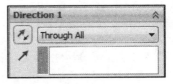

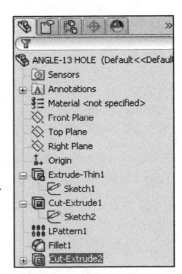

185) Click the **top horizontal edge** of the Extrude-Thin1 feature for Direction1. Edge<1> is displayed in the Pattern Direction box. The Direction arrow points to the right. If required, click the **Reverse Direction** button

186) Enter **3.000**in, **[76.20]** for Spacing.

187) Enter **3** for Number of Instances. Note: Cut-Extude2 (Seed feature) is displayed in the Features to Pattern box.

188) Click **OK** ✔ from the Linear Pattern PropertyManager. LPattern2 is displayed in the FeatureManager.

189) Click **Isometric view** ⬡ from the Heads-up View toolbar.

190) Click **Shaded With Edges** ⬜ from the Heads-up View toolbar.

Save the ANGLE-13HOLE part.

191) Click **Save** 💾.

Activity: ANGLE-13HOLE Part-Third Extruded Cut

Insert a new sketch for the third Extruded Cut Feature.

192) Select the Sketch plane. Right-click the **front face** of Extrude-Thin1.

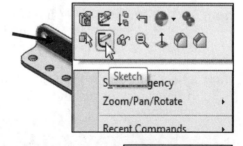

193) Click **Sketch** ⌇ from the Context toolbar. The Sketch toolbar is displayed.

194) Click **Front view** ⬒ from the Heads-up View toolbar.

195) Click **Hidden Lines Removed** ⬜ from the Heads-up View toolbar.

Sketch a vertical centerline.

196) Click the **Centerline** ⋮ Sketch tool. The Insert Line PropertyManager is displayed.

197) Click the **Origin** ⤬ .

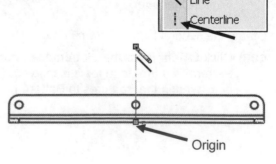

198) Click a **vertical position** above the top horizontal line as illustrated.

199) Click **Tools**, **Sketch Tools**, **Dynamic Mirror** from the Menu bar.

200) Click the **centerline** in the Graphics window.

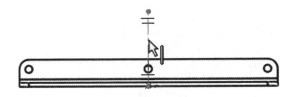

Sketch a rectangle.

201) Click **Wireframe** ⬚ from the Heads-up View toolbar.

Apply the Straight Slot Sketch tool. Sketch a straight slot using two end points and a point for height.

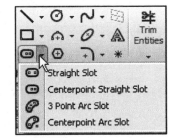

202) Click the **Straight Slot** ⬭ Sketch tool from the Consolidated Slot toolbar. Do not align the rectangle first point and second point to the center points of Lpattern1.

203) Click the **first point** of the rectangle to the left of the Origin as illustrated.

204) Click the **second point** directly to the right.

205) Click the **third point** to create the slot as illustrated. View the two slots on the model.

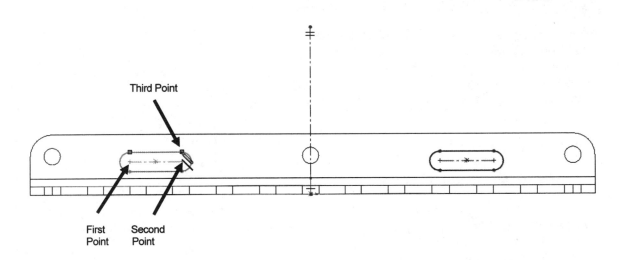

206) Click **OK** ✔ from the Slot PropertyManager.

Deactivate the Dynamic Mirror tool.
207) Click **Tools**, **Sketch Tools**, **Dynamic Mirror** from the Menu bar.

Add a Concentric relation.
208) Zoom in on the centerline.

209) Click the **top end point** of the centerline.

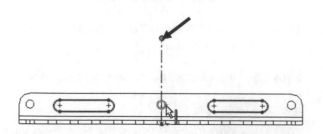

210) Hold the **Ctrl** key down.

211) Click the **circumference** of the circle.

212) Release the **Ctrl** key.

213) Click **Concentric** from the Add Relations box.

The endpoint of the centerline is positioned in the center of the circle. Note: Right-click Clear Selections to remove selected entities from the Add Relations box.

Add an Equal relation.
214) Click the circumference of the **circle**.

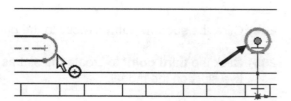

215) Hold the **Ctrl** key down.

216) Click the **left arc** of the first rectangle.

217) Release the **Ctrl** key.

218) Click **Equal** ⁼ from the Add Relations box. The arc radius is equal to the circle radius.

Add a Horizontal relation.
219) Click the **top end point** of the centerline as illustrated.

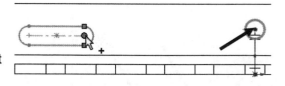

220) Hold the **Ctrl** key down.

221) Click the **center point** of the left arc of the first rectangle.

222) Release the **Ctrl** key.

223) Click **Horizontal** ━ from the Add Relations box.

224) Click **OK** ✓ from the Properties PropertyManager.

The right arc is horizontally aligned to the left arc due to symmetry from the Sketch Mirror tool.

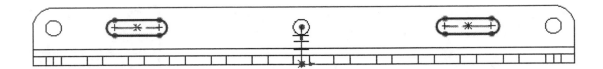

Add dimensions. Dimension the distance between the two slots.

225) Click the **Smart Dimension** Sketch tool.

226) Click the **right arc center point** of the left slot.

227) Click the **left arc center point** of the right slot.

228) Click a **position** above the top horizontal line.

229) Enter **1.000**in, **[25.40]** in the Modify dialog box.

230) Click the **Green Check mark** .

231) Click the **left center point** of the left arc.

232) Click the **right center point** of the left arc.

233) Click a **position** above the top horizontal line.

234) Enter **2.000**in, **[50.80]** in the Modify dialog box.

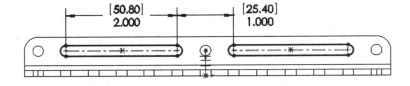

235) Click the **Green Check mark** . The black sketch is fully defined.

236) Click **Isometric view** from the Heads-up View toolbar.

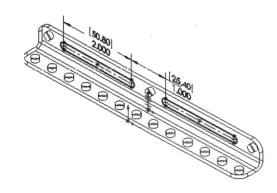

The Origin and Tangent edges are displayed for educational purposes.

Insert an Extruded Cut Feature.

237) Click **Extruded Cut** from the Features toolbar. The Cut-Extrude PropertyManager is displayed.

238) Select **Through All** for End Condition in Direction1. The direction arrow points to the back.

239) Click **OK** ✔ from the Extrude PropertyManager. Cut-Extrude3 is displayed in the FeatureManager.

240) Click **Shaded With Edges** 🗔 from the Heads-up View toolbar.

Save the ANGLE-13HOLE part.

241) Click **Save** 💾. The ANGLE-13HOLE is complete. All sketches in the FeatureManager should be fully defined.

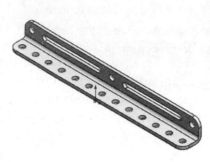

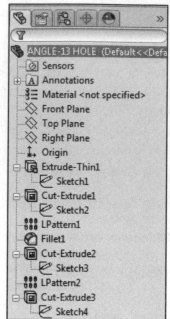

🔅 Model about the origin, it provides a point of reference.

🔅 The dimension between the two slots is over-defined if the arc center points are aligned to the center points of the LPattern1 feature. An over-defined sketch is displayed in red, in the FeatureManager.

🔅 The mouse pointer displays a blue dashed line when horizontal and vertical sketch references are inferred.

🔅 Add relations, then dimensions. This will keep the user from having too many unnecessary dimensions. This helps to show the design intent of the model. Dimension what geometry you intent to modify or adjust.

🔅 Right-click and drag in the Graphics area to display the mouse gesture wheel. Customize the default commands for a sketch, part, assembly or drawing document.

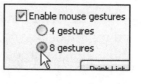

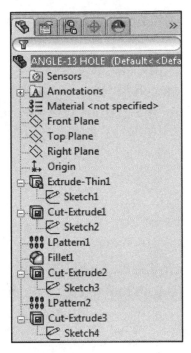

Review the ANGLE-13HOLE Part

The ANGLE-13HOLE part utilized an open L-Shaped profile sketched on the Right Plane. The Extruded Thin feature with the Mid Plane option located the part symmetrical to the Right Plane. The first Extruded Cut feature created the first hole sketched on the top face of the Extruded Thin feature.

The first Linear Pattern feature created an array of 13 holes along the bottom horizontal edge. The Fillet feature rounded the four corners. The second Extruded Cut feature created a hole on the Front face. The second Linear Pattern feature created an array of 3 holes along the top horizontal edge. The third Extruded Cut feature created two slot cuts using the Straight Slot Sketch tool.

Additional details on Extruded Base/Thin, Extruded Cut, Linear Pattern, Fillet, Mirror Entities, Add Relations, Slot, Straight Slot, Centerline, Line, Rectangle, and Smart Dimensions are available in Help. Keywords: Extruded Boss/Base - Thin, Extruded Cut, Patterns, Fillet, Sketch Entities, Sketch tools, and dimensions.

TRIANGLE Part

The TRIANGLE part is a multipurpose supporting plane.

The TRIANGLE is manufactured from .090in, [2.3] aluminum. The TRIANGLE contains numerous features.

Utilize symmetry and Sketch tools to simplify the geometry creation.

The center points of the slots and holes locate key geometry for the TRIANGLE.

Utilize sketched construction geometry to locate the center points.

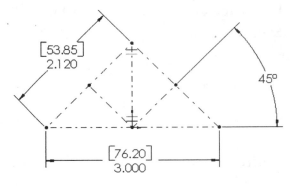

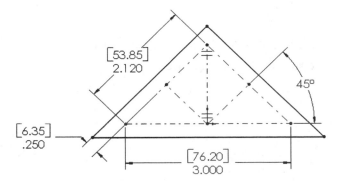

Construction geometry is not calculated in the extruded profile.

Utilize the Sketch Offset tool and Sketch Fillet to create the sketch profile for the Extruded Boss/Base 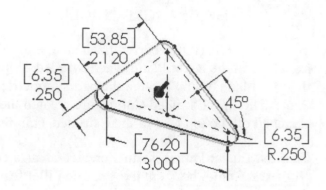 (Boss-Extrude1) feature.

Utilize the Dynamic Mirror Sketch tool and the Circle Sketch tool to create the first Extruded Cut feature.

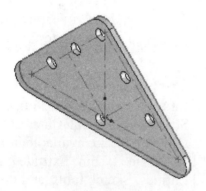

Utilize the Corner Rectangle, Trim, and the Tangent Arc Sketch tools to create the second Extruded Cut feature left bottom slot.

Note: A goal of this book is to expose the new user to different tools and methods. You can also apply the Straight Slot Sketch tool and eliminate steps.

Utilize the Mirror feature to create the right bottom slot.

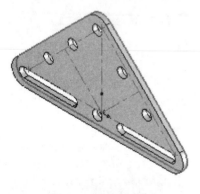

Utilize the Straight Slot Sketch tool to create the third Extruded Cut feature.

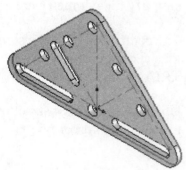

Utilize the Circular Pattern 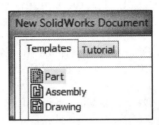 feature to create the three radial slot cuts.

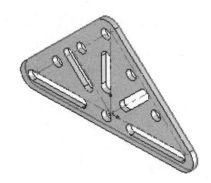

Activity: TRIANGLE Part-Mirror, Offset, and Fillet Sketch Tools

Create a New part.

242) Click **New** ⬜ from the Menu bar. The Templates tab is the default tab.

243) Double-click **Part**. The Part FeatureManager is displayed.

Save the part.
244) Click **Save As** from the drop-down Menu bar.

245) Select **SW-TUTORIAL-2013** for the Save in file folder.

246) Enter **TRIANGLE** for File name.

247) Enter **TRIANGLE** for Description.

248) Click **Save**. The TRIANGLE FeatureManager is displayed.

Set the dimensioning standard and part units.
249) Click **Options** 🗒, **Document Properties** tab from the Menu bar.

250) Select **ANSI** from the Overall drafting standard box.

251) Click **Units**.

252) Click **IPS**, [**MMGS**] for Unit system.

253) Select **.123**, [**.12**] for Length units Decimal places.

254) Select **None** for Angular units Decimal places.

255) Click **OK** to set the document units.

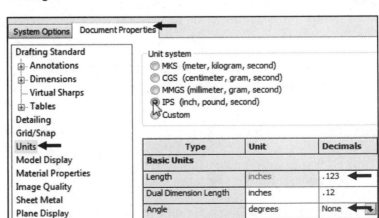

Insert a new sketch for the Extruded Base feature.

256) Right-click **Front Plane** from the FeatureManager.

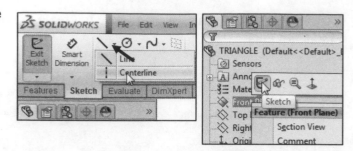

257) Click **Sketch** ⌐ from the Context toolbar. The Sketch toolbar is displayed.

Sketch a vertical centerline.

258) Click the **Centerline** ┆ Sketch tool.

259) Click the **Origin** ↧. Click a vertical **position** above the Origin as illustrated.

Deselect the Centerline Sketch tool.
260) Right-click **Select**.

Sketch a Mirrored profile.
261) Click **Tools**, **Sketch Tools**, **Dynamic Mirror** from the Menu bar.

262) Click the **centerline** in the Graphics window.

263) Click the **Centerline** ┆ Sketch tool.

264) Click the **Origin** ↧.

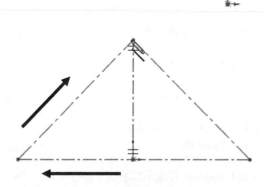

Origin

265) Click a **position** to the left of the Origin to create a horizontal line.

266) Click the **top end point** of the vertical centerline to complete the triangle as illustrated.

267) Right-click **End Chain** to end the line segment. The Centerline tool is still active.

268) Click the **Origin** ↧.

269) Click a **position** coincident with the right-angled centerline. *Do not select the Midpoint*.

270) Right-click **End Chain** to end the line segment.

Deactivate the Dynamic Mirror Sketch tool.
271) Click **Tools**, **Sketch Tools**, **Dynamic Mirror** from the Menu bar.

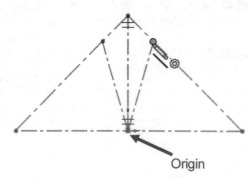

Origin

Add a dimension.

272) Click **Smart Dimension** ✎ from the Sketch toolbar.

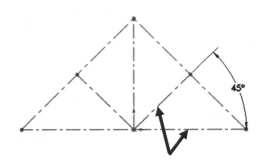

273) Click the **right horizontal** centerline.

274) Click the **inside right** centerline.

275) Click a **position** between the two lines.

276) Enter **45**deg in the Modify dialog box for the angular dimension.

277) Click the **Green Check mark** ✔ in the Modify dialog box.

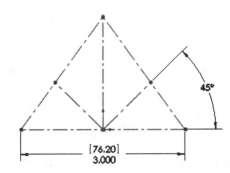

278) Click the **horizontal centerline**.

279) Click a position **below** the centerline.

280) Enter **3.000**in, **[76.20]**.

281) Click the **Green Check mark** ✔ in the Modify dialog box.

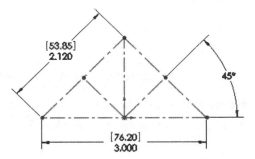

282) Click the **left angled** centerline.

283) Click **position** aligned to the left angled centerline.

284) Enter **2.120**in, **[53.85]**.

285) Click the **Green Check mark** ✔ in the Modify dialog box.

Offset the sketch

286) Right-click **Select** in the Graphics window.

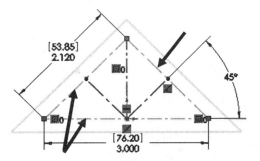

287) Hold the **Ctrl** key down.

288) Click the **three outside centerlines**; Line2, Line4, and Line5 are displayed in the Selected Entities box.

289) Release the **Ctrl** key.

290) Click the **Offset Entities** ⇗ Sketch tool.

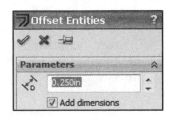

291) Enter **.250**in, **[6.35]** for Offset Distance. The yellow Offset direction is outward.

292) Click **OK** ✔ from the Offset Entities PropertyManager.

Three profile lines are displayed. The centerlines are on the inside.

Insert the Sketch Fillet.

293) Click **Sketch Fillet** ⌐⁺ from the Sketch toolbar. The Sketch Fillet PropertyManager is displayed.

294) Enter **.250**in, **[6.35]** for Radius.

295) Click the **three outside corner points**.

296) Click **OK** ✔ from the Sketch Fillet PropertyManager.

297) Click **OK** ✔ from the Sketch Fillet PropertyManager.

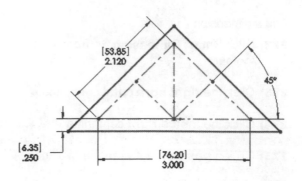

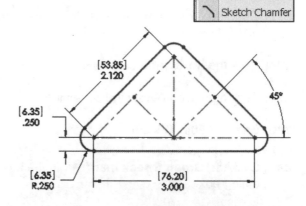

Activity: TRIANGLE Part-Extruded Boss/Base Feature

Extrude the sketch. Create the Boss-Extrude1 feature.

298) Click **Extruded Boss/Base** 🔲 from the Features toolbar. Blind is the default End Condition in Direction1.

299) Enter **.090**in, **[2.3]** for Depth in Direction 1. The direction arrow points to the front.

300) Click **OK** ✔ from the Boss-Extrude PropertyManager. Boss-Extrude1 is displayed in the FeatureManager.

Save the TRIANGLE part.

301) Click **Isometric view** 🧊 from the Heads-up View toolbar.

302) Click **Save** 💾.

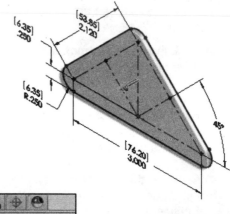

💡 Insert centerlines and relations to build sketches that are referenced by multiple features.

Display Sketch1.

303) Expand Boss-Extrude1 in the FeatureManager.

304) Right-click **Sketch1**.

305) Click **Show**.

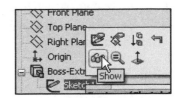

Activity: TRIANGLE Part-First Extruded Cut Feature

Insert a new sketch for the first Extruded Cut.

306) Right-click the **front face** of Boss-Extrude1. This is your Sketch plane.

307) Click **Sketch** ✏ from the Context toolbar. The Sketch toolbar is displayed.

308) Click **Front view** 🗔 from the Heads-up View toolbar.

309) Click the **Circle** ⊘ Sketch tool. The Circle PropertyManager is displayed.

310) Sketch a **circle** centered at the Origin.

311) Sketch a **circle** centered at the endpoint of the vertical centerline as illustrated.

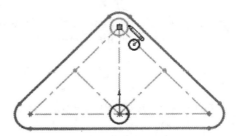

Sketch a vertical centerline.

312) Click the **Centerline** ┊ Sketch tool.

313) Click the **Origin** ⊾ .

314) Click the **center point** of the top circle.

Deselect the Centerline Sketch tool.

315) Right-click **Select**.

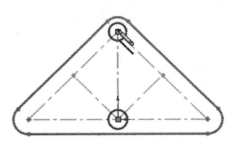

Sketch a Mirrored profile.

316) Click **Tools**, **Sketch Tools**, **Dynamic Mirror** from the Menu bar.

317) Click the **centerline** in the Graphics window.

318) Click the **Circle** ⊘ Sketch tool. The Circle PropertyManager is displayed.

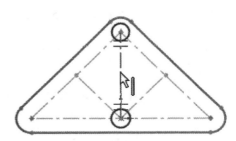

319) Sketch a **circle** on the left side of the centerline, coincident with the left centerline, in the lower half of the triangle.

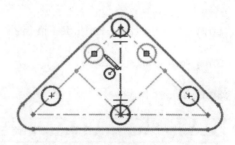

320) Sketch a **circle** on the left side of the centerline, coincident with the left centerline, in the upper half of the triangle. Right-click **Select**.

321) Deactivate the Dynamic Mirror tool. Click **Tools**, **Sketch Tools**, **Dynamic Mirror** from the Menu bar.

Add an Equal relation.
322) Click a **circle**. Hold the **Ctrl** key down.

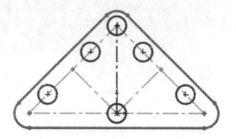

323) Click the five other **circles**. Release the **Ctrl** key.

324) Click **Equal** ═ from the Add Relations box.

Add a dimension.
325) Click the **Smart Dimension** ⬦ Sketch tool.

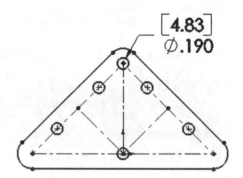

326) Click the circumference of the **top circle**. Click a **position** off the TRIANGLE.

327) Enter **.190**in, [**4.83**].

328) Click the **Green Check mark** ✔ in the Modify dialog box.

Create the aligned dimensions.
329) Click the bottom **left point**. Click the **center point** of the bottom left circle.

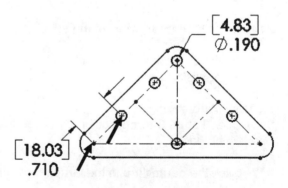

330) Click a **position** aligned to the angled centerline.

331) Enter **.710**in, [**18.03**]. Click the **Green Check mark** ✔ in the Modify dialog box.

332) Click the **bottom left point**.

333) Click the **center point** of the top left circle as illustrated.

334) Click a **position** aligned to the angled centerline.

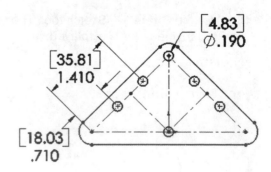

335) Enter **1.410**in, [**35.81**].

336) Click the **Green Check mark** ✔ in the Modify dialog box.

Insert an Extruded Cut Feature.

337) Click **Extruded Cut** 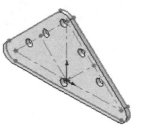 from the Features toolbar. The Cut-Extrude PropertyManager is displayed.

338) Select **Through All** for the End Condition in Direction1.

339) Click **OK** ✔ from the Cut-Extrude PropertyManager. Cut-Extrude1 is displayed in the FeatureManager.

340) Click **Isometric view** from the Heads-up View toolbar.

341) Click **Save** .

Activity: TRIANGLE Part-Second Extruded Cut Feature

Insert a new slot sketch for the second Extruded Cut.

342) Right-click the **front face** of Boss-Extrude1 for the Sketch plane.

343) Click **Sketch** ✏ from the Context toolbar. The Sketch toolbar is displayed.

344) Click **Front view** from the Heads-up View toolbar.

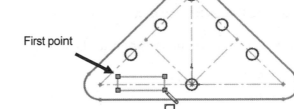

345) Click the **Corner Rectangle** ☐ tool from the Consolidated Sketch toolbar. Note: The purpose of this book is to teach you different tools and methods. You can also apply the Straight Slot Sketch tool and eliminate many of the next steps.

346) Sketch a **rectangle** to the left of the Origin as illustrated.

First point

Trim the vertical lines.

347) Click the **Trim Entities** ✂ Sketch tool. The Trim PropertyManager is displayed.

348) Click **Trim to closest** in the Options box. The Trim to closest ✂ icon is displayed. Click the **left vertical** line of the rectangle.

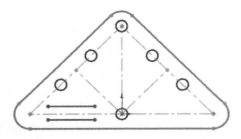

349) Click the **right vertical** line of the rectangle.

350) Click **OK** ✔ from the Trim PropertyManager.

Sketch the Tangent Arcs.

351) Click the **Tangent Arc**  Sketch tool from the Consolidated Sketch toolbar. The Arc PropertyManager is displayed.

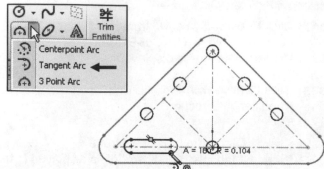

352) Sketch a **180° arc** on the left side.

353) Sketch a **180° arc** on the right side.

354) Click **OK** ✔ from the Arc PropertyManager.

Add an Equal relation.
355) Click the **right arc**.

356) Hold the **Ctrl** key down.

357) Click the **bottom center circle**.

358) Release the **Ctrl** key.

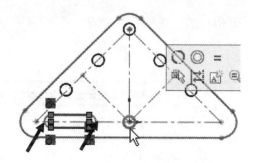

359) Click **Equal** = from the Add Relations box.

360) Click **OK** ✔ from the Properties PropertyManager.

Add a Coincident relation.
361) Press the **f** key to fit the model to the Graphics window.

362) Click the **center point** of the left arc.

363) Hold the **Ctrl** key down.

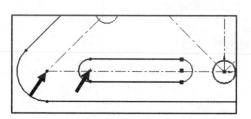

364) Click the **left lower point** as illustrated.

365) Release the **Ctrl** key.

366) Click **Coincident** ⟋ from the Add Relations box.

Add a Tangent relation.
367) Click the **bottom horizontal** line.

368) Hold the **Ctrl** key down. Click the **first arc tangent**.

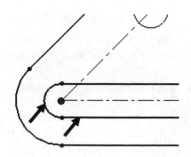

369) Release the **Ctrl** key.

370) Click **Tangent** ⟋ from the Add Relations box.

371) Click **OK** ✔ from the Properties PropertyManager.

Add a dimension.

372) Click the **Smart Dimension**  Sketch tool.

373) Click the **left center point** of the left arc.

374) Click the **right center point** of the right arc.

375) Click a **position** below the horizontal line.

376) Enter **1.000**in, [25.40] in the Modify dialog box.

377) Click the **Green Check mark** ✓.

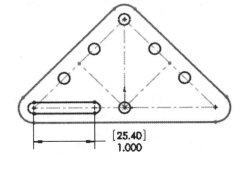

Insert an Extruded Cut feature.

378) Click **Isometric view** 🟦 from the Heads-up View toolbar.

379) Click **Extruded Cut** 🔲 from the Features toolbar. The Cut-Extrude PropertyManager is displayed.

380) Select **Through All** for End Condition in Direction 1.

381) Click **OK** ✓ from the Cut-Extrude PropertyManager. Cut-Extrude2 is displayed in the FeatureManager.

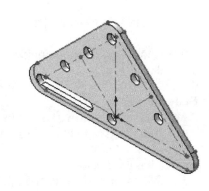

382) Click **Save** 💾. Cut-Extrude2 is highlighted in the FeatureManager.

Activity: TRIANGLE Part-Mirror Feature

Mirror the Cut-Extrude2 feature.

383) Click **Mirror** 🔳 from the Features toolbar. The Mirror PropertyManager is displayed. Cut-Extrude2 is displayed in the Feature to Mirror box.

384) Click **Right Plane** from the fly-out TRIANGLE FeatureManager. Right Plane is displayed in the Mirror Face/Plane box.

385) Check the **Geometry Pattern** box.

386) Click **OK** ✓ from the Mirror PropertyManager. Mirror1 is displayed in the FeatureManager.

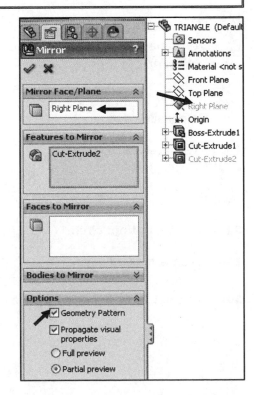

Activity: TRIANGLE Part-Third Extruded Cut Feature

Insert a new sketch for the third Extruded Cut feature.
387) Right-click the **front face** of Boss-Extrude1 for the Sketch plane.

388) Click **Sketch** from the Context toolbar. The Sketch toolbar is displayed.

389) Click **Front view** from the Heads-up View toolbar.

Sketch a Straight Slot.
390) Click the **Straight Slot** Sketch tool from the Consolidated Rectangle toolbar. The Straight Slot icon is displayed.

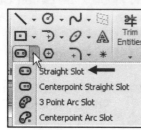

391) Click a **position** coincident with the left angled centerline as illustrated.

Sketch the second point.
392) Click a **position** aligned to the centerline. A dashed blue line is displayed.

Sketch the third point.
393) Click a **position** above the inside left centerline. The Straight Slot sketch is displayed.

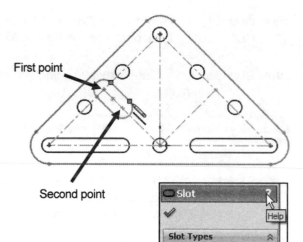

First point

Second point

Click the Question mark in the PropertyManager to obtain additional information on the tool.

394) Click **OK** from the Slot PropertyManager.

Add an Equal relation.
395) Click the **left arc**.

396) Hold the **Ctrl** key down.

397) Click the **bottom circle**.

398) Release the **Ctrl** key.

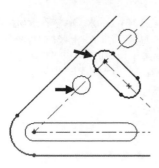

399) Click **Equal** = from the Add Relations box.

Add a dimension.

400) Click the **Smart Dimension** ✧ Sketch tool.

401) Click the **left center point** of the left arc.

402) Click the **right center point** of the right arc.

403) Click a **position** below the horizontal line.

404) Enter **.560**in, **[14.22]** in the Modify dialog box.

405) Click the **Green Check mark** ✅. The sketch is fully defined.

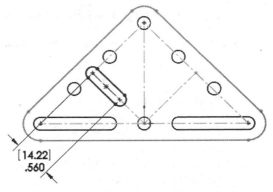

Insert an Extruded Cut Feature.

406) Click **Isometric view** 🔷 from the Heads-up View toolbar.

407) Click **Extruded Cut** 🔲 from the Features toolbar. The Cut-Extrude PropertyManager is displayed.

408) Select **Through All** for the End Condition in Direction 1.

409) Click **OK** ✅ from the Cut-Extrude PropertyManager. Cut-Extrude3 is displayed in the FeatureManager.

Save the model.

410) Click **Save** 💾.

Display the Temporary Axis.

411) Click **View**; check **Temporary Axes** from the Menu bar.

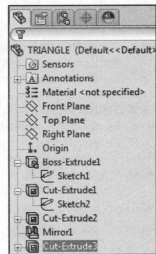

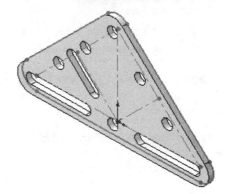

Activity: TRIANGLE Part-Circular Pattern Feature

Insert a Circular Pattern feature.

412) Click **Circular Pattern** 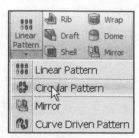 from the Features Consolidated toolbar. The Circular Pattern PropertyManager is displayed. Cut-Extrude3 is displayed in the Features to Pattern box.

413) Click the **Temporary Axis** displayed through the center hole located at the Origin. The Temporary Axis is displayed as Axis <1> in the Pattern Axis box.

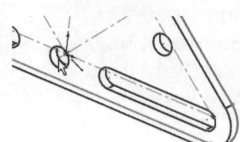

414) Enter **90**deg for Angle.

415) Enter **3** for Number of Instances.

416) Check the **Equal spacing** box. If required, click **Reverse Direction**.

417) Click **OK** ✔ from the Circular Pattern PropertyManager. CirPattern1 is displayed in the FeatureManager.

Hide Sketch1.
418) **Expand** Boss-Extrude1 from the FeatureManager.

419) Right-click **Sketch1**.

420) Click **Hide**.

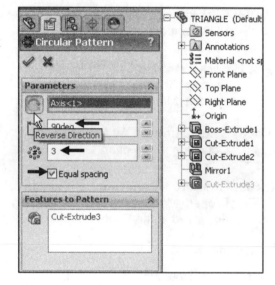

Save the TRIANGLE part and deactivate the Temporary Axes.

421) Click **Isometric view** 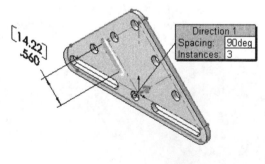 from the Heads-up View toolbar.

422) Click **View**; uncheck **Temporary Axes** from the Menu bar.

423) Click **Save** 🖫 . The TRIANGLE part is complete.

🔆 Model about the origin, this is great because it provides a point of reference.

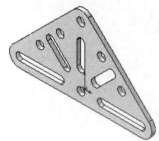

Review the TRIANGLE Part

The TRIANGLE part utilized a Boss-Extrude1 feature. A triangular shape profile was sketch on the Front Plane. Symmetry and construction geometry sketch tools to locate center points for slots and holes.

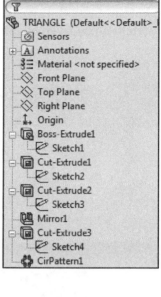

The Sketch Fillet tool created rounded corners for the profile. The Sketch Mirror and Circle Sketch tools were utilized to create the Extruded Cut features.

The Corner Rectangle, Sketch Trim, and Tangent Arc tools were utilized to create the second Extruded Cut feature, left bottom slot. The Mirror feature was utilized to create the right bottom slot.

The Parallelogram and Tangent Arc Sketch tools were utilized to create the third Extruded Cut feature. The Circular Pattern feature created the three radial slot cuts. The following Geometric relations were utilized: *Equal*, *Parallel*, *Coincident* and *Tangent*.

Additional details on Rectangle, Circle, Tangent Arc, Parallelogram, Mirror Entities, Sketch Fillet, Offset Entities, Extruded Boss/Base, Extruded Cut, Mirror and Circular Pattern are available in SolidWorks Help.

SCREW Part

The SCREW part is a simplified model of a 10-24 x 3/8 Machine screw. Screws, nuts and washers are classified as fasteners. An assembly contains hundreds of fasteners. Utilize simplified versions to conserve model and rebuild time.

Machine screws are described in terms of the following:
- Nominal diameter - Size 10.

- Threads per inch - 24.

- Length - 3/8.

Simplified version

Screw diameter, less than ¼ inch, is represented by a size number. Size 10 refers to a diameter of .190 inch. Utilize the SCREW part to fasten components in the FRONT-SUPPORT assembly.

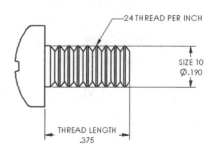

The SCREW part utilizes a Revolved Base ⚙ feature to add material. The Revolved Boss/Base feature requires a centerline and sketch on a Sketch plane. A Revolved feature requires an angle of revolution. The sketch is revolved around the centerline.

Sketch a centerline on the Front Sketch plane.

Sketch a closed profile.

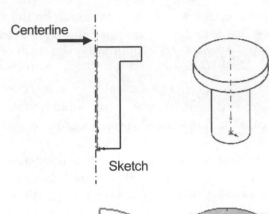

Revolve the sketch 360 degrees.

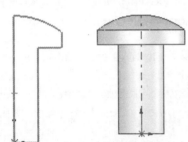

Utilize the Edit Sketch tool to modify the sketch. Utilize the Sketch Trim and Tangent Arc tool to create a new profile.

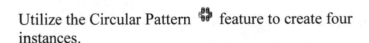

Utilize an Extruded Cut 🔲 feature sketched on the Front Plane. This is the seed feature for the Circular Pattern.

Utilize the Circular Pattern ⊛ feature to create four instances.

Apply the Fillet 🔲 feature to round edges and faces. Utilize the Fillet feature to round the top edge.

Apply the Chamfer 🔲 feature to bevel edges and faces. Utilize a Chamfer feature to bevel the bottom face.

Note: Utilize an M5 Machine screw for metric units.

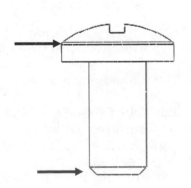

Activity: SCREW Part-Documents Properties

Create a New part.

424) Click **New** ⬜ from the Menu bar. The Templates tab is the default tab. Double-click **Part**.

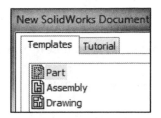

Save the part.

425) Click **Save As** from the drop-down Menu bar. Select **SW-TUTORIAL-2013** for the Save in file folder.

426) Enter **SCREW** for File name.

427) Enter **MACHINE SCREW 10-24x3/8** for Description.

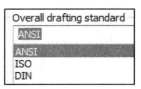

428) Click **Save**. The SCREW FeatureManager is displayed.

Set the dimensioning standard and part units.

429) Click **Options** 🗒, **Documents Properties** tab from the Menu bar.

430) Select **ANSI** from the Overall drafting standard box.

431) Click **Units**. Select **IPS**, **[MMGS]** for Unit system.

432) Select **.123**, **[.12]** for Length units Decimal places.

433) Select **None** for Angular units Decimal places.

434) Click **OK**.

Activity: SCREW Part-Revolved Feature

Insert a Revolved feature sketched on the Front Plane. The Front Plane is the default Sketch plane.

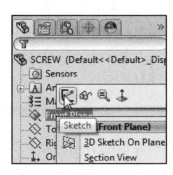

Insert a new sketch.

435) Right-click **Front Plane** from the FeatureManager.

436) Click **Sketch** ⌐ from the Context toolbar. The Sketch toolbar is displayed.

437) Click the **Centerline** ⁝ Sketch tool. The Insert Line PropertyManager is displayed.

Sketch a vertical centerline.

438) Click the **Origin** ↳. Click a **position** directly above the Origin as illustrated.

🔆 Press the **z** key to Zoom out in the Graphics window.

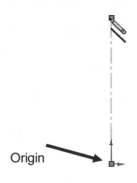

Origin ➡

439) Right-click **End Chain** to end the centerline.

Add a dimension.
440) Click the **Smart Dimension** 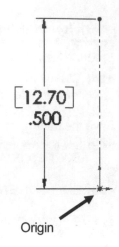 Sketch tool.

441) Click the **centerline**. Click a **position** to the left.

442) Enter **.500**in, [**12.70**]. Click the **Green Check mark** ✓ .

Fit the sketch to the Graphics Window.
443) Press the **f** key.

Sketch the profile.
444) Click the **Line** ＼ Sketch tool.

Sketch the first horizontal line.

445) Click the **Origin** ⊹ . Click a **position** to the right of the Origin.

Sketch the first vertical line.
446) Click a position **above** the horizontal line endpoint.

447) Sketch the second **horizontal line**.

448) Sketch the second **vertical line**. The top point of the vertical line is collinear with the top point of the centerline.

449) Sketch the third **horizontal line**. The left endpoint of the horizontal line is coincident with the top point of the centerline.

450) Right-click **Select** to deselect the Line Sketch tool.

Add a Horizontal relation.
451) Click the **top** most right point. Hold the **Ctrl** key down.

452) Click the **top** most left point. Release the **Ctrl** key.

453) Click **Horizontal** ▬ from the Add Relations box.

454) Click **OK** ✓ from the Properties PropertyManager.

Add a dimension.
455) Click the **Smart Dimension** 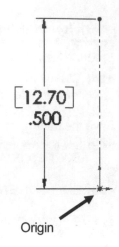 Sketch tool. Create the first diameter dimension.

456) Click the **centerline** in the Graphics window.

457) Click the **first vertical line**.

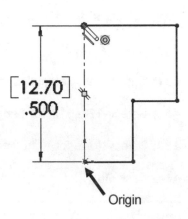

Origin

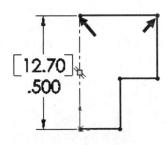

458) Click a **position** to the left of the Origin to create a diameter dimension.

459) Enter **.190**in, [**4.83**].

460) Click the **Green Check mark** 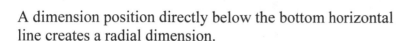.

A diameter dimension for a Revolved sketch requires a centerline, profile line, and a dimension position to the left of the centerline.

A dimension position directly below the bottom horizontal line creates a radial dimension.

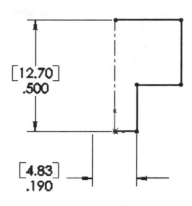

Create the second diameter dimension.
461) Click the **centerline** in the Graphics window.

462) Click the **second vertical line**.

463) Click a **position** to the left of the Origin to create a diameter dimension.

464) Enter **.373**in, [**9.47**].

Create a vertical dimension.
465) Click the **first vertical line**.

466) Click a **position** to the right of the line.

467) Enter **.375**in, [**9.53**].

Center the dimension text.
468) Click the **.190**in, [**4.83**] dimension.

469) Drag the **text** between the two extension lines.

470) Click the **.373**in, [**9.47**] dimension.

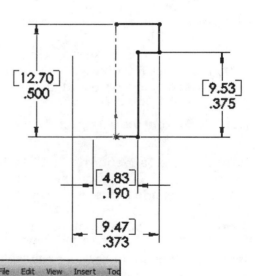

471) Drag the **text** between the two extension lines. If required, click the **blue arrow dots** to flip the arrows inside the extension lines.

472) Right-click **Select** to deselect the Smart Dimension Sketch tool.

Select the Centerline for axis of revolution.
473) Click the **vertical centerline** as illustrated.

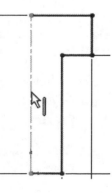

Revolve the sketch.

474) Click **Revolved Boss/Base** ⊕ from the Features toolbar.

475) Click **Yes**. The Revolve PropertyManager is displayed.

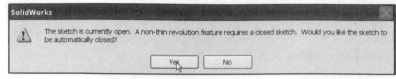

The "Yes" button causes a vertical line to be automatically sketched from the top left point to the Origin. The Graphics window displays the Isometric view and a preview of the Revolved Base feature.

The Revolve PropertyManager displays 360 degrees for the Angle of Revolution.

476) Click **OK** ✔ from the Revolve PropertyManager.

The FeatureManager displays the Revolve1 name for the first feature. The Revolved Boss/Base feature requires a centerline, sketch, and an angle of revolution. A solid Revolved Boss/Base feature requires a closed sketch. Draw the sketch on one side of the centerline.

The SCREW requires a rounded profile. Edit the Revolved Base sketch. Insert a Tangent Arc.

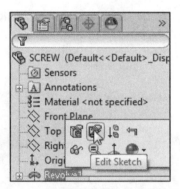

Edit the Revolved Base sketch.
477) Right-click **Revolve1** in the FeatureManager. Click **Edit Sketch** from the Context toolbar.

478) Click **Front view** 🔲 from the Heads-up View toolbar.

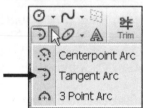

479) Click the **Tangent Arc** ⤵ Sketch tool.

480) Click the **top centerline** point as illustrated.

481) Drag the **mouse pointer** to the right and downward.

482) Click a **position** collinear with the right vertical line, below the midpoint. The arc is displayed tangent to the top horizontal line.

Deselect the Tangent Arc Sketch tool.
483) Right-click **Select**.

Delete unwanted geometry.
484) Click the **Trim Entities** ✂ Sketch tool. The Trim PropertyManager is displayed.

485) Click **Trim to closest** from the Options box. The Trim to closest icon is displayed.

Origin

486) Click the **right top vertical line** as illustrated.

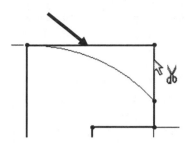

487) Click the **top horizontal line** as illustrated. The two lines are removed.

488) Click **OK** ✔ from the Trim PropertyManager. Note: You may still view lines until you exit the sketch.

Add a dimension.

489) Click the **Smart Dimension** ✧ Sketch tool.

490) Click the **arc**.

491) Click a **position** above the profile.

492) Enter **.304**in, [**7.72**].

493) Click the **Green Check mark** ✔ . The sketch should be fully defined, if not add dimension as illustrated.

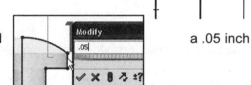

a .05 inch

494) Click **Exit Sketch** from the Sketch toolbar.

495) Click **Save** 💾 .

The SCREW requires an Extruded Cut feature on the Front Plane. Utilize the Convert Entities Sketch tool to extract the Revolved Base top arc edge for the profile of the Extruded Cut.

Activity: SCREW Part-Extruded Cut Feature

Insert a new sketch for the Extruded Cut feature.
496) Right-click **Front Plane** from the FeatureManager.

497) Click **Sketch** ⌐ from the Context toolbar. The Sketch toolbar is displayed.

498) Click the **top arc** as illustrated. The mouse pointer displays the silhouette edge icon for feedback.

499) Click the **Convert Entities** ⬚ Sketch tool.

500) Click **OK** ✔ from the Convert Entities PropertyManager.

501) Click the **Line** ╲ Sketch tool.

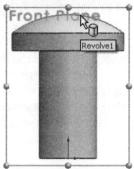

502) Sketch a **vertical line**. The top endpoint of the line is coincident with the arc, vertically aligned to the Origin.

503) Sketch a **horizontal line**. The right end point of the line is coincident with the arc. Do not select the arc midpoint. Right-click **Select**.

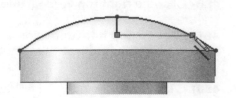

504) Click **Isometric view** from the Heads-up View toolbar.

505) Click the **Trim Entities** Sketch tool. The Trim PropertyManager is displayed.

506) Click **Power trim** from the Options box.

507) Click a position to the **left** side of the arc.

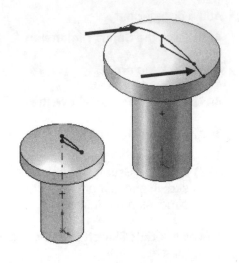

508) Drag the mouse pointer to **intersect** the left arc line.

509) Click a position to the **right** side of the right arc.

510) Drag the mouse pointer to **intersect** the right arc line.

511) Click **OK** from the Trim PropertyManager.

Add a dimension.

512) Click the **Smart Dimension** Sketch tool.

513) Click the **vertical line**.

514) Click a **position** to the right of the profile.

515) Enter .030in, [0.76].

516) Click the **Green Check mark** .

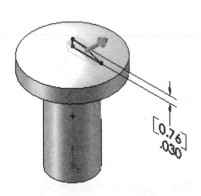

Insert an Extruded Cut Feature.

517) Click **Isometric view** from the Heads-up View toolbar.

518) Click **Extruded Cut** from the Features toolbar. The Cut-Extrude PropertyManager is displayed.

519) Select **Mid Plane** for the End Condition in Direction 1.

520) Enter .050in, [1.27] for Depth.

521) Click **OK** from the Cut-Extrude PropertyManager. Cut-Extrude1 is displayed in the FeatureManager.

Activity: SCREW Part-Circular Pattern Feature

Insert the Circular Pattern feature.

522) Click **View**; check **Temporary Axes** from the Menu bar. The Temporary Axis is required for the Circular Pattern feature.

523) Click **Circular Pattern** 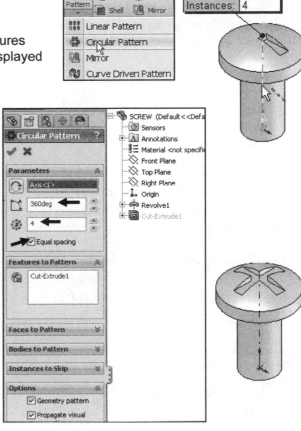 from the Features Consolidated toolbar. Cut-Extrude1 is displayed in the Features to Pattern box.

524) Click the **Temporary Axis** in the Graphics window. Axis<1> is displayed in the Pattern Axis box.

525) Check the **Equal spacing** box.

526) Enter **360**deg for Angle.

527) Enter **4** for Number of Instances.

528) Click **OK** ✔ from the Circular Pattern PropertyManager. CirPattern1 is displayed in the FeatureManager.

Save the model.

529) Click **Save** 💾.

🔅 Use Symmetry. When possible and if it makes sense, model objects symmetrically about the origin.

Activity: SCREW Part-Fillet Feature

Insert the Fillet feature.

530) Click the **top circular edge** as illustrated.

531) Click **Fillet** 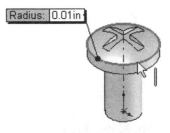 from the Features toolbar. The Fillet PropertyManager is displayed.

532) Click the **Manual** tab. Edge<1> is displayed in the Items to Fillet box.

533) Enter .**010**in, [.**25**] for Radius.

534) Click **OK** ✔ from the Fillet PropertyManager. Fillet1 is displayed in the FeatureManager.

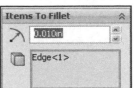

Activity: SCREW Part-Chamfer Feature

Insert the Chamfer feature.
535) Click the **bottom circular edge**.

536) Click **Chamfer** from the Features Consolidated toolbar. Edge<1> is displayed in the Items to Chamfer box.

537) Enter .050in, **[1.27]** for Distance.

538) Click **OK** ✔ from the Chamfer PropertyManager. Chamfer1 is displayed in the FeatureManager.

🔆 Simplify the part. Save rebuild time. Suppress features that are not required in the assembly.

A suppressed feature is not displayed in the Graphics window. A suppressed feature is removed from any rebuild calculations.

Suppress the Fillet and Chamfer feature.
539) Hold the **Ctrl** key down.

540) Click **Fillet1** and **Chamfer1** from the FeatureManager.

541) Release the **Ctrl** key.

542) Right-click **Suppress** 📥 Suppress from the Context toolbar. Note: Suppressed features are displayed in light gray in the FeatureManager.

Deactivate the Temporary Axes in the Graphics window.
543) Click **View**; uncheck **Temporary Axes** from the Menu bar.

Save the SCREW part.
544) Click **Isometric view** 📦 from the Heads-up View toolbar.

545) Click **Save** 💾.

Close all open documents.
546) Click **Window**, **Close All** from the Menu bar.

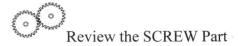 Review the SCREW Part

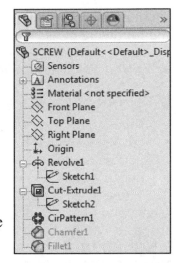

The Revolved Boss/Base feature was utilized to create the SCREW part. The Revolved Boss/Base feature required a centerline sketched on the Front Sketch plane and a closed profile. The sketch was revolved 360 degrees to create the Base feature for the SCREW part.

Edit Sketch was utilized to modify the sketch. The Sketch Trim and Tangent Arc tools created a new profile.

The Extruded Cut feature was sketched on the Front Plane. The Circular Pattern feature created four instances. The Fillet feature rounded the top edges.

The Chamfer feature beveled the bottom edge. The Fillet and Chamfer are suppressed to save rebuild time in the assembly. Note: Suppressed features are displayed in light gray in the FeatureManager.

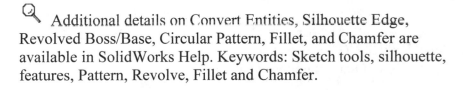 Additional details on Convert Entities, Silhouette Edge, Revolved Boss/Base, Circular Pattern, Fillet, and Chamfer are available in SolidWorks Help. Keywords: Sketch tools, silhouette, features, Pattern, Revolve, Fillet and Chamfer.

The Origin and Tangent edges are displayed for educational purposes.

Think design intent. When do you use the various End Conditions and Geometric sketch relations? What are you trying to do with the design? How does the component fit into an Assembly?

Mate to the first part added to the assembly. If you mate to the first part or base part of the assembly and decide to change its orientation later, all the parts will move with it.

FRONT-SUPPORT Assembly

The FRONT-SUPPORT assembly consists of
the following parts:

- ANGLE-13HOLE part

- TRIANGLE part

- HEX-STANDOFF part

- SCREW part

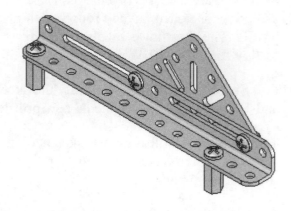

Create the FRONT-SUPPORT assembly.
Insert the ANGLE-13HOLE part. The
ANGLE-13HOLE part is fixed to the
FRONT-SUPPORT Origin. Insert the first
HEX-STANDOFF part.

Utilize Concentric and Coincident mates to assemble the HEX-STANDOFF to the left
hole of the ANGLE-13HOLE part. Insert the second HEX-STANDOFF part.

Utilize Concentric and Coincident mates to assemble the HEX-STANDOFF to the third
hole from the right side. Insert the TRIANGLE part. Utilize Concentric, Distance, and
Parallel mates to assemble the TRIANGLE. Utilize Concentric/Coincident SmartMates to
assemble the four SCREWS. Note: Other mate types can be used.

Activity: FRONT-SUPPORT Assembly-Insert ANGLE-13HOLE

Create a new assembly.

547) Click **New** ⬜ from the Menu bar.

548) Double-click **Assembly** from the Templates tab. The Begin
Assembly PropertyManager is displayed. Note: The Begin
Assembly PropertyManager is displayed if the Start command
when creating new assembly box is checked.

549) Click the **Browse** button.

550) Browse to the **SW-TUTORIAL-2013** folder on your hard drive.

551) Click the **Filter Parts (*.prt, *sldprt)** button from the Open dialog
box.

552) Double-click the **ANGLE-13HOLE** part.

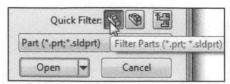

Fix the first component to the Origin.

553) Click **OK** ✔ from the Begin Assembly PropertyManager. The first component is fixed to the Origin (f).

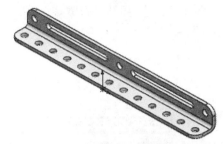

Save the assembly.

554) Click **Save As** from the drop-down Menu bar.

555) Select **SW-TUTORIAL-2013** for the Save in file folder.

556) Enter **FRONT-SUPPORT** for File name.

557) Enter **FRONT SUPPORT ASSEMBLY** for Description.

558) Click **Save**. The FRONT-SUPPORT assembly FeatureManager is displayed.

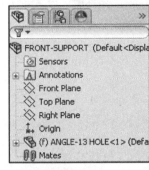

Set the dimensioning standard and assembly units.

559) Click **Options** 🗒, **Document Properties** tab from the Menu bar.

560) Select **ANSI** from the Overall drafting standard box.

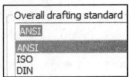

Set document units.

561) Click **Units**.

562) Select **IPS**, [**MMGS**] for Unit system.

563) Select **.123**, [**.12**] for Length units Decimal places.

564) Select **None** for Angular units Decimal places.

565) Click **OK**.

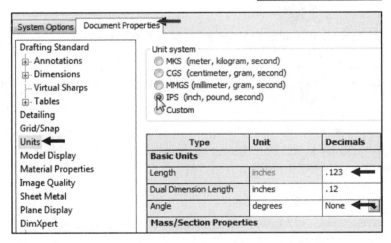

The ANGLE-13HOLE name in the FeatureManager displays an (f) symbol. The (f) symbol indicates that the ANGLE-13HOLE component is fixed to the FRONT-SUPPORT assembly Origin. The component cannot move or rotate.

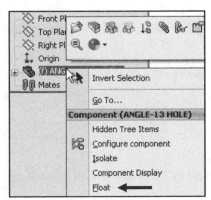

💡 To remove the fixed state, Right-click a component name in the FeatureManager. Click **Float**. The component is free to move.

Display the Isometric view.

566) Click **Isometric view** from the Heads-up View toolbar.

Save the assembly.

567) Click **Save** .

Activity: FRONT-SUPPORT Assembly-Inset HEX-STANDOFF

Insert the HEX-STANDOFF part.

568) Click the **Insert Components** Assembly tool. The Insert Component PropertyManager is displayed.

569) Click the **Browse** button.

570) Browse to the **SW-TUTORIAL-2013** folder on your hard drive. Click the **Filter Parts (*.prt, *sldprt)** button from the Open dialog box.

571) Double-click **HEX-STANDOFF** from the SW-TUTORIAL 2013 folder.

572) Click a **position** near the left top hole as illustrated.

Enlarge the view.
573) **Zoom in** on the front left side of the assembly.

Move the component.
574) Click and drag the **HEX-STANDOFF** component below the ANGLE-13HOLE left hole.

The HEX-STANDOFF name in the FeatureManager displays a (-) minus sign. The minus sign indicates that the HEX-STANDOFF part is free to move.

Insert a Concentric mate.

575) Click the **Mate** Assembly tool. The Mate PropertyManager is displayed.

576) Click the **left inside cylindrical hole face** of the ANGLE-13HOLE component.

577) Click inside the **cylindrical hole face** of the HEX-STANDOFF component. The selected faces are displayed in the Mate Selections box. Concentric is selected by default.

578) Click the **Green Check mark** .

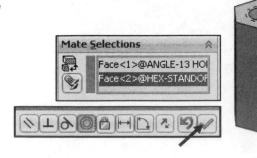

579) Click and drag the **HEX-STANDOFF** component below the ANGLE-13HOLE component until the top face is displayed.

Insert a Coincident mate.
580) Click the **HEX-STANDOFF top face**.

581) Press the **Up Arrow key** approximately 5 times to view the bottom face of the ANGLE-13HOLE component.

582) Click the **ANGLE-13HOLE bottom face**. The selected faces are displayed in the Mate Selections box. Coincident Mate is selected by default.

583) Click the **Green Check mark** ✔.

584) Click **Isometric view** 🔲 from the Heads-up View toolbar.

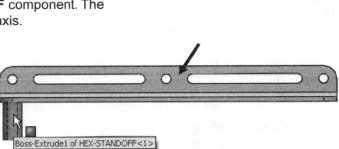

585) Click and drag the **HEX-STANDOFF** component. The HEX-STANDOFF rotates about its axis.

Insert a Parallel mate.
586) Click **Front view** 🔲 from the Heads-up View toolbar.

587) Click the **HEX-STANDOFF front face**.

588) Click the **ANGLE-13HOLE front face**. The selected faces are displayed in the Mate Selections box. A Mate message is displayed.

589) Click **Parallel** ⟍.

590) Click the **Green Check mark** ✔.

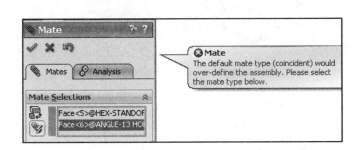

591) Click **OK** ✔ from the Mate PropertyManager.

Display the created mates.
592) **Expand** the Mates folder in the FRONT-SUPPORT FeatureManager. Three mates are displayed between the ANGLE-13HOLE component and the HEX-STANDOFF component. The HEX-STANDOFF component is fully defined.

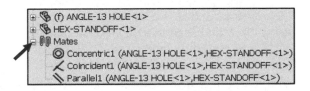

Save the FRONT-SUPPORT assembly.

593) Click **Save** 🖫 .

Insert the second HEX-STANDOFF part.
594) Hold the **Ctrl** key down.

595) Click and drag the **HEX-STANDOFF<1>**

(f) ANGLE-13 HOLE<1> name from the FeatureManager into the FRONT-SUPPORT assembly Graphics window.

596) Release the **mouse pointer** below the far right hole of the ANGLE-13HOLE component.

597) Release the **Ctrl** key. HEX-STANDOFF<2> is displayed in the Graphics window and listed in the FeatureManager.

🔅 The number <2> indicates the second instance or copy of the same component. The instance number increments every time you insert the same component. If you delete a component and then reinsert the component in the same SolidWorks session, the instance number increments by one.

Enlarge the view.
598) Zoom in on the right side of the assembly.

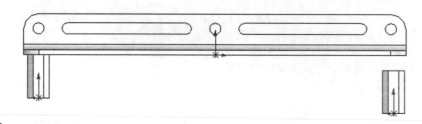

Insert a Concentric mate.
599) Click the **Mate** 🖉 Assembly tool. The Mate PropertyManager is displayed.

600) Click the **third hole cylindrical face** from the right ANGLE-13HOLE component.

601) Click inside the **cylindrical hole face** of the second HEX-STANDOFF component. Concentric is selected by default.

602) Click the **Green Check mark** ✔ .

Move the second HEX-STANDOFF part.
603) Click and drag the **HEX-STANDOFF** component below the ANGLE-13HOLE component until its top face is displayed.

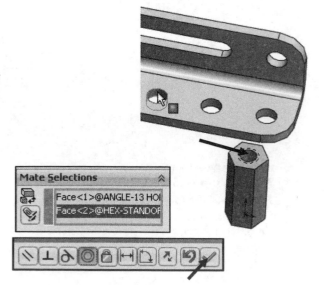

Insert a Coincident mate.

604) Click the **second HEX-STANDOFF** top face.

605) Press the **up arrow key** approximately 5 times to view the bottom face of the ANGLE-13HOLE component.

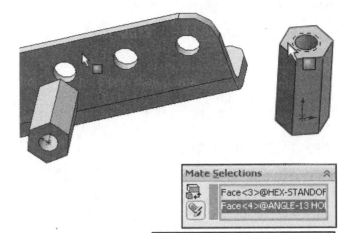

606) Click the **ANGLE-13HOLE bottom face**. The selected faces are displayed in the Mate Selections box. Coincident Mate is selected by default.

607) Click the **Green Check mark** ✓ .

Insert a Parallel mate.

608) Click **Front view** Heads-up View toolbar.

609) Click the **front face** of the second HEX-STANDOFF.

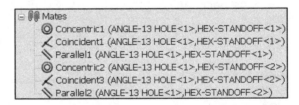

610) Click the **front face** of the ANGLE-13HOLE. A Mate message is displayed.

611) Click **Parallel** .

612) Click the **Green Check mark** ✓ .

613) Click **OK** ✓ from the Mate PropertyManager.

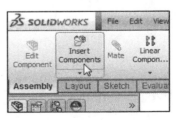

Display the created mates.

614) **Expand** the Mates folder in the FRONT-SUPPORT FeatureManager. Three mates are displayed between the ANGLE-13HOLE component and the second HEX-STANDOFF component. The second HEX-STANDOFF is fully defined.

Activity: FRONT-SUPPORT Assembly-Insert the TRIANGLE

Insert the TRIANGLE part.

615) Click **Isometric view** from the Heads-up View toolbar.

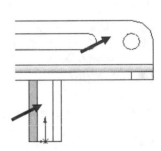

616) Click the **Insert Components** Assembly tool. The Insert Component PropertyManager is displayed.

617) Click the **Browse** button. Browse to the **SW-TUTORIAL-2013** folder on your hard drive.

618) Click the **Filter Parts (*.prt, *sldprt)** button from the Open dialog box.

619) Double-click **TRIANGLE**.

620) Click a **position** in back of the ANGLE-13HOLE
component as illustrated.

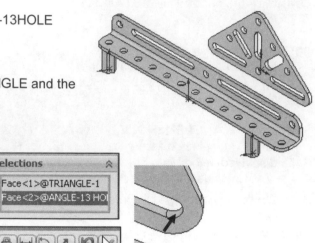

Enlarge the view.
621) Zoom in on the right side of the TRIANGLE and the
ANGLE-13HOLE.

Insert a Concentric mate.

622) Click the **Mate** ✎ Assembly
tool. The Mate
PropertyManager is
displayed.

623) Click the **inside right
arc face** of the
TRAINGLE.

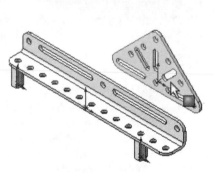

624) Click the **inside right arc face** of the ANGLE-
13HOLE slot. Concentric mate is selected by
default. Note: Utilize the Undo button if the mate is
not correct.

625) Click the **Green Check mark** ✓ .

Fit the model to the Graphics window.
626) Press the **f** key.

Insert a Distance mate.
627) Click the **front face** of the TRIANGLE.

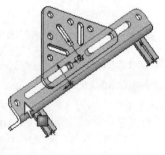

628) Press the **left Arrow key** approximately 5 times to view
the back face of the ANGLE-13HOLE component.

629) Click the **back face** of the ANGLE-13HOLE component.

630) Click **Distance** ⊢⊣ from the Mate dialog box.

631) Enter **0**.

632) Click the **Green Check mark** ✓ .

🔆 A Distance Mate of 0
provides additional flexibility
compared to a Coincident mate. A
Distance mate value can be
modified.

Insert a Parallel mate.

633) Click **Bottom view** ⊞ from the Heads-up View toolbar.

634) Click the **narrow bottom face** of the TRIANGLE.

635) Click the **bottom face** of the ANGLE-13HOLE. The selected faces are displayed in the Mate Selections box. A Mate message is displayed.

636) Click **Parallel** ⟍.

637) Click the **Green Check mark** ✔.

638) Click **OK** ✔ from the Mate PropertyManager.

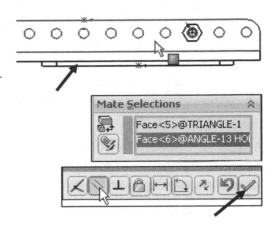

Display the Isometric view.

639) Click **Isometric view** ⬡ from the Heads-up View toolbar.

View the created mates.

640) Expand the Mates folder. View the created mates.

Save the FRONT-SUPPORT assembly.

641) Click **Save** 💾.

Assemble the four SCREW parts with SmartMates.

A SmartMate is a mate that automatically occurs when a component is placed into an assembly.

The mouse pointer displays a SmartMate feedback symbol when common geometry and relationships exist between the component and the assembly.

SmartMates are Concentric, Coincident, or Concentric and Coincident.

A Concentric SmartMate assumes that the geometry on the component has the same center as the geometry on an assembled reference.

Mating entities	Type of mate	Pointer
2 linear edges	Coincident	
2 planar faces	Coincident	
2 vertices	Coincident	
2 conical faces, or 2 temporary axes, or 1 conical face and 1 temporary axis	Concentric	
2 circular edges (peg-in-hole SmartMates). The edges do not have to be complete circles.	Concentric (conical faces) - and - Coincident (adjacent planar faces)	
2 circular patterns on flanges (flange SmartMates).	Concentric and coincident	

As the component is dragged into place, the mouse pointer provides various feedback icons. The SCREW utilizes a Concentric and Coincident SmartMate. Assemble the first SCREW. The circular edge of the SCREW mates Concentric and Coincident with the circular edge of the right slot of the TRIANGLE.

Activity: FRONT-SUPPORT Assembly-Inset the SCREW

Insert the SCREW part.

642) Click **Open** from the Menu bar.

643) Double-click **SCREW** from the SW-TUTORIAL-2013 folder. The SCREW PropertyManager is displayed.

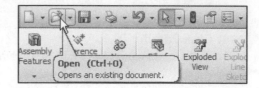

Display the SCREW part and the FRONT-SUPPORT assembly.

644) Click **Window**, **Tile Horizontally** from the Menu bar. **Zoom in** on the right side of the FRONT-SUPPORT assembly. Note: Work between the two tile windows.

Insert the first SCREW.

645) Click and drag the **circular edge** of the SCREW part into the FRONT-SUPPORT assembly Graphic window.

646) Release the mouse pointer on the **top 3ʳᵈ circular hole edge** of the ANGLE-13HOLE. The mouse pointer

displays the
Coincident/Concentric
circular edges icon.

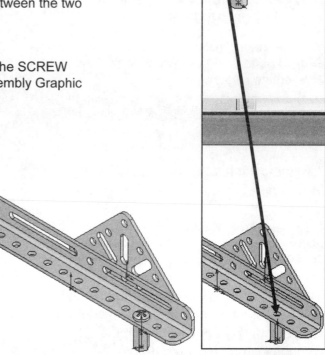

Reference geometry defines the shape or form of a surface or a solid. Reference geometry includes planes, axes, coordinate systems, and points.

Use the Pack and Go option to save an assembly or drawing with references. The Pack and Go tool saves either to a folder or creates a zip file to email. View SolidWorks help for additional information

Insert the second SCREW.
647) Zoom in on the right side of the FRONT-SUPPORT assembly.

648) Click and drag the **circular edge** of the SCREW part into the FRONT-SUPPORT assembly Graphic window.

649) Release the mouse pointer on the **right arc edge** of the ANGLE-13HOLE. The mouse pointer displays the Coincident/Concentric circular edges icon.

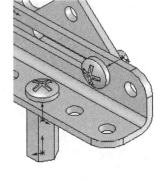

Insert the third SCREW part.
650) Zoom in on the left side of the FRONT-SUPPORT assembly

651) Click and drag the **circular edge** of the SCREW part into the FRONT-SUPPORT Assembly Graphic window.

652) Release the mouse pointer on the **left arc edge** of the ANGLE-13HOLE. The mouse pointer displays the Coincident/Concentric circular edges icon.

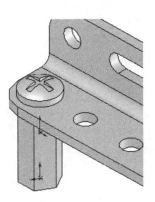

Insert the forth SCREW part.
653) Zoom in on the bottom circular edge of the ANGLE-13HOLE.

654) Click and drag the **circular edge** of the SCREW part into the FRONT-SUPPORT Assembly Graphic window.

655) Release the mouse pointer on the **bottom circular edge** of the ANGLE-13HOLE. The mouse pointer displays the Coincident/Concentric circular edges icon.

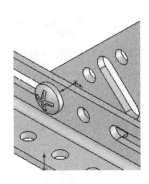

656) Close the SCREW part window.

657) Maximize the FRONT-SUPPORT assembly window.

Display the Isometric view.
658) Click **Isometric view** from the Heads-up View toolbar.

Deactivate the Origins.
659) Click **View**; uncheck **Origins** from the Menu bar menu.

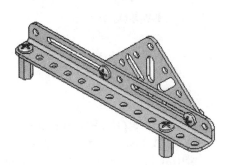

Save the FRONT-SUPPORT assembly.

660) Click **Save** 💾 .

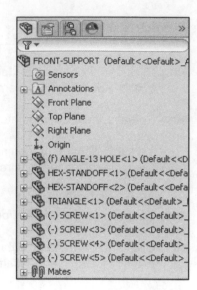

Select the Ctrl-Tab keys to quickly alternate between open SolidWorks documents.

Close all open parts and assemblies.
661) Click **Windows**, **Close All** from the Menu bar.

The FRONT-SUPPORT assembly is complete.

Display the Mates in the FeatureManager to check that the components and the mate types correspond to the design intent.

When a component is in the Lightweight 🪶 state, only a subset of its model data is loaded in memory. The remaining model data is loaded on an as-needed basis.

Review the FRONT-SUPPORT Assembly.

The ANGLE-13HOLE part was the first part inserted into the FRONT-SUPPORT assembly. The ANGLE-13HOLE part was fixed to the FRONT-SUPPORT Origin.

Concentric, Coincident, and Parallel mates were utilized to assemble the HEX-STANDOFF to the ANGLE-13HOLE. *Concentric*, *Distance*, and *Parallel* mates were utilized to assemble the TRIANGLE to the ANGLE-13HOLE. The *Concentric/Coincident* SmartMate was utilized to mate the four SCREW parts to the FRONT-SUPPORT assembly.

Chapter Summary

In this chapter you created four parts; HEX-STANDOFF, ANGLE-13HOLE, TRIANGLE and SCREW utilizing the Top, Front, Right Planes and the FRONT-SUPPORT assembly.

You obtained the knowledge of the following SolidWorks features: Extruded Boss/Base, Extruded Thin, Extruded Cut, Revolved Boss/Base, Hole Wizard, Linear Pattern, Circular Pattern, Fillet, and Chamfer. You also applied sketch techniques with various Sketch tools: Line, Circle, Corner Rectangle, Centerline, Dynamic Mirror, Straight Slot, Trim Entities, Polygon, Tangent Arc, Sketch Fillet, Offset Entities and Convert Entities.

You utilized centerlines as construction geometry to reference dimensions and relationships. You incorporated the four new parts to create the FRONT-SUPPORT assembly. Concentric, Distance, and Parallel mates were utilized to assemble the TRIANGLE to the ANGLE-13HOLE. The Concentric/Coincident SmartMate was utilized to mate the four SCREW parts to the FRONT-SUPPORT assembly.

The default location for storing drawing sheet formats is:

- **Windows XP** - C:Documents and Settings\All Users\ApplicationData\SolidWorks \ version\lang\language\sheetformat

- **Windows 7** - C:ProgramData\SolidWorks\version\lang\language\sheetformat

- **Windows Vista** - C:ProgramData\SolidWorks\version\lang\language\sheetformat

To change the default location, click Tools, Options, System Options, File Locations. In Show folder for, select Sheet Formats.

Chapter Terminology

Utilize SolidWorks Help for additional information on the terms utilized in this project.

Assembly: An assembly is a document which contains components, features, and other sub-assemblies. When a part is inserted into an assembly it is called a component. Components are mated together. The filename extension for a SolidWorks assembly file name is .SLDASM.

Component: A part or sub-assembly within an assembly.

Convert Entities: Converts model entities or sketch entities into sketch segments on the current sketch plane.

Features: Features are geometry building blocks. Features add or remove material. Features are created from sketched profiles or from edges and faces of existing geometry.

Instance Number: The instance number increments every time you insert the same component or mate. If you delete a component or mate and then reinsert the component or mate in the same SolidWorks session, the instance number increments by one.

Mates: A mate is a Geometric relation between components in an assembly.

Mirror Entities: Sketch tool that mirrors sketch geometry to the opposite side of a sketched centerline.

Offset Entities: Insert sketch entities by offsetting faces, edges, curves, construction geometry by a specified distance on the current sketch plane.

Orthographic Projection: Orthographic projection is the process of projecting views onto parallel planes with ⊥ projectors. The default reference planes are the Front, Top and Right Planes.

Part: A part is a single 3D object made up of features. The filename extension for a SolidWorks part file name is .SLDPRT.

Plane: To create a sketch, choose a plane. Planes are flat and infinite. They are represented on the screen with visible edges. The Front, Top and Right Planes were utilized as Sketch planes for parts in this chapter.

Relation: A relation is a geometric constraint between sketch entities or between a sketch entity and a plane, axis, edge or vertex.

Sketch: The name to describe a 2D or 3D profile is called a sketch. 2D Sketches are created on flat faces and planes within the model. Typical geometry types are lines, arcs, rectangles, circles and ellipses.

SmartMates: A SmartMate is a mate that automatically occurs when a component is placed into an assembly and references geometry between that component and the assembly.

Standard Views: Front, Back, Right, Left, Top, Bottom and Isometric are Standard views utilized to orient the model. Note: Third Angle Projection is used in this book.

Suppress features: A suppress feature is not displayed in the Graphics window. A suppress feature is removed from any rebuild calculations.

Trim Entities: Sketch tool that removes highlighted geometry.

Chapter Features

Chamfer: A Chamfer feature creates bevels on selected edges and faces.

Circular Pattern: A Circular Pattern feature repeats features or faces about an axis in a circular array. A Circular Pattern requires and axis, number of instances, and the angle of revolution.

Extruded Boss/Base: A Boss-Extrude1 feature is the first feature in a part. The Extruded Boss/Base feature starts with either a 2D or 3D sketch. An Extruded Boss feature (Boss-Extrude2) occurs after the Extruded Base (Boss-Extrude1) feature. The Extruded Boss/Base feature adds material by extrusion. Steps to create an Extruded Boss/Base Feature:

- Select the Sketch plane; Sketch the profile 2D or 3D; Add dimensions and Geometric relations; Select Extruded Boss/Base from the Features toolbar; Select an End Condition and/or options; Enter a depth; Click OK from the Boss-Extrude PropertyManager.

Extruded Cut: The Extruded Cut feature removes material from a solid. The Extruded Cut feature performs the opposite function of the Extruded Boss/Base feature. The Extruded Cut feature starts with either a 2D or 3D sketch and removes material by extrusion. Steps to create an Extruded Cut Feature:

- Select the Sketch plane; Sketch the profile, 2D or 3D; Add dimensions and Geometric relations; Select Extruded Cut from the Features toolbar; Select an End Condition and/or options; Enter a depth; Click OK from the Cut-Extrude PropertyManager.

Extruded Thin: The Extruded Thin feature adds material of constant thickness. The Extruded Thin feature requires an open profile.

Fillet: The Fillet feature creates a rounded internal or external face on a part. You can fillet all edges of a face, selected sets of faces, selected edges or edge loops.

Hole Wizard: The Hole Wizard feature creates either a 2D or 3D sketch for the placement of the hole in the FeatureManager. You can consecutively place multiple holes of the same type. The Hole Wizard creates 2D sketches for holes unless you select a nonplanar face or click the 3D Sketch button in the Hole Position PropertyManager.

Hole Wizard creates two sketches. The first sketch is the revolved cut profile of the selected hole type and the second sketch - center placement of the profile. Both sketches should be fully defined.

Linear Pattern: A Linear Pattern repeats features or geometry in an array. A Linear Patten requires the number of instances and the spacing between instances. Steps to create a Linear Pattern Feature:

- Select the feature/s to repeat (Seed feature); Select Linear Pattern from the Feature toolbar; Enter Direction of the pattern; Enter Number of pattern instances in each direction; Enter Distance between pattern instances; Optional: Pattern instances to skip; Click OK from the Linear Pattern PropertyManager.

Mirror: The Mirror feature mirrors features or faces about a selected plane. Select the features to copy and a plane about which to mirror them. If you select a planar face on the model, you mirror the entire model about the selected face.

Revolved Boss/Base: The Revolved Boss/Base feature adds material by revolving one or more profiles around a centerline. Create Revolved boss/bases, Revolved cuts, or Revolved surfaces. The Revolve feature can be a solid, a thin feature, or a surface.

Questions

1. Identify the three default Reference planes used in SolidWorks.

2. True or False. Sketches are created only on the Front Plane.

3. Identify the sketch tool required to create a hexagon.

4. Describe the profile required for an Extruded Thin feature.

5. Mirror Entities, Offset Entities, Sketch Fillet, and Trim Entities are located in the _____ toolbar.

6. List the six orthographic principle views in a drawing _____, _____, _____, _____, _____, _____,

7. Identify the type of Geometric relations that can be added to a sketch.

8. Describe the difference between a Circular Pattern feature and a Linear Pattern feature.

9. Describe the difference between a Fillet feature and a Chamfer feature.

10. Identify the function of the Hole Wizard feature.

11. Four 10-24X3/8 Machine Screws are required in the FRONT-SUPPORT assembly. The diameter is _____. The threads per inch are _____. The length is _____.

12. Describe the difference between a Distance mate and a Coincident mate.

13. True or False. A fixed component cannot move in an assembly.

14. Describe the procedure to remove the fix state, (f) of a component in an assembly.

15. Determine the procedure to rotate a component in an assembly.

16. Describe the procedure to resolve a Lightweight component in an assembly.

17. Describe the procedure to resolve a Lightweight assembly.

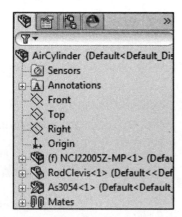

Exercises

Exercise 2.1: HEX-NUT Part

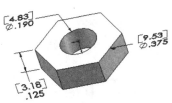
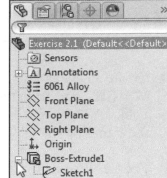

Create an ANSI, IPS HEX-NUT part. Apply 6061 Alloy material. Apply the following dimensions:

- Depth: .125 in, [3.18].

- Inside hole diameter: .190in, [4.83].

- Outside diameter: .375in, [9.53].

Use the Top Plane as the Sketch plane.

Exercise 2.2: FRONT-SUPPORT-2 Assembly

Create an ANSI, IPS FRONT-SUPPORT-2 assembly.

- Name the new assembly FRONT-SUPPORT-2.

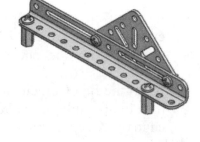

- Insert the FRONT-SUPPORT assembly. The FRONT-SUPPORT assembly was created in this Chapter. Note: The FRONT-SUPPORT assembly is provided in the Chapter 2 Homework folder on the DVD. Copy all parts to your folder on the computer. Do not work directly from the DVD.

- Fix the FRONT-SUPPORT assembly to the Origin.

- Insert the first HEX-NUT (Exercise 2.1) into the FRONT-SUPPORT-2 assembly.

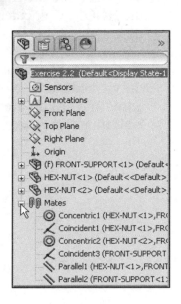

- Insert a Concentric mate and Coincident mate,

- Insert the second HEX-NUT part.

- Insert a Concentric mate and Coincident mate.

Note: You can also insert a Parallel mate between the HEX-NUT parts and the FRONT-SUPPORT assembly.

Exercise 2.3: Weight-Hook Assembly

Create an ANSI, IPS Weight-Hook assembly. The Weight-Hook assembly has two components: WEIGHT and HOOK.

- Create a new assembly document. Copy and insert the WEIGHT part from the Chapter 2 Homework folder in the book DVD. Note: Do not use the components directly from the folder on the DVD. Copy all parts to your computer.

- Fix the WEIGHT to the Origin as illustrated in the Assem1 FeatureManager.

- Insert the HOOK part from the Chapter2 - Homework folder into the assembly.

- Insert a Concentric mate between the inside top cylindrical face of the WEIGHT and the cylindrical face of the thread. Concentric is the default mate.

- Insert the first Coincident mate between the top edge of the circular hole of the WEIGHT and the top circular edge of Sweep1, above the thread.

- Coincident is the default mate. The HOOK can rotate in the WEIGHT.

- Fix the position of the HOOK. Insert the second Coincident mate between the Right Plane of the WEIGHT and the Right Plane of the HOOK. Coincident is the default mate.

- Expand the Mates folder and view the created mates. Note: Tangent edges and origins are displayed for educational purposes.

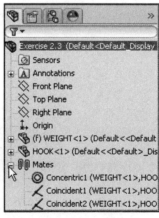

Exercise 2.4: Weight-Link Assembly

Create an ANSI, IPS Weight-Link assembly. The Weight-
Link assembly has two components and a sub-assembly:
Axle component, FLATBAR component, and the Weight-
Hook sub-assembly that you created in Exercise 2.4. Note:
Tangent edges and origins are displayed for educational
purposes.

- Create a new assembly document. Copy and insert the
  Axle part from the Chapter 2 Homework folder in the
  book DVD. Note: Do not use the parts / components
  directly from the folder on the DVD. Copy all parts
  and components to your computer from the DVD.

- Fix the Axle component to the Origin.

- Copy and insert the FLATBAR part from the
  Chapter2 - Homework folder in the book DVD. Note:
  Do not use the parts / components directly from the
  folder on the DVD. Copy all parts and components to
  your computer from the DVD.

- Insert a Concentric mate between the Axle cylindrical
  face and the FLATBAR inside face of the top circle.

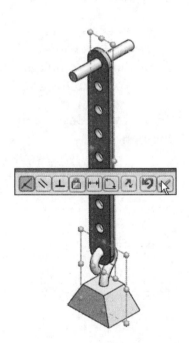

- Insert a Coincident mate between the Front Plane of
  the Axle and the Front Plane of the FLATBAR.

- Insert a Coincident mate between the Right Plane of
  the Axle and the Top Plane of the FLATBAR.
  Position the FLATBAR as illustrated.

- Insert the Weight-Hook sub-assembly that you created
  in Exercise 2.3.

🔅 Determine the static and dynamic behavior of mates in
each sub-assembly before creating the top level assembly.

🔅 Use the Pack and Go option to save an assembly or
drawing with references. The Pack and Go tool saves either to
a folder or creates a zip file to e-mail. View SolidWorks help
for additional information.

- Insert a Tangent mate between the inside bottom cylindrical face of the FLATBAR and the top circular face of the HOOK, in the Weight-Hook assembly. Tangent mate is selected by default.

- Insert a Coincident mate between the Front Plane of the FLATBAR and the Front Plane of the Weight-Hook sub-assembly. Coincident mate is selected by default. The Weight-Hook sub-assembly is free to move in the bottom circular hole of the FLATBAR.

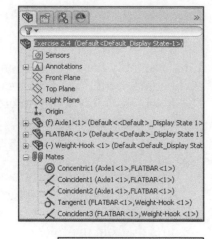

Exercise 2.5: Binder Clip

Create a simple Gem® binder clip. You see this item every day.

Create an ANSI - IPS assembly. Create two components - Binder and Binder Clip.

Apply material to each component and address all needed mates. Think about where you would start.

What is your Base Sketch for each component?

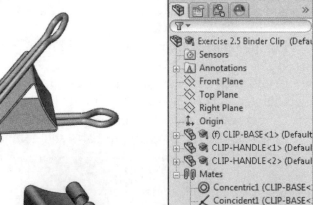

What are the dimensions? Measure all dimensions (approximately) from a small or large Gem binder clip.

You are the designer.

View SolidWorks Help or Chapter 4 on the Swept Base feature to create the Binder Clip handle.

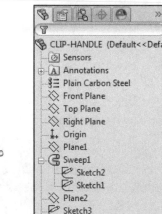

☼ Determine the static and dynamic behavior of mates in each sub-assembly before creating the top level assembly.

Exercise 2.6: Limit Mate (Advanced Mate)

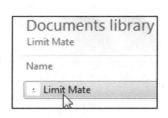

- Open the assembly (Limit Mate) from the Chapter 2 - Homework/Limit Mate folder located on the DVD in the book.

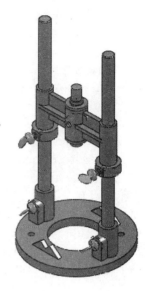

- Copy the assembly (components and sub-assemblies) to your working folder. Do not work directly from the DVD.

- Insert a Limit Mate to restrict the movement of the Slide Component - lower and upper movement. (Use the Measure tool to obtain maximum and minimum distances).

- Use SolidWorks Help for additional information.

A Limit Mate is an Advanced Mate type. Limit mates allow components to move within a range of values for distance and angle mates. You specify a starting distance or angle as well as a maximum and minimum value.

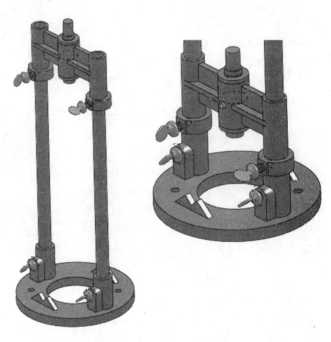

- Save the model and move the Slide to view the results in the Graphics window. Think about how you would use this mate type in other assemblies.

Use the Pack and Go option to save an assembly or drawing with references. The Pack and Go tool saves either to a folder or creates a zip file to e-mail. View SolidWorks help for additional information.

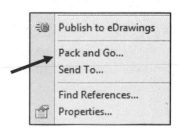

Exercise 2.7: Screw Mate (Mechanical Mate)

- Open the assembly (Screw Mate) from the Chapter 2 - Homework/Screw Mate folder located on the DVD in the book.

- Copy the assembly (components and sub-assemblies) to your working folder. Do not work directly from the DVD.

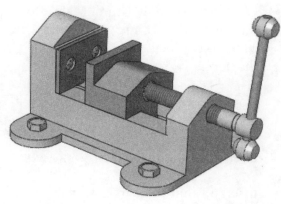

- Insert a Screw mate between the inside Face of the Base and the Face of the vice and any other mates that are required. A Screw is a Mechanical Mate type. View the avi file for proper movement.

A Screw mate constrains two components to be concentric, and also adds a pitch relationship between the rotation of one component and the translation of the other. Translation of one component along the axis causes rotation of the other component according to the pitch relationship. Likewise, rotation of one component causes translation of the other component. Use SolidWorks Help if needed.

Note: Use the Select Other tool (See SolidWorks Help if needed) to select the proper inside faces and to create the Screw mate for the assembly.

- Rotate the handle and view the results. Think about how you would use this mate type in other assemblies.

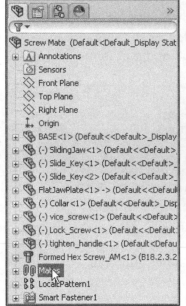

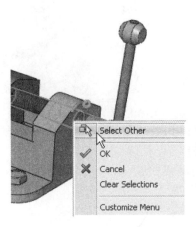

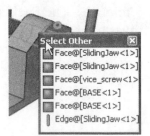

Exercise 2.8: Angle Mate

- Open the assembly (Angle Mate) from the Chapter 2 - Homework/ Angle Mate folder located on the DVD in the book.

- Copy the assembly (components and sub-assemblies) to your working folder. Do not work directly from the DVD.

- Move the Handle in the assembly. The Handle is free to rotate. Set the angle of the Handle. Insert an Angle mate (165 degrees) between the Handle and the Side of the valve using Planes. An Angle mate places the selected items at the specified angle to each other.

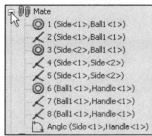

- The Handle has a 165-degree Angle mate to restrict flow through the valve. Think about how you would use this mate type in other assemblies.

Exercise 2.8A: Angle Mate (Cont:)

Open the SolidWorks FlowXpress Tutorial under the Design Evaluation Simulation folder. Follow the directions.

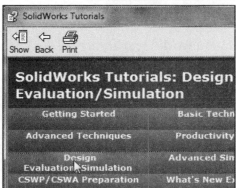

Create two end caps (lids) for the ball value using the Top-down Assembly method. Note: The Reference - In-Content symbols in the FeatureManager.

- Modify the Appearance of the body to observe the changes - enhance visualization. Apply the Select-other tool to obtain access to hidden faces and edges

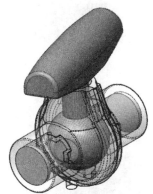

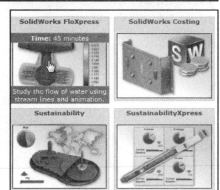

Exercise 2.9: Symmetric Mate (Advanced Mate)

- Open the assembly (Symmetric Mate) from the Chapter 2 - Homework/Symmetric Mate folder located on the DVD in the book.

- Copy the assembly (components and sub-assemblies) to your working folder. Do not work directly from the DVD.

- Insert a Symmetric Mate for the Guild Rollers. Think about how you would use this mate type in other assemblies.

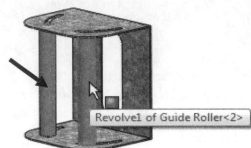
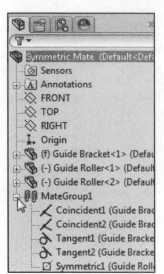

Exercise 2.10: Gear Mate (Mechanical mate)

View the ppt present on Gears located in the Chapter 2 - Homework/Gear folder on the DVD in the book.

Gears using SolidWorks

Instructors Name
Course Number

Copyright-Planchard 2011

Create the Gear assembly as illustrated below. All needed information is provided in the ppt. Create all needed components and mates. Use the SolidWorks Toolbox. The SolidWorks Toolbox is an add-in.

View the avi file in the Chapter 2 - Homework/Gear folder for proper movement.

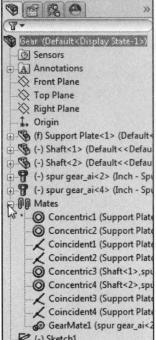

Exercise 2.11: Slider Part

Create the part from the illustrated A-ANSI - MMGS Third Angle Projection drawing below: Front, Top, Right and Isometric views.

Note: The location of the Origin.

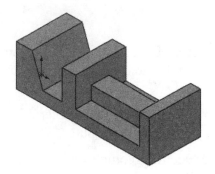

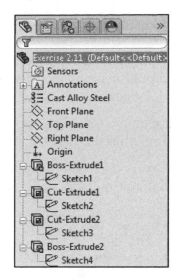

- Apply Cast Alloy steel for material.

- The part is symmetric about the Front Plane.

- Calculate the Volume of the part and locate the Center of mass.

Think about the steps that you would take to build the model. Do you need the Right view for manufacturing? Does it add any important information?

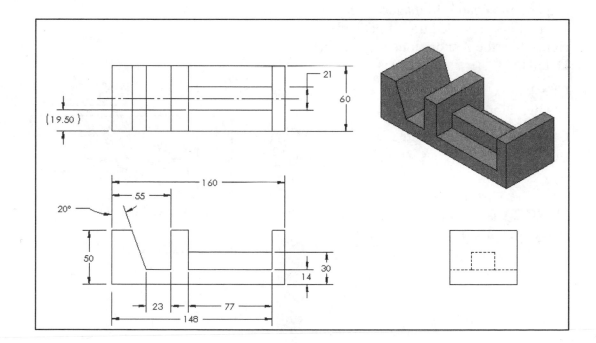

Exercise 2.12: Cosmetic Thread Part

Apply a Cosmetic thread: 1/4-20x2 UNC. A cosmetic thread represents the inner diameter of a thread on a boss or the outer diameter of a thread.

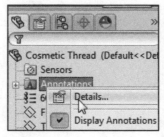

Open the Cosmetic thread part model from the Chapter 2 Homework folder on the DVD. Copy the part to your computer.

Create a Cosmetic thread. Produce the geometry of the thread. Click the bottom edge of the part as illustrated.

Click Insert, Annotations, Cosmetic Thread from the Menu bar menu. View the Cosmetic Thread PropertyManager. Edge<1> is displayed.

Select Blind for End Condition.

Enter 1.00 for depth.

Enter .200 for min diameter.

Enter ¼-20-2 UNC 2A in the Thread Callout box.

Click OK ✔ from the Cosmetic Thread FeatureManager.

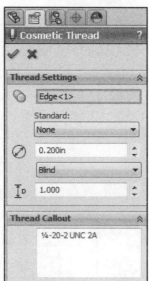

Expand the FeatureManager. View the Cosmetic Thread feature. If needed, right-click the Annotations folder, click Details.

Check the Cosmetic threads, and Shaded cosmetic threads box.

Click OK. View the cosmetic thread on the model.

☀ The Thread Callout: ¼-20-2UNC 2A is automatically inserted into a drawing document, if the drawing document is in the ANSI drafting standard.

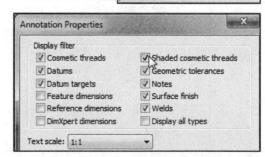

Exercise 2.13: Hole - Block

Create the Hole-Block ANSI - IPS part using the Hole Wizard feature as illustrated. Create the Hole-Block part on the Front Plane.

The Hole Wizard 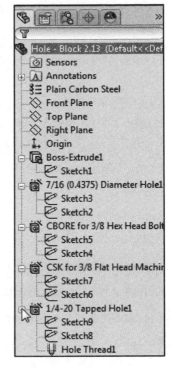 feature creates either a 2D or 3D sketch for the placement of the hole in the FeatureManager.

You can consecutively place multiple holes of the same type. The Hole Wizard creates 2D sketches for holes unless you select a non-planar face or click the 3D Sketch button in the Hole Position PropertyManager.

Hole Wizard creates two sketches. The first sketch is the revolved cut profile of the selected hole type and the second sketch - center placement of the profile. Both sketches should be fully defined.

Create a rectangular prism 2 inches wide by 5 inches long by 2 inches high on the top surface of the prism, place four holes, 1 inch apart

- Hole #1: Simple Hole Type: Fractional Drill Size, 7/16 diameter, End Condition: Blind, 0.75 inch deep.
- Hole #2: Counterbore hole Type: for 3/8 inch diameter Hex bolt, End Condition: Through All.
- Hole #3: Countersink hole Type: for 3/8 inch diameter Flat head screw, 1.5 inch deep.
- Hole #4: Tapped hole Type, Size ¼-20, End Condition: Blind -1.0 inch deep.

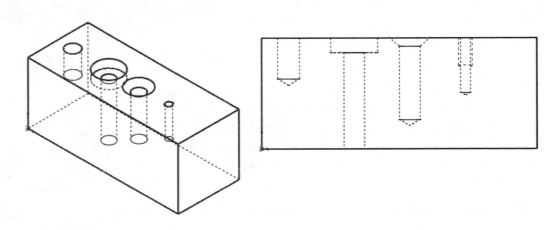

Exercise 2.14: Hole Wizard Part

Apply the 3D sketch placement method as illustrated in the FeatureManager. Insert and dimension a hole on a cylindrical face.

Open Hole Wizard 2-14 from the Chapter 2 Homework folder on the DVD. Note: Do not use the part / component directly from the folder on the DVD. Copy it first to your folder.

Note: With a 3D sketch, press the Tab key to move between planes.

Click the Hole Wizard 🖲 Features tool. The Hole Specification PropertyManager is displayed.

Select the Counterbore Hole Type.

Select ANSI Inch for Standard.

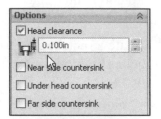

Select Socket Head Cap Screw for fastener Type.

Select 1/4 for Size. Select Normal for Fit.

Select Through All for End Condition.

Enter .100 for Head clearance in the Options box.

Click the Positions Tab. The Hole Position PropertyManager is displayed.

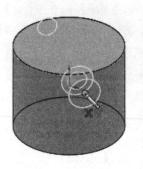
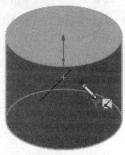

Click the 3D Sketch button. SolidWorks displays a 3D interface with the Point ✗Ẏ⟍ tool active.

🔆 When the Point tool is active, wherever you click, you will create a point.

Click the cylindrical face of the model as illustrated. The selected face is displayed in orange. This indicates that an OnSurface sketch relations will be created between the sketch point and the cylindrical face. The hole is displayed in the model.

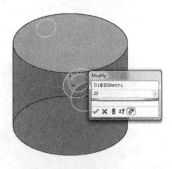

Insert a dimension between the top face and the Sketch point.

Click the Smart Dimension ✧ Sketch tool.

Click the top flat face of the model and the sketch point.

Enter .25in.

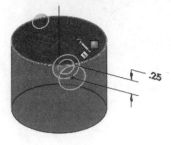

Locate the point angularly around the cylinder. Apply construction geometry.

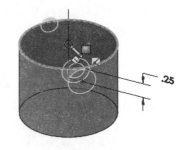

Activate the Temporary Axes. Click View; check the Temporary Axes box from the Menu bar toolbar.

Click the Line ＼ Sketch tool. Note: 3D sketch is still activated.

Ctrl+click the top flat face of the model. This moves the red space handle origin to the selected face. This also constrains any new sketch entities to the top flat face. Note the mouse

pointer ✎⬚ ＜ icon.

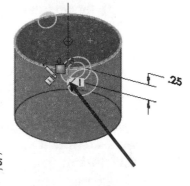

Move the mouse pointer near the center of the activated top flat face as illustrated. View the small black circle. The circle indicates that the end point of the line will pick up a Coincident relation.

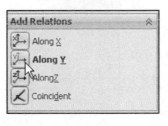

Click the center point of the circle.

Sketch a line so it picks up the **AlongZ sketch relation**. The cursor displays the relation to be applied. **This is a very important step!**

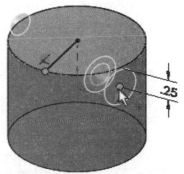

Create an AlongY sketch relation between the centerpoint of the hole on the cylindrical face and the endpoint of the sketched line as illustrated.

Click OK ✔ from the Properties PropertyManager.

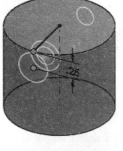

Click OK ✔ from the Hole Position PropertyManager.

Expand the FeatureManager and view the results. The two sketches are fully defined.

Close the model.

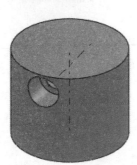

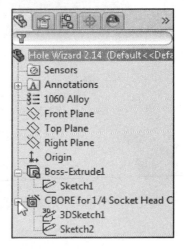

You can create a second sketched line and insert an angle dimension between the two lines. This process is used to control the position of the centerpoint of the hole on the cylindrical face as illustrated. Insert an AlongY sketch relation between the centerpoint of the hole on the cylindrical face and the end point of the second control line. Control the hole position with the angular dimension. Note: With a 3D sketch, press the Tab key to move between planes.

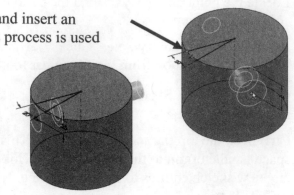

Exercise 2.15: DFMXpress

Apply the DFMXpress Wizard. DFMXpress is an analysis tool that validates the manufacturability of SolidWorks parts. Use DFMXpress to identify design areas that may cause problems in fabrication or increase the costs of production.

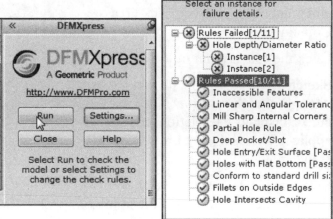

- Open the ROD Part from the Chapter 2 Homework folder on the DVD. Note: Do not use the part / component directly from the folder on the DVD. Copy all parts and components to your computer from the DVD.

- Click the Evaluate tab in the CommandManager.

- Click DFMXpress Analysis Wizard.

- Click the RUN button.

- Expand each folder. View the results.

- Make any needed changes and save the ROD. Use other models that you created and apply DFMXpress Wizard.

Exercise 2.16: Counter Weight Assembly

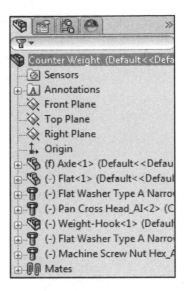

Create the Counter Weight assembly as illustrated using SmartMates and Standard mates. All components are supplied in the Chapter 2 - Homework/Counter-Weight folder on the DVD.

Copy all components to your working folder. The Counter Weight consists of the following items:

- Weight-Hook sub-assembly

- Weight

- Eye Hook

- Axle component (f). Fixed to the origin.

- Flat component

- Flat Washer Type A (from the SolidWorks Toolbox)

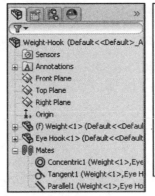

- Pan Cross Head Screw (from the SolidWorks Toolbox)

- Flat Washer Type A (from the SolidWorks toolbox)

- Machine Screw Nut Hex (from the SolidWorks Toolbox)

Apply SmartMates with the Flat Washer Type A Narrow_AI, Machine Screw Nut Hex_AI and the Pan Cross Head_AI components.

Use a Distance mate to fit the Axle in the middle of the Flat. Note a Symmetric mate could replace the Distance mate.

Think about the design of the assembly.

Apply all needed Lock mates.

The symbol (f) represents a fixed component. A fixed component cannot move and is locked to the assembly Origin.

Exercise 2.17: AIR RESERVOIR SUPPORT AND PLATE Assembly

The project team developed a concept sketch of the PNEUMATIC TEST MODULE assembly. Develop the AIR RESERVOIR SUPPORT AND PLATE assembly.

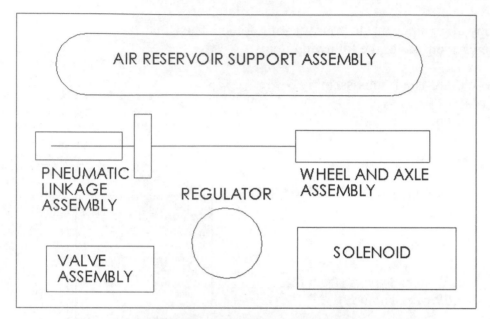

PNEUMATIC TEST MODULE Assembly Layout

Create three new parts:

- FLAT-PLATE

- IM15-MOUNT

- ANGLE-BRACKET

The Reservoir is a purchased part. The assembly file is available from the DVD in the book.

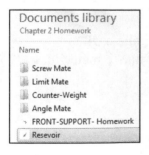

SMC AIR RESERVOIR

AIR RESERVOIR SUPPORT Assembly
Courtesy of Gears Educational Systems & SMC
Corporation of America

- Create a new assembly named AIR RESERVOIR SUPPORT AND PLATE.

- Two M15-MOUNT parts and two ANGLE-BRACKET parts hold the SMC AIR RESERVOIR.

- The ANGLE-BRACKET parts are fastened to the FLAT-PLATE.

Exercise 2.17a: FLAT-PLATE Part

Create the FLAT-PLATE Part on the Top Plane. The FLAT-PLATE is machined from .090, [2.3] 6061 Alloy flat stock. The default units are inches.

Utilize the Top Plane for the Sketch plane.

Locate the Origin at the Midpoint of the left vertical line.

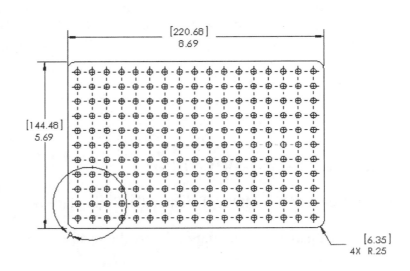

The 8.690, [220.68mm] x 5.688, [144.48mm] FLAT PLATE contains a Linear Pattern of ⌀.190, [4.83mm] Thru holes.

The Holes are equally spaced, .500, [12.7mm] apart.

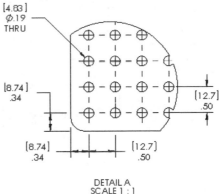

DETAIL A
SCALE 1 : 1

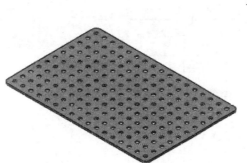

Determine the maximum number of holes contained in the FLAT-PLATE.

Maximum # of holes_____.

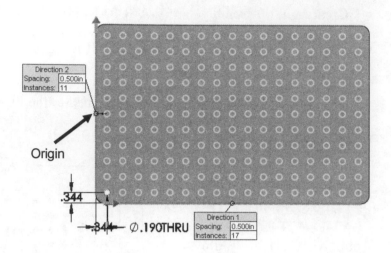

- Utilize a Linear Pattern in two Directions to create the holes.

- Utilize the Geometric Pattern Option.

Exercise 2.17b: IM15-MOUNT Part

- Create the IM15-MOUNT part on the Right plane.

- Center the part on the Origin. Utilize the features in the FeatureManager.

- The IM15-MOUNT Part is machined from 0.060, [1.5mm] 6061 Alloy flat stock. The default units are inches.

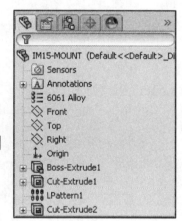

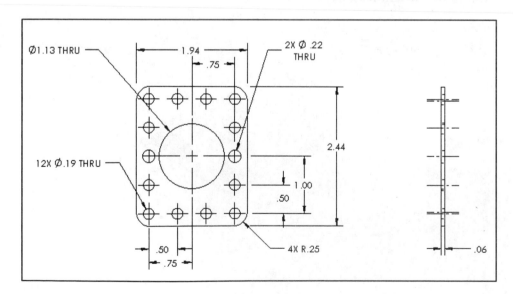

Exercise 2.17c: ANGLE BRACKET Part

- Create the ANGLE BRACKET part.

- The Extruded Base (Boss-Extrude1) feature is sketched with an L-Shaped profile on the Right Plane. The ANGLE BRACKET Part is machined from 0.060, [1.5mm] 6061 Alloy flat stock. The default units are inches.

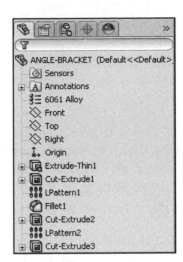

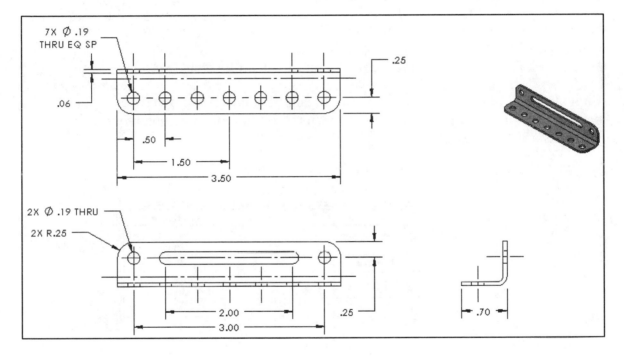

Exercise 2.17d: Reservoir Assembly

The Reservoir stores compressed air. Air is pumped through a Schrader Valve into the Reservoir.

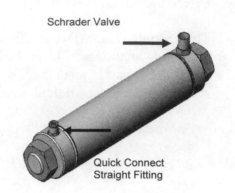

Schrader Valve

A Quick Connect Straight Fitting is utilized to supply air to the Pneumatic Test Module Assembly. Quick Connect Fittings allow air tubing to be assembled and disassembled without removing the fitting.

Quick Connect
Straight Fitting

Reservoir and Fittings
Courtesy of SMC Corporation of America and
Gears Educational Systems

Copy the Pneumatic Components folder from the DVD in the book to the SW-TUTORIAL folder.

Open the part, Reservoir from the Pneumatics Components folder or from the Chapter 2 Homework folder. The Reservoir default units are in millimeters (MMGS).

Engineers and designers work in metric and english units. Always verify your units for parts and other engineering data. In pneumatic systems, common units for volume, pressure and temperature are defined in the below table.

Magnitude	Metric Unit (m)	English (e)
Mass	kg	pound
	g	ounce
Length	m	foot
	m	yard
	mm	inch
Temperature	°C	°F
Area, Section	m ^{2}	sq.ft
	cm ^{2}	sq.inch
Volume	m ^{3}	cu.yard
	cm ^{3}	cu.inch
	dm ^{3}	cu.ft.
Volume Flow	m ^{3}n / min	scfm
	dm ^{3}n /min (ℓ/min)	scfm
Force	N	pound force (ℓbf.)
Pressure	bar	ℓbf./sq.inch (psi)

Common Metric and English Units

The ISO unit of pressure is the Pa (Pascal). $1Pa = 1N/m$.

Exercise 2.17e: AIR RESERVOIR SUPPORT AND PLATE Assembly

Create the AIR RESERVOIR SUPPORT AND PLATE assembly. Note: There is more than one solution for the mate types illustrated below.

The FLAT-PLATE is the first component in the AIR RESERVOIR SUPPORT AND PLATE assembly. Insert the FLAT-PLATE. The FLAT-PLATE is fixed to the Origin.

- Insert the ANGLE BRACKET.

- Mate the ANGLE BRACKET to the FLAT-PLATE. The bottom flat face of the ANGLE BRACKET is coincident to the top face of the FLAT-PLATE.

- The center hole of the ANGLE BRACKET is concentric to the upper left hole of the FLAT-PLATE.

- The first hole of the ANGLE bracket is concentric with the hole in the 8th row, 1st column of the FLAT-PLATE.

- Insert the IM15-MOUNT.

- Mate the IM15-MOUNT. The IM15-MOUNT flat back face is coincident to the flat inside front face of the ANGLE BRACKET.

- The bottom right hole of the IM15-MOUNT is concentric with the right hole of the ANGLE BRACKET.

- The bottom edge of the IM15-MOUNT is parallel to bottom edge of the ANGLE BRACKET.

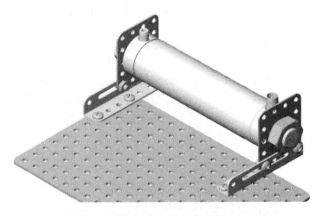

AIR RESERVOIR SUPPORT AND PLATE Assembly
Courtesy of SMC Corporation of America

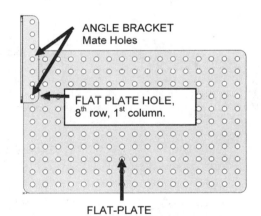

- Insert the Reservoir Assembly.

- Mate the Reservoir Assembly. The conical face of the Reservoir is concentric to the IM15-MOUNT center hole.

- The left end cap of the Reservoir Assembly is coincident to the front face of the IM15-MOUNT.

- The Hex Nut flat face is parallel to the top face of the FLAT-PLATE.

- Insert the second ANGLE BRACKET.

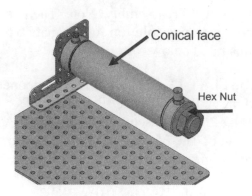

- Mate the ANGLE BRACKET to the FLAT-PLATE. The bottom flat face of the ANGLE BRACKET is coincident to the top face of the FLAT-PLATE.

- The center hole of the ANGLE BRACKET is concentric with the hole in the 11th row, 13th column of the FLAT-PLATE.

- The first hole of the ANGLE bracket is concentric with the hole in the 8th row, 13th column of the FLAT-PLATE.

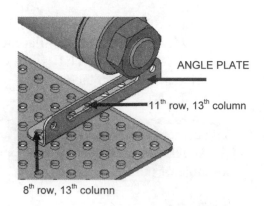

- Insert the second IM15-MOUNT.

- Mate the IM15-MOUNT to the outside face of the ANGLE BRACKET. The bottom right hole of the IM15-MOUNT is concentric with the right hole of the ANGLE BRACKET.

- The top edge of the IM15-MOUNT is parallel to the top edge of the ANGLE BRACKET.

- Save the assembly. Insert the required SCREWS. The AIR RESERVOIR SUPPORT AND PLATE assembly is complete.

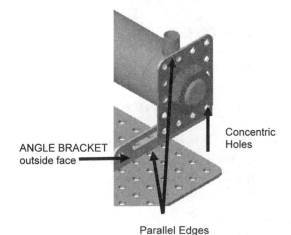

Chapter 3

Fundamentals of Drawing

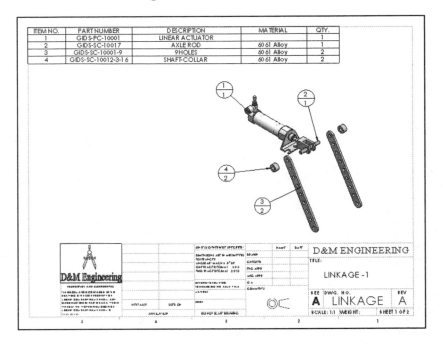

ITEM NO.	PART NUMBER	DESCRIPTION	MATERIAL	QTY.
1	GIDS-PC-10001	LINEAR ACTUATOR		1
2	GIDS-SC-10017	AXLE ROD	6061 Alloy	1
3	GIDS-SC-10001-9	9HOLES	6061 Alloy	2
4	GIDS-SC-10012-3-16	SHAFT-COLLAR	6061 Alloy	2

Below are the desired outcomes and usage competencies based on the completion of Chapter 3.

Desired Outcomes:	Usage Competencies:
• CUSTOM-A Sheet Format. • A-ANSI-MM Drawing Template.	• Ability to create a Custom Sheet Format, Drawing Template, Company logo and Title block.
• FLATBAR configurations. • FLATBAR part drawing. • LINKAGE assembly drawing. • FLATBAR-SHAFTCOLLAR assembly.	• Understand Standard, Isometric, Detail, Section and Exploded views. • Knowledge of the View Palette. • Ability to incorporate a Bill of Materials with Custom Properties.
	• Proficiency to create and edit drawing dimensions and annotations. • Aptitude to create a Design Table.

Notes:

Chapter 3 - Fundamentals of Drawing

Chapter Objective

Create a FLATBAR drawing with a customized Sheet Format and a Drawing Template containing a Company logo and Title block.

Obtain an understanding to display the following views with the ability to insert, add, and edit dimensions and annotations:

- Standard: Top, Front and Right

- Isometric, Detail, Section and Exploded

Create a LINKAGE assembly drawing with a Bill of Materials. Obtain knowledge to develop and incorporate a Bill of Materials with Custom Properties. Create a FLATBAR-SHAFTCOLLAR assembly.

On the completion of this chapter, you will be able to:

- Create a customized Sheet Format.

- Generate a custom Drawing Template.

- Produce a Bill of Materials with Custom Properties.

- Develop various drawing views.

- Reposition views on a drawing.

- Move dimensions in the same view.

- Apply Edit Sheet Format mode and Edit Sheet mode.

- Modify the dimension scheme.

- Create a Parametric drawing note.

- Link notes in the Title block to SolidWorks properties.

- Generate an Exploded view.

- Create and edit a Design Table.

Chapter Overview

Generate two drawings in this chapter:

- FLATBAR part drawing and a LINKAGE assembly drawing.

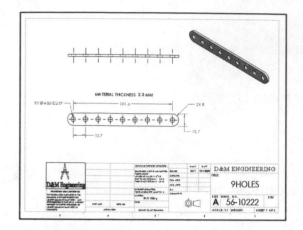 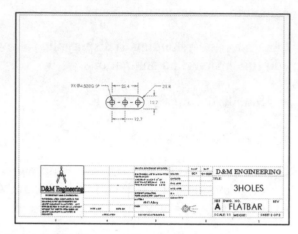

The FLATBAR drawing utilizes a custom Drawing Template and a custom Sheet Format. The FLATBAR drawing contains two sheets:

- Sheet1 contains a Front, Top and Isometric view with dimensions and a linked Parametric note.

- Sheet2 contains the 3HOLE configuration of the FLATBAR. Configurations are created with a Design Table.

The LINKAGE assembly drawing contains two sheets:

- Sheet1 contains the LINKAGE assembly in an Exploded view with a Bill of Materials.

- Sheet2 contains the AirCylinder assembly with a Section view, Detail view, and a Scale view.

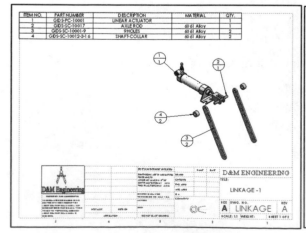 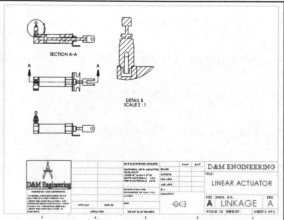

Create the FLATBAR-SHAFTCOLLAR assembly.
Utilize a Design Table to create four new
configurations of the assembly.

🔅 Tangent edges are displayed for educational
purposes.

There are two major design modes used to develop
a drawing:

- *Edit Sheet Format*

- *Edit Sheet*

The *Edit Sheet Format* mode provides the ability to:

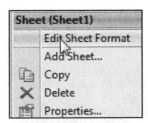

- Change the Title block size and text headings.

- Incorporate a Company logo.

- Add Custom Properties and text.

The *Edit Sheet* mode provides the ability to:

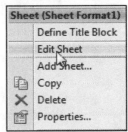

- Add or modify views

- Add or modify dimensions

- Add or modify notes

Drawing Template and Sheet Format

The foundation of a SolidWorks drawing is the Drawing
Template. Drawing size, drawing standards, company
information, manufacturing and or assembly requirements,
units and other properties are defined in the Drawing Template.

The Sheet Format is incorporated into the Drawing Template.
The Sheet Format contains the border, Title block information,
Revision block information, Company name and or Logo
information, Custom Properties, and SolidWorks Properties.

Custom Properties and SolidWorks Properties are shared
values between documents. Utilize an A-size Drawing
Template with Sheet format for the FLATBAR drawing and
LINKAGE assembly drawing.

During the initial SolidWorks installation, you are requested to select either the ISO or ANSI drafting standard. ISO is typically a European drafting standard and uses First Angle Projection. The book is written using the ANSI (US) overall drafting standard and Third Angle Projection for drawings.

Views from the part or assembly are inserted into the SolidWorks drawing.

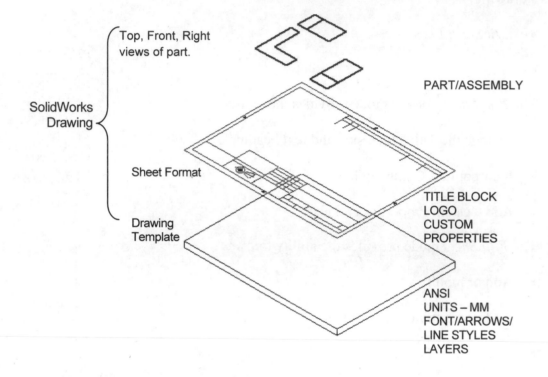

Create Sheet Formats for different parts types. Example: sheet metal parts, plastic parts, and high precision machined parts.

Create Sheet Formats for each category of parts that are manufactured with unique sets of title block notes.

Note: The Third Angle Projection scheme is illustrated in this chapter.

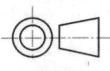

Third Angle
Projection icon

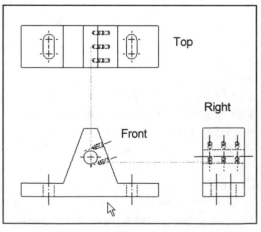

Third Angle Projection

For non-ANSI dimension standards, the dimensioning techniques are the same, even if the displayed arrows and text size are different. For printers supporting millimeter paper sizes, select A4 (ANSI) Landscape (297mm × 210mm).

The default Drawing Templates contain predefined Title block Notes linked to Custom Properties and SolidWorks Properties.

Activity: New Drawing

Create a New drawing. Close all parts and drawings.

1) Click **Windows**, **Close All** from the Menu bar.

2) Click **New** ⬜ from the Menu bar.

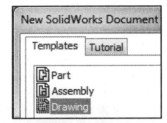

3) Double-click **Drawing** from the Templates tab.

4) Select **A (ANSI) Landscape**. If needed uncheck the Only show standard formats box.

5) Click **OK** from the Sheet Format/Size box.

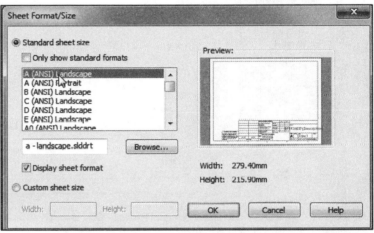

6) If required, click **Cancel** ✖ from the Model View PropertyManager. The Draw FeatureManager is displayed.

🔅 A new drawing invokes the Model View PropertyManager if the Start Command When Creating New Drawing option is checked.

The A (ANSI) Landscape paper is displayed in a new Graphics window. The sheet border defines the drawing size, 11″ × 8.5″ or (279.4mm × 215.9mm).

🔅 View the Sheet properties, right-click Properties in the drawing sheet. View the Sheet Properties dialog box. Click OK to return to the drawing sheet.

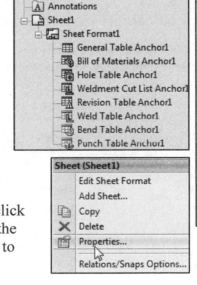

Draw1 is the default drawing name. Sheet1 is the default first Sheet name. For an active drawing document, the *View Layout*, *Annotation*, *Sketch*, *Evaluate* and *Office Products* tabs are displayed in the CommandManager.

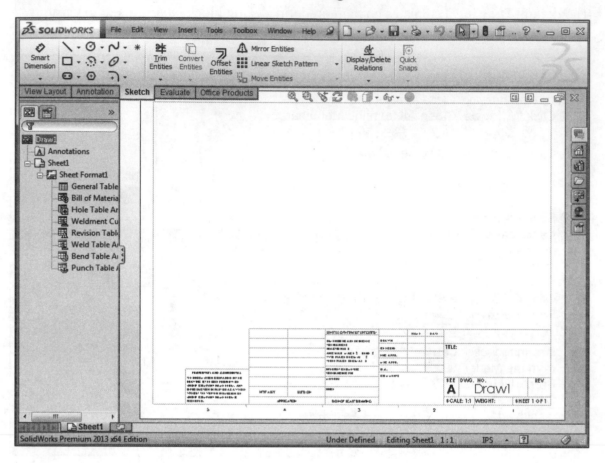

Utilize the CommandManager tabs or individual toolbars to access the needed tools in this chapter.

Set the Sheet Properties.

7)   Right-click in the **Graphics window**.

8)   Click **Properties**. The Sheet Properties are
          displayed. Enter Sheet Scale **1:1**.

9)   Check the **Third angle** box for Type of
          projection. Click **OK** from the Sheet Properties
          dialog box.

Activity: Drawing-Document Properties

Set the drawing document properties.

10)   Click **Options** [icon], **Document Properties** tab
           from the Menu bar.

11)   Select **ANSI** for Overall drafting standard from
           the drop-down menu.

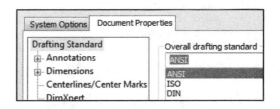

12)   Click **Units**.

13)   Click **MMGS** (millimeter, gram,
           second) for Unit system.

14)   Select **.12** for Length units
           Decimal places.

15)   Select **None** for Angular units
           Decimal places.

View the available Document
Properties options. Click each
folder under the Document
Properties tab.

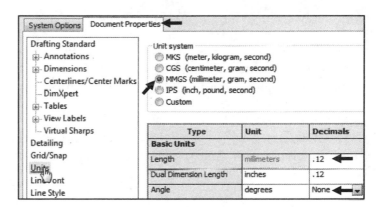

  Available Document Properties are document dependent.

Companies develop drawing format standards and use specific
text height for Metric and English drawings. Numerous
engineering drawings use the following format:

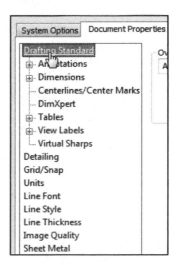

- *Font*: Century Gothic - All capitals.

- *Text height*: 3mm for drawings up to B Size, 17in. × 22in.

- *Text height*: 5mm for drawings larger than B Size, 17in ×
   22in.

- *Arrow heads*: Solid filled; with a 1:3 ratio - width to height.

Set the dimension font.
16)   Click **Annotations** folder as illustrated.

17)   Click the **Font** button. The Choose Font dialog box is displayed.

Set the dimension text height.
18)   Click the **Units** box from the Choose Font dialog box.

19)   Enter **3.0**mm for Height.

20)   Click **OK** from the Choose Font dialog box.

Set the arrow size.
21)   Click the **Dimensions** folder as illustrated.

22)   Enter **1**mm for arrow Height.

23)   Enter **3**mm for arrow Width.

24)   Enter **6**mm for arrow Length.

25)   Click **OK** from the Document Properties dialog box.

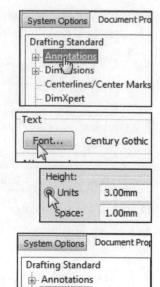

There are three dimension style type buttons: Outside, Inside, and Smart. Smart is the default option.

Check the Dual dimensions display box to display dual dimensions for your model or drawing.

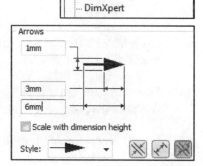

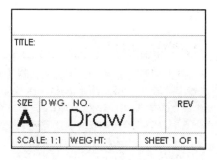

Title Block

The Title block contains text fields linked to System Properties and Custom Properties. System Properties are determined from the SolidWorks documents. Custom Property values are assigned to named variables.

Save time. Utilize System Properties and define Custom Properties in your Sheet Formats.

System Properties Linked to fields in default Sheet Formats:	Custom Properties of drawings linked to fields in default Sheet Formats:		Custom Properties of parts and assemblies linked to fields in default Sheet Formats:
SW-File Name (in DWG. NO. field):	CompanyName:	EngineeringApproval:	Description (in TITLE field):
SW-Sheet Scale:	CheckedBy:	EngAppDate:	Weight:
SW-Current Sheet:	CheckedDate:	ManufacturingApproval:	Material:
SW-Total Sheets:	DrawnBy:	MfgAppDate:	Finish:
	DrawnDate:	QAApproval:	Revision:
	EngineeringApproval:	QAAppDate:	

The Title block is located in the lower right hand corner of Sheet1. The Drawing contains two modes:

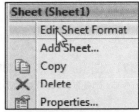

1. *Edit Sheet Format*

2. *Edit Sheet*

Insert views and dimensions in the Edit Sheet mode. Modify the Sheet Format text, lines or title block information in the Edit Sheet Format mode.

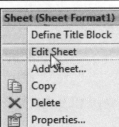

The CompanyName Custom Property is located in the title block above the TITLE box. There is no value defined for CompanyName. A small text box indicates an empty field.

Define a value for the Custom Property CompanyName. Example: D&M ENGINEERING.

Activity: Title Box

Activate the Edit Sheet Format Mode.
26)   Right-click in **Sheet1**.

27)   Click **Edit Sheet Format**. The Title block lines turn blue.

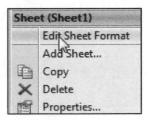

View the right side of the Title block.

28)   Click the **Zoom to Area** tool from the Heads-up View toolbar.

29)   **Zoom in** on the Title block.

30) Click the **Zoom to Area** tool to deactivate.

Define CompanyName Custom Property.

31) Position the **mouse pointer** in the middle of the box above the TITLE box as illustrated.

32) Click **File**, **Properties** from the Menu bar. The Summary Information dialog box is displayed.

33) Click the **Custom** tab.

34) Click inside the **Property Name** box.

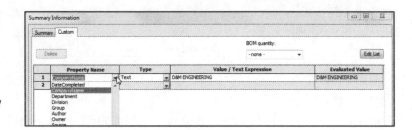

35) Click the **drop down arrow** in the Property Name box.

36) Select **CompanyName** from the Property menu.

37) Enter **D&M ENGINEERING** (or your company name) in the Value/Text Expression box.

38) Click inside the **Evaluated Value** box. The CompanyName is displayed in the Evaluated Value box.

39) Click **OK** from the dialog box.

40) Move your **mouse pointer** in the center of the block as illustrated. The Custom Property, $PRP: "COMPANYNAME", is displayed in the Title block.

Modify the font size.

41) Double-click the **D&M ENGINEERING** text. The Formatting dialog box is displayed.

42) Click the **drop down arrows** to set the Text Font and Height from the Formatting toolbar.

43) Click the **Style buttons** and **Justification buttons** to modify the selected text.

44) **Close** the Formatting dialog box. Click **OK** from the Note PropertyManager.

Click a position outside the selected text box to save and exit the text.

The Tolerance block is located in the Title block. The Tolerance block provides information to the manufacturer on the minimum and maximum variation for each dimension on the drawing. If a specific tolerance or note is provided on the drawing, the specific tolerance or note will override the information in the Tolerance block.

General tolerance values are based on the design requirements and the manufacturing process.

Create Sheet Formats for different part types; examples: sheet metal parts, plastic parts, and high precision machined parts. Create Sheet Formats for each category of parts that are manufactured with unique sets of Title block notes.

Modify the Tolerance block in the Sheet Format for ASME Y14.5 machined, millimeter parts. Delete unnecessary text. The FRACTIONAL text refers to inches. The BEND text refers to sheet metal parts. The Three Decimal Place text is not required for this millimeter part in the chapter.

Modify the Tolerance Note.
45) Double-click the text **INTERPRET GEOMETRIC TOLERANCING PER:**

46) Enter **ASME Y14.5**.

47) Click **OK** ✔ from the Note PropertyManager.

48) Double-click inside the **Tolerance block** text. The Formatting dialog box and the Note PropertyManager is displayed.

49) Delete the text **INCHES**.

50) Enter **MILLIMETERS**.

51) Delete the line **FRACTIONAL** ±.

52) Delete the text **BEND** ±.

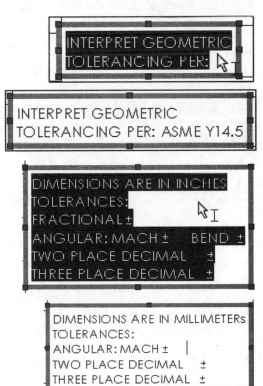

53) Click a **position** at the end of the  ANGULAR: MACH ± line.

54) Enter **0**.

55) Click the **Add Symbol** button from the Text Format box. The Symbols dialog box is displayed.

56) Select **Degree** from the Symbols dialog box.

57) Click **OK** from the Symbols dialog box.

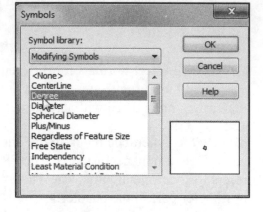

58) Enter **30'** for minutes of a degree.

Modify the TWO and THREE PLACE DECIMAL LINES.
59) Delete the **TWO** and **THREE PLACE DECIMAL lines**.

60) Enter **ONE PLACE DECIMAL ± 0.5**.

61) Enter **TWO PLACE DECIMAL ± 0.15**.

62) Click **OK** ✔ from the Note PropertyManager.

Fit the drawing to the Graphics window.
63) Press the **f** key.

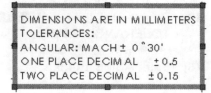

Save Draw1.

64) Click **Save** 💾. Accept the default name.

65) Click **Save** from the Save As box.

 Draw1 is the first default drawing file name.

Various symbols are available through the Symbol dialog box. The ± symbol is located in the Modify Symbols list. The ± symbol is sometimes displayed as <MOD-PM>. The degree symbol ° is sometimes displayed as <MOD-DEG>.

Interpretation of tolerances is as follows:

- The angular dimension 110° is machined between 109.5° and 110.5°.

- The dimension 2.5 is machined between 2.0 and 3.0.

- The dimension 2.05 is machined between 1.90 and 2.20.

Company Logo

A Company logo is normally located in the Title block of the drawing. You can create your own Company logo or copy and paste an existing picture.

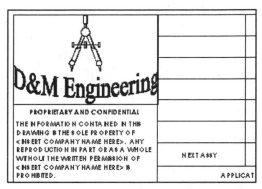

The Logo.jpeg file is enclosed on the DVD in the book. Copy all folders and files from the DVD to your hard drive. Do not work directly from the DVD. Insert the Company logo in the Edit Sheet Format mode.

If you have your own Logo, use it for the drawing and skip the process of copying it from the DVD.

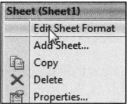

Activity: Company Logo

Insert a Company Logo.

66) Copy the folder **LOGO** from the DVD to your folder. Note: If you have your own Logo, use it for the drawing and skip the process of copying it from the DVD.

67) Click **Insert, Picture** from the Menu bar. The Open dialog box is displayed.

68) Select **\LOGO\Logo.jpg**.

69) Click **Open**. The Sketch Picture PropertyManager is displayed.

70) Drag the picture handles to size the **picture** to the left side of the Title block. Note: Text was added to the picture.

71) Click **OK** ✔ from the Sketch Picture PropertyManager.

Text can be added to create a custom logo. You can insert a picture or an object.

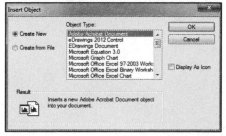

Return to the Edit Sheet mode.

72) Right-click in the **Graphics window**.

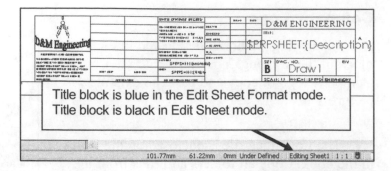

Title block is blue in the Edit Sheet Format mode.
Title block is black in Edit Sheet mode.

73) Click **Edit Sheet**. The Title block is displayed in black.

Fit the Sheet Format to the Graphics window.

74) Press the **f** key.

Draw1 displays Editing Sheet1 in the Status bar. The Title block is displayed in black when in Edit Sheet mode.

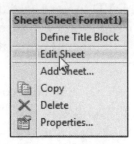

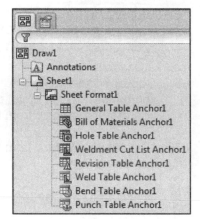

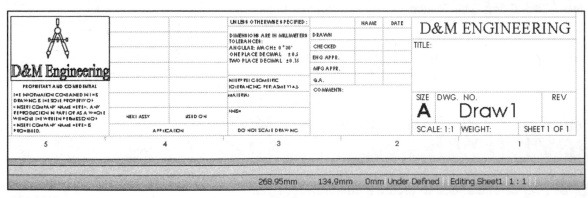

Save Sheet Format and Save As Drawing Template

Save the drawing document in the Graphics window in two forms: Sheet Format and Drawing Template. Save the Sheet Format as a custom Sheet Format named CUSTOM-A. Use the CUSTOM-A Sheet Format for the drawings in this chapter. The Sheet Format file extension is .slddrt.

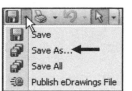

The Drawing Template can be displayed with or without the Sheet Format. Combine the Sheet Format with the Drawing Template to create a custom Drawing Template named A-ANSI-MM. Utilize the Save As option to save a Drawing Template. The Drawing Template file extension is .drwdot.

Always select the Save as type option first, then select the Save in folder to avoid saving in default SolidWorks installation directories.

The System Options, File Locations, Document Templates option is only valid for the current session of SolidWorks in some network locations. Set the File Locations option in order to view the SW-TUTORIAL-2013 tab in the New Document dialog box.

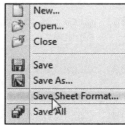

Activity: Save Sheet Format and Save As Drawing Template

Save the Sheet Format.

75) Click **File**, **Save Sheet Format** from the Menu bar. The Save Sheet Format dialog box is displayed.

The default Sheet Format folder is called SolidWorks 2013 on a new installation. Do not select this folder. The file extension for Sheet Format is .slddrt.

76) Select **SW-TUTORIAL-2013** for the Save in folder.

77) Enter **CUSTOM-A** for File name.

78) Click **Save** from the Save Sheet Format dialog box.

Save the Drawing Template.
79) Click **Save As** from the Menu bar.

80) Click **Drawing Templates (*.drwdot)** from the Save as type box.

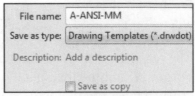

81) Select **SW-TUTORIAL-2013** for the Save in folder.

82) Enter **A-ANSI-MM** for File name.

83) Click **Save**.

The A-ANSI-MM.drwdot drawing template is displayed in the Graphics window. Add the SW-TUTORIAL-2013 folder to the File Locations Document Template System Option.

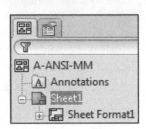

Set System Options - File Locations. Note: Only do this if you are working on your system - not a public computer in a lab.
84) Click **Options** [icon] , **File Locations** from the Menu bar.

85) Click **Add**.

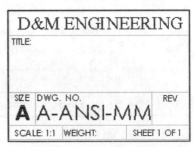

86) Select the **SW-TUTORIAL-2013** folder.

87) Click **OK** from the Browse for Folder menu.

88) Click **OK** to exit System Options.

89) Click **Yes**.

Close all files.
90) Click **Windows, Close All** from the Menu bar.

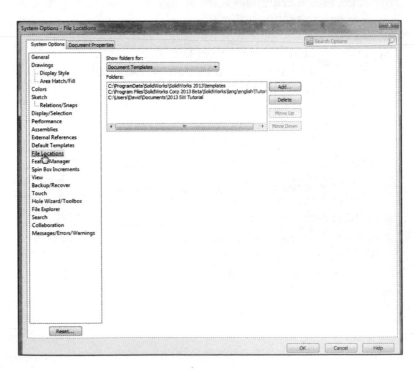

Create a New drawing.

91)   Click **New** ⬚ from the Menu bar.

92)   Select the **SW-TUTORIAL-2013** tab.

93)   Double-click the **A-ANSI-MM** Drawing Template.

94)   If required, click **Cancel** ✖ from the Model View PropertyManager. Draw2 is displayed in the Graphics window.

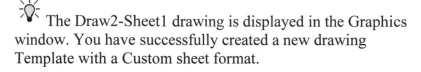

🔆 The Draw2-Sheet1 drawing is displayed in the Graphics window. You have successfully created a new drawing Template with a Custom sheet format.

Close all files.
95)   Click **Windows**, **Close All** from the Menu bar.

🔆 Combine customize Drawing Templates and Sheet Formats to match your company's drawing standards. Save the empty Drawing Template and Sheet Format separately to reuse information.

🔍 Additional details on Drawing Templates, Sheet Format and Custom Properties are available in SolidWorks Help Topics. Keywords: Documents (templates, properties) Sheet Formats (new, new drawings, note text), Properties (drawing sheets), Customize Drawing Sheet Formats.

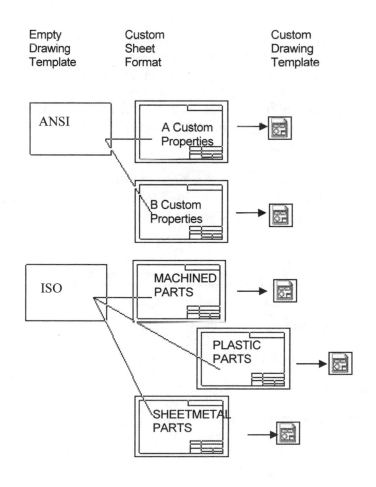

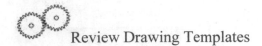 Review Drawing Templates

The Custom Drawing Template was created from the default Drawing Template. You modified Sheet Properties and Document Properties to control the Sheet size, Scale, Annotations and Dimensions.

The Sheet Format contained a Title block and Custom Property information. You inserted a Company Logo and modified the Title block.

The Save Sheet Format option was utilized to save the CUSTOM-A.slddrt Sheet Format. The Save As option was utilized to save the A-ANSI-MM.drwdot template.

The Sheet Format and Drawing Template were saved in the SW-TUTORIAL-2013 folder.

FLATBAR Drawing

A drawing contains part views, geometric dimensioning and tolerances, notes and other related design information. When a part is modified, the drawing automatically updates. When a dimension in the drawing is modified, the part is automatically updated.

Create the FLATBAR drawing from the FLATBAR part. Display the Front, Top, Right, and Isometric views. Utilize the Model View tool from the View Layout toolbar.

Insert dimensions from the part. Utilize the Insert Model Items tool from the Annotation toolbar. Insert and modify dimensions and notes.

Insert a Parametric note that links the dimension text to the part depth. Utilize a user defined Part Number. Define the part material with the Material Editor. Add Custom Properties for Material and Number.

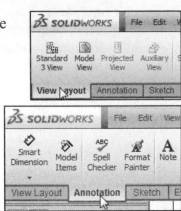

Activity: FLATBAR Drawing-Open the FLATBAR Part

Open the FLATBAR part. Note: The FLATBAR part was created in Chapter 1.

96)   Click **Open** from the Menu bar.

97)   Select the **SW-TUTORIAL-2013** folder.

98)   Select **Part** for file type.

99)   Double-click **FLATBAR**. The FLATBAR FeatureManager is displayed.

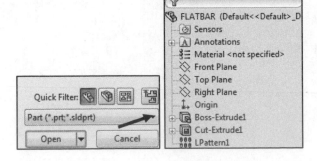

Create a New drawing.

100) Click **New** ⬜ from the Menu bar.

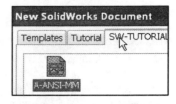

101) Select the **SW-TUTORIAL-2013** tab.

102) Double-click **A-ANSI-MM**.

The Model View PropertyManager is displayed if the Start command when creating new drawing box is checked. If the Model View PropertyManager is not displayed, click the Model View tool from the View Layout toolbar.

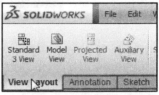

The FLATBAR ⚡ **FLATBAR** part icon is displayed in the Open documents box. Drawing view names are based on the part view orientation. The Front view is the first view inserted into the drawing. The Top view and Right view are projected from the Front view.

Insert the Front, Top and Right view.

103) Click **Next** ↻ from the Model View PropertyManager.

104) Check the **Create multiple views** box.

De-activate the Isometric view.
105) Click the ***Isometric** icon from the Standard views box.

106) Click ***Front**, ***Top** and ***Right** view from the Standard views box.

107) Click **OK** ✔ from the Model View PropertyManager. Click **Yes**. The three views are displayed on Sheet1.

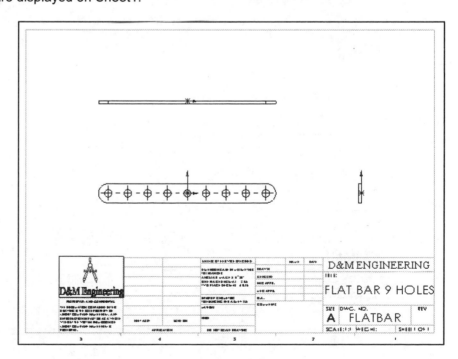

A part cannot be inserted into a drawing when the *Edit Sheet Format* is selected. You are required to be in the *Edit Sheet* mode.

Insert an Isometric view using the View Palette.

108) Click the **View Palette** ▦ tab on the right side of the Graphics window.

109) Select **FLATBAR** from the View Palette drop-down menu as illustrated. View the available views.

110) Click and drag the **Isometric view** in the top right corner as illustrated.

111) Click **OK** ✔ from the Drawing View PropertyManager.

*Isometric

Click the View Palette tab in the Task Pane. Click the drop-down arrow to view any active documents or click the Browse button to locate a document. Click and drag the desired view/views into the active drawing sheet.

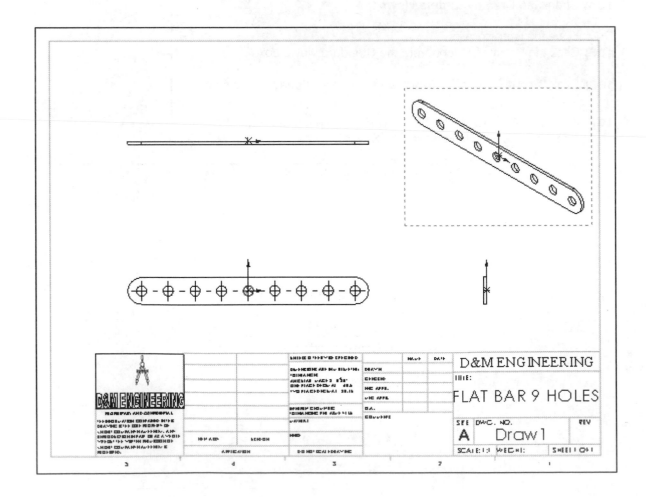

Modify the Sheet Scale.
112) Right-click a **position** inside the Sheet1 boundary.

113) Click **Properties**. The Sheet Properties dialog box is displayed.

114) Enter **1:1** for Sheet Scale.

115) Click **OK** from the Sheet Properties dialog box.

If needed, hide the Origins.
116) Click **View**; uncheck **Origins** from the Menu bar.

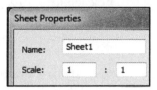

Save the drawing.
117) Click **Save As** from the Menu bar.

118) Enter **FLATBAR** in the SW-TUTORIAL-2013 folder.

119) Click **Save**.

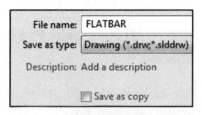

120) Click **Save** 💾 .

Text in the Title block is linked to the Filename and Description created in the part. The DWG. NO. text box utilizes the Property, $PRP:"SW-File Name" passed from the FLATBAR part to the FLATBAR drawing.

The Title text box utilizes the Property, $PRPSHEET: "Description".

The filename FLATBAR is displayed in the DWG. NO. box. The Description FLATBAR 9 HOLE is displayed in the Title box. The FLATBAR drawing contains three Principle views (Standard views): Front, Top, Right and an Isometric view.

Insert drawing views as follows:

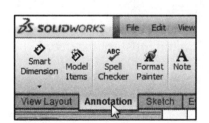

- Utilize the Model View tool.

  o Drag a part into the drawing to create three Standard views.

  o Predefine views in a custom Drawing Template.

  o Drag a hyperlink through Internet Explorer.

- Drag an active part view from the View Palette.
The View Palette is located in the Task Pane. With
an open part, drag the selected view into the active
drawing sheet.

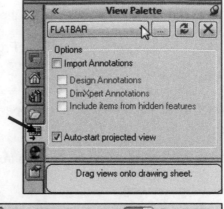

The View Palette populates when you:

- Click Make Drawing from Part/Assembly.

- Browse to a document from the View Palette.

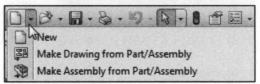

- Select from a list of open documents in the
View Palette.

Move Views and Properties of the Sheet

Move Views on Sheet1 to create
space for additional Drawing View
placement.

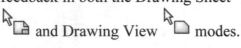

The mouse pointer provides
feedback in both the Drawing Sheet

and Drawing View   modes.

The mouse pointer displays the Drawing Sheet   icon when the Sheet properties and
commands are executed.

The mouse pointer displays the Drawing View   icon when the View properties and
commands are executed.

View the mouse pointer icon for feedback to select
Sheet, View, and Component and Edge properties in the
Drawing.

Use the Pack and Go option to save an assembly or
drawing with references. The Pack and Go tool saves
either to a folder or creates a zip file to e-mail. View
SolidWorks help for additional information.

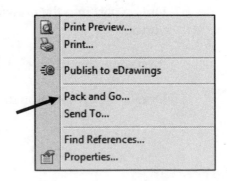

Sheet Properties

- Sheet Properties display properties of the selected

  sheet. Right-click in the sheet boundary 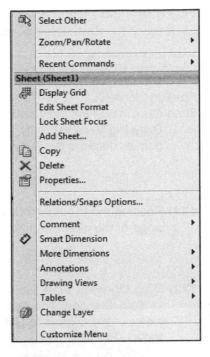 to view
  the available commands.

View Properties

- View Properties display properties of the selected view.

  Right-click inside the view boundary. Modify the
  View Properties in the Display Style box or the View
  Toolbar.

Component Properties

- Component Properties display properties of the
  selected component. Right-click to on the face of the

  component 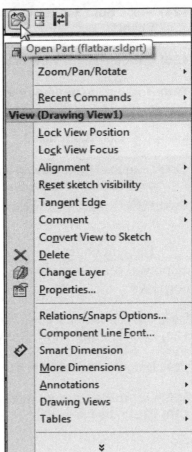. View the available options.

Edge Properties

- Edge Properties display properties of the selected

  geometry. Right-click on an edge inside the view
  boundary. View the available options.

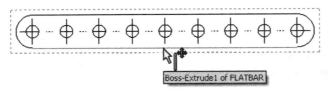

Reposition the views on the drawing. Provide approximately 25mm - 50mm between each view for dimension placement.

Activity: FLATBAR Drawing-Position Views

Position the views.

121) Click inside the view boundary of **Drawing View1** (Front). The mouse pointer displays the Drawing View

     icon.

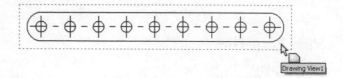

122) Position the **mouse pointer** on the edge of the view boundary until the

    Drawing View   icon is displayed.

123) Drag **Drawing View1** in an upward vertical direction. The Top and Right views move aligned to Drawing View1 (Front).

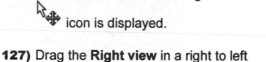

124) Press **Shift + Z** key to Zoom in on Sheet1.

125) Click the **Right view** boundary.

126) Position the **mouse pointer** on the edge of the view until the Drawing Move View

     icon is displayed.

127) Drag the **Right view** in a right to left direction towards the Front view.

💡 Tangent edges are displayed for educational purposes.

Move the Top view in a downward vertical direction.
128) Click the **Top view**, "Drawing View3" boundary.

129) Drag the **Top view** in a downward direction towards Drawing View1.

Fit Sheet1 to the Graphics window.
130) Press the **f** key.

Detail Drawing

The design intent of this project is to work with dimensions inserted from parts and to incorporate them into the drawings. Explore methods to move, hide and recreate dimensions to adhere to a drawing standard.

There are other solutions to the dimensioning schemes illustrated in this project. Detail drawings require dimensions, annotations, tolerance, materials, Engineering Change Orders, authorization, etc. to release the part to manufacturing and other notes prior to production.

Review a hypothetical "worse case" drawing situation. You just inserted dimensions from a part into a drawing. The dimensions, extensions lines and arrows are not in the correct locations. How can you address the position of these details? Answer: Dimension to an ASME Y14.5M standard.

No.	Situation:
1	Extension line crosses dimension line. Dimensions not evenly spaced.
2	Largest dimension placed closest to profile.
3	Leader lines overlapping.
4	Extension line crossing arrowhead.
5	Arrow gap too large.
6	Dimension pointing to feature in another view. Missing dimension – inserted into Detail view (not shown).
7	Dimension text over centerline, too close to profile.
8	Dimension from other view – leader line too long.
9	Dimension inside section lines.
10	No visible gap.
11	Arrows overlapping text.
12	Incorrect decimal display with whole number (millimeter), no specified tolerance.

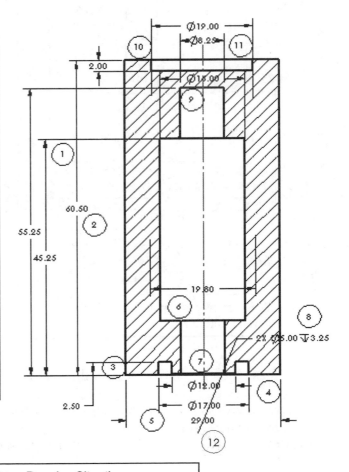

Worse Case Drawing Situation

The ASME Y14.5M standard defines an engineering drawing standard.

Review the twelve changes made to the drawing to meet
the standard.

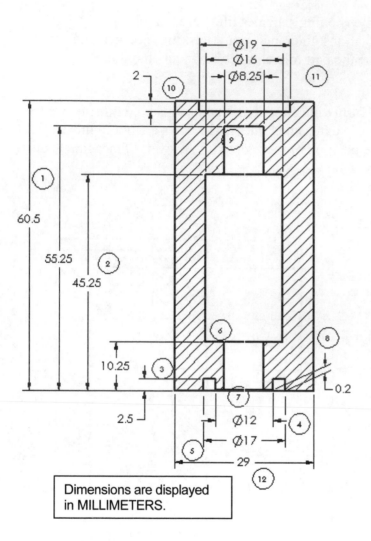

Dimensions are displayed
in MILLIMETERS.

No.	Preferred Application of the Dimensions:
1	Extension lines do not cross unless situation is unavoidable. Stagger dimension text.
2	Largest dimension placed farthest from profile. Dimensions are evenly spaced and grouped.
3	Arrow heads do not overlap.
4	Break extension lines that cross close to arrowhead.
5	Flip arrows to the inside.
6	Move dimensions to the view that displays the outline of the feature. Insure that all dimensions are accounted for.
7	Move text off of reference geometry (centerline).
8	Drag dimensions into their correct view boundary. Create reference dimensions if required. Slant extension lines to clearly illustrate feature.
9	Locate dimensions outside off section lines.
10	Create a visible gap between extension lines and profile lines.
11	Arrows do not overlap the text.
12	Whole numbers displayed with no zero and no decimal point (millimeter).

Apply these dimension practices to the FLATBAR and other drawings in this project.

A Detailed drawing is used to manufacture a part. A mistake on a drawing can cost your
company substantial loss in revenue. The mistake could result in a customer liability
lawsuit.

Dimension and annotate your parts clearly to avoid common problems and mistakes.

Dimensions and Annotations

Dimensions and annotations are inserted from the part. The annotations are not in the correct location. Additional dimensions and annotations are required.

Dimensions and annotations are inserted by selecting individual features, views or the entire sheet. Select the entire sheet. Insert Model Items command from the Annotations toolbar.

Activity: FLATBAR Drawing-Dimensions and Annotations

Insert dimensions.

131) Click **Sheet1** in the center of the drawing. The mouse pointer displays the Sheet icon.

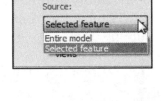

132) Click the **Annotation** tab from the CommandManager.

133) Click the **Model Items** tool from the Annotation toolbar. The Model Items PropertyManager is displayed. The Import items into all views option is checked.

134) Select **Entire model** from the Source box.

135) Click **OK** from the Model Items PropertyManager. Dimensions are inserted into the drawing.

Remove Trailing zeroes.

136) Click **Options**, **Document Properties** tab from the Menu bar.

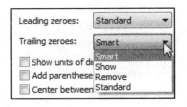

137) Click the **Dimensions** folder.

138) Select **Remove** for the Trailing zeroes drop-down menu.

139) Click **OK** from the Document Properties - Dimensions dialog box.

Dimensions are inserted into the drawing. The dimensions MAY NOT BE in the correct location with respect to the feature lines. Move them later in the chapter and address extension line gaps (5mm).

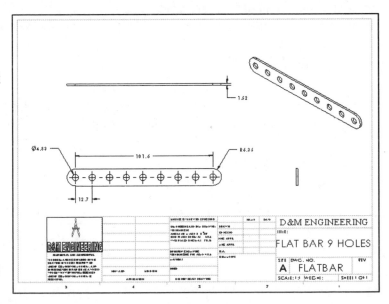

The dimensions and text in the next section have been enlarged for visibility. Drawing dimension location is dependent on: *Feature dimension creation* and *Selected drawing views.*

Move dimensions within the same view. Use the mouse pointer to drag dimensions and leader lines to a new location. Leader lines reference the size of the profile. A gap must exist between the profile lines and the leader lines. Shorten the leader lines to maintain a drawing standard. Use the blue Arrow buttons to flip the dimension arrows.

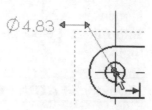

Plan ahead for general drawing notes. Notes provide relative part or assembly information. Example: Material type, material finish, special manufacturing procedure or considerations, preferred supplier, etc.

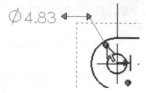

Below are a few helpful guidelines to create general drawing notes:

- Use capitol letters

- Use left text justification

- Font size should be the same as the dimension text

Create Parametric notes by selecting dimensions in the drawing. Example: Specify the material thickness of the FLATBAR as a note in the drawing. If the thickness is modified, the corresponding note is also modified.

Hide superfluous feature dimensions. Do not delete feature dimensions. Recall hidden dimension with the View, Show Annotations command. Move redundant, dependent views outside the sheet boundary.

Move the linear dimensions in Drawing View1, (Front).
140) Click the vertical dimension text **101.6**. The dimension text turns blue.

141) Drag the **dimension text** downward.

142) Click the horizontal dimension **12.7**.

143) Drag the **text** approximately 10mm's from the profile. The smallest linear dimensions are closest to the profile.

144) Click the radial dimension **R6.35**.

145) Drag the **text** diagonally off the profile if required.

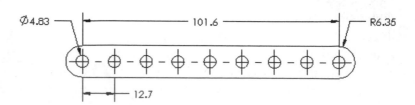

Modify dimension text.

146) Click the diameter dimension **4.83**. It turns blue. The Dimension PropertyManager is displayed.

147) Click inside the **Dimension Text** box.

148) Enter **9X** before <MOD-DIAM>. Enter **EQ SP** after <DIM>.

149) Click **OK** ✔ from the Dimension PropertyManager.

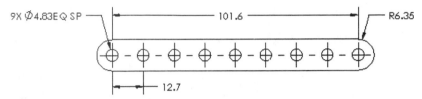

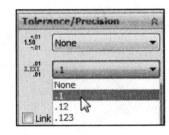

💡 Inserted dimensions can be moved from one drawing view to another. Hold the Shift key down. Click and drag the dimension text from one view into the other view boundary. Release the Shift key.

Modify the precision of the material thickness.

150) Click the depth dimension text **1.52** in the Top view.

151) Select **.1** from the Unit Precision drop-down menu.

152) Click **OK** ✔ from the Dimension PropertyManager. The text displays 1.5.

Insert a Parametric note.

153) Click the **Annotation** tab from the CommandManager.

154) Click the **Note** **A** tool from the Annotation toolbar. The Note icon is displayed.

155) Click a **position** above Front view.

156) Enter **MATERIAL THICKNESS**.

157) Click the depth dimension text **1.5** in the Top view. The variable name for the dimension is displayed in the text box.

158) Enter **MM**.

159) Click **OK** ✔ from the Note PropertyManager.

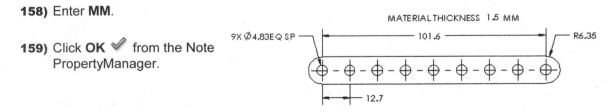

Hide superfluous dimensions.
160) Right-click the **1.5** dimension text in the Top view.

161) Click **Hide**.

Hide the Right view.
162) Right-click the **Right view** boundary.

163) Click **Hide**. Note: If required, expand the drop-down menu. The Right view is not displayed in the Graphics window.

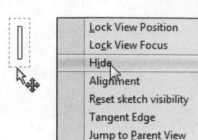

164) Click **OK** ✔ from the Drawing View PropertyManager.

Fit the model to the drawing and address all needed extension line gaps.
165) Press the **f** key.

Save the drawing.

166) Click **Save** 🖫.

Locate the Top view off of Sheet1.
167) Click and drag the **Top view boundary** off of the Sheet1 boundary as illustrated.

Views and notes outside the sheet boundary do not print. The Parametric note is controlled through the FLATBAR Boss-Extrude1 feature depth. Modify the depth to update the note.

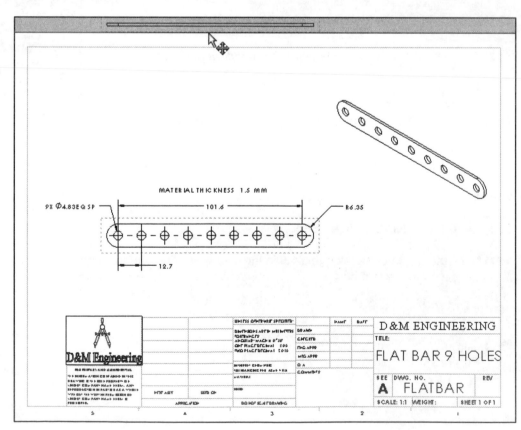

Open the FLATBAR part.
168) Right-click inside the **Front view** boundary.

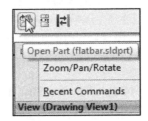

169) Click **Open Part**. The FLATBAR part is displayed.

Modify the Boss-Extrude1 depth dimension.
170) Click **Boss-Extrude1** from the FeatureManager.

171) Click **.060**in, [1.52].

172) Enter **2.3MM** as illustrated. Note: You need to enter MM.

173) Click **inside** the Graphics window.

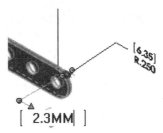

174) Click **Save** 🖫 .

Return to the drawing.
175) Click **Window**, **FLATBAR - Sheet1** from the Menu bar. The
Parametric note is updated to reflect the dimension change in
the part.

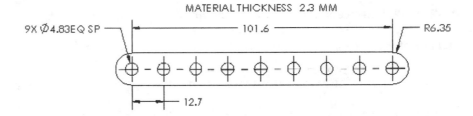

The FLATBAR drawing references the FLATBAR
part. Do not delete the part or move the part location.
Work between multiple documents:

- Press Ctrl-Tab to toggle between open SolidWorks
  documents.

- Right-click inside the Drawing view boundary.
  Select Open Part.

- Right-click the part icon in the FeatureManager.
  Select Open Drawing.

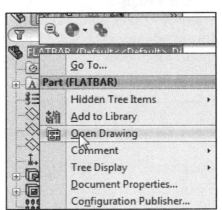

☼ Commands are accessed through the toolbars and
drop-down menus. Commands are also accessed with a
right-click in the Graphics window and
FeatureManager.

A majority of FLATBAR drawing dimensions are inserted from the FLATBAR part. An overall dimension is required to dimension the slot shape profile. Add a dimension in the drawing.

Add a dimension to Drawing View1.

176) Click the **Smart Dimension** ✒ tool from the Annotation toolbar. The Autodimension tab is selected by default.

177) Click the **Smart dimensioning** box.

178) Click the **top horizontal line** of the FLATBAR.

179) Click the **bottom horizontal line** of the FLATBAR.

180) Click a **position** to the right of the Front view as illustrated.

Modify the Radius text.
181) Click the **R6.36** dimension text.

182) Delete **R<DIM>** in the Dimension Text box.

183) Click **Yes** to confirm dimension override.

184) Enter **2X R** for Dimension text. Do not enter the radius value.

185) Click **OK** ✔ from the Dimension PropertyManager.

186) Insert all needed **extension line gaps (5mm)** as illustrated.

Save the FLATBAR drawing.
187) Click **Save** 💾 .

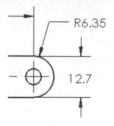

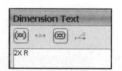

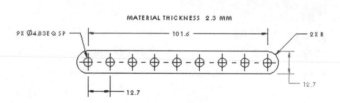

💡 Click the dimension Palette rollover button 🖉 to display the dimension palette. Use the dimension palette in the Graphics window to save mouse travel to the Dimension PropertyManager. Click on a dimension in a drawing view, and modify it directly from the dimension palette.

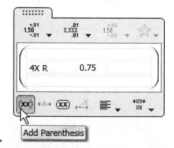

Part Number and Document Properties

Engineers manage the parts they create and modify. Each part requires a Part Number and Part Name. A part number is a numeric representation of the part. Each part has a unique number. Each drawing has a unique number. Drawings incorporate numerous part numbers or assembly numbers.

There are software applications that incorporate unique part numbers to create and perform:

- Bill of Materials

- Manufacturing procedures

- Cost analysis

- Inventory control / Just in Time, JIT

You are required to procure the part and drawing numbers from the documentation control manager. Utilize the following prefix codes to categorize created parts and drawings. The part name, part number and drawing numbers are as follows:

Category:	Prefix:	Part Name:	Part Number:	Drawing Number:
Machined Parts	56-	FLATEPLATE	GIDS-SC-10001-9	56-10222
		AXLE	GIDS-SC-10017	56-10223
		SHAFT-COLLAR	GIDS-SC-10012-3-16	56-10224
Purchased Parts	99-	AIRCYLINDER	99-FBM8x1.25	999-101-8
Assemblies	10-	LINKAGE ASM	GIDS-SC-1000	10-10123

Link notes in the Title block to SolidWorks Properties. Properties are variables shared between documents and applications.

The machined parts are manufactured from Aluminum. Specify the Material Property in the part. Link the Material Property to the drawing title block. Create a part number that is utilized in the Bill of Materials. Create additional notes in the title block to complete the drawing.

Activity: FLATBAR Drawing-Part Number and Document Properties

---

Return to the FLATEBAR part.
188) Right-click in the **Front view** boundary.

189) Click **Open Part**.

190) Right-click **Material** in the FLATBAR FeatureManager.

191) Click **Edit Material**. The Material dialog box is displayed.

192) **Expand** the Aluminum Alloys folder.

193) Select **2014 Alloy**. View the material properties.

194) Click the **Apply** button.

195) Click **Close**. The 2014 Alloy is displayed in the FeatureManager.

Save the FLATBAR.

196) Click **Save** 🖫 .

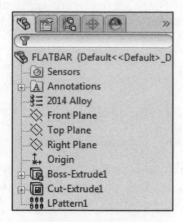

Define the part number property for the BOM.

197) Click the FLATBAR **ConfigurationManager** 🔧 tab.

198) Right-click **Default**.

199) Click **Properties**. The Configuration Properties PropertyManager is displayed.

200) Click **User Specified Name** from the drop-down box under Document Name.

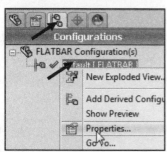

201) Enter **GIDS-SC-10001-9** in the Part number text box.

Define a material property.
202) Click the **Custom Properties** button.

203) Click inside the **Property Name** box.

204) Click the **down arrow**.

205) Select **Material** from the Property Name list.

206) Click inside the **Value / Text Expression** box.

207) Click the **down arrow**.

208) Select **Material**.

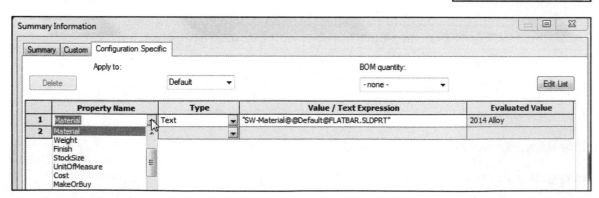

Define the Number Property.
209) Click inside the **second Property Name** box.

210) Click the **down arrow**. Select **Number** from the Name list.

211) Click inside the **Value / Text Expression** box.

212) Enter **56-10222** for Drawing Number.

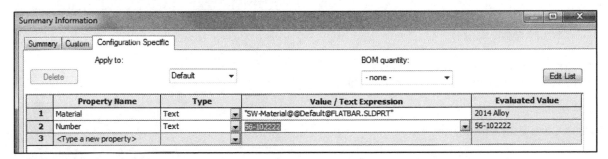

213) Click **OK** from the Summary Information dialog box.

214) Click **OK** ✔ from the Configuration Properties
PropertyManager.

Return to the FeatureManager.
215) Click the FLATBAR **FeatureManager** 🖑 tab.

Save the FLATBAR part.
216) Click **Save** 🖫.

Return to the drawing.
217) Click **Windows**, **FLATBAR - Sheet1** from the
Main menu.

The Material Property is inserted into the Title
block.

INTERPRET GEOMETRIC
TOLERANCING PER: ASME Y14.5

MATERIAL
2014 Alloy

Activity: FLATBAR Drawing-Linked Note

Create a Linked Note.
218) Right-click in **Sheet1**.

219) Click **Edit Sheet Format**.

220) **Zoom in** on the lower right corner of the drawing.

221) Double-click on the DWG. NO. text **FLATBAR**. The Note
PropertyManager is displayed.

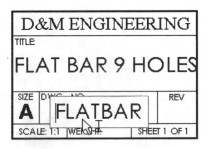

222) Click **Link to Property**  from the Text Format box.

223) Select **Model in view specified in sheet properties**.

224) Select **Number** from the Link to Property drop-down menu.

225) Click **OK** from the Link to Property box.

226) Click **OK** ✓ from the Note PropertyManager.

Return to the drawing sheet.
227) Right-click a **position** in the Graphics window.

228) Click **Edit Sheet**.

229) If needed, **remove all Tangent Edges** from the Top and Isometric view.

230) Address **all extension line gaps (5mm)** as illustrated below

Save the FLATBAR drawing.

231) Click **Save** 💾.

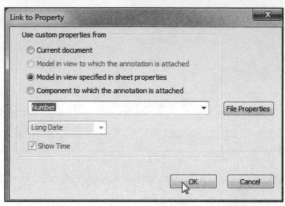

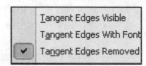

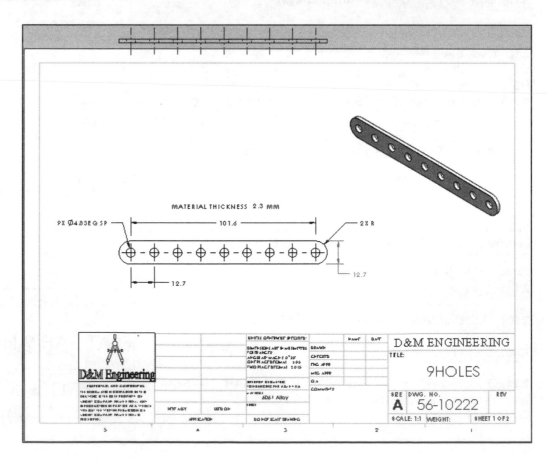

Custom Properties such as Revision and Drawn By are created in the chapter exercises.

Additional details on Drawing Views, New Drawing, Details, Dimensions, Dimensions and Annotations are available in SolidWorks Help.

Keywords: Drawing Views (overview), Drawing Views (model), Move (drawing views), Dimensions (circles, extension lines, inserting into drawings, move, parenthesis), Annotations Hole Callout, Centerline, Center Mark, Properties, and Sheet format.

 Review the FLATBAR Drawing

You created the FLATBAR drawing with the A-ANSI-MM Drawing Template. The FLATBAR drawing utilized the FLATBAR part with the Model View tool and the View Palette tool.

The Model View PropertyManager provided the ability to insert new views of a document. You selected the Front, Top and Right, view. You applied the View Palette to insert an Isometric view.

You moved the views by dragging the blue view boundary. You inserted part dimensions and annotations into the drawing with the Insert Model Items tool. Dimensions were moved to new positions. Leader lines and dimension text were repositioned. Annotations were edited to reflect the dimension standard.

You created a Parametric note that referenced part dimensions in the drawing text. Aluminum 2014 was assigned in the FLATBAR part. The Material Custom Property and Number Custom Property were assigned in the FLATBAR part and referenced in the drawing Title block.

Know inch/mm decimal display. The ASME Y14.5 standard states:

- *For millimeter dimensions < 1, display the leading zero. Remove trailing zeros.*

- *For inch dimensions < 1, delete the leading zero. The dimension is displayed with the same number of decimal places as its tolerance.*

Note: The FLATBAR drawing linked Title block notes to Custom Properties in the drawing and in the part. The additional drawings in this project utilize drawing numbers linked to the model file name. The Title of the drawing utilizes a Note.

Use the Pack & Go option to save an assembly or drawing with references. The Pack & Go tool saves either to a folder or creates a zip file to e-mail. View SolidWorks help for additional information.

LINKAGE Assembly Drawing - Sheet1

The LINKAGE assembly drawing Sheet 1 utilizes the LINKAGE assembly. Add an Exploded view and a Bill of Materials to the drawing.

Create an Exploded view in the LINKAGE assembly. The Bill of Materials reflects the components of the LINKAGE assembly. Create a drawing with a Bill of Materials. Perform the following steps:

- Create a new drawing with the custom A-ANSI-MM size Drawing Template with the CUSTOM-A sheet format.

- Create and display the Exploded view of the LINKAGE assembly.

- Insert the Exploded view of the assembly into the drawing.

- Insert a Bill of Materials.

- Label each component with Balloon text.

Activity: LINKAGE Assembly Drawing-Sheet1

Close all parts and drawings.
232) Click **Windows**, **Close All** from the Menu bar.

Create a New drawing.
233) Click **New** ☐ from the Menu bar.

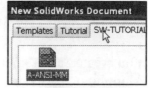

234) Double-click **A-ANSI-MM** from the SW-TUTORIAL-2013 tab. The Model View PropertyManager is displayed.

Open the LINKAGE assembly.
235) Click the **Browse** button.

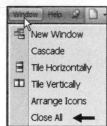

236) Select **Assembly** for file type in the SW-TUTORIAL-2013 folder.

237) Double-click **LINKAGE**. Note: Single view is selected by default.

238) Click **Isometric view** from the Standard views box.

239) Select **Shaded With Edges** 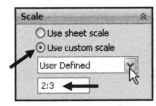 from the Display Style box.

240) Check the **Use custom scale** box.

241) Select **User Defined** from the drop down menu.

242) Enter **2:3** for Scale.

243) Click a **position** on the right side of Sheet1 as illustrated.

244) Click **OK** ✔ from the Drawing View1 PropertyManager.

Deactivate the Origins if needed.
245) Click **View**; uncheck **Origin** from the Menu bar.

Save the LINKAGE assembly drawing.

246) Click **Save** 💾. Accept the default file name.

247) Click **Save**.

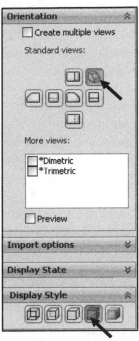

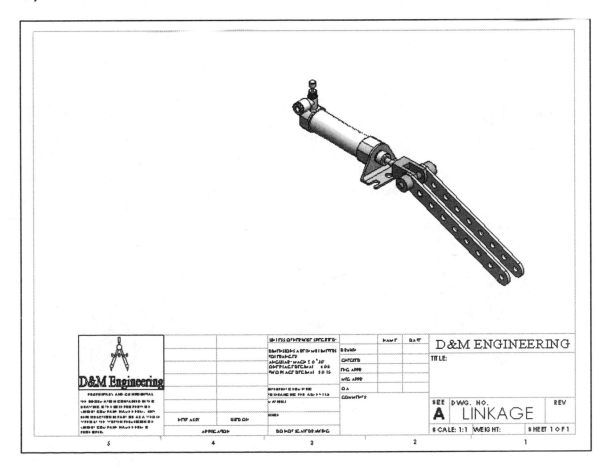

Display modes for a Drawing view are similar to a part document. The 3D Drawing View 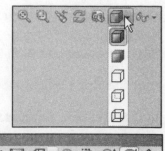 tool provides the ability to manipulate the model view in 3D, to select a difficult face, edge, or point.

Wireframe and Shaded Display modes provide the best graphic performance. Mechanical details require Hidden Lines Visible display and Hidden Lines Removed display. Select Shaded/Hidden Lines Removed to display Auxiliary Views to avoid confusion.

Tangent Edges Visible provides clarity for the start of a Fillet edge. Tangent Edges Removed provides the best graphic performance.

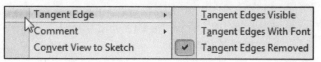

Right-click in the view boundary to access the Tangent Edge options.

Utilize the Lightweight Drawing option to improve performance for large assemblies.

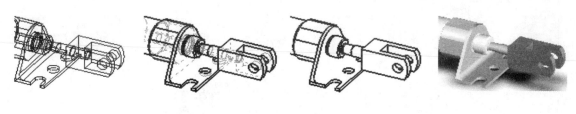

| Wireframe | Hidden Lines Visible | Hidden Lines Removed | Shaded |

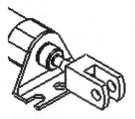 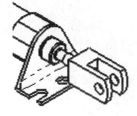 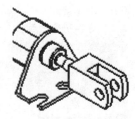

| Tangent Edges Visible | Tangent Edges With Font | Tangent Edges Removed |

To address Tangent lines views:

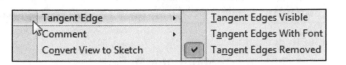

- Right-click in a Drawing view.

- Click Tangent Edge.

- Click a Tangent Edge view option.

Return to the LINKAGE assembly.
248) Right-click inside the **Isometric view** boundary.

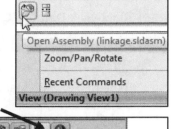

249) Click **Open Assembly**. The LINKAGE assembly is displayed.

250) Click the **ConfigurationManager** tab.

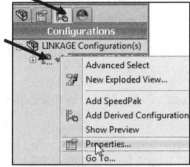

251) Right-click **Default [LINKAGE]**.

252) Click **Properties**. The Configuration Properties PropertyManager is displayed.

253) Select **User Specified Name** from the Part number displayed when used in Bill of Materials.

254) Enter **GIDS-SC-1000** in the Part number text box.

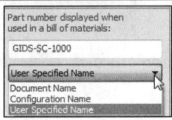

255) Click **OK** ✔ from the Configuration Properties PropertyManager.

256) Click the LINKAGE **FeatureManager** tab.

257) Click **Save** .

Exploded View

The Exploded View illustrates how to assemble the components in an assembly. Create an Exploded View with four steps. Click and drag components in the Graphics window.

The Manipulator icon ⤝ indicates the direction to explode. Select an alternate component edge for the Explode direction. Drag the component in the Graphics window or enter an exact value in the Explode distance box.

Manipulate the top-level components in the assembly. Access the Explode view option as follows:

- Right-click the configuration name in the ConfigurationManager.

- Select the Exploded View tool in the Assembly toolbar.

- Select Insert, Exploded View from the Menu bar.

Activity: LINKAGE Assembly Drawing-Exploded View

Insert an Exploded view.

258) Click the **ConfigurationManager** ⊡ tab.

259) Right-click **Default [GIDS-SC-1000]**.

260) Click **New Exploded view**
🔧 New Exploded View…. The
Explode PropertyManager is
displayed.

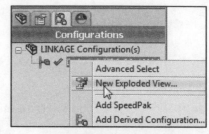

Create Explode Step 1. Use the distance
box option.
261) Click the back **SHAFT-COLLAR**
as illustrated.

262) Enter **50**mm in the Explode
distance box.

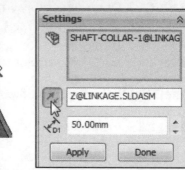

263) Click **Apply**. The SHAFT-COLLAR
moves 50mms to the back of the
model. If required, click the **Reverse direction**
button.

264) Click **Done**. Explode Step1 is created.

Create Explode Step 2. Use the Manipulator icon.
265) Click the front **SHAFT-COLLAR** in the
Graphics window as illustrated.

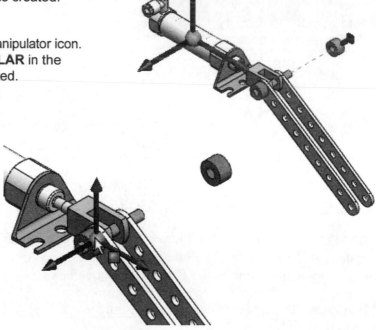

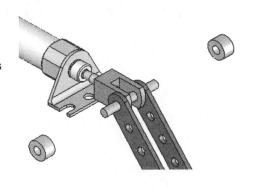

266) Drag the blue/orange **Manipulator icon** to the front of the assembly approximately 50mms.

267) Click **inside** the Graphics window. Explode Step2 is created.

Create Explode Step 3.
268) Click the **back FLATBAR** in the Graphics window as illustrated.

269) Drag the blue/orange **Manipulator icon** to the back of the assembly. Explode Step3 is created.

Create Explode Step 4.
270) Click the **front FLATBAR** in the Graphics window.

271) Drag the blue/orange **Manipulator icon** to the front of the assembly. Explode Step4 is created.

272) Click **inside** the Graphics window.

273) Expand each Explode Step to review.

274) Click **OK** from the Explode PropertyManager.

Save the LINKAGE part in the Exploded State.
275) Click **Save** .

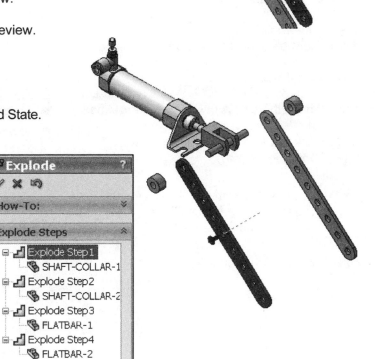

Activity: LINKAGE Assembly Drawing-Animation

Animate the Exploded view.
276) Expand Default [GIDS-SC-1000].

277) Right-click **ExplView1** in the ConfigurationManager.

278) Click **Animate collapse** to play the animation. View the Animation.

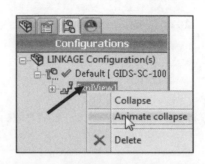

Return the Exploded view in its collapsed state.
279) Close ☒ the Animation Controller dialog box.

Return to the Assembly FeatureManager
280) Click the LINKAGE **FeatureManager** tab.

281) Click **Save** 💾 .

Open the LINKAGE drawing.
282) Click **Window, LINKAGE - SHEET1** from the Menu bar.

Display the Exploded view in the drawing.
283) Right-click inside the **Isometric view**.

284) Click **Properties**.

285) Check the **Show in exploded state** box.

286) Click **OK** from the Drawing Views Properties box.

287) Click **OK** ✓ from the Drawing View1 PropertyManager. View the exploded state in the drawing on Sheet1.

288) Rebuild 🔨 the model.

Bill of Materials

A Bill of Materials (BOM) is a table inserted into a drawing to keep a record of the parts used in an assembly. The default BOM template contains the Item Number, Quantity, Part No. and Description. The default Item number is determined by the order in which the component is inserted into the assembly. Quantity is the number of instances of a part or assembly.

Part No. is determined by the following: file name, default and the User Defined option, Part number used by the Bill of Materials. Description is determined by the description entered when the document is saved.

Activity: LINKAGE Assembly Drawing-Bill of Materials

Create a Bill of Materials.

289) Click inside the **Isometric view** boundary.

290) Click the **Annotation** tab from the CommandManager.

291) Click the **Bill of Materials** tool from the Consolidated Tables toolbar. The Bill of Materials PropertyManager is displayed.

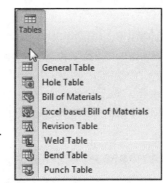

292) Select **bom-material** for Table Template.

293) Select **Top Level only** for BOM Type.

294) Click **OK** from the Bill of Materials PropertyManager.

295) Double-click a position in the **upper left corner** of the Sheet1.

296) Click a **position** in Sheet1.

	A	B	C	D	E
1	ITEM NO.	PART NUMBER	DESCRIPTION	MATERIAL	QTY.
2	1	Flexible	LINEAR ACTUATOR		1
3	2	AXLE	AXLE ROD		1
4	3	FLATBAR	9 HOLES	2014 Alloy	2
5	4	SHAFT-COLLAR	SHAFT-COLLAR		2

The Bill of Materials requires some editing. The AXLE and SHAFT-COLLAR PART NUMBER values are not defined. The current part file name determines the PART NUMBER value.

The current part description determines the DESCRIPTION values. Redefine the PART NUMBER for the Bill of Materials. Note: You will also scale the LINKAGE assembly.

Modify the AXLE Part number.
297) Right-click the **AXLE** part in the LINKAGE drawing. Click **Open Part**. The AXLE FeatureManager is displayed.

298) Click the AXLE **ConfigurationManager** tab.

299) Right-click **Default [AXLE]** in the ConfigurationManager.

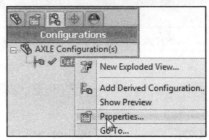

300) Click **Properties**. Select **User Specified Name** from the Configuration Properties dialog box.

301) Enter **GIDS-SC-10017** for the Part Number to be utilized in the Bill of Materials. Click **OK** ✔ from the Configuration Properties PropertyManager.

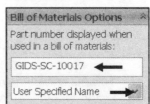

302) **Return** to the FeatureManager. Click **Save** 🖫.

Return to the LINKAGE drawing.
303) Click **Window**, **LINKAGE - Sheet1** from the Menu bar.

Modify the SHAFT-COLLAR PART NUMBER.
304) Right-click the front **SHAFT-COLLAR** part in the LINKAGE drawing as illustrated.

305) Click **Open Part**. The SHAFT-COLLAR FeatureManager is displayed.

306) Click the SHAFT-COLLAR **ConfigurationManager** tab.

307) Right-click **Default [SHAFT-COLLAR]** from the ConfigurationManager.

308) Click **Properties**. Select the **User Specified Name** from the Configuration Properties box.

309) Enter **GIDS-SC-10012-3-16** for the Part Number in the Bill of Materials. Click **OK** ✔ from the Configuration Properties PropertyManager.

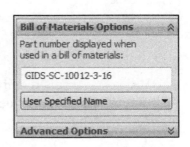

310) **Return** to the FeatureManager. Click **Save** 🖫.

Double-click the values in the BOM table (Keep Link) to directly edit the Custom Property of the Part/Assembly.

Return to the LINKAGE assembly drawing.
311) Click **Window**, **LINKAGE - Sheet1** from the Menu bar.

312) Rebuild the drawing and update the BOM.

Modify the LINKAGE assembly scale.
313) Click inside the **Isometric view** boundary.

314) Enter **1:2** for Scale.

315) Click **OK** ✅ from the Drawing View1 PropertyManager.

316) Click **Save** 💾.

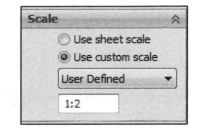

ITEM NO.	PART NUMBER	DESCRIPTION	MATERIAL	QTY.
1	GIDS-PC-10001	LINEAR ACTUATOR		1
2	GIDS-SC-10017	AXLE ROD		1
3	GIDS-SC-10001-9	FLAT BAR 9 HOLES	2014 Alloy	2
4	GIDS-SC-10012-3-16	SHAFT-COLLAR		2

Note: As an exercise, complete the Bill of Materials. Label each component with a unique item number. The item number is placed inside a circle. The circle is called Balloon text. List each item in a Bill of Materials table. Utilize Auto Balloon to apply Balloon text to all BOM components.

The Circle Split Line option contains the Item Number and Quantity. Item number is determined by the order listed in the assembly FeatureManager. Quantity lists the number of instances in the assembly.

Activity: LINKAGE Assembly Drawing-Automatic Balloons

Insert the Automatic Balloons.
317) Click inside the **Isometric view** boundary of the LINKAGE.

318) Click the **Auto Balloons** 🎈 tool from the Annotation toolbar. The Auto Balloon PropertyManager is displayed. Accept the defaults. Note: The Insert Magnet line option. Inserts one or more magnetic lines when Pattern type is not Circular.

319) Click **OK** ✅ from the Auto Balloon PropertyManager.

Reposition the Balloon text.
320) Click and drag each **Balloon** to the desired position. Click and drag the **Balloon arrowhead** to reposition the arrow on a component edge.

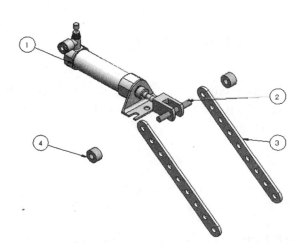

321) Click **OK** ✔ from the Balloon PropertyManager.

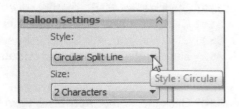

Display Item Number/Quantity.
322) Ctrl-Select the **four Balloon text** in the Graphics window. The Balloon PropertyManager is displayed.

323) Select **Circular Split Line** for Style.

324) Click **OK** ✔ from the Balloon PropertyManager.

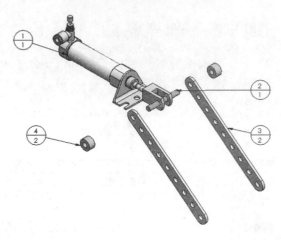

Save the LINKAGE assembly drawing.
325) Click **Save** 🖫 .

Select the BOM table in the drawing and Right-click Properties to modify entries and display table parameters.

LINKAGE Assembly Drawing - Sheet2

A drawing consists of one or more sheets. Utilize the Model View tool in the View Layout toolbar to insert the AirCylinder assembly. The LINKAGE drawing Sheet2 displays the Front view and Top view of the AirCylinder assembly.

Insert a Section View to display the internal features of the AirCylinder. Insert a Detail View to display an enlarged area of the AirCylinder.

Activity: LINKAGE Assembly Drawing-Sheet2

Add Sheet2.
326) Right-click in the Graphics window.

327) Click **Add Sheet**. Sheet2 is displayed.

328) Right-click in Sheet2.

You can also add a sheet by clicking the Add Sheet icon in the lower left corner of the Graphics window.

329) Click **Properties**. Enter **1:2** for Scale.

Select the CUSTOM-A Sheet Format.
330) Click **Browse** from the Sheet Properties box.

331) Select the **SW-TUTORIAL-2013** folder.

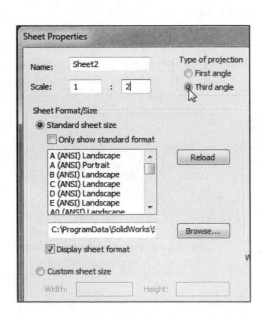

332) Double-click **CUSTOM-A**.

333) Click **OK** from the Sheet Properties box. Sheet 2 of 2 is displayed in the Graphics window.

Insert the AirCylinder assembly.
334) Click the **View Layout** tab from the CommandManager.

335) Click the **Model View** 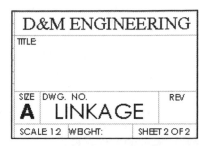 tool from the View Layout toolbar. The Model View PropertyManager is displayed.

336) Click the **Browse** button.

337) Double-click the **AirCylinder** assembly from the SW-TUTORIAL-2013 folder.

338) Check the **Create multiple views** box.

339) Click **Top view** as illustrated in the Standard views box. Note: Front view is selected by default. Both views should be active.

340) Click **OK** ✔ from the Model View PropertyManager.

Save Sheet2.
341) Click **Save** 🖫.

💡 Drawing sheets are ordered as they are created. The names are displayed in the FeatureManager design tree and as Excel-style tabs at the bottom of the Graphics window. Activate a sheet by right-clicking in the FeatureManager design tree and clicking Activate or click the tab name.

Modify the Title Name font size.
342) Right-click in the Graphics window.

343) Click **Edit Sheet Format**.

344) Double-click on the Title: **LINEAR ACTUATOR**.

345) Resize the text to the Title block. Enter **5mm** for text height. Click inside the **Graphics window**.

346) Right-click in the Graphics window.

347) Click **Edit Sheet**.

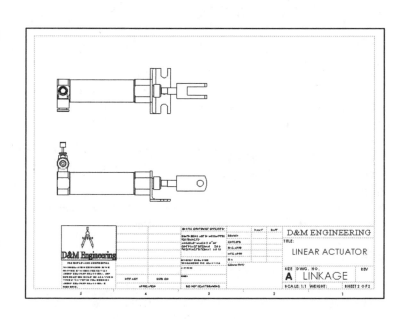

Section views display the interior features. Define a cutting plane with a sketched line in a view perpendicular to the Section view. Create a full Section view by sketching a section line in the Top view. Detailed views enlarge an area of an existing view. Specify location, shape and scale. Create a Detail view from a Section view at a 2:1 scale.

Activity: LINKAGE Assembly Drawing-Sheet2 Section view

Add a Section View to the drawing.
348) Click inside the **Drawing View3** boundary.

349) Click the **Section View** ↕ tool from the View Layout toolbar. The Section View PropertyManager is displayed.

350) Click the **Section** tab from the PropertyManager.

351) Click the **Horizontal** Cutting Line button.

352) Click the **midpoint** of the model as illustrated.

Position Section View A-A.
353) Click **OK** from the Section View dialog box.

354) Click a **location** above the Top view. The section arrows point upward.

355) If needed, check the **Flip direction** box.

356) Click **OK** ✔ from the Section View PropertyManager.

Fit the views to the drawing.
357) Press the **f** key.

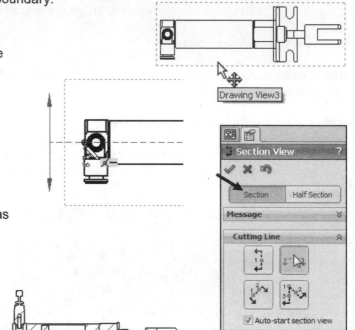

SECTION A-A

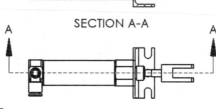

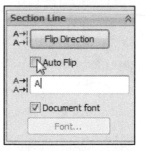

Activity: LINKAGE Assembly Drawing-Sheet2 Detail view

Add a Detail view to the drawing.
358) Click inside the **Section View** boundary. The Section View A-A PropertyManager is displayed.

359) Zoom in to enlarge the view.

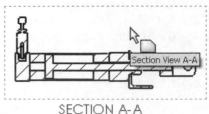

SECTION A-A

360) Click the **Detail View** 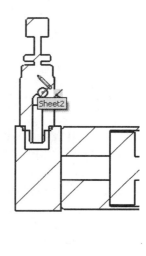 tool from the View Layout toolbar. The Circle Sketch tool is selected.

361) Click the **center** of the air fitting on the left side in the Section View as illustrated.

362) Sketch a **Circle** to encompass the air fitting.

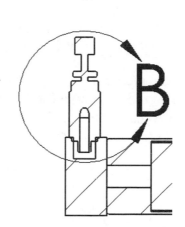

363) If required, enter **B** for Detail View Name in the Label text box.

Position Detail View B.
364) Press the **f** key.

365) Click a **location** on Sheet2 to the right of the SECTION View.

366) Enter **2:1** for Scale.

367) Click **OK** ✔ from the Detail View B PropertyManager.

💡 Select a view boundary before creating Projected Views, Section Views or Detail Views.

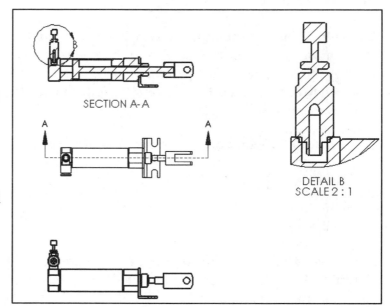

SECTION A-A

DETAIL B
SCALE 2 : 1

Move views if required.
368) Click and drag the **view boundary** to allow for approximately 1 inch, [25mm] spacing between views.

Save the LINKAGE assembly drawing.

369) Click **Save** 💾.

Close all parts and assemblies.
370) Click **Window, Close All** from the Menu bar.

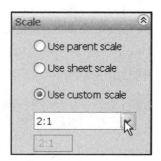

🔍 Additional details on Exploded View, Notes, Properties, Bill of Materials, Balloons, Section View and Detail View are available in SolidWorks Help. Keywords: Exploded, Notes, Properties (configurations), Bill of Materials, Balloons, Auto Balloon, Section and Detail.

 Review the LINKAGE Assembly Drawing

The LINKAGE Assembly drawing consisted of two sheets. Sheet1 contained an Exploded view. The Exploded view was created in the LINKAGE assembly.

The Bill of Materials listed the Item Number, Part Number, Description, Material and Quantity of components in the assembly. Balloons were inserted to label top level components in the LINKAGE assembly. You developed Custom Properties in the part and utilized the Properties in the drawing and Bill of Materials.

Sheet2 contained the Front view, Top view, Section view and Detail view of the AirCylinder assembly.

Design Tables

A Design Table is a spreadsheet used to create multiple configurations in a part or assembly. The Design Table controls the dimensions and parameters in the part. Utilize the Design Table to modify the overall length and number of holes in each FLATBAR.

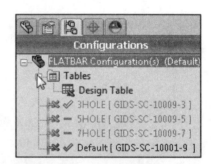

Create three configurations of the FLATBAR:

- 3HOLE

- 5HOLE

- 7HOLE

Utilize the Design Table to control the Part Number and Description in the Bill of Materials. Insert the custom parameter $PRP@DESCRIPTION into the Design Table. Insert the system parameter $PARTNUMBER into the Design Table.

Activity: FLATBAR Part-Design Table

Open the FLATBAR part.

371) Click **Open** 📂 from the Menu bar.

372) Double-click the **FLATBAR** part from the SW-TUTORIAL-2013 folder. The FLATBAR FeatureManager is displayed.

Insert a Design Table.

373) Click **Insert**, **Tables**, **Design Table** from the Menu bar. The Auto-create option is selected. Accept the default settings.

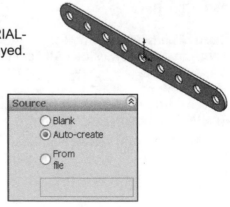

374) Click **OK** ✔ from the Design Table PropertyManager.

Select the input dimension.
375) Hold the **Ctrl key** down.

376) Click the **D1@Sketch1**, **D2@Sketch1**, **D1@Boss-Extude1**, **D1@Sketch2**, **D3@LPattern1** and **D1@LPattern1** from the Dimensions box.

377) Release the **Ctrl key**.

378) Click **OK** from the Dimensions dialog box.

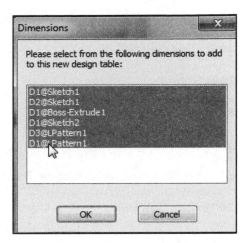

The illustrated dimension variable names in the Dimensions dialog box will be different if sketches or features were deleted when creating the FLATBAR part.

The input dimension names and default values are automatically entered into the Design Table. The Design Table displays the Primary Units of the Part. Example: Inches. The value Default is entered in Cell A3.

The values for the FLATBAR are entered in Cells B3 through G9. The FLATBAR length is controlled in Column B. The Number of Holes is controlled in Column G.

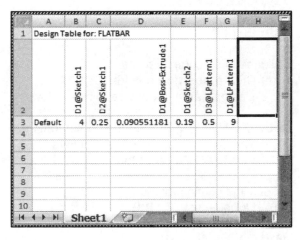

Enter the three configuration names.
379) Click **Cell A4**.

380) Enter **3HOLE**.

381) Click **Cell A5**.

382) Enter **5HOLE**.

383) Click **Cell A6**.

384) Enter **7HOLE**.

385) Click Cell **D3**.

386) If needed, enter **0.09** to round off the Thickness value.

Enter the dimension values for the 3HOLE configuration.
387) Click **Cell B4**. Enter **1**.

388) Click **Cell G4**. Enter **3**.

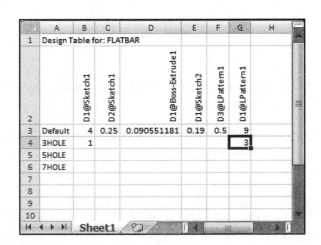

Enter the dimension values for the 5HOLE configuration.
389) Click **Cell B5**.

390) Enter **2**.

391) Click **Cell G5**.

392) Enter **5**.

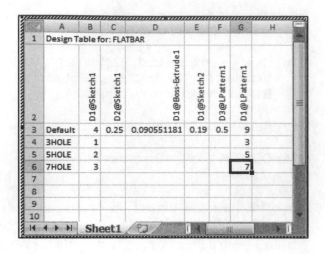

Enter the dimension values for the 7HOLE configuration.
393) Click **Cell B6**.

394) Enter **3**.

395) Click **Cell G6**.

396) Enter **7**.

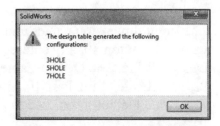

Build the three configurations.
397) Click a **position** outside the EXCEL Design Table in the Graphics window.

398) Click **OK** to generate the configurations. The Design Table icon is displayed in the FLATBAR FeatureManager.

Display the configurations.
399) Double-click **3HOLE**.

400) Double-click **5HOLE**.

401) Double-click **7HOLE**.

402) Double-click **Default**.

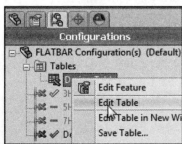

403) Click **Save** 💾 .

Edit the Design Table.
404) Right-click **Design Table** in the ConfigurationManager.

405) Click **Edit Table**. The Add Rows and Columns dialog box is displayed.

406) Click **Cancel** from the Add Rows and Columns dialog box.

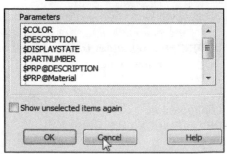

Columns C through G are filled with the default FLATBAR values.

Enter parameters for DESCRIPTION and PARTNUMBER. Custom Properties begin with the prefix, "$PRP@". SolidWorks Properties begin with the prefix, "$".

Enter DESCRIPTION custom Property.
407) Double-click **Cell H2**.

408) Enter **$PRP@DESCRIPTION**.

409) Click **Cell H3**. Enter **9HOLES**.

410) Click **Cell H4**. Enter **3HOLES**.

411) Click **Cell H5**. Enter **5HOLES**.

412) Click **Cell H6**. Enter **7HOLES**.

Enter the PARTNUMBER Property.
413) Double-click **Cell I2**.

414) Enter **$PARTNUMBER**.

415) Click **Cell I3**.

416) Enter **GIDS-SC-10009-9**.

417) Click **Cell I4**.

418) Enter **GIDS-SC-10009-3**.

419) Click **Cell I5**.

420) Enter **GIDS-SC-10009-5**.

421) Click **Cell I6**.

422) Enter **GIDS-SC-10009-7**.

423) Click a **position** in the Graphics window to update the Design Table. View the updated ConfigurationManager.

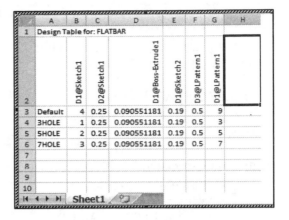

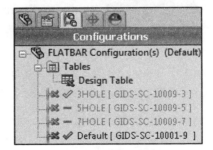

Activity: FLATBAR Drawing - Sheet2

Select configurations in the drawing. The Properties option in the Drawing view displays a list of configuration names.

Open the FLATBAR drawing.

424) Click **Open** 📩 from the Menu bar.

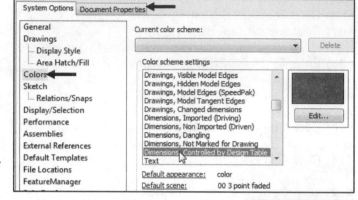

425) Double-click the **FLATBAR drawing** from the SW-TUTORIAL-2013 folder. The FLATBAR drawing is displayed. The dimensions tied to the Design table are displayed in a different color. The dimension color is controlled from the System Options, Colors section.

Copy the Front view.

426) Click inside the FLATBAR **Front view** boundary. Press **Ctrl C**.

427) **Right-click** in the Graphics window. Click **Add Sheet**. Sheet2 is displayed.

428) Right-click **Properties**. Click **Browse** from the Sheet Properties dialog box.

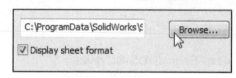

429) Double-click **CUSTOM-A** Sheet Format from the SW-TUTORIAL-2013 folder.

430) Click **OK** from the Sheet Properties box.

Paste the Front view from Sheet1.

431) Click a **position** inside the Sheet2 boundary.

432) Press **Ctrl V**. The Front view is displayed.

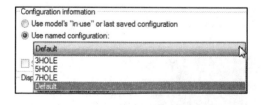

Display the 3HOLE FLATBAR configuration on Sheet2.

433) Right-click inside the **Front view** boundary.

434) Click **Properties**.

435) Select **3HOLE** from the Use named configuration list.

436) Click **OK** from the Drawing View Properties dialog box. The 3HOLE FLATBAR configuration is displayed.

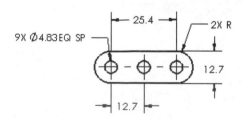

437) Right-click inside the **Drawing View** boundary.

438) Click **Open Part**.

439) Double-click the **3HOLE** configuration from the ConfigurationManager tab.

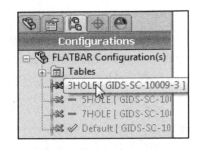

Return to the FLATBAR Drawing Sheet2.
440) Click **Window**, **FLATBAR - Sheet2** from the Menu bar.

441) Click on the **9X** dimension text in the Graphics window. The Dimension PropertyManager is displayed.

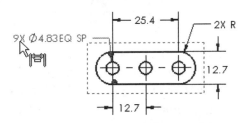

442) Replace the 9X dimension text with **3X** in the Dimension Text box as illustrated.

443) Click **OK** ✔ from the Dimension PropertyManager.

444) **Align** all dimension text as illustrated below.

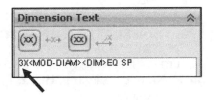

445) Address **all extension line gaps**.

Save the FLATBAR Sheet2 drawing.

446) Click **Save** 🖫.

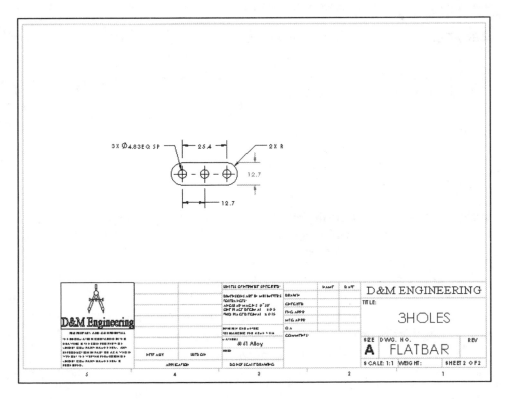

The 5HOLE and 7HOLE configurations are explored as an exercise. Combine the FLATBAR configurations with the SHAFT-COLLAR part to create three different assemblies. Select configuration in the assembly. The Properties in the FeatureManager option displays a list of configuration names.

The FLATBAR-SHAFTCOLLAR assembly contains a FLATBAR fixed to the assembly Origin and a SHAFTCOLLAR mated to the FLATBAR left hole. The default configuration utilizes the FLATBAR-9HOLE part.

Design Tables exist in the assembly. Utilize a Design Table to control part configurations, 3HOLE, 5HOLE and 7HOLE. Utilize the Design Table to Control Suppress/Resolve state of a component in an assembly. Insert the parameter $STATE into the Design Table.

Activity: FLATBAR-SHAFTCOLLAR Assembly

Return to the Default FLATBAR configuration.
447) Right-click in the **3HOLE FLATBAR** view boundary.

448) Click **Open Part**.

449) Click the **ConfigurationManager** tab.

450) Double-click the **Default** configuration.

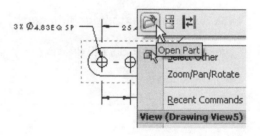

451) Click the **FeatureManager** tab. The FLATBAR (Default) FeatureManager is displayed.

452) Click **Save**.

Create the FLATBAR-SHAFTCOLLAR assembly.
453) Click **New** from the Menu bar.

454) Double-click **Assembly** from the Templates tab. The Begin Assembly PropertyManager is displayed. FLATBAR is an active document. FLATBAR is displayed in the Open documents box.

455) Click **FLATBAR** from the Open documents box.

456) Click **OK** from the Begin Assembly PropertyManager. The FLATBAR is fixed to the Origin.

Save the FLATBAR-SHAFTCOLLAR assembly.

457) Click **Save** 💾 .

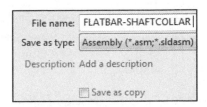

458) Enter **FLATBAR-SHAFTCOLLAR** for Assembly name.

459) Click **Save**.

Insert the SHAFTCOLLAR part.

460) Click the **Insert Components** 🗗 tool from the Assembly toolbar. The Insert Component PropertyManager is displayed.

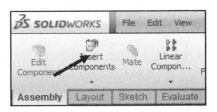

461) Click **BROWSE**.

462) Double-click the **SHAFT-COLLAR** part.

463) Click a **position** to the front left of the FLATBAR as illustrated in the Graphics window.

Fit the model to the Graphics window.
464) Press the **f** key.

465) Click **Save** 💾 .

Mate the SHAFTCOLLAR.

466) Click the **Mate** 🖉 tool from the Assembly toolbar. The Mate PropertyManager is displayed.

Insert a Concentric mate.
467) Click the **left hole face** of the FLATBAR.

468) Click the outside **cylindrical face** of the SHAFT-COLLAR. The selected faces are displayed in the Mate Selections box. Concentric is selected by default.

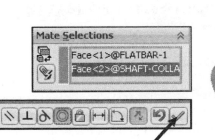

469) Click the **Green Check mark** ✔ .

Insert a Coincident mate.
470) Click the **back flat face** of the SHAFT-COLLAR.

471) Click the **front face** of the FLATBAR as illustrated. Coincident ⟨ is selected by default.

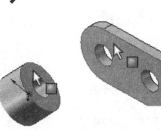

472) Click the **Green Check mark** ✔ .

473) Click **OK** ✔ from the Mate PropertyManager.

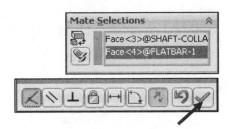

Insert and mate the second SHAFT-COLLAR to the right hole.

474) Click the **Insert Components** 📷 tool from the Assembly toolbar. The Insert Component PropertyManager is displayed.

475) Click the **Browse** button.

476) Double-click the **SHAFT-COLLAR** part.

477) Click a **position** to the front right of the FLATBAR as illustrated.

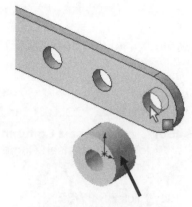

Mate the second SHAFTCOLLAR.

478) Click the **Mate** ✎ tool from the Assembly toolbar. The Mate PropertyManager is displayed.

Insert a Concentric mate.

479) Click the **right hole face** of the FLATBAR.

480) Click the outside **cylindrical face** of the SHAFT-COLLAR. Concentric is selected by default.

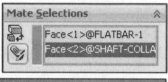

481) Click the **Green Check mark** ✔ .

Insert a Coincident mate.

482) Click the **back flat face** of the SHAFT-COLLAR.

483) Click the **front face** of the FLATBAR. Coincident ⚞ is selected by default.

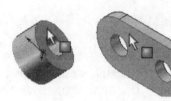

484) Click the **Green Check mark** ✔ .

485) Click **OK** ✔ from the Mate PropertyManager.

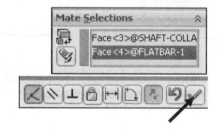

Save the FLATBAR-SHAFTCOLLAR assembly.

486) Click **Save** 💾 .

The FLATBAR-SHAFTCOLLAR FeatureManager displays the Default configuration of the FLATBAR in parenthesis, FLATBAR<1> (Default).

The instance number, <1> indicates the first instance of the FLATBAR. Note: Your instance number will be different, if you delete the FLATBAR and then reinsert into the assembly. The exact instance number is required for the Design Table.

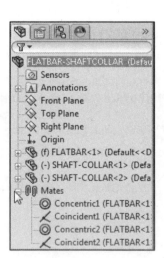

Create a Design Table that contains three new configurations. Each configuration utilizes a different FLATBAR configuration. Control the Suppress/Resolve State of the second SHAFT-COLLAR.

Insert a Design Table.

487) Click **Insert**, **Tables**, **Design Table** from the Menu bar. The Auto-create option is selected by default.

488) Click **OK** ✔ from the Design Table PropertyManager.

Enter the Design Table values.

489) Default is displayed in Cell A3. Click **Cell A4**.

490) Enter **NO SHAFT-COLLAR**.

491) Double-click **CELL B2**.

492) Enter **$STATE@SHAFT-COLLAR<2>**.

493) Click **Cell B3**.

494) Enter **R** for Resolved.

495) Click **Cell B4**.

496) Enter **S** for Suppressed.

497) Click a **position** outside the Design Table in the Graphics window.

498) Click **OK** to display the NO SHAFT-COLLAR configuration.

Display the configurations.

499) Click the **ConfigurationManager** tab.

500) Double-click the **NO SHAFT-COLLAR** configuration. The second SHAFT-COLLAR is suppressed in the Graphics window.

501) Double-click the **Default** configuration. The second SHAFT-COLLAR is resolved. Both SHAFT-COLLARs are displayed in the Graphics window.

💡 Tangent edges are displayed for educational purposes.

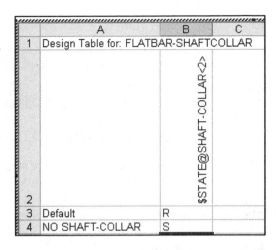

	A	B	C
1	Design Table for: FLATBAR-SHAFTCOLLAR		
2		$STATE@SHAFT-COLLAR<2>	
3	Default	R	
4	NO SHAFT-COLLAR	S	

Insert FLATBAR configurations.
502) Right-click **Design Table**.

503) Click **Edit Table**.

504) Click **Cancel** from the Add Rows and Columns dialog box.

Enter Configuration names.
505) Click **Cell A5**. Enter **3HOLE FLATBAR**.

506) Click **Cell A6**. Enter **5HOLE FLATBAR**.

507) Click **Cell A7**. Enter **7HOLE FLATBAR**.

Enter STATE values.
508) Click **Cell B5**. Enter **S** for Suppress.

509) Click Cell **B6**. Enter **S**.

510) Click **Cell B7**. Enter **S**.

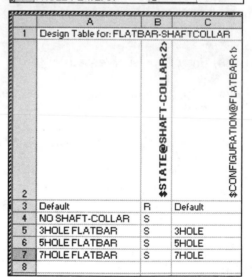

Enter Design Table values.
511) Double-click **Cell C2**.

512) Enter **$CONFIGURATION@FLATBAR<1>**.

513) Click **Cell C5**.

514) Enter **3HOLE**.

515) Click **Cell C6**.

516) Enter **5HOLE**.

517) Click **Cell C7**.

518) Enter **7HOLE**.

519) Click a **position** in the Graphics window to exit.

520) Click **OK** to create the three configurations.

Display the configurations.
521) Double-click the **3HOLE FLATBAR** configuration.

522) Double-click the **5HOLE FLATBAR** configuration.

523) Double-click the **7HOLE FLATBAR** configuration.

524) Double-click the **Default** configuration.

525) Click the **Assembly FeatureManager**  tab.

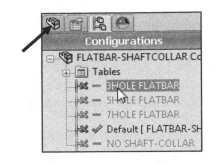

Save the FLATBAR-SHAFTCOLLAR assembly.
526) Click **Isometric view** from the Heads-up View toolbar.

527) Click **Save** .

Close all documents.
528) Click **Windows**, **Close All** from the Menu bar.

Always return to the Default configuration in the assembly. Control the individual configuration through properties of a view in a drawing and properties of a component in the assembly.

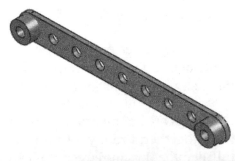

To modify configuration specific notes or dimensions in an assembly drawing, the configuration in the assembly must be the active configuration.

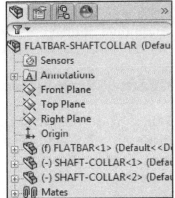

If an assembly or component is loaded in a Lightweight state, right-click the **assembly name** or **component name** from the FeatureManager. Click **Set Lightweight to Resolved**.

Additional details on Design Tables and Configurations are available in SolidWorks Help.

Chapter Summary

You created two drawings: the FLATBAR drawing and the LINKAGE assembly drawing. The drawings contained Standard views, a Detail view, a Section view and an Isometric view.

The drawings utilized a Custom Sheet Format and a Custom Drawing Template. The Sheet Format contained the Company logo and Title block information.

The FLATBAR drawing consisted of two Sheets: Sheet1 and Sheet2. You obtained an understanding of displaying views with the ability to insert, add, and modify dimensions. You used two major design modes in the drawings: Edit Sheet Format and Edit Sheet.

The LINKAGE assembly drawing contained two sheets. Sheet1 contained an Exploded view and a Bill of Materials. The Properties for the Bill of Materials were developed in each part and assembly. Sheet2 utilized a Detail view and a Section view of the AirCylinder assembly.

You created three configurations of the FLATBAR part with a Design Table. The Design Table controlled parameters and dimensions of the FLATBAR part. You utilized these three configurations in the FLATBAR-SHAFTCOLLAR assembly.

Drawings are an integral part of the design process. Part, assemblies and drawings all work together. From your initial design concepts, you created parts and drawings that fulfilled the design requirements of your customer.

Additional SolidWorks examples are provided in the text **Drawing and Detailing with SolidWorks**, Planchard & Planchard, SDC Publications.

Chapter Terminology

Bill of Materials (BOM): A BOM is an EXCEL table in a drawing that lists the item, quantity, part number and description of the components in an assembly. Balloon labels are placed on items in the drawing that correspond to the number in the table. A BOM template controls additional information such as Material or Cost.

Center marks: Represents two perpendicular intersecting centerlines.

Design Table: A Design Table is a spreadsheet used to create multiple configurations in a part or assembly. The Design Table controls the dimensions and parameters in the part.

Detailed view: Detailed views enlarge an area of an existing view. Specify location, shape, and scale.

Drawing file name: Drawing file names end with a .slddrw suffix.

Drawing Layers: Contain dimensions, annotations and geometry.

Drawing Sheets: The "paper sheets" used to hold the views, dimensions and annotations and create the drawing.

Drawing Template: The foundation of a SolidWorks drawing is the Drawing Template. Drawing size, drawing standards, company information, manufacturing and or assembly requirements, units and other properties are defined in the Drawing Template. In this chapter, the Drawing Template contained the drawing Size and Document Properties.

Edit Sheet Format Mode: Provides the ability to:

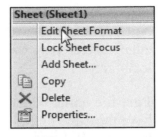

- Change the Title block size and text headings.

- Incorporate a Company logo.

- Add a drawing, design or company text.

Remember: A part cannot be inserted into a drawing when the Edit Sheet Format mode is selected.

Edit Sheet Mode: Provides the ability to:

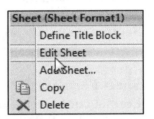

- Add or modify views.

- Add or modify dimensions.

- Add or modify text.

General Notes: Below are a few helpful guidelines to create general drawing notes:

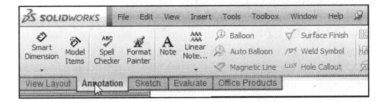

- Use capitol letters.

- Use left text justification.

- Font size should be the same as the dimension text.

Hole Callout: The Hole Callout function creates additional notes required to dimension the holes.

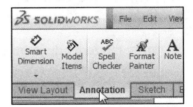

Hole Centerlines: Are composed of alternating long and short dash lines. The lines identify the center of a circle, axes or other cylindrical geometry.

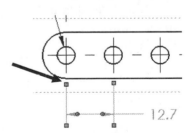

Insert Model Items: The tool utilized to insert part dimensions and annotations into drawing views. The Insert Model Items tool is located in the Annotate toolbar.

Leader lines: Reference the size of the profile. A gap must exist between the profile lines and the leader lines.

Model View: The tool utilized to insert named views into a drawing. The Model View tool is located in the Layout View toolbar.

Multiple Drawing Sheets: The drawing can have multiple sheets, if required. To create an additional sheet, use Add Sheet. The size and format of the new sheet is copied from the original but can be edited and changed.

Notes: Notes can be used to add text with leaders or as a stand-alone text string. If an edge, face or vertex is selected prior to adding the note, a leader is created to that location.

Part file name: Part file names end with a .sldprt suffix. Note: A drawing or part file can have the same prefix. A drawing or part file cannot have the same suffix. Example: Drawing file name: FLATBAR.slddrw. Part file name: FLATBAR.sldprt

Section view: Section views display the interior features. Define a cutting plane with a sketched line in a view perpendicular to the Section view.

Sheet Format: The Sheet Format is incorporated into the Drawing Template. The Sheet Format contains the border, title block information, revision block information, company name and or logo information, Custom Properties and SolidWorks Properties. In this chapter the Sheet Format contained the title block information.

Title block: Contains vital part or assembly information. Each company can have a unique version of a title block.

View Appearance: There are two important factors that affect the appearance of views:

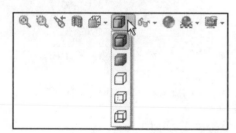

1. Whether the view is shown wireframe, hidden lines removed, or hidden lines visible.

2. How tangent edges on entities such as fillets are displayed.

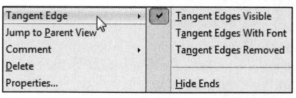

Use the Pack and Go option to save an assembly or drawing with references. The Pack and Go tool saves either to a folder or creates a zip file to e-mail. View SolidWorks help for additional information.

Questions

1. Describe a Bill of Materials and its contents.

2. Name the two major design modes used to develop a drawing in SolidWorks.

3. True or False. Units, Dimensioning Standards, Arrow size, Font size are modified in the Options, Document Properties section.

4. How do you save a Sheet Format?

5. Identify seven components that are commonly found in a title block.

6. Describe the procedure to insert an Isometric view to the drawing?

7. In SolidWorks, drawing file names end with a _____ suffix. Part file names end with a _____ suffix.

8. True or False. In SolidWorks, if a part is modified, the drawing is updated with a Rebuild command.

9. True or False. In SolidWorks, when a dimension in the drawing is modified, the part is updated with a Rebuild command.

10. Name three guidelines to create General Notes on a drawing.

11. True or False. Most engineering drawings use the following font: Times New Roman - All small letters.

12. What are Leader lines? Provide an example.

13. Describe the key differences between a Detail view and a Section view on a drawing.

14. Identify the procedure to create an Exploded view.

15. Describe the purpose of a Design Table in a part and in an assembly.

16. Review the Design Intent section in the Introduction. Identify how you incorporated design intent into the drawing.

17. Identify how you incorporate design intent into configurations with a Design Table.

18. Review the Keyboard Short Cut keys in the Appendix. Identify the Short Cut keys you incorporated into this chapter.

19. Discuss why a part designed in inch units would utilize a drawing detailed in millimeter units.

Exercises

Exercise 3.1: FLATBAR - 3 HOLE Drawing

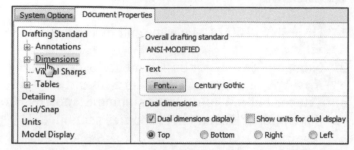

Note: Dimensions are enlarged for clarity. Utilize inch, millimeter, or dual dimensioning.

- Create the A (ANSI) Landscape IPS Third Angle Projection FLATBAR - 3HOLE drawing. First create the part from the drawing - then create the drawing. Use the default A (ANSI) Landscape Sheet Format/Size.

- Insert a Shaded Isometric view. No Tangent Edges displayed.

- Insert a Front and Top view. Insert dimensions. Address all needed extension line gaps. Insert 3X – EQ. SP. Insert the Company and Third Angle Projection icon. Add a Parametric Linked Note for MATERIAL THICKNESS.

- Hide the Thickness dimension in the Top view. Insert needed Centerlines. Insert the correct drawing views display modes.

- Insert Custom Properties for Material (2014 Alloy), DRAWNBY, DRAWNDATE, COMPANYNAME, etc.

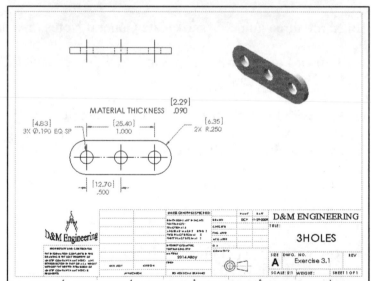

Exercise 3.2: CYLINDER Drawing

Create the A (ANSI) Landscape IPS - Third Angle CYLINDER drawing.

- First create the part from the drawing; then create the drawing. Use the default A (ANSI) Landscape Sheet Format/Size.

- Insert the Front and Right view as illustrated. Insert dimensions. Address all needed extension line gaps. Think about the proper view for your dimensions.

- Insert Company and Third Angle projection icons. The Third Angle Projection icon is available in the homework folder.

- Insert needed Centerlines and Center Marks. Insert the correct drawing views display modes.

- Insert Custom Properties: Material, Description, DrawnBy, DrawnDate, CompanyName, etc. Note: Material is AISI 1020.

- Utilize the Mass Properties tool from the Evaluate toolbar to calculate the volume and mass of the CYLINDER part. Set decimal places to 4 under the Options button in the Mass Properties dialog box.

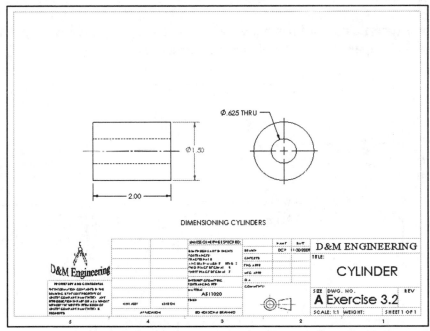

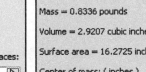

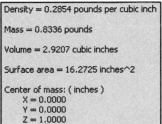

Exercise 3.3: PRESSURE PLATE Drawing

Create the A (ANSI) Landscape IPS - Third Angle PRESSURE
PLATE drawing.

- First create the part from the drawing; then create the
  drawing. Use the default A (ANSI) Landscape Sheet
  Format/Size.

- Insert the Front and Right view as illustrated. Insert
  dimensions. Address all needed extension line gaps. Insert
  the correct drawing views display modes. Think about the proper view for your
  dimensions.

- Insert Company and Third Angle projection icons. The Third Angle Projection icon is
  available in the homework folder.

- Insert needed Centerlines and Center Marks.

- Insert Custom Properties: Material, Description, DrawnBy, DrawnDate,
  CompanyName, etc. Note: Material is 1060 Alloy.

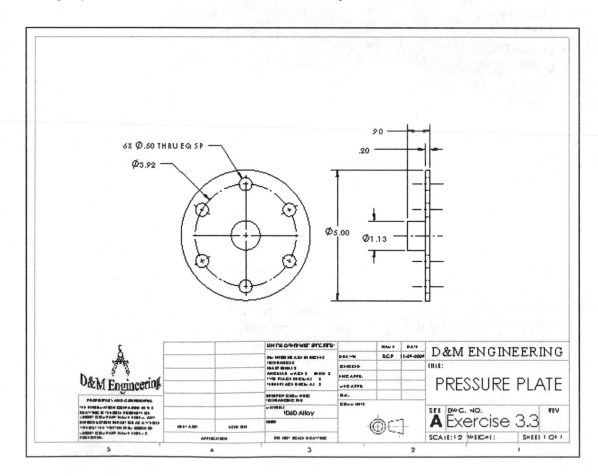

Exercise 3.4: LINKS Assembly Drawing

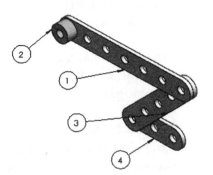

- Create the LINK A-ANSI assembly. Utilize three different FLATBAR configurations and a SHAFT-COLLAR.

- Create the LINK assembly drawing as illustrated. Use the default A (ANSI) Landscape Sheet Format/Size.

- Insert Company and Third Angle projection icons. The icons are available in the homework folder. Remove all Tangent Edges.

- Insert Custom Properties: Description, DrawnBy, DrawnDate, CompanyName, etc.

- Insert a Bill of Materials as illustrated with Balloons.

ITEM NO.	PART NUMBER	DESCRIPTION	QTY.
1	GIDS-SC-10009-7	7HOLES	1
2	GIDS-SC-10012-3-16	SHAFT-COLLAR	1
3	GIDS-SC-10009-5	5HOLES	1
4	GIDS-SC-10009-3	3HOLES	1

D&M Engineering

PROPRIETARY AND CONFIDENTIAL

THE INFORMATION CONTAINED IN THIS DRAWING IS THE SOLE PROPERTY OF <INSERT COMPANY NAME HERE>. ANY REPRODUCTION IN PART OR AS A WHOLE WITHOUT THE WRITTEN PERMISSION OF <INSERT COMPANY NAME HERE> IS PROHIBITED.

		UNLESS OTHERWISE SPECIFIED:		NAME	DATE	**D&M ENGINEERING**
DIMENSIONS ARE IN INCHES TOLERANCES: FRACTIONAL± ANGULAR: MACH± BEND ± TWO PLACE DECIMAL ± THREE PLACE DECIMAL ±	DRAWN	DCP	11-3D-2DDF	TITLE:
	CHECKED			
	ENG APPR.			**LINK**
	MFG APPR.			
INTERPRET GEOMETRIC TOLERANCING PER:	Q.A.			
MATERIAL	COMMENTS:			
NEXT ASSY	USED ON	FINISH				SIZE DWG. NO. REV **A Exercise 3.4**
APPLICATION		DO NOT SCALE DRAWING			SCALE: 1:1 WEIGHT: SHEET 1 OF 1

Exercise 3.5: PLATE-1 Drawing

Create the A (ANSI) Landscape MMGS - Third Angle
PLATE-1 drawing.

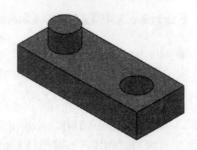

- First create the part from the drawing; then create the
  drawing. Use the default A (ANSI) Landscape Sheet
  Format/Size.

- Insert the Front and Right view as illustrated. Insert dimensions. Address all needed
  extension line gaps. Insert the correct drawing views display modes. Think about the
  proper view for your dimensions!

- Insert Company and Third Angle projection icons. The icons are available in the
  homework folder.

- Insert needed Centerlines and Center Marks.

- Insert Custom Properties: Material, Description, DrawnBy, DrawnDate,
  CompanyName, etc. Note: Material is 1060 Alloy.

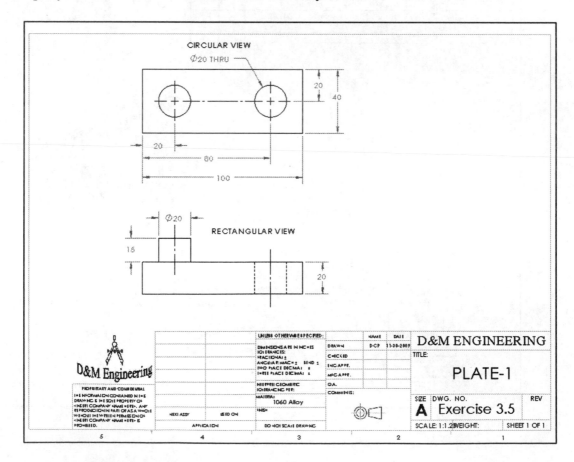

Exercise 3.6: FLATE-PLATE Drawing

Create the A (ANSI) Landscape IPS - Third Angle
PLATE-1 drawing.

- First create the part from the drawing; then create the
  drawing. Use the default A (ANSI) Landscape Sheet
  Format/Size. Remove all Tangent Edges.

- Insert the Front, Top, Right and Isometric view as illustrated. Insert dimensions.
  Address all needed extension line gaps. Insert the correct drawing views display
  modes. Think about the proper view for your dimensions!

- Insert Company and Third Angle projection icons. The icons are available in the
  homework folder.

- Insert needed Centerlines and Center Marks.

- Insert Custom Properties: Material, Description, DrawnBy, DrawnDate,
  CompanyName, Hole Annotation, etc. Note: Material is 1060 Alloy

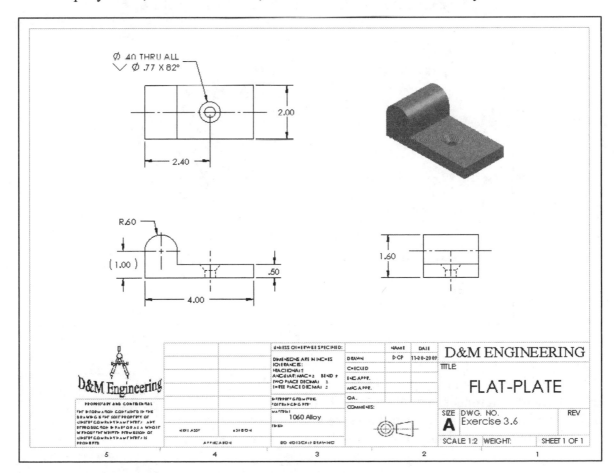

Exercise 3.7: **LINKAGE-2 Drawing**

- Create a new A-ANSI drawing named, LINKAGE-2.

- Insert an Isometric view, shaded view of the LINKAGE-2 Assembly created in the Chapter 1 exercises.

- Define the PART NO. Property and the DESCRIPTION Property for the AXLE, FLATBAR- 9HOLE, FLATBAR - 3HOLE and SHAFT COLLAR.

- Save the LINKAGE-2 assembly to update the properties. Return to the LINKAGE-2 Drawing. Insert a Bill of Materials with Auto Balloons as illustrated.

- Insert the Company and Third Angle Projection icon. Insert Custom Properties for DRAWNBY, DRAWNDATE and COMPANYNAME

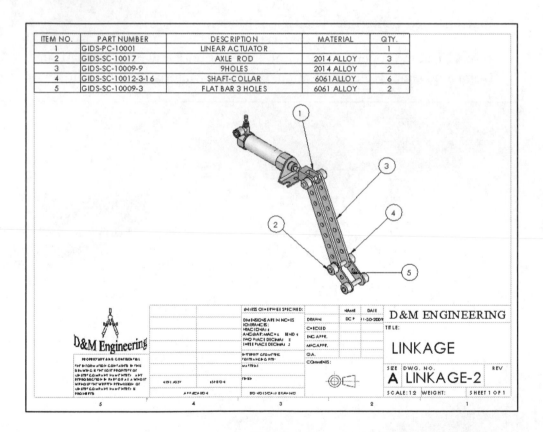

ITEM NO.	PART NUMBER	DESCRIPTION	MATERIAL	QTY.
1	GIDS-PC-10001	LINEAR ACTUATOR		1
2	GIDS-SC-10017	AXLE ROD	2014 ALLOY	3
3	GIDS-SC-10009-9	9HOLES	2014 ALLOY	2
4	GIDS-SC-10012-3-16	SHAFT-COLLAR	6061 ALLOY	6
5	GIDS-SC-10009-3	FLAT BAR 3 HOLES	6061 ALLOY	2

Use the Pack and Go option to save an assembly or drawing with references. The Pack and Go tool saves either to a folder or creates a zip file to e-mail. View SolidWorks help for additional information.

Exercise 3.8: CAM Drawing

- Create the A (ANSI) Landscape IPS - Third Angle drawing from the below information. First create the part from the provided information, and then create the drawing.

- Use the default A (ANSI) Landscape Sheet Format/Size. Remove all Tangent Edges.

- Insert a Front, Top, Right and Isometric view.

- Insert all needed drawing view dimensions, annotations, local and general notes, title block information, gaps, etc.

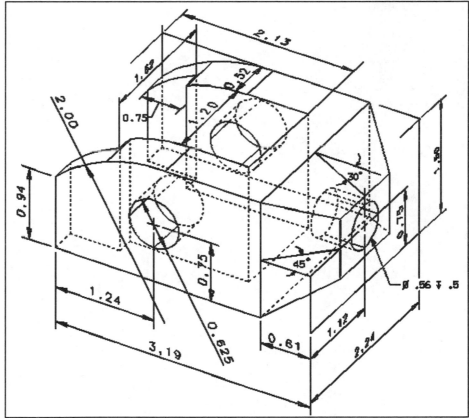

Notes:

Chapter 4

Advanced Features

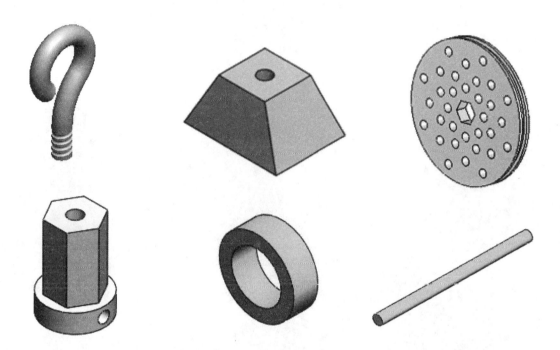

Below are the desired outcomes and usage competencies based on the completion of Chapter 4.

Desired Outcomes:	Usage Competencies:

• Six parts for the PNEUMATIC-TEST-MODULE assembly:
   o WEIGHT
   o HOOK
   o WHEEL
   o HEX-ADAPTER
   o AXLE-3000
   o SHAFTCOLLAR-500
	• Apply the following Advanced modeling features: Plane, Lofted Base, Extruded Cut, Swept Base, Dome, Helix and Spiral, Swept Cut, Extruded Boss/Base, Revolved Cut, Extruded Cut, Circular Pattern, Axis, Instant3D and Hole Wizard.
	
	• Reuse geometry.
	
	• Modify existing parts to create new parts with the Save as copy command.

Notes:

Chapter 4 - Advanced Features

Chapter Objective

Obtain an understanding to create parts for the configuration of the PNEUMATIC-TEST-MODULE assembly. Attain the ability to reuse geometry by modifying existing parts and to create new parts. Knowledge of the following SolidWorks features: *Extruded Boss/Base, Extruded Cut, Dome, Plane, Axis, Lofted Boss/Base, Swept Boss/Base, Helix and Spiral Swept Cut, Revolved Cut, Hole Wizard, Instant3D and Circular Pattern.*

Create six individual parts:

- WEIGHT

- HOOK

- WHEEL

- HEX-ADAPTER

- AXLE-3000

- SHAFTCOLLAR-500

In Chapter 5, develop a working understanding with multiple documents in an assembly. Build on sound assembly modeling techniques that utilize symmetry, component patterns, and mirrored components.

Create five assemblies:

- 3HOLE-SHAFTCOLLAR assembly

- 5HOLE-SHAFTCOLLAR assembly

- WHEEL-FLATBAR assembly

- WHEEL-AND-AXLE assembly

- PNEUMATIC-TEST-MODULE assembly

On the completion of this chapter, you will be able to:

- Create new parts and copy parts with the Save As command to reuse similar geometry.

- Utilize Construction geometry in a sketch.

- Apply the following SolidWorks features:

    o Extruded Boss/Base

    o Extruded Cut

    o Dome

    o Plane

    o Lofted Boss/Base

    o Swept Boss/Base

    o Swept Cut

    o Revolved Cut

    o Hole Wizard

    o Helix and Spiral

    o Axis

    o Circular Pattern

    o Instant3D

Chapter Overview

Six additional parts are required for the final
PNEUMATIC-TEST-MODULE assembly. Each
part explores various modeling techniques.

Create three new parts in this chapter:

- WEIGHT

- HOOK

- WHEEL

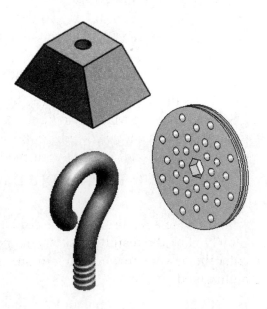

The WEIGHT and HOOK parts were applied
in the Chapter 2 exercises. See Chapter 2
Homework folder on the DVD in the book.

Utilize the Save As command and modify existing parts that were created in the previous chapters to create three additional parts for the PNEUMATIC-TEST-MODULE assembly.

- HEX-ADAPTER

- AXLE-3000

- SHAFTCOLLAR-500

The HEX-ADAPTER part utilizes modified geometry from the HEX-STANDOFF part.

The AXLE-3000 part utilizes modified geometry from the AXLE part.

HEX-STANDOFF

The SHAFTCOLLAR-500 part utilizes modified geometry from the SHAFT-COLLAR part.

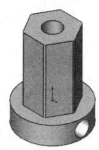

HEX-
ADAPTER

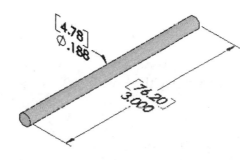

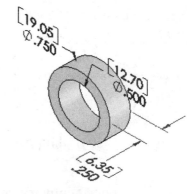

Press the **g** key to activate the Magnifying glass tool. Use the Magnifying glass tool to inspect a model and make selections without changing the overall view of your model in the Graphics window.

Rename a feature or sketch for clarity. Slowly click the feature or sketch name twice and enter the new name when the old one is highlighted.

WEIGHT Part

The WEIGHT part is a machined part. Utilize
the Loft 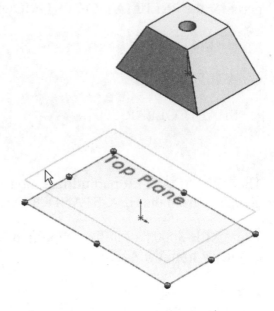 feature. Create a Loft by blending
two or more profiles. Each profile is sketched
on a separate plane.

Create Plane1. Offset Plane1 from the Top
Plane.

Sketch a rectangle for the first profile on the
Top Plane.

Sketch a square for the second profile on
Plane1.

Select the corner of each profile to create the Loft
feature.

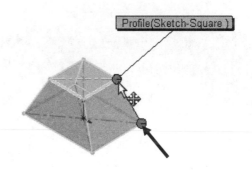

Utilize the Instant3D tool to create an Extruded
Cut 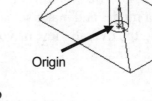 feature to create a Though All hole centered
on the top face of the Loft feature.

☀ Reference geometry defines the shape or form
of a surface or a solid. Reference geometry includes
planes, axes, coordinate systems, and points.

☀ When using the Instant3D tool, you lose the ability to
select an End Conditions to maintain design intent.

All parts in this chapter utilize a custom part template. Create the custom part template from the default part template. Save the Custom Part template in the SW-TUTORIAL-2013 folder.

Activity: Create the WEIGHT Part

Create a New part template.

1) Click **New** ⬚ from the Menu bar.

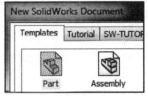

2) Double-click **Part** from the Templates tab. The Part FeatureManager is displayed.

Set the Dimensioning standard.

3) Click **Options** , **Document Properties** tab from the Menu bar.

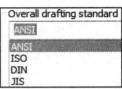

4) Select **ANSI** from the Overall drafting standard drop-down menu.

Set document units.

5) Click **Units**.

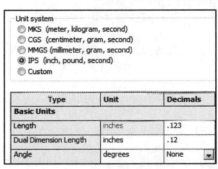

6) Select **IPS**, [**MMGS**] for Unit system.

7) Select **.123**, [**.12**] for Linear units Decimal places.

8) Select **None** for Angular units Decimal places.

Set Leader arrow direction.

9) Click **Dimensions**.

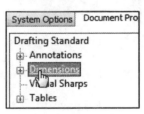

10) Check the **Smart** box as illustrated.

11) Click **OK** from the Document Properties - Detailing - Dimensions dialog box.

Save the Part template.

12) Click **Save As** from the drop-down Menu bar.

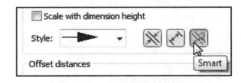

13) Select **Part Templates (*.prtdot)** for Save as type.

14) Select **SW-TUTORIAL-2013** for Save in folder.

15) Enter **PART-ANSI-IN**, [PART-ANSI-MM] for File name.

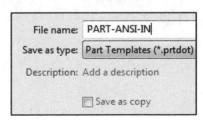

16) Click **Save**.

17) Click **File**, **Close** from the Menu bar.

Create a New part.

18) Click **New** 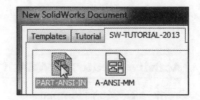 from the Menu bar.

19) Click the **SW-TUTORIAL-2013** tab.

20) Double-click **PART-ANSI-IN**, [PART-ANSI-MM]. The Part FeatureManager is displayed.

Save the part.

21) Click **Save As** from the drop-down Menu bar.

22) Select the **SW-TUTORIAL-2013** folder.

23) Enter **WEIGHT** for File name.

24) Enter **WEIGHT** for Description.

25) Click **Save**.

Insert Plane1.

26) Right-click **Top Plane** from the FeatureManager.

27) Click **Show**. The Top Plane is displayed in the Graphics window. Note: In a new installation, Planes and Origins may be displayed by default.

28) Hold the **Ctrl** key down.

29) Click the **boundary** of the Top Plane as illustrated.

30) Drag the **mouse pointer** upward.

31) Release the **mouse pointer**.

32) Release the **Ctrl** key. The Plane PropertyManager is displayed. Top Plane is displayed in the First Reference box.

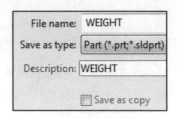

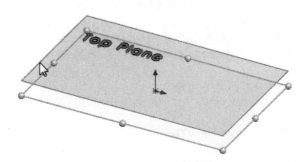

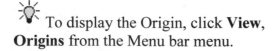 To display the Origin, click **View**, **Origins** from the Menu bar menu.

33)   Enter **.500**in, **[12.70]** for Distance.

34)   Click **OK** ✔ from the Plane PropertyManager.

Plane1 is displayed in the Graphics window and is listed in the FeatureManager. Plane1 is offset from the Top Plane.

A Loft feature requires two sketches. The first sketch, Sketch1 is a rectangle sketched on the Top Plane centered about the Origin ⬑. The second sketch, Sketch2 is a square sketched on Plane1 centered about the Origin.

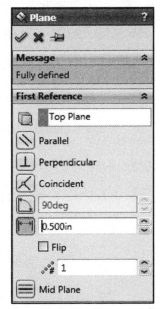

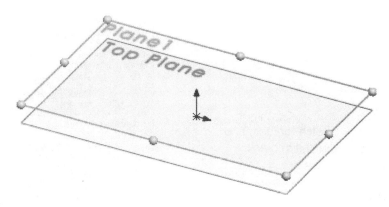

Create Sketch1 in the Top Plane.
35)   Right-click **Top Plane** from the FeatureManager.

36)   Click **Sketch** ⬕ from the Context toolbar. The Sketch toolbar is displayed.

37)   Click **Center Rectangle** ⬛ from the Consolidated Sketch tool. The Center Rectangle icon is displayed.

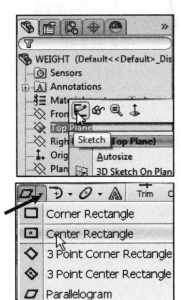

38)   Click the **Origin** ⬑ as illustrated.

39)   Click a **position** to the top right.

🔅 The Center Rectangle tool provides the ability to sketch a rectangle located at a center point, in this case the Origin. This eliminates the need for centerlines to the Origin with a Midpoint geometric relation.

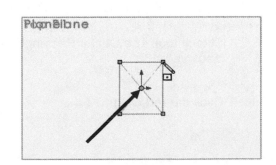

Add dimensions.

40) Click the **Smart Dimension** ✐ Sketch tool.

41) Click the **top horizontal** line.

42) Click a **position** above the line.

43) Enter **1.000**in, [25.40].

44) Click the **Green Check mark** ✔.

45) Click the **right vertical** line.

46) Click a **position** to the right.

47) Enter **.750**in, [19.05].

48) Click the **Green Check mark** ✔.

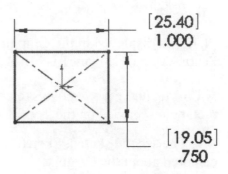

Close Sketch1.

49) Click **Exit Sketch** ⤶ from the Sketch toolbar. The sketch is fully defined and is displayed in black.

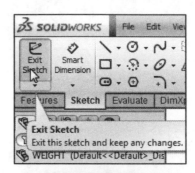

Rename Sketch1.

50) Rename **Sketch1** to **Sketch-Rectangle**.

Save the part

51) Click **Save** 💾.

Display an Isometric view.

52) Click **Isometric view** ⬦ from the Heads-up View toolbar.

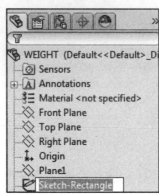

Create Sketch2 on Plane1. Plane1 is your Sketch plane.

53) Right-click **Plane1** from the FeatureManager. Plane1 is your Sketch plane.

54) Click **Sketch** ⤶ from the Context toolbar. The Sketch toolbar is displayed.

55) Click the **Center Rectangle** ▣ Consolidated

Sketch tool. The Center Rectangle ▣ icon is displayed.

56) Click the **red Origin** ↳.

57)   Click a **position** as illustrated.

58)   Right-click **Select** to de-select the Center Rectangle tool.

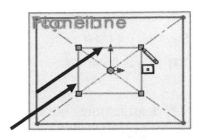

Add an Equal relation between the left vertical line and the top horizontal line.

59)   Click the **left vertical line** of the rectangle.

60)   Hold the **Ctrl** key down.

61)   Click the **top horizontal line** of the rectangle.

62)   Release the **Ctrl** key.

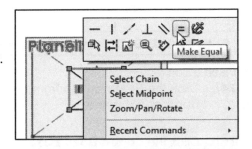

63)   Right-click **Make Equal** = from the Context toolbar.

64)   Click **OK** ✔ from the Properties PropertyManager.

Add a dimension.

65)   Click the **Smart Dimension** ✎ Sketch tool.

66)   Click the **top horizontal** line.

67)   Click a **position** above the line.

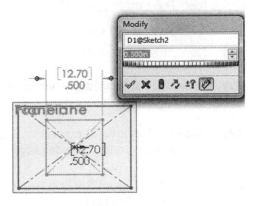

68)   Enter **.500**in, [**12.70**].

69)   Click the **Green Check mark** ✔ .

Close Sketch2.

70)   Click **Exit Sketch** ↙ from the Sketch toolbar.
             Sketch2 is fully defined and is displayed in black.

71)   Click **Isometric view** ⬛ from the Heads-up View
             toolbar. View the results in the Graphics window.

💡 If you did not select the Origin, insert a Coincident relation between the rectangle and the Origin to fully define Sketch2.

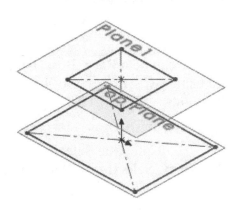

💡 Think design intent. When do you use the various End Conditions and Geometric sketch relations? What are you trying to do with the design? How does the component fit into an Assembly?

Rename Sketch2.

72) Rename **Sketch2** to **Sketch-Square**.

Save the WEIGHT part.

73) Click **Save** 🖫.

💡 Loft features are comprised of multiple sketches. Name sketches for clarity.

Activity: WEIGHT Part-Loft Feature

Insert a Loft feature.

74) Click the **Features** tab from the CommandManager.

75) Click the **Lofted Boss/Base** 🛢 Feature tool. The Loft PropertyManager is displayed.

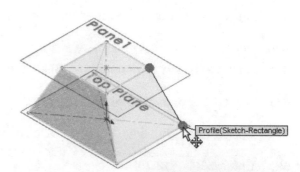

76) Clear the **Profiles** box.

77) Click the **back right corner** of Sketch-Rectangle as illustrated.

78) Click the **back right corner** of Sketch-Square. Sketch-Rectangle and Sketch-Square are displayed in the Profiles box.

79) Click **OK** ✔ from the Loft PropertyManager. Loft1 is displayed in the FeatureManager.

80) Hide all planes.

💡 A Loft feature creates transitions between profiles. A Loft feature can be a Base, Boss, Cut, or Surface. Create a Loft feature by using two or more profiles. Only the first and last profiles can be points.

💡 To display the Selection Filter toolbar, click **View, Toolbars, Selection Filter**. The Selection Filter is displayed.

💡 To clear a Filter icon ⬚▽, click **Clear All Filters** from the Selection Filter toolbar.

81) **Expand** Loft1 in the FeatureManager. Sketch-Rectangle and Sketch-Square are the two sketches that contain the Loft feature.

82) **Zoom in** on the Loft1 feature.

Activity: WEIGHT Part-Instant3D - Extruded Cut Feature

Insert a New sketch for the Extruded Cut feature.

83) Right-click the **top square face** of the Loft1 feature for the Sketch plane.

84) Click **Sketch** ✏ from the Context toolbar. The Sketch toolbar is displayed.

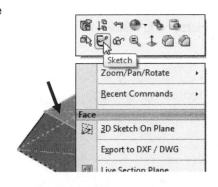

85) Click the **Circle** ⊙ Sketch tool. The circle ⊙ icon is displayed.

86) Click the **Origin** ⌐ as illustrated.

87) Click a **position** to the right of the Origin as illustrated.

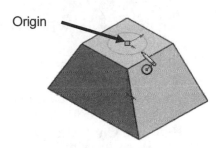

Add a dimension.

88) Click the **Smart Dimension** ⌀ Sketch tool.

89) Click the **circumference** of the circle.

90) Click a **position** in the Graphics window above the circle to locate the dimension.

91) Enter **.150**in, [**3.81**] in the Modify box.

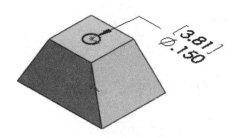

Insert an Extruded feature using the Instant3D tool.

92) **Exit** the Sketch. By default, Instant3D is active.

93) Click the **diameter** of the circle, Sketch3 as illustrated. A green arrow is displayed.

94) Click the **Arrow head** and drag it below the model.

95) Click a **position** on the Instant3D ruler. The Extrude feature is displayed in the FeatureManager.

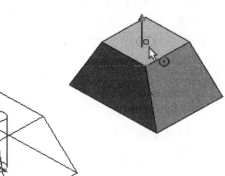

96) Click **Wireframe** ⬜ from the Heads-up View toolbar. View the Extrude feature.

Rename the Extrude feature.

97) Rename the **Extrude** feature to **Hole-for-Hook** as illustrated.

Save the WEIGHT part.

98) Click **Isometric view** from the Heads-up View toolbar.

99) Click **Shaded With Edges** from the Heads-up View toolbar.

100) Click **Save** . The WEIGHT part is complete.

 Rename a feature or sketch for clarity. Slowly click the feature or sketch name twice and enter the new name when the old one is highlighted.

Review the WEIGHT Part

The WEIGHT part was created with the Loft feature. The Loft feature required two planes: Top Plane and Plane1. Profiles were sketched on each plane. Profiles were selected to create the Loft feature.

An Extruded Cut feature was created using the Instant3D tool to create a Through All center hole in the WEIGHT.

When using the Instant3D tool, you lose the ability to select various End Conditions to insert design intent.

HOOK Part

The HOOK part fastens to the WEIGHT part. The HOOK is created with a Swept Boss/Base feature.

The Swept Boss/Base feature adds material by moving a profile along a path. A simple Swept feature requires two sketches. The first sketch is called the path. The second sketch is called the profile.

The profile and path are sketched on perpendicular planes.

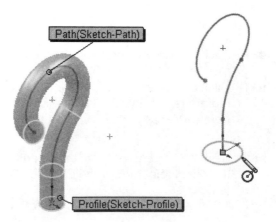

Create the HOOK part with a Swept Base feature.

The Swept Base feature uses:

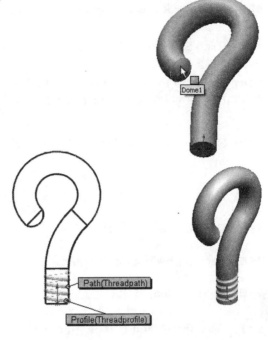

- A path sketched on the Right Plane.

- A profile sketched on the Top Plane.

Utilize the Dome feature ⬚ tool to create a spherical feature on a circular face.

Utilize the Swept Cut feature ▤ tool to create the thread for the HOOK part as illustrated. The Swept Cut feature removes material.

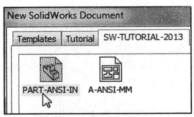

☀ Reference geometry defines the shape or form of a surface or a solid. Reference geometry includes planes, axes, coordinate systems, and points.

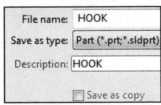

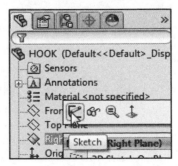

Activity: Create the HOOK Part

Create the New part.

101) Click **New** ⬚ from the Menu bar.

102) Select the **SW-TUTORIAL-2013** tab.

103) Double-click **PART-ANSI-IN**, [PART-ANSI-MM].

Save the part.

104) Click **Save** 🖫.

105) Select the **SW-TUTORIAL-2013** folder.

106) Enter **HOOK** for File name.

107) Enter **HOOK** for Description.

108) Click **Save**. The HOOK FeatureManager is displayed.

The Swept feature requires two sketches. Sketch1 is the Sweep Path sketched on the Right Plane. Sketch2 is the Sweep Profile sketched on the Top Plane.

Sketch the Sweep Path.
109) Right-click **Right Plane** from the FeatureManager.

110) Click **Sketch** ⊾ from the Context toolbar.

111) Click the **Line** ╲ Sketch tool. The Insert Line
PropertyManager is displayed.

112) Sketch a **vertical line** from the Origin ⌙ as illustrated.

Origin

Add a dimension.
113) Click the **Smart Dimension** ⟨⟩ Sketch tool.

114) Click the **vertical line**.

115) Click a **position** to the right.

116) Enter .250in, [6.35].

[6.35]
.250

117) Click the **Green Check mark** ✅ .

Fit the model to the Graphics window.
118) Press the **f** key.

Create the Centerpoint arc.
119) Click the **Centerpoint Arc** ⟳ Sketch
tool from the Consolidated Sketch

toolbar. The Centerpoint Arc ⟳ icon is
displayed.

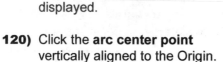

Arc center
point

120) Click the **arc center point**
vertically aligned to the Origin.

[6.35]
.250

121) Click the **arc start point** as
illustrated.

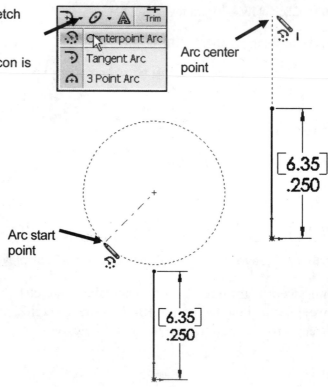

Arc start
point

[6.35]
.250

122) Move the **mouse pointer** clockwise approximately 260°.

123) Click a point **horizontally aligned** to the arc start point.

124) Click the **3 Point Arc** ⌒ Sketch tool from the Consolidated Sketch toolbar. The Arc PropertyManager is displayed.

125) Click the **vertical line endpoint**.

126) Click the **center point arc endpoint**.

127) Drag and pull the center of the **3 Point Arc downwards**.

128) Click the center of the **center point arc line** as illustrated.

129) Click **OK** ✔ from the Arc PropertyManager.

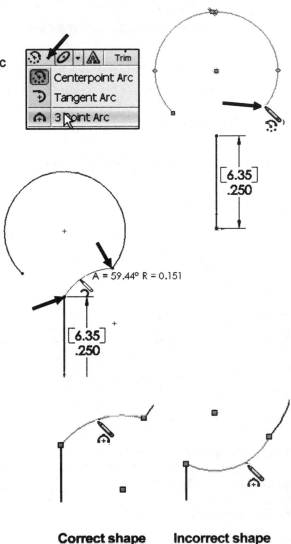

🔅 It is important to draw the correct shape with the 3 Point Arc tool as illustrated.

Add a Vertical relation between the Origin and the center point of the arc.

130) Click the **Origin** ⌐.

131) Hold the **Ctrl** key down.

132) Click the **center point** of the Center point arc.

133) Release the **Ctrl** key.

134) Click **Vertical** | from the Add Relations box.

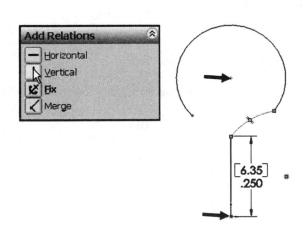

Correct shape   **Incorrect shape**

Add a Horizontal relation.
135) Click the **start point** of the Center point arc.

136) Hold the **Ctrl** key down.

137) Click the **end point** of the Center point arc.

138) Release the **Ctrl** key.

139) Click **Horizontal** — from the Add Relations box.

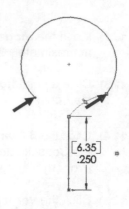

Add a Tangent relation.
140) Click the **vertical line**.

141) Hold the **Ctrl** key down.

142) Click the **3 Point Arc**.

143) Release the **Ctrl** key.

144) Click **Tangent** from the Add Relations box.

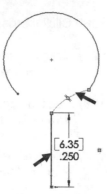

Add a second Tangent relation.

145) Click the **3 Point Arc**.

146) Hold the **Ctrl** key down.

147) Click the **Center point arc**.

148) Release the **Ctrl** key.

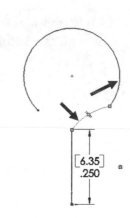

149) Click **Tangent** from the Add Relations box.

Add dimensions.
150) Click the **Smart Dimension** Sketch tool.

151) Click the **3 Point Arc**.

152) Click a **position** to the left.

153) Enter .500in, [**12.70**].

154) Click the **Green Check mark** .

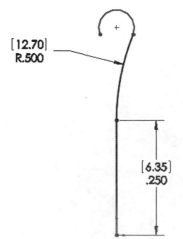

Dimension the overall length of the sketch.
155) Click the **top of the arc**.

156) Click the **Origin** 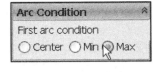.

157) Click a **position** to the right of the profile. Accept the default dimension.

158) Click the **Green Check mark** ✓ .

159) Click the **Leaders** tab in the Dimension PropertyManager.

Modify the Arc condition.
160) Click the **First arc condition: Max**.

161) Click **OK** ✓ from the Dimension PropertyManager.

Modify the overall length.
162) Double-click the default **dimension**.

163) Enter **1.000**in, [**25.40**].

164) Click the **Green Check mark** ✓ .

Fit the model to the Graphics window.
165) Press the **f** key.

166) Move the **dimensions** to the correct location.

By default, the Dimension tool utilizes the center point of an arc or circle. Select the circle profile during dimensioning. Utilize the Leaders tab in the Dimension PropertyManager to modify the arc condition to Minimum or Maximum.

Close the sketch.

167) Click **Exit Sketch** ⤴ from the Sketch toolbar.

168) Rename **Sketch1** to **Sketch-Path**.

Save the HOOK.
169) Click **Save** 💾 .

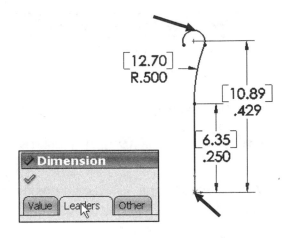

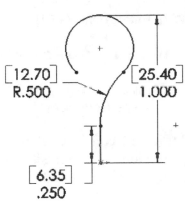

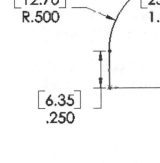

Center point

Minimum   Maximum
Arc Conditions

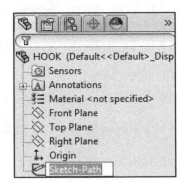

Activity: HOOK Part-Sweep Profile

Create the Sweep profile (cross section).

170) Click **Isometric view** 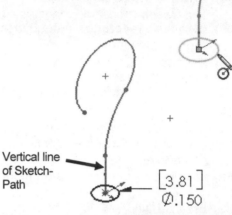. Right-click **Top Plane** from the FeatureManager.

171) Click **Sketch** from the Context toolbar.

172) Click the **Circle** Sketch tool. The Circle PropertyManager is displayed.

173) Click the **Origin**. Click a **position** to the right of the Origin.

Add a dimension.

174) Click the **Smart Dimension** Sketch tool.

175) Click the **circumference** of the small circle.

176) Click a **position** diagonally to the right.

177) Enter **.150**in, [**3.81**].

178) Click the **Green Check mark**.

179) Click **OK** from the Dimension PropertyManager.

Vertical line of Sketch-Path

$$\begin{bmatrix} 3.81 \end{bmatrix}$$
$$\varnothing.150$$

A Pierce Geometric relation positions the center of the cross section on the sketched path. The center point of the small circle pierces the sketch-path, (vertical line).

Add a Pierce relation.

180) Click the **Origin**.

181) Hold the **Ctrl** key down.

182) Click the **vertical line** of the Sketch-Path.

183) Release the **Ctrl** key.

184) Click **Pierce** from the Add Relations box.

185) Click **OK** from the Properties PropertyManager

Close the sketch.

186) Click **Exit Sketch** from the Sketch toolbar.

187) Rename **Sketch2** to **Sketch-Profile**.

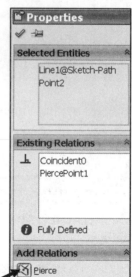

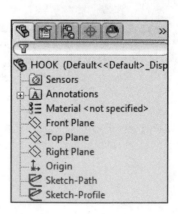

Save the part.

188) Click **Save** 💾.

Activity: HOOK Part-Swept Base Feature

Insert a Swept feature.

189) Click **Sketch-Profile** in the FeatureManager.

190) Click the **Swept Boss/Base** 🗗 Features tool. The Sweep PropertyManager is displayed. Sketch-Profile is displayed in the Profile box.

191) **Expand** HOOK from the fly-out FeatureManager.

192) Click inside the **Path** box.

193) Click **Sketch-Path** from the fly-out FeatureManager. Sketch-Path is displayed in the Path box.

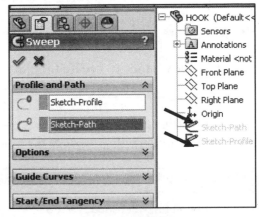

194) Click **OK** ✔ from the Sweep PropertyManager. Sweep1 is displayed in the FeatureManager.

Save the HOOK part.

195) Click **Save** 💾.

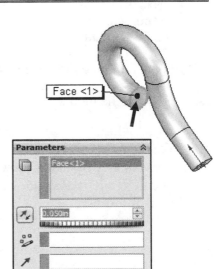

💡 Sketch the path, sketch the profile or cross section for the Swept Base feature. Pierce the profile at the start of the path trajectory.

Activity: HOOK Part-Dome Feature

Insert a Dome feature.

196) **Rotate** the model with the middle mouse button.

197) Click the **flat face** of the Sweep1 feature in the Graphics window as illustrated.

198) Click the **Dome** 🔵 Features tool. The Dome PropertyManager is displayed. Face<1> is displayed in the Parameters box.

199) Enter .050in, [**1.27**] for Distance.

200) Click **OK** ✔ from the Dome PropertyManager. Dome1 is displayed in the FeatureManager.

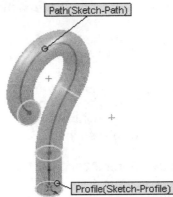

The HOOK requires threads. Use the Swept Cut feature to create the required threads. The thread requires a spiral path. The path is called the Threadpath. The thread requires a sketched profile. The circular cross section is called the Threadprofile.

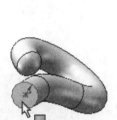

There are numerous steps required to create a thread. The thread is not flush with the bottom face. Use an offset plane to start the thread. Create a new offset Sketch plane, ThreadPlane.

Use the below steps to create the thread: Note: Steps on threads for plastic parts, springs, and coils. **1.)** *Create a new plane for the thread.* **2.)** *Create the spiral path.* **3.)** *Create a large cross section circular profile to improve visibility.* **4.)** *Pierce the cross section circular profile to the spiral path.* **5.)** *Dimension the circular profile.* **6.)** *Create the Swept feature.*

Activity: HOOK Part-Threads with Swept Cut Feature

Create the Offset Reference Plane.
201) **Rotate** the model with the middle mouse button.

202) Click the **bottom circular** face of Sweep1. Do not click the Origin.

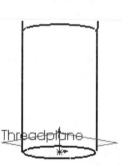

203) Click **Insert**, **Reference Geometry**, **Plane** from the Menu bar. The Plane PropertyManager is displayed. Face<1> is displayed in the Selections box.

204) Enter **.020**in, **[0.51]** for Distance.

205) Check the **Flip** box. Plane1 is located above the Top Plane.

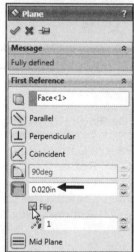

206) Click **OK** ✔ from the Plane PropertyManager. Plane1 is displayed in the FeatureManager.

207) Rename **Plane1** to **Threadplane**.

208) **Rebuild** the model.

🔅 You can also access the Plane PropertyManager by using the Consolidated Reference Geometry drop-down menu from the Features toolbar.

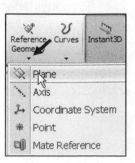

Display the Isometric view.

209) Click **Isometric view**  from the Heads-up View toolbar.

210) Click **Hidden Lines Removed** from the Heads-up View toolbar.

Create the Thread path.
211) **Rotate** and **Zoom in** on the bottom of Sweep1.

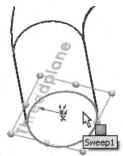

212) Right-click **Threadplane** from the FeatureManager.

213) Click **Sketch** from the Context toolbar.

214) Click the **bottom** of Sweep1 as illustrated.

215) Click the **Convert Entities** Sketch tool.

216) Click **OK** from the PropertyManager.

Create the Thread Path.
217) Click **Insert**, **Curve**, **Helix/Spiral** from the Menu bar. The Helix/Spiral PropertyManager is displayed.

218) Enter .**050**in, [**1.27**] for Pitch.

219) Check the **Reverse direction** box.

220) Enter **4** for Revolutions. Enter **0**deg for the Start angle. Click the **Clockwise** box.

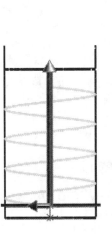

221) Click **OK** from the Helix/Spiral PropertyManager. Helix/Spiral1 is displayed in the FeatureManager.

222) Rename **Helix/Spiral1** to **Threadpath**.

223) Click **Isometric view** from the Heads-up View toolbar.

224) Click **Save**.

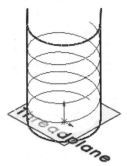

You can also access the Helix/Spiral PropertyManager through the Consolidated Curves drop-down menu from the Features toolbar.

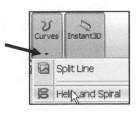

Create the Thread Profile, (cross section).

225) Right-click **Right Plane** from the FeatureManager.

226) Click **Sketch**  from the Context toolbar. The Sketch toolbar is displayed.

227) Click **Right view** from the Heads-up View toolbar.

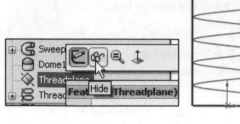

228) Right-click **Threadplane** from the FeatureManager.

229) Click **Hide** from the Context toolbar.

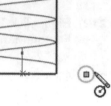

230) Click the **Circle** ⊘ Sketch tool. The Circle PropertyManager is displayed.

231) Sketch a **circle** to the right of the profile as illustrated.

De-select the Circle Sketch tool.
232) Right-click **Select**.

Add a Pierce relation.
233) Click the **Threadpath** at the start of the helical curve as illustrated.

234) Hold the **Ctrl** key down.

235) Click the **center point** of the circle.

236) Release the **Ctrl** key. The Properties PropertyManager is displayed. The selected sketch entities are displayed in the Properties box.

237) Click **Pierce** from the Add Relations box.

238) Click **OK** ✔ from the Properties PropertyManager. View the results.

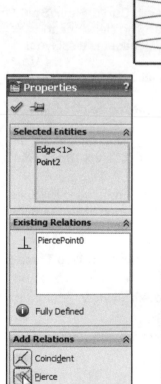

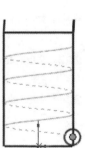

Add a dimension.

239) Click the **Smart Dimension** Sketch tool.

240) Click the **circumference**.

241) Click a **position** off the profile.

242) Enter .030in, [0.76].

243) Click the **Green Check mark** .

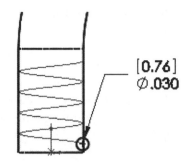

[0.76]
Ø.030

Close the sketch.
244) Click **Exit Sketch** from the Sketch toolbar.

245) Click **Isometric view** from the Heads-up View toolbar.

246) Rename **Sketch3** to **Threadprofile**.

247) Click **Threadprofile** in the FeatureManager.

Insert the Swept Cut feature.

248) Click **Swept Cut** from the Features toolbar. The Cut-Sweep PropertyManager is displayed. Threadprofile is displayed in the Profile box.

249) Click inside the **Path** box.

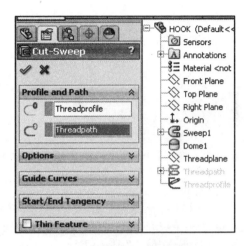

250) Click **Threadpath** from the fly-out FeatureManager. Threadpath is displayed in the Path box.

251) Click **OK** from the Cut-Sweep PropertyManager. Cut-Sweep1 is displayed in the FeatureManager.

252) Rename **Cut-Sweep1** to **Thread**.

When you create a new part or assembly, the three default Planes (Front, Right and Top) are align with specific views. The Plane you select for the Base sketch determines the orientation of the part.

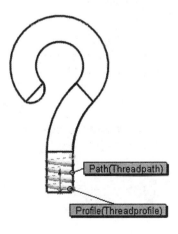

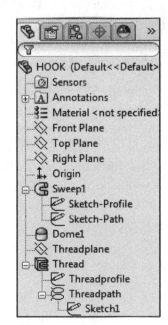

Save the HOOK part.

253) Click **Shaded** ⬛ from the Heads-up View toolbar.

254) **Remove** all Tangent Edges.

255) Click **Save** 💾. The HOOK part is complete.

🔅 Utilize Insert, Feature from the Menu bar to select other Feature tools which are not located on the Features tab in the CommandManager.

🔅 Utilize Tools, Customize, Command, Features to modify the Features toolbar.

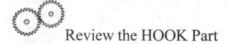 Review the HOOK Part

The HOOK part was created with two Swept features. A Swept Base feature added material by moving a profile along a path. The Swept feature required two sketches. The first sketch was called the path. The path was sketched on the Right Plane. The second sketch was called profile. The profile was sketched on the Top Plane. The path and profile were sketched on perpendicular planes. The path was sweep along the profile to create the Swept Base feature.

The Dome feature created a spherical face on the end of the Swept Base feature.

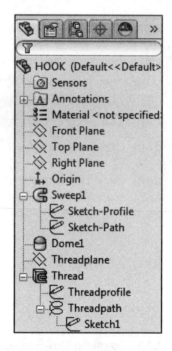

A Swept Cut feature removed material to create the thread. The thread required a spiral path and a circular profile. The path was created on a reference plane, parallel to the Top Plane. The path utilized a Helical Curve. The thread required a sketched profile. This circular cross section was sketched perpendicular to the Front Plane. The thread profile was pierced to the thread path.

🔍 Additional details on Loft, Swept, Swept Cut, Helix and Spiral, Relations, Pierce and Reference planes are available in SolidWorks Help.

🔅 It's considered best practice to fully define all sketches in the model. However; there are times when this is not practical. Generally when using the spline tool to create a complex freeform shape.

WHEEL Part

The WHEEL part is a machined part.

Create the WHEEL part with the Extruded Boss/Base feature 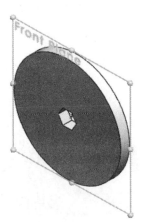 tool. Utilize the Mid Plane option to center the WHEEL on the Front Plane.

Utilize the Revolved Cut feature 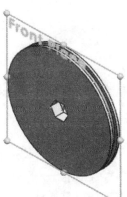 tool to remove material from the WHEEL and to create a groove for a belt.

The WHEEL contains a complex pattern of holes. Apply the Extruded Cut feature 🔲 tool.

Simplify the geometry by dividing the four holes into two Extruded Cut features.

The first Extruded Cut feature contains two small circles sketched on two bolt circles. The bolt circles utilize Construction geometry.

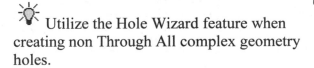

🔅 Utilize the Hole Wizard feature when creating non Through All complex geometry holes.

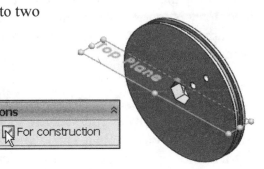

The second Extruded Cut feature 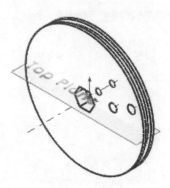 utilizes two small circles sketched on two bolt circles. The bolt circles utilize Construction geometry.

Utilize the Circular Pattern Feature 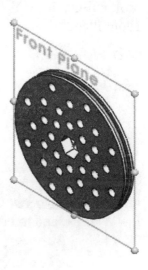 tool. The two Extruded Cut features are contained in the Circular Pattern. Revolve the Extruded Cut features about the Temporary Axis located at the center of the Hexagon.

Create a Reference Axis. The Reference Axis is utilized in the WHEEL-AXLE assembly.

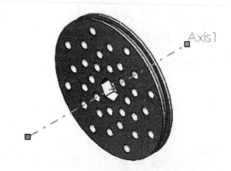

🔆 Construction geometry is used only to assist in creating the sketch entities and geometry that are ultimately incorporated into the part. Construction geometry is ignored when the sketch is used to create a feature. Construction geometry uses the same line style as centerlines.

🔆 You can utilize the Hole Wizard feature tool instead of the Cut-Extrude feature tool, or use the Instant3D tool to create a Through All hole for any part. See SolidWorks Help for additional information.

Activity: WHEEL Part

Create the New part.

256) Click **New** ⬜ from the Menu bar.

257) Click the **SW-TUTORIAL-2013** tab.

258) Double-click **PART-ANSI-IN**, [PART-ANSI-MM].

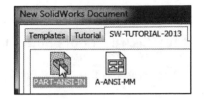

Save the part.

259) Click **Save** 🖫.

260) Select the **SW-TUTORIAL-2013** folder.

261) Enter **WHEEL** for File name.

262) Enter **WHEEL** for Description.

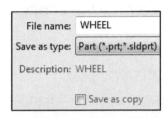

263) Click **Save**. The WHEEL FeatureManager is displayed.

Insert the sketch for the Extruded Base feature.

264) Right-click **Front Plane** from the FeatureManager.

265) Click **Sketch** ✎ from the Context toolbar. The Sketch toolbar is displayed.

266) Click the **Circle** ⊙ Sketch tool. The Circle PropertyManager is displayed.

267) Click the **Origin** ↳ as illustrated.

268) Click a **position** to the right of the Origin.

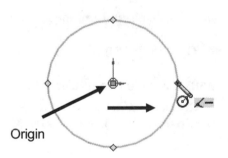

Insert a polygon.

269) Click the **Polygon** ⬡ Sketch tool. The Polygon PropertyManager is displayed.

270) Click the **Origin** ↳.

271) Drag and click the **mouse pointer** horizontally to the right of the Origin to create the hexagon as illustrated.

272) Click **OK** ✔ from the Polygon PropertyManager.

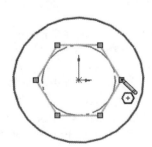

De-select the Polygon Sketch tool.

273) Right-click **Select**.

Add a Horizontal relation.

274) Click the **Origin**.

275) Hold the **Ctrl** key down.

276) Click the **right point** of the hexagon.

277) Release the **Ctrl** key.

278) Right-click **Make Horizontal** ━ from the Context toolbar.

279) Click **OK** ✓ from the Properties PropertyManager.

Add dimensions.

280) Click the **Smart Dimension** ✧ Sketch tool.

281) Click the **circumference** of the large circle.

282) Click a **position** above the circle.

283) Enter **3.000**in, [**76.20**].

284) Click the **Green Check mark** ✓.

285) Click the **circumference** of the inscribed circle for the Hexagon.

286) Click a **position** above the Hexagon.

287) Enter **.438**in, [**11.13**].

288) Click the **Green Check mark** ✓.

Activity: WHEEL Part-Extruded Boss/Base Feature

Insert an Extruded Boss/Base feature.

289) Click **Extruded Boss/Base** 🗔 from the Features toolbar. The Boss-Extrude PropertyManager is displayed.

290) Select **Mid Plane** for End Condition in Direction 1.

291) Enter **.250**in, [**6.35**] for Depth.

292) Click **OK** ✓ from the Boss-Extrude PropertyManager. Boss-Extrude1 is displayed in the FeatureManager.

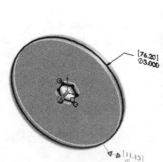

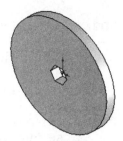

Fit the model to the Graphics window.

293) Press the **f** key.

Save the WHEEL part.

294) Click **Save** 💾.

Activity: WHEEL Part-Revolved Cut Feature

Insert a new sketch for the Revolved Cut feature.

295) Right-click **Right Plane** from the FeatureManager.

296) Click **Sketch** ✎ from the Context toolbar. The Sketch toolbar is displayed.

297) Click **Right view** ⬚ from the Heads-up View toolbar.

Sketch the axis of revolution.

298) Click the **Centerline** ⁞ Sketch tool from the Consolidated Sketch toolbar. The Insert Line PropertyManager is displayed.

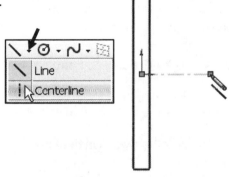

299) Click the **Origin** ↳.

300) Click a **position** horizontally to the right of the Origin.

De-select the sketch tool.

301) Right-click **Select**.

302) **Zoom in** on the top edge.

Sketch the profile.

303) Click the **Line** ╲ Sketch tool.

304) Sketch the **first vertical line** as illustrated.

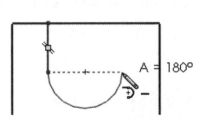

305) Click the **Tangent Arc** ⟳ Sketch tool. The Arc PropertyManager is displayed.

306) Click the **end point** of the vertical line.

307) Sketch a **180° arc** as illustrated.

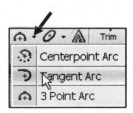

De-select the sketch tool.

308) Right-click **Select** in the Graphics window.

309) Click the **Line** ⟍ Sketch tool.

310) Sketch the **second vertical line** as illustrated. The end point of the line is Coincident with the top horizontal edge of Extrude1.

311) Sketch a **horizontal line** collinear with the top edge to close the profile.

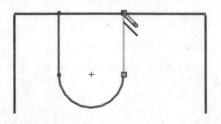

Add a Vertical relation.
312) Right-click **Select** in the Graphics window.

313) Click the **Origin** ↳ from the FeatureManager.

314) Hold the **Ctrl** key down. Click the **center point** of the arc.

315) Release the **Ctrl** key.

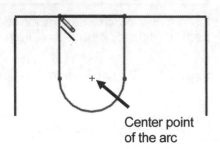

Center point
of the arc

316) Click **Vertical** | from the Add Relations box.

Add an Equal relation.
317) Click the **left vertical** line. Hold the **Ctrl** key down.

318) Click the **right vertical** line.

319) Release the **Ctrl** key.

320) Click **Equal** from the Add Relations box.

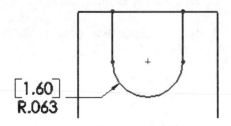

Add dimensions.
321) Click the **Smart Dimension** ✎ Sketch tool.

322) Click the **arc**.

323) Click a position to the **left** of the profile.

324) Enter .063in, [**1.6**].

325) Click the **Green Check mark** ✔ .

326) Click the **right vertical line**.

327) Click a position to the **right** of the profile.

328) Enter .078in, [**1.98**].

329) Click the **Green Check mark** ✔ . The sketch should be fully defined.

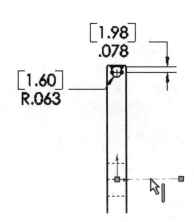

If needed, add a Collinear relation.
330) Click the **horizontal line**. Hold the **Ctrl** key down.

331) Click the **horizontal silhouette edge** as illustrated. *Note the feedback icon*.

332) Release the **Ctrl** key.

333) Click **Collinear** ✐ from the Add Relations box.

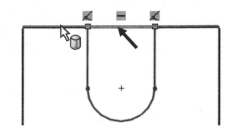

Fit the model to the Graphics window.
334) Press the **f** key.

De-select the sketch tool.
335) Right-click **Select** in the Graphics window.

Activity: WHEEL Part-Revolved Cut Feature

Insert a Revolved Cut feature.
336) Select the Axis of Revolution. Click the **centerline** in the Graphics window as illustrated.

337) Click **Revolved Cut** 🔲 from the Features toolbar. The Cut-Revolve PropertyManager is displayed. The Cut-Revolve PropertyManager displays 360 degrees for Direction 1 Angle.

338) Click **OK** ✓ from the Cut-Revolve PropertyManager. Cut-Revolve1 is displayed in the FeatureManager.

Save the WHEEL part.

339) Click **Save** 🖫.

Four bolt circles, spaced 0.5in, [12.7] apart locate the 8 - ∅.190, [4.83] holes. Simplify the situation. Utilize two Extruded Cut features on each bolt circle.

Position the first Extruded Cut feature hole on the first bolt circle and third bolt circle.

Position the second Extruded Cut feature hole on the second bolt circle and forth bolt circle.

Activity: WHEEL Part- First Extruded Cut Feature

Display the Top Plane.

340) Right-click **Top Plane** from the FeatureManager.

341) Click **Show** 👁 from the Context toolbar.

342) Click **Front view** 📦 from the Heads-up View toolbar.

343) Click **Hidden Lines Visible** 📦 from the Heads-up View toolbar.

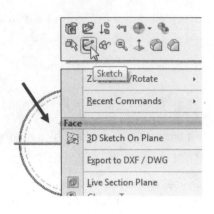

Insert a new sketch for the first Extruded Cut feature.

344) Right-click the **Boss-Extrude1 front face** as illustrated.

345) Click **Sketch** ✏ from the Context toolbar. The Sketch toolbar is displayed.

Create the first construction bolt circle.

346) Click the **Circle** ⊙ Sketch tool. The Circle PropertyManager is displayed.

347) Click the **Origin** ↳.

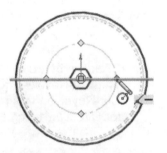

348) Click a **position** to the right of the hexagon as illustrated.

349) Check the **For construction** box.

Create the second construction bolt circle.

350) Click the **Origin** ↳.

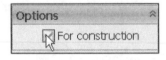

351) Click a **position** to the right of the first construction bolt circle as illustrated.

352) Check the **For construction** box. The two bolt circles are displayed with Construction style lines.

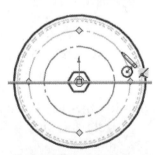

💡 Construction geometry is used only to assist in creating the sketch entities and geometry that are ultimately incorporated into the part. Construction geometry is ignored when the sketch is used to create a feature. Construction geometry uses the same line style as centerlines.

De-select the circle Sketch tool.

353) Right-click **Select**.

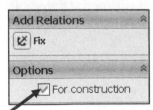

Insert a centerline.

354) Click the **Centerline** ⋮ Sketch tool. The Insert Line PropertyManager is displayed.

355) Sketch a **45° centerline** (approximately) from the Origin to the second bolt circle as illustrated.

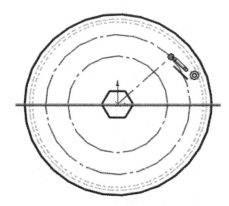

Sketch the two circle profiles.

356) Click the **Circle** ⊘ Sketch tool. The Circle PropertyManager is displayed.

357) Sketch a **circle** at the intersection of the centerline and the first bolt circle.

358) Sketch a **circle** at the intersection of the centerline and the second bolt circle.

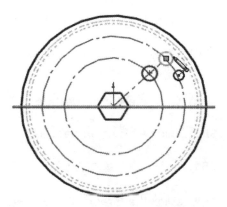

De-select the Circle Sketch tool.
359) Right-click **Select** in the Graphics window.

Note: An Intersection relation is created between three entities: the center point of the small circle, the centerline, and the bolt circle.

Add an Equal relation.
360) Click the **first circle**.

361) Hold the **Ctrl** key down.

362) Click the **second circle**.

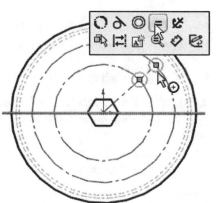

363) Release the **Ctrl** key.

364) Right-click **Make Equal** = from the Context toolbar.

Add dimensions.
365) Click the **Smart Dimension** ⌀ Sketch tool.

366) Click the **first construction circle**.

367) Click a **position** above the profile.

368) Enter **1.000**in, **[25.4]**.

369) Click the **Green Check mark** ✔.

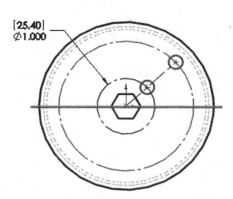

370) Click the **second construction circle**.

371) Click a **position** above the profile.

372) Enter **2.000**in, **[50.80]**.

373) Click the **Green Check mark** ✔.

374) Click the **second small circle**.

375) Click a **position** above the profile.

376) Enter **.190**in, **[4.83]**.

377) Click the **Green Check mark** ✔.

378) Click **Top Plane** from the fly-out FeatureManager.

379) Click the **45° centerline**.

380) Click a **position** between the two lines.

381) Enter **45**deg for angle.

382) Click the **Green Check mark** ✔.

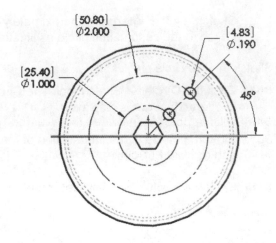

Note: If the sketch is not fully defined, you may need to add an Intersection relation between the center point of the small circle, the centerline, and the bolt circle.

Insert an Extruded Cut feature.

383) Click **Extruded Cut** 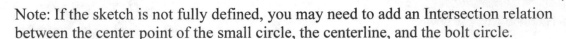 from the Features toolbar. The Cut-Extrude PropertyManager is displayed. Select **Through All** for the End Condition in Direction 1.

384) Click **OK** ✔ from the Cut-Extrude PropertyManager. Cut-Extrude1 is displayed in the FeatureManager.

Activity: WHEEL Part- Second Extruded Cut Feature

Insert a new sketch for the second Extruded Cut feature.
385) Right-click the **Boss-Extrude1** front face.

386) Click **Sketch**  from the Context toolbar.

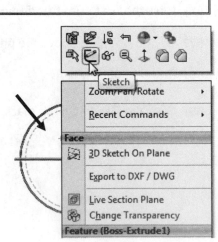

Sketch two additional Construction line bolt circles, 1.500in, [38.1] and 2.500in, [63.5]. Create the first Construction bolt circle.

387) Click the **Circle** 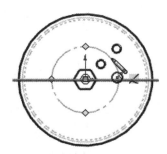 Sketch tool. The Circle PropertyManager is displayed.

388) Click the **Origin** ⌐.

389) Click a **position** between the two small circles.

390) Check the **For construction** box.

Create the second additional construction bolt circle.

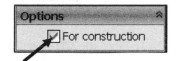

391) Click the **Origin** ⌐.

392) Click a **position** to the right of the large construction bolt circle as illustrated.

393) Check the **For construction** box from the Circle PropertyManager. The two bolt circles are displayed with the two construction lines.

Insert a centerline.

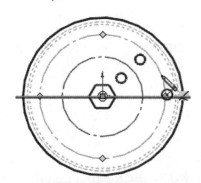

394) Click the **Centerline** Sketch tool. The Insert Line PropertyManager is displayed.

395) Sketch a **22.5° centerline** to the right from the Origin to the second bolt circle as illustrated.

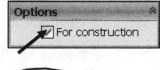

396) Select **.1** from the Unit Precision box.

397) Click **Hidden Lines Removed** ⬚ from the Heads-up View toolbar.

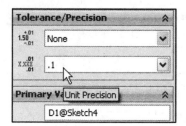

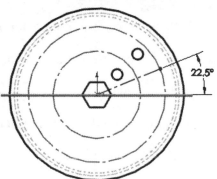

Sketch the two circle profiles.

398) Click the **Circle** ⊘ Sketch tool. The Circle PropertyManager is displayed

399) Sketch a **circle** at the intersection of the centerline and the first bolt circle.

400) Sketch a **circle** at the intersection of the centerline and the second bolt circle.

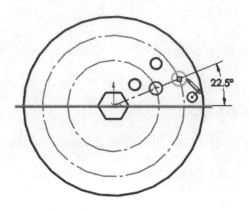

De-select the Circle Sketch tool.
401) Right-click **Select**.

Add an Equal relation.
402) Click the **first circle**.

403) Hold the **Ctrl** key down.

404) Click the **second circle**. Release the **Ctrl** key.

405) Right-click **Make Equal** ＝ from the shortcut toolbar.

Add dimensions.
406) Click the **Smart Dimension** ⟡ Sketch tool. The Smart Dimension ⟡ icon is displayed.

407) Click the **first construction circle**.

408) Click a **position** above the profile.

409) Enter **1.500**in, **[38.1]**.

410) Click the **second construction circle**.

411) Click a **position** above the profile.

412) Enter **2.500**in, **[63.5]**.

413) Click the **small circle** as illustrated.

414) Click a **position** above the profile.

415) Enter **.190**in, **[4.83]**.

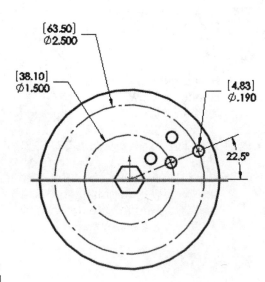

💡 If the sketch is not fully defined, you may need to add an Intersection relation between the center point of the small circle, the centerline, and the bolt circle.

Insert an Extruded Cut feature.

416) Click **Extruded Cut**  from the Features toolbar. The Cut-Extrude PropertyManager is displayed.

417) Select **Through All** for End Condition in Direction 1.

418) Click **OK** ✔ from the Cut-Extrude PropertyManager. Cut-Exturde2 is displayed in the FeatureManager.

419) Click **Save** 🖫.

View the Temporary Axes.
420) Click **View**; check **Temporary Axes** from the Menu bar.

Activity: WHEEL Part-Circular Pattern Feature

Insert a Circular Pattern.

421) Click **Isometric view** from the Heads-up View toolbar.

422) Click **Circular Pattern** from the Consolidated Features toolbar. The Circular Pattern PropertyManager is displayed.

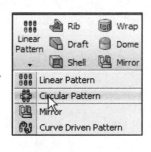
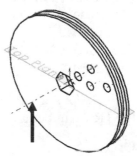

423) Click **inside** the Pattern Axis box.

424) Click the **Temporary Axis** in the Graphics window at the center of the Hexagon. Axis<1> is displayed in the Pattern Axis box.

425) Click the **Equal spacing** box.

426) Enter **360**deg for Angle.

427) Enter **8** for Number of Instances.

428) Click inside the **Features to Pattern** box.

429) Click **Cut-Extrude1** and **Cut-Extrude2** from the fly-out FeatureManager. Cut-Extrude1 and Cut-Extrude2 are displayed in the Features to Pattern box.

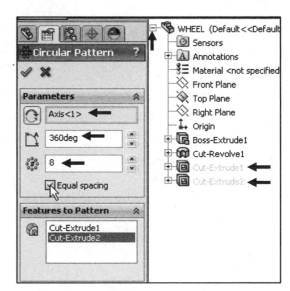

430) Check the **Geometry pattern** box.

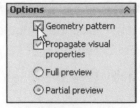

431) Click **OK** ✅ from the Circular Pattern PropertyManager. CirPattern1 is displayed in the FeatureManager.

Save the WHEEL part.

432) Click **Save** 🖫.

Utilize a Reference Axis to locate the WHEEL in the PNEUMATIC-TEST-MODULE assembly. The Reference Axis is located in the FeatureManager and Graphics window. The Reference Axis is a construction axis defined between two planes.

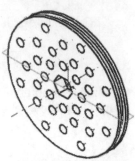

Insert a Reference axis.

433) Click the **Axis** tool from the Reference Geometry Consolidated Features toolbar. The Axis PropertyManager is displayed.

434) Click **Top Plane** from the fly-out FeatureManager.

435) Click **Right Plane** from the fly-out FeatureManager. The selected planes are displayed in the Selections box.

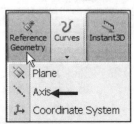

436) Click **OK** ✅ from the Axis PropertyManager. Axis1 is displayed in the FeatureManager.

Axis1 is positioned through the Hex Cut centered at the Origin.

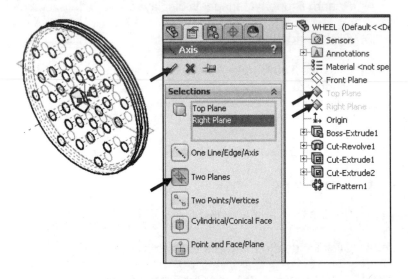

437) Click and drag the **Axis1 handles** outward to extend the length on both sides as illustrated.

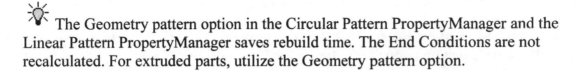

Save the WHEEL part.

438) Click **Isometric view**.

439) Click **View**; uncheck **Temporary Axes** from the Menu bar.

440) **Hide** all Planes.

441) Click **Shaded With Edges** from the Heads-up View toolbar.

442) Click **Save**.

The Geometry pattern option in the Circular Pattern PropertyManager and the Linear Pattern PropertyManager saves rebuild time. The End Conditions are not recalculated. For extruded parts, utilize the Geometry pattern option.

Sketched lines, arcs or circles are modified from profile geometry to construction geometry. Select the geometry in the sketch. Check the For construction box option.

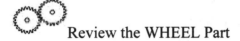 Review the WHEEL Part

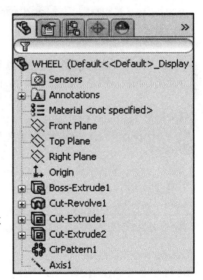

The WHEEL part was created with the Extruded Boss/Base feature. You sketched a circular sketch on the Front Plane and extruded the sketch with the Mid Plane option.

A Revolved Cut feature removed material from the WHEEL and created the groove. The Revolved Cut feature utilized an arc sketched on the Right Plane. A sketched centerline was required to create the Revolved Cut feature.

The WHEEL contained a complex pattern of holes. The first Extruded Cut feature contained two small circles sketched on two bolt circles. The bolt circles utilized construction geometry. Geometric relationships and dimensions were used in the sketch. The second Extruded Cut feature utilized two small circles sketched on two bolt circles.

The two Extruded Cut features were contained in one Circular Pattern and revolved about the Temporary Axis. The Reference Axis was created with two perpendicular planes. Utilize the Reference Axis, Axis1 in the WHEEL-AXLE assembly.

Modify a Part

Conserve design time and cost. Modify existing parts
and assemblies to create new parts and assemblies.
Utilize the Save as copy tool to avoid updating the
existing assemblies with new file names.

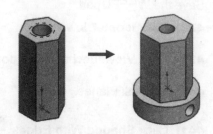

The HEX-STANDOFF part was created in Chapter 2.
The HEX-ADAPTER is required to fasten the WHEEL
to the AXLE. Start with the HEX-STANDOFF part.

Utilize the Save As command and enter the HEX-ADAPTER for the new file name.
Important: Check the Save as copy check box. The HEX-ADAPTER is the new part
name. Open the HEX-ADAPTER. Modify the dimensions of the Extruded Base feature.

Utilize Edit Definition to modify the Hole Wizard Tap Hole to a Standard Hole. Insert an
Extruded Boss/Base feature to create the head of the HEX-ADAPTER.

Insert an Extruded Cut feature. Sketch a circle on the Right Plane. Extrude the circle in
Direction1 and Direction2 with the Through All End Condition option. Note: You can
use the Hole Wizard feature with a 3D Sketch.

Feature order determines the internal geometry of the Hole. If the Hole feature is created
before the Extrude2-Head feature, the Through All End Condition will extend through
the Boss-Extrude1 feature.

If the Hole feature is created after the Extrude2-Head feature, the Through All End
Condition will extend through the Boss-Extrude1 feature and the Extrude2-Head feature.

Modify feature order by dragging feature names in the FeatureManager. Utilize the Save
As command to create the AXLE3000 part from the AXLE part.

Utilize the Save As command to create the SHAFTCOLLAR-500 part from the SHAFT-
COLLAR part. Save the HEX-STANDOFF as the HEX-ADAPTER part.

Activity: HEX-ADAPTER Part

Create the HEX-ADAPTER.

443) Click **Open** 📂 from the Menu bar.

444) Select **Filer Parts (*.prt; *.sldprt)** for file type from the
SW-TUTORIAL-2013 folder.

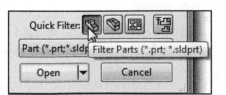

445) Double-click **HEX-STANDOFF**. The HEX-STANDOFF
FeatureManager is displayed.

446) Click **Save As** from the drop-down Menu bar.

447) Select the **SW-TUTORIAL-2013** folder.

448) Enter **HEX-ADAPTER** for File name.

449) Enter **HEX-ADAPTER** for Description.

450) Check the **Save as copy** box.

451) Click **Save**.

452) Click **File**, **Close** from the Menu bar.

Open the HEX-ADAPTER.
453) Click **Open** 📂 from the Menu bar.

454) Double-click **HEX-ADAPTER** from the SW-TUTORIAL-2013 folder. The HEX-ADAPTER FeatureManager is displayed.

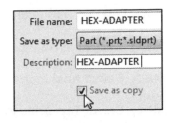

Modify the Boss-Extrude1 dimensions.
455) Double-click **Boss-Extrude1** from the FeatureManager.

456) Click **.735**in, [**18.67**].

457) Enter **.700**in, [**17.78**] for depth.

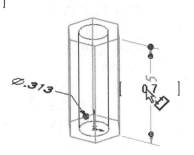

458) Click **.313**in, [**7.95**].

459) Enter **.438**in, [**11.13**] for diameter.

Modify the #10-24 Tapped Hole1 feature.
460) Right-click **#10-24 Tapped Hole1** from the FeatureManager.

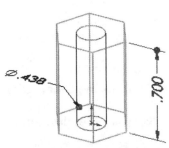

461) Click **Edit Feature** 📷 from the Context toolbar. The Hole Specification PropertyManager is displayed.

💡 The Hole Specification PropertyManager is part of the Hole Wizard tool located in the Features toolbar.

The Type tab is selected by default.

462) Select the **Hole** tab from the Hole Specification box.

463) Select **Ansi Inch** for Standard.

464) Select **Tap Drills** for Type.

465) Select **#10-24** for Size.

466) Select **Through All** for End Condition.

467) Click **OK** ✅ from the Hole Specification PropertyManager. The Tap Hole is modified.

Insert a sketch for the Extruded Boss feature.

468) Press the **Up Arrow key** approximately four times.

469) Right-click the **bottom hexagonal face** of the Boss-Extrude1 feature as illustrated. Note: The face icon feedback symbol.

470) Click **Sketch** ✏ from the Context toolbar.

471) Click **Bottom view** 🖾 from the Heads-up View toolbar.

472) Click the **Circle** ⊘ Sketch tool. The Circle PropertyManager is displayed.

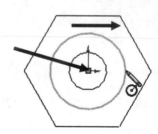

473) Click the **Origin** ⅃ as illustrated.

474) Click a **position** in the Graphics window to the right of the Origin.

Add a dimension.

475) Click the **Smart Dimension** ♢ Sketch tool.

476) Click the **circumference** of the circle.

477) Click a **position** above the circle to locate the dimension.

478) Enter **.625**in, **[15.88]** in the Modify dialog box.

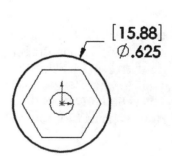

Fit the model to the Graphics window.

479) Press the **f** key.

Activity: HEX-ADAPTER Part-Extruded Boss/Base Feature

Extrude the sketch to create the Extruded Boss/Base feature.

480) Click **Isometric view**  from the Heads-up View toolbar.

481) Click **Extruded Boss/Base** from the Features toolbar. The Boss-Extrude PropertyManager is displayed.

482) Enter **.200**in, **[6.35]** for Depth. The Direction arrow points downward. Flip the **Direction arrow** if required.

483) Click **OK** from the Boss-Extrude PropertyManager. Boss-Extrude2 is displayed in the FeatureManager.

484) Rename **Boss-Extrude2** to **Extrude2-Head**.

485) Click **Save**.

Rename a feature or sketch for clarity. Slowly click the feature or sketch name twice and enter the new name when the old one is highlighted.

Activity: HEX-ADAPTER Part-Extruded Cut Feature

Insert a new sketch for the Extruded Cut on the Right Plane.

486) Right-click **Right Plane** from the FeatureManager.

487) Click **Sketch** from the Context toolbar.

488) Click **Right view** from the Heads-up View toolbar. Note the location of the Origin.

489) Click the **Circle** Sketch tool. The Circle PropertyManager is displayed.

490) Sketch a **circle** below the Origin. The center point is vertically aligned to the Origin as illustrated. If required, add a Vertical relation between the center point of the circle and the Origin.

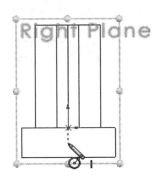

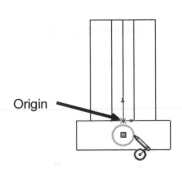

Origin

Add dimensions.

491) Click the **Smart Dimension** ✏️ Sketch tool.

492) Click the **middle horizontal edge**.

493) Click the **center point** of the circle.

494) Click a **position** to the right of the profile.

495) Enter **.100**in, [**2.54**].

496) Click the **Green Check mark** ✅.

497) Click the **circumference** of the circle.

498) Click a **position** below the profile.

499) Enter **.120**in, [**3.95**].

500) Click the **Green Check mark** ✅.

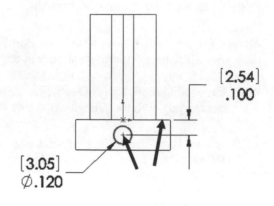

Insert an Extruded Cut feature.

501) Click **Extruded Cut** 📋 from the Features toolbar. The Cut-Extrude PropertyManager is displayed.

502) Select **Through All** for End Condition in Direction 1.

503) Check the **Direction 2** box.

504) Select **Through All** for End Condition in Direction 2.

505) Click **OK** ✅ from the Cut-Extrude PropertyManager.

506) Click **Isometric view** 🔲 from the Heads-up View toolbar.

507) Rename the feature to **Extrude3-SetScrew**.

Save the HEX-ADAPTER part.

508) Click **Save** 💾.

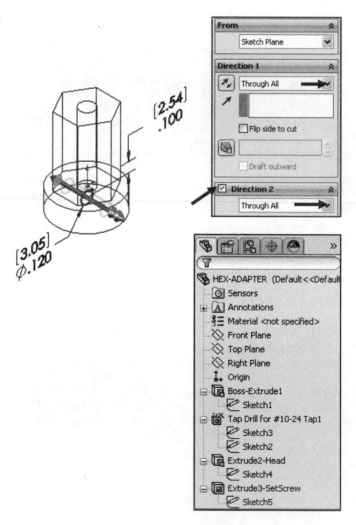

The Through All End Condition is required to penetrate both the Boss-Extrude1 and Extrude2 features. Reorder features in the FeatureManager. Position the Extrude2 feature before the Tap Drill for # 10-24 Tap 1 feature in the FeatureManager.

Reorder the Features.
509) Click and drag **Extrude2-Head** from the FeatureManager upward as illustrated.

510) Click a **position** below Boss-Extrude1. The Through All End Condition option for the Tap Drill for # 10-24 Tap 1 feature creates a hole through both Boss-Extrude1 and Extrude2.

Display a Section view.
511) Click **Front Plane** from the FeatureManager.

512) Click **Section view** from the Heads-up View toolbar in the Graphics window. The Section View PropertyManager is displayed. View the results.

513) Click **OK** ✅ from the Section View PropertyManager.

Display the full view.
514) Click **Section view** from the Heads-up View toolbar in the Graphics window.

515) Click **Shaded With Edges** 📦 from the Heads-up View toolbar.

Save the HEX-ADAPTER.
516) Click **Save** 💾. Note the location of the Origin in the model.

Close all documents.
517) Click **Windows**, **Close All** from the Menu bar.

🔅 Utilize the Save As command and work on the copied version of the document before making any changes to the original. Keep the original document intact.

🔅 Tangent edges and Origins are displayed for educational purposes in this book.

Origin

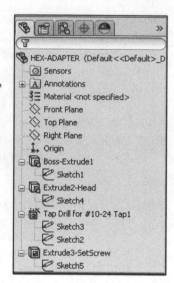

Review the HEX-ADAPTER Part

The HEX-ADAPTER part was created by utilizing the Save As, and the Save as copy command with the HEX-STANDOFF part. The Boss-Extrude1 feature dimensions were modified. Edit Definition was utilized to modify the Hole type from the Hole Wizard feature.

An Extruded Boss feature added material. An Extruded Cut feature, sketched on the Right Plane with the Through All End Condition for both Direction1 and Direction2, created a hole through the Extruded Boss feature. Reordering features in the FeatureManager modified the Hole. Utilizing existing geometry saved time with the Save as copy command. The original part and its references to other assemblies are not affected with the Save as copy command.

You require additional work before completing the PNEUMATIC-TEST-MODULE assembly. The AXLE and SHAFT-COLLAR were created in Chapter 1. Utilize the Save as copy command to save the parts.

Additional details on Save (Save as copy), Reorder (features), Section View PropertyManager are available in SolidWorks Help.

Utilize Design Table configurations for the AXLE part and SHAFT-COLLAR part developed in the previous chapter.

Note: The AXLE-3000 part and SHAFT-COLLAR-500 part utilize the Save as copy option in the next section. Utilize the Save as copy components or the configurations developed with Design Tables in Chapter 3 for the WHEEL-AXLE assembly.

Activity: AXLE-3000 Part

Create the AXLE-3000 part from the AXLE part.

518) Click **Open** from the Menu bar.

519) Double-click **AXLE** from the SW-TUTORIAL-2013 folder. The AXLE FeatureManager is displayed.

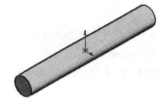

520) Click **Save As** from the drop-down Menu bar.

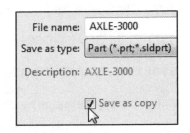

521) Select the **SW-TUTORIAL-2013** folder.

522) Enter **AXLE-3000** for File name.

523) Enter **AXLE-3000** for Description.

524) Check the **Save as copy** check box.

525) Click **Save**.

Close the AXLE part
526) Click **File**, **Close** from the Menu bar.

Open AXLE-3000 part.
527) Click **Open** 📁 from the Menu bar.

528) Double-click **AXLE-3000** from the SW-TUTORIAL-2013 folder. The AXLE-3000 FeatureManager is displayed.

Modify the depth dimension.
529) Double-click the **cylindrical face** in the Graphics window. Dimensions are displayed.

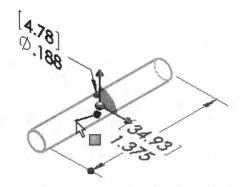

530) Click **1.375**in, **[34.93]**.

531) Enter **3.000**in, **[76.20]**.

Fit the model to the Graphics window.
532) Press the **f** key.

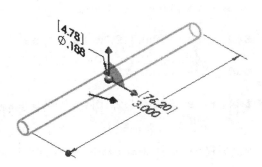

Save the AXLE-3000 part.
533) Click **Save** 💾.

534) Click **inside** the Graphics window.

Activity: SHAFTCOLLAR-500 Part

Create the SHAFTCOLLAR-500 part.
535) Click **Open** 📁 from the Menu bar.

536) Double-click **SHAFT-COLLAR** from the SW-TUTORIAL-2013 folder.

537) Click **Save As** from the Menu bar.

538) Enter **SHAFT-COLLAR-500** for File name.

539) Enter **SHAFT-COLLAR-500** for Description.

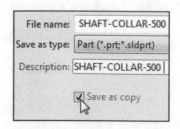

540) Click **Save as copy** check box.

541) Click **Save**.

Close the SHAFT-COLLAR part.
542) Click **File**, **Close** from the Menu bar.

Open the SHAFT-COLLAR-500 part.
543) Click **Open** 📂 from the Menu bar.

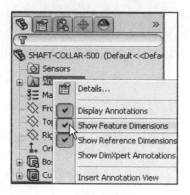

544) Double-click **SHAFT-COLLAR-500** from the SW-TUTORIAL-2013 folder. SHAFT-COLLAR-500 is displayed in the Graphics window.

Modify the diameter dimensions.
545) Right-click **Annotations** in the FeatureManager.

546) Check the **Show Feature Dimensions** box.

547) Press the **f** key to fit the model to the graphics area.

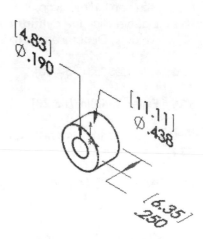

548) Click **.438**in, **[11.11]**.

549) Enter **.750**in, **[19.05]** for outside diameter.

550) Click **.190**in, **[4.83]**.

551) Enter **.500**in, **[12.70]** for inside diameter. View the results.

552) Right-click **Annotations** in the FeatureManager.

553) Uncheck the **Show Feature Dimensions** box.

554) **Rebuild** the model.

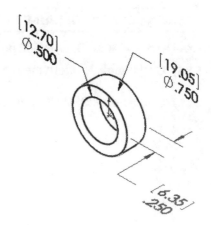

Fit the model to the Graphics window.
555) Press the **f** key.

Save the SHAFT-COLLAR-500 part.
556) Click **Save** 🔲.

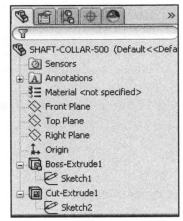

Close all documents.
557) Click **Windows**, **Close All** from the Menu
bar.

🔆 Press the **s** key in the Graphics window.
A Context Pop-up features toolbar is
displayed. The features toolbar displays the
last few feature tools applied.

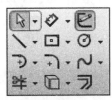

🔆 Select the types of Annotations that you
want to display and set text scale and other
Annotations options. In the FeatureManager design
tree, right-click the **Annotations** folder, and click
details. View the options from the Annotation
Properties dialog box.

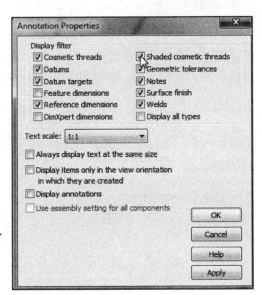

🔆 Rename a feature or sketch for clarity. Slowly
click the feature or sketch name twice and enter the
new name when the old one is highlighted.

🔆 Add relations, then dimensions. This will
keep the user from having too many unnecessary
dimensions. This helps to show the design intent of
the model. Dimension what geometry you intent to
modify or adjust.

Chapter Summary

In this chapter, you created six parts. The WEIGHT part utilized the Plane feature, Lofted Base feature and the Extruded Cut (Instant3D tool) feature. The HOOK part utilized the *Swept Base feature, Dome feature, Plane feature, Helix and Spiral feature, and Swept Cut* feature. The WHEEL part utilized the *Extruded Base feature, Revolved Cut feature, Extruded Cut feature, Circular Pattern feature and Axis* feature.

The second three parts utilized existing parts created in early chapter. The HEX-ADAPTER part, AXLE-3000 part and the SHAFTCOLLAR-500 part utilized existing part geometry along with the Hole Wizard feature.

You applied the following Sketch tools in this chapter: *Circle, Line, Centerline, Tangent Arc, Polygon, Smart Dimension, Center Rectangle, Centerpoint Arc, 3 Point Arc and Convert Entities*.

Chapter Terminology

Circular Pattern: A Circular Pattern repeats features or geometry in a polar array. A Circular Patten requires an axis of revolution, the number of instances and an angle.

ConfigurationManager: The ConfigurationManager on the left side of the Graphics window is utilized to create, select, and view the configurations of parts and assemblies.

Dome: A Dome feature creates a spherical or elliptical feature from a selected face.

Loft: A Loft feature blends two or more profiles. Each profile is sketched on a separate plane.

Mirror Component: A mirror component creates a mirrored or copied part or assembly. A mirrored component is sometimes called a "right-hand" version of the original "left hand" version.

Replace: The Replace command substitutes one or more open instances of a component in an assembly with a different component.

Revolved Cut: A Revolved Cut removes material. A sketched profile is revolved around a centerline. The Revolved Cut requires a direction and an angle of revolution.

Swept Boss/Base: A Swept Boss/Base feature adds material by moving a profile along a path. A basic Swept feature requires two sketches. The first sketch is called the path. The second sketch is called profile. The profile and path are sketched on perpendicular planes.

Swept Cut: A Swept Cut feature removes material by moving a profile along a path. A basic Swept feature requires two sketches. The first sketch is called the path. The second sketch is called profile. The profile and path are sketched on perpendicular planes.

Questions

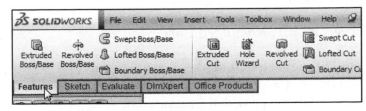

1. What is the minimum number of profiles and planes required for a Loft feature?

2. A Swept Boss/Base feature requires a _____ and a _____.

3. Describe the differences between a Loft feature and a Swept feature.

4. Identify the three default reference planes in an assembly.

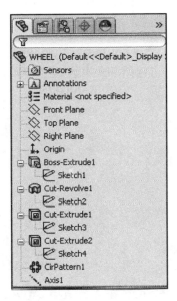

5. True of False. A Revolved-Cut feature (Cut-Revolve1) requires an axis of revolution.

6. True or False. A Circular Pattern contains only one feature to pattern.

7. Describe the difference between a Swept Boss/Base feature and a Swept Cut feature.

8. Identify the type of Geometric relations that can be added to a sketch.

9. What function does the Save as copy check box perform when saving a part under a new name?

10. True or False. Never reuse geometry from one part to create another part.

Exercises

Exercise 4.1: Advanced Part

Build the illustrated model. Calculate the volume of the part and locate the Center of mass with the provided information.

Three holes are displayed with an Ø1.00in.

Set the document properties for the model.

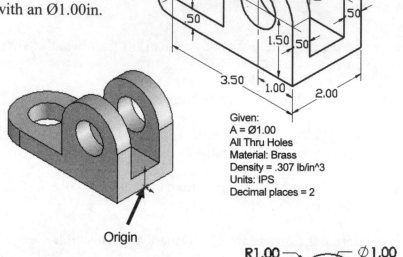

Tangent edges and Origin are displayed for educational purposes.

Given:
A = Ø1.00
All Thru Holes
Material: Brass
Density = .307 lb/in^3
Units: IPS
Decimal places = 2

Origin

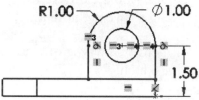

Exercise 4.2: Advanced Part

Build the illustrated model. Calculate the overall mass of the part and locate the Center of mass with the provided information. Insert a Revolved Base feature and Extruded Cut feature to build this part.

Note: Select the Front Plane as the Sketch plane. Apply the Centerline Sketch tool for the Revolve1 feature. Insert the required geometric relations and dimensions. Sketch1 is the profile for the Revolve1 feature.

Origin

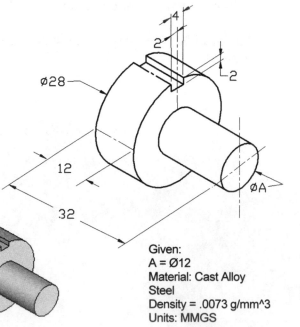

Given:
A = Ø12
Material: Cast Alloy Steel
Density = .0073 g/mm^3
Units: MMGS

Exercise 4.3: Advanced Part

Build the illustrated model. Calculate the overall mass of the part and locate the Center of mass with the provided information. Insert the required geometric relations and dimensions.

Note: Insert two features: Extruded Base and Revolved Boss.

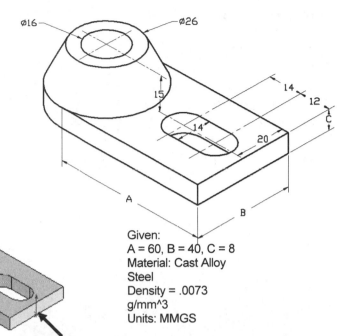

Given:
A = 60, B = 40, C = 8
Material: Cast Alloy Steel
Density = .0073 g/mm^3
Units: MMGS

Origin

Exercise 4.4: Advanced Part

Build the illustrated model. Calculate the overall mass of the part and locate the Center of mass with the provided information.

Think about the various features that create the model. Insert the required geometric relations and dimensions.

Apply symmetry. Create the left half of the model first, and then apply the Mirror feature.

Tangent Edges and Origin are displayed for educational purposes.

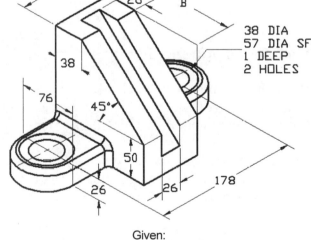

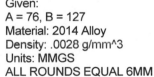

38 DIA
57 DIA SF
1 DEEP
2 HOLES

Given:
A = 76, B = 127
Material: 2014 Alloy
Density: .0028 g/mm^3
Units: MMGS
ALL ROUNDS EQUAL 6MM

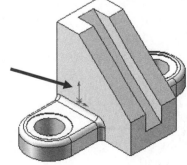

Origin

Exercise 4.5: Advanced Part

Build the illustrated model.
Calculate the overall mass of
the part and locate the Center
of mass with the provided
information.

Think about the various
features that create the part.

Apply reference
construction planes to build
the circular features. Insert
the required geometric
relations and
dimensions.

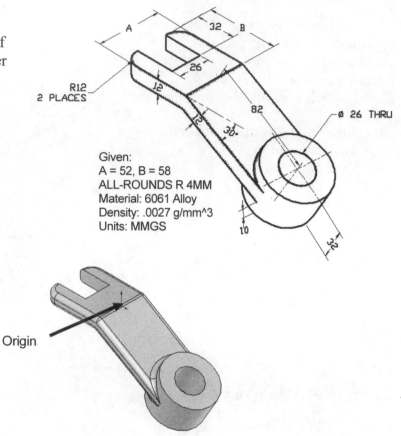

Given:
A = 52, B = 58
ALL-ROUNDS R 4MM
Material: 6061 Alloy
Density: .0027 g/mm^3
Units: MMGS

Origin

Exercise 4.6: Advanced Part

Build the illustrated model. Build this model.
Calculate the volume of the part and locate the
Center of mass with the provided information.

Think about the various features that create this
model. Insert the required geometric relations
and dimensions.

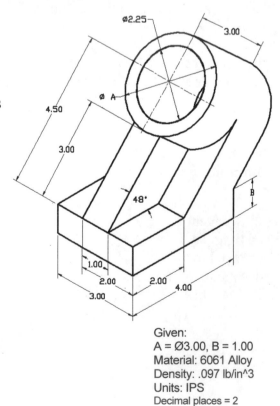

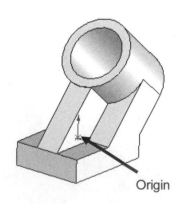

Origin

Given:
A = Ø3.00, B = 1.00
Material: 6061 Alloy
Density: .097 lb/in^3
Units: IPS
Decimal places = 2

Exercise 4.7: Advanced Part

Build the illustrated model.

Calculate the overall mass and locate the Center of mass of the illustrated model.

Think about the steps that you would take to build the illustrated part.

Identify the location of the part Origin.

Review the provided dimensions and annotations in the part illustration.

🔆 Tangent edges and Origin are displayed for educational purposes.

🔆 Use Symmetry. When possible and if it makes sense, model objects symmetrically about the origin.

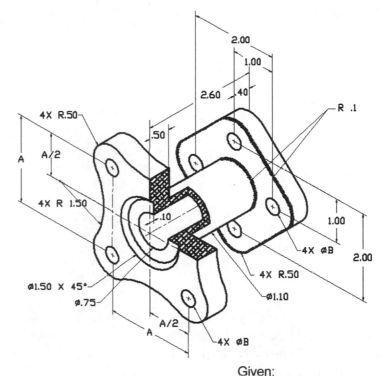

Given:
A = 2.00, B = Ø.35
Material: 1060 Alloy
Density: 0.097 lb/in^3
Units: IPS
Decimal places = 2

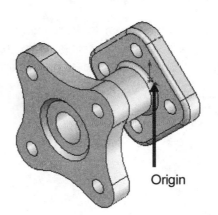

Origin

Exercise 4.8: Traditional Ice cream cone

Create a traditional Ice Cream Cone as illustrated. Create an ANSI - IPS model.

This is a common item that you see all of the time. Think about where you would start.

Think about the design features that create this model. Why does the cone use ribs?

Ribs are used for structural integrity.

Use a standard Cake Ice Cream Cone and measure all dimensions (approximately). Do your best.

View the sample FeatureManager. Your FeatureManager can (should) be different. This is just ONE way to create this part. You are the designer. Be creative. Create your own ice cream cone design.

Below are a few sample models from my Freshman Engineering class.

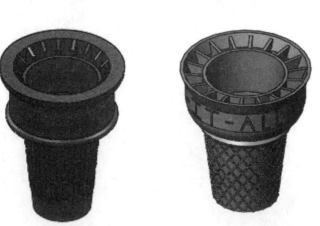

Below are a few sample models from my
Freshman Engineering (Cont:).

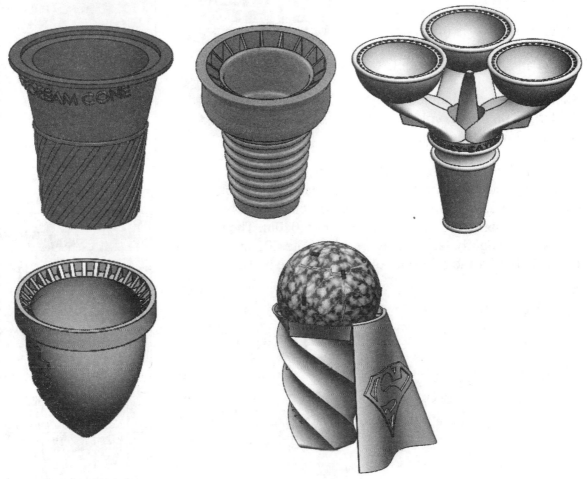

Exercise 4.9: Gem® Paper clip

Create a simple paper clip. You see
this common item every day. Create
an ANSI - IPS model. Apply
material to the model.

Think about where you would start.
What is your Base Sketch?

What are the dimensions? Measure
or estimate all needed dimensions
from a small gem paper clip. You
are the designer.

Note: The paper clip uses a circle as
the profile and (lines and arcs) as the
path.

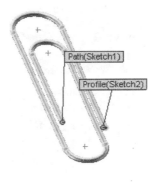

Exercise 4.10: Anvil Spring

Create a Variable Pitch Helix. Create an Anvil Spring with 6 coils, two active as illustrated.

Create an ANSI - IPS model.

Sketch a circle, Coincident to the Origin on the Top plane with a .235in dimension.

Create a Variable Pitch Helix/Spiral. Enter the following information as illustrated in the Region Parameters table. The spring has 6 coils. Coils 1,2,5 & 6 are the closed ends of the spring. The spring will have a diameter of .020in. The pitch needs to be slightly larger than the wire. Enter .021in for Pitch. Enter .080in for the free state of the two active coils.

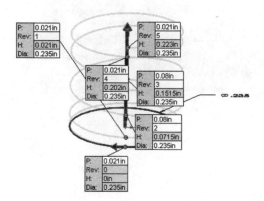

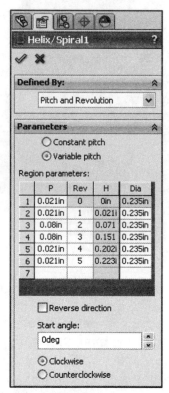

Region parameters:

	P	Rev	H	Dia
1	0.021in	0	0in	0.235in
2	0.021in	1	0.021i	0.235in
3	0.08in	2	0.071	0.235in
4	0.08in	3	0.151	0.235in
5	0.021in	4	0.202i	0.235in
6	0.021in	5	0.223i	0.235in
7				

Second, create the profile (circle .021in) for the spring and add a Pierce relation (do not select the endpoint of the path).

Third, create the Sweep feature (path & profile).

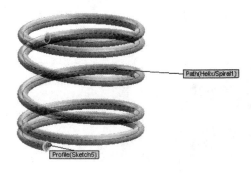

Exercise 4.11: Bottle

Create the container as illustrated.
Create an ANSI - IPS model.

You see this common item every day.

Apply material to the model.

Think about where you would start.

What is your Base Sketch?

What is your Base Feature?

What are the dimensions?

View the sample FeatureManager.
Your FeatureManager can (should) be
different. This is just ONE way to create this part. You are the
designer. Be creative. Estimate any needed dimension.

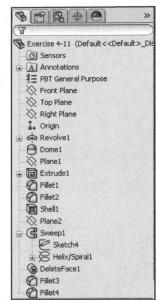

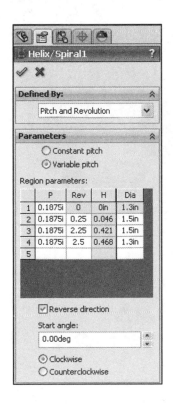

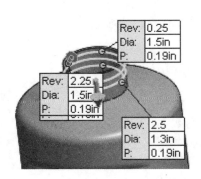

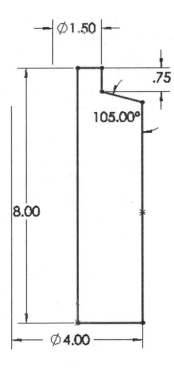

Exercise 4.12: Explicit Equation Driven Curve tool

Create an Explicit Equation Driven Curve on the Front plane. Revolve the curve. Calculate the volume of the solid.

Create a New part. Use the default ANSI, IPS Part template.

Create a 2D Sketch on the Front Plane.

Active the Equation Driven Curve Sketch  tool from the Consolidated drop-down menu.

Enter the Equation y_x as illustrated.

Enter the parameters x_1, x_2 that defines the lower and upper bound of the equation as illustrated. View the curve in the Graphics window.

Size the curve in the Graphics window. The Sketch is under defined.

Insert three lines to close the profile as illustrated. Fully define your sketch. Enter dimensions and any needed geometric relation.

Create the Revolved feature. View the results in the Graphics window. Revolve1 is displayed. Utilize the Section tool, parallel with the Right plane to view how each cross section is a circle.

Apply Brass for material.

Calculate the volume of the part using the Mass Properties tool. View the results. Also note the surface area and the Center of mass.

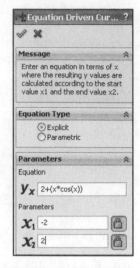

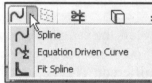

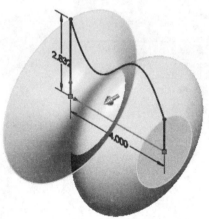

Mass = 16.10 pounds

Volume = 52.43 cubic inches

Surface area = 103.20 square inches

Center of mass: (inches)
　X = 2.07
　Y = 0.00
　Z = -0.00

💡 You can create parametric (in addition to explicit) equation-driven curves in both 2D and 3D sketches.

💡 Use regular mathematical notation and order of operations to write an equation. x_1 and x_2 are for the beginning and end of the curve. Use the transform options at the bottom of the PropertyManager to move the entire curve in x-, y- or rotation. To specify $x = f(y)$ instead of $y = f(x)$, use a 90 degree transform.

Exercise 4.13: Curve Through XYZ Points tool

The Curve Through XYZ Points 𝒰 feature provides the ability to either type in (using the Curve File dialog box) or click Browse and import a text file with x-, y-, z-, coordinates for points on a curve.

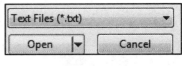

A text file can be generated by any program which creates columns of numbers. The Curve 𝒰 feature reacts like a default spline that is fully defined.

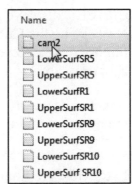

Create a curve using the Curve Through XYZ Points tool. Import the x-, y-, z- data.

Verify that the first and last points in the curve file are the same for a closed profile.

Create a new part.

Click the Curve Through XYZ Points 𝒰 tool from the Features CommandManager. The Curve File dialog box is displayed.

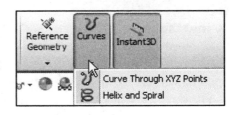

Import the curve data. Click Browse from the
Curve File dialog box.

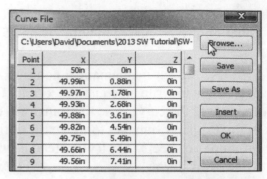

Browse to the downloaded folder location:
Chapter 4 - Homework folder. Note: Copy all
information from the DVD to your working
folder. Set file type to Text Files.

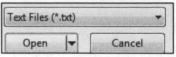

Double-click cam2.text. View the data in the
Curve File dialog box. View the sketch in the
Graphics window. Review the data points in the
dialog box.

Click OK from the Curve File dialog box.

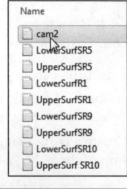

Fix the Curve to the Graphics window.

Curve1 is displayed in the FeatureManager. You created a
curve using the Curve Through XYZ Points tool with
imported x-, y-, z- data from a
cam program.

This Curve can now be used to
create a sketch (closed profile). In
this case a cam.

Let's view the final model using
the imported Curve.

Close the existing model.

Open the Curve Through XYZ
points model from the Chapter 4
- Homework folder to view the
final model.

Think about how you can use this
tool for other classes.

Exercise 4.14: Advanced Part

Build the illustrated model below.

Calculate the overall mass of the model. Units - IPS. Decimal places: 2. Material: AISI 304.

Think about the steps that you would take to build the illustrated part.

Insert the required geometric relations and dimensions.

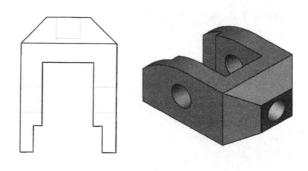

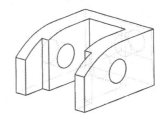

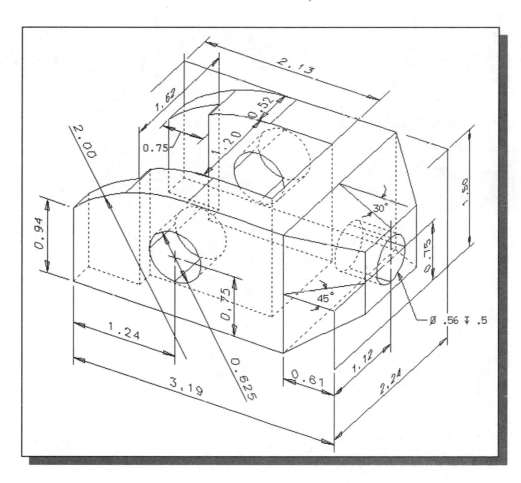

Notes:

Chapter 5

PNEUMATIC-TEST-MODULE and Final ROBOT Assembly

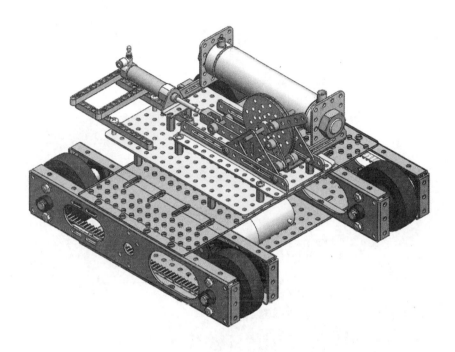

Below are the desired outcomes and usage competencies based on the completion of Chapter 5.

Desired Outcomes:	Usage Competencies:

• Create five sub-assemblies:
  o WHEEL-AND-AXLE
  o WHEEL-FLATBAR
  o 3HOLE-SHAFTCOLLAR
  o 5HOLE-SHAFTCOLLAR
  o PNEUMATIC-TEST-MODULE
• Create the final ROBOT assembly
	• Reuse geometry.
	
	• Apply Standard Mate types.
	
	• Modify existing assemblies to create new assemblies.
	
	• Utilize the following Assembly tools: Mate, Linear Component Pattern, Feature Driven Component Pattern, Mirror Components, Replace Components, and AssemblyXpert.
	
	• Work with multiple documents in an assembly.

Notes:

Chapter 5 - PNEUMATIC-TEST-MODULE and ROBOT Assembly

Chapter Objective

Develop a working understanding with multiple documents in an assembly. Build on sound assembly modeling techniques that utilize symmetry, component patterns and mirrored components.

Create five sub-assemblies and the final ROBOT assembly:

- 3HOLE-SHAFTCOLLAR sub-assembly

- 5HOLE-SHAFTCOLLAR sub-assembly

- WHEEL-FLATBAR sub-assembly

- WHEEL-AND-AXLE sub-assembly

- PNEUMATIC-TEST-MODULE sub-assembly

- ROBOT final assembly

On the completion of this chapter, you will be able to:

- Utilize various Assembly techniques

- Suppress and hide components

- Create new assemblies and copy assemblies to reuse similar parts

- Use the following Assembly tools:

  o Insert Component

  o Standard Mates: Concentric, Coincident and Parallel

  o Linear Component Pattern

  o Feature Driven Component Pattern

  o Circular Component Pattern

  o Mirror Components

  o Replace Components

  o AssemblyXpert

Chapter Overview

Create the 3HOLE-SHAFTCOLLAR sub-assembly.

Utilize the 3HOLE-SHAFTCOLLAR sub-assembly to create the 5HOLE-SHAFTCOLLAR sub-assembly.

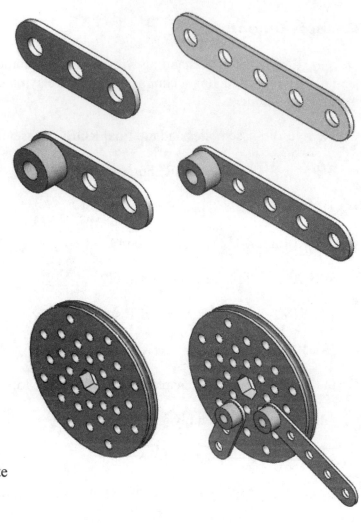

The WHEEL-FLATBAR sub-assembly contains the following items:

- 3HOLE-SHAFTCOLLAR assembly

- 5HOLE-SHAFTCOLLAR assembly

- WHEEL part

Mate to the first component added to the assembly. If you mate to the first component or base component of the assembly and decide to change its orientation later, all the components will move with it.

Remove Tangent edges. Click Display/Selections from the Options dialog box, check the Removed box as illustrated.

Determine the static and dynamic behavior of mates in each sub-assembly before creating the top level assembly.

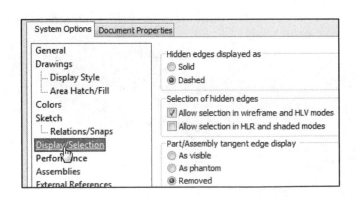

The WHEEL-AND-AXLE assembly contains the following items:

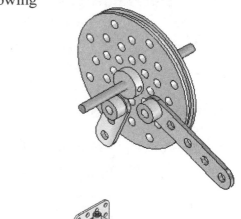

- WHEEL-FLATBAR assembly

- AXLE-3000 part

- SHAFTCOLLAR-500 part

- HEX-ADAPTER part

Combine the created new assemblies and parts to develop the PNEUMATIC-TEST-MODULE assembly.

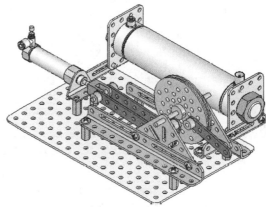

Create the final ROBOT assembly. Insert the Robot-platform assembly, PNEUMATIC-TEST-MODULE assembly, basic_integration assembly and the HEX-STANDOFF components.

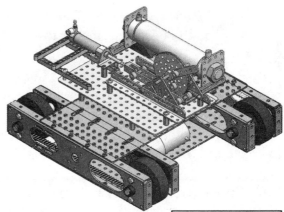

All assemblies and components for the final ROBOT assembly are located on the DVD under the Chapter 5 Models folder. Do not work directly from the DVD. Copy all needed files to your hard drive.

Tangent edges and Origins are displayed for educational purpose.

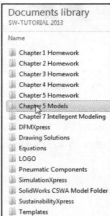

Use the Pack and Go option to save an assembly or drawing with references. The Pack and Go tool saves either to a folder or creates a zip file to e-mail. View SolidWorks help for additional information.

Assembly Techniques

Assembly modeling requires practice and time. Below are a few helpful techniques to address Standard Mates. These techniques are utilized throughout the development of all assemblies.

Mating Techniques:
• Plan your assembly and sub-assemblies in an assembly layout diagram. Group components together to form smaller sub-assemblies.
• Utilize symmetry in an assembly. Utilize Mirror Component and Component Pattern to create multiple instances (copies) of components. Reuse similar components with Save as copy and configurations.
• Use the Zoom and Rotate commands to select the geometry in the Mate process. Zoom to select the correct face.
• Apply various colors to features and components to improve display.
• Activate Temporary Axes and Show Planes when required for Mates, otherwise Hide All Types from the View menu.
• Select Reference planes from the FeatureManager for complex components. Expand the FeatureManager to view the correct plane.
• Remove display complexity. Hide components when visibility is not required.
• Suppress components when Mates are not required. Group fasteners at the bottom of the FeatureManager. Suppress fasteners and their assembly patterns to save rebuild time and file size.
• Utilize Section views to select internal geometry.
• Use the Move Component and Rotate Component commands before Mating. Position the component in the correct orientation.
• Create additional flexibility in a Mate. Distance Mates are modified in configurations and animations. Rename Mates in the FeatureManager.
• Verify the position of the components. Use Top, Front, Right and Section views.

PNEUMATIC TEST MODULE Layout

The PNEUMATIC TEST MODULE assembly is comprised of four major sub-assemblies:

- LINKAGE assembly

- RESERVOIR assembly

- FRONT-SUPPORT assembly

- WHEEL-AND-AXLE assembly

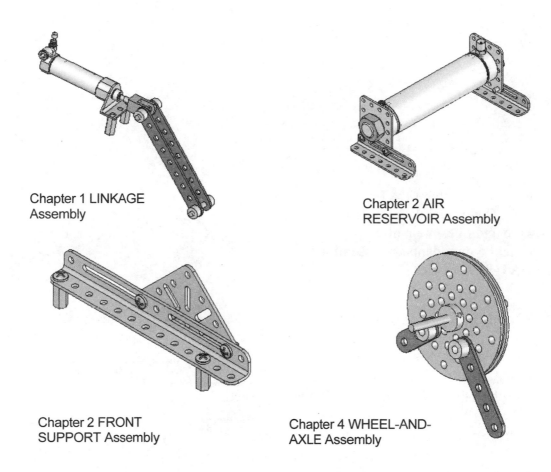

Chapter 1 LINKAGE
Assembly

Chapter 2 AIR
RESERVOIR Assembly

Chapter 2 FRONT
SUPPORT Assembly

Chapter 4 WHEEL-AND-
AXLE Assembly

There are over one hundred components in the PNEUMATIC TEST MODULE assembly. Complex assemblies require planning. The Assembly Layout diagram provides organization for a complex assembly by listing sub-assemblies and parts.

Review the Assembly Layout diagram for the PNEUMATIC TEST MODULE assembly.

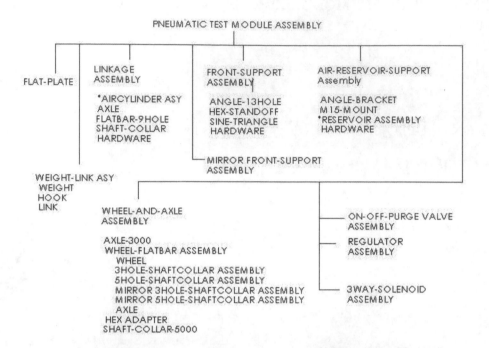

Physical space on the FLAT-PLATE is at a premium. Determine the requirements for hardware and placement after the mechanical components are assembled to the FLAT-PLATE part.

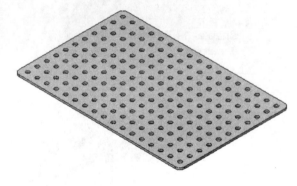

The FLAT-PLATE was created in the Chapter 2 exercises. The FLAT-PLATE is available on the enclosed DVD in the book under the Chapter 5 Models folder. If needed, copy the FLAT-PLATE from the DVD to your working SW-TUTORIAL-2013 folder.

The LINKAGE assembly, FRONT-SUPPORT assembly and the AIR-RESERVOIR SUPPORT assembly were created in Chapter 1 and 2. The ON-OFF-PURGE VALVE assembly, REGULATOR assembly and the 3WAY SOLENOID VALVE assembly require additional hardware and

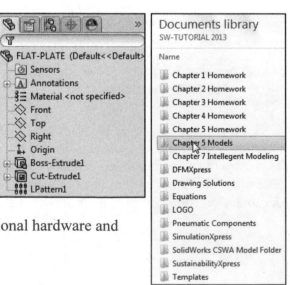

are addressed in the chapter exercises.

The WHEEL-FLATBAR assembly consists of the following:

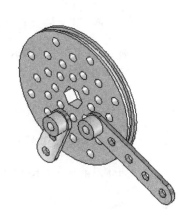

- WHEEL part

- 3HOLE-SHAFTCOLLAR assembly

- 5HOLE-SHAFTCOLLAR assembly

FLATBAR Sub-assembly

There are two similar sub-assemblies contained in the WHEEL-FLATBAR assembly:

- 3HOLE-SHAFTCOLLAR assembly

- 5HOLE-SHAFTCOLLAR assembly

Create the 3HOLE-SHAFTCOLLAR assembly. Utilize parts and mating techniques developed in Chapter 1.

Utilize the Save as copy command and create the 5HOLE-SHAFTCOLLAR assembly.

Combine the 3HOLE-SHAFTCOLLAR assembly, 5HOLE-SHAFTCOLLAR assembly and the WHEEL part to create the WHEEL-FLATBAR assembly.

The FLATBAR-3HOLE and FLATBAR 5HOLE parts were created in the Chapter 1 exercises. If needed, copy the models from the Chapter 5 models folder on the DVD to your working folder on your hard drive.

Activity: 3HOLE-SHAFTCOLLAR Assembly

Create the 3HOLE-SHAFTCOLLAR assembly.

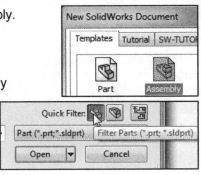

1) Click **New** from the Menu bar.

2) Double-click **Assembly** from the Templates tab. The Begin Assembly PropertyManager is displayed.

3) Click the **Browse** button.

4) Browse to the **SW-TUTORIAL-2013/Chapter 5 Models** folder.

5) Select **Filter Parts (*.prt;*.sldprt)** for Quick Filter.

6) Double-click **FLATBAR-3HOLE**. The FLATBAR-3HOLE part is located in the Chapter 5 Models folder on the DVD. If you want to create this part, follow the below procedure; otherwise, skip the next few steps.

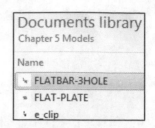

7) Click **Open** 📂 from the Menu bar.

8) Double-click **FLATBAR** from the SW-TUTORIAL-2013 folder.

9) Click **Save As** from the drop-down Menu bar.

10) Select the **SW-TUTORIAL-2013** folder.

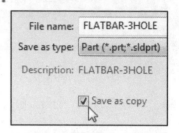

11) Enter **FLATBAR-3HOLE** for File name.

12) Enter **FLATBAR-3HOLE** for Description.

13) Check the **Save as copy** box.

14) Click **Save**.

15) **Close** the FLATBAR model.

16) Click **Open** 📂 from the Menu bar.

17) Double-click **FLATBAR-3HOLE** from the SW-TUTORIAL-2013 folder.

18) Right-click **LPATTERN1** from the FeatureManager.

19) Click **Edit Feature** from the Context toolbar. The LPattern1 PropertyManager is displayed.

20) Enter **3** in the Number of Instances.

21) Click **OK** ✔ from the LPattern1 PropertyManager. Note: If needed, delete the Design Table in the CommandManager.

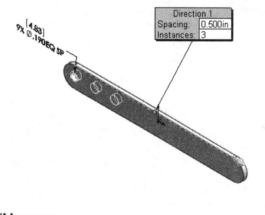

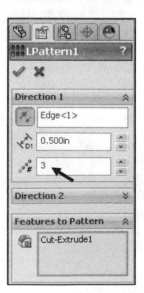

22) Click **Boss-Extrude1** from the FeatureManager. View the dimensions in the Graphics window.

23) Click the **4.000**in, [**101.60**] dimension.

24) Enter **1.000**in, [**25.4**].

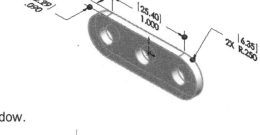

25) Click **Cut-Extrude1** from the FeatureManager. View the dimensions in the Graphics window.

26) Click the **9X** dimension text in the Graphics window. The Dimension PropertyManager is displayed.

27) Delete the **9X** text in the Dimension Text box.

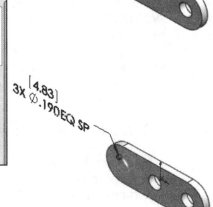

28) Enter **3X** in the Dimension Text box.

29) Click **OK** ✔ from the Dimension PropertyManager.

30) Click **Save** 💾.

31) Click **New** from the Main menu.

32) Double-click **Assembly** from the Templates tab. The Begin Assembly PropertyManager is displayed.

33) Double-click **FLATBAR-3HOLE.**

34) Click **OK** ✔ from the Begin Assembly PropertyManager. The FLATBAR-3HOLE is fixed to the Origin.

Save the assembly.

35) Click **Save As** from the drop-down Menu bar.

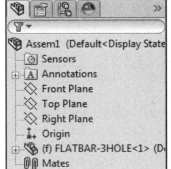

🔅 Tangent edges and Origin are displayed for educational purpose.

36)   Enter **3HOLE-SHAFTCOLLAR** for File name.

37)   Enter **3HOLE-SHAFTCOLLAR** for Description.

38)   Click **Save**.

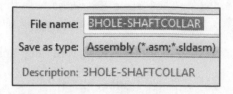

Save the 3HOLE-SHAFTCOLLAR assembly.

39)   Click **Save** 💾.

Utilize a Concentric/Coincident 🖱️ SmartMate between the SHAFT-COLLAR and the FLATBAR-3HOLE.

Open the **SHAFT-COLLAR** part.

40)   Click **Open** 📂 from the Menu bar.

41)   Double-click **SHAFT-COLLAR** from the SW-TUTORIAL-2013 folder. SHAFT-COLLAR is the current document name.

42)   Press the **Left Arrow** key approximately 5 times to rotate the SHAFT-COLLAR to view the back circular edge.

43)   Click **Window, Tile Horizontally** from the Menu bar.

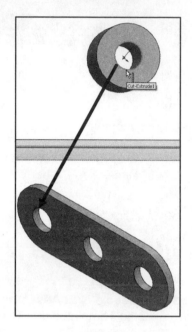

44)   Drag the **back circular edge** of the SHAFT-COLLAR to the left circular hole edge of the FLATBAR-3HOLE in the Assembly Graphics window as illustrated. The mouse pointer displays the Concentric/Coincident 🖱️ icon.

45)   **Release** the mouse button. Note: Select the back circular edge of the SHAFT-COLLAR, not the face.

Save the 3HOLE-SHAFTCOLLAR assembly.

46)   **Close** ✕ the SHAFT-COLLAR window.

47)   **Maximize** ☐ the 3HOLE-SHAFTCOLLAR assembly.

Fit the model to the Graphics window.

48)   Press the **f** key.

49)   Click **Save** 💾.

Create the 5HOLE-SHAFTCOLLAR assembly. Utilize the Save As command with the Save as copy option. Recover from Mate errors.

Save the 3HOLE-SHAFTCOLLAR assembly as the 5HOLE-SHAFTCOLLAR assembly.

50) Click **Save As** from the drop-down Menu bar.

51) Check the **Save as copy** box.

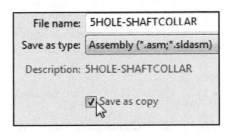

52) Enter **5HOLE-SHAFTCOLLAR** for File name.

53) Enter **5HOLE-SHAFTCOLLAR** for Description.

54) Click **Save**.

Close the model.

55) Click **File**, **Close** from the Menu bar.

Open the new assembly.

56) Click **Open** from the Menu bar.

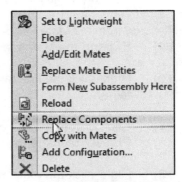

57) Select **Assembly** for file type.

58) Double-click **5HOLE-SHAFTCOLLAR**. The 5HOLE-SHAFTCOLLAR FeatureManager is displayed.

59) Right-click **FLATBAR-3HOLE** from the FeatureManager.

60) **Expand** the Pop-up menu if needed.

61) Click **Replace Components**. The Replace PropertyManager is displayed.

62) Click the **Browse** button.

63) Double-click **FLATBAR-5HOLE**. Note: The FLATBAR-5HOLE part is located in the Chapter 5 Models folder on the DVD. Copy all parts to your hard drive. Use the parts from your hard drive.

64) Check the **Re-attach mates** box.

65) Click **OK** from the Replace PropertyManager. The Mate Entities PropertyManager and the Wants Wrong dialog box is displayed. There are two red Mate error marks displayed in the Mate Entities box.

66) The What's Wrong dialog box is displayed. Recover from the Mate errors. Click **Close** from the What's Wrong dialog box.

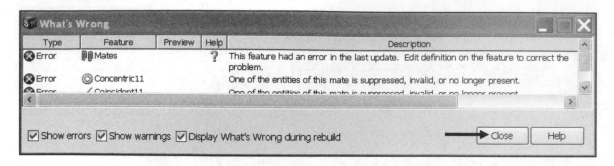

67) Click **OK** ✔ from the Mated Entities PropertyManager.

68) Click **Close** from the What's Wrong dialog box. View the location of the SHAFT-COLLAR in the Graphics window.

Recover from the Mate errors.
69) **Expand** the Mates folder from the FeatureManager.

70) Right-click the first mate, **Concentric #** from the Mates folder.

71) Click **Edit Feature** from the Context toolbar. The Mate PropertyManager is displayed.

72) Right-click the **Mate Face error** in the Mate Selections box as illustrated.

73) Click **Delete**.

74) Click the **inside face** of the left hole of the FLATBAR as illustrated. Concentric is selected by default.

75) Click the **Green Check mark** ✔ .

76) Click **OK** ✔ from the Mate PropertyManager.

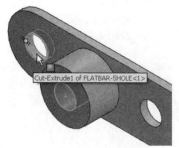

77) Right-click the second mate, **Coincident #** from the Mates folder.

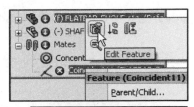

78) Click **Edit Feature** from the Context toolbar. The Mate PropertyManager is displayed.

79) Right-click the **Mate Face error** in the Mate Selections box as illustrated.

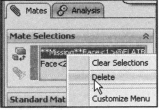

80) Click **Delete** as illustrated.

81) Click the **front face** of the FLATBAR as illustrated. The selected faces are displayed in the Mate Selections box. Coincident is selected by default.

82) Click **OK** if needed from the dialog box. Click the **Green Check mark** ✔.

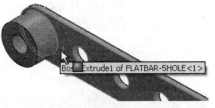

83) Click **OK** ✔ from the Mate PropertyManager.

84) **Expand** the Mate folder from the FeatureManager. View the created mates.

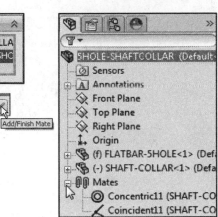

🔅 The Mate Entities box will list red X's if the faces, edges or planes are not valid. Expand the Mate Entities and select new references in the Graphics window to redefine the mates.

The FLATBAR-3HOLE is replaced with the FLATBAR-5HOLE part. The Mates are updated.

Fit the model to the Graphics window.
85) Press the **f** key.

Save the 5HOLE-SHAFTCOLLAR assembly.
86) Click **Isometric view** 📦 from the Heads-up View toolbar.

87) Click **Save** 💾.

🔅 Incorporate symmetry into the assembly.

🔅 Divide large assemblies into smaller sub-assemblies.

WHEEL-FLATBAR Assembly

The WHEEL-FLATBAR assembly consists of the following
components:

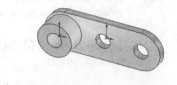

- 3HOLE-SHAFTCOLLAR assembly

- 5HOLE-SHAFTCOLLAR assembly

- WHEEL part

Create the WHEEL-FLATBAR assembly. Mate the
3HOLE-SHAFTCOLLAR assembly 67.5 degrees
counterclockwise from the Top Plane.

The 3HOLE-SHAFTCOLLAR assembly is concentric
with holes on the second and forth bolt
circle.

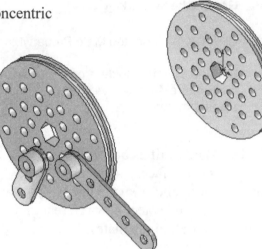

Mate the 5HOLE-SHAFTCOLLAR
assembly 22.5 degrees clockwise from
the Top Plane.

The 5HOLE-SHAFTCOLLAR assembly
is concentric with holes on the second
and forth bolt circle.

Tangent edges and Origins are
displayed for educational purpose.

Remove the fixed state. Right-click
the component name in the
FeatureManager. Click **Float**. The
component is free to move.

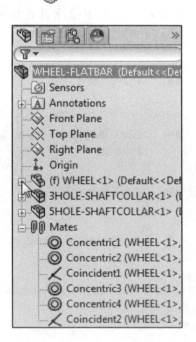

Activity: WHEEL-FLATBAR Assembly

Create the WHEEL-FLATBAR assembly.

88)   Click **New** ⬜ the Menu bar.

89)   Double-click **Assembly** from the Templates tab. The Begin Assembly PropertyManager is displayed.

Insert the WHEEL.

90)   Click the **Browse** button.

91)   Browse to the **SW-TUTORIAL-2013** folder.

92)   Select **Filter Parts (*.prt;*.sldprt)** for Quick Filter.

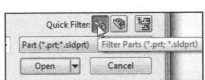

93)   Double-click **WHEEL**.

94)   Click **OK** ✔ from the Begin Assembly PropertyManager. The WHEEL part is fixed to the assembly Origin. If needed, click View, Origins from the Menu bar menu to displayed the Origin in the Graphics window.

Save the assembly.

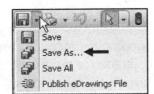

95)   Click **Save As** from the drop-down Menu bar.

96)   Select the **SW-TUTORIAL-2013** folder.

97)   Enter **WHEEL-FLATBAR** for File name.

98)   Enter **WHEEL-FLATBAR** for Description.

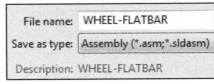

99)   Click **Save**.

Display the Top Plane in the Front view.

100)   Click **Front view** ⬜ from the Heads-up View toolbar. View the WHEEL part.

Locate the first set of holes from the Right plane (-Y-axis). Left Hole1 and Left Hole2 are positioned on the second and forth bolt circle, 22.5° from the Right plane. Select Left Hole1. The x, y, z coordinates, -.287, -.693, .125 are displayed.

$$Tan^{-1} (-.287/.693) = 22.5°$$

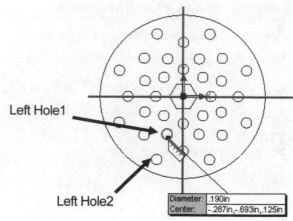

As an exercise, utilize the Measure tool to determine the center-to-center distance between the Left Hole1 and Left Hole2. The center-to-center distance is .500in.

Insert two Concentric mates between Left Hole1 and Left Hole2 and the 3HOLE-SHAFTCOLLAR assembly holes. The FLATBAR-3HOLE center-to-center distance is also .500in.

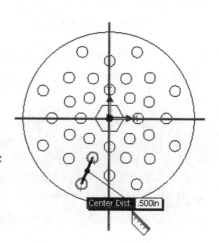

To determine tolerance issues, utilize two Concentric mates between components with mating cylindrical geometry. If the mating components center-to-center distance is not exact, a Mate error is displayed on the second Concentric mate.

Insert a Coincident mate between the back face of the 3HOLE-SHAFTCOLLAR assembly and the front face of the WHEEL.

Right Hole1 and Right Hole2 are 22.5° from the Top Plane.

Insert two Concentric mates between Right Hole1 and Right Hole2 and the 5HOLE-SHAFTCOLLAR assembly holes.

Insert a Coincident mate between the back face of the 5HOLE-SHAFTCOLLAR assembly and the front face of the WHEEL.

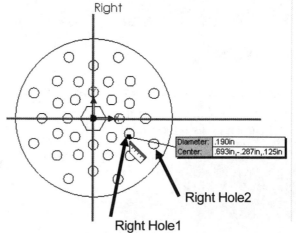

Activity: WHEEL-FLATBAR Assembly-Insert 3HOLE-SHAFTCOLLAR Assembly

---

Insert the 3HOLE-SHAFTCOLLAR assembly.

101) Click **Isometric view** 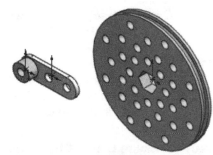 from the Heads-up View toolbar.

102) Click **Insert Components** from the Assembly toolbar. The Insert Components PropertyManager is displayed.

103) Click the **Browse** button.

104) Browse to the **SW-TUTORIAL-2013** folder.

105) Select **Filter Assemblies (*.asm;*.sldasm)** for Quick Filter.

106) Double-click the **3HOLE-SHAFTCOLLAR** assembly.

107) Click a **position** to the left of the WHEEL as illustrated.

Move and rotate the 3HOLE-SHAFTCOLLAR component.

108) Click the front face of the **3HOLE-SHAFTCOLLAR**.

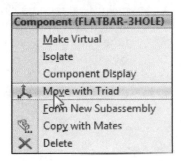

109) Right-click **Move with Triad**.

110) Hold the **left mouse button** down on the X-axis (red).

111) Drag the **component** to the left. View the ruler.

112) Hold the **right mouse button** down on the Z-axis (blue).

113) Drag the **component** and rotate it about the Z-axis. View the ruler.

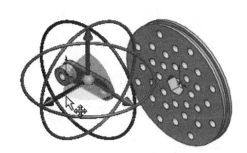

114) **Position** the component until the SHAFT-COLLAR part is approximately in front of the WHEEL Left Hole1.

115) Release the **right mouse** button.

116) Click a **position** in the Graphics window to deselect the face.

Insert the required mates.

117) Click the **Mate** ✎ tool from the Assembly toolbar. The Mate PropertyManager is displayed.

Insert a Concentric mate.

118) Click the **back top inside cylindrical face** of the SHAFT-COLLAR.

119) Click the **WHEEL Left Hole1** cylindrical face as illustrated. Concentric is selected by default. The selected faces are displayed in the Mate Selections box.

120) Click the **Green Check mark** ✔.

Insert the second Concentric mate.

121) Click the **back middle inside cylindrical face** of the FLATBAR.

122) Click the **WHEEL Left Hole2** inside cylindrical face as illustrated. Concentric is selected by default. The selected faces are displayed in the Mate Selections box.

123) Click the **Green Check mark** ✔.

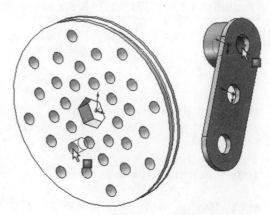

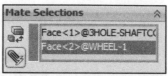

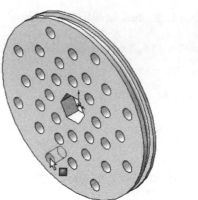

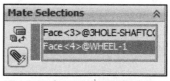

Insert a Coincident mate.

124)   Click the **FLATBAR-3HOLE back** face.

125)   Click the front face of the **WHEEL**. Coincident is selected by default.

126)   Click the **Green Check mark** ✔.

127)   Click **OK** ✔ from the Mate PropertyManager.

128)   Click **Front view** ▱ from the Heads-up View toolbar.

Save the WHEEL-FLATBAR assembly.

129)   Click **Save** 💾.

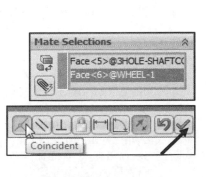

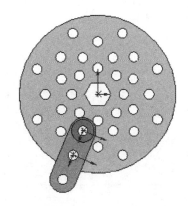

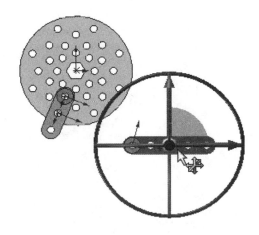

Mate Selections
- Face<5>@3HOLE-SHAFTC(
- Face<6>@WHEEL-1

Coincident

Activity: WHEEL-FLATBAR Assembly-Insert 5HOLE-SHAFTCOLLAR Assembly

Insert the 5HOLE-SHAFTCOLLAR assembly.

130)   Click **Insert Components** 🖼 from the Assembly toolbar. The Insert Components PropertyManager is displayed.

131)   Click the **Browse** button.

132)   Double-click the **5HOLE-SHAFTCOLLAR** assembly from the SW-TUTORIAL-2013 folder.

133)   Click a **position** to the right of the WHEEL.

Move the 5HOLE-SHAFTCOLLAR component.

134)   Click the **5HOLE-SHAFTCOLLAR** front face.

135)   Right-click **Move with Triad**.

136)   Hold the **left mouse button** down on the X-axis (red). Drag the **component** to the right. View the results.

137)   Click **Isometric view** 🞓 from the Heads-up View toolbar.

138)   Click **inside** the Graphics window.

Mate the 5HOLE-SHAFTCOLLAR assembly.

139) Click the **Mate** ✎ tool from the Assembly toolbar. The Mate PropertyManager is displayed.

Insert a Concentric mate.

140) Click the **back inside cylindrical face** of the first hole on the FLATBAR-5HOLE assembly.

141) Click the **WHEEL Right Hole1** cylindrical face. Concentric is selected by default.

142) Click the **Green Check mark** ✔.

Insert a Concentric mate.

143) **Move** the 5HOLE-SHAFTCOLLAR to view the back side.

144) Click the **back inside cylindrical** face of the second hole on the FLATBAR-5HOLE assembly.

145) Click the **WHEEL Right Hole2** cylindrical face. Concentric is selected by default.

146) Click the **Green Check mark** ✔.

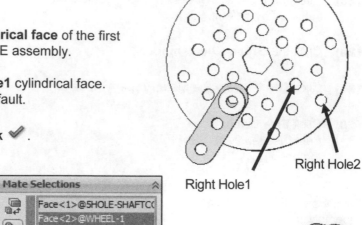

Right Hole2

Right Hole1

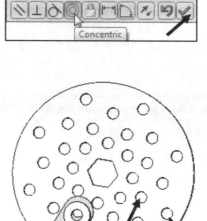

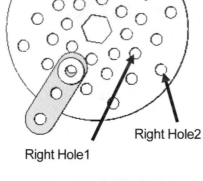

Right Hole2

Right Hole1

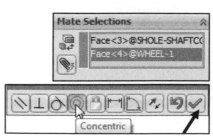

Insert a Coincident mate.

147) Click the **back face** of the FLATBAR-5HOLE.

148) Click the **front face** of the WHEEL. Coincident is the selected by default.

149) Click the **Green Check mark** ✔.

150) Click **OK** ✔ from the Mate PropertyManager.

De-activate the Origins.

151) Click **View**; uncheck **Origin** from the Menu bar.

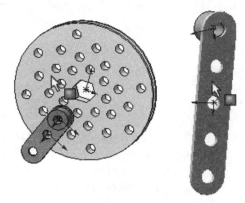

Measure the angle between the 3HOLE-SHAFTCOLLAR assembly and the 5HOLE-SHAFTCOLLAR assembly.

152) Click **Front view** 🔲 from the Heads-up View toolbar.

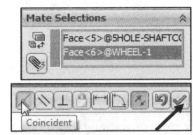

153) Click the **Measure** ⬛ Measure... tool from the Evaluate tab in the CommandManager. The Measure dialog box is displayed.

154) Select the **two inside edges** of the FLATBAR assemblies. View the results.

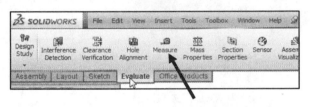

155) If required, click the **Show XYZ Measurements button**. The items are perpendicular.

🔅 The Measure tool provides the ability to display dual units. Click the **Units/ Precision** mm in icon from the Measure dialog box. Set the desired units.

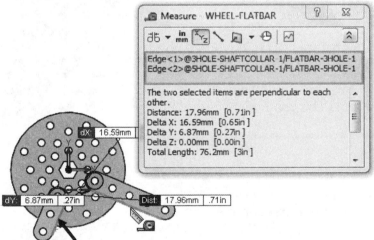

156) **Close** the Measure dialog box.

Apply the AssemblyXpert tool. The AssemblyXpert tool displays statistics and checks the health of the current assembly.

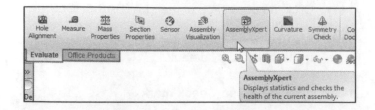

157) Click the **AssemblyXpert** tool in the Evaluate toolbar. The AssemblyXpert dialog box is displayed. Review the Status and description for the assembly.

158) Click **OK** from the AssemblyXpert dialog box.

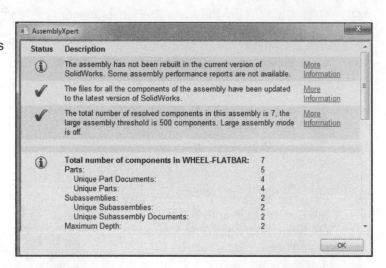

Fit the model to the Graphics window.

159) Press the **f** key.

160) Click **Isometric view** from the Heads-up View toolbar.

Save the WHEEL-FLATBAR assembly.

161) Click **Save**.

To remove the fixed state, Right-click the component name in the FeatureManager. Click **Float**. The component is free to move.

Mate to the first component added to the assembly. If you mate to the first component or base component of the assembly and decide to change its orientation later, all the components will move with it.

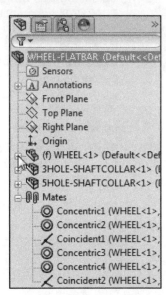

WHEEL-AND-AXLE Assembly

The WHEEL-AND-AXLE assembly contains the following items:

- WHEEL-FLATBAR assembly

- AXLE-3000 part

- SHAFTCOLLAR-500 part

- HEX-ADAPTER part

Create the WHEEL-AND-AXLE assembly. The AXLE-3000 part is the first component in the assembly. A part or assembly inserted into a new assembly is called a component. The WHEEL-FLATBAR assembly rotates about the AXLE part.

Combine the created new assemblies and parts to develop the PNEUMATIC-TEST-MODULE assembly.

Activity: WHEEL-AND-AXLE Assembly

Create the WHEEL-AND-AXLE assembly.

162) Click **New** from the Menu bar.

163) Double-click **Assembly** from the Templates tab. The Begin Assembly PropertyManager is displayed.

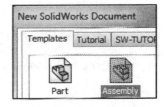

Insert the AXLE-3000 part.

164) Click the **Browse** button.

165) Browse to the **SW-TUTORIAL-2013** folder.

166) Select **Filter Parts (*.prt;*.sldprt)** for Quick Filter.

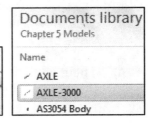

167) Double-click **AXLE-3000**. Note: AXLE-3000 is located in the Chapter 5 Models folder on the DVD.

168) Click **OK** from the Begin Assembly PropertyManager. The AXLE-3000 part is fixed to the assembly Origin.

Save the assembly.

169) Click **Save As** from the drop-down Menu bar.

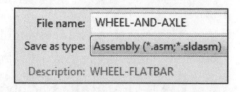

170) Enter **WHEEL-AND-AXLE** for File name in the SW-TUTORIAL-2013 folder.

171) Enter **WHEEL-AND-AXLE** for Description.

172) Click **Save**.

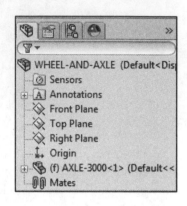

Insert a Coincident mate between the Axis of the AXLE-3000 and the Axis of the WHEEL. Insert a Coincident mate between the Front Plane of the AXLE-3000 and the Front Plane of the WHEEL. The WHEEL-FLATBAR assembly rotates about the AXLE-3000 axis.

Display the Temporary Axes.

173) Click **View**; check **Temporary Axes** from the Menu bar.

Insert the WHEEL-FLATBAR assembly.

174) Click **Insert Components** from the Assembly toolbar. The Insert Components PropertyManager is displayed.

175) Click the **Browse** button.

176) Double-click the **WHEEL-FLATBAR** assembly from the SW-TUTORIAL-2013 folder.

177) Click a **position** to the right of AXLE-3000.

View the Reference WHEEL Axis.

178) Click **View**; check **Axes** from the Menu bar.

179) If needed, click **View**; uncheck **Origins** from the Menu bar.

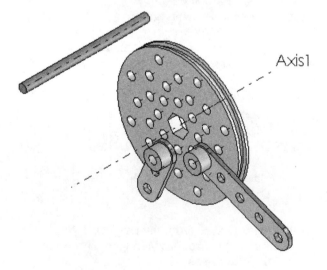

🔆 Reference geometry defines the shape or form of a surface or a solid. Reference geometry includes planes, axes, coordinate systems, and points.

Insert a Coincident mate.

180) Click the **Mate** ✎ tool from the Assembly toolbar. The Mate PropertyManager is displayed.

181) Click **Axis1** in the Graphics window.

182) Click the **AXLE-3000 Temporary Axis**. Coincident is selected by default.

183) Click the **Green Check mark** ✔ .

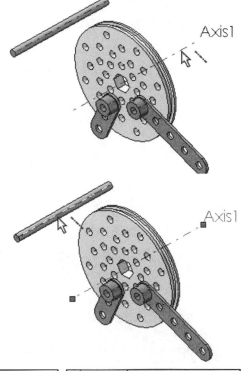

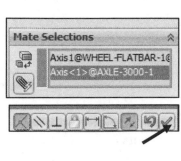

Insert a Coincident mate.

184) **Expand** WHEEL-AND-AXLE from the fly-out FeatureManager.

185) **Expand** AXLE-3000 from the fly-out FeatureManager.

186) Click **Front Plane** of AXLE-3000<1>.

187) **Expand** WHEEL from the fly-out FeatureManager.

188) Click **Front Plane** of the WHEEL. Coincident is selected by default.

189) Click the **Green Check mark** ✔ ..

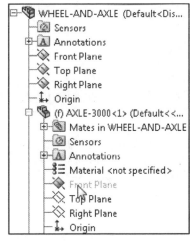

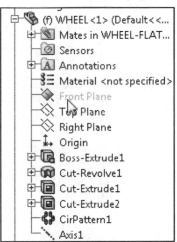

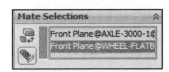

190) Click **OK** ✔ from the Mate PropertyManager.

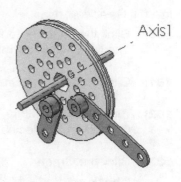

Rotate the WHEEL-FLATBAR assembly about AXLE-3000.
191) Click and drag the **WHEEL** around AXLE-3000.

Save the WHEEL-AND-AXLE assembly.

192) Click **Save** 💾.

Activity: WHEEL-AND-AXLE Assembly-Insert the HEX-ADAPTER Part

Insert the HEX-ADAPTER part.

193) Click the **Insert Components** 🗏 tool from the Assembly toolbar. The Insert Component PropertyManager is displayed.

194) Click the **Browse** button.

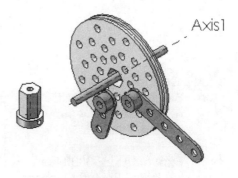

195) Browse to the **SW-TUTORIAL-2013** folder.

196) Select **Filter Parts (*.prt;*.sldprt)** for Quick Filter.

197) Double-click **HEX-ADAPTER**.

198) Click a **position** to the left of the WHEEL as illustrated. The HEX-ADAPTER is displayed in the FeatureManager.

199) **Expand** the Mates folder. View the created mates for the assembly. View the inserted components: AXLE-3000, WHEEL-FLATBAR and HEX-ADAPTER.

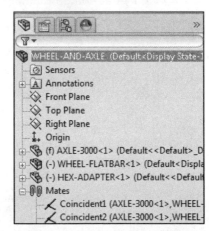

Insert a Concentric mate. Mate the HEX-ADAPTER.

200) Click the **Mate** ✎ tool from the Assembly toolbar. The Mate PropertyManager is displayed.

201) Click the **HEX-ADAPTER** cylindrical face as illustrated.

202) Click the **AXLE-3000** cylindrical face as illustrated. Concentric is selected by default. The selected faces are displayed in the Mate Selections box.

203) Click **Aligned** ⊕⊕ from the Concentric1 PropertyManager to flip the HEX-ADAPTER, if required.

204) Click **OK** ✔ from the Concentric PropertyManager.

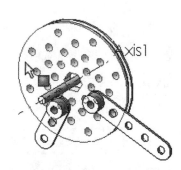

Insert a Coincident mate.

205) Click the **front face** of the WHEEL.

206) Press the **left arrow key** to rotate the model.

207) Click the **flat back circular face** of the HEX-ADAPTER as illustrated. Coincident is selected by default.

208) Click the **Green Check mark** ✔ .

Insert a Parallel mate.

209) **Rotate** the WHEEL-AND-AXLE assembly to view the back bottom edge of the HEX-ADAPTER.

210) **Zoom in** on the back bottom edge of the HEX-ADAPTER.

211) Click the **back bottom edge** of the WHEEL. Note: Do not select the midpoint.

212) Click the **top edge** of the HEX-ADAPTER. Do not select the midpoint. The selected edges are displayed in the Mate Selections box.

213) Click **Parallel** ⦦ as illustrated.

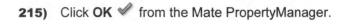

214) Click the **Green Check mark** ✓.

215) Click **OK** ✓ from the Mate PropertyManager.

Fit the model to the Graphics window.
216) Press the **f** key.

217) Click **Isometric view** 🎲 from the Heads-up View toolbar.

View the created mates.
218) **Expand** the Mates folder.

Save the WHEEL-AND-AXLE assembly.

219) Click **Save** 💾.

Activity: WHEEL-AND-AXLE Assembly-Insert SHAFTCOLLAR-500 Part

Insert the SHAFTCOLLAR-500 part.

220) Click the **Insert Components** 🖼 tool from the Assembly toolbar. The Insert Component PropertyManager is displayed.

221) Click the **Browse** button.

222) Browse to the **SW-TUTORIAL-2013** folder.

223) Double-click **SHAFTCOLLAR-500**.

224) Click a **position** behind the WHEEL-AND-AXLE assembly as illustrated.

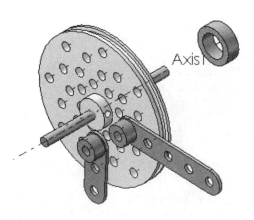

Insert a Concentric mate.

225) Click **View**; uncheck **Temporary Axes** from the Menu bar.

226) Click **View**; uncheck **Axes** from the Menu bar.

227) Click the **Mate** ✎ tool from the Assembly toolbar. The Mate PropertyManager is displayed.

228) Click the **inside cylindrical face** of the SHAFTCOLLAR-500 part.

229) Click the **cylindrical face** of the AXLE-3000 part. Concentric is selected by default.

230) Click the **Green Check mark** ✔.

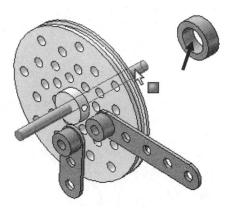

Insert a Coincident mate.

231) Click the **front face** of the SHAFTCOLLAR-500 part.

232) Click the **back face** of the WHEEL. Coincident is selected by default.

233) Click the **Green Check mark** ✔.

234) Click **OK** ✔ from the Mate PropertyManager.

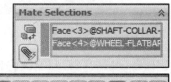

Display an Isometric view.

235) Click **Isometric view** ▣ from the Heads-up View toolbar.

View the created Mates.

236) **Expand** the Mates folder. View the created mates.

Save the WHEEL-AND-AXLE assembly.

237) Click **Save** 🖫.

Close all files.

238) Click **Windows**, **Close All** from the Menu bar.

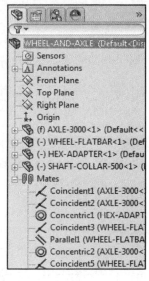

 Determine the static and dynamic behavior of mates in each sub-assembly before creating the top level assembly.

 Review the WHEEL-AND-AXLE Assembly

You combined the WHEEL-FLATBAR sub assembly, the AXLE-3000 part, the HEX-ADAPTER part and the SHAFTCOLLAR-500 part to create the WHEEL-AND-AXLE assembly.

The WHEEL-FLATBAR sub-assembly rotated about the AXLE-3000 part. The WHEEL-FLATBAR assembly combined the 3HOLE-SHAFTCOLLAR assembly and the 5HOLE-SHAFTCOLLAR assembly. The 5HOLE-SHAFTCOLLAR assembly was created from the 3HOLE-SHAFTCOLLAR assembly by replacing the FLATBAR component and recovering from two Mate errors. Additional components are added to the WHEEL-AND-AXLE assembly in the chapter exercises.

PNEUMATIC-TEST-MODULE Assembly

Create the PNEUMATIC-TEST-MODULE assembly. The first component is the

FLAT-PLATE. The FLAT-PLATE is fixed to the Origin ⌐. The FLAT-PLATE part was created in the Chapter 2 exercises: and is located on the enclosed DVD and supports the other components. Do not work directly from the DVD. Copy all needed files to your hard drive.

Modify the LINKAGE assembly. Insert the HEX-STANDOFF part. Insert the LINKAGE assembly into the PNEUMATIC-TEST-MODULE assembly.

Insert the AIR-RESERVOIR-SUPPORT assembly. Utilize the Linear Component Pattern, and Feature Driven Component Pattern tools. Insert the FRONT-SUPPORT assembly. Utilize the Mirror Components tool to create a mirrored version of the FRONT-SUPPORT assembly.

Insert the WHEEL-AND-AXLE assembly. Utilize Component Properties and create a Flexible State. Utilize the ConfigurationManager to select the Flexible configuration for the AirCylinder assembly.

Work between multiple part and sub-assembly documents to create the final assembly.

Activity: PNEUMATIC-TEST-MODULE Assembly

Create the PNEUMATIC-TEST-MODULE assembly.

239) Click **New** ☐ from the Menu bar.

240) Double-click **Assembly** from the Templates tab. The Begin Assembly PropertyManager is displayed.

Insert the FLAT-PLATE part.
241) Click the **Browse** button.

242) Browse to the **SW-TUTORIAL-2013/ Chapter 5 Models** folder.

243) Double-click **FLAT-PLATE**. Note: FLAT-PLATE is located in the Chapter 5 Models folder on the DVD. Do not work directly from the DVD. Copy all needed files to your hard drive.

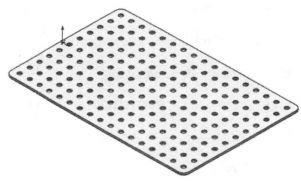

244) Click **OK** ✓ from the Begin Assembly PropertyManager. FLAT-PLATE is fixed to the Origin.

Save the assembly.
245) Click **Save As** from the drop-down Menu bar.

246) Enter **PNEUMATIC-TEST-MODULE** for File name.

247) Enter **PNEUMATIC-TEST-MODULE** for Description.

248) Click **Save**.

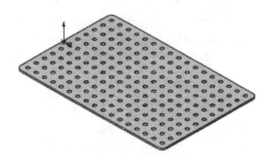

Click **View, Origins** from the Menu bar menu to display the Origin in the Graphics window.

Activity: Modify the LINKAGE Assembly

Modify the LINKAGE assembly created in Chapter 1.

249) Click **Open** 📂 from the Menu bar.

250) Select **Assembly** for file type from the SW-TUTORIAL-2013 folder.

251) Double-click **LINKAGE**. The LINKAGE assembly is displayed.

Insert the HEX-STANDOFF part into the LINKAGE assembly.

252) Click the **Insert Components** 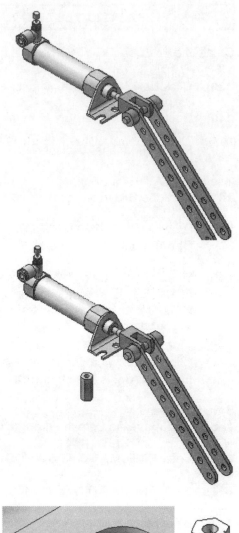 tool from the Assembly toolbar. The Insert Component PropertyManager is displayed.

253) Click the **Browse** button.

254) Browse to the **SW-TUTORIAL-2013** folder.

255) Double-click **HEX-STANDOFF**.

256) Click a **position** to the front of the half Slot Cut as illustrated.

View the Temporary Axes.

257) Click **View**; check **Temporary Axes** from the Menu bar.

258) Click **View**; check **Axes** from the Menu bar.

Insert a Coincident mate.

259) Click the **Mate** tool from the Assembly toolbar. The Mate PropertyManager is displayed.

260) Click the **HEX-STANDOFF** tapped hole Temporary Axis.

261) Click the **half Slot Cut Axis1**. The selected entities are displayed in the Mate Selections box. Coincident is selected by default.

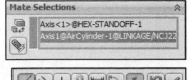

262) Click the **Green Check mark** .

Reference geometry defines the shape or form of a surface or a solid. Reference geometry includes planes, axes, coordinate systems, and points.

Insert a Coincident mate.
263)   Click the **HEX-STANDOFF** top face.

264)   Click the **BRACKET bottom face**.
Coincident is selected by default.
The selected faces are displayed in
the Mate Selections box.

265)   Click the **Green Check mark** ✔.

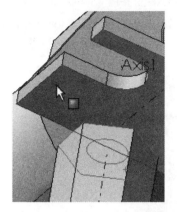
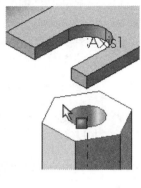

Insert a Parallel mate.
266)   Click the **HEX-STANDOFF** front
face.

267)   Click the **BRACKET front face**. The
selected faces are displayed in the
Mate Selections box.

268)   Click **Parallel** ＼ as illustrated.

269)   Click the **Green Check mark** ✔.

270)   Click **OK** ✔ from the Mate
PropertyManager.

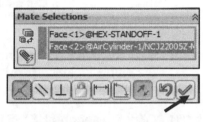

Fit the model to the Graphics window.
271)   Press the **f** key.

272)   Click **Isometric
view** 🔲 from the
Heads-up View
toolbar.

273)   Click **Save** 💾.

View the created Mates.
274)   **Expand** the Mates
folder. View the
created mates.

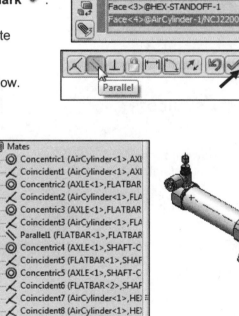
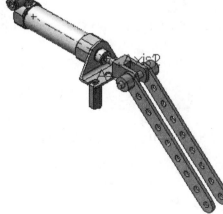

Insert the second HEX-STANDOFF.

275) Click the **Insert Components** tool from the Assembly toolbar. The Insert Component PropertyManager is displayed.

276) Click the **Browse** button.

277) Browse to the **SW-TUTORIAL-2013** folder.

278) Double-click **HEX-STANDOFF**.

279) Click a **position** to the back right of the back half Slot Cut as illustrated.

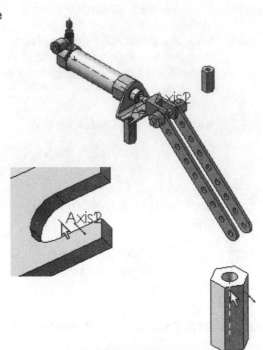

Insert a Concentric mate.

280) Click the **Mate** tool from the Assembly toolbar. The Mate PropertyManager is displayed.

281) Click the **second HEX-STANDOFF** Tapped Hole Temporary Axis.

282) Click the **back half Slot Cut Axis1**. Coincident is selected by default.

283) Click the **Green Check mark**.

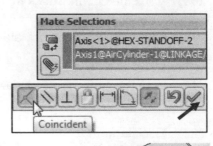

Insert a Coincident mate.

284) Click the **second HEX-STANDOFF top** face.

285) Click the **BRACKET bottom face**. Coincident is selected by default.

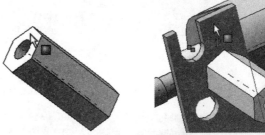

286) Click the **Green Check mark**.

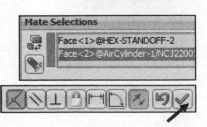

Insert a Parallel mate.

287) Click the **second HEX-STANDOFF** face as illustrated.

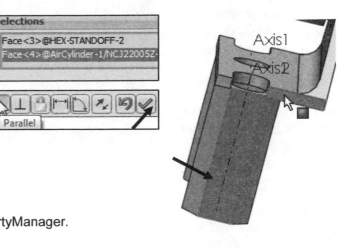

288) Click the **BRACKET back right** face.

289) Click **Parallel** ⟍ as illustrated.

290) Click the **Green Check mark** ✔ .

291) Click **OK** ✔ from the Mate PropertyManager.

💡 Use Selection Filter toolbar to select the correct face, edge, axis, etc.

Fit the model to the Graphics window.

292) Press the **f** key. Click **Isometric view** ▢ from the Heads-up View toolbar.

293) Click **Save** 💾 .

In the Chapter 1 exercises, you created the LINKAGE-2 assembly. Insert the second AXLE. Insert the two SHAFT-COLLAR parts as an exercise at the end of this chapter.

Insert the second AXLE.

294) Click the **Insert Components** tool from the Assembly toolbar.

295) Click the **Browse** button.

296) Browse to the **SW-TUTORIAL-2013** folder.

297) Double-click **AXLE**.

298) Click a **position** to the front bottom of the FLATBAR as illustrated.

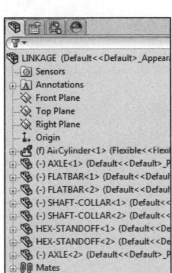

Insert a Concentric mate.

299) Click the **Mate** ✎ Assembly tool. The Mate
PropertyManager is displayed.

300) Click the **second AXLE cylindrical** face.

301) Click the **FLATBAR bottom hole** face as
illustrated. Concentric is selected by default.

302) Click the **Green Check mark** ✔.

Insert a Coincident mate.

303) Click the second **AXLE Front
Plane** from the fly-out
FeatureManager.

304) Click the **LINKAGE assembly
Front Plane** from the fly-out
FeatureManager. Coincident is
selected by default. The selected
Front Planes are displayed in the
Mate Selections box.

305) Click the **Green Check mark** ✔.

306) Click **OK** ✔ from the Mate
PropertyManager.

Fit the model to the Graphics window.

307) Press the **f** key.

308) Click **Isometric view** 📦
from the Heads-up View
toolbar.

Save the LINKAGE assembly.

309) Click **Save** 💾.

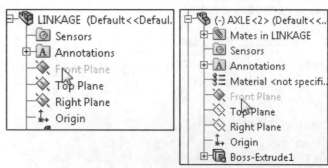

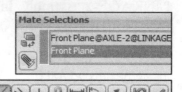

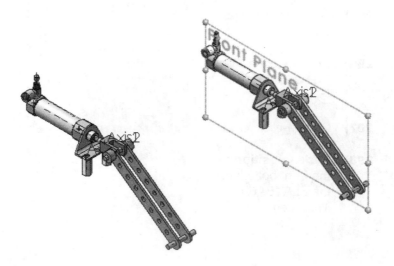

Insert the first SHAFT-COLLAR on the second AXIS.

310)   Click the **Insert Components** 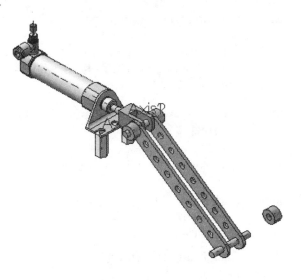 Assembly tool.

311)   Click the **Browse** button.

312)   Browse to the **SW-TUTORIAL-2013** folder.

313)   Double-click **SHAFT-COLLAR**.

314)   Click a **position** to the back of the second AXLE as illustrated.

Enlarge the view.

315)   Zoom-in on the **SHAFT-COLLAR** and the **AXLE** to enlarge the view.

Insert a Concentric mate.

316)   Click the **Mate** Assembly tool. The Mate PropertyManager is displayed.

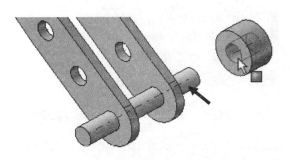

317)   Click the inside **hole face** of the SHAFT-COLLAR.

318)   Click the **long cylindrical face** of the AXLE. Concentric is selected by default. The selected faces are displayed in the Mate Selections box.

319)   Click the **Green Check mark** .

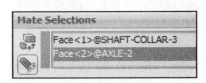

Insert a Coincident mate.

320) Click the **front face** of the SHAFT-COLLAR.

321) Press the **left arrow key** approximately 5 times to rotate the model to view the back face of the first FLATBAR.

322) Click the **back face** of the FLATBAR. Coincident is selected by default.

323) Click the **Green Check mark** 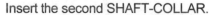 .

324) Click **OK** from the Mate PropertyManager.

Display the Isometric view.

325) Click **Isometric view** from the Heads-up View toolbar.

Insert the second SHAFT-COLLAR.

326) Click the **Insert Components** Assembly tool. The Insert Component PropertyManager is displayed.

327) Click the **Browse** button.

328) Browse to the **SW-TUTORIAL-2013** folder.

329) Double-click **SHAFT-COLLAR**.

330) Click a **position** to the front of the AXLE as illustrated.

Enlarge the view.

331) **Zoom in** on the second SHAFT-COLLAR and the AXLE to enlarge the view.

Insert a Concentric mate.

332) Click the **Mate** Assembly tool. The Mate PropertyManager is displayed.

333) Click the inside **hole face** of the second SHAFT-COLLAR. Note: The icon face feedback symbol.

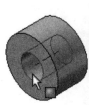

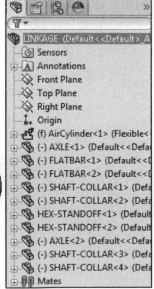

334) Click the **long cylindrical face** of the AXLE. Concentric is selected by default.

335) Click the **Green Check mark** ✅ .

Insert a Coincident mate.

336) Press the **f** key to fit the model to the Graphics window.

337) **Zoom in** on the front face of the second FLATBAR.

338) Click the **front face** of the second FLATBAR.

339) Click the **back face** of the second SHAFT-COLLAR. Coincident is selected by default.

340) Click the **Green Check mark** ✅ .

341) Click **OK** ✅ from the Mate PropertyManager.

Display the Isometric view.

342) Click **Isometric view** 🧊 from the Heads-up View toolbar.

Save the LINKAGE assembly.

343) **Rebuild** the model.

344) Click **View**; uncheck **Axis** from the Menu bar.

345) Click **View**; uncheck **Temporary Axis** from Menu bar.

346) Click **Save** 💾 . Note: As an exercise, insert SCREWs between the AirCylinder assembly and the two HEX-STANDOFFs as illustrated.

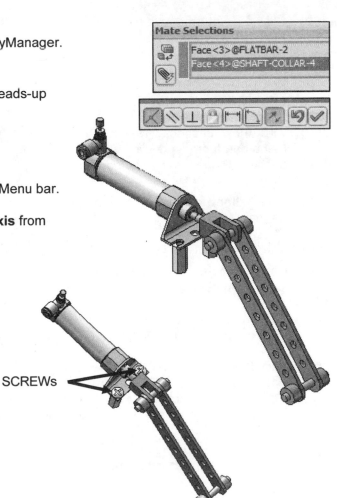

SCREWs

Activity: PNEUMATIC-TEST - MODULE-Insert LINKAGE Assembly

Insert the LINKAGE assembly into the PNEUMATIC-TEST-MODULE assembly.

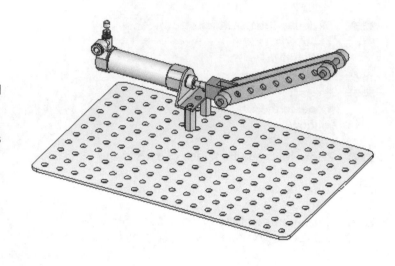

347) Click **Window**, **Tile Horizontally** from the Menu bar. Note: The PNEUMATIC-TEST-MODULE assembly should be open.

348) Rotate the two **FLATBARs** approximately 45°.

349) Click and drag the **LINKAGE** 🗇 LINKAGE assembly icon into the PNEUMATIC-TEST-MODULE assembly.

350) Click a **position** above the FLAT-PLATE as illustrated.

351) **Maximize** the PNEUMATIC-TEST-MODULE Graphics window.

352) Click **View**; uncheck **Origins** from the Menu bar. If required, click View; uncheck Planes from the Menu bar.

353) Click **Trimetric view** 🔲 from the Heads-up View toolbar.

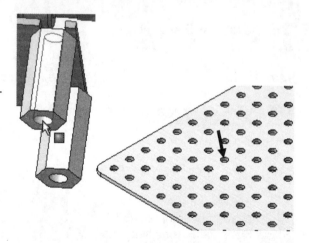

Insert a Concentric mate.

354) Click the **Mate** 🖎 Assembly tool. The Mate PropertyManager is displayed.

355) Click the **Front HEX-STANDOFF Tapped** inside hole face as illustrated.

356) Click the **FLAT-PLATE Hole** face in the 5th row, 4th column as illustrated. Concentric is selected by default. The selected faces are displayed in the Mate Selections box.

357) Click the **Green Check mark** ✅.

Mate Selections

Face<1>@LINKAGE-1/HEX
Face<2>@FLAT-PLATE-1

Concentric

Insert a Parallel mate.

358) Click the **PNEUMATIC-TEST-MODULE Front Plane** from the fly-out FeatureManager.

359) Click the **LINKAGE assembly Front Plane** from the fly-out FeatureManager.

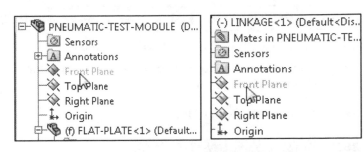

360) Click **Parallel**. Click the **Green Check mark** .

Insert a Coincident mate.

361) Click the **Front HEX-STANDOFF** bottom face.

362) Click the **FLAT-PLATE top face**. Coincident is selected by default.

363) Click the **Green Check mark** .

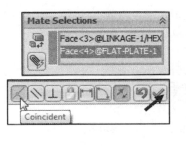

364) Click **OK** from the Mate PropertyManager.

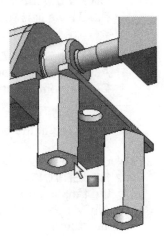

Display the Isometric view.

365) Click **Isometric view** from the Heads-up View toolbar.

Save the PNEUMATIC-TEST-MODULE assembly.

366) Click **Save** .

The LINKAGE assembly is fully defined, and located on the FLAT-PLATE part. Insert the AIR-RESERVOIR-SUPPORT assembly. The AIR-RESERVOIR-SUPPORT assembly was created in the Chapter 2 exercises. Note: The AIR-RESERVOIR SUPPORT is also located on the DVD in the book.

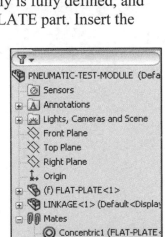

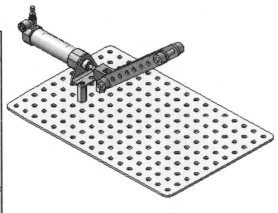

Activity: PNEUMATIC-TEST-MODULE Insert AIR-RESERVOIR-SUPPORT

Insert the AIR-RESERVOIR-SUPPORT assembly.

367) Click the **Insert Components** Assembly tool. The Insert Component PropertyManager is displayed.

368) Click the **Browse** button.

369) Browse to the **SW-TUTORIAL-2013/Chapter 5 Models** folder.

370) Double-click the **AIR-RESERVOIR-SUPPORT** assembly. Note: The AIR-RESERVOIR SUPPORT assembly is supplied on the DVD in the book: Chapter 5 models folder.

371) Click a **position** above the FLAT-PLATE as illustrated.

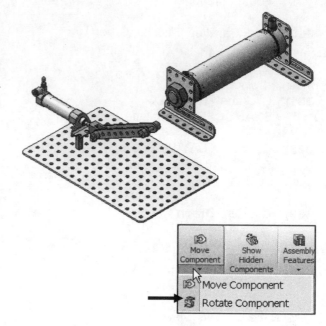

372) Click the **Rotate Component** Assembly tool. The Rotate Component PropertyManager is displayed. The Rotate icon is displayed in the Graphics window.

373) Click and drag the **AIR-RESERVOIR-SUPPORT** until the tank is parallel with the AirCylinder assembly as illustrated.

374) Click **OK** from the Rotate Component PropertyManager.

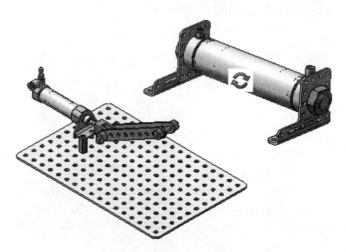

Insert a Concentric mate.

375) Click the **Mate**  Assembly tool. The Mate PropertyManager is displayed.

376) Click the **FLAT-PLATE back left** inside hole face as illustrated.

377) Click the fourth **ANGLE-BRACKET** inside hole face. Concentric is selected by default.

378) Click the **Green Check mark** .

Insert a Coincident mate.

379) Click the **ANGLE-BRACKET bottom face**.

380) Click the **FLAT-PLATE top face**. Coincident is selected by default.

381) Click the **Green Check mark** .

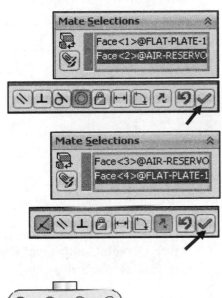

Insert a Parallel mate.

382) Click **Left view** from the Heads-up View toolbar.

383) Click the **ANGLE-BRACKET** narrow face.

384) Click the **FLAT-PLATE narrow face**.

385) Click **Parallel** .

386) Click the **Green Check mark** .

387) Click **OK** from the Mate PropertyManager.

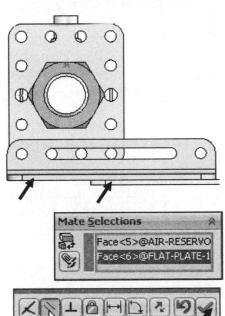

Display the Isometric view.

388) Click **Isometric view** 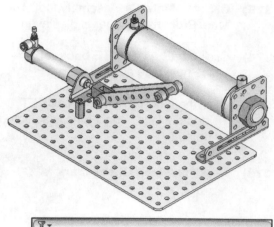 from the Heads-up View toolbar.

Save the PNEUMATIC-TEST-MODULE assembly.

389) Click **Save** .

Component Patterns in the Assembly

There are three methods to define a pattern in an assembly.

- *Linear*

- *Circular*

- *Feature Driven*

A Linear / Circular Component pattern utilizes geometry in the assembly to arrange instances in a Linear or Circular pattern.

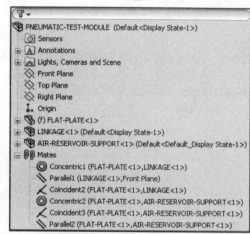

A Feature Driven Component Pattern utilizes an existing feature pattern.

The SCREW part fastens the ANGLE-BRACKET part to the FLAT-PLATE part. Mate one SCREW to the first instance on the ANGLE-BRACKET Linear Pattern.

Utilize the Feature Driven Component Pattern tool to create instances of the SCREW. Suppress the instances.

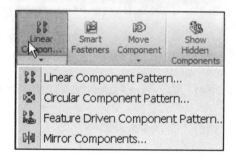

Utilize the Linear Component Pattern tool to copy the Feature Driven Pattern of SCREWS to the second ANGLE-BRACKET part.

Drag the part by specific geometry to create a mate.

Activity: PNEUMATIC-TEST-MODULE-Component Pattern

Open the SCREW part.

390) Click **Open** from the Menu bar.

391) Double-click **SCREW** from the SW-TUTORIAL-2013 folder.

392) Un-suppress the **Fillet1** and **Chamfer1** feature.

393) Click **Window**, **Tile Horizontally** to display the SCREW and the PNEUMATIC-TEST-MODULE assembly.

Insert and mate the SCREW.

394) Click the **bottom circular edge** of the SCREW.

395) Drag the **SCREW** into the PNEUMATIC-TEST-MODULE assembly window. Note: Zoom in on the top circular edge of the ANGLE-BRACKET left hole.

396) Release the mouse pointer on the **top circular edge** of the ANGLE-BRACKET left hole. The mouse pointer displays the Coincident/Concentric feedback symbol.

397) **Return** to the PNEUMATIC-TEST-MODULE assembly window. Click **Left view** from the Heads-up View toolbar.

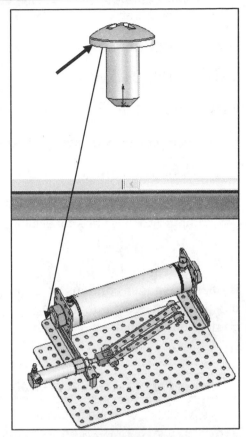

The SCREW part is position in the left hole with a Coincident/Concentric mate.

Create a Feature Driven Component Pattern.

398) Click the **Feature Driven Component Pattern** tool from the Consolidate Assembly toolbar. The Feature Driven PropertyManager is displayed.

399) Click the **SCREW** component in the Graphics window. SCREW<1> is displayed in the Components to Pattern box.

400) Click inside the **Driving Feature** box. **Expand** the AIR-RESERVOIR-SUPPORT assembly in the PNEUMATIC-TEST-MODULE fly-out FeatureManager.

401) **Expand** ANGLE-BRACKET <1>.

402) Click **LPattern1** in the fly-out FeatureManager. Note: The SCREW is the seed feature.

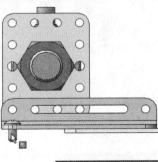

403) Click **OK** ✔ from the Feature Driven PropertyManager. Six instances are displayed in the Graphics window. DerivedLPattern1 is displayed in the FeatureManager.

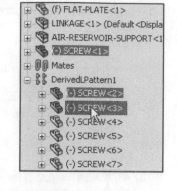

404) Click **SCREW<1>** from the FeatureManager.

405) Hold the **Ctrl** key down.

406) **Expand** DerivedLPattern1 from the FeatureManager.

407) Click the first two entries: **SCREW<2>** and **SCREW<3>**.

408) Release the **Ctrl** key.

409) Right-click **Suppress**. The first three SCREWs are not displayed.

💡 The Feature Driven PropertyManager contains an option to skip instances of a feature component in a pattern.

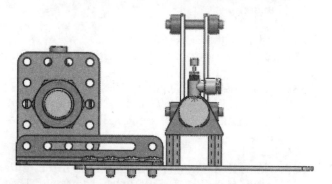

Activity: PNEUMATIC-TEST-MODULE-Linear Component Pattern

Create a Linear Component Pattern.

410) Click **Front view** 🗗 from the Heads-up View toolbar.

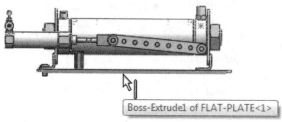

Boss-Extrude1 of FLAT-PLATE<1>

411) Click the **Linear Component Pattern** ░░ tool from the Assembly toolbar. The Linear Pattern PropertyManager is displayed.

412) Click inside the **Pattern Direction** box for Direction 1.

413) Click the long front edge of the **FRONT-PLATE** as illustrated. Edge<1> is displayed in the Pattern Direction box. The direction arrow points to the right.

414) Enter **177.80**mm, [7in] for Spacing.

415) Enter **2** for Instances.

416)　Click inside the **Components to Pattern** box.

417)　Click **DerivedLPattern1** from the fly-out FeatureManager.

418)　Click **OK** ✔ from the Linear Pattern PropertyManager.

419)　Click **Top view** ⬛ from the Heads-up View toolbar. View the results.

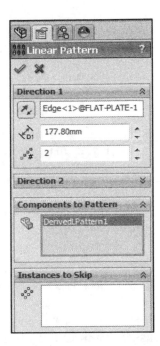

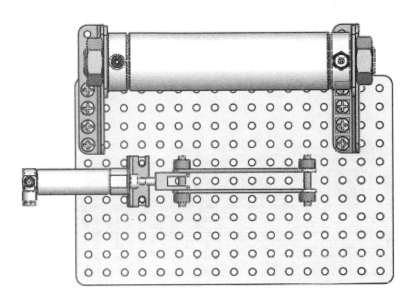

The Linear Component Pattern feature is displayed in the second ANGLE-BRACKET part. LocalLPattern1 is displayed in the FeatureManager.

Save the PNEUMATIC TEST MODULE assembly.

420)　Click **Isometric view** ⬛ from the Heads-up View toolbar. View the FeatureManager and the created features in their states.

421)　Click **Save** 💾.

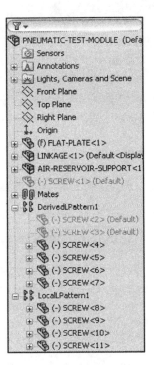

Hide the AIR-RESERVOIR-SUPPORT
assembly.

422) Right-click **AIR-RESERVOIR-
SUPPORT<1>** in the
FeatureManager.

423) Click **Hide components**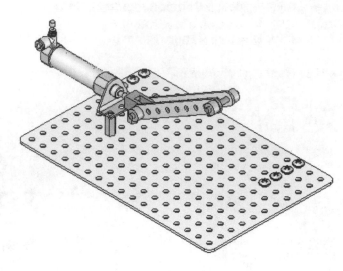
Note: Utilize the Show
components tool to display a
component that has been hidden.

Hide the LINKAGE assembly.

424) Right-click **LINKAGE<1>** in the
FeatureManager.

425) Click **Hide components** .

Insert the FRONT-SUPPORT
assembly into the PNEUMATIC-
TEST-MODULE assembly. Mate the
FRONT-SUPPORT assembly to the
FLAT-PLATE part.

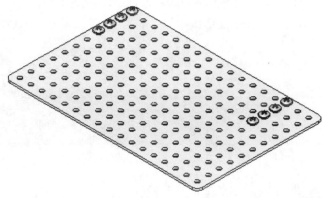

Utilize the Mirror Components tool to
create a mirrored copy of the
FRONT-SUPPORT assembly.

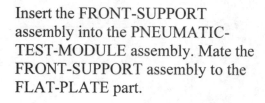 You can create new components
by mirroring existing part or sub-
assembly components. The new components can either be
a copy or a mirror of the original components. A mirrored
component is sometimes called a "right-hand" version of
the original "left-hand" version.

Access the Mirror Components tool from the
Consolidated Linear Component Pattern drop-down
menu.

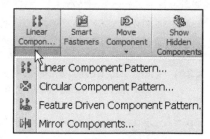

Activity: PNEUMATIC-TEST-MODULE-Insert FRONT-SUPPORT Assembly

---

Insert and mate the FRONT-SUPPORT assembly.

426) Click the **Insert Components** tool from the Assembly toolbar. The Insert Component
PropertyManager is displayed.

427) Click the **Browse** button.

428) Double-click **FRONT-SUPPORT**.

Hide the SCREWs in the FRONT-SUPPORT.

429) Click a **position** above the FLAT-PLATE as illustrated.

430) Right-click **FRONT-SUPPORT** in the FeatureManager.

431) Click **Open Assembly**.

432) **Hide** the SCREW parts and HEX-NUTS if required in the assembly.

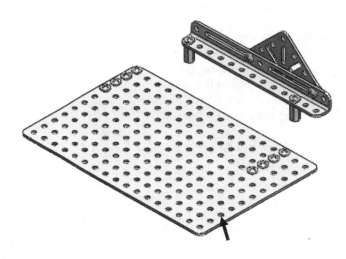

433) Click **Save** 💾.

Return to the PNEUMATIC-TEST-MODULE assembly.

434) Press **Ctrl Tab**.

435) Select the **PNEUMATIC-TEST-MODULE** document.

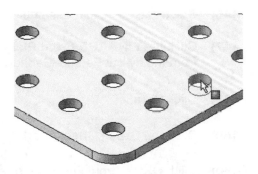

436) Click **Save** 💾.

437) Click **Yes** to the Message, "Save the document and referenced models now?"

The PNEUMATIC-TEST-MODULE is displayed. The SCREW and HEX-NUT components are hidden in the FRONT-SUPPORT assembly.

Insert a Concentric mate.

438) Click the **Mate** ✎ Assembly tool. The Mate PropertyManager is displayed.

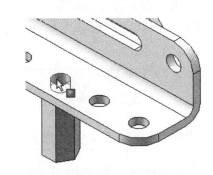

439) Click the **FLAT-PLATE hole face** in the 3rd row, right most column (17th column).

440) Click the **HEX-STANDOFF Tapped Hole as** illustrated. Concentric is selected by default.

441) Click the **Green Check mark** ✔.

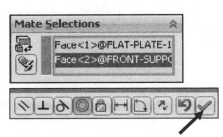

Insert a Coincident mate.

442) Click the bottom face of the **HEX-STANDOFF** part.

443) Click the top face of the **FLAT-PLATE**. The selected faces are displayed in the Mate Selections box. Coincident is selected by default.

444) Click the **Green Check mark** ✔.

Insert a Parallel mate.

445) Click the **FRONT-SUPPORT Front Plane** from the fly-out FeatureManager.

446) **Show** the LINKAGE assembly.

447) Click the **LINKAGE Front Plane** from the fly-out FeatureManager.

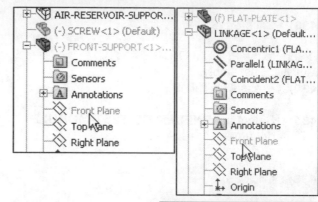

448) Click **Parallel** ⟍.

449) Click the **Green Check mark** ✔.

450) Click **OK** ✔ from the Mate PropertyManager.

451) **Hide** the LINKAGE assembly.

Save the PNEUMATIC-TEST-MODULE assembly.

452) Click **Save** 💾.

Mirrored Components

Create new components by mirroring existing parts or sub-assemblies. New components are created as copied geometry or mirrored geometry.

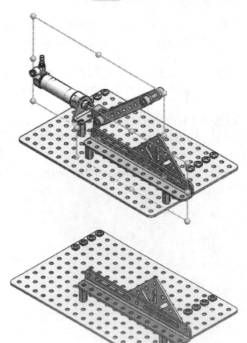

A mirrored component is sometimes called a "right-hand" version of the original "left hand" version.

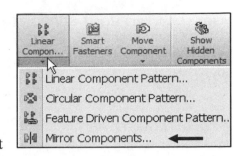

The copied or mirrored component changes, when the original component is modified.

A mirrored component creates a new document. The default document prefix is mirror. A copied component does not create a new document.

Suppressed components in the original sub-assembly are not mirrored or copied. The SCREW parts in the FRONT-SUPPORT assembly are not copied.

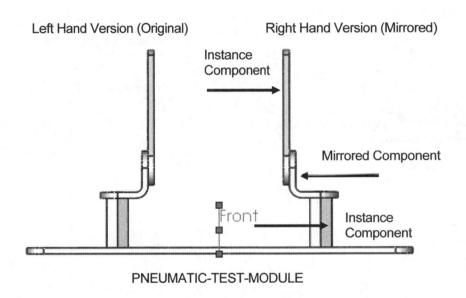

Left Hand Version (Original)   Right Hand Version (Mirrored)

Instance Component

Mirrored Component

Front

Instance Component

PNEUMATIC-TEST-MODULE

Activity: PNEUMATIC-TEST-MODULE Assembly: Mirrored Component

Insert a Mirrored Component.

453) Click the **Mirror Components** 🔲 tool from the Consolidated Assembly toolbar. The Mirror Components PropertyManager is displayed.

Step 1: The Selections box is displayed. Select face/plane to mirror about and the components to be mirrored.

454) **Expand** the PNEUMATIC-TEST-MODULE fly-out FeatureManager.

455) Click the **FLAT-PLATE Front Plane**. The Front Plane is displayed in the Mirror plane box.

456) Click the **FRONT-SUPPORT** assembly from the fly-out FeatureManager.

457) Click **Next** 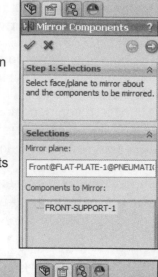. The FRONT-SUPPORT assembly is displayed in the Components to Mirror box.

Step 2: Verify the orientation of the components to be mirrored and adjust accordingly using the buttons below.

458) Click the **Create opposite hand version** button. View the results in the Graphics window.

459) Click **Next** .

Step 3: The mirrored components selected in step 2 need new geometries. This may be new files or new configurations in existing files. Specify the new configuration or file name using the options below.

460) Click **OK** from the Mirror Components PropertyManager.

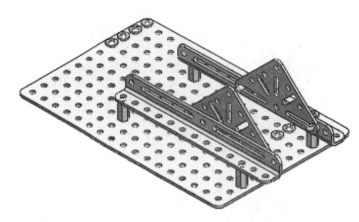

Select suppressed components and their mates to be mirrored in the Components to Mirror box.

The MirrorFRONT-SUPPORT, TRIANGLE, ANGLE-13HOLE, and SCREW components are mated.

Utilize the Fix option to mate the MirrorFRONT-SUPPORT to its current location in the PNEUMATIC-TEST-MODULE. No other mates are required.

Activity: PNEUMATIC-TEST-MODULE-Fix the MIRRORFRONT-SUPPORT

Fix the MirrorFRONT-SUPPORT.

461) Right-click **MirrorFRONT-SUPPORT** from the FeatureManager.

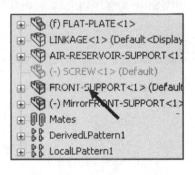

462) Click **Fix**. The MirrorFRONT assembly is fixed in the PNEUMATIC-TEST-MODULE assembly. The MirrorFRONT-SUPPORT does not move or rotate.

Display the LINKAGE assembly.
463) Right-click **LINKAGE** in the FeatureManager.

464) Click **Show components**.

Save the PNEUMATIC-TEST-MODULE assembly.

465) Click **Save** 💾.

Reuse geometry in the assembly. Utilize the Mirror Component tool to create a left and right version of parts and assemblies.

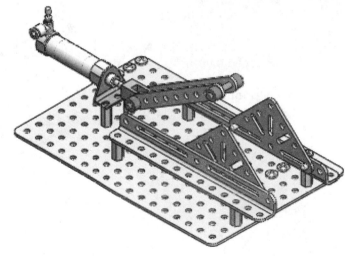

Component Properties

Component Properties control the flexibility of the sub-assembly when inserted into an assembly. Components do not translate or rotate after insertion into the assembly.

The FLATBAR parts in the LINKAGE assembly do not rotate after insertion into the PNEUMATIC TEST MODULE assembly. The LINKAGE assembly is in the Rigid State.

Insert the WHEEL-AND-AXLE assembly into the PNEUMATIC-TEST-MODULE assembly. Modify the Mate state of the LINKAGE assembly from the Rigid State to the Flexible State. The LINKAGE assembly is free to rotate.

Modify the Mate State of the AirCylinder assembly from the Rigid State to the Flexible State. The AirCylinder assembly is free to translate.

By default, when you create a sub-assembly, it is rigid. Within the parent assembly, the sub-assembly acts as a single unit and its components do not move relative to each other.

Activity: PNEUMATIC-TEST-MODULE Assembly-Insert WHEEL-AND-AXLE Assembly

Insert the WHEEL-AND-AXLE assembly.

466) Click the **Insert Components** tool from the Assembly toolbar. The Insert Component PropertyManager is displayed.

467) Click the **Browse** button.

468) Browse to the **WHEEL-AND-AXLE** assembly.

469) Click a **position** above the FLAT-PLATE part as illustrated.

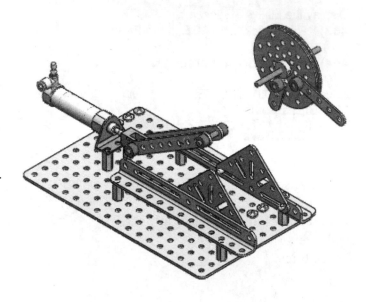

Insert a Concentric mate.

470) Click the **Mate**  tool from the Assembly toolbar.

471) Click the **AXLE-3000 cylindrical** face.

472) Click the inside **TRIANGLE top hole** face. The selected faces are displayed in the Mate Selections box. Concentric is selected by default.

473) Click the **Green Check mark** 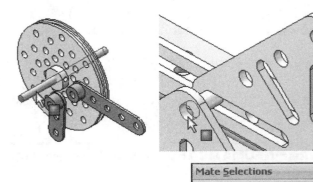.

Insert a Coincident mate.

474) Click the **WHEEL-AND-AXLE Front Plane** from the fly-out FeatureManager.

475) Click the **LINKAGE Front Plane** from the fly-out FeatureManager. Coincident is selected by default.

476) Click the **Green Check mark** .

477) Click **OK** from the Mate PropertyManager.

A Concentric mate is required between the left hole of the FLATBAR-3HOLE and right AXLE of the LINKAGE assembly.

DO NOT INSERT A CONCENTRIC MATE AT THIS TIME.

A Concentric mate will result in Mate errors.

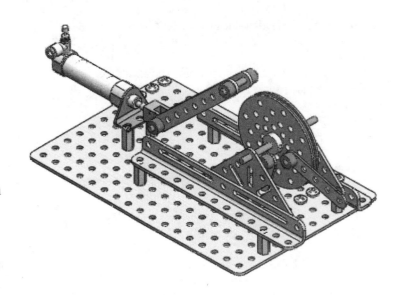

The WHEEL-AND-AXLE is free to rotate in the PNEUMATIC-TEST-MODULE assembly. The LINKAGE assembly interferes with the WHEEL-AND-AXLE. The LINKAGE assembly is not free to rotate or translate. Mate errors will occur.

Sub-assemblies within the LINKAGE assembly are in a Rigid Mate state when inserted into the PNEUMATIC-TEST-MODULE assembly. Remove the Rigid Mate state and insert a Concentric mate between the LINKAGE assembly and the WHEEL-AND-AXLE.

Activity: PNEUMATIC-TEST-MODULE Assembly-Remove Rigid state

Remove the Rigid State.

478) Right-click the **LINKAGE** assembly from the FeatureManager.

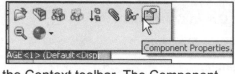

479) Click **Component Properties** from the Context toolbar. The Component Properties dialog box is displayed.

480) Check **Flexible** in the Solve as box.

481) Click **OK** from the Component Properties dialog box. Note the icon next to the LINKAGE assembly in the FeatureManager.

482) Right-click the **AirCylinder** assembly from the FeatureManager.

483) Click **Component Properties**.

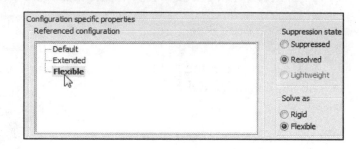

484) Check **Flexible** in the Solve as box.

485) Click **Flexible** in the Referenced configuration box.

486) Click **OK** from the Component Properties dialog box.

Hide the FRONT-SUPPORT assembly.

487) Right-click **FRONT-SUPPORT** from the FeatureManager.

488) Click **Hide components**.

Move the LINKAGE assembly.

489) Click and drag the **front FLATBAR-9HOLE** downward. The FLATBAR-9HOLE rotates about the left AXLE.

490) Click a **position** below the WHEEL-AND-AXLE. Click **inside** the Graphics window to deselect.

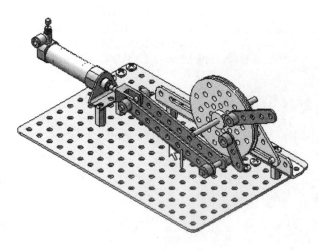

Insert a Concentric mate.

491) Click the **Mate** ✎ tool from the Assembly toolbar.

492) Click the second bottom **AXLE** face of the LINKAGE assembly.

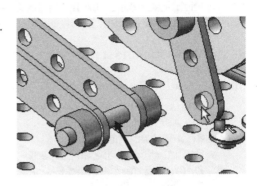

493) Click the **bottom hole** of the FLATBAR-3HOLE as illustrated. Concentric is the default.

494) Click the **Green Check mark** ✔.

495) Click **OK** ✔ from the Mate PropertyManager.

Save the PNEUMATIC-TEST-MODULE assembly.

496) Click **Isometric view** ⬦ from the Heads-up View toolbar.

497) Click **Save** 💾.

The AirCylinder assembly is inserted in a Rigid state by default. The AirCylinder contains three configurations:

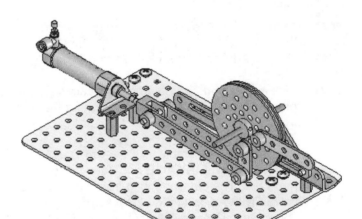

- Default

- Extended

- Flexible

Open the AirCylinder assembly. Modify the configuration to Flexible.

Open the LINKAGE assembly. Modify the AirCylinder Component Properties from Default to Flexible.

Activity: PNEUMATIC-TEST-MODULE Assembly - Review AirCylinder Configurations

Review the AirCylinder configurations.

498) Right-click **LINKAGE** from the PNEUMATIC-TEST-MODULE FeatureManager.

499) Click **Open Assembly** from the Context toolbar.

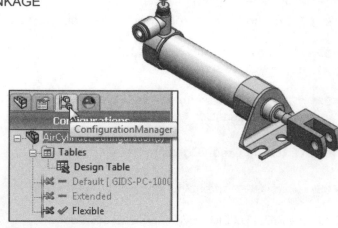

500) Right-click **AirCylinder** in the LINKAGE FeatureManager.

501) Click **Open Assembly**.

502) Click the **Configuration Manager** tab at the top of the AirCylinder FeatureManager. Three configurations are displayed: *Default*, *Extended* and *Flexible*. The current Default configuration sets the Piston Rod at 0 mm.

Display the Extended Configuration.
503) Double-click **Extended**. The Piston Rod of the AirCylinder extends 25mm.

Display the Flexible Configuration.
504) Double-click **Flexible**.

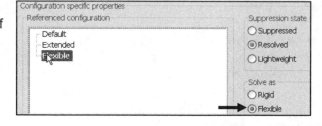

505) Click the **Rod-Clevis** in the Graphics window.

506) Click and drag the **Piston Rod** from left to right.

507) Click a **position** near its original location. The AirCylinder remains in the Flexible configuration for the rest of this project.

Update the LINKAGE assembly.
508) Click **Window**, **LINKAGE** from the Menu bar. The current configuration of the AirCylinder part in the LINKAGE assembly is Default. Modify the configuration.

509) Right-click **AirCylinder** from the LINKAGE assembly FeatureManager.

510) Click **Component Properties**.

511) Click **Flexible** for Solve as.

512) Click **Flexible** for Referenced configuration.

513) Click **OK**. The AirCylinder displays the Flexible configuration next to its name in the FeatureManager.

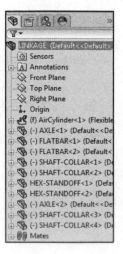

Update the PNEUMATIC-TEST-MODULE.
514) Click **Window**, **PNEUMATIC-TEST-MODULE** assembly from the Menu bar.

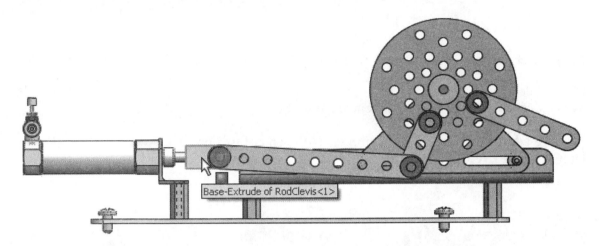

Move the ROD-CLEVIS.
515) Click and drag the **ROD-CLEVIS** to the right. The WHEEL rotates in a counterclockwise direction.

516) Click and drag the **ROD-CLEVIS** to the left. The WHEEL rotates in a clockwise direction.

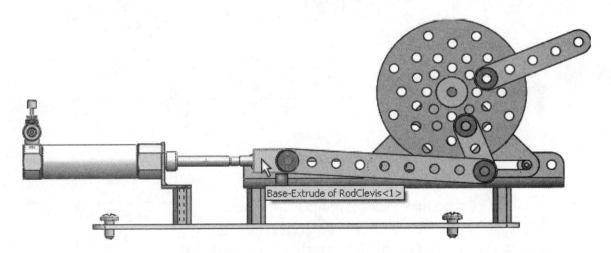

Display the AIR-RESERVOIR-SUPPORT assembly.
517) Right-click **AIR-RESERVOIR-SUPPORT** in the FeatureManager.

518) Click **Show components**.

Display the second FRONT-SUPPORT assembly.
519) Right-click **FRONT-SUPPORT** in the FeatureManager.

520) Click **Show components**.

521) **Display** the SCREWs in the FRONT-SUPPORT.

Save the PNEUMATIC-TEST-MODULE.
522)   Click **Isometric view** from the Heads-up View toolbar.

523)   Click **Save** .

524)   Click **Yes** to update referenced documents.

Close all documents.
525)   Click **Windows**, **Close All** from the Menu bar.

Explore additional parts and assemblies at the end of this project. Add the WEIGHT, HOOK and FLATBAR parts.

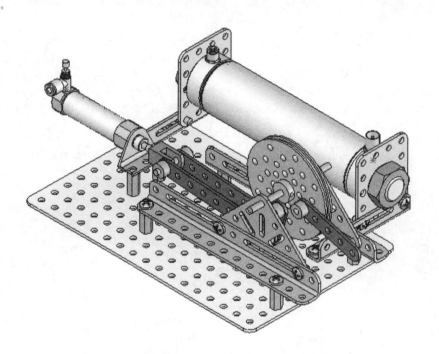

A Rebuild icon maybe displayed in the Assembly FeatureManager and a flexible rebuild icon at the sub-assembly level when the AirCylinder assembly is in the Flexible state.

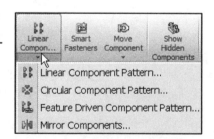

Additional details on Show components, Hide components, Linear Component Pattern, Circular Component Pattern, Feature Driven Component Pattern, Mirror Components, Configurations, Configuration Manager are available in SolidWorks Help. Select Help, SolidWorks Help topics.

Review the PNEUMATIC-TEST-MODULE Assembly

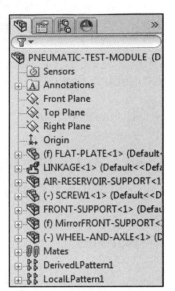

The PNEUMATIC TEST MODULE assembly was created by combining five major mechanical sub-assemblies.

The PNEUMATIC TEST MODULE assembly utilized the FLAT-PLATE as the first component. The LINKAGE assembly, AIR-RESERVOIR-SUPPORT assembly, FRONT-SUPPORT assembly, MirrorFRONT-SUPPORT assembly and the WHEEL-AND-AXLE assembly were mated to the FLAT-PLATE part.

Work at the lowest assembly level. The LINKAGE assembly required two HEX-STANDOFF parts. The HEX-STANDOFF components were inserted into the LINKAGE assembly. The LINKAGE assembly was inserted into the PNEUMATIC-TEST-MODULE assembly.

The AIR-RESERVOIR-SUPPORT assembly was inserted into the PNEUMATIC-TEST-MODULE assembly. The SCREW component utilized a Feature Driven Component Pattern tool and the Linear Component Pattern tool to create multiple copies.

The FRONT-SUPPORT assembly was inserted into the PNEUMATIC-TEST-MODULE assembly. The Mirror Components tool created a mirrored version of the FRONT-SUPPORT assembly.

The WHEEL-AND-AXLE assembly was inserted into the PNEUMATIC-TEST-MODULE assembly. Component Properties created a Flexible state mate.

 The LINKAGE assembly, "AirCylinder" is in a Flexible state.

In the next section, create the final ROBOT assembly. Either use your created assemblies and components, or use the created assemblies and components provided in the Chapter 5 Models folder on the enclosed DVD.

 Work from your hard drive. Copy all folders from the DVD to your hard drive.

Final ROBOT Assembly

The final ROBOT assembly is comprised of three major sub-assemblies and the HEX-STANDOFF component:

- Robot Platform assembly

- PNEUMATIC-TEST-MODULE assembly

- Basic_integration assembly

- 4 - HEX-STANDOFF components

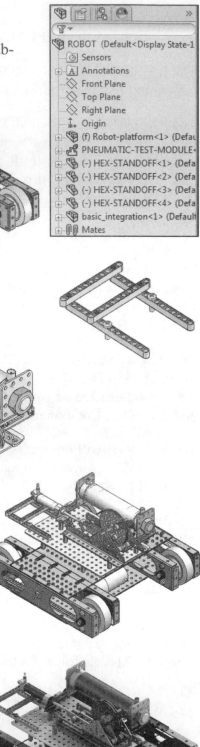

The LINKAGE assembly is in a Flexible state.

A Rebuild icon may be displayed in the final ROBOT Assembly FeatureManager and a flexible rebuild icon at the sub-assembly level when the AirCylinder assembly is in the Flexible state.

All assemblies and components for the final ROBOT assembly are provided in the Chapter 5 models folder on the enclosed DVD.

As an exercise apply PhotoView 360 to render the final ROBOT assembly.

Combine the created new assemblies and components to develop the final ROBOT assembly. In this next section, work from the Chapter 5 Models folder located on the DVD in the book. If needed, copy all models from to the DVD to your hard drive. Create the SW-TUTORIAL-2013/Chapter 5 Models folder.

Note: Step-by-step instructions are not provided in this section for the mates.

Activity: Create the ROBOT Assembly

Create the final ROBOT assembly.

526) Click **New** ☐ from the Menu bar.

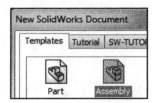

527) Double-click **Assembly** from the Templates tab. The Begin Assembly PropertyManager is displayed.

Insert the Robot-platform assembly.
528) Click the **Browse** button.

529) Browse to the **SW-TUTORIAL-2013/ Chapter 5 Models** folder. The Chapter 5 models folder is supplied on the DVD in the book. Work from your hard drive.

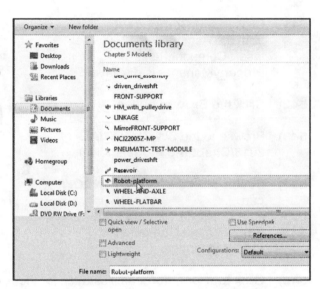

530) Double-click **Robot-platform**. *If needed click NO if a component is missing and the system wants you to find it. This will not change the final assembly.*

531) Click **OK** ✔ from the Begin Assembly PropertyManager. The Robot-platform is fixed to the assembly Origin.

Save the Assembly.
532) Click **Save As** from the drop-down Menu bar.

533) Enter **ROBOT** for File name in the SW-TUTORIAL-2013 /Chapter 5 models folder.

534) Enter **Final ROBOT Assembly** for Description.

535) Click **Save**.

Insert the PNEUMATIC-TEST-MODULE assembly.

536) Click **Insert Components** 🗐 from the Assembly toolbar. The Insert Components PropertyManager is displayed.

537) Click the **Browse** button.

538) Browse to the **SW-TUTORIAL-2013/ Chapter 5 Models** folder.

539) Double-click the **PNEUMATIC-TEST-MODULE** assembly.

540) Click a **position** above the Robot-platform.

If an assembly or component is loaded in a Lightweight state, right-click the **assembly name** or **component name** from the FeatureManager. Click **Set Lightweight to Resolved**.

Insert 4 HEX-STANDOFF components.

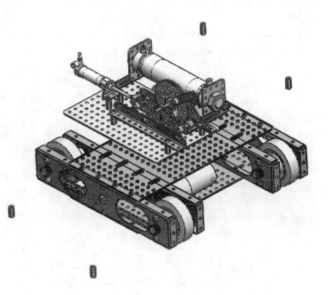

541) Click **Insert Components** from the Assembly toolbar. The Insert Components PropertyManager is displayed.

542) Click the **Browse** button.

543) Browse to the **SW-TUTORIAL-2013/Chapter 5 models** folder.

544) Double-click the **HEX-STANDOFF** part.

545) **Pin** the Insert Components PropertyManager.

546) Click **four positions** as illustrated for the four HEX-STANDOFF components.

547) **Un-Pin** the Insert Components PropertyManager.

548) Click **OK** from the Insert Components PropertyManager.

Insert Coincident and Concentric mates between the four HEX-STANDOFF components and the PNEUMATIC-TEST-MODULE and the Robot-platform as illustrated. View the location of the HEX-STANDOFF components on the PNEUMATIC-TEST-MODULE assembly.

View the location of the HEX-STANDOFF
components on the Robot-platform as
illustrated.

549) **Expand** the Mates folder. View the
created mates.

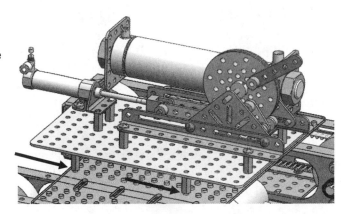

Insert the basic_integration assembly.

550) Click the **Browse** button.

551) Browse to the **SW-TUTORIAL-
2013/Chapter 5 models** folder. Do
not work directly from the DVD.
Copy all needed files to your hard
drive.

552) Double-click the
basic_integration assembly.

553) Click a position to the **left** of the assembly
as illustrated.

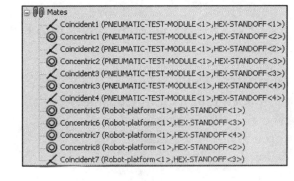

Insert Coincident and Concentric mates
between the two screws in the
basic_integration assembly and the
PNEUMATIC-TEST-MODULE
assembly.

554) **Expand** the Mates folder. View the
created mates.

Save the ROBOT assembly.

555) Click **Save** 💾. You are finished with
the final ROBOT assembly.

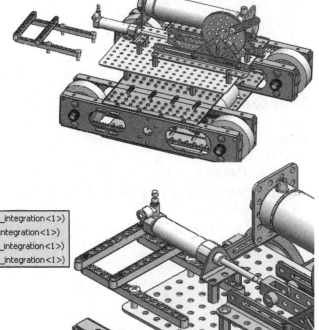

Chapter Summary

In this chapter, you created and worked with multiple documents in sub-assemblies and assemblies. You developed sound assembly modeling techniques that utilized Standard mates, fixed components, symmetry, component patterns and mirrored components.

The WHEEL-AND-AXLE assembly combined the WHEEL-FLATBAR assembly with the AXLE-3000 part, SHAFTCOLLAR-500 part and HEX-ADAPTER part.

The WHEEL-FLATBAR assembly combined the 3HOLE-SHAFTCOLLAR assembly and 5HOLE-SHAFTCOLLAR assembly.

The PNEUMATIC-TEST-MODULE assembly combined four major mechanical sub-assemblies. The final ROBOT assembly was comprised of three major sub-assemblies and the HEX-STANDOFF component.

Organize your assemblies. For an exercise, create an assembly Layout Diagram of the final ROBOT assembly to determine the grouping of components and assemblies.

As an exercise apply PhotoView 360 to render the final ROBOT assembly.

Chapter Terminology

Mates: A mate is a Geometric relationship between components in an assembly.

Circular Pattern: A Circular Pattern repeats features or geometry in a polar array. A Circular Patten requires an axis of revolution, the number of instances and an angle.

Component Pattern: There are two methods to define a component pattern in an assembly. A Derive Component Pattern utilizes an existing feature pattern. A Local Component pattern utilizes geometry in the assembly to arrange instances in a Linear or Circular pattern.

Component Properties: The properties of a component, part or assembly are controlled through Component Properties. The Rigid/Flexible Mate State property and Configuration property were explored in this project. Component Properties are used to define visibility and color.

ConfigurationManager: The ConfigurationManager on the left side of the Graphics window is utilized to create, select, and view the configurations of parts and assemblies.

Dome: A Dome feature creates a spherical or elliptical feature from a selected face.

Loft: A Loft feature blends two or more profiles. Each profile is sketched on a separate plane.

Mirror Component: A mirror component creates a mirrored or copied part or assembly. A mirrored component is sometimes called a "right-hand" version of the original "left hand" version.

Replace: The Replace command substitutes one or more open instances of a component in an assembly with a different component.

Revolved Cut: A Revolved Cut removes material. A sketched profile is revolved around a centerline. The Revolved Cut requires a direction and an angle of revolution.

Swept: A Swept feature adds/removes material by moving a profile along a path. A basic Swept feature requires two sketches. The first sketch is called the path. The second sketch is called profile. The profile and path are sketched on perpendicular planes.

Questions

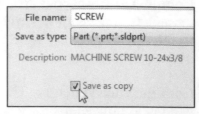

1. What function does the Save as copy check box perform when saving a part under a new name?

2. True or False. Never reuse geometry from one part to create another part.

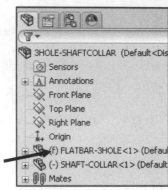

3. Describe 5 Assembly techniques utilized in this chapter.

4. True or False. A fixed (f) component cannot move and is locked to the Origin.

5. Describe the purpose of an Assembly Layout diagram.

6. Describe the difference between a Feature Driven Component Pattern and a Linear Component Pattern.

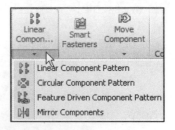

7. Describe the difference between copied geometry and mirrored geometry utilizing the Mirror Components tool.

8. True of False. An assembly contains one or more configurations.

9. Review the Design Intent section in the Introduction. Identify how you incorporated design intent into the assembly.

10. Review the Keyboard Short Cut keys in the Appendix. Identify the Short Cut keys you incorporated into this chapter. What is the g key used for?

Project assemblies below were created by students in my Freshman Engineering CAD class.

Chapter 5 Homework

Name

- Bench Vice Assembly Project
- Butterfly Valve Assembly Project
- Drill Guide Assembly Project
- Kant Twist Clamp Assembly Project
- Pipe Vice Assembly Project
- Pulley Assembly Project
- Quick Acting Clamp Assembly Project
- Radial Engine Assembly Project
- Shock Assembly Project
- Welder Arm Assemlby Project

Exercises

Exercise 5.1: Butterfly Valve Assembly Project

Copy the components from the Chapter 5
Homework/Butterfly Valve Assembly Project folder
located on the DVD. View all components.

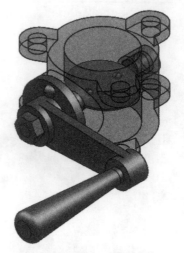

Create an ANSI IPS Butterfly Valve assembly document.
Insert all needed components and mates to assemble the
assembly and to simulate proper movement per the
provided avi file located in the folder. You are the
designer. Address all tolerancing and dimension
modifications. Use Standard, Advanced and Mechanical
Mates. Create and insert any additional components if
needed.

Create a C-ANSI Landscape - Third Angle Isometric Exploded
Drawing document with Explode lines of the assembly using
your knowledge of SolidWorks. Insert a BOM with Balloons.
Insert all needed General notes and Custom Properties in the
Title Block.

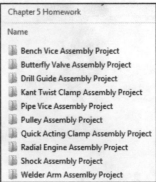

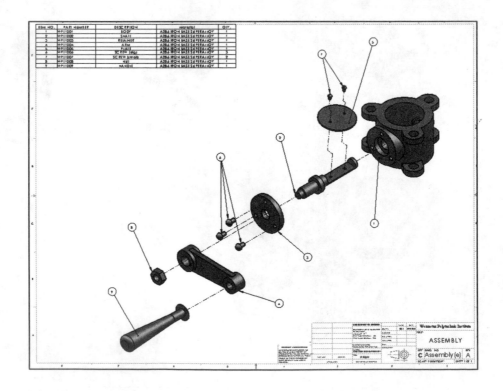

Exercise 5.2: Shock Assembly Project

Copy the components from the Chapter 5 Homework/Shock Assembly Project folder located on the DVD. View all components.

Create an ANSI IPS Shock assembly document. Insert all needed components and mates to assemble the assembly and to simulate proper movement per the provided avi file located in the folder. You are the designer. Address all tolerancing and dimension modifications if needed. Be creative. Use Standard, Advanced and Mechanical Mates. Create and insert any additional components if needed.

Create a C-ANSI Landscape - Third Angle Isometric Exploded Drawing document with Explode lines of the assembly using your knowledge of SolidWorks. Insert a BOM with Balloons. Insert all needed General notes in the Title Block.

Chapter 5 Homework

Name

- Bench Vice Assembly Project
- Butterfly Valve Assembly Project
- Drill Guide Assembly Project
- Kant Twist Clamp Assembly Project
- Pipe Vice Assembly Project
- Pulley Assembly Project
- Quick Acting Clamp Assembly Project
- Radial Engine Assembly Project
- Shock Assembly Project
- Welder Arm Assemlby Project

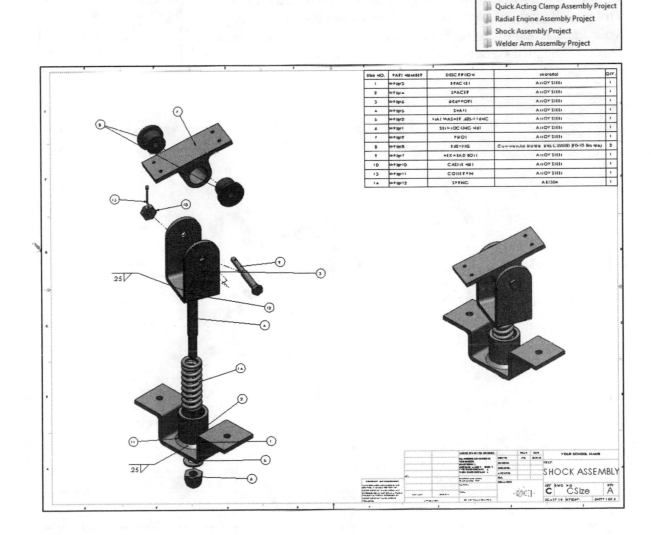

Exercise 5.3: Quick Acting Clamp Assembly Project

Copy the components from the Chapter 5 Homework/Quick Acting Clamp Assembly Project folder located on the DVD. View all components.

Create an ANSI IPS Quick Acting Clamp assembly document. Insert all needed components and mates to assemble the assembly and to simulate proper movement per the provided avi file located in the folder.

You are the designer. Address all tolerancing and dimension modifications if needed. Be creative. Use Standard, Advanced and Mechanical Mates. Create and insert any additional components if needed.

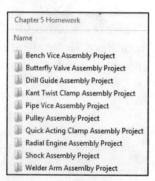

Create a C-ANSI Landscape - Third Angle Isometric Exploded Drawing document with Explode lines of the assembly using your knowledge of SolidWorks. Insert a BOM with Balloons. Insert all needed General notes in the Title Block.

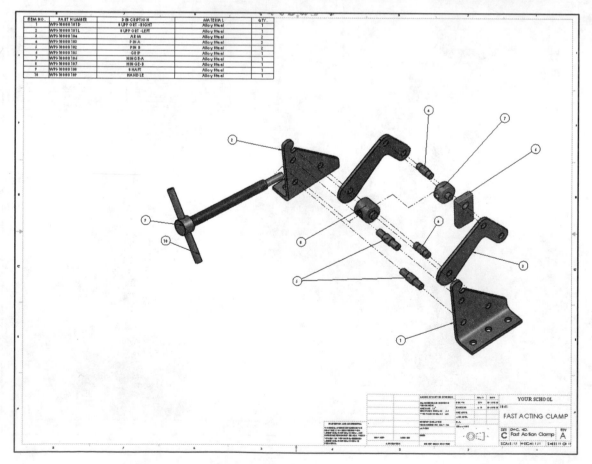

ITEM NO.	PART NUMBER	DESCRIPTION	MATERIAL	QTY.
1	WPF10000101D	SUPPORT-RIGHT	Alloy Steel	1
2	WPF10000101L	SUPPORT-LEFT	Alloy Steel	1
3	WPF10000104	ARM	Alloy Steel	2
4	WPF10000102	PIN A	Alloy Steel	2
5	WPF10000103	PIN B	Alloy Steel	2
6	WPF10000105	GRIP	Alloy Steel	1
7	WPF10000106	HINGE-A	Alloy Steel	1
8	WPF10000107	HINGE-B	Alloy Steel	1
9	WPF10000108	SHAFT	N.A.	1
10	WPF10000109	HANDLE	Alloy Steel	1

Chapter 5 Homework

Name

- Bench Vice Assembly Project
- Butterfly Valve Assembly Project
- Drill Guide Assembly Project
- Kant Twist Clamp Assembly Project
- Pipe Vice Assembly Project
- Pulley Assembly Project
- Quick Acting Clamp Assembly Project
- Radial Engine Assembly Project
- Shock Assembly Project
- Welder Arm Assemlby Project

YOUR SCHOOL

FAST ACTING CLAMP

Exercise 5.4: Drill Guide Assembly Project

Copy the components from the Chapter 5
Homework/Drill Guide Assembly Project folder
located on the DVD. View all components.

Create an ANSI IPS Drill Guide assembly document.
Insert all needed components and mates to assemble
the assembly and to simulate proper movement per the
provided avi file located in the folder. You are the
designer. Address all tolerancing and dimension
modifications if needed. Be creative. Use Standard,
Advanced and Mechanical Mates. Create and insert
any additional components if needed.

Create a C-ANSI Landscape - Third Angle Isometric
Exploded Drawing document with Explode lines of
the assembly using your knowledge of SolidWorks.
Insert a BOM with Balloons. Insert all needed General
notes in the Title Block.

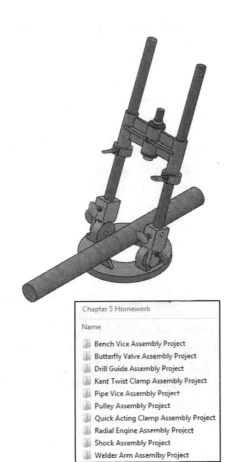

Chapter 5 Homework

Name

- Bench Vice Assembly Project
- Butterfly Valve Assembly Project
- Drill Guide Assembly Project
- Kant Twist Clamp Assembly Project
- Pipe Vice Assembly Project
- Pulley Assembly Project
- Quick Acting Clamp Assembly Project
- Radial Engine Assembly Project
- Shock Assembly Project
- Welder Arm Assemlby Project

ITEM NO.	PART NUMBER	DESCRIPTION	MATERIAL	QTY.
1	WPI-1000-01	BASE	2014 ALLOY	1
2	WPI-1000-02	ROTATOR	PLAIN CARBON STEEL	2
3	WPI-1000-03	ROD GUIDE	CAST ALLOY STEEL	2
4	WPI-1000-04	SLIDE	2014 ALLOY	1
5	WPI-1000-05	COLLAR	2014 ALLOY	2
6	WPI-1000-06	BUSHING	ALUMINUM BRONZE	2
7	WPI-1000-07	RETAINING RING B27.1 - NA2-45	ALLOY STEEL	2
8	WPI-1000-08	DRILL ADAPTOR	PLAIN CARBON STEEL	1
9	WPI-1000-09	THUMB SCREW .25-20x0.51 TYPE B, FLAT POINT-C	2014 ALLOY	4

Exercise 5.5: Pulley Assembly Project

Copy the components from the Chapter 5 Homework/Pulley Assembly Project folder located on the DVD. View all components.

Create an ANSI Pulley assembly document. Insert all needed components and mates to assemble the assembly and to simulate proper movement per the provided avi file located in the folder.

You are the designer. Address all tolerancing and dimension modifications if needed. Be creative. Use Standard, Advanced and Mechanical Mates.

Create and insert any additional components if needed.

Create a C-ANSI Landscape - Third Angle Isometric Exploded Drawing document with Explode lines of the assembly using your knowledge of SolidWorks. Insert a BOM with Balloons. Insert all needed General notes in the Title Block.

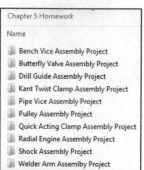

Chapter 5 Homework

Name

- Bench Vice Assembly Project
- Butterfly Valve Assembly Project
- Drill Guide Assembly Project
- Kant Twist Clamp Assembly Project
- Pipe Vice Assembly Project
- Pulley Assembly Project
- Quick Acting Clamp Assembly Project
- Radial Engine Assembly Project
- Shock Assembly Project
- Welder Arm Assemlby Project

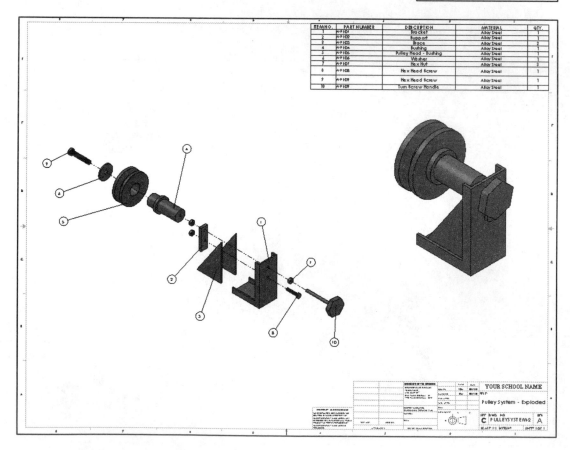

Exercise 5.6: Welder Arm Assembly Project

Copy the components from the Chapter 5 Homework/Welder Arm Assembly Project folder located on the DVD. View all components.

Create an ANSI Welder Arm assembly document. Insert all needed components and mates to assemble the assembly and to simulate proper movement per the provided avi file located in the folder. You are the designer. Address all tolerancing and dimension modifications if needed. Be creative. Use Standard, Advanced and Mechanical Mates. Create and insert any additional components if needed.

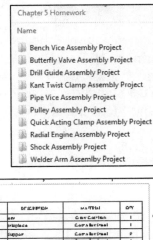

Create a C-ANSI Landscape - Third Angle Isometric Exploded Drawing document with Explode lines of the assembly using your knowledge of SolidWorks. Insert a BOM with Balloons. Insert all needed General notes in the Title Block.

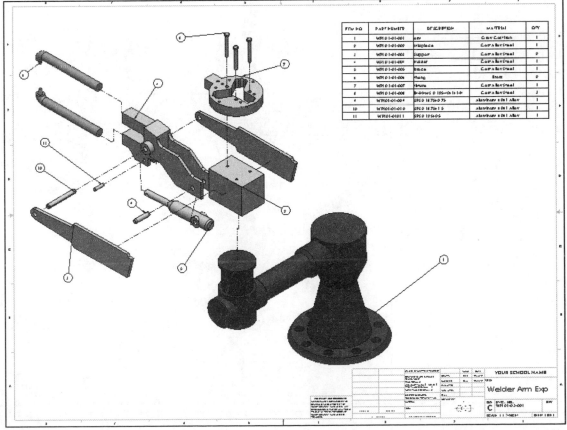

Exercise 5.7: Radial Engine Assembly Project

Copy the components from the Chapter 5 Homework/Radial Engine Assembly Project folder located on the DVD. View all components.

Create an ANSI Radial Engine assembly document. Insert all needed components and mates to assemble the assembly and to simulate proper movement per the provided avi file located in the folder.

You are the designer. Address all tolerancing and dimension modifications if needed. Be creative.

Use Standard, Advanced and Mechanical Mates.

Create and insert any additional components if needed.

Create a C-ANSI Landscape - Third Angle Isometric Exploded Drawing document with Explode lines of the assembly using your knowledge of SolidWorks.

Insert a BOM with Balloons. Insert all needed General notes in the Title Block.

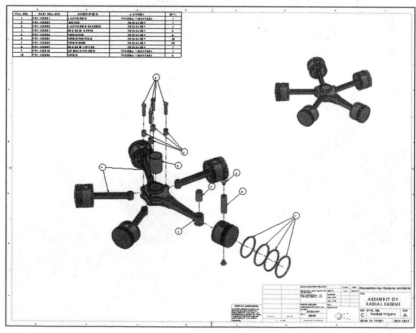

Exercise 5.8: Bench Vice Assembly Project

Copy the components from the Chapter 5 Homework/Bench Vice Assembly Project folder located on the DVD. View all components.

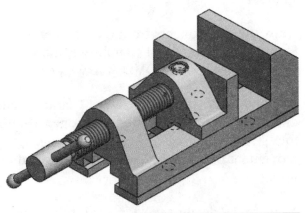

Create an ANSI IPS Bench Vice assembly document. Insert all needed components and mates to assemble the assembly and to simulate proper movement per the provided avi file located in the folder.

You are the designer. Address all tolerancing and dimension modifications if needed. Use Standard, Advanced and Mechanical Mates.

Create and insert any additional components if needed.

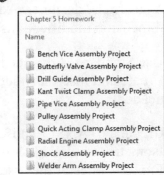

Chapter 5 Homework

Name

- Bench Vice Assembly Project
- Butterfly Valve Assembly Project
- Drill Guide Assembly Project
- Kant Twist Clamp Assembly Project
- Pipe Vice Assembly Project
- Pulley Assembly Project
- Quick Acting Clamp Assembly Project
- Radial Engine Assembly Project
- Shock Assembly Project
- Welder Arm Assemlby Project

Create a C-ANSI Landscape - Third Angle Isometric Exploded Drawing document with Explode lines of the assembly using your knowledge of SolidWorks.

Insert a BOM with Balloons. Insert all needed General notes and Custom Properties in the Title Block.

ITEM NO.	PART NUMBER	DESCRIPTION	MATERIAL	QTY.
1	WPI - 0001	Base	Alloy Steel	1
2	WPI - 0002	Base Plate	Alloy Steel	2
3	WPI - 0003	Vice Jaw	Alloy Steel	1
4	WPI - 0004	Clamping Plate	Alloy Steel	1
5	WPI - 0005	Jaw Screw	Alloy Steel	1
6	WPI - 0006	Screw Bar	Alloy Steel	1
7	WPI - 0007	Bar Globes	Alloy Steel	2
8	WPI-008	Hex Screw M6x1.0x14-14WN	Alloy Steel	4
9	WPI-0009	Bolt	Alloy Steell	1
10	WPI- 00019	Blot1	Alloy Steel	2

			NAME	DATE	MAIN MACHINE
UNLESS OTHERWISE SPECIFIED:		DRAWN	DSP	7-4-2021	
DIMENSIONS ARE IN INCHES TOLERANCES: FRACTIONALS ANGULAR: MACHS BEND ± TWO PLACE DECIMAL ± THREE PLACE DECIMAL ±		CHECKED			TITLE: ARBOR PRESS
		ENG APPR.			
		MFG APPR.			
INTERPRET GEOMETRIC TOLERANCING PER:		Q.A.			
PROPRIETARY AND CONFIDENTIAL	MATERIAL	COMMENTS:			SIZE A	DWG. NO. 10-344	REV
THE INFORMATION CONTAINED IN THIS DRAWING IS THE SOLE PROPERTY OF <INSERT COMPANY NAME HERE>. ANY REPRODUCTION IN PART OR AS A WHOLE WITHOUT THE WRITTEN PERMISSION OF <INSERT COMPANY NAME HERE> IS PROHIBITED.	FINISH				
	NEXT ASSY	USED ON		SCALE: 1:3	WEIGHT:	SHEET 1 OF 1
	APPLICATION		DO NOT SCALE DRAWING		

Exercise 5.9: Kant Twist Clamp Assembly Project

Copy the components from the Chapter 5 Homework/Kant Twist Clamp Assembly Project folder located on the DVD. View all components.

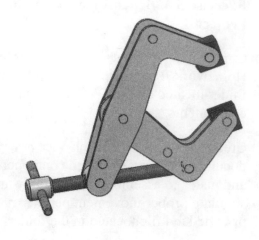

Create an ANSI IPS Kant Twist Clamp assembly document. Insert all needed components and mates to assemble the assembly and to simulate proper movement per the provided avi file located in the folder.

You are the designer. Address all tolerancing and dimension modifications if needed.

Use Standard, Advanced and Mechanical Mates. Create and insert any additional components if needed.

Create a C-ANSI Landscape - Third Angle Isometric Exploded Drawing document with Explode lines of the assembly using your knowledge of SolidWorks.

Insert a BOM with Balloons. Insert all needed General notes and Custom Properties in the Title Block.

Chapter 5 Homework

Name

- Bench Vice Assembly Project
- Butterfly Valve Assembly Project
- Drill Guide Assembly Project
- Kant Twist Clamp Assembly Project
- Pipe Vice Assembly Project
- Pulley Assembly Project
- Quick Acting Clamp Assembly Project
- Radial Engine Assembly Project
- Shock Assembly Project
- Welder Arm Assemlby Project

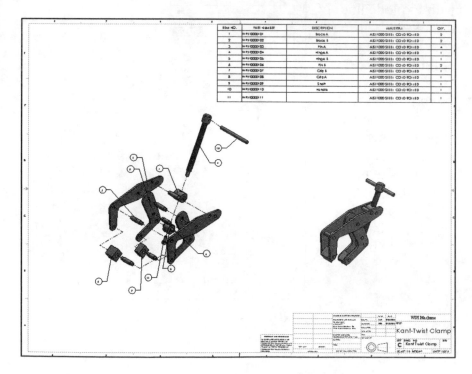

Chapter 6

SolidWorks SimulationXpress, Sustainability, and DFMXpress

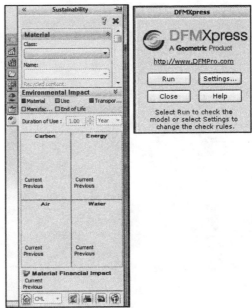

Below are the desired outcomes and usage competencies based on the completion of Chapter 6.

Desired Outcomes:	Usage Competencies:
• Understand and navigate SolidWorks SimulationXpress analysis. • Awareness of SolidWorks Sustainability and SustainabilityXpress. • Knowledge of SolidWorks DFMXpress.	• Utilize SolidWorks SimulationXpress Wizard. • Apply SolidWorks SimulationXpress to a simple part. • Display and understand the four environmental impact factors. • Generate a customer report and find suitable alternative materials. • Apply SolidWorks DFMXpress Wizard.

Notes:

Chapter 6 - SimulationXpress, Sustainabilty, and DFMXpress

Chapter Objective

Execute a SolidWorks SimulationXpress analysis on a simple part. Determine if the part can support an applied load under a static load condition.

Perform a SolidWorks SustainabilityXpress analysis on a part. View the environmental impact calculated in four key areas: *Carbon Footprint, Energy Consumption, Air Acidification* and *Water Eutrophication*. Material and Manufacturing process region and Usage region are used as input variables. Compare similar materials and environmental impacts on the base line design.

Implement DFMXpress on a part. DFMXpress is an analysis tool that validates the manufacturability of SolidWorks parts. Use DFMXpress to identify design areas that *may cause problems* in fabrication or increase the costs of production.

On the completion of this chapter, you will be able to:

- Implement a SolidWorks SimulationXpress analysis on a simple part.
- Apply SustainabilityXpress to a part.
- View the four key environmental impact areas:
  - Carbon Footprint
  - Energy Consumption
  - Air Acidification
  - Water Eutrophication
- Generate a Customer sustainability report and locate suitable alternative materials
- Perform a DFMXpress analysis on a simple part

SolidWorks SimulationXpress

SimulationXpress is a Finite Element Analysis (FEA) tool incorporated into SolidWorks. SimulationXpress calculates the displacement and stress in a part based on material, restraints and static loads.

When loads are applied to a part, the part tries to absorb its effects by developing internal forces. Stress is the intensity of these internal forces. Stress is defined in terms of Force per unit Area: $Stress = \dfrac{f}{A}$.

Different materials have different stress property levels. Mathematical equations derived from Elasticity theory and Strength of Materials are utilized to solve for displacement and stress. These analytical equations solve for displacement and stress for simple cross sections.

Example: Bar or Beam. In complicated parts, a computer based numerical method such as Finite Element Analysis is used.

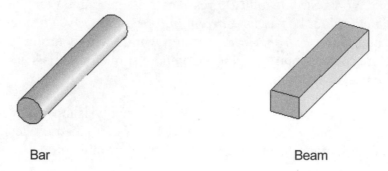

Bar　　　　　　　　　　　　　　　　　　　　Beam

SimulationXpress utilizes linear static analysis based on the Finite Element Method. The Finite Element Method is a numerical technique used to analyze engineering designs. FEM divides a large complex model into numerous smaller models. A model is divided into numerous smaller segments called elements.

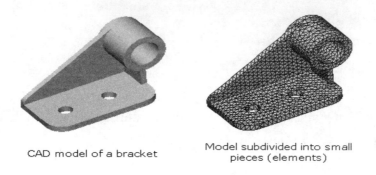

CAD model of a bracket　　　　　Model subdivided into small
　　　　　　　　　　　　　　　　pieces (elements)

SimulationXpress utilizes a tetrahedral element containing 10 nodes. Each node contains a series of equations. SimulationXpress develops the equations governing the behavior of each element. The equations relate displacement to material properties, restraints, "boundary conditions" and applied loads.

☀ SimulationXpress organizes a large set of simultaneous algebraic equations.

The Finite Element Analysis (FEA) equation is:

$[K]\{U\} = \{F\}$ where:

1. $[K]$ is the structural stiffness matrix.

2. $\{U\}$ is the vector of unknown nodal displacements.

3. $\{F\}$ is the vector of nodal loads.

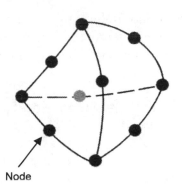

Node

SimulationXpress determines the X, Y, and Z displacement at each node. This displacement is utilized to calculate strain.

Tetrahedral Element

Strain is defined as the ratio of the change in length, δL to the original length, L.

Stress is proportional to strain in a Linear Elastic Material.

The Elastic Modulus (Young's Modulus) is defined as stress divided by strain.

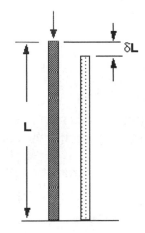

Strain = δ L / L

Compression Force Applied
Original Length L
Change in Length δL

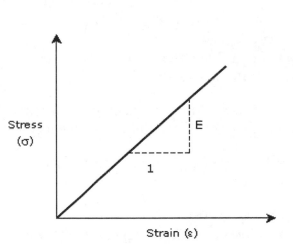

Elastic Modulus is the ratio of Stress to Strain for Linear Elastic Materials.

SimulationXpress determines the stress for each element based on the Elastic Modulus of the material and the calculated strain.

The Stress versus Strain Plot for a Linearly Elastic Material provides information about a material.

The Elastic Modulus, E is the stress required to cause one unit of strain. The material behaves linearly in the Elastic Range.

The material remains in the Elastic Range until it reaches the elastic limit.

The point EL is the elastic limit. The material begins Plastic deformation.

The point Y is called the Yield Point. The material begins to deform at a faster rate. The material behaves non-linearly in the Plastic Range. The point U is called the ultimate tensile strength. Point U is the maximum value of the non-linear curve. Point U represents the maximum tensile stress a material can handle before a facture or failure. Point F represents where the material will fracture.

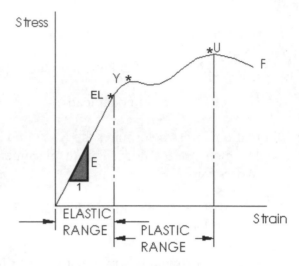

Stresss versus Strain Plot
Linearly Elastic Material

Designers utilize maximum and minimum stress calculations to determine if a part is safe. SimulationXpress reports a recommended Factor of Safety during the analysis.

The SimulationXpress Factor of Safety is a ratio between the material strength and the calculated stress.

The von Mises stress is a measure of the stress intensity required for a material to yield. The SimulationXpress Results plot displays von Mises stress.

A Newton is defined as the force acting on a mass of one kilogram at a location where the acceleration due to gravity is 1m/s^2. Weight equals mass * gravity. Weight is a Force.

$$1 \, newton = \frac{1 \, kg - m}{s^2}$$

SimulationXpress guides you through various default steps to define fixtures, loads, material properties, analyze the model, and view the results and the optional Optimization process.

The SimulationXpress interface consists of the following Menus:

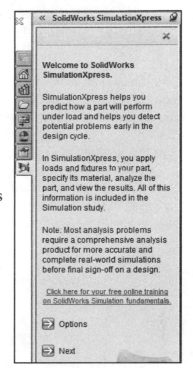

- **Welcome**: Informs the user about SolidWorks SimulationXpress. Provides the ability to set units and a save in folder location for the results.

- **Fixtures**: Provides the ability to apply restraints or fixtures to selected entities of the part. This keeps the part from moving when loads are applied. Faces with fixtures are treated as perfectly rigid. This may cause unrealistic results when the fixture is in the vicinity of: *Fixed Holes*, *Fixed vs. Supported* and *Fixed vs. Attached Parts*.

- **Loads**: Provides the ability to apply either a *force* or *pressure* to the selected entity of the part. Loads are assumed to be uniform and constant when using SimulationXpress.

- **Material**: Provides the ability to assign material to the part. SimulationXpress requires that part's material to predict how it will respond to loads. SimulationXpress assumes that the material deforms in a linear fashion with increasing load.

- **Run**: Provides the ability to run the simulation and to mesh the study. The results are based on the specified study criterion.

- **Result**: Examine the animation of the part's response to verify that the correct loads and fixtures were applied. The Results folder in the SimulationXpress Study displays the following:

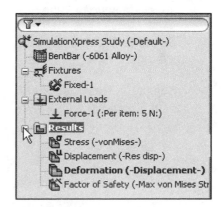

  - Stress (-vonMises-)

  - Displacment (-Res disp-)

  - Deformation (-Displacement-)

  - Factor of Safety (-Max von Mises Stress-)

- *Optimize*: Optimizes a model dimension based on a specified criterion. This is an optional step.

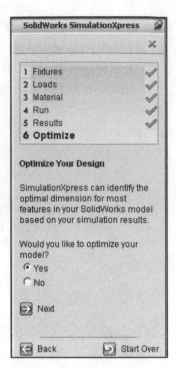

The book is design to expose the new user to many tools, techniques and procedures. It may not always use the most direct tool or process.

Run the SimulationXpress wizard: Analyzes the Bent Bar part.

Note: Use the model from the SimulationXpress folder located on the DVD in the book.

Activity: SolidWorks SimulationXpress - Analyze the BentBar Part

Start a SolidWorks SimulationXpress session.

1) Open the **BentBar** part from the SW-TUTORIAL-2013/SimulationXpress folder.

2) Click **SimulationXpress Analysis Wizard** from the Evaluate tab. The Welcome box is displayed.

3) Click the **Options** button to select the system units and to specify a save in folder.

4) Select **SI (MMGS)** for unit system.

5) Select the **Results location** - your file folder.

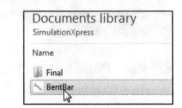

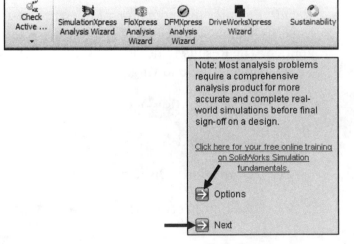

6) Click **OK** from the SimulationXpress Options dialog box.

Add a Fixture. Fix the part to apply a load.

7) Click **Next**. Apply fixtures to keep the part from moving.

8) Click **Add a fixture**. The Fixture PropertyManager is displayed.

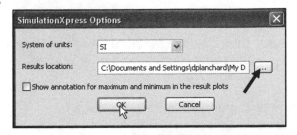

☀ You can specify multiple sets of fixtures (restraints) for a part. Each set of fixtures can have multiple faces.

9) Fix the Faces. Select the **two illustrated end faces** of the Bent Bar as illustrated. Face1 and Face2 are displayed.

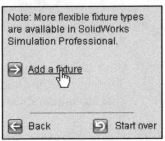

10) Click **OK** ✔ from the Fixture PropertyManager. Fixed-1 is displayed in the Study tree.

Add a uniform/constant load (force) to the part. SolidWorks SimulationXpress assumes that all loads are applied slowly. Conditions such as shock loading, vibration and fatigue require SolidWorks Simulation. SolidWorks Simulation is an Add-In.

11) Click **Next**.

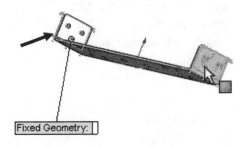

12) Click **Add a force**. The Force PropertyManager is displayed.

13) Click **SI** for units.

14) Click the **top flat face** of the Bent Bar as illustrated. Note: The edges of the Bent Bar are fixed. The direction of the applied force is displayed. The direction is downward and is normal to the selected face.

15) Enter **5**N for Force Value.

16) Click **OK** ✔ from the Force PropertyManager. Force-1 is displayed in the Study tree. View your options to edit, go back, etc.

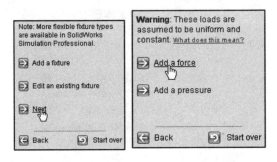

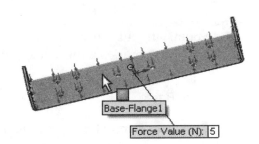

Apply material to the part.
17) Click **Next**.

18) Click **Choose Material**. View the Material dialog box. This is the same information available when adding material to a part in SolidWorks.

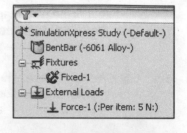

19) **Expand** the Aluminum Alloys folder.

20) Select **6061 Alloy**. View the available material information.

21) Click **Apply**.

22) Click **Close**. A green check mark is displayed in the Study tree. This indicates that material is applied.

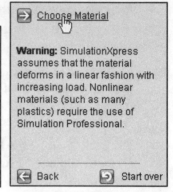

☀ Brittle materials do not have a specific yield point and hence it is not recommended to use the yield strength to define the limit stress for the criterion.

☀ You can apply multiple pressures to a single face or to multiple faces. SimulationXpress applies pressure loads normal to each face.

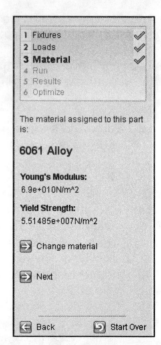

Run the analysis.
23) Click **Next**. View your options.

24) Click **Change settings**. This option provides the ability to modify the element size and element tolerance during the mesh period to analyze the part. The smaller the element size and element tolerance, the longer it will take to calculate. Accept the default conditions.

☀ Specifying a smaller mesh element size provides a more accurate result.

25) Click **Back**.

26) Click **Run Simulation**. View the animation in the Graphics window and the SimulationXpress Study tree. The Results folder displays: *Stress, Displacement, Deformation,* and *Factor of Safety*.

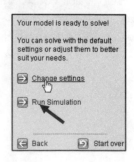

27) Click **Stop animation**.

28) **Double-click each folder** (Stress, Displacement, Deformation, and Factor of Safety) in the Results section of the Study tree to view the graph. Explore your options. End viewing the Factor of Safety graph.

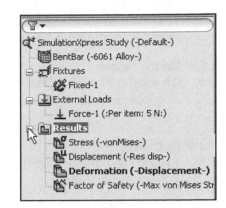

29) Click the **Yes, continue** button. The result is displayed. The Factor of safety for the specified parameters is approximately 24. What does this mean? This indicates that the current design is safe or maybe overdesigned.

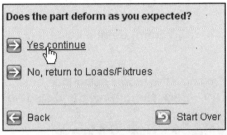

☀ The FOS plot displays in red, where the FOS is less than 1. The plot displays in blue, where the FOS is greater than one.

☀ The Factor of Safety is a ratio between the material strength and the calculated stress.

Interpretation of factor of safety values:

- A factor of safety less than 1.0 at a location indicates that the material at that location has yielded and that the design is not safe.

- A factor of safety of 1.0 at a location indicates that the material at that location has just started to yield.

- A factor of safety greater than 1.0 at a location indicates that the material at that location has not yielded.

- The material at a location will start to yield if you apply new loads equal to the current loads multiplied by the resulting factor of safety.

View the area of the model with a FOS of 3 or below.
30) Enter **3**.

31) Click the **Show where factor of safety (FOS) is below**. View the results. Note: The color red indicates areas below 3.

32) Click **Done Viewing results**.

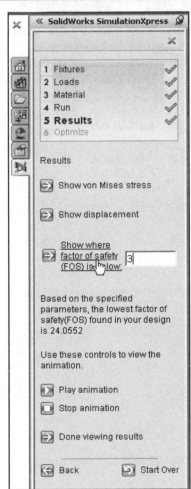

33) There are two kinds of reports that you can generate. As an exercise, generate a report. Click **Next**.

Optimize the model.
34) Check the **Yes** box. Click **Next**. The Add Parameters dialog box and Optimization table is displayed.

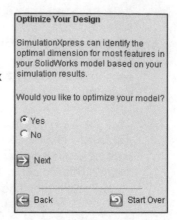

Select a Dimension.
35) **Rotate** the part and click the Sheet metal part thickness of **2.5mm** as illustrated.

36) Click **OK** from the Add Parameters dialog. View the updated Optimization table. Accept the Min (1.25mm) and Max (3.75mm) default values.

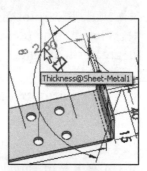

Optimize the model using the Factor of Safety.
37) Click **Next**. View the dialog box.

38) Click **Next**. Set the Constraint in the next step.

39) Click **Specify the constraint**.

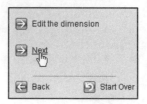

40) Select **Factor of Safety** from the Constraints drop-down menu as illustrated.

41) Accept the default: Is greater than. Enter **6** in the for Min of Factor of Safety box.

42) Click **Next**.

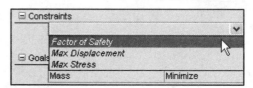

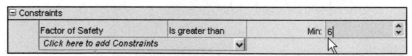

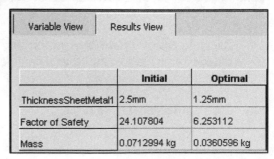

	Initial	Optimal
ThicknessSheetMetal1	2.5mm	1.25mm
Factor of Safety	24.107804	6.253112
Mass	0.0712994 kg	0.0360596 kg

43) Click **Run the optimization** button. Note: This may take 2- 3 minutes. View the results. Results may vary depending on system setup and mesh type. To optimal the value of 1.25mm, the Factor of Safety would be approximately 6. You have the option to select the Initial Value, or to select the Optimal Value.

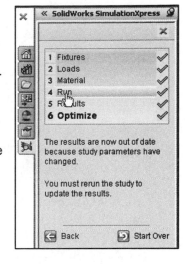

44) Check the **Optimal Value** box.

45) Click **Next**. The results are now out of date because study parameters have changed. You must rerun the study to update the plot results.

46) Click **Run** in the Wizard window.

Re-run the Simulation.
47) Click **Run Simulation**.

The SolidWorks SimulationXpress Wizard window is updated. Generate a Report as an exercise.

48) Click **Generate report**.

49) View your options. **Fill out** the needed fields.

50) **Close** the report.

51) **Save** the part.

52) Click **Sheet-Metal1** in the FeatureManager. View the new updated thickness.

53) **Close** the model.

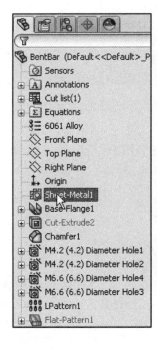

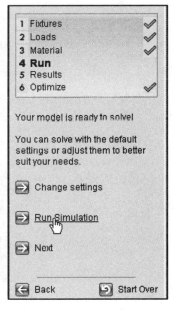

Use the Study Optimization table to select Variables, Constraints and Goals when performing the Optimize procedure in SimuationXpress.

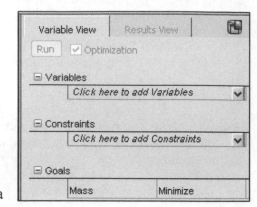

 Here are a few tips in performing the analysis. Remember you are dealing with thousands or millions of equations. These tips are a starting point. Every analysis situation is unique.

- Utilize symmetry. If a part is symmetric about a plane, utilize one half of the model for analysis. If a part is symmetric about two planes, utilize one fourth of the model for analysis.

- Suppress small fillets and detailed features in the part.

- Avoid parts that have aspect ratios over 100.

- Utilize consistent units.

- Estimate an intuitive solution based on the fundamentals of stress analysis techniques.

- Factor of Safety is a guideline for the designer. The designer is responsible for the safety of the part.

Additional information on SolidWorks SimulationXpress is located in SolidWorks Help. Additional analysis tools for static, dynamic, thermal and fluid analysis are also available in SolidWorks.

Review of SolidWorks SimulationXpress

SolidWorks SimulationXpress is a Finite Element tool that calculates stress, displacement and FOS based on Fixtures, Loads, and material on a part. You utilized SolidWorks SimulationXpress to analysis the stress, displacement and FOS on a part.

You assigned the Material to be Aluminum, added fixtures and applied a force of 5Ns. Based on the inputs, the results provided visual representation of displacement and von Mises stress. See SolidWorks Help for additional information.

SolidWorks Sustainability

Sustainable engineering is the integration of social, environmental, and economic conditions into a product or process. Soon all design will be Sustainable Design.

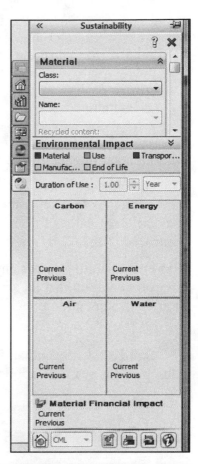

SolidWorks Sustainability allows students and designers to be environmentally conscious about their designs.

Every license of SolidWorks obtains a copy of SustainabilityXpress. SustainabilityXpress calculates environmental impact on a part in four key areas: *Carbon Footprint, Energy Consumption, Air Acidification and Water Eutrophication.*

Material and Manufacturing process region and Transportation Usage region are used as input variables. Two SolidWorks Sustainability products are available: *SolidWorks SustainabilityXpress* and *SolidWorks Sustainability.*

SolidWorks SustainabilityXpress: Handles part documents and is included in the core software.

SolidWorks Sustainability: Provides the following functions:

- Same functions as SustainabilityXpress.

- Life Cycle Assessment (LCA) of assemblies.

- Configuration support:

    o Save inputs and results per configuration.

- Expanded reporting capabilities for assemblies.

- Specify amount & type of energy consumed during use.

- Assembly - Assemble all of the finished parts to create the final product.

- Product Use - Examine the total intended lifespan of product.

- End of Life - Once the product reaches the end of its useful life, how is it disposed of:

  o Recycled

  o Incinerated

  o Landfill

- Financial Impact - View the material financial impact of a part.

You can choose either CML or TRACI as the impact assessment methodologies to display the environmental impact of your study. TRACI uses different values for air acidification and water eutrophication compared to the CML methodology used in SolidWorks Sustainability.

Run SustainabilityXpress and analyzes a part. Display the four environmental impact factors, view suitable alternative materials, compare their environmental impact factors and generate a customer report.

💡 SolidWorks Sustainability is included in the SolidWorks Educational edition and is separate application in the SolidWorks commercial edition.

Life Cycle Assessment

Life Cycle Assessment is a method to quantitatively assess the environmental impact of a product throughout its entire lifecycle, from the procurement of the raw materials, through the production, distribution, use, disposal and recycling of that product.

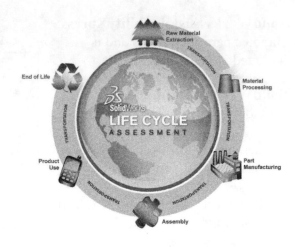

- **Raw Material Extraction:**

  o Planting, growing, and harvesting of trees

  o Mining of raw ore (example: bauxite)

  o Drilling and pumping of oil

- **Material Processing** - The processing of raw materials into engineered materials:

  o Oil into Plastic

  o Iron into Steel

  o Bauxite into Aluminum

- **Part Manufacturing** - Processing of material into finished parts:
  - ○ Injection molding
  - ○ Milling and Turning
  - ○ Casting
  - ○ Stamping
- **Assembly** - Assemble all of the finished parts to create the final product
- **Product Use** - End consumer uses product for intended lifespan of product
- **End of Life** - Once the product reaches the end of its useful life, how is it disposed of:
  - ○ Landfill
  - ○ Recycled
  - ○ Incinerated

Environmental Impact

SolidWorks Sustainability / SustainabilityXpress calculates environmental impact on a part in four key areas: *Carbon Footprint*, *Total Energy*, *Air Acidification*, and *Water Eutrophication*.

- **Carbon Footprint:** A measure of carbon-dioxide and other greenhouse gas emissions such as methane (in CO_2 equivalent units, CO_{2e}) which contributes to emissions, predominantly caused by burning fossil fuels. Global warming Potential (GWP) is also commonly referred to as a carbon footprint.

- **Energy Consumption:** A measure of the non-renewable energy sources associated with the part's lifecycle in nits of Mega Joules (MJ). This impact includes not only the electricity of fuels used during the product's lifecycle, but also the upstream energy required to obtain and process these fuels, and the embodied energy of materials which would be released if burned. Energy Consumed is expressed as the net calorific value of energy demand from non-renewable resources (petroleum, natural gas, etc.).

Efficiencies in energy conversion (power, heat, steam, etc.) are taken into account.

- **Air Acidification:** Sulfur dioxide, nitrous oxides other acidic emissions to air cause an increase in the acidity of rain water, which in turn acidifies lakes and soil. These acids can make the land and water toxic for plants and aquatic life. Acid rain can also slowly dissolve man-made building materials such as concrete. This impact is typically measured in nits of either kg sulfur dioxide equivalent SO_{2e} or moles H+ equivalent.

- **Water Eutrophication:** When an over abundance of nutrients are added to a water ecosystem, Eutrophication occurs, nitrogen and phosphorous from waste water and agricultural fertilizers causes an overabundance of algae to bloom, which then depletes the water of oxygen and results in the death of both plant and animal life. This impact is typically measured in either kg phosphate equivalent (PO_{4e}) or kg nitrogen (N) equivalent.

You can estimate the relative financial impact of your material choices based on the financial impact per unit mass associated with each material. The material financial impact is the mass of the parts in the model multiplied by the financial impact property for each part material.

The SolidWorks materials database includes default financial impact values. When you select materials from the database, the financial impact of your choices is shown in the Environmental Impact section of the Sustainability task pane.

In the Find Similar Material dialog box, you can use the financial impact value as a search category to locate materials that meet your physical and environmental requirements with a lower cost impact.

If you use custom materials, you can add the Financial Impact property to assign valuesto the financial impacts of the materials.

When a part is painted, the surface area of the part is used to determine the amount of paint and the environmental impact of painting the part.

References

It is very important to understand definitions and how SolidWorks information is obtained on the above areas for baseline calculations and comparative calculations. The following standards and agencies were used in the development cycles of this tool:

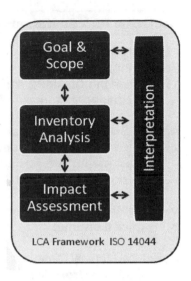

- **Underlying LCA Technology: PE International:**
  - o 20 years of LCA experience
  - o LCA international database
  - o GaBi 4 - leading software application for product sustainability
  - o www.pe-international.com
- **International LCA Standards:**
  - o Environmental Management Life Cycle Assessment Principles and Framework ISO 14040/44 www.iso.org
- **US EPA LCA Resources:**
  - o http://www.epa.gov/nrmrl/lcaccess/

SolidWorks Sustainability Methodology

The following chart was created to provide a visualization of the Methodology used in SolidWorks Sustainability. Note the Input variables and the Output areas along with the ability to create and send a customer report are based on your selected decisions.

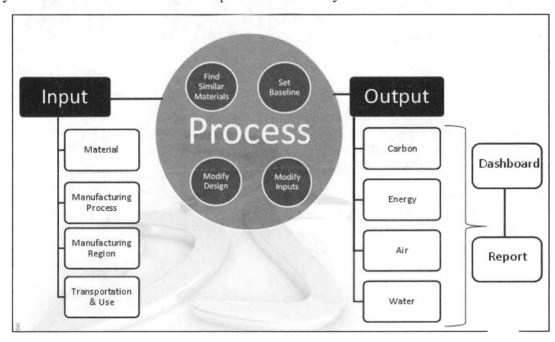

Activity: Run Sustainability/SustainabilityXpress - Analyze a simple part

Close all parts, assemblies and drawings. Run Sustainability / SustainabilityXpress. Perform a simple analysis on a part.

1) Open the **CLAMP2** part from the SW-TUTORIAL-2013/ SustainabilityXpress folder.

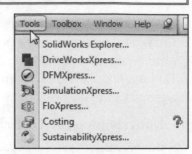

Activate SustainabilityXpress.

2) Click **Tools**, **SustainabilityXpress/Sustainability** from the Main menu. The Sustainability Wizard is displayed in the Task Pane area.

View the SolidWorks Sustainability dialog box.

3) Click **Continue**.

Select the Material Class.

4) Click the **Drop-down arrow** under Class. View your options.

5) Select **Steel** from the drop-down menu as illustrated.

Select the Material Name. Material Name is Class dependent.

6) Click the **Drop-down arrow** under Name. View your options.

7) Select **Stainless Steel (ferritic)** from the drop-down menu as illustrated.

Select the Manufacturing Region. Each region produces energy by different method combinations. Impact of a kWh is different for each region. Example methods include: Fossil Fuels, Nuclear and Hydro-electric.

8) Position the **mouse pointer** over the map. View your available options.

9) Click **Asia** as illustrated.

Select Build to last Period.

10) Select **10 years** as illustrated.

Select Manufacturing Process. Manufacturing Process is Material Name dependent.

11) Select **Milled** from the drop-down menu. View the provided information on energy and scrap rate.

Select the Use region.

12) Position the **mouse pointer** over the map. View your available options.

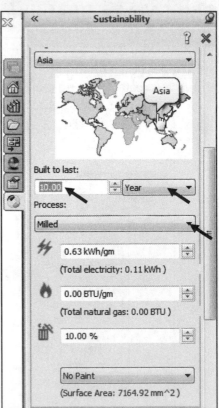

13) Click **North America**.

View the provided Transportation modes.

14) Accept the default: **Boat**. This option estimates the environmental impacts associated with transporting the product from its manufacturing location to its use location.

View the provided information on End of Life.

15) **Accept** the default.

Set Duration of Use period.

16) Select **10 years**.

Set your design Baseline. A Baseline is required to comprehend the environmental impact of the original design.

17) Click the **Set Baseline** tool from the bottom of the Environmental Impact screen. The Environmental Impact of this part is displayed. The Environmental Impact is calculated in four key areas: *Carbon Footprint, Energy Consumption, Air Acidification* and *Water Eutrophication*.

18) Position the **mouse pointer** over the Carbon box. View Factor percentage. 75.05% represents the Material percentage of the total Carbon footprint of the part (0.871kg).

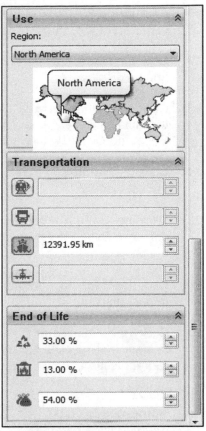

75.05% represents the Material percentage of the Energy footprint of the part.

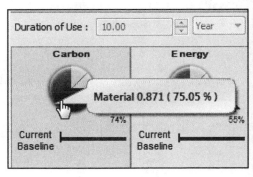

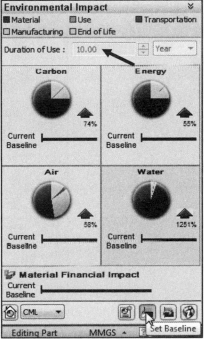

19) Click inside the **Carbon** box to display a Baseline bar chart of the Carbon Footprint. View the results.

20) Click the **Home** icon to return to the Environmental Impact display.

21) Click inside the **Energy** Consumption impact screen to display a Baseline bar chart of Energy Consumption. View the results.

22) Click the **Home** icon to return to the Environmental Impact display.

23) Click inside the **Air** Consumption impact screen to display a Baseline bar chart of Air Acidification. View the results.

24) Click the **Home** icon to return to the Environmental Impact display.

25) Click inside the **Water** Consumption impact screen to display a Baseline bar chart of Water Eutrophication. View the results.

26) Click the **Home** icon to return to the Environmental Impact display.

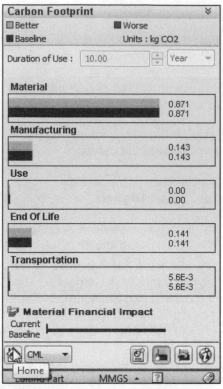

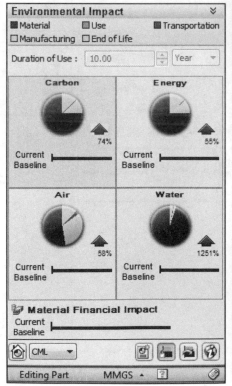

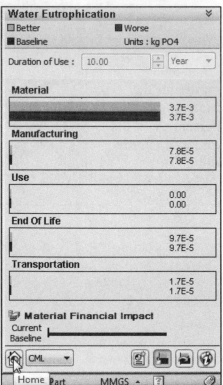

In the next section, compare the baseline design to a different Material Class, Name and Manufacturing Process. Let's compare the present material Stainless Steel (ferritic) to Nylon 6/10.

Select a new Material Class.

27) Click the **Drop-down arrow** under Class. View your options.

28) Select **Plastics** from the drop-down menu.

Select a new Material Name.

29) Click the **Drop-down arrow** under Name. View your options.

30) Select **Nylon 6/10** from the drop-down menu.

Select a new Manufacturing Process.

31) Select **Injection Molded** from the drop-down menu. Note: the energy and scrap changes. Asia is selected for Manufacturing Region and North America is selected for Use region.

View the results.

32) Changing the material from **Stainless Steel (ferritic)** to **Nylon 6/10** and the manufacturing process from Milled to Injection Molded had a positive impact in all categories, but a further material change may provide a better result.

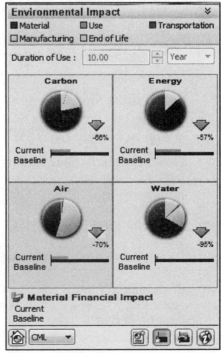

Find a similar material and compare the Environmental Impact to
Nylon 6/10. This function is a real time saver.

33) Click the **Find Similar** button as illustrated. The Find Similar
Material dialog box is displayed.

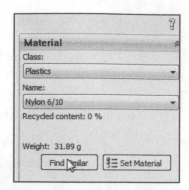

34) Click the **Value (-any-)** drop-down arrow. View your options.

35) Select **Plastics**. You can perform a general search or
customize your search on physical properties of the material.

Select a Similar Material from the provided list. You can find
similar materials based on the following Properties: *Material
Class, Thermal Expansion Coefficient, Specific Heat, Density,
Elastic Modulus, Shear Modulus, Thermal Conductivity,
Poissons Ratio, Tensile Strength and Yield Strength*. The
definitions are listed at the end of the chapter.

SolidWorks Simulation provides the ability to search on
various materials properties. Select either Greater than, Less
than or approximately from the drop-down menu.

36) Click the **Find Similar** button as illustrated. SolidWorks
provides a full list of comparable materials that you can
further refine.

37) Check the **ABS** material box.

38) Check the **Nylon 101** material box.

39) Click **inside the top left box (Show All)** as
illustrated. The selected materials are displayed with
their properties.

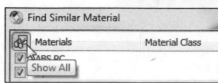

View the Environment Impact for the alternative materials.

40) Click the **ABS PC** material row as illustrated. View the results. The material is lower in Carbon Footprint, Energy Consumption, Air Acidification and Water Eutrophication than Nylon 6/10.

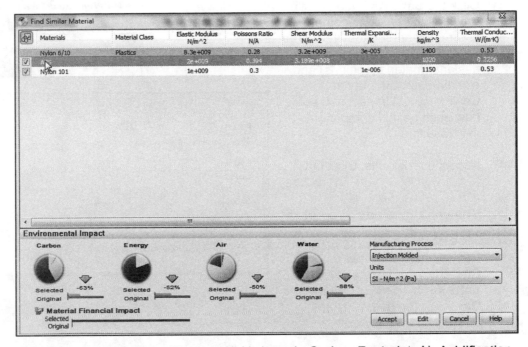

41) Click the **Nylon 101** material row. The material is lower in Carbon Footprint, Air Acidification and Water Eutrophication but higher in Energy Consumption than Nylon 6/10. You decide to stay with Nylon 6/10 due to cost and other design issues.

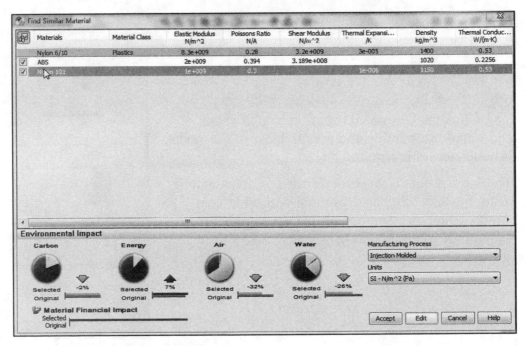

42) Click the **Cancel** button from the Find Similar Material dialog box.

Run a Report.

43) Click the **Save As** button as illustrated. SolidWorks provides the ability to communicate this report information throughout your organization. Sustainability generates a report that will compare designs (material, regions) and explain each category of Environmental Impact and show how each design compares to the Base line.

44) Accept the defaults. Click **OK**.

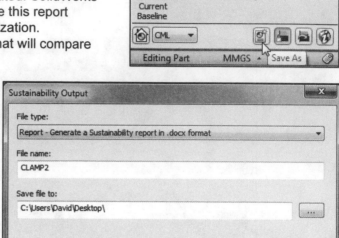

You can't generate a report if Microsoft Word is running.

45) Review the Generated report. **Ctrl -Click here for alternative units such as Miles Driven In a Car.** View the results. Note: Internet access is required

Click here for alternative units such as Miles Driven In A Car

46) **View the Glossary** in the report section and the other hyperlinks for additional information.

Close the Report and Part.
47) **Close** the report.

48) **Close** the part.

Click the Online information icon to obtain additional information and comparisons of the model. Internet access is required.

The same process can be performed on an assembly using Sustainability as illustrated with additional inputs. Click on a component in an assembly to display the Material dialog box.

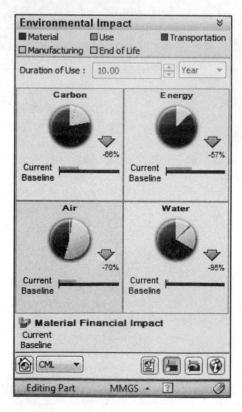

SolidWorks DFMXpress

DFMXpress is an analysis tool that validates the manufacturability of SolidWorks parts. Use DFMXpress to identify design areas that may cause problems in fabrication or increase the costs of production.

The DFMXpress tool uses a Wizard. Run the DFMXpress Wizard. Analyze a simple part. View the results.

Activity: SolidWorks DFMXpress - Analyze the AXLE and ROD Part

Close all documents.
1)   Click **Window**, **Close All** from the Menu bar.

Open the AXLE part.
2)   Open the **AXLE** part from the SW-TUTORIAL-2013/DFMXpress folder. The AXLE FeatureManager is displayed. Note: The folder is located on the DVD in the book. Copy all models to your local hard drive.

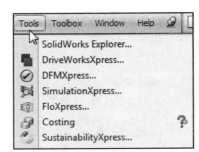

Activate DFMXpress.
3)   Click **Tools**, **DFMXpress**. View the DFMXpress wizard in the Task Pane location.

4)   Click the **Settings** button.

5)   **View** the optional settings in DFMXpress.

6)   Click the **Back** button to return to the Main menu.

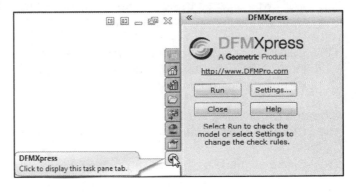

Run the DFMXpress wizard on the AXLE part.
7)   Click the **Run** button.

8)   **Expand** each folder. View the results.

9)   Click on each **red check mark**. The hole in the AXLE was created with an Extruded Cut feature (failed due to flat bottom). Use the Hole Wizard to create holes for Manufacturing. Use caution for depth to diameter ratio.

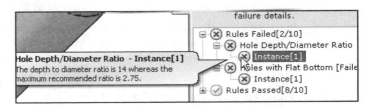

10) Click on each **green check mark**. Review the information. This is a very useful tool to use for manufacturing guidelines.

Close the DFMXpress Wizard.

11) Click the **Close** button.

Open the ROD part.

12) Open the **ROD** part from the SW-TUTORIAL-2013/DFMXpress folder. The ROD FeatureManager is displayed. Note: The folder is located on the DVD in the book. Copy all models to your local hard drive.

Activate DFMXpress.

13) Click **Tools**, **DFMXpress**. View the DFMXpress wizard in the Task Pane location.

Run the DFMXpress wizard on the ROD part.

14) Click the **Run** button.

15) **Expand** each folder. View the results.

16) Click on each **red check mark**. The hole in the ROD was created using the Hole Wizard feature. Use caution for depth to diameter ratio.

17) Click on each **green check mark**. Review the information. This is a very useful tool to use for manufacturing guidelines.

Close the DFMXpress Wizard.

18) Click the **Close** button.

19) **Close** all models.

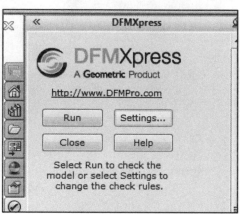

Review the DFMXpress Wizard

DFMXpress is an analysis tool that validates the manufacturability of SolidWorks parts. Use DFMXpress to identify design areas that may cause problems in fabrication or increase the costs of production.

The DFMXpress tool uses a Wizard. Run the DFMXpress Wizard. Analyze a simple part. View the results.

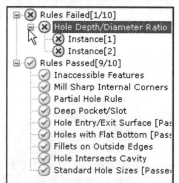

Project Summary

You performed a SolidWorks SimulationXpress analysis on a part with a Force load. You applied material, set loads and fixtures. Run the optimization tool as an exercise.

You then applied SolidWorks SustainabilityXpress to a part. Every license of SolidWorks obtains a copy of SolidWorks SustainabilityXpress. SustainabilityXpress calculates environmental impact on a model in four key areas: *Carbon Footprint, Energy Consumption, Air Acidification and Water Eutrophication.*

Material and Manufacturing process region and Transportation Usage region are used as input variables.

You applied material, manufacturing process and selected the manufacturing process region and the part transportation and usage region. You then viewed the environmental impact of your design.

You viewed suitable alternative materials, re-ran the environmental impact study and compared their environmental impact factors in all four categories. A customer report was generated.

You used DFMXpress to identify design areas that may cause problems in fabrication or increase the costs of production. The DFMXpress tool uses a Wizard.

Notes:

Chapter 7

Intelligent Modeling Techniques

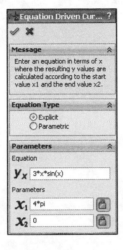

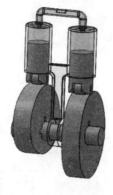

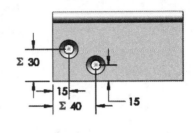

Below are the desired outcomes and usage competencies based on the completion of Chapter 7.

Project Desired Outcomes:	Usage Competencies:
• Utilize and understand various Design Intent tools and Intelligent Modeling Techniques.	• Apply Design Intent and Intelligent Modeling Techniques in a Sketch, Feature, Part, Plane, Assembly and Drawing.
• Awareness of the Equation Driven Sketch Curve tool.	• Create Explicit Dimension Driven and Parametric Equation Driven Curves. • Generate curves using the Curve Through XYZ Points tool for a NACA aerofoil and CAM data text file.
• Knowledge of the SolidWorks Xpert tools.	• Apply SketchXpert, DimXpert and FeatureXpert.

Notes:

Chapter 7 - Intelligent Modeling Techniques

Chapter Objective

Understand some of the available tools in SolidWorks to perform intelligent modeling. Intelligent modeling is incorporating design intent into the definition of the sketch, feature, part, and assembly or drawing document. Intelligent modeling is most commonly addressed through design intent using a:

- Sketch:
    - Geometric relations
    - Fully defined Sketch tool
    - SketchXpert
    - Equations:
        - Explicit Dimension Driven
        - Parametric Driven Curve
    - Curves:
        - Curve Through XYZ Points:
        - Projected Composite
- Feature:
    - End Conditions:
        - Blind, Through All, Up to Next, Up to Vertex, Up to Surface, Offset from Surface, Up to Body and Mid Plane
    - Along a Vector
    - FeatureXpert (Constant Radius)
    - Symmetry:
        - Mirror
- Plane
- Assembly:
    - Symmetry (Mirror / Pattern)
    - Assembly Visualization
    - SolidWorks Sustainability
    - MateXpert
- Drawing:
    - DimXpert (Slots, Pockets, Machined features, etc.)

This chapter uses short step-by-step tutorials to practice and reinforce the subject matter and objectives. Learn by doing, not just by reading! All needed models for this chapter are located on the DVD in the book.

Design Intent

What is design intent? All designs are created for a purpose. Design intent is the intellectual arrangement of features and dimensions of a design. Design intent governs the relationship between sketches in a feature, features in a part and parts in an assembly or drawing document.

The SolidWorks definition of design intent is the process in which the model is developed to accept future modifications. Models behave differently when design changes occur.

Design for change! Utilize geometry for symmetry, reuse common features, and reuse common parts. Build change into the following areas that you create: sketch, feature, part, assembly and drawing.

Design Intent is how your part reacts as parameters are modified. Example: If you have a hole in a part that must always be .125≤ from an edge, you would dimension to the edge rather than to another point on the sketch. As the part size is modified, the hole location remains .125≤ from the edge.

Sketch

In SolidWorks, relations between sketch entities and model geometry, in either 2D or 3D sketches, are an important means of building in design intent. In this chapter - we will only address 2D sketches.

Apply design intent in a sketch as the profile is created. A profile is determined from the Sketch Entities. Example: Rectangle, Circle, Arc, Point, Slot etc.

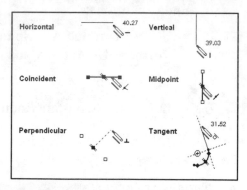

Develop design intent as you sketch with Geometric relations. Sketch relations are geometric constraints between sketch entities or between a sketch entity and a plane, axis, edge, or vertex. Relations can be added automatically or manually.

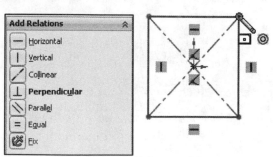

As you sketch, allow SolidWorks to automatically add relations. Automatic relations rely on:

- Inferencing
- Pointer display
- Sketch snaps and Quick Snaps

After you sketch, manually add relations using the Add Relations tool, or edit existing relations using the Display/Delete Relations tool.

Fully Defined Sketch

Sketches are generally in one of the following states:

- Under defined
- Fully defined
- Over defined

Although you can create features using sketches that are not fully defined, it is a good idea to always fully define sketches for production models. Sketches are parametric, and if they are fully defined, changes are predictable. However, sketches in drawings, although they follow the same conventions as sketches in parts, do not need to be fully defined since they are not the basis of features.

SolidWorks provides a tool to help the user fully define a sketch. The Fully Defined Sketch tool provides the ability to calculate which dimensions and relations are required to fully define under defined sketches or selected sketch entities. You can access the Fully Define Sketch tool at any point and with any combination of dimensions and relations already added. See Chapter 5 for additional information.

Your sketch should include some dimensions and relations before you use the Fully Define Sketch tool.

The Fully Defined Sketch tool uses the Fully Define Sketch PropertyManager. The Fully Define Sketch PropertyManager provides the following selections:

- *Entities to Fully Define*. The Entities to Filly Define box provides the following options:

  - **All entities in sketch**. Fully defines the sketch by applying combinations of relations and dimensions.

  - **Selected entities**. Provides the ability to select sketch entities.

    - **Entities to Fully Define**. Only available when the Selected entities box is checked. Applies relations and dimensions to the specified sketch entities.

  - **Calculate**. Analyzes the sketch and generates the appropriate relations and dimensions.

- *Relations*. The Relations box provide the following selections:

  - **Select All**. Includes all relations in the results.

  - **Deselect All**. Omits all relations in the results.

  - **Individual relations**. Include or exclude needed relations. The available relations are: **Horizontal, Vertical, Collinear, Perpendicular, Parallel, Midpoint, Coincident, Tangent, Concentric** and **Equal radius/Length**.

- *Dimensions*. The Dimensions box provides the following selections:

  - **Horizontal Dimensions**. Displays the selected Horizontal Dimensions Scheme and the entity used as the Datum - Vertical Model Edge, Model Vertex, Vertical Line or Point for the dimensions. The available options are: **Baseline, Chain** and **Ordinate**.

  - **Vertical Dimensions.** Displays the selected Vertical Dimensions Scheme and the entity used as the Datum - Horizontal Model Edge, Model Vertex, Horizontal Line or Point for the dimensions. The available options are: **Baseline, Chain** and **Ordinate**.

  - **Dimension**. Below sketch and Left of sketch is selected by default. Locates the dimension. There are four selections: **Above sketch, Below the sketch, Right of sketch** and **Left of sketch**.

Activity: Fully Defined Sketch

Close all parts, assemblies and drawings. Apply the Fully Defined Sketch tool. Modify the dimension reference location in the sketch profile with control points.

1)   Open **Fully Defined Sketch 7-1** from the SW-TUTORIAL-2013/Chapter 7 Intelligent Modeling folder. View the FeatureManager. Sketch1 is under defined.

2)   **Edit** ✎ Sketch1. The two circles are equal and symmetrical about the y axis. The rectangle is centered at the origin.

3)   Click the **Fully Define Sketch** ✎ tool from the Consolidated Display/Delete Relations drop-down menu. The Fully Defined Sketch PropertyManager is displayed.

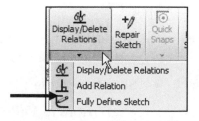

4)   The All entities in the sketch are selected by default. Click **Calculate**. View the results. Sketch1 is fully defined to the origin.

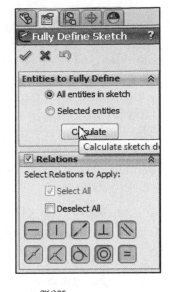

5) Click **OK** ✔ from the PropertyManager. Drag all dimensions off the profile.

6) Modify the **vertical dimension to 50mms** and the **diameter dimension to 25mms** as illustrated. SolidWorks suggests a dimension scheme to create a fully defined sketch.

7) Click **View**; uncheck **Sketch Relations** from the Main menu.

Modify the dimension reference location in the sketch profile with control points.

8) Click the **90**mm dimension in the Graphic window.

9) Click and drag the **left control point** as illustrated.

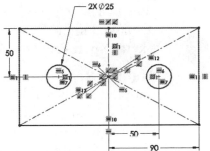

10) Release the mouse pointer on the **left vertical line** of the profile. View the new dimension reference location of the profile.

11) Repeat the same procedure for the horizontal **50mm** dimension. Select the new reference location to the left hole diameter as illustrated.

12) **Close** the model. View the results.

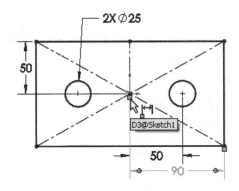

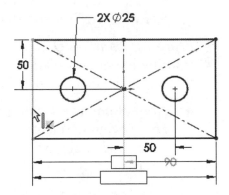

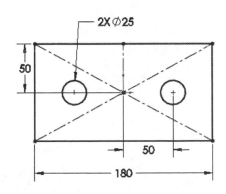

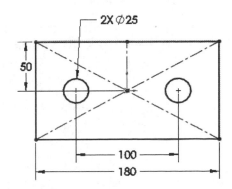

SketchXpert

SketchXpert resolves conflicts in over defined sketches and proposes possible solution sets. Color codes are displayed in the SolidWorks Graphics window to represent the sketch states. The SketchXpert tool uses the SketchXpert PropertyManager. The SketchXpert PropertyManager provides the following selections:

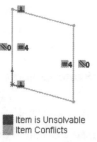

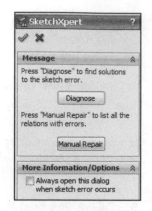

- *Message*. The Message box provides access to the following selections:

  - **Diagnose**. The Diagnose button generates a list of solutions for the sketch. The generated solutions are displayed in the Results section of the SketchXpert PropertyManager.

  - **Manual Repair**. The Manual Repair button generates a list of all relations and dimensions in the sketch. The Manual Repair information is displayed in the Conflicting Relations/Dimensions section of the SketchXpert PropertyManager.

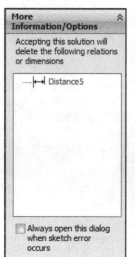

- *More Information/Options*. Provides information on the relations or dimensions that would be deleted to solve the sketch.

  - **Always open this dialog when sketch error occurs**. Selected by default. Opens the dialog box when a sketch error is detected.

- *Results*. The Results box provides the following selections:

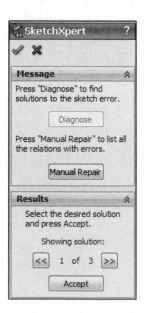

  - **Left or Right arrows**. Provides the ability to cycle through the solutions. As you select a solution, the solution is highlighted in the Graphics window.

  - **Accept**. Applies the selected solution. Your sketch is no longer over-defined.

- *More Information/Options*. The More Information/Options box provides the following selections:

  - **Diagnose**. The Diagnose box displays a list of the valid generated solutions.

  - **Always open this dialog when sketch error occurs**. Selected by default. Opens the dialog box when a sketch error is detected.

- *Conflicting Relations/Dimensions*. The Conflicting Relations/Dimensions box provides the ability to select a displayed conflicting relation or dimension. The select item is highlight in the Graphics window. The options include:

  - **Suppressed**. Suppresses the relation or dimension.

  - **Delete**. Removes the selected relation or dimension.

  - **Delete All**. Removes all relations and dimensions.

  - **Always open this dialog when sketch error occurs**. Selected by default. Opens the dialog box when a sketch error is detected.

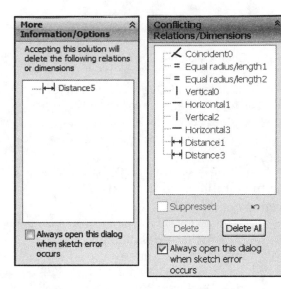

Activity: SketchXpert

Close all parts, assemblies and drawings. Create an over defined sketch. Apply SketchXpert to select a solution.

1) Open **SketchXpert 7-1** from the SW-TUTORIAL-2013/ Chapter 7 Intelligent Modeling folder. View the FeatureManager. Sketch1 is under defined.

2) Edit 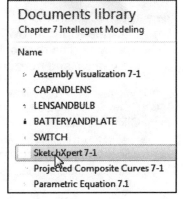 Sketch1. The two circles are equal and symmetrical about the y axis. The rectangle is centered at the origin. Insert a dimension to create an over defined sketch.

3) Click **Smart Dimension** .

4) Add a dimension to the **left vertical line**. This makes the sketch over-defined. The Make Dimension Driven dialog box is displayed.

5)   Check the **Leave this dimension driving** box option.

6)   Click **OK**. The Over Defined warning is displayed.

7)   Click the **red Over Defined** message. The SketchXpert PropertyManager is displayed.

Color codes are displayed in the Graphics window to represent the sketch states.

8)   Click the **Diagnose** button. The Diagnose button generates a list of solutions for your sketch. You can either accept the first solution or click the Right arrow key in the Results box to view the section solution. The first solution is to delete the vertical dimension of 105mm.

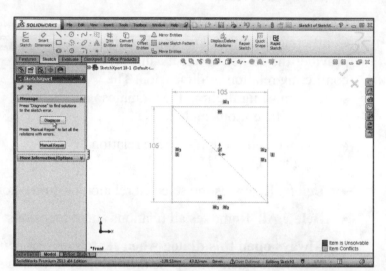

View the Second solution.
9)   Click the **Right arrow** key in the Results box. The second solution is displayed. The second solution is to delete the horizontal dimension of 105mm.

View the Third solution.
10)   Click the **Right arrow** key in the Results box. The third solution is displayed. The third solution is to delete the Equal relation between the vertical and horizontal lines.

Accept the Second solution.
11)   Click the **Left arrow** key to obtain the second solution.

12)   Click the **Accept** button. The SketchXpert tool resolves the over-defined issue. A message is displayed.

13)   Click **OK** ✅ from the SketchXpert PropertyManager.

14)   **Rebuild** 🔘 the model. View the results.

15)   **Close** the model.

Equations

Dimension driven by equations

You want to design a hinge assembly that you can modify easily to make similar assemblies. You need an efficient way to create two matching hinge pieces and a pin for a variety of hinge assembly sizes.

Some analysis and planning can help you develop a design that is flexible, efficient, and well defined. You can then adjust the size as needed, and the hinge assembly still satisfies the design intent.

In the following example, one hole is fixed, one is driven by an equation (Equations create a mathematical relations between dimensions), and the other two are mirrored. As the size of the hinge changes, the holes remain properly spaced along the length and width of the model.

If you modify the height or length hinge dimension, the screw holes maintain the mathematical relation design intent.

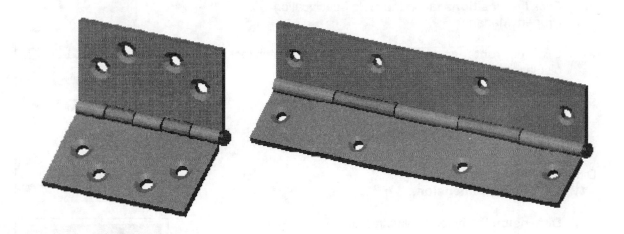

You can add comments to equations to document your design intent. Place a single quote (') at the end of the equation, then enter the comment. Anything after the single quote is ignored when the equation is evaluated. Example: "D2@Sketch1" = "D1@Sketch1" / 2 ' height is 1/2 width. You can also use comment syntax to prevent an equation from being evaluated. Place a single quote (') at the beginning of the equation. The equation is then interpreted as a comment, and it is ignored. See SolidWorks Help for additional information.

Activity: Equation

Close all parts, assemblies and drawings. Create two driven equations. Insert two Countersink holes. To position each hole on the hinge, one dimension is fixed, and the other is driven by an equation.

1)   Open the **Hinge 7-1** part from the SW-TUTORIAL-2013/ Chapter 7 Intelligent Modeling folder.

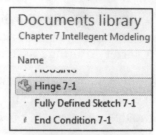

Add Screw holes using the Hole Wizard.

2)   Click **Hole Wizard** from the Features toolbar. The Hole Specification PropertyManager is displayed.

3)   Click **Countersink** for Hole Type as illustrated.

4)   Select **Ansi Metric** for Standard. Accept the default Type.

5)   Select **M8** for Size from the drop-down menu.

6)   Select **Through All** for End Condition.

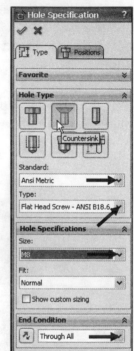

Place the location of the holes.

7)   Click the **Positions** tab in the Hole Specification PropertyManager.

8)   Click the **front face** of the model. The Point Sketch tool is displayed.

9)   Click to **place the holes** approximately as shown.

10) **De-select** the Point Sketch tool.

Dimension the holes.

11) Click **Smart Dimension**.

12) **Dimension** the holes as illustrated.

13) Click **OK** from the Hole Position PropertyManager.

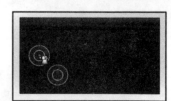

14) Click **OK** from the Hole Specification PropertyManager. View the new feature in the FeatureManager.

Add equations to control the locations of the screw Countersink holes. First; add an equation to control the location of one of the points. Create an equation that sets the distance between the point and the bottom edge to one-half the height of the hinge.

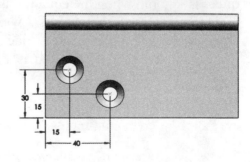

15) Right-click **Sketch5**. Click **Edit Sketch**.

16) Double-click **Extruded-Thin1** from the FeatureManager. Dimensions are displayed in the Graphics window.

17) Click **Tools**, **Equations** from the Menu bar. The Equations, Global Variables, and Dimensions dialog box is displayed.

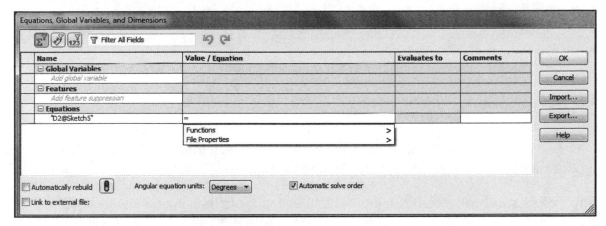

18) Click inside the **first empty** cell under Equations.

19) Click the **30mm** dimension in the Graphics window. An = sign is displayed in the Value / Equation cell.

20) Click the **60mm** dimension in the Graphics window.

21) Enter **/2** in the dialog box to complete the dimension.

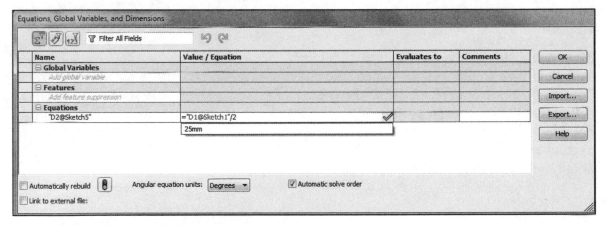

22) Press the **Tab** key. This equation sets the distance between the point and the bottom edge to one-half the height of the hinge.

Create the second equation. Add an equation to control the location of the other point.

23) Click inside the **first empty** cell under Equations.

24) Click the **40mm** dimension from the Graphics window. An = sign is displayed in the Value / Equation cell.

25) Click the **120mm** dimension for the base.

26) Enter **/3** in the dialog box to complete the dimension.

27) Press the **Tab** key. View the active equations. This sets the distance between the point and the side edge to one-third the length of the hinge.

⊟ **Equations**		
"D1@Sketch5"	= "D1@Sketch1" / 2	30mm
"D3@Sketch5"	= "D1@Extrude-Thin1" / 3	40mm
Add equation		

28) Click **OK** from the Equations dialog box. View the equations in the Graphics window.

29) **Exit** the Sketch. **Close** the model.

💡 For additional information, view the below link. The initial and final model and a .ppt presentation are enclosed on the DVD in the Equation folder.

http://blogs.solidworks.com/teacher/2012/11/equations-help-using-solidworks.html

Equation Driven Curve

SolidWorks provides the ability to address Explicit and Parametric equation types.

Explicit Equation Driven Curve

Explicit provides the ability to define x values for the start and endpoints of the range. Y values are calculated along the range of x values.

Mathematical equation can be inserted into a sketch. Utilize parenthesis to manage the order of operations. For example, calculate the volume of a solid bounded by a curve as illustrated. The region bounded by the equation y = 2+xcosx, and the x-axis, over the interval x = -2 to x = 2, is revolved about the x-axis to generate a solid.

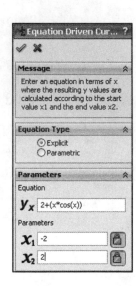

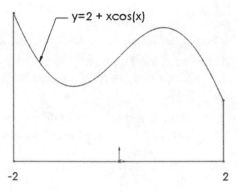

$y = 2 + x\cos(x)$

-2   2

Activity: Explicit Equation Driven Curve

Create an Explicit Equation Driven Curve on the Front plane. Revolve the curve. Add material. Calculate the volume of the solid.

1) Create a **New** ☐ part. Use the default ANSI, IPS Part template.

Create a 2D Sketch on the Front Plane.

2) Right-click **Sketch** from the Front Plane in the FeatureManager. The Sketch toolbar is displayed. Front Plane is your Sketch plane.

3) Click the **Equation Driven Curve Sketch** ⁿ𝟤 tool from the Consolidated drop-down menu. The Equation Driven Curve PropertyManager is displayed.

4) Enter the **Equation y_x** as illustrated.

5) Enter the **parameters x_1, x_2** that defines the lower and upper bound of the equation as illustrated.

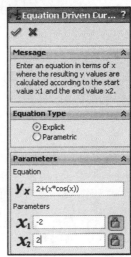

6) Click **OK** ✔ from the Equation Driven Curve Sketch PropertyManager. View the curve in the Graphics window. Size the curve in the Graphics window. The Sketch is under defined.

7) Insert **three lines to close** the profile as illustrated.

8) Insert the **required dimensions** and any needed geometric relations to fully define the sketch.

Create a Revolved feature.

9) Click the **horizontal line**.

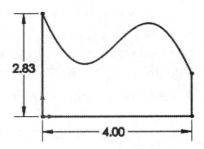

10) Click the **Revolved Boss/Base** ⊕ tool from the Feature toolbar. 360 degrees is the default.

11) Click **OK** ✔ from the PropertyManager. View the results in the Graphics window. Revolve1 is displayed. Utilize the Section tool, parallel with the Right plane to view how each cross section is a circle.

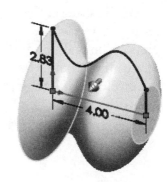

12) Apply **Brass** for material.

13) Calculate the **volume** of the part using the Mass Properties tool. View the results. Also note the surface area and the Center of mass.

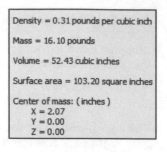

Density = 0.31 pounds per cubic inch

Mass = 16.10 pounds

Volume = 52.43 cubic inches

Surface area = 103.20 square inches

Center of mass: (inches)
  X = 2.07
  Y = 0.00
  Z = 0.00

14) **Save** the model.

15) Name the model **Explicit Equation Driven Curve 7-1**.

16) **Close** the model.

You can create parametric (in addition to explicit) equation-driven curves in both 2D and 3D sketches.

Use regular mathematical notation and order of operations to write an equation. x_1 and x_2 are for the beginning and end of the curve. Use the transform options at the bottom of the PropertyManager to move the entire curve in x-, y- or rotation. To specify $x = f(y)$ instead of $y = f(x)$, use a 90 degree transform.

View the .mp4 files located on the DVD in the book to better understand the potential of the Equation Driven Curve tool. The first one: *Calculating Area of a region bounded by two curves (secx)^2 and sin x* in SolidWorks - the second one: *Determine the Volume of a Function Revolved Around the x Axis* in SolidWorks.

Parametric Equation Driven Curve

The Parametric option of Equation Driven Curve can be utilize to represent two parameters, x- and y-, in terms of a third variable, t.

In the illustration below, a string is wound about a fixed circle of radius 1, and is then unwound while being held taught in the x-y-plane. The end point of the string, P traces an involute of the circle. The initial point (1,0) is on the x- axis and the string is tangent to the circle at Q. The angle, t is measured in radians from the positive x- axis.

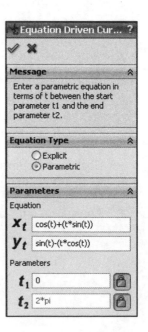

Equation Driven Cur... ?

Message

Enter a parametric equation in terms of t between the start parameter t1 and the end parameter t2.

Equation Type

○ Explicit
⊙ Parametric

Parameters

Equation

x_t cos(t)+(t*sin(t))

y_t sin(t)-(t*cos(t))

Parameters

t_1 0

t_2 2*pi

Use the Equation Driven Curve, Parametric option to illustrate how the parametric equations $x = \cos t + t \sin t$ and $y = \sin t - t \cos t$ represents the involute of the circle from $t = 0$ to $t = 2\pi$.

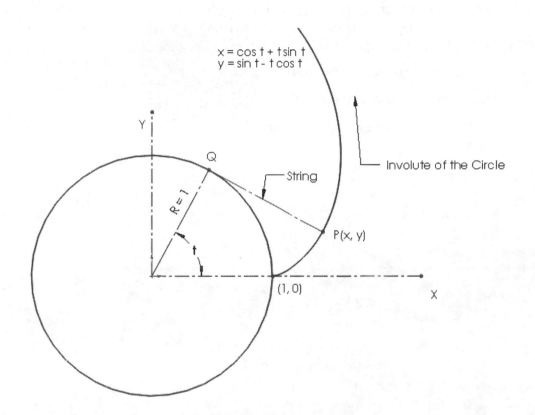

Rename a feature or sketch for clarity. Slowly click the feature or sketch name twice and enter the new name when the old one is highlighted.

Activity: Parametric Equation Driven Curve

Close all parts, assemblies and drawings. Create a Parametric Equation Driven Curve.

1) Open the **Parametric Equation 7.1** part from the SW-TUTORIAL-2013/Chapter 7 Intelligent Modeling folder. The circle of radius 1 is displayed.

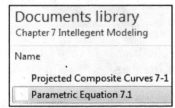

2) **Edit** Sketch1 from the FeatureManager.

Activate the Equation Driven Curve tool.

3) Click **Tools**, **Sketch Entities**, **Equation Driven Curve** from the Menu bar. The Equation Driven Curve PropertyManager is displayed.

4) Click **Parametric** in the Equation Type dialog box.

5)   Enter the parametric equations for x_t and y_t as illustrated.

6)   Enter t_1 and t_2 as illustrated.

You can also utilize sketch parameters in the equation. For example, the diameter dimension DIA2 is represented as "D2@Sketch2". The equation can be multiplied by the diameter.

X = "D2@Sketch2"*(cos(t)+(t*sin(t)))

Y = "D2@Sketch2"*(sin(t)-(t*cos(t)))

7)   Click **OK** ✔ from the PropertyManager. View the results in the Graphics window.

8)   **Close** the model.

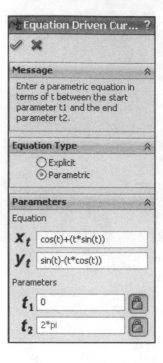

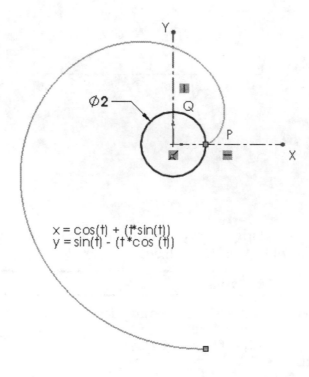

$$x = \cos(t) + (t*\sin(t))$$
$$y = \sin(t) - (t*\cos(t))$$

Curves

Another intelligent modeling technique is to apply the Curve Through XYZ Points feature. This feature provides the ability to either type in (using the Curve File dialog box) or click Browse and import a text file with x-, y-, z-, coordinates for points on a curve.

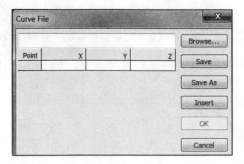

Generate the text file by any program which creates columns of numbers. The Curve 𝒰 feature reacts like a default spline that is fully defined.

It is highly recommend that you insert a few extra points on either end of the curve to set end conditions or tangency in the Curve File dialog box.

Imported files can have an extension of either *.sldcrv or *.text. The imported data: x-, y-, z-, must be separated by a space, a comma, or a tab.

The National Advisory Committee for Aeronautics (NACA) developed airfoil shapes for aircraft wings. The shape of the aerofoil is defined by parameters in the numerical code that can be entered into equations to generate accurate cross-sections.

Activity: Curve Through XYZ Points

Create a curve using the Curve Through XYZ Points tool and the Composite curve tool.
Import the x-, y-, z- data for an NACA aerofoil file for various cross sections.

1)   Create a **New** part. Use the default ANSI, MMGS Part template.

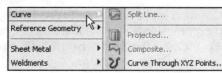

Browse to select the imported x-, y-, z- data.
2)   Click **Insert**, **Curve**, **Curve Through XYZ Points** from the Menu bar. The Curve File dialog box is displayed.

3)   **Browse** to the SW-TUTORIAL-2013/Chapter 7 Intelligent Modeling folder.

4)   Select **Text Files (*.txt)** for file type.

5)   Double-click **LowerSurfSR5.txt**. View the results in the Curve File dialog box.

6)   Click **OK** from the Curve File dialog box. Curve1 is displayed in the FeatureManager.

7)   **Repeat** the above procedure to create Curve2 from the UpperSurfSR5.txt file. Both the Lower and Upper curves are on the same Z plane. They are separate entities.

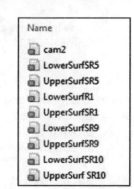

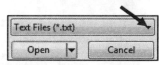

Point	X	Y	Z	
1	0mm	0mm	187.81mm	Save
2	2.91mm	-3.32mm	187.81mm	
3	5.81mm	-4.53mm	187.81mm	Save As
4	11.62mm	-5.79mm	187.81mm	
5	17.43mm	-6.37mm	187.81mm	Insert
6	23.24mm	-6.65mm	187.81mm	
7	31.06mm	-6.89mm	187.81mm	OK
8	46.48mm	-6.37mm	187.81mm	
9	58.1mm	-5.81mm	187.81mm	Cancel

Use the Composite curve tool to join the Lower and Upper curves.

8)   Click **Insert**, **Curve**, **Composite** from the Menu bar.

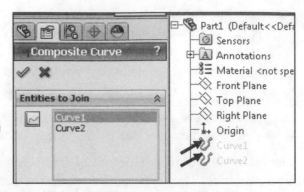

9)   Select **Curve1** and **Curve2** from the FeatureManager as illustrated. Both curves are displayed in the Entities to Join box.

10)   Click **OK** ✔ from the PropertyManager. View the results in the FeatureManager.

11)   **Close** the model.

Activity: Curve Through XYZ Points - Second Tutorial

Create a curve using the Curve Through XYZ Points tool. Import the x-, y-, z- data from a cam program. Verify that the first and last points in the curve file are the same for a closed profile.

1)   Open **Curve Through XYZ points 7-2** from the SW-TUTORIAL-2013/Chapter 7 Intelligent Modeling folder.

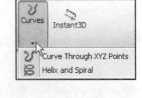

2)   Click the **Curve Through XYZ Points** ʊ tool from the Features CommandManager. The Curve File dialog box is displayed.

Import curve data. Additional zero points were added on either end of the curve to set end conditions.

3)   Click **Browse** from the Curve File dialog box. Browse to the SW-TUTORIAL-2013/Chapter 7 Intelligent Modeling folder.

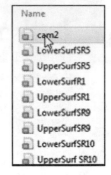

4)   Set file type to **Text Files**.

5)   Double-click **cam2.text**. View the data in the Curve File dialog box. View the sketch in the Graphics window. Review the data points in the dialog box.

6)   Click **OK** from the Curve File dialog box. Curve1 is displayed in the FeatureManager. Use the curve to create a fully defined base sketch of a cam. Let's view the final results.

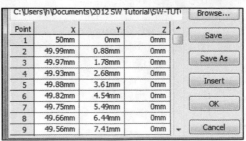

Point	X	Y	Z
1	50mm	0mm	0mm
2	49.99mm	0.88mm	0mm
3	49.97mm	1.78mm	0mm
4	49.93mm	2.68mm	0mm
5	49.88mm	3.61mm	0mm
6	49.82mm	4.54mm	0mm
7	49.75mm	5.49mm	0mm
8	49.66mm	6.44mm	0mm
9	49.56mm	7.41mm	0mm

7)   **Close** the model.

8)   Open **Curve Through XYZ points 7-3** from the SW-TUTORIAL-
2013/Chapter 7 Intelligent Modeling folder to view the final Cam model.
Curve1 is used to fully defined Sketch1.

9)   **Close** the model.

Activity: Projected Composite Curves

Create a plane and sketch for two composite curves. Note: Before you create a Loft feature, you must
insert a plane for each curve and add additional construction geometry to the sketch.

1)   Open the **Projected Composite Curves 7-1** part from the SW-TUTORIAL-2013/Chapter 7
Intelligent Modeling folder. Two NACA aerofoil profiles are displayed created from x-, y-, z-
data.

Create a reference plane through each point of the composite curve.

2)   Click **Insert**, **Reference Geometry**, **Plane** from the Menu bar. The Plane PropertyManager
is displayed.

3)   Click **Front Plane** for
First Reference from the
fly-out FeatureManager.

4)   Click the **end point** of
CompCurve1 in the
Graphics window as
illustrated for Second
Reference. The Plane is
fully defined.

5)   Click **OK** from the
Plane PropertyManager.
Plane1 is displayed in the
FeatureManager.

Create a Reference Plane
through CompCurve 2, parallel
to Plane1.

6)   Click **Insert**, **Reference
Geometry**, **Plane** from
the Menu bar. The Plane
PropertyManager is
displayed. Plane1 is the
First Reference.

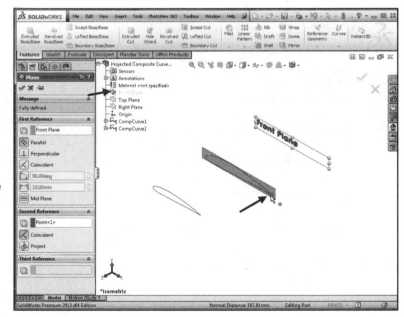

7) Click the **end point** of CompCurve2 in the Graphics window as illustrated,

8) Click **OK** ✔ from the Plane PropertyManager. Plane2 is displayed in the FeatureManager.

9) **Rename** Plane1 to PlaneSR5.

10) **Rename** Plane2 to PlaneSR9. When preparing multiple cross sections it is important to name the planes for clarity and future modification in the design.

Convert CompCurve1 to Plane SR5 and CompCurve2 to Plane SR9.

11) Right-click **PlaneSR5** from the FeatureManager.

12) Click **Sketch** ⎿ from the Context toolbar.

13) Click the **Convert Entities** ⬜ Sketch tool.

14) Click **CompCurve1** from the fly-out FeatureManager in the Graphics window.

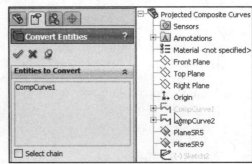

15) Click **OK** ✔ from the Convert Entities PropertyManager.

16) Click **Exit Sketch**.

17) **Rename** Sketch1 to SketchSR5.

18) Right-click **PlaneSR9** from the FeatureManager.

19) Click **Sketch** ⎿ from the Context toolbar.

20) Click the **Convert Entities** ⬜ Sketch tool.

21) Click **CompCurve2** from the fly-out FeatureManager in the Graphics window.

22) Click **OK** ✔ from the Convert Entities PropertyManager.

23) Click **Exit Sketch**.

24) **Rename** Sketch2 to SketchSR9.

25) Display an **Isometric** view.

26) **Show** Front Plane. View the results in the Graphics window.

27) **Close** the model.

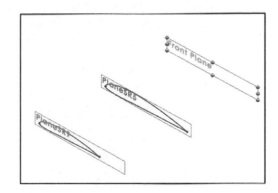

To save time in developing a series of curves, sketches can be copied and rotated.

Feature - End Conditions

Build design intent into a feature by addressing End Conditions (Blind, Through All, Up to Next, Up to Vertex, Up to Surface, Offset from Surface, Up to Body and Mid Plane) symmetry, feature selection, and the order of feature creation.

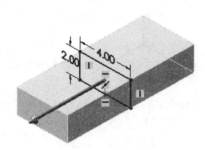

Example A: The Extruded Base feature remains symmetric about the Front Plane. Utilize the Mid Plane End Condition option in Direction 1. Modify the depth, and the feature remains symmetric about the Front Plane.

Example B: Create 34 teeth in the model. Do you create each tooth separate using the Extruded Cut feature? No.

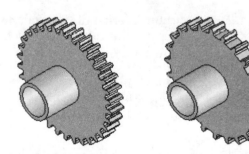

Create a single tooth and then apply the Circular Pattern feature. Modify the Circular Pattern from 32 to 24 teeth. Think about Design Intent when you apply an End Condition in a feature during modeling. The basic End Conditions are:

- *Blind* - Extends the feature from the selected sketch plane for a specified distance - default End Condition.

- *Through All* - Extends the feature from the selected sketch plane through all existing geometry.

- *Up to Next* - Extends the feature from the selected sketch plane to the next surface that intercepts the entire profile. The intercepting surface must be on the same part.

- *Up To Vertex* - Extends the feature from the selected sketch plane to a plane that is parallel to the sketch plane and passing through the specified vertex.

- *Up To Surface* - Extends the feature from the selected sketch plane to the selected surface.

- *Offset from Surface* - Extends the feature from the selected sketch plane to a specified distance from the selected surface.

- *Up To Body* - Extends the feature up to the selected body. Use this option with assemblies, mold parts, or multi-body parts.

- *Mid Plane* - Extends the feature from the selected sketch plane equally in both directions.

Activity: End Condition options

Create Extruded Cut features using various End Condition options. Think about Design Intent of the model.

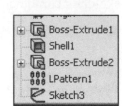

1)   Open **End Condition 7-1** from the SW-TUTORIAL-2013/Chapter 7 Intelligent Modeling folder. The FeatureManager displays two Extrude features, a Shell feature, and a Linear Pattern feature.

2)   Click the **circumference of the front most circle**. Sketch3 is highlighted in the FeatureManager.

Create an Extruded Cut feature using the Selected Contours and Through All option.

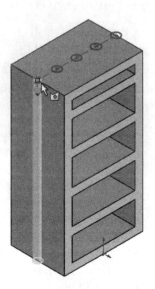

3)   Click **Extruded Cut** 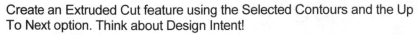 from the Features toolbar. The Cut-Extrude PropertyManager is displayed.

4)   **Expand** the Selected Contours box.

5)   Click the **circumference of the front most circle**. Sketch3-Contour<1> is displayed in the Selected Contours box. The direction arrow points downward, if not click the Reverse Direction button.

6)   Select **Through All** for End Condition in Direction 1. Only the first circle of your sketch is extruded.

7)   Click **OK** ✔ from the Cut-Extruded PropertyManager. Cut-Extrude1 is displayed in the FeatureManager.

Create an Extruded Cut feature using the Selected Contours and the Up To Next option. Think about Design Intent!

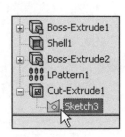

8)   Click **Sketch3** from the FeatureManager.

9)   Click **Extruded Cut** from the Features toolbar. The Cut-Extrude PropertyManager is displayed.

10) **Expand** the Selected Contours box.

11) Click the **circumference of the second circle** from the left. Sketch3-Contour<1> is displayed in the Selected Contours box.

12) Select **Up To Next** for End Condition in Direction 1. Only the second circle of your sketch is extruded.

13) Click **OK** ✅ from the Cut-Extrude PropertyManager. Cut-Extrude2 is displayed in the FeatureManager.

14) **Rotate** your model and view the created cut through the first plate.

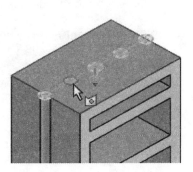

Create an Extruded Cut feature using the Selected Contours and the Up To Vertex option.

15) Click **Sketch3** from the FeatureManager.

16) Click the **Extruded Cut** 🔲 Features tool. The Cut-Extrude PropertyManager is displayed.

17) **Expand** the Selected Contours box.

18) Click the **circumference of the third circle** from the left. Sketch3-Contour<1> Is displayed in the Selected Contours box.

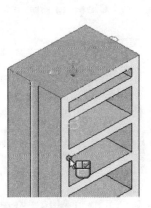

19) Select **Up To Vertex** for End Condition in Direction 1. Only the third circle of your sketch is extruded.

20) Select a **vertex point below** the second shelf as illustrated. Vertex<1> is displayed in the Vertex box in Direction 1.

21) Click **OK** ✅ from the PropertyManager. Cut-Extrude3 is displayed in the FeatureManager. The third circle has an Extruded Cut feature through the top two shelves.

Create an Extruded Cut feature using the Selected Contours and the Offset From Surface option.

22) Click **Sketch3** from the FeatureManager.

23) Click the **Extruded Cut** 🔲 Features tool.

24) **Expand** the Selected Contours box.

25) Click the circumference of the **fourth circle** from the left. Sketch3-Contour<1> is displayed in the Selected Contours box.

26) Select **Offset From Surface** for End Condition in Direction 1.

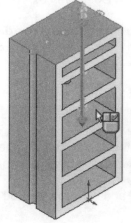
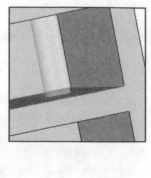

27) Click the **face** of the third shelf. Face<1> is displayed in the Face/Plane box in Direction1.

28) Enter **60**mm for Offset Distance.

29) Click the **Reverse offset** box if required.

30) Click **OK** ✅ from the PropertyManager. Cut-Extrude4 is displayed in the FeatureManager.

31) Click **Isometric** view. View the created features.

32) **Close** the model.

Along a Vector

In engineering design, vectors are utilized in modeling techniques. In an extrusion, the sketch profile is extruded perpendicular to the sketch plane. The Direction of Extrusion Option allows the profile to be extruded normal to the vector.

Activity: Along a Vector

Utilize a vector, created in a separate sketch, and the Direction of Extrusion to modify the extruded feature.

1) Open **Along Vector** 7-1 from the SW-TUTORIAL-2013/Chapter 7 Intelligent Modeling folder. View the model in the Graphics window. The current sketch profile is extruded normal to the Top Sketch Plane.

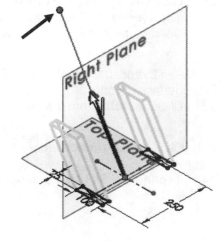

2) Edit **Boss-Extrude1** from the FeatureManager. The Boss-Extrude1 PropertyManager is displayed.

3) Select **Up to Vertex** for End Condition in Direction 1.

4) Click the **top endpoint** of Sketch Vector.

5)   Click inside the **Direction of Extrusion** box.

6)   Click **Sketch Vector** from the Graphics window as illustrated. The feature is extruded along the Sketch Vector normal to the Sketch Profile.

7)   Click **OK** ✓ from the Boss-Extrude1 PropertyManager. View the results in the Graphics window.

8)   **Close** the part.

FeatureXpert (Constant Radius)

FeatureXpert manages the interaction between fillet and draft features when features fail. The FeatureXpert, manages fillet and draft features for you so you can concentrate on your design. See Xperts Overview in SolidWorks Help for additional information.

When you add or make changes to constant radius fillets and neutral plane drafts that cause rebuild errors, the **What's Wrong** dialog appears with a description of the error. Click **FeatureXpert** in the dialog to run the FeatureXpert to attempt to fix the error.

The FeatureXpert can change the feature order in the FeatureManager design tree or adjust the tangent properties so a part successfully rebuilds. The FeatureXpert can also, to a lesser extent, repair reference planes that have lost references.

Supported features:

- *Constant radius fillets*
- *Neutral plane drafts*
- *Reference planes*

Unsupported items:

- *Other types of fillets or draft features.*

- *Mirror or pattern features. When mirror or pattern features contain a fillet or draft feature, the FeatureXpert cannot manipulate those features in the mirrored or patterned copies.*

- *Library features. Fillet or draft features in a library feature are ignored by the FeatureXpert and the entire Library feature is treated as one rigid feature.*

- *Configurations and Design Tables. The FeatureXpert is not available for parts that contain these items.*

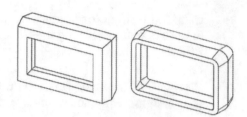

Utilize symmetry, feature order and reusing common features to build design intent into a part. Example A: Feature order. Is the entire part symmetric? Feature order affects the part.

Apply the Shell feature before the Fillet feature and the inside corners remain perpendicular.

Symmetry

An object is symmetrical when it has the same exact shape on opposite sides of a dividing line (or plane) or about a center or axis. The simplest type of Symmetry is a "Mirror" as we discussed above in this chapter.

Symmetry can be important when creating a 2D sketch, a 3D feature or an assembly. Symmetry is important because:

- Mirrored shapes have symmetry where points on opposite sides of the dividing line (or mirror line) are the same distance away from the mirror line.

- For a 2D mirrored shape, the axis of symmetry is the mirror line.

- For a 3D mirrored shape, the symmetry is about a plane.

- Molded symmetrical parts are often made using a mold with two halves, one on each side of the axis of symmetry.

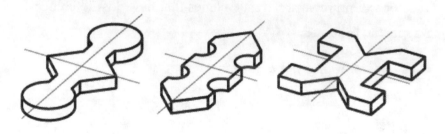

- The axis or line where two mold parts join is called a parting line.

- When items are removed from a mold, sometimes a small ridge of material is left on the object. Have you ever notice a parting line on a molded object such as your toothbrush or a screwdriver handle?

Parting line

Bodies to Mirror

When a model contains single point entities, the pattern and mirror features may create disjoint geometry and the feature will fail. For example, a cone contains a single point at its origin. To mirror the cone about a plane would create disjoint geometry. To resolve this issue, utilize Bodies to Pattern option.

Activity: Bodies to Mirror

Create a Mirror feature with the Top plane and utilize the Body to Mirror option.

1)   Open **Bodies to Mirror 7-1** from the SW-TUTORIAL-2013/
     Chapter 7 Intelligent Modeling folder. View the model in the
     Graphics window.

2)   Select **Mirror** ⬚ from the Features toolbar. The Mirror
     PropertyManager is displayed.

3)   **Expand** the Bodies to Mirror dialog box.

4)   Click the **face of the Cone** in the Graphics window. Note
     the icon feedback symbol.

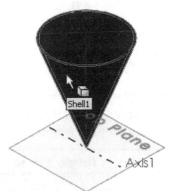

5)   Click inside the **Mirror Face/Plane** dialog box.

6)   Click **Top Plane** from the fly-out FeatureManager.

7)   Uncheck the **Merge solids** box. (You cannot merge these
     two cones at a single point).

8)   Click **OK** ✓ from the Mirror
     PropertyManager. View the results in the
     Graphics window. Mirror1 is displayed in the
     FeatureManager.

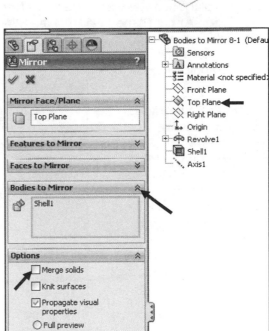

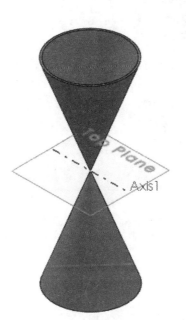

Planes

Certain types of models are better suited to design automation than others. When setting up models for automation, consider how they fit into an assembly and how the parts might change when automated.

Create planes so that sketches and features can be referenced to them (coincident, up to surface, etc.) This provides the ability to dimension for the plane to be changed and the extrusion extended with it. When placed in an assembly, other components can be mated to a plane so that they move with consideration to the parts altered.

Incorporating planes into the design process prepares the model for future changes. As geometry becomes more complex, additional sketch geometry(construction lines, circles) or reference geometry (axis, planes) may be required to construct planes.

For example, a sketched line coincident with the silhouette edge of the cone provides a reference to create a plane through to the outer cone's face. An axis, a plane and an angle creates a new plane through the axis at a specified angle.

Activity: Angle Plane

Create a plane at a specified angle through an axis.

1) Open **Angle Planes 7-1** from the SW-TUTORIAL-2013/Chapter 7 Intelligent Modeling folder. View the model in the Graphics window.

Create an Angle Plane.

2) Click **Insert, Reference Geometry, Plane** from the Menu bar. The Plane PropertyManager is displayed.

3) Click **Axis1** in the Graphics window as illustrated. Axis1 is displayed in the First Reference box.

4) Click **Right Plane** from the fly-out FeatureManager. Right Plane is displayed in the Second Reference box.

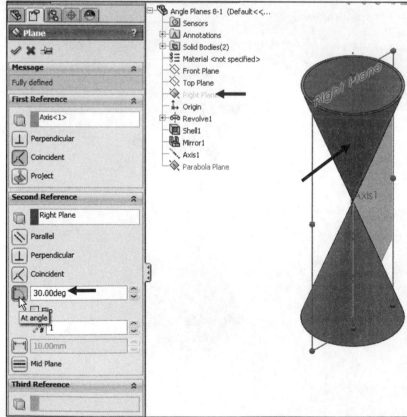

Set the angle of the Plane.

5) Click the **At angle** box.

6) Enter **30** for Angle. The Plane is fully defined.

7) Click **OK** ✅ from the Plane PropertyManager. Plane1 is displayed in the FeatureManager.

8) **Close** the Model.

As geometry becomes more complex in mechanical design, planes and conical geometry can be combined to create circular, elliptical, parabolic and hyperbolic sketches with the Intersection Curve Sketch Curve.

Conic Sections and Planes

Conic sections are paths traveled by planets, satellites, electrons and other bodies whose motions are driven by inverse-square forces. Once the path of a moving body is known, information about its velocity and forces can be derived. Using planes to section cones creates circular, elliptical, parabolic, hyperbolic and other cross sections are utilized in engineering design.

The Intersection Curve tool provides the ability to open a sketch and create a sketched curve at the following kinds of intersections: a plane and a surface or a model face, two surfaces, a surface and a model face, a plane and the entire part, and a surface and the entire part.

Activity: Conic Section

Apply the Intersection Curve tool. Create a sketched curve

1) Open **Conic Section 7-1** from the SW-TUTORIAL-2013/ Chapter 7 Intelligent Modeling folder. View the model in the Graphics window. Create a Sketch.

2) Right-click **Plane1 Circle** from the FeatureManager.

3) Click **Sketch** ↳ from the Context toolbar. The Sketch toolbar is displayed in the CommandManager.

4) Click **Tools, Sketch Tools, Intersection Curve** from the Menu bar. The Intersection Curve PropertyManager is displayed.

5) Click the **top face** of the cone as illustrated. Face<1> is displayed in the Selected Entities dialog box.

6) Click **OK** ✅ from the Intersection Curve PropertyManager. Click **OK** ✅ .

7)   Click **Exit Sketch**.

8)   **Hide** Plane1 Circle. The intersection of the cone with the plane creates a circle. **Close** the model. You can use the resulting sketched intersection curve in the same way that you use any sketched curve.

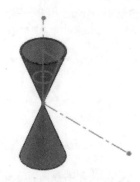

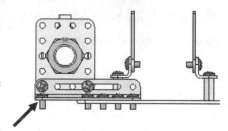

Assembly

Utilizing symmetry, reusing common parts and using the Mate relation between parts builds the design intent into an assembly. For example: Reuse geometry in an assembly. The assembly contains a linear pattern of holes. Insert one screw into the first hole. Utilize the Component Pattern feature to copy the machine screw to the other holes.

Assembly Visualization

In an assembly, the designer selects material based on cost, performance, physical properties, manufacturing processes, and sustainability.

The Assembly Visualization tool provides the ability to rank components based on the values of their custom properties, and activate a spectrum of colors that reflects the relative values of the properties for each component. The default custom properties are: *SW-Density, SW-Mass, SW-Material, SW-Rebuild Time, SW-Surface Area, SW-Volume, Description, PartNo, Quantity*

Additional predefined properties are available for selection. New view modes are available for grouping and ungrouping components in the list.

You can select the following component properties from the drop-down list in the Custom Column dialog box: *Converted to current version, Excluded from BOM (instance-specific), External references, Flexible subassemblies (instance-specific), Fully mated (instance-specific).*

To reduce the weight in the overall assembly, first review the component with the greatest mass. Alternative materials or changes to the geometry that still meet safely requirements may save in production and shipping costs.

When comparing mass, volume and other properties with assembly visualization, utilize similar units.

Activity: Assembly Visualization

Apply the Assembly Visualization tool to an assembly. View your options

1)   Open **Assembly Visualization 7-1** from the SW-
     TUTORIAL-2013/Chapter 7 Intelligent Modeling
     folder. View the assembly in the Graphics window.
     Material was assigned to each component in the
     assembly.

2)   Click the **Assembly Visualization** tool from the
     Evaluate Tab in the CommandManager. The
     Assembly Visualization PropertyManager is
     displayed.

3)   Click the **expand arrow** to the right of Mass as
     illustrated to display the default visualization
     properties. Mass is selected by default.

4)   **Explore** the available tabs and SolidWorks Help for
     additional information.

5)   **Close** the model.

SolidWorks Sustainability - Assembly

With SolidWorks Sustainability you can determine Life Cycle Assessment (LCA)
properties for a part or assembly. By integrating Life Cycle Assessment (LCA) into the
design process, you can see how decisions about material, manufacturing, and location
(where parts are manufactured and where they are used) influence a design's
environmental impact. You specify various parameters that SolidWorks Sustainability
uses to perform a comprehensive evaluation of all the steps in a design's life. LCA
includes:

- Ore extraction from the earth

- Material processing

- Part manufacturing

- Assembly

- Product usage by the end consumer

- End of Life (EOL) - Landfill, recycling, and
  incineration

- All the transportation that occurs between and
  within each of these steps

By combining SolidWorks Sustainability and Assembly Visualization, you can determine the components in the assembly that contain the greatest carbon footprint and review materials with similar properties to reduce CO_2 emissions. See chapter on SolidWorks Sustainability and SolidWorks Help for additional information.

You need SolidWorks Professional or SolidWorks Premium to access SolidWorks Sustainability for an assembly. Every license of SolidWorks 2013 provides access to SolidWorks SustainabilityXpress for a part

MateXpert

The MateXpert is a tool that provides the ability to identify mate problems in an assembly. You can examine the details of mates that are not satisfied, and identify groups of mates which over define the assembly. If the introduction of a component leads to multiple mate errors, it may be easier to delete the component, review the design intent, reinsert the component and then apply new mates. See SolidWorks Help for additional information.

Drawing

Utilize dimensions, tolerance and notes in parts and assemblies to build the design intent into a drawing.

Example A: Tolerance and material in the drawing. Insert an outside diameter tolerance +.000/-.002 into the Pipe part. The tolerance propagates to the drawing.

Define the Custom Property Material in the Part. The Material Custom Property propagates to your drawing.

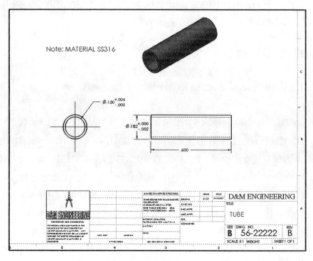

DimXpert

DimXpert for parts is a set of tools you use to apply dimensions and tolerances to parts according to the requirements of the ASME Y14.41-2003 standard.

DimXpert dimensions show up in a different color to help identify them from model dims and reference dims. DimXpert dims are the dimensions that are used when calculating tolerance stack-up using TolAnalyst.

DimXpert applies dimensions in drawings so that manufacturing features (patterns, slots, pockets, etc.) are fully-defined.

DimXpert for parts and drawings automatically recognize manufacturing features. What are manufacturing features? Manufacturing features are *not SolidWorks features*. Manufacturing features are defined in 1.1.12 of the ASME Y14.5M-1994 Dimensioning and Tolerancing standard as: "The general term applied to a physical portion of a part, such as a surface, hole or slot.

The DimXpertManager provides the following selections:
Auto Dimension Scheme ✦, **Show Tolerance Status** 𝜎ᶜ,
Copy Scheme ✦, **TolAnalyst Study** ◫.

💡 Care is required to apply DimXpert correctly on complex surfaces or with some existing models. See SolidWorks help for detail information on DimXpert with complex surfaces.

Activity: DimXpert 7-1

Apply the DimXpert tool. Apply Prismatic and Geometric options

1)   Open **DimXpert 7-1** from the SW-TUTORIAL-2013/Chapter 7 Intelligent Modeling folder.

2)   Click the **DimXpertManager** tab as illustrated.

3)   Click the **Auto Dimension Scheme** tab from the DimXpertManager. The Auto Dimension Scheme PropertyManager is displayed.

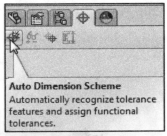

4)   Click the **Prismatic** box.

5)   Click the **Geometric** box.

Select the Primary Datum.

6)   Click the **front face** of the model. Plane1 is displayed in the Primary Datum box.

Select the Secondary Datum.

7)   Click **inside** the Secondary Datum box.

8)   Click the **left face** of the model. Plane2 is displayed in the Secondary Datum box.

Select the Tertiary Datum.

9)   Click **inside** the Tertiary Datum box.

10)   Click the **bottom face** of the model. Plane3 is displayed in the Tertiary Datum box. Accept the default options.

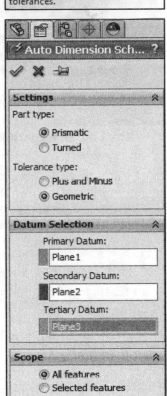

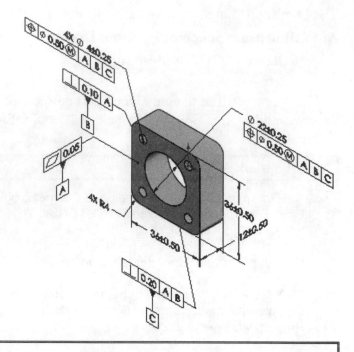

11) Click **OK** ✔ from the Auto Dimension Scheme PropertyManager. View the results in the Graphics window and in the DimXpertManager.

12) **Close** all models. Do not save the updates.

🔅 Right-click Delete to delete the Auto Dimension Scheme in the DimXpert PropertyManager.

Activity: DimXpert 7-2

Apply DimXpert: Geometric option. Edit a Feature Control Frame.

1) Open **DimXpert 7-2** from the SW-TUTORIAL-2013/Chapter 7 Intelligent Modeling folder.

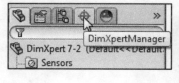

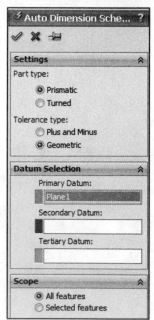

2) Click the **DimXpertManager** ⊕ tab.

3) Click the **Auto Dimension Scheme** tool from the DimXpertManager. The Auto Dimension PropertyManager is displayed. Prismatic and Plus and Minus is selected by default. In this section, you will select the Geometric option.

🔅 DimXpert: Geometric option provides the ability to locate axial features with position and circular runout tolerances. Pockets and surfaces are located with surface profiles.

4) Click the **Geometric** box as illustrated. Note: the Prismatic box is checked.

Create the Primary Datum.

5) Click the **back face** of the model. Plane1 is displayed in the Primary Datum box.

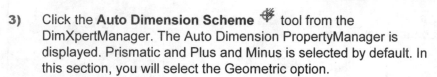

Select the Secondary Datum.

6) Click **inside** the Secondary Datum box.

7) Click the **left face** of the model. Plane2 is displayed in the Secondary Datum box.

Select the Tertiary Datum.

8) Click **inside** the Tertiary Datum box.

9) Click the **top face** of the model. Plane3 is displayed in the Tertiary Datum box.

10) Click **OK** ✅ from the Auto Dimension PropertyManager.

11) Click **Isometric view** from the Heads-up View toolbar. View the Datum's, Feature Control Frames, and Geometric tolerances. All features are displayed in green.

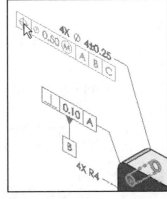

Edit a Feature Control Frame.

12) **Double-click** the illustrated Position Feature Control Frame. The Properties dialog box is displayed.

Modify the 0.50 tolerance.

13) Click **inside** the Tolerance 1 box.

14) **Delete** the existing text.

15) Enter **0.25**.

16) Click **OK** from the Properties dialog box.

17) **Repeat** the above procedure for the second Position Feature Control Frame. View the results.

18) **Close** the model. Do not save the model.

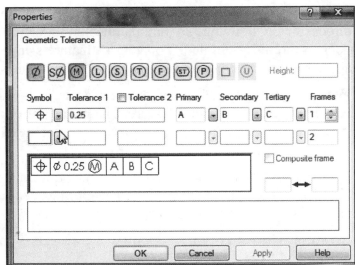

Project Summary

In this project, you performed short step by step tutorials to understanding some of the available tools in SolidWorks to perform intelligent modeling. Intelligent modeling is incorporating design intent into the definition of the Sketch, Feature, Part and Assembly or Drawing document.

All designs are created for a purpose. Design intent is the intellectual arrangement of features and dimensions of a design. Design intent governs the relationship between sketches in a feature, features in a part and parts in an assembly or drawing document.

The SolidWorks definition of design intent is the process in which the model is developed to accept future modifications. Models behave differently when design changes occur.

You create Explicit Dimension Driven and Parametric Equation Driven Curves and generated curves using the Curve Through XYZ Points tool for a NACA aerofoil and CAM data text file.

You also applied SketchXpert, DimXpert and FeatureXpert.

🔆 View the .mp4 files located on the DVD in the book to better understand the potential of the Equation Driven Curve tool.

Definitions

DimXpert: DimXpert speeds the process of adding reference dimensions by applying dimensions in drawings so that manufacturing features, such as patterns, slots, and pockets, are fully-defined. You select a feature's edge to dimension, then DimXpert applies all associated dimensions in that drawing view for the feature.

Feature: The first feature you create in a part is the base. This feature is the basis on which you create the other feature. The base feature can be an extrusion, a revolve, a sweep, a loft, thickening of a surface, or a sheet metal flange. However, most base feature are extrusions.

FeatureXpert: The FeatureXpert, manages fillet and draft features. The FeatureXpert can change the feature order in the FeatureManager design tree or adjust the tangent properties so a part successfully rebuilds.

Involute: The path of the endpoint of a cord as it is pulled straight (held taut) and unwrapped from a circular disk.

Sketch: The sketch is the basis for a 3D model. Create a sketch on any of the default planes (**Front Plane**, **Top Plane**, and **Right Plane**), or a created plane.

SketchXpert: SketchXpert resolves over-defined sketches and proposes possible solution sets.

Xperts: The SolidWorks Xperts are tools that help novices use SolidWorks like experts, without having to understand the details of the software. The Xperts take care of the details of software functionality. Using Xperts, you can focus on your design intent while the Xperts focus on what the software should do to achieve it.

Notes:

CHAPTER 8 - CSWA INTRODUCTION AND DRAFTING COMPETENCIES

Introduction

DS SolidWorks Corp. offers various types of certification. Each stage represents increasing levels of expertise in 3D CAD: *Certified SolidWorks Associate CSWA, Certified SolidWorks Professional CSWP and Certified SolidWorks Expert CSWE* along with specialty fields in Simulation, Sheet Metal, Weldments, Molds, Surfacing, and Sustainable Design.

The CSWA Certification indicates a foundation in and apprentice knowledge of 3D CAD design and engineering practices and principles. The main requirement for obtaining the CSWA certification is to take and pass the on-line proctored 180 minute exam (minimum of 165 out of 240 points).

The CSWA exam consists of fourteen questions in five categories. Passing this exam provides students the chance to prove their knowledge and expertise and to be part of a worldwide industry certification standard.

The following five categories and subject areas:

- *Drafting Competencies*: (Three questions - multiple choice - 5 points each).

    - Questions on general drawing views: Projected, Section, Break, Crop, Detail, Alternate Position, etc.

- *Basic Part Creation and Modification*: (Two questions - one multiple choice / one single answer - 15 points each).

    - Sketch Planes:

A00006: Drafting Competencies - To create drawing view 'B' it is necessary to select drawing view 'A' and insert which SolidWorks view type?

Screen shot from the exam

B22001: Basic Part (Hydraulic Cylinder Half) - Step 1
Build this part in SolidWorks.
(Save part after each question in a different file in case it must be reviewed)

Unit system: MMGS (millimeter, gram, second)
Decimal places: 2
Part origin: Arbitrary
All holes through all unless shown otherwise.
Material: Aluminium 1060 Alloy

Screen shot from the exam

- Front, Top, Right
- 2D Sketching:
  - Geometric Relations and Dimensioning
- Extruded Boss/Base Feature
- Extruded Cut feature
- Modification of Basic part

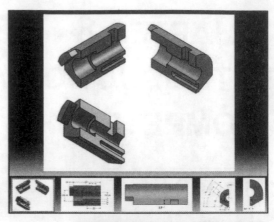

In the *Basic Part Creation and Modification* category there is a dimension modification.

- *Intermediate Part Creation and Modification*: (Two questions - one multiple choice / one single answer - 15 points each).
  - Sketch Planes:
    - Front, Top, Right
  - 2D Sketching:
    - Geometric Relations and Dimensioning
  - Extruded Boss/Base Feature
  - Extruded Cut Feature
  - Revolved Boss/Base Feature
  - Mirror and Fillet Feature
  - Circular and Linear Pattern Feature
  - Plane Feature
  - Modification of Intermediate Part:
    - Sketch, Feature, Pattern, etc.
  - Modification of Intermediate part
- *Advanced Part Creation and Modification:* (Three questions - one multiple choice / two single answers - 15 points each).
  - Sketch Planes:
    - Front, Top, Right, Face, Created Plane, etc.
    - 2D Sketching or 3D Sketching

D12801: Intermediate Part (Wheel) - Step 1
Build this part in SolidWorks.
(Save part after each question in a different file in case it must be reviewed)

Unit system: MMGS (millimeter, gram, second)
Decimal places: 2
Part origin: Arbitrary
All holes through all unless shown otherwise.
Material: Aluminium 1060 Alloy

A = 134.00
B = 890.00

Note: All geometry is symmetrical about the plane represented by the line labeled F"" in the M-M Section View.

What is the overall mass of the part (grams)?

Screen shots from the exam

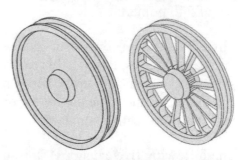

C12801: Advanced Part (Bracket) - Step 1
Build this part in SolidWorks.
(Save part after each question in a different file in case it must be reviewed)

Unit system: MMGS (millimeter, gram, second)
Decimal places: 2
Part origin: Arbitrary
All holes through all unless shown otherwise.
Material: AISI 1020 Steel
Density = 0.0079 g/mm^3

A = 64.00
B = 20.00
C = 26.50

What is the overall mass of the part (grams)?

Screen shots from the exam

- Sketch Tools:
    - Offset Entities, Convert Entitles, etc.
- Extruded Boss/Base Feature
- Extruded Cut Feature
- Revolved Boss/Base Feature
- Mirror and Fillet Feature
- Circular and Linear Pattern Feature
- Shell Feature
- Plane Feature
- More Difficult Geometry Modifications
- *Assembly Creation and Modification*: (Two different assemblies - four questions - two multiple choice / two single answers - 30 points each).
    - Insert the first (fixed) component
    - Insert all needed components
    - Standard Matcs
    - Modification of key parameters in the assembly

Download the needed components in a zip folder during the exam to create the assembly.

Note: To apply for CSWA Provider status for your institution, go to **www.solidWorks.com/cswa** and fill out the CSWA Provider application. It is as easy as that.

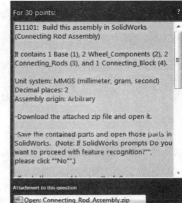

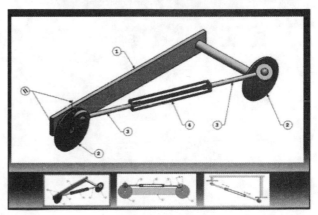

Screen shots from the exam

A total score of 165 out of 240 or better is required to obtain your CSWA Certification.

You are allowed to answer the questions in any order you prefer. Use the Summary Screen during the CSWA exam to view the list of all questions you have or have not answered.

During the exam, use the control keys at the bottom of the screen to:

- *Show the Previous the Question.*

- *Reset the Question.*

- *Show the Summary Screen.*

- *Move to the Next Question.*

Do NOT use feature recognition when you open the downloaded components for the assembly in the CSWA exam. This is a timed exam. Manage your time. You do not need this information.

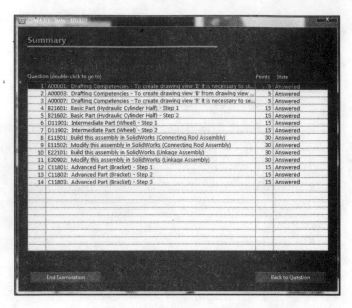

Screen shot from the exam

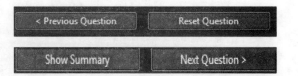

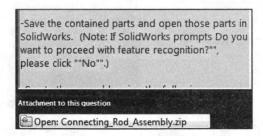

Screen shots from the exam

During the exam, SolidWorks provides the ability to click on a detail view below (as illustrated) to obtain additional details and dimensions during the exam.

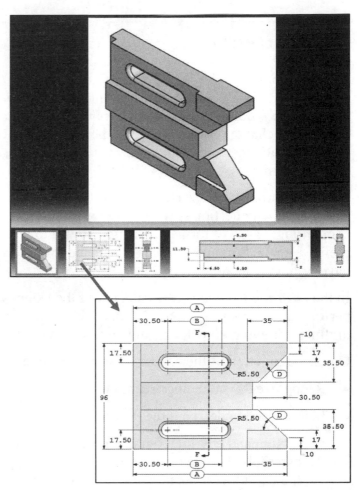

☀ No Simulation (CosmosXpress) questions are on the CSWA exam at this time.

☀ No Sheetmetal questions are on the CSWA exam at this time.

☀ FeatureManager names were changed through various revisions of SolidWorks. Example: Extrude1 vs. Boss-Extrude1. These changes do not affect the models or answers in this book.

☀ No Surface questions are on the CSWA exam at this time.

Screen shots from the exam

☀ For additional detail exam information see The **Official Guide to Certified SolidWorks Associate Exams: CSWA, CSDA, and CSWSA-FEA** book. This book is written to assist the SolidWorks user to pass the associate level exams. Information is provided to aid a person to pass the Certified SolidWorks Associate (CSWA), Certified Sustainable Design Associate (CSDA) and the Certified SolidWorks Simulation Associate Finite Element Analysis (CSWSA FEA) exams. The primary goal of this book is not only to help you pass the exams, but also to ensure that you understand and comprehend the concepts and implementation details of the process.

Objectives

Drafting Competencies is one of the five categories *(Drafting Competencies, Basic Part Creation and Modification, Intermediate Part Creation and Modification, Advance Part Creation and Modification, and Assembly Creation and Modification)* on the CSWA exam. This chapter covers the general concepts, symbols and terminology used in the exam and then the core element *(Drafting Competencies)* which is aligned to the new CSWA exam.

There are three questions (total) on the CSWA exam in the *Drafting Competencies* category. Each question is worth five (5) points. The three questions are in a multiple choice single answer format. You are allowed to answer the questions in any order you prefer. Use the Summary Screen during the exam to view the list of all questions you have or have not answered.

In the *Drafting Competencies* category of the exam, you are **not required** to create or perform an analysis on a part, assembly, or drawing but you are required to have general drafting / drawing knowledge and understanding of various drawing view methods.

On the completion of the chapter, you will be able to:

- Recognize 3D modeling techniques:

- Identify and understand the procedure for the following:

  - Assign and edit material to a part, Apply the Measure tool to a part or an assembly, Locate the Center of mass, and Principal moments of inertia relative to the default coordinate location, and Origin.

- Calculate the overall mass and volume of a part

- Identify the process of creating a simple drawing from a part or an assembly

- Identify the procedure to create a named drawing view:

  - Projected view, Section view, Break view, Crop view, Detail, Alternate Position view, etc.

- Specify Document Properties: Select Unit System, and Set Precision

In the *Basic Part Creation and Modification, Intermediate Part Creation and Modification, Advanced Part Creation and Modification and Assembly Creation and Modification* categories, you are required to read and interpret various types of drawing views and understand various types of drawing annotations.

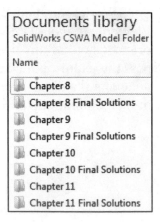

All SolidWorks models for the next few chapters (initial and final) are provided on the DVD in the book. Copy the folders and model files to your local hard drive. Do not work directly from the DVD.

Procedure to Create a Named Drawing view

You need the ability to identify the procedure to create a named drawing view: *Standard 3 View, Model View, Projected View, Auxiliary View, Section View, Detail View, Broken-out Section, Break, Crop View and Alternate Position View.*

Create a Section view in a drawing by cutting the parent view with a section line. The section view can be a straight cut section or an offset section defined by a stepped section line. The section line can also include concentric arcs.

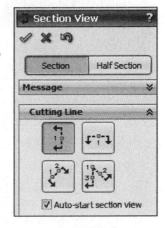

Create an Aligned section view in a drawing through a model, or portion of a model, that is aligned with a selected section line segment. The Aligned Section view is similar to a Section View, but the section line for an aligned section comprises two or more lines connected at an angle.

Create a Detail view in a drawing to show a portion of a view, usually at an enlarged scale. This detail may be of an orthographic view, a non-planar (isometric) view, a section view, a crop view, an exploded assembly view, or another detail view.

☀ Crop any drawing view except a Detail view, a view from which a Detail view has been created, or an Exploded view. To create a Crop view, sketch a closed profile such as a circle or spline. The view outside the closed profile disappears as illustrated.

☀ Create a Detail view in a drawing to display a portion of a view, usually at an enlarged scale. This detail may be of an orthographic view, a non-planar (isometric) view, a Section view, a Crop view, an Exploded assembly view, or another Detail view.

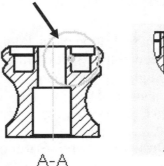

A-A

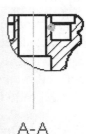

A-A

Tutorial: Drawing Named Procedure 8-1

Identify the drawing name view and understand the procedure to create the name view.

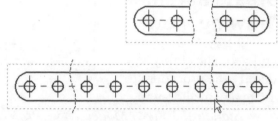

1. **View** the illustrated drawing views. The top drawing view is a Break view. The Break view is created by adding a break line to a selected view.

Broken views make it possible to display the drawing view in a larger scale on a smaller size drawing sheet. Reference dimensions and model dimensions associated with the broken area reflect the actual model values.

In views with multiple breaks, the Break line style must be the same.

Tutorial: Drawing Named Procedure 8-2

Identify the drawing name view and understand the procedure to create the name view.

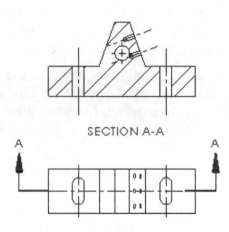

1. **View** the illustrated drawing views. The right drawing view is a Section View. The Section view is created by cutting the parent view with a cutting section line.

Create a Section view in a drawing by cutting the parent view with a section line. The section view can be a straight cut section or an offset section defined by a stepped section line. The section line can also include Concentric arcs.

Tutorial: Drawing Named Procedure 8-3

Identify the drawing name view and understand the procedure to create the name view.

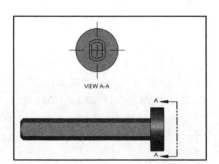

1. **View** the illustrated drawing views. The Top drawing view is an Auxilary view of the Front view. Select a reference edge to create an Auxiliary view.

An Auxiliary view is similar to a Projected view, but it is unfolded normal to a reference edge in an existing view.

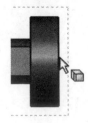

Tutorial: Drawing Named Procedure 8-4

Identify the drawing name view and understand the procedure to create the name view.

1. **View** the illustrated drawing views. The right drawing view is an Aligned Section view of the bottom view. The Section view is created by using two lines connected at an angle. Create an Aligned Section view in a drawing through a model, or portion of a model, that is aligned with a selected section line segment.

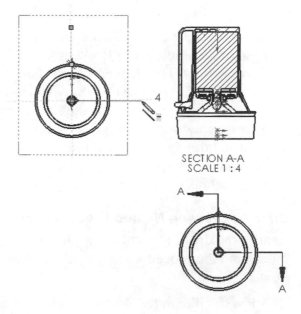

SECTION A-A
SCALE 1 : 4

🔆 The Aligned Section view is very similar to a Section View, with the exception that the section line for an aligned section comprises of two or more lines connected at an angle.

Tutorial: Drawing Named Procedure 8-5

Identify the drawing name view and understand the procedure to create the name view.

1. **View** the illustrated drawing views. The left drawing view is a Detail view of the Section view. The Detail view is created by sketching a circle with the Circle Sketch tool. Click and drag for the location.

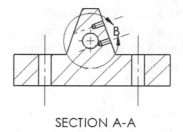

SECTION A-A

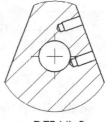

DETAIL B
SCALE 1 : 1

🔆 The Detail view ⃝A tool provides the ability to add a Detail view to display a portion of a view, usually at an enlarged scale.

🔆 To create a profile other than a circle, sketch the profile before clicking the Detail view tool. Using a sketch entity tool, create a closed profile around the area to be detailed.

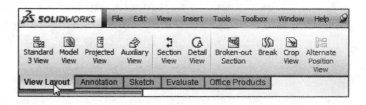

Tutorial: Drawing Named Procedure 8-6

Identify the drawing name view and understand the procedure to create the name view.

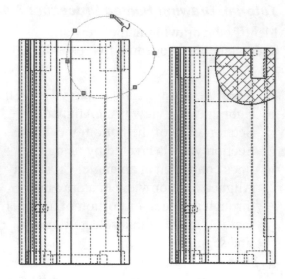

1. **View** the illustrated drawing views. The right drawing view is a Broken-out Section view. The Broken-out Section View is part of an existing drawing view, not a separate view. Create the Broken-out Section view with a closed profile, usually by using the Spline Sketch tool. Material is remove to a specified depth to expose inner details.

Tutorial: Drawing Named Procedure 8-7

Identify the drawing name view and understand the procedure to create the name view.

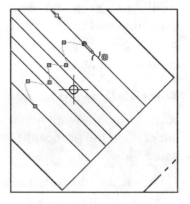

1. **View** the illustrated drawing view. The top drawing view is a Crop view. The Crop view is created by a closed sketch profile such as a circle, or spline as illustrated.

The Crop View provides the ability to crop an existing drawing view. You cannot use the Crop tool on a Detail view, a view from which a Detail view has been created, or an Exploded view.

Use the Crop tool to save steps. Example: instead of creating a Section View and then a Detail view, then hiding the unnecessary Section view, use the Crop tool to crop the Section view directly.

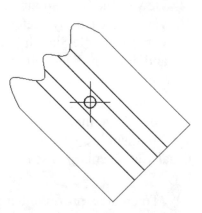

☀ In the exam; you are allowed to answer the questions in any order. Use the Summary Screen during the exam to view the list of all questions you have or have not answered.

Tutorial: Drawing Named Procedure 8-8

Identify the drawing name view and understand the procedure to create the name view.

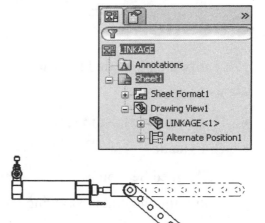

1. **View** the illustrated drawing view. The drawing view is an Alternate Position View.

   The Alternate Position view tool ⊞ provides the ability to superimpose an existing drawing view precisely on another. The alternate position is displayed with phantom lines.

☀ Use the Alternate Position view is display the range of motion of an assembly. You can dimension between the primary view and the Alternate Position view. You can not use the Alternate Position view tool with Broken, Section, or Detail views.

Summary

Drafting Competencies is one of the five categories on the CSWA exam. There are three questions on the CSWA exam in this category. Each question is worth five (5) points. The three questions are in a multiple choice single answer format.

Spend no more than 10 minutes on each question in this category. This is a timed exam. Manage your time.

Basic Part Creation and Modification and *Intermediate Part Creation and Modification* is the next chapter in this book. This chapter covers the knowledge to create and modify models for these categories from detailed dimensioned illustrations.

The complexity of the models along with the features progressively increases throughout the chapter to simulate the final types of model that could be provided on the exam.

☀ For additional detail exam information see The **Official Guide to Certified SolidWorks Associate Exams: CSWA, CSDA, and CSWSA-FEA** book. This book is written to assist the SolidWorks user to pass the associate level exams. Information is provided to aid a person to pass the Certified SolidWorks Associate (CSWA), Certified Sustainable Design Associate (CSDA) and the Certified SolidWorks Simulation Associate Finite Element Analysis (CSWSA FEA) exams. The primary goal of this book is not only to help you pass the exams, but also to ensure that you understand and comprehend the concepts and implementation details of the process.

Questions

1. Identify the illustrated Drawing view.

- A: Projected

- B: Alternative Position

- C: Extended

- D: Aligned Section

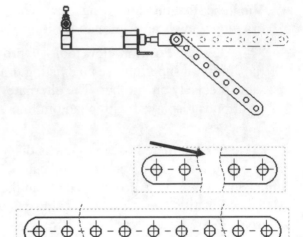

2. Identify the illustrated Drawing view.

- A: Crop

- B: Break

- C: Broken-out Section

- D: Aligned Section

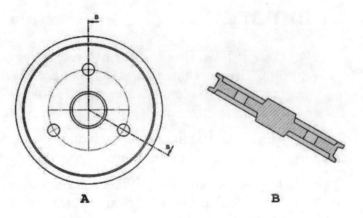

3. Identify the illustrated Drawing view.

- A: Section

- B: Crop

- C: Broken-out Section

- D: Aligned

4. Identify the view procedure. To create the following view, you need to insert a:

- A: Rectangle Sketch tool

- B: Closed Profile: Spline

- C: Open Profile: Circle

- D: None of the above

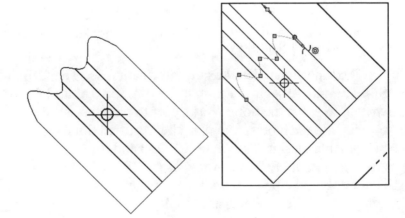

5. Identify the view procedure. To create the following view, you need to insert a:

- A: Open Spline

- B: Closed Spline

- C: 3 Point Arc

- D: None of the above

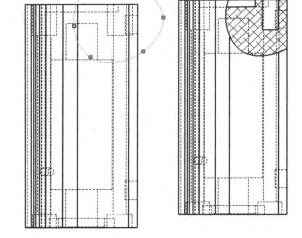

6. Identify the illustrated view type.

- A: Crop

- B: Section

- C: Projected

- D: Detail

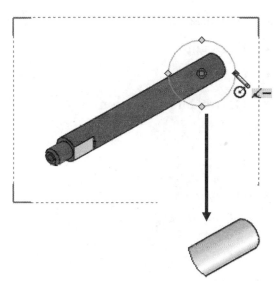

7. To create View B from Drawing View A insert which View type?

- A: Crop

- B: Section

- C: Aligned Section

- D: Projected

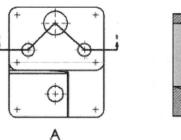

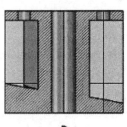

A   B

8. To create View B it is necessary to sketch a closed spline on View A and insert which View type?

- A: Broken out Section

- B: Detail

- C: Section

- D: Projected

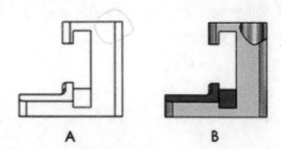

A   B

9. To create View B it is necessary to sketch a closed spline on View A and insert which View type?

- A: Horizontal Break

- B: Detail

- C: Section

- D: Broken out Section

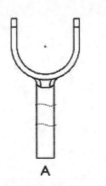

A   B

CHAPTER 9 - BASIC PART AND INTERMEDIATE PART CREATION AND MODIFICATION

Objectives

Basic Part Creation and Modification and Intermediate Part Creation and Modification are two of the five categories on the CSWA exam. This chapter covers the knowledge to create and modify models for these categories from detailed dimensioned illustrations.

There are two questions on the CSWA exam in the *Basic Part Creation and Modification* category. One question is in a multiple choice single answer format and the other question (Modification of the model) is in the fill in the blank format. Each question is worth fifteen (15) points for a total of thirty (30) points. You are required to build a model, with six or more features and to answer a question either on the overall mass, volume, or the location the Center of mass for the created model relative to the default part Origin location. You are then requested to modify the part and answer a fill in the blank format question.

There are two questions on the CSWA exam in the *Intermediate Part Creation and Modification* category. One question is in a multiple choice single answer format and the other question (Modification of the model) is in the fill in the blank format. Each question is worth fifteen (15) points for a total of thirty (30) points. You are required to build a model, with six or more features and to

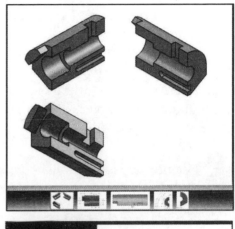

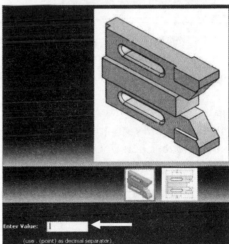

Screen shots from the exam

answer a question either on the overall mass, volume, or the location the Center of mass for the created model relative to the default part Origin location. You are then requested to modify the model and answer a fill in the blank format question.

The main difference between the *Basic Part Creation and Modification* category and the *Intermediate Part Creation and Modification* or the *Advance Part Creation and Modification* category is the complexity of the sketches and the number of dimensions and geometric relations along with an increase in the number of features.

On the completion of the chapter, you will be able to:

- Read and understand an Engineering document used in the CSWA exam:

  - Identify the Sketch plane, part Origin location, part dimensions, geometric relations, and design intent of the sketch and feature

- Build a part from a detailed dimensioned illustration using the following SolidWorks tools and features:

  - 2D & 3D sketch tools, Extruded Boss/Base, Extruded Cut, Fillet, Mirror, Revolved Base, Chamfer, Reference geometry, Plane, Axis, Calculate the overall mass and volume of the created part, and Locate the Center of mass for the created part relative to the Origin

The complexity of the models along with the features progressively increases throughout this chapter to simulate the final types of models that would be provided on the exam.

FeatureManager names were changed through various revisions of SolidWorks. Example: Extrude1 vs. Boss-Extrude1. These changes do not affect the models or answers in this book.

Read and understand an Engineering document

What is an Engineering document? In SolidWorks a part, assembly or drawing is referred to as a document. Each document is displayed in the Graphics window.

During the exam, each question will display an information table on the left side of the screen and drawing information on the right. Read the provided information and apply it to the drawing. Various values are provided on each question.

If you don't find your answer (within 1%) in the multiple choice single answer format section - recheck your solid model for precision and accuracy.

All SW models (initial and final) are provided on the DVD in the book. Copy the folders and model files to your local hard drive. Do not work directly from the DVD.

Modify the part in SolidWorks.

Unit system: MMGS (millimeter, gram, second)
Decimal places: 2
Part origin: Arbitrary
All holes through all unless shown otherwise.
Material: Aluminium 1060 Alloy
Density = 0.0027 g/mm^3

Modify the part using the following variable values:

A = 140.00
B = 50.00
C = 55 degrees

Note: Assume all unshown dimensions are the same as in the previous question.

What is the overall mass of the part (grams)?

Screen shot from the exam

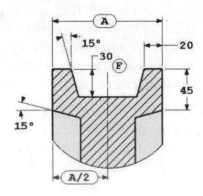

N

Build a Basic Part from a detailed illustration

Tutorial: Volume / Center of Mass 9-1

Build this model. Calculate the volume of the part and locate the Center of mass with the provided information.

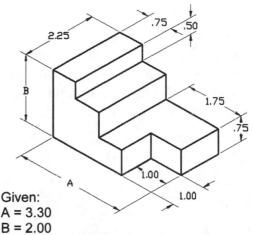

1. **Create** a New part in SolidWorks.

2. **Build** the illustrated dimensioned model. The model displays all edges on perpendicular planes. Think about the steps to build the model. Insert two features: Extruded Base (Boss-Extrude1) and Extruded Cut (Cut-Extrude1). The part Origin is located in the front left corner of the model. Think about your Base Sketch plane. Keep your Base Sketch simple.

Given:
A = 3.30
B = 2.00
Material: 2014 Alloy
Density = .101 lb/in^3
Units: IPS
Decimal places = 2

3. **Set** the document properties for the model.

4. Create **Sketch1**. Select the Front Plane as the Sketch plane. Sketch1 is the Base sketch. Sketch1 is the profile for the Extruded Base (Boss-Extrude1) feature. Insert the required geometric relations and dimensions.

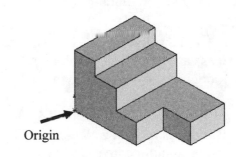

Origin

5. Create the **Extruded Base** feature. Boss-Extrude1 is the Base feature. Blind is the default End Condition in Direction 1. Depth = 2.25in. Identify the extrude direction to maintain the location of the Origin.

6. Create **Sketch2**. Select the Top right face as the Sketch plane for the second feature. Sketch a square. Sketch2 is the profile for the Extruded Cut feature. Insert the required geometric relations and dimensions.

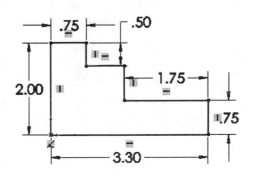

7. Create the **Extruded Cut** feature. Select Through All for End Condition in Direction 1.

8. **Assign** 2014 Alloy material to the part. Material is required to locate the Center of mass.

9. **Calculate** the volume. The volume = 8.28 cubic inches.

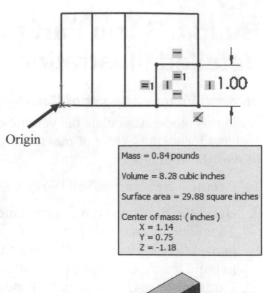

Origin

🔅 There are numerous ways to build the models in this chapter. A goal is to display different design intents and techniques.

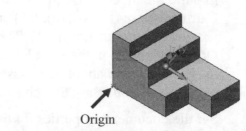

Mass = 0.84 pounds

Volume = 8.28 cubic inches

Surface area = 29.88 square inches

Center of mass: (inches)
  X = 1.14
  Y = 0.75
  Z = -1.18

10. **Locate** the Center of mass. The location of the Center of mass is derived from the part Origin.

- X: 1.14 inches

- Y: 0.75 inches

- Z: -1.18 inches

11. **Save** the part and name it Volume-Center of mass 9-1.

12. **Close** the model.

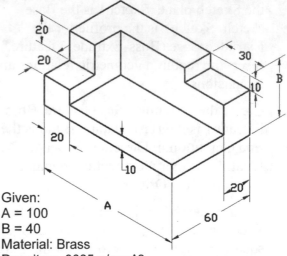

Origin

🔅 The principal axes and Center of mass are displayed graphically on the model in the Graphics window.

Tutorial: Volume / Center of Mass 9-2

Build this model. Calculate the volume of the part and locate the Center of mass with the provided information.

1. **Create** a New part in SolidWorks.

2. **Build** the illustrated dimensioned model. The model displays all edges on perpendicular planes. Think about the steps that are required to build this model. Remember, there are numerous ways to create the models in this chapter.

Given:
A = 100
B = 40
Material: Brass
Density = .0085 g/mm^3
Units: MMGS

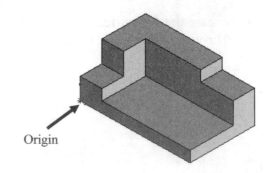

Origin

The CSWA exam is timed. Work efficiently.

View the provided Part FeatureManagers. Both FeatureManagers create the same illustrated model. In Option1, there are four sketches and four features (Extruded Base and three Extruded Cuts) that are used to build the model.

In Option2, there are three sketches and three features (Extruded Boss/Base) that are used to build the model. Which FeatureManager is better? In a timed exam, optimize your time and use the least amount of features through mirror, pattern, symmetry, etc.

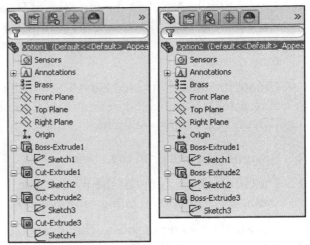

Use Centerlines to create symmetrical sketch elements and revolved features, or as construction geometry.

Create the model using the Option2 Part FeatureManager.

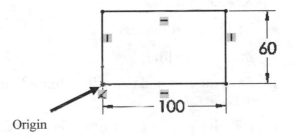

Origin

3. **Set** the document properties for the model.

4. Create **Sketch1**. Select the Top Plane as the Sketch plane. Sketch a rectangle. Insert the required dimensions.

5. Create the **Extruded Base** feature. Boss-Extrude1 is the Base feature. Blind is the default End Condition in Direction 1. Depth = 10mm.

Origin

6. Create **Sketch2**. Select the back face of Boss-Extrude1.

7. Select **Normal To** view. Sketch2 is the profile for the second Extruded Boss/Base feature. Insert the required geometric relations and dimensions as illustrated.

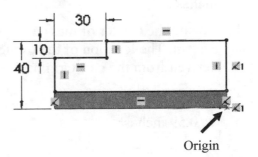

8. Create the second Extruded Boss/Base feature (**Boss-Extrude2**). Blind is the default End Condition in Direction 1. Depth = 20mm. Note the direction of the extrude, towards the front of the model.

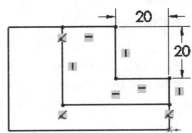

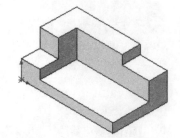

9. Create **Sketch3**. Select the left face of Boss-Extrude1 as the Sketch plane. Sketch3 is the profile for the third Extrude feature. Insert the required geometric relations and dimensions.

10. Create the third Extruded Boss/Base feature (**Boss-Extrude3**). Blind is the default End Condition in Direction 1. Depth = 20mm.

11. **Assign** Brass material to the part.

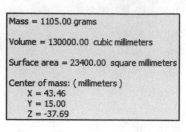

12. **Calculate** the volume of the model. The volume = 130,000.00 cubic millimeters.

13. **Locate** the Center of mass. The location of the Center of mass is derived from the part Origin.

- X: 43.46 millimeters

- Y: 15.00 millimeters

- Z: -37.69 millimeters

14. **Save** the part and name it Volume-Center of mass 9-2.

15. **Calculate** the volume of the model using the IPS unit system. The volume = 7.93 cubic inches.

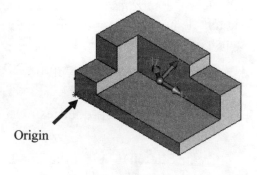

Origin

16. **Locate** the Center of mass using the IPS unit system. The location of the Center of mass is derived from the part Origin.

- X: 1.71 inches

- Y: 0.59 inches

- Z: -1.48 inches

16. **Save** the part and name it Volume-Center of mass 9-2-IPS.

17. **Close** the model.

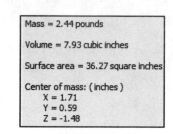

There are numerous ways to create the models in this chapter. A goal is to display different design intents and techniques.

All SW models (initial and final) are provided on the DVD in the book. Copy the folders and model files to your local hard drive. Do not work directly from the DVD.

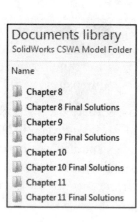

Tutorial: Mass-Volume 9-3

Build this model. Calculate the overall mass of the illustrated model with the provided information.

1. **Create** a New part in SolidWorks.

2. **Build** the illustrated model. The model displays all edges on perpendicular planes. Think about the steps required to build the model. Apply the Mirror Sketch tool to the Base sketch. Insert an Extruded Base (Boss-Extrude1) and Extruded-Cut (Cut-Extrude1) feature.

3. **Set** the document properties for the model.

🔆 To activate the Mirror Sketch tool, click **Tools**, **Sketch Tools**, **Mirror** from the Menu bar menu. The Mirror PropertyManager is displayed.

4. Create **Sketch1**. Select the Front Plane as the Sketch plane. Apply the Mirror Sketch tool. Select the construction geometry to mirror about as illustrated. Select the Entities to mirror. Insert the required geometric relations and dimensions.

🔆 Construction geometry is ignored when the sketch is used to create a feature. Construction geometry uses the same line style as centerlines.

🔆 When you create a new part or assembly, the three default Planes (Front, Right and Top) are align with specific views. The Plane you select for the Base sketch determines the orientation of the part.

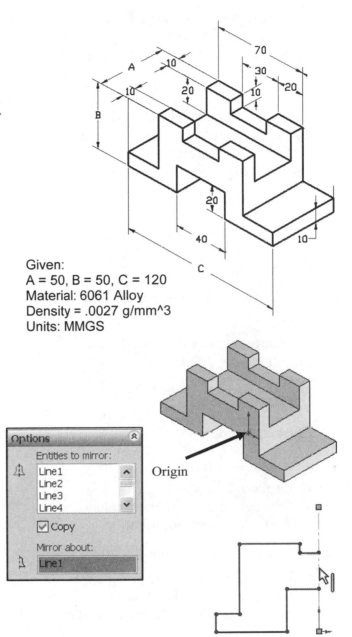

Given:
A = 50, B = 50, C = 120
Material: 6061 Alloy
Density = .0027 g/mm^3
Units: MMGS

Origin

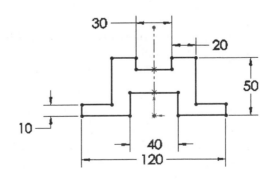

5. Create the **Boss-Extrude1** feature. Boss-Extrude1 is the Base feature. Apply the Mid Plane End Condition in Direction 1 for symmetry. Depth = 50mm.

6. Create **Sketch2**. Select the right face for the Sketch plane. Sketch2 is the profile for the Extruded Cut feature. Insert the required geometric relations and dimensions. Apply construction geometry.

7. Create the **Extruded Cut** feature. Through All is the selected End Condition in Direction 1.

8. **Assign** 6061 Alloy material to the part.

9. **Calculate** the overall mass. The overall mass = 302.40 grams.

10. **Save** the part and name it Mass-Volume 9-3.

11. **Close** the model.

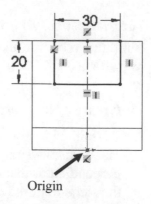

Origin

Mass = 302.40 grams

Volume = 112000.00 cubic millimeters

Surface area = 26200.00 square millimeters

Center of mass: (millimeters)
    X = 0.00
    Y = 19.20
    Z = 0.00

Tutorial: Mass-Volume 9-4

Build this model. Calculate the overall mass of the part and locate the Center of mass with the provided information.

1. **Create** a New part in SolidWorks.

2. **Build** the illustrated model. All edges of the model are not located on Perpendicular planes. Think about the steps required to build the model. Insert two features: Extruded Base (Boss-Extrude1) and Extruded Cut (Cut-Extrude1).

3. **Set** the document properties for the model.

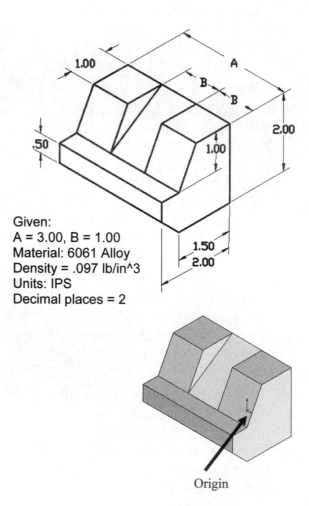

Given:
A = 3.00, B = 1.00
Material: 6061 Alloy
Density = .097 lb/in^3
Units: IPS
Decimal places = 2

Origin

4. Create **Sketch1**. Select the Right Plane as the Sketch plane. Apply construction geometry. Insert the required geometric relations and dimensions.

5. Create the **Extruded Base** feature. Boss-Extrude1 is the Base feature. Apply symmetry. Select Mid Plane as the End Condition in Direction 1. Depth = 3.00in.

6. Create **Sketch2**. Select the Right Plane as the Sketch plane. Select the Line Sketch tool. Insert the required geometric relations. Sketch2 is the profile for the Extruded Cut feature.

7. Create the **Extruded Cut (Cut-Extrude1)** feature. Apply symmetry. Select Mid Plane as the End Condition in Direction 1. Depth = 1.00in.

8. **Assign** 6061 Alloy material to the part.

9. **Calculate** overall mass. The overall mass = 0.87 pounds.

10. **Locate** the Center of mass. The location of the Center of mass is derived from the part Origin.

- X: 0.00 inches

- Y: 0.86 inches

- Z: 0.82 inches

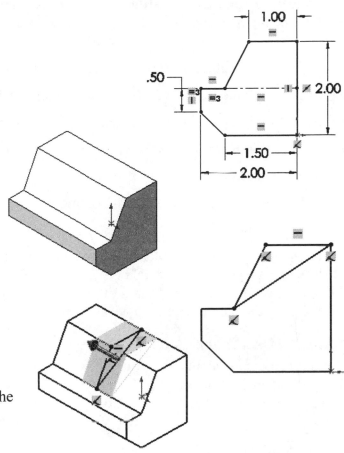

Mass = 0.87 pounds

Volume = 8.88 cubic inches

Surface area = 28.91 square inches

Center of mass: (inches)
    X = 0.00
    Y = 0.86
    Z = 0.82

In this category an exam question could read: Build this model. Locate the Center of mass with respect to the part Origin.

- A: X = 0.10 inches, Y = -0.86 inches, Z = -0.82 inches

- B: X = 0.00 inches, Y = 0.86 inches, Z = 0.82 inches

- C: X = 0.15 inches, Y = -0.96 inches, Z = -0.02 inches

- D: X = 1.00 inches, Y = -0.89 inches, Z = -1.82 inches

The correct answer is B.

11. **Save** the part and name it Mass-Volume 9-4.

12. **Close** the model.

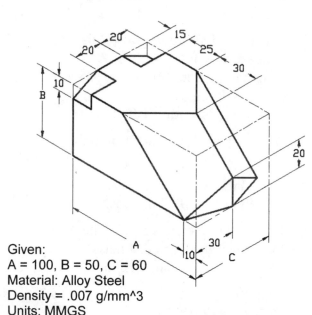

Origin

As an exercise, modify the Mass-Volume 9-4 part using the MMGS unit system. Assign Nickel as the material. Calculate the overall mass. The overall mass of the part = 1236.20 grams. Save the part and name it Mass-Volume 9-4-MMGS.

Tutorial: Mass-Volume 9-5

Build this model. Calculate the overall mass of the part and locate the Center of mass with the provided information.

1. **Create** a New part in SolidWorks.

2. **Build** the illustrated model. Insert five sketches and five features to build the model: Extruded Base, three Extruded Cut features and a Mirror feature.

⌇⌇ There are numerous ways to build the models in this chapter. A goal is to display different design intents and techniques.

3. **Set** the document properties for the model.

4. Create **Sketch1**. Select the Front Plane as the Sketch plane. Sketch a rectangle. Insert the required dimensions. The part Origin is located in the lower left corner of the sketch.

Given:
A = 100, B = 50, C = 60
Material: Alloy Steel
Density = .007 g/mm^3
Units: MMGS

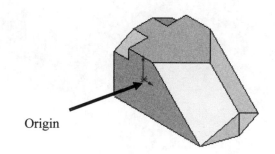

Origin

5. Create the **Extruded Base (Boss-Extrude1)** feature. Apply symmetry. Select the Mid Plane End Condition for Direction 1. Depth = 60mm.

6. Create **Sketch2**. Select the left face of Boss-Extrude1 as the Sketch plane. Insert the required geometric relations and dimensions.

7. Create the first **Extruded Cut** feature. Blind is the default End Condition in Direction 1. Depth = 15mm. Note the direction of the extrude feature.

8. Create **Sketch3**. Select the bottom face of Boss-Extrude1 for the Sketch plane. Insert the required geometric relations and dimension.

9. Create the second **Extruded Cut** feature. Blind is the default End Condition in Direction 1. Depth = 20mm.

10. Create **Sketch4**. Select Front Plane as the Sketch plane. Sketch a diagonal line. Sketch4 is the direction of extrusion for the third Extruded Cut feature. Insert the required dimension.

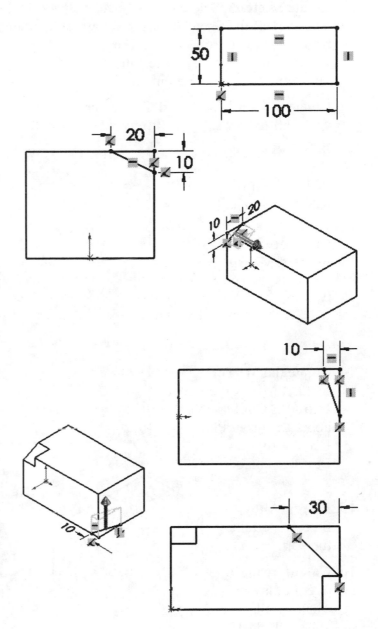

11. Create **Sketch5**. Select the top face of Boss-Extrude1 as the Sketch plane. Sketch5 is the sketch profile for the third Extruded Cut feature. Apply construction geometry. Insert the required geometric relations and dimensions.

12. Create the third **Extruded Cut** feature. Select Through All for End Condition in Direction 1.

13. Select **Sketch4** in the Graphics window for Direction of Extrusion. Line1@Sketch4 is displayed in the Cut-Extrude PropertyManager.

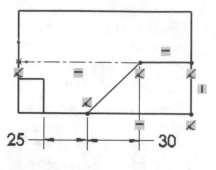

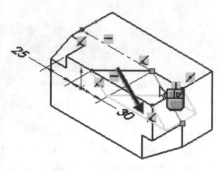

14. Create the **Mirror** feature. Mirror the three Extruded Cut features about the Front Plane. Use the fly-out FeatureManager.

15. **Assign** Alloy Steel material to the part.

16. **Calculate** the overall mass. The overall mass = 1794.10 grams.

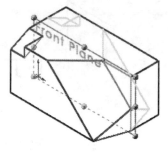

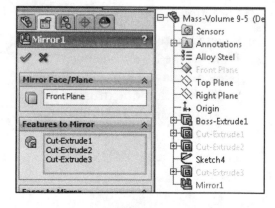

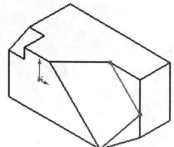

17. **Locate** the Center of mass. The location of the Center of mass is derived from the part Origin.

- X = 41.17 millimeters

- Y = 22.38 millimeters

- Z = 0.00 millimeters

View the triad location of the Center of mass for the part.

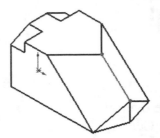

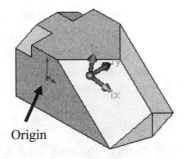

18. **Save** the part and name it Mass-Volume 9-5.

19. **Close** the model.

🔆 Set document precision from the Document Properties dialog box or from the Dimension PropertyManager. You can also address: Callout value, Tolerance type, and Dimension Text symbols in the Dimension PropertyManager.

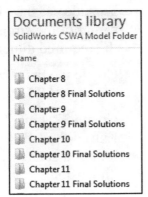

Origin

🔆 You are allowed to answer the questions in any order you prefer. Use the Summary Screen during the CSWA exam to view the list of all questions you have or have not answered.

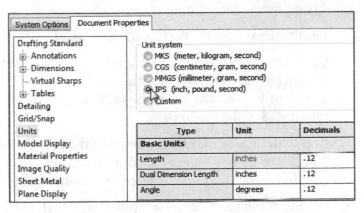

🔆 There are no Surfacing or Boundary feature questions on the CSWA exam at this time.

Build Additional Basic Parts

Tutorial: Mass-Volume 9-6

Build this model. Calculate the overall mass of the part and locate the Center of mass with the provided information.

1. **Create** a New part in SolidWorks.

2. **Build** the illustrated model. Think about the required steps to build this part. Insert four features: Extruded Base, two Extruded Cuts, and a Fillet.

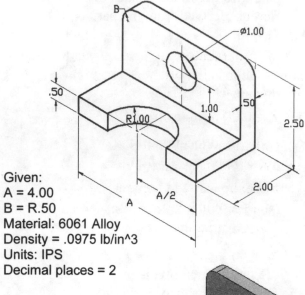

Given:
A = 4.00
B = R.50
Material: 6061 Alloy
Density = .0975 lb/in^3
Units: IPS
Decimal places = 2

There are numerous ways to build the models in this chapter. A goal is to display different design intents and techniques.

3. **Set** the document properties for the model.

4. Create **Sketch1**. Select the Right Plane as the Sketch plane. The part Origin is located in the lower left corner of the sketch. Insert the required geometric relations and dimensions.

5. Create the **Extruded Base (Boss-Extrude1)** feature. Apply symmetry. Select the Mid Plane End Condition for Direction 1. Depth = 4.00in.

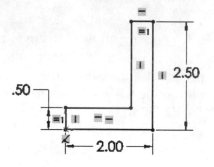

6. Create **Sketch2**. Select the top flat face of Boss-Extrude1 as the Sketch plane. Sketch a circle. The center of the circle is located at the part Origin. Insert the required dimension.

7. Create the first **Extruded Cut** feature. Select Through All for End Condition in Direction 1.

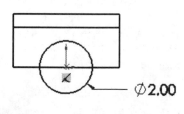

8. Create **Sketch3**. Select the front vertical face of Extrude1 as the Sketch plane. Sketch a circle. Insert the required geometric relations and dimensions.

9. Create the second **Extruded Cut** feature. Select Through All for End Condition in Direction 1.

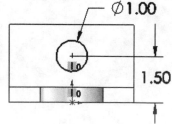

10. Create the **Fillet** feature. Constant radius is selected by default. Fillet the top two edges as illustrated. Radius = .50in.

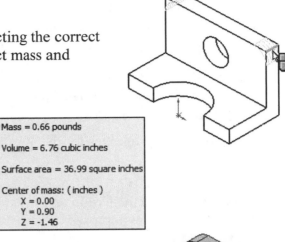

Radius: 0.5in

💡 A Fillet feature removes material. Selecting the correct radius value is important to obtain the correct mass and volume answer in the exam.

11. **Assign** the defined material to the part.

12. **Calculate** the overall mass. The overall mass = 0.66 pounds.

13. **Locate** the Center of mass. The location of the Center of mass is derived from the part Origin.

Mass = 0.66 pounds

Volume = 6.76 cubic inches

Surface area = 36.99 square inches

Center of mass: (inches)
    X = 0.00
    Y = 0.90
    Z = -1.46

- X: 0.00 inches

- Y: 0.90 inches

- Z: -1.46 inches

In this category an exam question could read: Build this model. Locate the Center of mass relative to the part Origin.

- A: X = -2.63 inches, Y = 4.01 inches, Z = -0.04 inches

- B: X = 4.00 inches, Y = 1.90 inches, Z = -1.64 inches

- C: X = 0.00 inches, Y = 0.90 inches, Z = -1.46 inches

- D: X = -1.69 inches, Y = 1.00 inches, Z = 0.10 inches

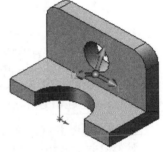

The correct answer is C. Note: Tangent edges and Origin is displayed for educational purposes.

14. **Save** the part and name it Mass-Volume 9-6.

15. **Close** the model.

As an exercise, calculate the overall mass of the part using the MMGS unit system, and assign 2014 Alloy material to the part.

Mass = 310.17 grams

Volume = 110774.26 cubic millimeters

Surface area = 23865.83 square millimeters

Center of mass: (millimeters)
    X = 0.00
    Y = 22.83
    Z = -37.11

The overall mass of the part = 310.17 grams. Save the part and name it Mass-Volume 9-6-MMGS.

Tutorial: Mass-Volume 9-7

Build this model. Calculate the overall mass of the part and locate the Center of mass with the provided information.

1. **Create** a New part in SolidWorks.

2. **Build** the illustrated model. Insert two features: Extruded Base (Boss-Extrude1) and Revolved Boss.

3. **Set** the document properties for the model.

🔆 Tangent edges and the Origin are displayed for educational purposes.

4. Create **Sketch1**. Select the Top Plane as the Sketch plane. Apply construction geometry. Apply the Tangent Arc and Line Sketch tool. Insert the required geometric relations and dimensions.

5. Create the **Extruded Base** feature. Blind is the default End Condition. Depth = 8mm.

6. Create **Sketch2**. Select the Front Plane as the Sketch plane. Apply construction geometry for the Revolved Boss feature. Insert the required geometric relations and dimension.

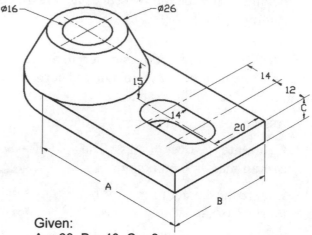

Given:
A = 60, B = 40, C = 8
Material: Cast Alloy Steel
Density = .0073 g/mm^3
Units: MMGS

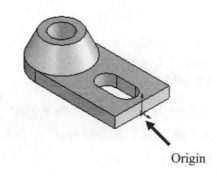

Origin

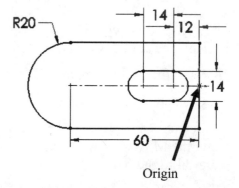

Origin

7. Create the **Revolved Boss** feature. The default angle is 360deg. Select the centerline for Axis of Revolution.

8. **Assign** the defined material to the part.

9. **Calculate** the overall mass. The overall mass = 229.46 grams.

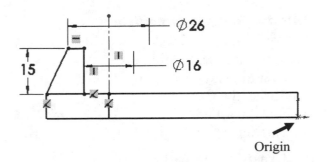

Origin

10. **Locate** the Center of mass. The location of the Center of mass is derived from the part Origin.

- X = -46.68 millimeters

- Y = 7.23 millimeters

- Z = 0.00 millimeters

In this category an exam question could read: Build this model. What is the overall mass of the part?

- A: 229.46 grams

- B: 249.50 grams

- C: 240.33 grams

- D: 120.34 grams

The correct answer is A.

11. **Save** the part and name it Mass-Volume 9-7.

12. **Close** the model.

☼ Tangent edges and Origin is displayed for educational purposes.

☼ When you create a new part or assembly, the three default Planes (Front, Right and Top) are align with specific views. The Plane you select for the Base sketch determines the orientation of the part.

Mass = 229.46 grams

Volume = 31433.02 cubic millimeters

Surface area = 9459.63 square millimeters

Center of mass: (millimeters)
  X = -46.68
  Y = 7.23
  Z = 0.00

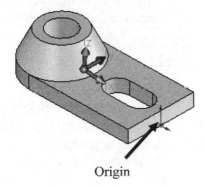

Origin

Tutorial: Basic/Intermediate Part 9-1

Build this model. Calculate the overall mass of the part and locate the Center of mass with the provided information.

1. **Create** a New part in SolidWorks.

2. **Build** the illustrated model. Think about the various features that create the part. Insert seven features and a plane to build this part: Extruded-Thin1, Boss-Extrude1, Cut-Extrude1, Cut-Extrude2 and three Fillets. Apply reference construction planes to build the circular features.

3. **Set** the document properties for the model.

4. Create **Sketch1**. Select the Front Plane as the Sketch plane. Apply construction geometry as the reference line for the 30deg angle. Insert the required geometric relations and dimensions. Note the location of the Origin.

5. Create the **Extrude-Thin1** feature. This is the Base feature. Apply symmetry. Select Mid Plane for End Condition in Direction 1 to maintain the location of the Origin. Depth = 52mm. Thickness = 12mm.

⌖ Use the Thin Feature option to control the extrude thickness, not the Depth.

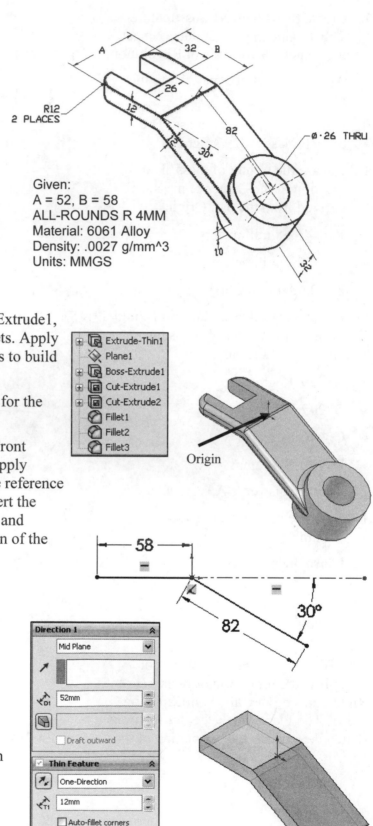

Given:
A = 52, B = 58
ALL-ROUNDS R 4MM
Material: 6061 Alloy
Density: .0027 g/mm^3
Units: MMGS

6. Create **Plane1**. Plane1 is the Sketch plane for the Extruded Boss (Boss-Extrude1) feature. Select the midpoint and the top face as illustrated. Plane1 is located in the middle of the top and bottom faces. Select Parallel Plane at Point for option.

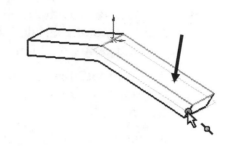

🔅 Plane1 uses the Depth dimension of 32mm.

7. Create **Sketch2**. Select Plane1 as the Sketch plane. Use the Normal To view tool. Sketch a circle to create the Extruded Boss feature. Insert the required geometric relations.

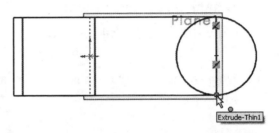

🔅 The Normal To view tool rotates and zooms the model to the view orientation normal to the selected plane, planar face, or feature.

8. Create the **Extruded Boss** feature. Apply Symmetry. Select Mid Plane for End Condition in Direction 1. Depth = 32mm.

9. Create **Sketch3**. Select the top circular face of Boss-Extrude1 as the Sketch plane. Sketch a circle. Insert the required geometric relation and dimension.

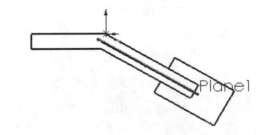

🔅 There are numerous ways to create the models in this chapter. A goal is to display different design intents and techniques.

10. Create the first **Extruded Cut** feature. Select Through All for End Condition in Direction 1.

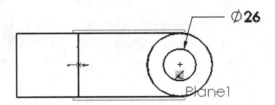

11. Create **Sketch4**. Select the top face of Extrude-Thin1 as the Sketch plane. Apply construction geometry. Insert the required geometric relations and dimensions.

12. Create the second **Extruded Cut** feature. Select Through All for End Condition in Direction 1.

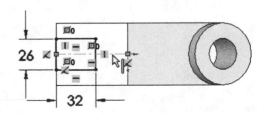

13. Create the **Fillet1** feature. Fillet the left and right edges of Extrude-Thin1 as illustrated. Radius = 12mm.

14. Create the **Fillet2** feature. Fillet the top and bottom edges of Extrude-Thin1 as illustrated. Radius = 4mm.

15. Create the **Fillet3** feature. Fillet the rest of the model; six edges as illustrated. Radius = 4mm.

16. **Assign** the defined material to the part.

17. **Calculate** the overall mass of the part. The overall mass = 300.65 grams.

18. **Locate** the Center of mass. The location of the Center of mass is derived from the part Origin.

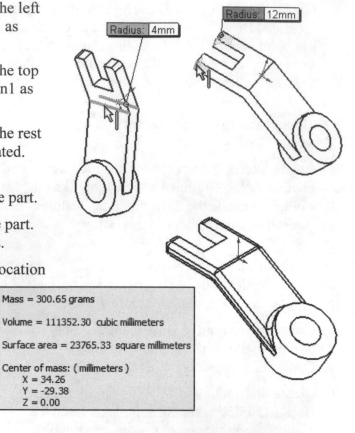

- X: 34.26 millimeters

- Y: -29.38 millimeters

- Z: 0.00 millimeters

```
Mass = 300.65 grams

Volume = 111352.30  cubic millimeters

Surface area = 23765.33  square millimeters

Center of mass: ( millimeters )
    X = 34.26
    Y = -29.38
    Z = 0.00
```

19. **Save** the part and name it Part-Modeling 9-1.

20. **Close** the model.

As an exercise, modify the Fillet2 and Fillet3 radius from 4mm to 2mm. Modify the Fillet1 radius from 12m to 10mm. Modify the material from 6061 Alloy to ABS.

Modify the Sketch1 angle from 30deg to 45deg. Modify the Extrude depth from 32mm to 38mm. Recalculate the location of the Center of mass with respect to the part Origin.

- X = 27.62 millimeters

- Y = -40.44 millimeters

- Z = 0.00 millimeters

21. **Save** the part and name it Part-Modeling 9-1-Modify.

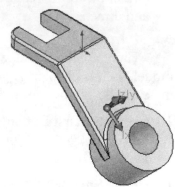

```
Mass = 123.60 grams

Volume = 121173.81  cubic millimeters

Surface area = 25622.46  square millimeters

Center of mass: ( millimeters )
    X = 27.62
    Y = -40.44
    Z = 0.00
```

In the exam; you are allowed to answer the questions in any order. Use the Summary Screen during the exam to view the list of all questions you have or have not answered.

Tutorial: Basic/Intermediate - Part 9-2

Build this model. Calculate the volume of the part and locate the Center of mass with the provided information.

1. **Create** a New part in SolidWorks.

2. **Build** the illustrated model. Think about the various features that create this model. Insert five features and a plane to build this part: Extruded Base, two Extruded Bosses, Extruded Cut and a Rib. Insert a reference plane to create the Boss-Extrude2 feature.

3. **Set** the document properties for the model.

4. Create **Sketch1**. Select the Top Plane as the Sketch plane. Sketch a rectangle. Apply two construction lines for an Intersection relation. Use the horizontal construction line as the Plane1 reference. Insert the required relations and dimensions.

5. Create the **Extruded Base** feature. Blind is the default End Condition in Direction 1. Depth = 1.00in. Note the extrude direction is downward.

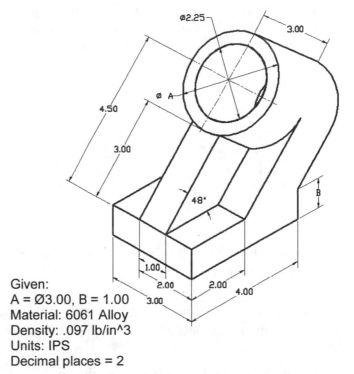

Given:
A = Ø3.00, B = 1.00
Material: 6061 Alloy
Density: .097 lb/in^3
Units: IPS
Decimal places = 2

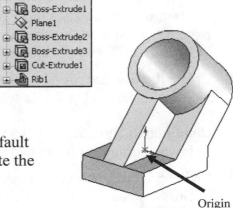

🔅 Create planes to aid in the modeling for the exam. Use planes to sketch, to create a section view, for a neutral plane in a draft feature, and so on.

🔅 The created plane is displayed 5% larger than the geometry on which the plane is created, or 5% larger than the bounding box. This helps reduce selection problems when planes are created directly on faces or from orthogonal geometry.

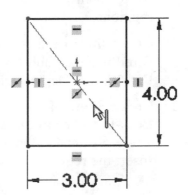

Origin

6. Create **Plane1**. Plane1 is the Sketch plane for the Extruded Boss feature. Show Sketch1. Select the horizontal construction line in Sketch1 and the top face of Boss-Extrude1. Angle = 48deg.

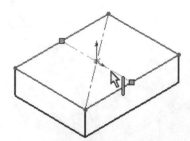
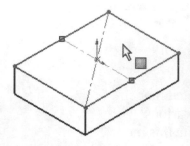

💡 Click **View, Sketches** from the Menu bar menu to displayed sketches in the Graphics window.

💡 The Normal To view tool rotates and zooms the model to the view orientation normal to the selected plane, planar face, or feature.

7. Create **Sketch2**. Select Plane1 as the Sketch plane. Create the Extruded Boss profile. Insert the required geometric relations and dimension. Note: Dimension to the front top edge of Boss-Extrude1 as illustrated.

8. Create the first **Extruded Boss** feature. Select the Up To Vertex End

    Condition in Direction 1. Select the back top right vertex point as illustrated.

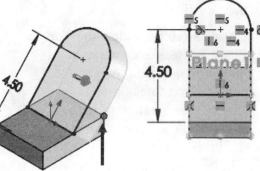

9. Create **Sketch3**. Select the back angled face of Boss-Extrude2 as the Sketch plane. Sketch a circle. Insert the required geometric relations.

10. Create the third **Extruded Boss** feature. Blind is the default End Condition in Direction 1. Depth = 3.00in.

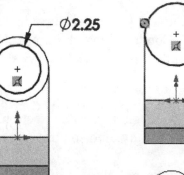

11. Create **Sketch4**. Select the front face of Boss-Extrude3 as the Sketch plane. Sketch a circle. Sketch4 is the profile for the Extruded Cut feature. Insert the required geometric relation and dimension.

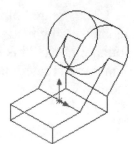

The part Origin is displayed in blue.

12. Create the **Extruded Cut** feature. Select Through All for End Condition in Direction 1.

13. Create **Sketch5**. Select the Right Plane as the Sketch plane. Insert a Parallel relation to partially define Sketch5. Sketch5 is the profile for the Rib feature. Sketch5 does not need to be fully defined. Sketch5 locates the end conditions based on existing geometry.

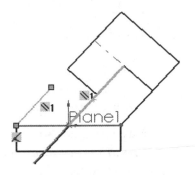

14. Create the **Rib** feature. Thickness = 1.00in.

The Rib feature is a special type of extruded feature created from open or closed sketched contours. The Rib feature adds material of a specified thickness in a specified direction between the contour and an existing part. You can create a rib feature using single or multiple sketches.

15. **Assign** 6061 Alloy material to the part.

16. **Calculate** the volume. The volume = 30.65 cubic inches.

17. **Locate** the Center of mass. The location of the Center of mass is derived from the part Origin.

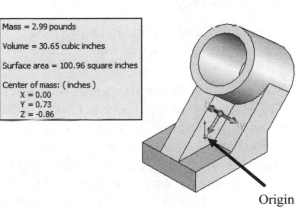

- X: 0.00 inches
- Y: 0.73 inches
- Z: -0.86 inches

18. **Save** the part and name it Part-Modeling 9-2.

19. **Close** the model.

As an exercise, modify the Rib1 feature from 1.00in to 1.25in. Modify the Extrude depth from 3.00in to 3.25in. Modify the material from 6061 Alloy to Copper.

Modify the Plane1 angle from 48deg to 30deg. Recalculate the volume of the part. The new volume = 26.94 cubic inches.

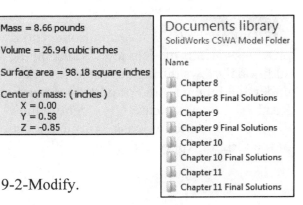

20. **Save** the part and name it Part-Modeling 9-2-Modify.

Summary

Basic Part Creation and Modification and Intermediate Part Creation and Modification is two of the five categories on the CSWA exam.

There are two questions on the CSWA exam in the *Basic Part Creation and Modification* category. One question is in a multiple choice single answer format and the other question (Modification of the model) is in the fill in the blank format. Each question is worth fifteen (15) points for a total of thirty (30) points.

There are two questions on the CSWA exam in the *Intermediate Part Creation and Modification* category. One question is in a multiple choice single answer format and the other question (Modification of the model) is in the fill in the blank format. Each question is worth fifteen (15) points for a total of thirty (30) points.

The main difference between the *Basic Part Creation and Modification* category and the *Intermediate Part Creation and Modification* or the *Advance Part Creation and Modification* category is the complexity of the sketches and the number of dimensions and geometric relations along with an increase in the number of features.

At this time, there are no modeling questions on the exam that requires you to use Sheet Metal, Loft, Surfacing or Swept features.

💡 For additional detail exam information see The **Official Guide to Certified SolidWorks Associate Exams: CSWA, CSDA, and CSWSA-FEA** book. This book is written to assist the SolidWorks user to pass the associate level exams. Information is provided to aid a person to pass the Certified SolidWorks Associate (CSWA), Certified Sustainable Design Associate (CSDA) and the Certified SolidWorks Simulation Associate Finite Element Analysis (CSWSA FEA) exams. The primary goal of this book is not only to help you pass the exams, but also to ensure that you understand and comprehend the concepts and implementation details of the process.

💡 During the CSWA exam; SolidWorks provides various model views. Click on the additional views during the exam to better understand the part and provided information. Read each question carefully. Identify the dimensions, center of mass, units and location of the Origin. Apply needed material.

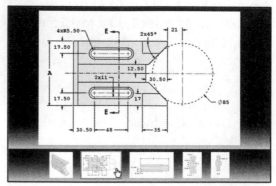

Screen shot from the exam

Questions

1. Build this model: Set document properties, identify the correct Sketch planes, apply the correct Sketch and Feature tools and apply material.

Calculate the overall mass of the part, volume, and locate the Center of mass with the provided illustrated information.

- Material: 6061 Alloy

- Units: MMGS

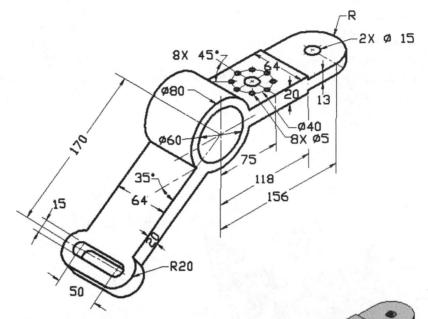

When you create a new part or assembly, the three default planes (Front, Right and Top) are align with specific views. The plane you select for the Base sketch determines the orientation of the part.

Origin

2. Build this model. Set document properties and identify the correct Sketch planes. Apply the correct Sketch and Feature tools, and apply material.

Calculate the overall mass of the part, volume, and locate the Center of mass with the provided information.

- Material: 6061 Alloy

- Units: MMGS

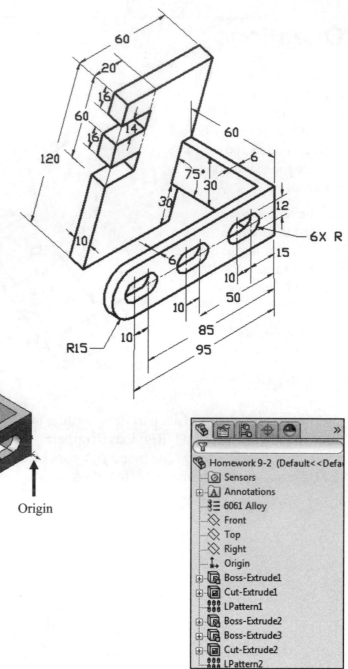

Origin

3. Build this model. Set document properties and identify the correct Sketch planes. Apply the correct Sketch and Feature tools, and apply material.

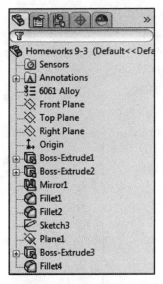

Calculate the overall mass of the part, volume, and locate the Center of mass with the provided information.

- Material: 6061

- Units: IPS

- View the provided drawing views for details

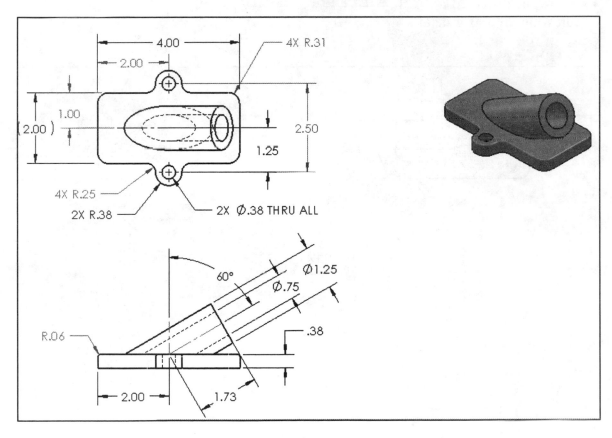

4. Build this model. Set document properties and identify the correct Sketch planes. Apply the correct Sketch and Feature tools, and apply material.

Calculate the overall mass of the part, volume, and locate the Center of mass with the provided information.

- Material: 6061

- Units: IPS

- View the provided drawing views for details

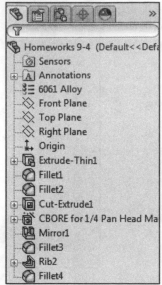

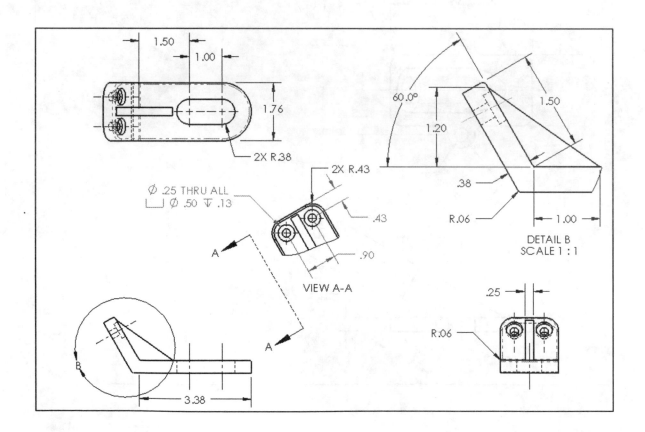

Sample screen shots from an older CSWA exam for a simple part. Click on the additional views to understand the part and to provide information. Read each question carefully. Understand the dimensions, center of mass and units. Apply needed materials.

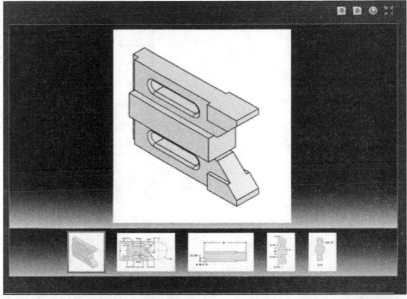

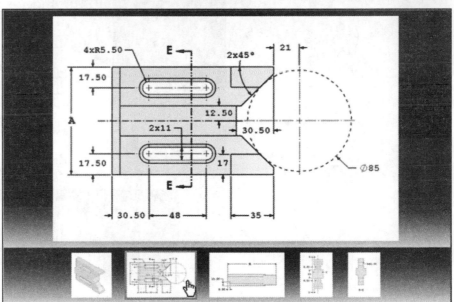

Screen shots from the exam

💡 Zoom in on the part or view if needed.

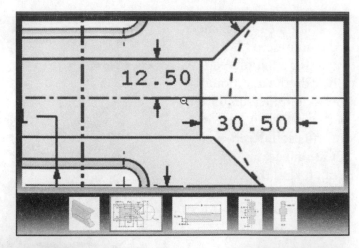

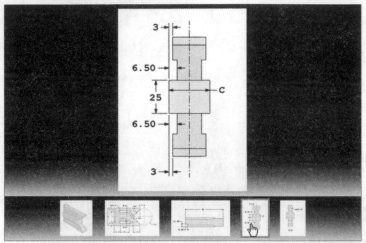

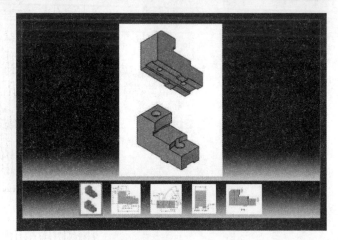

Screen shots from the exam

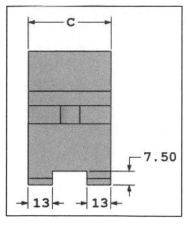

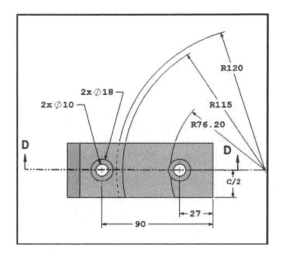

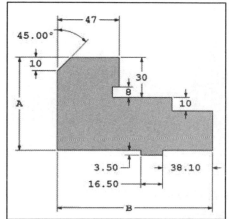

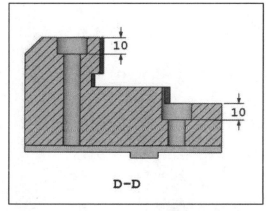

D-D

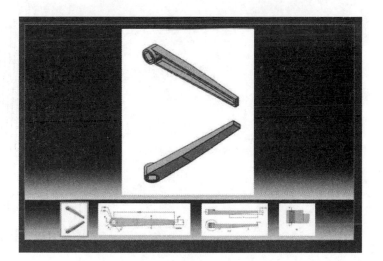

Screen shots from the exam

Notes:

CHAPTER 10 - ADVANCED PART CREATION AND MODIFICATION

Objectives

Advanced Part Creation and Modification is one of the five categories on the CSWA exam. The main difference between the *Advanced Part Creation and Modification* and the *Basic Part Creation and Modification* or the *Intermediate Part Creation and Modification* category is the complexity of the sketches and the number of dimensions and geometric relations along with an increase number of features.

There are three questions on the CSWA exam in this category. One question is in a multiple choice single answer format and the other two questions (Modification of the model) are in the fill in the blank format. Each question is worth fifteen (15) points for a total of fourth five (45) points.

You are required to build a model, with six or more features and to answer a question either on the overall mass, volume, or the location the Center of mass for the created model relative to the default part Origin location. You are then requested to modify the model and answer fill in the blank format questions.

Question (double-click to go to)	Points	State
1 A00004: Drafting Competencies - To create drawing view 'B' from drawing view ...	5	Answered
2 A00005: Drafting Competencies - To create drawing view 'B' it is necessary to sk...	5	Answered
3 A00006: Drafting Competencies - To create drawing view 'B' it is necessary to se...	5	Answered
4 B22001: Basic Part (Hydraulic Cylinder Half) - Step 1	15	Answered
5 B22002: Basic Part (Hydraulic Cylinder Half) - Step 2	15	Answered
6 D12801: Intermediate Part (Wheel) - Step 1	15	Answered
7 D12802: Intermediate Part (Wheel) - Step 2	15	Answered
8 E11101: Build this assembly in SolidWorks (Connecting Rod Assembly)	30	Answered
9 E11602: Modify this assembly in SolidWorks (Connecting Rod Assembly)	30	Answered
10 E21211: Build this assembly in SolidWorks (Linkage Assembly)	30	Answered
11 E20302: Modify this assembly in SolidWorks (Linkage Assembly)	30	Answered
12 C12801: Advanced Part (Bracket) - Step 1	15	Answered
13 C12802: Advanced Part (Bracket) - Step 2	15	Answered
14 C12803: Advanced Part (Bracket) - Step 3	15	Answered

For 15 points: ?

C12801: Advanced Part (Bracket) - Step 1
Build this part in SolidWorks.
(Save part after each question in a different file in case it must be reviewed)

Unit system: MMGS (millimeter, gram, second)
Decimal places: 2
Part origin: Arbitrary
All holes through all unless shown otherwise.
Material: AISI 1020 Steel
Density = 0.0079 g/mm^3

A = 64.00
B = 20.00
C = 26.50

What is the overall mass of the part (grams)?

Hint: If you don't find an option within 1% of your answer please re-check your solid model.

Screen shots from the exam

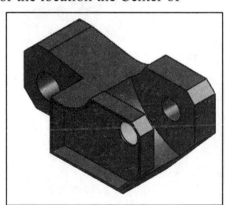

Screen shots from the exam

On the completion of the chapter, you will be able to:

- Specify Document Properties

- Interpret Engineering terminology

- Build an advanced part from a detailed dimensioned illustration using the following tools and features:

  - 2D & 3D Sketch tools, Extruded Boss/Base, Extruded Cut, Fillet, Mirror, Revolved Boss/Base, Linear & Circular Pattern, Chamfer and Revolved Cut

- Locate the Center of mass relative to the part Origin

- Create a coordinate system location

- Locate the Center of mass relative to a created Coordinate system

Build an Advanced part from a detailed dimensioned illustration

Tutorial: Advanced Part 10-1

An exam question in this category could read: Build this part. Calculate the overall mass and locate the Center of mass of the illustrated model.

1. **Create** a New part in SolidWorks.

2. **Build** the illustrated model. Insert seven features: Extruded Base, two Extruded Bosses, two Extruded Cuts, a Chamfer and a Fillet.

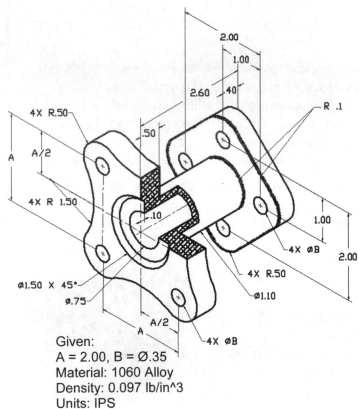

Given:
A = 2.00, B = Ø.35
Material: 1060 Alloy
Density: 0.097 lb/in^3
Units: IPS
Decimal places = 2

Think about the steps that you would take to build the illustrated part. Identify the location of the part Origin. Start with the back base flange. Review the provided dimensions and annotations in the illustration.

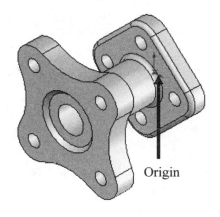
Origin

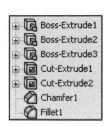

💡 The main difference between the *Advanced Part Creation and Modification* and the *Basic Part Creation and Modification* or the *Intermediate Part Creation and Modification* category is the complexity of the sketches and the number of dimensions and geometric relations along with an increase number of features.

💡 All SW models (initial and final) are provided on the DVD in the book. Copy the folders and model files to your local hard drive. Do not work directly from the DVD.

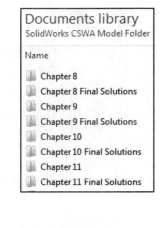

Documents library
SolidWorks CSWA Model Folder

Name

Chapter 8
Chapter 8 Final Solutions
Chapter 9
Chapter 9 Final Solutions
Chapter 10
Chapter 10 Final Solutions
Chapter 11
Chapter 11 Final Solutions

3. **Set** the document properties for the model.

4. Create **Sketch1**. Sketch1 is the Base sketch. Select the Front Plane as the Sketch plane. Apply construction geometry. Sketch a horizontal and vertical centerline. Sketch four circles. Insert an Equal relation. Insert a Symmetric relation about the vertical and horizontal centerlines. Sketch two top angled lines and a tangent arc. Apply the Mirror Sketch tool. Complete the sketch. Insert the required geometric relations and dimensions.

💡 In a Symmetric relation, the selected items remain equidistant from the centerline, on a line perpendicular to the centerline. Sketch entities to select: a centerline and two points, lines, arcs or ellipses.

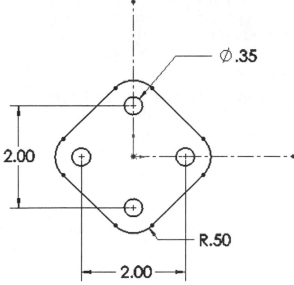

🔆 In the exam; you are allowed to answer the questions in any order. Use the Summary Screen during the exam to view the list of all questions you have or have not answered.

🔆 The Sketch Fillet tool rounds the selected corner at the intersection of two sketch entities, creating a tangent arc.

5. Create the **Extruded Base** feature. Boss-Extrude1 is the Base feature. Blind is the default End Condition in Direction 1. Depth = .40in.

6. Create **Sketch2**. Select the front face of Boss-Extrude1 as the Sketch plane. Sketch a circle. Insert the required geometric relation and dimension.

7. Create the first **Extruded Boss** feature. Blind is the default End Condition in Direction 1. The Extrude feature is the tube between the two flanges. Depth = 1.70in.
    Note: 1.70in = 2.60in - (.50in + .40in).

🔆 The complexity of the models along with the features progressively increases throughout this chapter to simulate the final types of parts that could be provided on the CSWA exam.

🔆 When you create a new part or assembly, the three default Planes (Front, Right and Top) are align with specific views. The Plane you select for the Base sketch determines the orientation of the part.

🔆 There are no Surfacing or Boundary feature questions on the CSWA exam at this time.

🔆 The book is design to expose the new user to many tools, techniques and procedures. It may not always use the most direct tool or process.

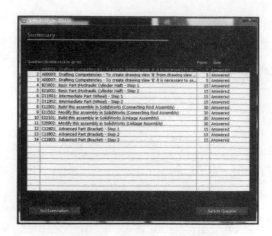

Screen shot from the exam

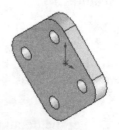

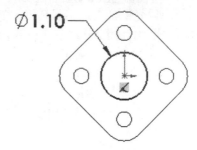

Ø1.10

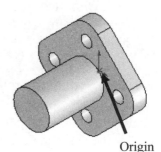

Origin

8. Create **Sketch3**. Select the front circular face of Boss-Extrude2 as the Sketch plane. Sketch a horizontal and vertical centerline. Sketch the top two circles. Insert an Equal and Symmetric relation between the two circles. Mirror the top two circles about the horizontal centerline. Insert dimensions to locate the circles from the Origin. Apply either the 3 Point Arc or the Centerpoint Arc Sketch tool. The center point of the Tangent Arc is aligned with a Vertical relation to the Origin. Complete the sketch.

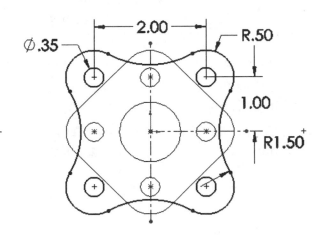

Use the Centerpoint Arc Sketch tool to create an arc from a: centerpoint, a start point, and an end point.

Apply the Tangent Arc Sketch tool to create an arc, tangent to a sketch entity.

The Arc PropertyManager controls the properties of a sketched Centerpoint Arc, Tangent Arc, and 3 Point Arc.

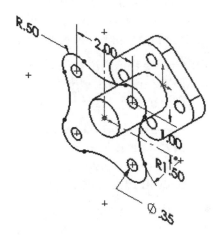

9. Create the second **Extruded Boss** feature. Blind is the default End Condition in Direction 1. Depth = .50in.

10. Create **Sketch4**. Select the front face of the Extrude feature as the Sketch plane. Sketch a circle. Insert the required geometric relation and dimension.

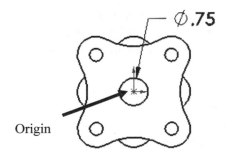

Origin

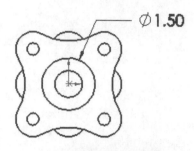

11. Create the first **Extruded Cut** feature. Select the Through All End Condition for Direction 1.

12. Create **Sketch5**. Select the front face of the Extrude feature as the Sketch plane. Sketch a circle. Insert the required geometric relation and dimension.

13. Create the second **Extruded Cut** feature. Blind is the default End Condition for Direction1. Depth = .10in.

14. Create the **Chamfer** feature. In order to have the outside circle 1.50in, select the inside edge of the sketched circle. Create an Angle distance chamfer. Distance = .10in. Angle = 45deg.

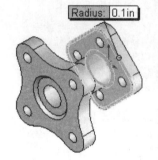

The Chamfer feature creates a beveled feature on selected edges, faces or a vertex.

15. Create the **Fillet** feature. Fillet the two edges as illustrated. Radius = .10in.

16. **Assign** 1060 Alloy material to the part. Material is required to calculate the overall mass of the part.

17. **Calculate** the overall mass. The overall mass = 0.59 pounds.

18. **Locate** the Center of mass. The location of the Center of mass is relative to the part Origin.

- X: 0.00

- Y: 0.00

- Z: 1.51

19. **Save** the part and name it Advanced Part 10-1.

20. **Close** the model.

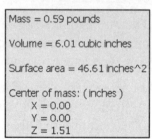

Mass = 0.59 pounds

Volume = 6.01 cubic inches

Surface area = 46.61 inches^2

Center of mass: (inches)
X = 0.00
Y = 0.00
Z = 1.51

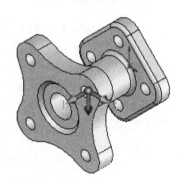

Tutorial: Advanced Part 10-2

An exam question in this category could read: Build this part. Calculate the overall mass and locate the Center of mass of the illustrated model.

1. **Create** a New part in SolidWorks.

2. **Build** the illustrated dimensioned model. Insert eight features: Extruded Base, Extruded Cut, Circular Pattern, two Extruded Bosses, Extruded Cut, Chamfer and Fillet.

Think about the steps that you would take to build the illustrated part. Review the provided information. Start with the six hole flange.

🔆 Tangent Edges are displayed for educational purposes.

3. **Set** the document properties for the model.

4. Create **Sketch1**. Sketch1 is the Base sketch. Select the Front Plane as the Sketch plane. Sketch two circles. Insert the required geometric relations and dimensions.

5. Create the **Extruded Base** feature. Blind is the default End Condition in Direction 1. Depth = 10mm. Note the direction of the extrude feature to maintain the Origin location.

6. Create **Sketch2**. Select the front face of Boss-Extrude1 as the Sketch plane. Sketch2 is the profile for first Extruded Cut feature. The Extruded Cut feature is the seed feature for the Circular Pattern. Apply construction reference geometry. Insert the required geometric relations and dimensions.

Given:
A = 70, B = 76
Material: 6061 Alloy
Density: .0027 g/mm^3
Units: MMGS

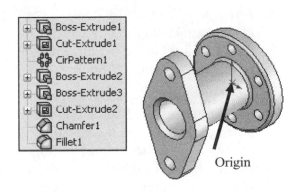

Origin

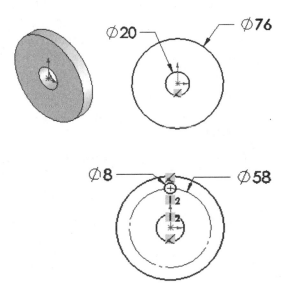

7. Create the **Extruded Cut** feature. Cut-Extrude1 is the first bolt hole. Select Through All for End Condition in Direction 1.

8. Create the **Circular Pattern** feature. Default Angle = 360deg. Number of instances = 6. Select the center axis for the Pattern Axis box.

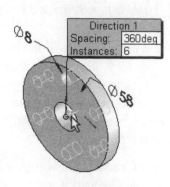

💡 The Circular Pattern PropertyManager is displayed when you pattern one or more features about an axis.

9. Create **Sketch3**. Select the front face of the Extrude feature as the Sketch plane. Sketch two circles. Insert a Coradial relation on the inside circle. The two circles share the same center point and radius. Insert the required dimension.

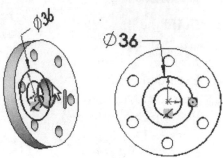

10. Create the first **Extruded Boss (Boss-Extrude2)** feature. The Boss-Extrude2 feature is the connecting tube between the two flanges. Blind is the default End Condition in Direction 1. Depth = 48mm.

11. Create **Sketch4**. Select the front circular face of Extrude3 as the Sketch plane. Sketch a horizontal and vertical centerline from the Origin. Sketch the top and bottom circles symmetric about the horizontal centerline. Dimension the distance between the two circles and their diameter. Create the top center point arc with the center point Coincident to the top circle. The start point and the end point of the arc are horizontal. Sketch the two top angled lines symmetric about the vertical centerline. Apply symmetry. Mirror the two lines and the center point arc about the horizontal centerline. Insert the left and right tangent arcs with a center point Coincident with the Origin. Complete the sketch.

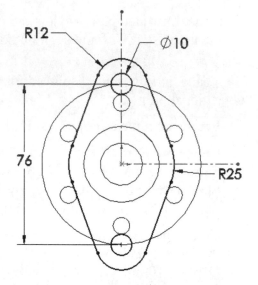

12. Create the second **Extruded Boss** (Boss-Extrude3) feature. Blind is the default End Condition in Direction 1. Depth = 12mm.

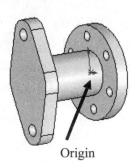

Origin

13. Create **Sketch5**. Select the front face of the Extrude feature as the Sketch plane. Sketch a circle. The part Origin is located in the center of the model. Insert the required dimension.

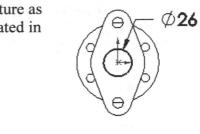

14. Create the second **Extruded Cut** feature. Blind is the default End Condition in Direction 1. Depth = 25mm.

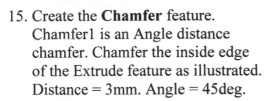

15. Create the **Chamfer** feature. Chamfer1 is an Angle distance chamfer. Chamfer the inside edge of the Extrude feature as illustrated. Distance = 3mm. Angle = 45deg.

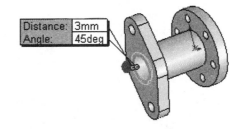

16. Create the **Fillet** feature. Fillet the two edges of Extrude1. Radius = 2mm.

17. **Assign** 6061 Alloy material to the part.

18. **Calculate** the overall mass of the part. The overall mass = 276.97 grams.

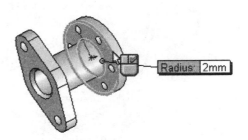

19. **Locate** the Center of mass. The location of the Center of mass is relative to the part Origin.

- X: 0.00 millimeters

- Y: 0.00 millimeters

- Z: 21.95 millimeters

20. **Save** the part and name it Advanced Part 10-2.

21. **Close** the model.

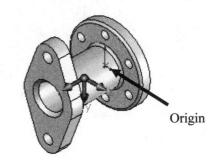

Origin

In the Advanced Part Modeling category, an exam question could read: Build this model. Locate the Center of mass with respect to the part Origin.

- A: X = 0.00 millimeters, Y = 0.00 millimeters, Z = 21.95 millimeters

- B: X = 21.95 millimeters, Y = 10.00 millimeters, Z = 0.00 millimeters

- C: X = 0.00 millimeters, Y = 0.00 millimeters, Z = -27.02 millimeters

- D: X= 1.00 millimeters, Y = -1.01 millimeters, Z = -0.04 millimeters

The correct answer is A.

Mass = 276.97 grams

Volume = 102579.75 cubic millimeters

Surface area = 29703.14 millimeters^2

Center of mass: (millimeters)
    X = 0.00
    Y = 0.00
    Z = 21.95

Calculate the Center of Mass Relative to a Created Coordinate System Location

In the Simple Part Modeling chapter, you located the Center of mass relative to the default part Origin. In the Advanced Part Modeling category, you may need to locate the Center of mass relative to a created coordinate system location. The exam model may display a created coordinate system location. Example:

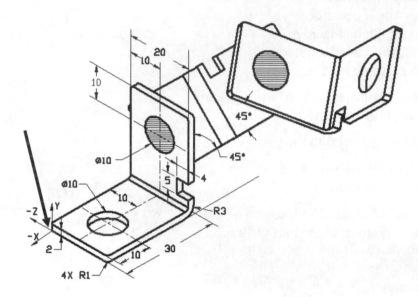

The SolidWorks software displays positive values for (X, Y, Z) coordinates for a reference coordinate system. The CSWA exam displays either a positive or negative sign in front of the (X, Y, Z) coordinates to indicate direction as illustrated, (-X, +Y, -Z).

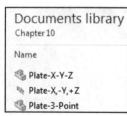

The following section reviews creating a Coordinate System location for a part.

Tutorial: Coordinate location 10-1

Use the Mass Properties tool to calculate the Center of mass for a part located at a new coordinate location through a point.

1. **Open** the Plate-3-Point part from the SolidWorks CSWA Folder\Chapter 10 location. View the location of the part Origin.

2. **Locate** the Center of mass. The location of the Center of mass is relative to the part Origin.

Documents library
Chapter 10

Name

Plate-X-Y-Z
Plate-X,-Y,+Z
Plate-3-Point

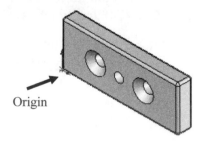

Origin

- X = 28 millimeters

- Y = 11 millimeters

- Z = -3 millimeters

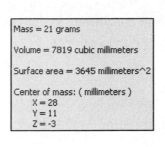

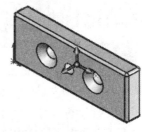

Create a new coordinate system location.
Locate the new coordinate system location
at the center of the center hole as
illustrated.

3. Right-click the **front face** of Base-Extrude.

4. Click **Sketch** from the Context toolbar.

5. Click the **edge** of the center hole as illustrated.

6. Click **Convert Entities** from the Sketch
   toolbar. The center point for the new
   coordinate location is displayed.

7. **Exit** the sketch. Sketch4 is displayed.

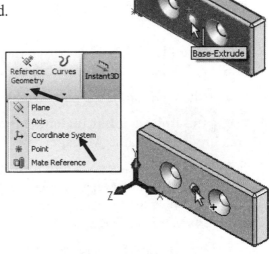

8. Click the **Coordinate System** tool from the
   Consolidated Reference Geometry toolbar.
   The Coordinate System PropertyManager is
   displayed.

9. Click the **center point** of the center hole in
   the Graphics window. Point2@Sketch4 is
   displayed in the Selections box as the
   Origin.

10. Click **OK** from the Coordinate System
    PropertyManager. Coordinate System1 is
    displayed.

11. **View** the new coordinate location at
    the center of the center hole.

View the Mass Properties of the part with
the new coordinate location.

12. Click the **Mass Properties** tool from
    the Evaluate tab.

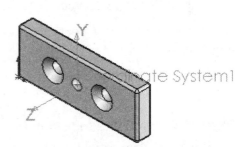

13. Select **Coordinate System1** from the
    Output box. The Center of mass
    relative to the new location is located
    at the following coordinates: X = 0
    millimeters, Y = 0 millimeters,
    Z = -3 millimeters

14. **Reverse** the direction of the axes as illustrated. On the CSWA exam, the coordinate system axes could be represented by: (+X, -Y, -Z).

15. **Close** the model.

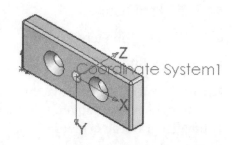

To reverse the direction of an axis, click its **Reverse Axis Direction** button in the Coordinate System PropertyManager.

Tutorial: Coordinate location 10-2

Create a new coordinate system location. Locate the new coordinate system at the top back point as illustrated.

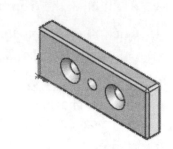

1. **Open** the Plate-X-Y-Z part from the SolidWorks CSWA Folder\Chapter 10 location.

2. **View** the location of the part Origin.

3. Drag the **Rollback bar** under the Base-Extrude feature in the FeatureManager.

4. Click the **Coordinate System** tool from the Consolidated Reference Geometry toolbar. The Coordinate System PropertyManager is displayed.

5. Click the **back left vertex** as illustrated.

6. Click the **top back horizontal** edge as illustrated. Do not select the midpoint.

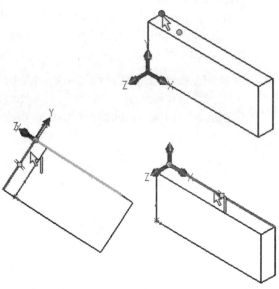

7. Click the **back left vertical** edge as illustrated.

8. Click **OK** from the Coordinate System PropertyManager. Coordinate System1 is displayed in the FeatureManager and in the Graphics window.

9. Drag the **Rollback bar** to the bottom of the FeatureManager.

10. **Calculate** the Center of mass relative to the new coordinate system.

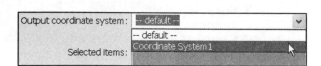

11. Select **Coordinate System1**. The Center of mass relative to the new location is located at the following coordinates:

- X = -28 millimeters

Y = -11 millimeters

Z = -4 millimeters

12. **Reverse** the direction of the axes as illustrated.

13. **Close** the model.

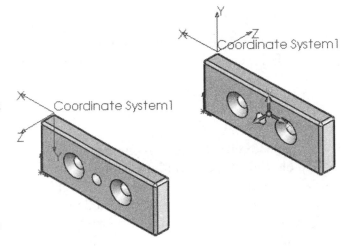

🔆 Define a Coordinate system for a part or assembly. Apply a Coordinate system with the Measure and Mass Properties tool.

Tutorial: Advanced Part 10-3

An exam question in this category could read: Build this part. Calculate the overall mass and locate the Center of mass of the illustrated model.

1. **Create** a New part in SolidWorks.

2. **Build** the illustrated dimensioned model. Insert thirteen features: Extrude-Thin1, Fillet, two Extruded Cuts, Circular Pattern, two Extruded Cuts, Mirror, Chamfer, Extruded Cut, Mirror, Extruded Cut and Mirror.

Think about the steps that you would take to build the illustrated part. Review the provided information. The depth of the left side is 50mm. The depth of the right side is 60mm.

🔆 There are numerous ways to build the models in this chapter. A goal is to display different design intents and techniques.

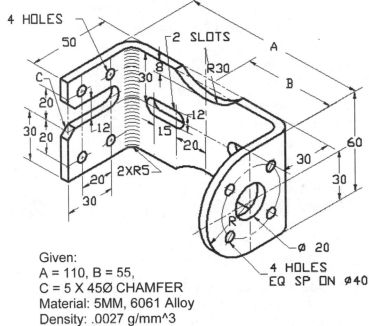

Given:
A = 110, B = 55,
C = 5 X 45Ø CHAMFER
Material: 5MM, 6061 Alloy
Density: .0027 g/mm^3
Units: MMGS
ALL HOLES 6MM

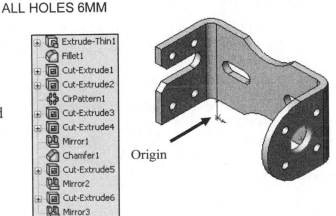

Origin

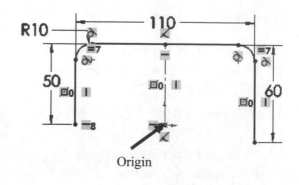

Origin

🔆 If the inside radius = 5mm and the material thickness = 5mm, then the outside radius = 10mm.

3. **Set** the document properties for the model.

4. Create **Sketch1**. Sketch1 is the Base sketch. Select the Top Plane as the Sketch plane. Apply the Line and Sketch Fillet Sketch tools. Apply construction geometry. Insert the required geometric relations and dimensions.

5. Create the **Extrude-Thin1** feature. Extrude-Thin1 is the Base feature. Apply symmetry in Direction 1. Depth = 60mm. Thickness = 5mm. Check the Auto-fillet corners box. Radius = 5mm.

🔆 The Auto-fillet corners option creates a round at each edge where lines meet at an angle.

6. Create the **Fillet** feature. Fillet1 is a full round fillet. Fillet the three illustrated faces: top, front and bottom.

7. Create **Sketch2**. Select the right face as the Sketch plane. Wake-up the center point. Sketch a circle. Insert the required relation and dimension.

8. Create the first **Extruded Cut** feature. Select Up To Next for the End Condition in Direction 1.

🔆 The Up To Next End Condition extends the feature from the sketch plane to the next surface that intercepts the entire profile. The intercepting surface must be on the same part.

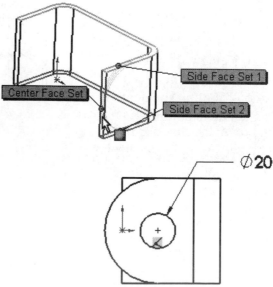

9. Create **Sketch3**. Select the right face as the Sketch plane. Create the profile for the second Extruded Cut feature. This is the seed feature for CirPattern1. Apply construction geometry to locate the center point of Sketch3. Insert the required relations and dimensions.

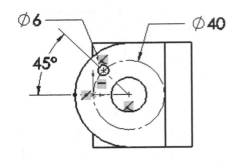

10. Create the second **Extruded Cut** feature. Select Up To Next for the End Condition in Direction 1.

11. Create the **Circular Pattern** feature. Number of Instances = 4. Default angle = 360deg.

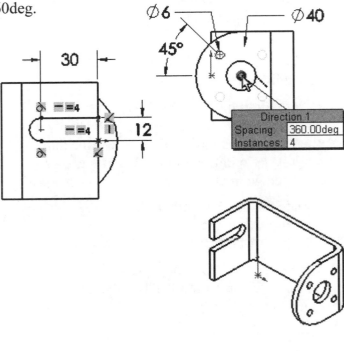

12. Create **Sketch4**. Select the left outside face of Extrude-Thin1 as the Sketch plane. Apply the Line and Tangent Arc Sketch tool to create Sketch4. Insert the required geometric relations and dimensions.

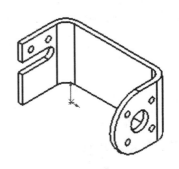

13. Create the third **Extruded Cut** feature. Select Up To Next for End Condition in Direction 1. The Slot on the left side of Extrude-Thin1 is created.

14. Create **Sketch5**. Select the left outside face of Extrude-Thin1 as the Sketch plane. Sketch two circles. Insert the required geometric relations and dimensions.

15. Create the forth **Extruded Cut** feature. Select Up To Next for End Condition in Direction 1.

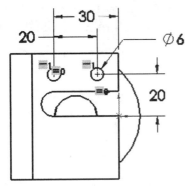

There are numerous ways to create the models in this chapter. A goal is to display different design intents and techniques

16. Create the first **Mirror** feature. Mirror the top two holes about the Top Plane.

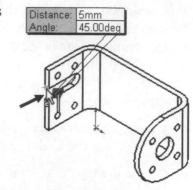

17. Create the **Chamfer** feature. Create an Angle distance chamfer. Chamfer the selected edges as illustrated. Distance = 5mm. Angle = 45deg.

18. Create **Sketch6**. Select the front face of Extrude-Thin1 as the Sketch plane. Insert the required geometric relations and dimensions.

19. Create the fifth **Extruded Cut** feature. Select Thought All for End Condition in Direction 1.

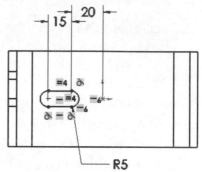

20. Create the second **Mirror** feature. Mirror Extrude5 about the Right Plane.

21. Create **Sketch7**. Select the front face of Extrude-Thin1 as the Sketch plane. Apply the 3 Point Arc Sketch tool. Apply the min First Arc Condition option. Insert the required geometric relations and dimensions.

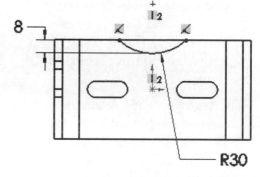

22. Create the last **Extruded Cut** feature. Through All is the End Condition in Direction 1 and Direction 2.

23. Create the third **Mirror** feature. Mirror the Extrude feature about the Top Plane as illustrated.

24. **Assign** the material to the part.

25. **Calculate** the overall mass of the part. The overall mass = 134.19 grams.

26. **Locate** the Center of mass relative to the part Origin:

- X: 1.80 millimeters

- Y: -0.27 millimeters

- Z: -35.54 millimeters

Mass = 134.19 grams

Volume = 49701.13 cubic millimeters

Surface area = 24415.20 millimeters^2

Center of mass: (millimeters)
    X = 1.80
    Y = -0.27
    Z = -35.54

27. **Save** the part and name it Advanced Part 10-3.

28. **Close** the model.

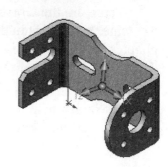

Tangent edges and Origin are displayed for educational purposes.

All questions on the exam are in a multiple choice single answer or fill in the blank format. In the Advanced Part Modeling category, an exam question could read: Build this model. Calculate the overall mass of the part with the provided information.

- A: 139.34 grams

- B: 155.19 grams

- C: 134.19 grams

- D: 143.91 grams

The correct answer is C.

☀ Use the Options button in the Mass Properties dialog box to apply custom settings to units.

Tutorial: Advanced Part 10-3A

An exam question in this category could read: Build this part. Locate the Center of mass. Note the coordinate system location of the model as illustrated.

Where do you start? Build the model as you did in the Tutorial: Advanced Part 10-3. Create Coordinate System1 to locate the Center of mass.

1. **Open** Advanced Part 10-3 that you created in the previous exercise.

Create the illustrated coordinate system location.

2. Show **Sketch2** from the FeatureManager design tree.

3. Click the **center point** of Sketch2 in the Graphics window as illustrated.

☀ Click on the additional views during the CSWA exam to better understand the part and provided information.

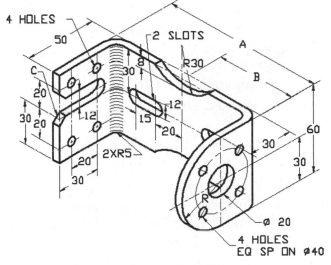

A = 110, B = 55, C = 5 X 45Ø CHAMFER
Material: 5MM, 6061 Alloy
Density: .0027 g/mm^3
Units: MMGS
ALL HOLES 6MM

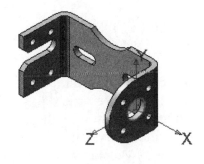

Coordinate system: +X, +Y, +Z

4. Click the **Coordinate System** tool from the Consolidated Reference Geometry toolbar. The Coordinate System PropertyManager is displayed. Point2@Sketch2 is displayed in the Origin box.

5. Click **OK** from the Coordinate System PropertyManager. Coordinate System1 is displayed

6. **Locate** the Center of mass based on the location of the illustrated coordinate system. Select Coordinate System1.

    - X: -53.20 millimeters

    - Y: -0.27 millimeters

    - Z: -15.54 millimeters

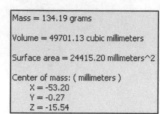

7. **Save** the part and name it Advanced Part 10-3A.

8. **Close** the model.

Tutorial: Advanced Part 10-3B

Build this part. Locate the Center of mass. View the location of the coordinate system. The coordinate system is located at the left front point of the model.

Build the illustrated model as you did in the Tutorial: Advanced Part 10-3. Create Coordinate System1 to locate the Center of mass for the model.

1. **Open** Advance Part 10-3 that you created in the previous exercise.

Create the illustrated coordinate system.

2. Click the **vertex** as illustrated for the Origin location.

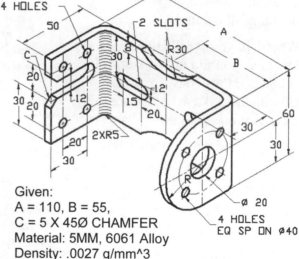

Given:
A = 110, B = 55,
C = 5 X 45Ø CHAMFER
Material: 5MM, 6061 Alloy
Density: .0027 g/mm^3
Units: MMGS
ALL HOLES 6MM

To reverse the direction of an axis, click the **Reverse Axis Direction** button in the Coordinate System PropertyManager.

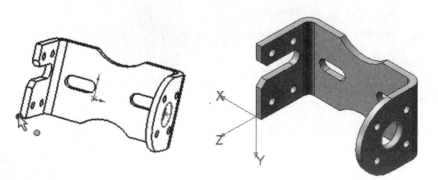

3. Click the **Coordinate System** tool from the Consolidated Reference Geometry toolbar. The Coordinate System PropertyManager is displayed. Vertex<1> is displayed in the Origin box.

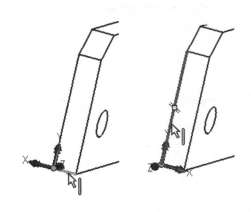

4. Click the **bottom horizontal edge** as illustrated. Edge<1> is displayed in the X Axis Direction box.

5. Click the **left back vertical edge** as illustrated. Edge<2> is displayed in the Y Axis Direction box.

6. Click **OK** from the Coordinate System PropertyManager. Coordinate System1 is displayed.

9. **Locate** the Center of mass based on the location of the illustrated coordinate system. Select Coordinate System1.

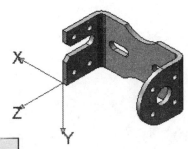

- X: -56.80 millimeters

- Y: -29.73 millimeters

- Z: -35.54 millimeters

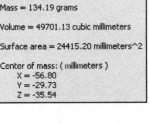

Mass = 134.19 grams

Volume = 49701.13 cubic millimeters

Surface area = 24415.20 millimeters^2

Center of mass: (millimeters)
   X = -56.80
   Y = -29.73
   Z = -35.54

10. **Save** the part and name it Advanced Part 10-3B.

11. **Close** the model.

In the Advanced Part Modeling category, an exam question could read: Build this model. Locate the Center of mass.

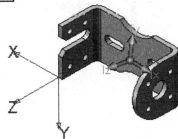

- A: X = -56.80 millimeters, Y = -29.73 millimeters, Z = -35.54 millimeters

- B: X = 1.80 millimeters, Y = -0.27 millimeters, Z = -35.54 millimeters

- C: X = -59.20 millimeters, Y = -0.27 millimeters, Z = -15.54 millimeters

- D: X= -1.80 millimeters, Y = 1.05 millimeters, Z = -0.14 millimeters

The correct answer is A.

Tutorial: Advanced Part 10-4

An exam question in this category could read: Build this part. Calculate the overall mass and locate the Center of mass of the illustrated model.

1. **Create** a new part in SolidWorks.

2. **Build** the illustrated dimensioned model. Insert twelve features and a Reference plane: Extrude-Thin1, two Extruded Bosses, Extruded Cut, Extruded Boss, Extruded Cut, Plane1, Mirror and five Extruded Cuts.

Think about the steps that you would take to build the illustrated part. Create an Extrude-Thin1 feature as the Base feature.

3. **Set** the document properties for the model. Review the given information.

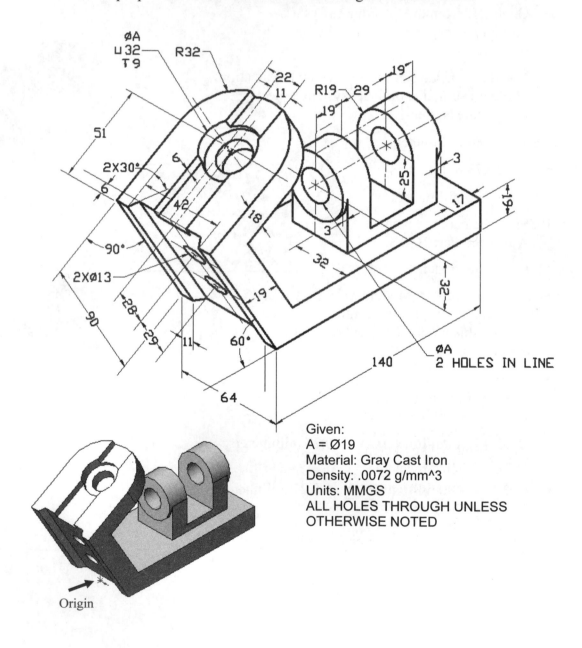

Given:
A = Ø19
Material: Gray Cast Iron
Density: .0072 g/mm^3
Units: MMGS
ALL HOLES THROUGH UNLESS
OTHERWISE NOTED

4. Create **Sketch1**. Sketch1 is the Base sketch. Select the Right Plane as the Sketch plane. Apply construction geometry. Insert the required geometric relations and dimensions. Sketch1 is the profile for Extrude-Thin1. Note the location of the Origin.

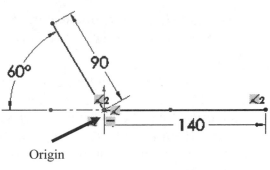

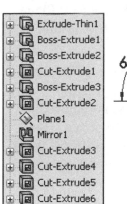

5. Create the **Extrude-Thin1** feature. Apply symmetry. Select Mid Plane as the End Condition in Direction 1. Depth = 64mm. Thickness = 19mm.

6. Create **Sketch2**. Select the top narrow face of Extrude-Thin1 as the Sketch plane. Sketch three lines: two vertical and one horizontal and a tangent arc. Insert the required geometric relations and dimensions.

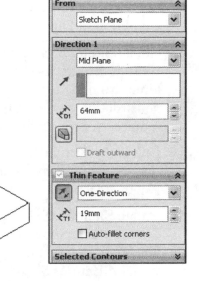

7. Create the **Boss-Extrude1** feature. Blind is the default End Condition in Direction 1. Depth = 18mm.

8. Create **Sketch3**. Select the Right Plane as the Sketch plane. Sketch a rectangle. Insert the required geometric relations and dimensions. Note: 61mm = (19mm - 3mm) x 2 + 29mm.

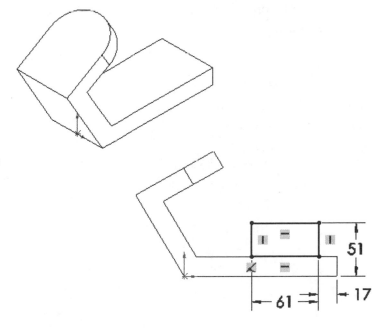

9. Create the **Boss-Extrude2** feature. Select Mid Plane for End Condition in Direction 1. Depth = 38mm. Note: 2 x R19.

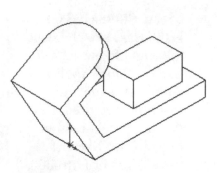

10. Create **Sketch4**. Select the Right Plane as the Sketch plane. Sketch a vertical centerline from the top midpoint of the sketch. The centerline is required for Plane1. Plane1 is a Reference plane. Sketch a rectangle symmetric about the centerline. Insert the required relations and dimensions. Sketch4 is the profile for Extrude3.

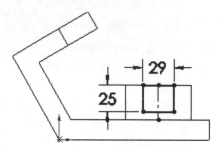

11. Create the first **Extruded Cut** feature. Extrude in both directions. Select Through All for End Condition in Direction 1 and Direction 2.

12. Create **Sketch5**. Select the inside face of the Extrude feature for the Sketch plane. Sketch a circle from the top midpoint. Sketch a construction circle. Construction geometry is required for future features. Complete the sketch.

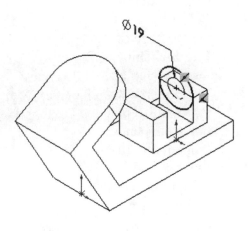

13. Create the **Extruded Boss** (Boss-Extrude3) feature. Blind is the default End Condition. Depth = 19mm.

14. Create **Sketch6**. Select the inside face for the Sketch plane. Show Sketch5. Select the construction circle in Sketch5. Apply the Convert Entities Sketch tool.

15. Create the second **Extruded Cut** feature. Select the Up To Next End Condition in Direction 1.

🔅 There are numerous ways to create the models in this chapter. A goal is to display different design intents and techniques

🔅 Tangent edges and Origin are displayed for educational purposes.

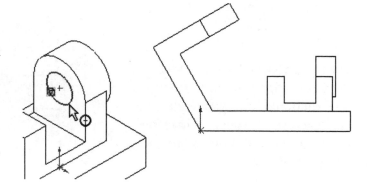

16. Create **Plane1**. Apply symmetry. Create Plane1 to mirror Cut-Extrude2 and Boss-Extrude3. Create a Parallel Plane at Point. Select the midpoint of Sketch4, and Face<1> as illustrated. Point1@Sketch4 and Face<1> is displayed in the Selections box.

17. Create the **Mirror** feature. Mirror Cut-Extrude2 and Boss-Extrude3 about Plane1.

The Mirror feature creates a copy of a feature, (or multiple features), mirrored about a face or a plane. You can select the feature or you can select the faces that comprise the feature.

18. Create **Sketch7**. Select the top front angled face of Extrude-Thin1 as the Sketch plane. Apply the Centerline Sketch tool. Insert the required geometric relations and dimensions.

19. Create the third **Extruded Cut** feature. Select Through All for End Condition in Direction 1. Select the angle edge for the vector to extrude as illustrated.

Click on the additional views during the CSWA exam to better understand the part and provided information. Read each question carefully. Identify the dimensions, center of mass and units. Apply needed material.

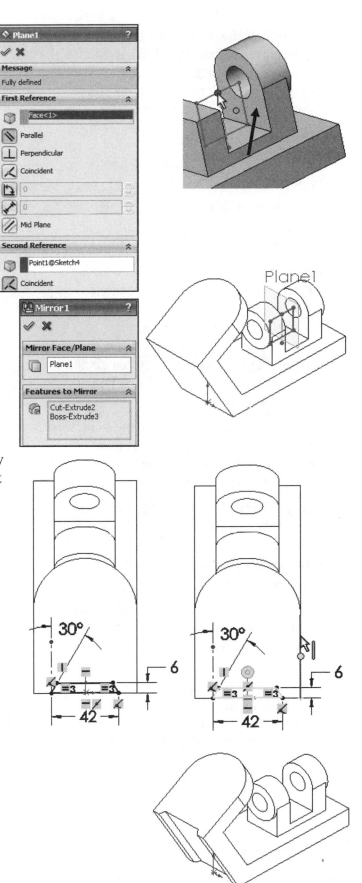

20. Create **Sketch8**. Select the top front angled face of Extrude-Thin1 as the Sketch plane. Sketch a centerline. Sketch two vertical lines and a horizontal line. Select the top arc edge. Apply the Convert Entities Sketch tool. Apply the Trim Sketch tool to remove the unwanted arc geometry. Insert the required geometric relations and dimension.

21. Create the forth **Extruded Cut** feature. Blind is the default End Condition in Direction 1. Depth = 6mm.

22. Create **Sketch9**. Create a Cbore with Sketch9 and Sketch10. Select the top front angled face of Extrude-Thin1 as illustrated for the Sketch plane. Extrude8 is the center hole in the Extrude-Thin1 feature. Sketch a circle. Insert the required geometric relations and dimension.

23. Create the fifth **Extrude Cut** feature. Blind is the default End Condition. Depth = 9mm. Note: This is the first feature for the Cbore.

24. Create **Sketch10**. Select the top front angled face of Extrude-Thin1 as the Sketch plane. Sketch a circle. Insert the required geometric relation and dimension. Note: A = Ø19.

25. Create the sixth **Extruded Cut** feature. Select the Up To Next End Condition in Direction 1. The Cbore is complete.

In the exam; you are allowed to answer the questions in any order. Use the Summary Screen during the exam to view the list of all questions you have or have not answered.

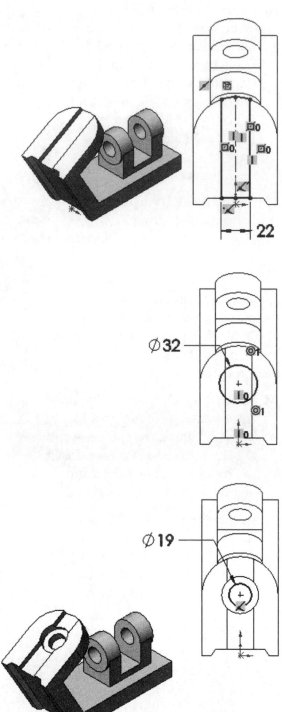

26. Create **Sketch11**. Select the front angle face of the Extrude feature for the Sketch plane. Sketch two circles. Insert the required geometric relations and dimensions.

27. Create the last **Extruded Cut** feature. Select the Up To Next End Condition in Direction 1.

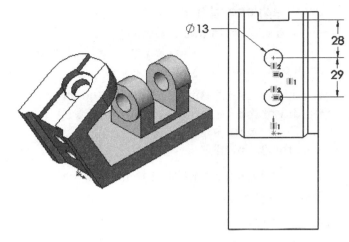

⋇ The FilletXpert manages, organizes, and reorders constant radius fillets.

⋇ The FilletXpert automatically calls the FeatureXpert when it has trouble placing a fillet on the specified geometry.

28. **Assign** the material to the part.

29. **Calculate** the overall mass of the part. The overall mass = 2536.59 grams.

30. **Locate** the Center of mass relative to the part Origin:

- X: 0.00 millimeters

- Y: 34.97 millimeters

- Z: -46.67 millimeters

31. **Save** the part and name it Advanced Part 10-4.

⋇ Due to software rounding, you may view a negative -0.00 coordinate location in the Mass Properties dialog box.

⋇ The book is design to expose the new user to many tools, techniques and procedures. It may not always use the most direct tool or process.

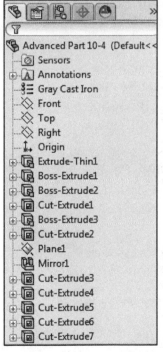

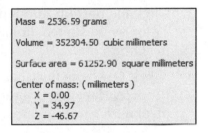

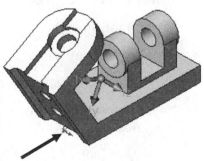

Origin

Tutorial: Advanced Part 10-4A

An exam question in this category could read:
Build this part. Locate the Center of mass for the illustrated coordinate system.

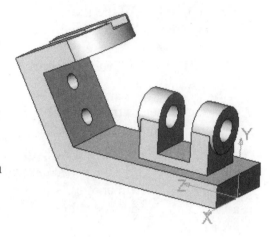

Where do you start? Build the illustrated model as you did in the Tutorial: Advanced Part 10-3. Create Coordinate System1 to locate the Center of mass for the model.

1. **Open** Advanced Part 10-4 that you created in the previous exercise.

Create the illustrated Coordinate system.

2. Click the **Coordinate System** tool from the Consolidated Reference Geometry toolbar. The Coordinate System PropertyManager is displayed.

3. Click the **bottom midpoint** of Extrude-Thin1 as illustrated. Point<1> is displayed in the Origin box.

4. Click **OK** from the Coordinate System PropertyManager. Coordinate System1 is displayed.

5. **Locate** the Center of mass based on the location of the illustrated coordinate system. Select Coordinate System1.

- X: 0.00 millimeters

- Y: 34.97 millimeters

- Z: 93.33 millimeters

6. **Save** the part and name it Advanced Part 10-4A.

7. **View** the Center of mass with the default coordinate system.

8. **Close** the model.

Mass = 2536.59 grams

Volume = 352304.50 cubic millimeters

Surface area = 61252.90 square millimeters

Center of mass: (millimeters)
   X = 0.00
   Y = 34.97
   Z = 93.33

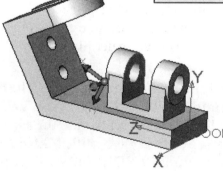

Coordinate System1

Summary

Advanced Part Creation and Modification is one of the five categories on the CSWA exam. The main difference between the *Advanced Part Creation and Modification* and the *Basic Part Creation and Modification* or the *Intermediate Part Creation and Modification* category is the complexity of the sketches and the number of dimensions and geometric relations along with an increase number of features.

There are three questions on the CSWA exam in this category. One question is in a multiple choice single answer format and the other two questions (Modification of the model) are in the fill in the blank format. Each question is worth fifteen (15) points for a total of forty-five (45) points. You are required to build a model, with six or more features and to answer a question either on the overall mass, volume, or the location the Center of mass for the created model relative to the default part Origin location. You are then requested to modify the model and answer a fill in the blank format question.

Assembly Creation and Modification (Bottom-up) is the next chapter in this book. Up to this point, a Basic Part, Intermediate Part or an Advanced part was the focus. The *Assembly Creation and Modification* category addresses an assembly with numerous sub-components. All subcomponents are provided to you on the exam. The next chapter covers the general concepts and terminology used in the *Assembly Creation and Modification* category and then addresses the core elements. Knowledge of Standard mates is required in this category.

There are four questions - Multiple Choice/Single Answer in the category. Each question is worth 30 points.

Click on the additional views during the CSWA exam to better understand the part and provided information. Read each question carefully. Identify the dimensions, center of mass and units. Apply needed material.

For additional detail exam information see The **Official Guide to Certified SolidWorks Associate Exams: CSWA, CSDA, and CSWSA-FEA** book. This book is written to assist the SolidWorks user to pass the associate level exams. Information is provided to aid a person to pass the Certified SolidWorks Associate (CSWA), Certified Sustainable Design Associate (CSDA) and the Certified SolidWorks Simulation Associate Finite Element Analysis (CSWSA FEA) exams. The primary goal of this book is not only to help you pass the exams, but also to ensure that you understand and comprehend the concepts and implementation details of the process.

Questions

1. In Tutorial, Advanced Part 10-1 you created the illustrated part. Modify the Base flange thickness from .40in to .50in. Modify the Chamfer feature angle from 45deg to 33deg. Modify the Fillet feature radius from .10in to .125in. Modify the material from 1060 Alloy to Nickel.

Calculate the overall mass of the part, volume, and locate the Center of mass with the provided information.

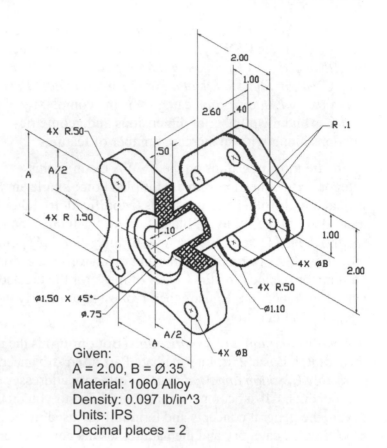

Given:
A = 2.00, B = Ø.35
Material: 1060 Alloy
Density: 0.097 lb/in^3
Units: IPS
Decimal places = 2

2. In Tutorial, Advanced Part 10-2 you created the illustrated part. Modify the CirPattern1 feature. Modify the number of instances from 6 to 8. Modify the seed feature from an 8mm diameter to a 6mm diameter.

Calculate the overall mass, volume, and the location of the Center of mass relative to the part Origin.

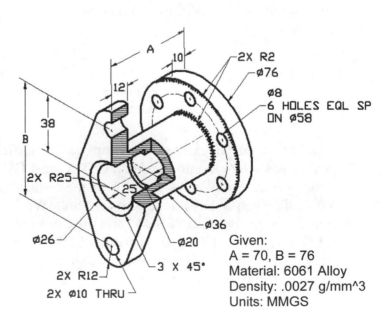

Given:
A = 70, B = 76
Material: 6061 Alloy
Density: .0027 g/mm^3
Units: MMGS

3. Build this illustrated model. Set document properties, identify the correct Sketch planes, apply the correct Sketch and Feature tools, and apply material.

Calculate the overall mass of the part, volume and locate the Center of mass with the provided information.

- Material: 6061 Alloy

- Units: MMGS

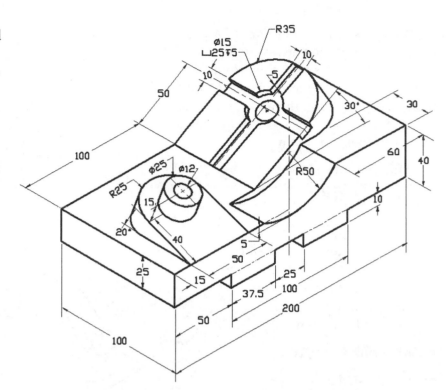

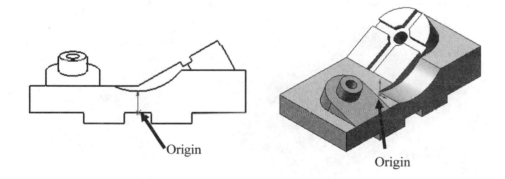

Origin

Origin

4. Build this illustrated model. Calculate the overall mass of the part, volume and locate the Center of mass with the provided information. Where do you start? Build the model, as you did in the above exercise. Create Coordinate System1 to locate the Center of mass for the model.

- Material: 6061 Alloy

- Units: MMGS

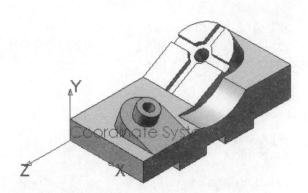

5. Build this illustrated model. Calculate the overall mass of the part, volume, and locate the Center of mass with the provided information.

- Material: 6061 Alloy

- Units: MMGS

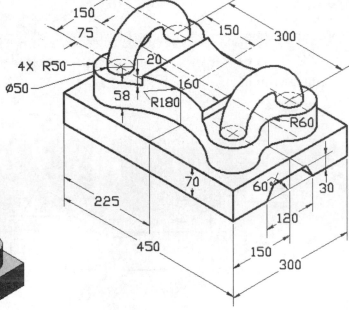

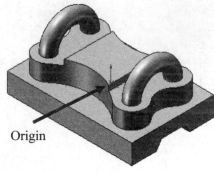

Origin

6. Build this model. Calculate the overall mass of the part, volume and locate the Center of mass with the provided information. Where do you start? Build the illustrated model, as you did in the above exercise. Create Coordinate System1 to locate the Center of mass for the model

- Material: 6061 Alloy

- Units: MMGS

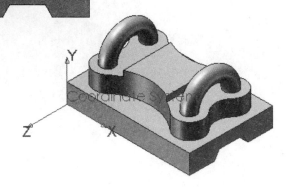

Sample screen shots from an older CSWA exam for an Advanced Modeling part. Click on the additional views to understand the part and provided information. Read each question carefully. Understand the dimensions, center of mass and units. Apply needed materials.

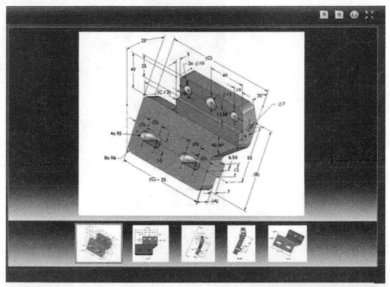

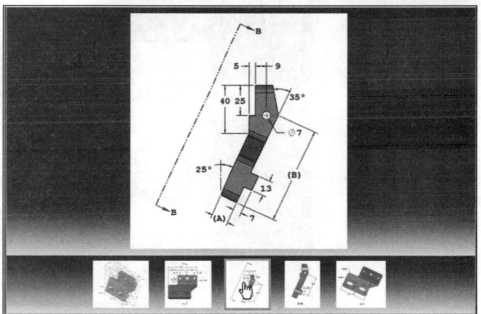

Screen shots from the exam

Zoom in on the part if needed.

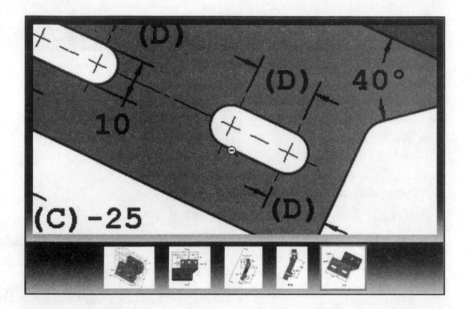

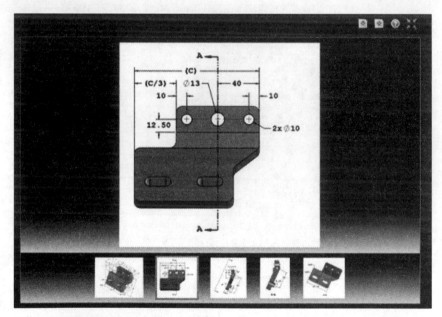

CHAPTER 11 - ASSEMBLY CREATION AND MODIFICATION

Objectives

Assembly Creation and Modification is one of the five categories on the CSWA exam. In the last two chapters, a Basic, Intermediate or Advanced model was the focus. The Assembly Creation and Modification (Bottom-up) category addresses an assembly with numerous components.

This chapter covers the general concepts and terminology used in Assembly modeling and then addresses the core elements that are aligned to the CSWA exam. Knowledge to insert Standard mates and to create a new Coordinate system location is required in this category.

There are four questions on the CSWA exam in the Assembly Creation and Modification category: (2) different assemblies - (4) questions - (2) multiple choice / (2) single answer - 30 points each.

You are required to download the needed components from a provided zip file and insert them correctly to create the assembly as illustrated. You are then requested to modify the assembly and answer fill in the blank format questions.

On the completion of the chapter, you will be able to:

- Specify Document Properties
- Identify the first fixed component in an assembly

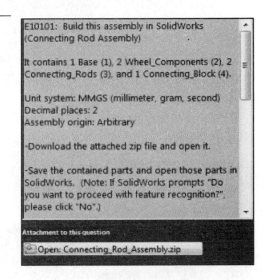

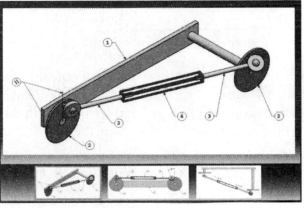

Screen shots from the CSWA exam

- Create a Bottom-up assembly with the following Standard mates:

  - Coincident, Concentric, Perpendicular, Parallel, Tangent, Distance, Angle, and Aligned, Anti-Aligned options

- Apply the Mirror Component tool

- Locate the Center of mass relative to the assembly Origin

- Create a Coordinate system location

- Locate the Center of mass relative to a created Coordinate system

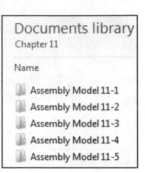

Components for the assembly are supplied in the exam. Copy all needed components for this chapter from the provided DVD in the book.

Assembly Modeling

There are two key Assembly Modeling techniques:

- Top-down, "In-Context" assembly modeling

- Bottom-up assembly modeling

In Top-down assembly modeling, one or more features of a part are defined by something in an assembly, such as a sketch or the geometry of another component. The design intent comes from the top, and moves down into the individual components, hence the name Top-down assembly modeling.

Mate the first component with respect to the assembly reference planes.

Bottom-up assembly modeling is a traditional method that combines individual components. Based on design criteria, the components are developed independently. The three major steps in a Bottom-up design approach are:

1. Create each part independent of any other component in the assembly.

2. Insert the parts into the assembly.

3. Mate the components in the assembly as they relate to the physical constraints of your design.

To modify a component in an assembly using the bottom-up assembly approach, you must edit the individually part.

Build an Assembly from a Detailed Dimensioned illustration

An exam question in this category could read: Build this assembly. Locate the Center of mass of the model with respect to the illustrated coordinate system. Set decimal place to 2.

The assembly contains the following: (1) Clevis component, (3) Axle components, (2) 5 Hole Link components, (2) 3 Hole Link components, and (6) Collar components. All holes Ø.190 THRU unless otherwise noted. Angle A = 150deg. Angle B = 120deg. Unit system: IPS.

Note: The location of the illustrated coordinate system: (+X, +Y, +Z).

In the exam, download the zip file of the components. Unzip the components. Do NOT use feature recognition when you open the downloaded components. This is a timed exam. You do not need the additional feature information.

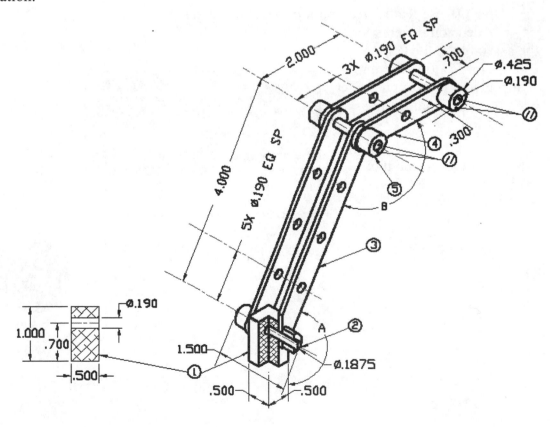

- Clevis, (Item 1): Material: 6061 Alloy. The two (5) Hole Link components are positioned with equal Angle mates, (150 deg) to the Clevis component.

- Axle, (Item 2): Material: AISI 304. The first Axle component is mated Concentric and Coincident to the Clevis. The second and third Axle components are mated Concentric and Coincident to the 5 Hole Link and the 3 Hole Link components respectively.

- 5 Hole Link, (Item 3): Material: 6061 Alloy. Material thickness = .100in. Radius = .250in. Five holes located 1in. on center. The 5 Hole Link components are position with equal Angle mates, (120 deg) to the 3 Hole Link components.

- 3 Hole Link, (Item 4): Material: 6061 Alloy. Material thickness = .100in. Radius = .250in. Three holes located 1in. on center. The 3 Hole Link components are positioned with equal Angle mates, (120 deg) to the 5 Hole Link components.

- Collar, (Item 5): Material: 6061 Alloy. The Collar components are mated Concentric and Coincident to the Axle and the 5 Hole Link and 3 Hole Link components respectively.

Think about the steps that you would take to build the illustrated assembly. Identify the first fixed component. Insert the required Standard mates.

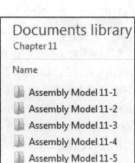

Locate the Center of mass of the model with respect to the illustrated coordinate system. In this example, start with the Clevis component.

Do NOT use feature recognition when you open the downloaded components for the assembly in the CSWA exam. This is a timed exam. Manage your time. You do not need the additional feature information.

View the .pdf on the DVD for a sample CSWA exam.

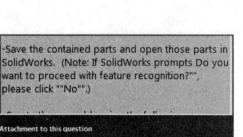

-Save the contained parts and open those parts in SolidWorks. (Note: If SolidWorks prompts Do you want to proceed with feature recognition?"", please click ""No"".)

Attachment to this question

Open: Connecting_Rod_Assembly.zip

Screen shots from the exam

Tutorial Assembly Model 11-1

Create the assembly. The illustrated assembly contains the following components: (1) Clevis component, (3) Axle components, (2) 5 Hole Link components, (2) 3 Hole Link components, and (6) Collar component s. All holes Ø.190 THRU unless otherwise noted. Angle A = 150deg, Angle B = 120deg. Set decimal place to 2. Unit system: IPS.

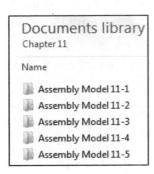

1. **Download** the needed components from the SolidWorks CSWA Model Folder/Chapter 11/Assembly Model 11-1 folder.

2. **Create** a new IPS assembly in SolidWorks. The created models are displayed in the Open documents box.

3. Click **Cancel** ✖ from the Begin Assembly PropertyManager. Assem1 is the default document name. Assembly documents end with the extension; .sldasm.

4. **Set** the document properties for the model.

5. **Insert** the Clevis part.

6. **Fix** the component to the assembly Origin. Click OK from the Insert Component PropertyManager. The Clevis is displayed in the Assembly FeatureManager and in the Graphics window.

💡 Fix the position of a component so that it cannot move with respect to the assembly Origin. By default, the first part in an assembly is fixed; however, you can float it at any time.

💡 Only insert the required mates (timed exam) to obtain the needed Mass properties information.

7. **Insert** the Axle part above the Clevis component as illustrated. Note the location of the Origin.

8. **Clear** the origin view from the Graphics window.

9. **Insert** a Concentric mate between the inside cylindrical face of the Clevis and the outside cylindrical face of the Axle. The selected face entities are displayed in the Mate Selections box. Concentric1 is created.

10. **Insert** a Coincident mate between the Right Plane of the Clevis and the Right Plane of the Axle. Coincident1 mate is created.

11. **Insert** the 5 Hole Link part. Locate and rotate the component as illustrated.

12. **Insert** a Concentric mate between the outside cylindrical face of the Axle and the inside cylindrical face of the 5 Hole Link. Concentric2 is created.

13. **Insert** a Coincident mate between the right face of the Clevis and the left face of the 5 Hole Link. Coincident2 is created.

14. **Insert** an Angle mate between the bottom face of the 5 Hole Link and the back face of the Clevis. Angle = 30deg. The selected faces are displayed in the Mate Selections box. Angle1 is created. Flip direction if needed.

Depending on the component orientation, select the Flip direction option and or enter the supplement of the angle.

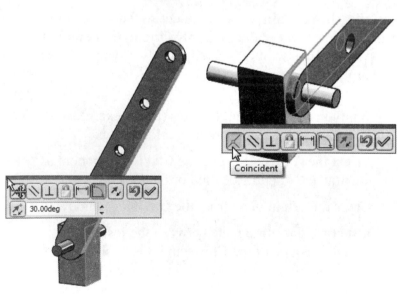

15. **Insert** the second Axle part. Locate the second Axle component near the end of the 5 Hole Link as illustrated.

16. **Insert** a Concentric mate between the inside cylindrical face of the 5 Hole Link and the outside cylindrical face of the Axle. Concentric3 is created.

17. **Insert** a Coincident mate between the Right Plane of the assembly and the Right Plane of the Axle. Coincident3 is created.

18. **Insert** the 3 Hole Link part. Locate and rotate the component as illustrated. Note the location of the Origin.

19. **Insert** a Concentric mate between the outside cylindrical face of the Axle and the inside cylindrical face of the 3 Hole Link. Concentric4 is created.

20. **Insert** a Coincident mate between the right face of the 5 Hole Link and the left face of the 3 Hole Link.

21. **Insert** an Angle mate between the bottom face of the 5 Hole Link and the bottom face of the 3 Hole Link. Angle = 60deg. Angle2 is created.

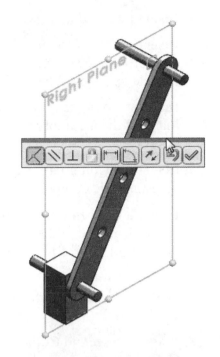

 Depending on the component orientation, select the Flip direction option and or enter the supplement of the angle when needed.

 Apply the Measure tool to check the angle.

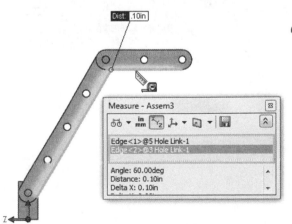

22. **Insert** the third Axle part.

23. **Insert** a Concentric mate between the inside cylindrical face of the 3 Hole Link and the outside cylindrical face of the Axle.

24. **Insert** a Coincident mate between the Right Plane of the assembly and the Right Plane of the Axle.

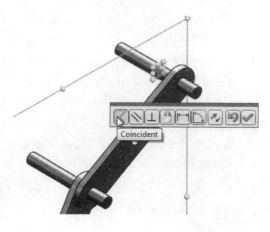

25. **Insert** the Collar part. Locate the Collar near the first Axle component.

26. **Insert** a Concentric mate between the inside cylindrical face of the Collar and the outside cylindrical face of the first Axle.

27. **Insert** a Coincident mate between the right face of the 5 Hole Link and the left face of the Collar.

28. **Insert** the second Collar part. Locate the Collar near the second Axle component

29. **Insert** a Concentric mate between the inside circular face of the second Collar and the outside circular face of the second Axle.

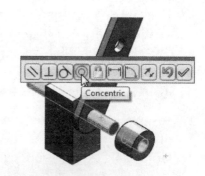

30. **Insert** a Coincident mate between the right face of the 3 Hole Link and the left face of the second Collar.

31. **Insert** the third Collar part. Locate the Collar near the third Axle component.

32. **Insert** a Concentric mate between the inside cylindrical face of the Collar and the outside cylindrical face of the third Axle.

33. **Insert** a Coincident mate between the right face of the 3 Hole Link and the left face of the third Collar.

34. **Mirror** the components. Mirror the three Collars, 5 Hole Link and 3 Hole Link about the Right Plane. If using an older version of SolidWorks, check the Recreate mates to new components box. Click Next in the Mirror Components PropertyManager. Check the Preview instanced components box.

☀ Click **Insert**, **Mirror Components** from the Menu bar menu or click the **Mirror Components** tool from the Linear Component Pattern Consolidated toolbar.

☀ If using an older release of SolidWorks, no check marks in the Components to Mirror box indicates that the components are copied. The geometry of a copied component is unchanged from the original, only the orientation of the component is different.

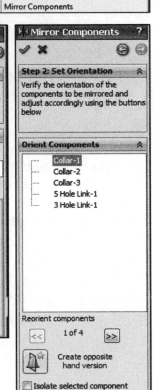

☀ If using an older release of SolidWorks, check marks in the Components to Mirror box indicates that the selected is mirrored. The geometry of the mirrored component changes to create a truly mirrored component.

Create the coordinate system location for the assembly.

35. Select the front right **vertex** of the Clevis component as illustrated.

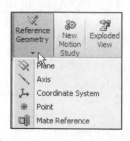

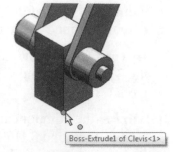

Boss-Extrude1 of Clevis<1>

36. Click the **Coordinate System** tool from the Reference Geometry Consolidated toolbar. The Coordinate System PropertyManager is displayed.

37. Click the **right bottom edge** of the Clevis component.

38. Click the **front bottom edge** of the Clevis component as illustrated.

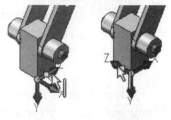

39. Address the **direction** for X, Y, Z as illustrated.

40. Click **OK** from the Coordinate System PropertyManager. Coordinate System1 is displayed

41. **Locate** the Center of mass based on the location of the illustrated coordinate system. Select Coordinate System1.

- X: 1.79 inches

- Y: 0.25 inches

- Z: 2.61 inches

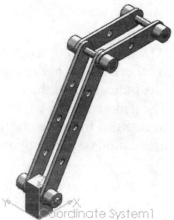

Coordinate System1

42. **Save** the part and name it Assembly Modeling 11-1.

43. **Close** the model.

🔆 There are numerous ways to create the models in this chapter. A goal in this text is to display different design intents and techniques.

🔆 If you don't find an option within 1% of your answer on the exam re-check your assembly.

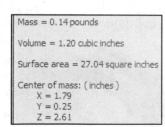

Mass = 0.14 pounds

Volume = 1.20 cubic inches

Surface area = 27.04 square inches

Center of mass: (inches)
  X = 1.79
  Y = 0.25
  Z = 2.61

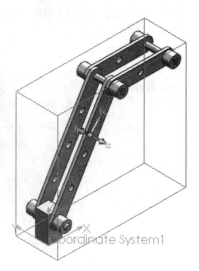

Coordinate System1

Tutorial: Assembly Model 11-2

An exam question in this category could read: Build this assembly. Locate the Center of mass of the model with the illustrated coordinate system. Set decimal place to 2. Unit system: MMGS.

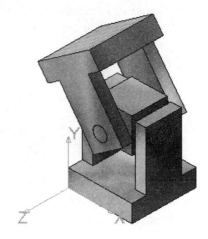

The assembly contains the following: (2) U-Bracket components, (4) Pin components and (1) Square block component.

- U-Bracket, (Item 1): Material: AISI 304. Two U-Bracket components are combined together Concentric to opposite holes of the Square block component. The second U-Bracket component is positioned with an Angle mate, to the right face of the first U-Bracket and a Parallel mate between the top face of the first U-Bracket and the top face of the Square block component. Angle A = 125deg.

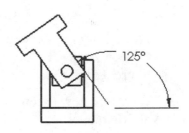

- Square block, (Item 2): Material: AISI 304. The Pin components are mated Concentric and Coincident to the 4 holes in the Square block, (no clearance). The depth of each hole = 10mm.

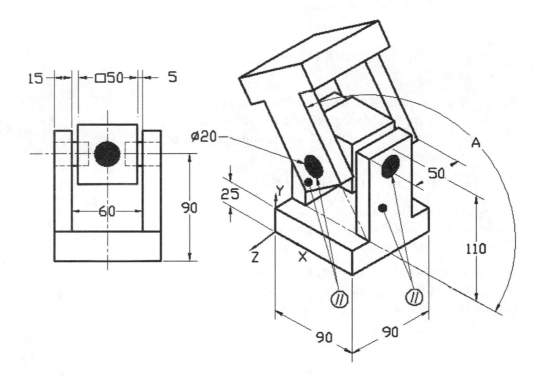

- Pin, (Item 3): Material: AISI 304. The Pin components are mated Concentric to the hole, (no clearance). The end faces of the Pin components are Coincident to the outer face of the U-Bracket components. The Pin component has a 5mm spacing between the Square block component and the two U-Bracket components.

Think about the steps that you would take to build the illustrated assembly. Identify the first fixed component. This is the Base component of the assembly. Insert the required Standard mates. Locate the Center of mass of the model with respect to the illustrated coordinate system. In this example, start with the U-Bracket part.

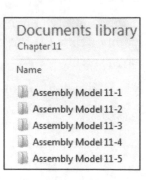

Create the assembly. The illustrated assembly contains the following: (2) U-Bracket components, (4) Pin components and (1) Square block component. Unit system: MMGS.

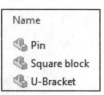

1. **Download** the needed components from the SolidWorks CSWA Model Folder/Chapter 11/Assembly Model 11-2 folder to create the assembly.

2. **Create** a new assembly in SolidWorks. The created models are displayed in the Open documents box.

3. Click **Cancel** ✖ from the Begin Assembly PropertyManager.

4. **Set** the document properties for the model.

5. **Insert** the first U-Bracket component into the assembly document.

6. **Fix** the component to the assembly Origin. Click OK from the PropertyManager. The U-Bracket is displayed in the Assembly FeatureManager and in the Graphics window.

7. **Insert** the Square block above the U-Bracket component as illustrated.

8. **Insert** the first Pin part. Locate the first Pin to the front of the Square block.

9. **Insert** the second Pin part. Locate the second Pin to the back of the Square block.

10. **Insert** the third Pin part. Locate the third Pin to the left side of the Square block. Rotate the Pin.

11. **Insert** the fourth Pin part. Locate the fourth Pin to the right side of the Square block. Rotate the Pin.

12. **Insert** a Concentric mate between the inside cylindrical face of the Square block and the outside cylindrical face of the first Pin. The selected face entities are displayed in the Mate Selections box. Concentric1 is created.

13. **Insert** a Coincident mate between the inside back circular face of the Square block and the flat back face of the first Pin. Coincident1 mate is created.

14. **Insert** a Concentric mate between the inside cylindrical face of the Square block and the outside cylindrical face of the second Pin. The selected face sketch entities are displayed in the Mate Selections box. Concentric2 is created.

15. **Insert** a Coincident mate between the inside back circular face of the Square block and the front flat face of the second Pin. Coincident2 mate is created.

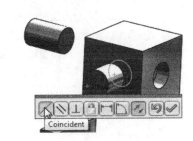

16. **Insert** a Concentric mate between the inside cylindrical face of the Square block and the outside cylindrical face of the third Pin. The selected face sketch entities are displayed in the Mate·Selections box. Concentric3 is created.

17. **Insert** a Coincident mate between the inside back circular face of the Square block and the right flat face of the third Pin. Coincident3 mate is created.

18. **Insert** a Concentric mate between the inside circular face of the Square block and the outside cylindrical face of the fourth Pin. The selected face entities are displayed in the Mate Selections box. Concentric4 is created.

19. **Insert** a Coincident mate between the inside back circular face of the Square block and the left flat face of the fourth Pin. Coincident4 mate is created.

20. **Insert** a Concentric mate between the inside right cylindrical face of the Cut-Extrude feature on the U-Bracket and the outside cylindrical face of the right Pin. Concentric5 is created.

21. **Insert** a Coincident mate between the Right Plane of the Square block and the Right Plane of the assembly. Coincident5 is created.

22. **Insert** the second U-Bracket part above the assembly. Position the U-Bracket as illustrated.

23. **Insert** a Concentric mate between the inside cylindrical face of the second U-Bracket component and the outside cylindrical face of the second Pin. The mate is created.

24. **Insert** a Coincident mate between the outside circular edge of the second U-Bracket and the back flat face of the second Pin. The mate is created.

☼ There are numerous ways to mate the models in this chapter. A goal is to display different design intents and techniques.

25. **Insert** an Angle mate between the top flat face of the first U-Bracket component and the front narrow face of the second U-Bracket component as illustrated. Angle1 is created. An Angle mate is required to obtain the correct Center of mass.

26. **Insert** a Parallel mate between the top flat face of the first U-Bracket and the top flat face of the Square block component.

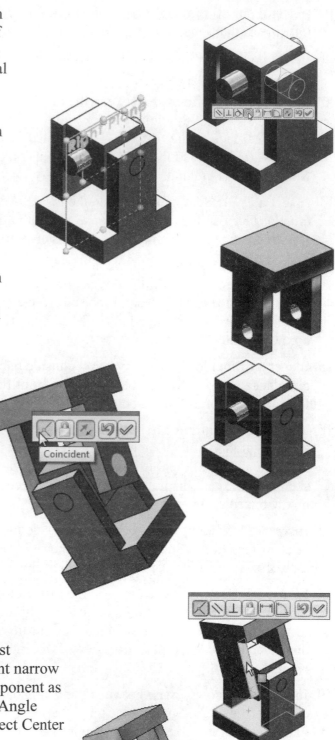

27. **Expand** the Mates folder and the components from the FeatureManager. View the created mates.

Create the coordinate location for the assembly.

28. Select the front **bottom left vertex** of the first U-Bracket component as illustrated.

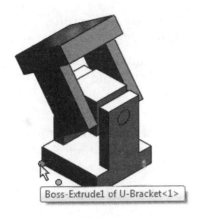

Boss-Extrude1 of U-Bracket<1>

29. Click the **Coordinate System** tool from the Reference Geometry Consolidated toolbar. The Coordinate System PropertyManager is displayed.

30. Click **OK** from the Coordinate System PropertyManager. Coordinate System1 is displayed.

31. **Locate** the Center of mass based on the location of the illustrated coordinate system. Select Coordinate System1.

- X: 31.54 millimeters

- Y: 85.76 millimeters

- Z: -45.00 millimeters

32. **Save** the part and name it Assembly Modeling 11-2.

33. **Close** the model.

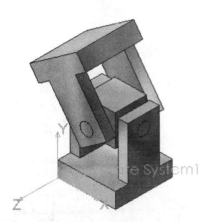

If you don't find an option within 1% of your answer on the exam re-check your assembly.

Click on the additional views during the CSWA exam to better understand the assembly/component. Read each question carefully. Identify the dimensions, center of mass and units. Apply needed material.

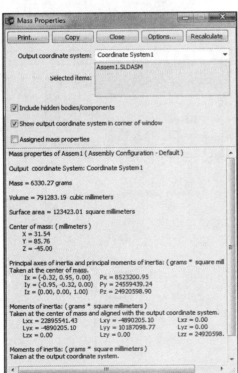

Tutorial: Assembly Model 11-3

An exam question in this category could read: Build this assembly. Locate the Center of mass using the illustrated coordinate system. Set decimal place to 2. Unit system: MMGS.

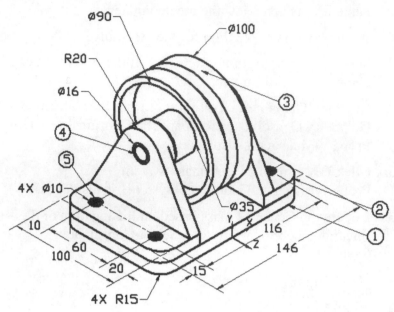

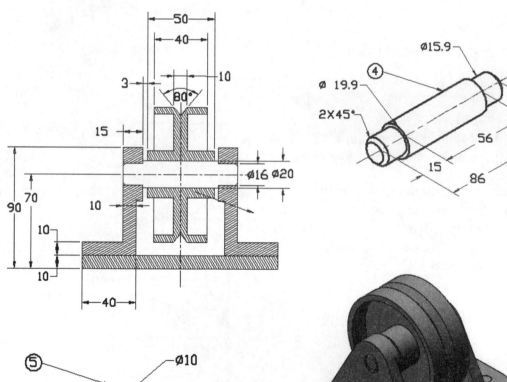

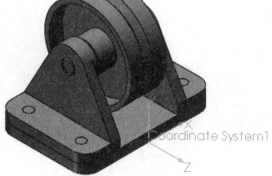

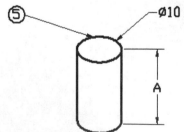

The assembly contains the following: (1) WheelPlate component, (2) Bracket100 components, (1) Axle40 component, (1) Wheel1 component and (4) Pin-4 components.

- WheelPlate, (Item 1): Material: AISI 304. The WheelPlate contains 4-Ø10 holes. The holes are aligned to the left Bracket100 and the right Bracket100 components. All holes are THRU ALL. The thickness of the WheelPlate = 10 mm.

- Bracket100, (Item 2): Material: AISI 304. The Bracket100 component contains 2-Ø10 holes and 1- Ø16 hole. All holes are through-all.

- Wheel1, (Item 3): Material AISI 304: The center hole of the Wheel1 component is Concentric with the Axle40 component. There is a 3mm gap between the inside faces of the Bracket100 components and the end faces of the Wheel hub.

- Axle40, (Item 4): Material AISI 304: The end faces of the Axle40 are Coincident with the outside faces of the Bracket100 components.

- Pin-4, (Item 5): Material AISI 304: The Pin-4 components are mated Concentric to the holes of the Bracket100 components, (no clearance). The end faces are Coincident to the WheelPlate bottom face and the Bracket100 top face.

Think about the steps that you would take to build the illustrated assembly. Identify the first fixed component. This is the Base component of the assembly. Insert the required Standard mates.

Locate the Center of mass of the illustrated model with respect to the referenced coordinate system.

The referenced coordinate system is located at the bottom, right, midpoint of the Wheelplate. In this example, start with the WheelPlate part.

1. **Download** the needed components from the SolidWorks CSWA Model Folder/Chapter 11/Assembly Model 11-3 folder to create the assembly.

2. **Create** a new assembly in SolidWorks. The created models are displayed in the Open documents box.

3. Click **Cancel** ✖ from the Begin Assembly PropertyManager.

4. **Set** the document properties for the assembly.

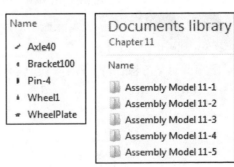

5. **Insert** the first component. Insert the WheelPlate. Fix the component to the assembly Origin. The WheelPlate is displayed in the Assembly FeatureManager and in the Graphics window. The WheelPlate component is fixed.

6. **Insert** the first Bracket100 part above the WheelPlate component as illustrated.

7. **Insert** a Concentric mate between the inside front left cylindrical face of the Bracket100 component and the inside front left cylindrical face of the WheelPlate. Concentric1 is created.

8. **Insert** a Concentric mate between the inside front right cylindrical face of the Bracket100 component and the inside front right cylindrical face of the WheelPlate. Concentric2 is created.

9. **Insert** a Coincident mate between the bottom flat face of the Bracket100 component and the top flat face of the WheelPlate component. Coincident1 is created.

10. **Insert** the Axle40 part above the first Bracket100 component as illustrated.

11. **Insert** a Concentric mate between the outside cylindrical face of the Axle40 component and the inside cylindrical face of the Bracket100 component. Concentric3 is created.

12. **Insert** a Coincident mate between the flat face of the Axle40 component and the front outside edge of the first Bracket100 component. Coincident2 is created.

🔅 To verify that the distance between holes of mating components is equal, utilize Concentric mates between pairs of cylindrical hole faces.

13. **Insert** the first Pin-4 part above the Bracket100 component.

14. **Insert** the second Pin-4 part above the Bracket100 component.

15. **Insert** a Concentric mate between the outside cylindrical face of the first Pin-4 component and the inside front left cylindrical face of the Bracket100 component. Concentric4 is created.

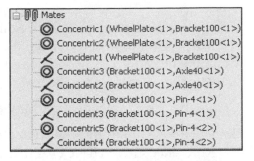

16. **Insert** a Coincident mate between the flat top face of the first Pin-4 component and the top face of the first Bracket100 component. Coincident3 is created.

17. **Insert** a Concentric mate between the outside cylindrical face of the second Pin-4 component and the inside front right cylindrical face of the Bracket100 component. Concentric5 is created.

18. **Insert** a Coincident mate between the flat top face of the second Pin-4 component and the top face of the first Bracket100 component. Coincident4 is created.

19. **Insert** the Wheel1 part as illustrated.

20. **Insert** a Concentric mate between the outside cylindrical face of Axle40 and the inside front cylindrical face of the Wheel1 component. Concentric6 is created.

21. **Insert** a Coincident mate between the Front Plane of Axle40 and the Front Plane of Wheel1. Coincident5 is created.

22. **Mirror** the components. Mirror the Bracket100, and the two Pin-4 components about the Front Plane.

Click **Insert**, **Mirror Components** from the Menu bar menu or click the **Mirror Components** tool from the Linear Component Pattern Consolidated toolbar.

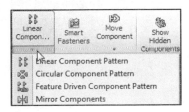

If using an older version of SolidWorks, click the Mirror Component tool from the Linear Component Pattern Consolidated toolbar to activate the Mirror Components PropertyManager.

Create the coordinate location for the assembly.

23. Click the **Coordinate System** tool from the Reference Geometry Consolidated toolbar. The Coordinate System PropertyManager is displayed.

24. **Select** the right bottom midpoint as the Origin location as illustrated.

25. **Select** the bottom right edge as the X axis direction reference as illustrated.

26. Click **OK** from the Coordinate System PropertyManager. Coordinate System1 is displayed.

27. **Locate** the Center of mass based on the location of the illustrated coordinate system. Select Coordinate System1.

- X: = 0.00 millimeters

- Y: = 37.14 millimeters

- Z: = -50.00 millimeters

If you don't find an option within 1% of your answer on the exam re-check your assembly.

28. **Save** the part and name it Assembly Modeling 11-3.

29. **Close** the model.

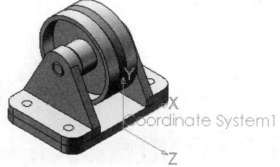

Mate the First Component with Respect to the Assembly Reference Planes

You can fix the position of a component so that it cannot move with respect to the assembly Origin. By default, the first part in an assembly is fixed - however, you can float it at any time.

It is recommended that at least one assembly component is either fixed, or mated to the assembly planes or Origin. This provides a frame of reference for all other mates, and prevents unexpected movement of components when mates are added.

Up to this point, you identified the first fixed component, and built the required Base component of the assembly. The component features were orientated correctly to the illustrated assembly. In the exam, what if you created the Base component where the component features were not orientated correctly to the illustrated assembly.

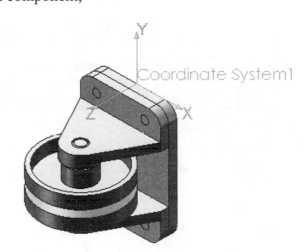

In the next tutorial, build the illustrated assembly. Insert the Base component, float the component, then mate the first component with respect to the assembly reference planes.

Complete the assembly with the components from the Tutorial: Assembly model 11-3. Set decimal place to 2.

Tutorial: Assembly Model 11-4

1. **Create** a new assembly in SolidWorks.

2. **Set** document settings. Set decimal place to 2. Unit system: MMGS.

3. **Insert** the illustrated WheelPlate part that you obtained from the DVD.

4. **Float** the WheelPlate component from the FeatureManager.

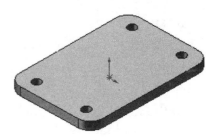

5. **Insert** a Coincident mate between the Front Plane of the assembly and the bottom flat face of the WheelPlate. Coincident1 is created.

6. **Insert** a Coincident mate between the Right Plane of the assembly and the Right Plane of the WheelPlate. Coincident2 is created.

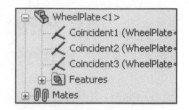

7. **Insert** a Coincident mate between the Top Plane of the assembly and the Front Plane of the WheelPlate. Coincident3 is created.

🔆 When the Base component is mated to three assembly reference planes, no component status symbol is displayed in the Assembly FeatureManager.

8. **Insert** the first Bracket100 part as illustrated. Rotate the component if required.

9. **Insert** a Concentric mate between the inside back left circular face of the Bracket100 component and the inside top left circular face of the WheelPlate. Concentric1 is created.

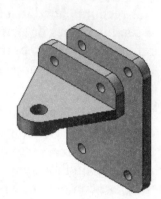

10. **Insert** a Concentric mate between the inside back right cylindrical face of the Bracket100 component and the inside top right cylindrical face of the WheelPlate. Concentric2 is created.

11. **Insert** a Coincident mate between the flat back face of the Bracket100 component and the front flat face of the WheelPlate component. Coincident4 is created.

12. **Insert** the Axle40 part as illustrated. Rotate the component if required.

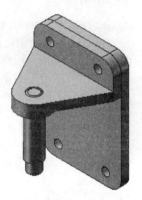

13. **Insert** a Concentric mate between the outside cylindrical face of the Axle40 component and the inside cylindrical face of the Bracket100 component. Concentric3 is created.

14. **Insert** a Coincident mate between the top flat face of the Axle40 component and the top outside circular edge of the Bracket100 component. Coincident5 is created.

15. **Insert** the first Pin-4 part above the Bracket100 component. Rotate the component.

16. **Insert** the second Pin-4 part above the Bracket100 component. Rotate the component.

17. **Insert** a Concentric mate between the outside cylindrical face of the first Pin-4 component and the inside front left cylindrical face of the Bracket100 component. Concentric4 is created.

18. **Insert** a Coincident mate between the flat front face of the first Pin-4 component and the top flat front face of the Bracket100 component. Coincident6 is created.

19. **Insert** a Concentric mate between the outside cylindrical face of the second Pin-4 component and the inside front right cylindrical face of the Bracket100 component. Concentric5 is created.

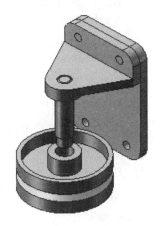

20. **Insert** a Coincident mate between the flat front face of the second Pin-4 component and the top flat front face of the Bracket100 component. Coincident7 is created.

21. **Insert** the Wheel1 part as illustrated.

22. **Insert** a Concentric mate between the outside cylindrical face of Axle40 and the inside top cylindrical face of the Wheel1 component. Concentric6 is created.

23. **Insert** a Coincident mate between the Right Plane of Axle40 and the Right Plane of the Wheel1 component. Coincident8 is created.

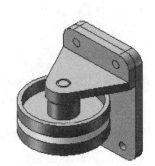

24. **Insert** a Coincident mate between the Front Plane of Axle40 and the Front Plane of the Wheel1 component. Coincident9 is created.

30. **Mirror** the components. Mirror the Bracket100, and the two Pin-4 components about the Top Plane. Do not check any components in the Components to Mirror box. Check the Recreate mates to new components box. Click Next in the PropertyManager. Check the Preview instanced components box.

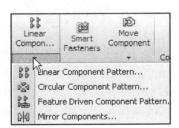

Create the coordinate location for the assembly.

31. Click the **Coordinate System** tool from the Reference Geometry Consolidated toolbar. The Coordinate System PropertyManager is displayed.

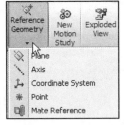

32. **Select** the top back midpoint for the Origin location as illustrated.

33. Click **OK** from the Coordinate System PropertyManager. Coordinate System1 is displayed.

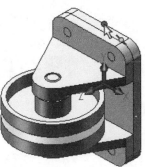

34. **Locate** the Center of mass based on the location of the illustrated coordinate system. Select Coordinate System1.

- X: = 0.00 millimeters

- Y: = -73.00 millimeters

- Z: = 37.14 millimeters

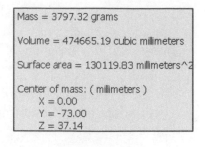

Mass = 3797.32 grams

Volume = 474665.19 cubic millimeters

Surface area = 130119.83 millimeters^2

Center of mass: (millimeters)
  X = 0.00
  Y = -73.00
  Z = 37.14

35. **Save** the part and name it Assembly Modeling 11-4.

36. **Close** the model.

In a multi choice format - the question is displayed as:

What is the center of mass of the assembly (millimeters)?

A) X = 0.00, Y = -73.00, Z = 37.14

B) X = 308.53, Y = -109.89, Z = -61.40

C) X = 298.66, Y = -17.48, Z = -89.22

D) X = 448.66, Y = -208.48, Z = -34.64

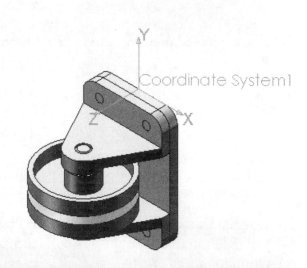

If you don't find an option within 1% of your answer on the exam re-check your assembly.

In the exam; you are allowed to answer the questions in any order. Use the Summary Screen during the exam to view the list of all questions you have or have not answered.

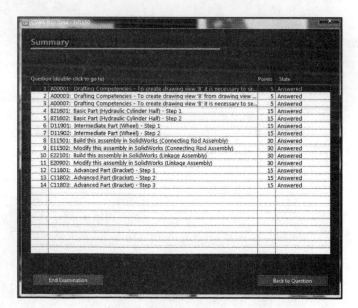

Tutorial: Assembly Model 11-5

An exam question in this category could read:

Build this assembly in SolidWorks (Chain Link Assembly). It contains 2 long_pins (1), 3 short_pins (2), and 4 chain_links (3).

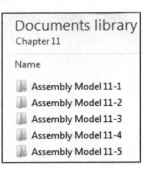

- Unit system: MMGS (millimeter, gram, second)

- Decimal places: 2

- Assembly origin: Arbitrary

Download the needed components from the SolidWorks CSWA Model Folder/Chapter 11/Assembly Model 11-5 folder to create the Assembly document.

IMPORTANT: Create the assembly with respect to the Origin as shown in the Isometric view. (This is important for calculating the proper Center of Mass). Create the assembly using the following conditions:

1. Pins are mated concentric to chain link holes (no clearance).

2. Pin end faces are coincident to chain link side faces.

A = 25 degrees, B = 125 degrees, C = 130 degrees

What is the center of mass of the assembly (millimeters)?

Hint: If you don't find an option within 1% of your answer please re-check your assembly.

A) X = 348.66, Y = -88.48, Z = -91.40

B) X = 308.53, Y = -109.89, Z = -61.40

C) X = 298.66, Y = -17.48, Z = -89.22

D) X = 448.66, Y = -208.48, Z = -34.64

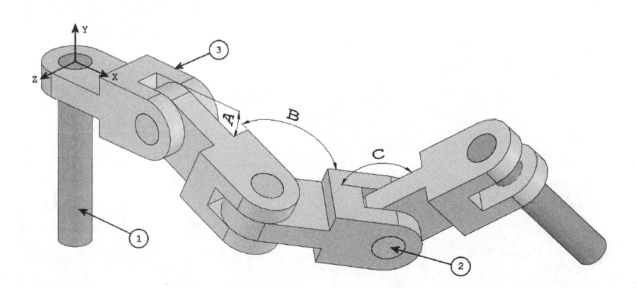

There are no step by step procedures in this section. Below are various Assembly FeatureManagers that created the above assembly and obtained the correct answer.

The correct answer is:

A) X = 348.66, Y = -88.48, Z = -91.40

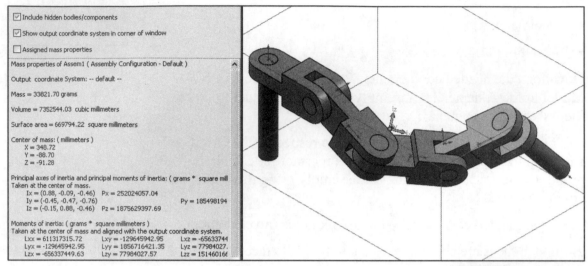

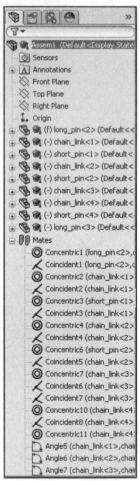

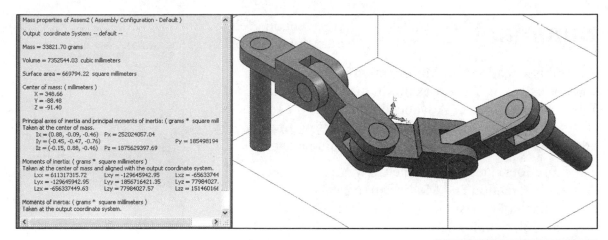

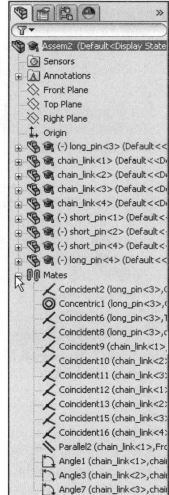

Summary

Assembly Creation and Modification is one of the five categories on the CSWA exam. In the last two chapters, a Basic, Intermediate or Advanced model was the focus. The Assembly Creation and Modification (Bottom-up) category addresses an assembly with numerous components.

There are four questions on the CSWA exam in the Assembly Creation and Modification category: (2) different assemblies - (4) questions - (2) multiple choice / (2) single answers - 30 points each.

You are required to download the needed components from a provided zip file and insert them correctly to create the assembly as illustrated. You are then requested to modify the assembly and answer fill in the blank format questions.

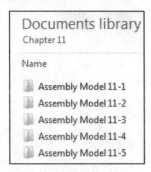

For additional detail exam information see The **Official Guide to Certified SolidWorks Associate Exams: CSWA, CSDA, and CSWSA-FEA** book. This book is written to assist the SolidWorks user to pass the associate level exams. Information is provided to aid a person to pass the Certified SolidWorks Associate (CSWA), Certified Sustainable Design Associate (CSDA) and the Certified SolidWorks Simulation Associate Finite Element Analysis (CSWSA FEA) exams. The primary goal of this book is not only to help you pass the exams, but also to ensure that you understand and comprehend the concepts and implementation details of the process.

At this time, Advance Mates and Mechanical Mates are not required for the CSWA exam.

Click on the additional views during the CSWA exam to better understand the assembly/component. Read each question carefully. Identify the dimensions, center of mass and units. Apply needed material.

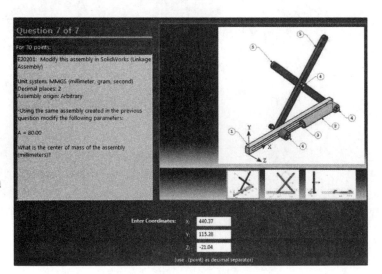

Questions

1: Build this ANSI MMGS assembly.

Calculate the overall mass and volume of the assembly.

Locate the Center of mass using the illustrated coordinate system.

The assembly contains the following: one Base100 component, one Yoke component, and one AdjustingPin component.

- Base100, (Item 1): Material 1060 Alloy. The distance between the front face of the Base100 component and the front face of the Yoke = 60mm.
- Yoke, (Item 2): Material 1060 Alloy. The Yoke fits inside the left and right square channels of the Base100 component, (no clearance). The top face of the Yoke contains a Ø12mm through all hole.
- AdjustingPin, (Item 3): Material 1060 alloy. The bottom face of the AdjustingPin head is located 40mm from the top face of the Yoke component. The AdjustingPin component contains an Ø5mm Though All hole.

The Coordinate system is located in the lower left corner of the Base100 component. The X axis points to the right.

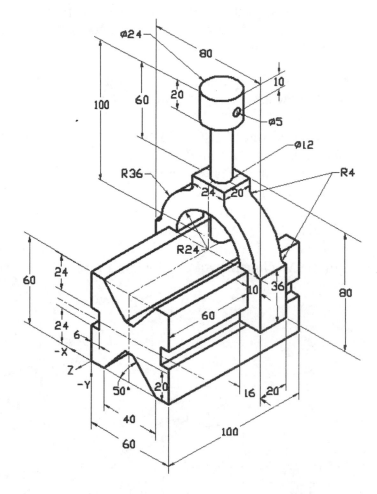

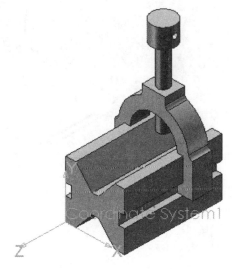

2. Build the assembly. Calculate the overall mass and volume of the assembly. Locate the Center of mass using the illustrated coordinate system. The assembly contains the following: three MachinedBracket components, and two Pin-5 components. Apply the MMGS unit system.

Insert the Base component, float the component, then mate the first component with respect to the assembly reference planes.

- MachinedBracket, (Item 1): Material 6061 Alloy. The MachineBracket component contains two Ø10mm through all holes. Each MachinedBracket component is mated with two Angle mates. The Angle mate = 45deg. The top edge of the notch is located 20mm from the top edge of the MachinedBracket.
- Pin-5, (Item 2): Material Titanium. The Pin-5 component is 5mms in length and equal in diameter. The Pin-5 component is mated Concentric to the MachinedBracket, (no clearance). The end faces of the Pin-5 component are Coincident with the outer faces of the MachinedBracket. There is a 1mm gap between the Machined Bracket components.

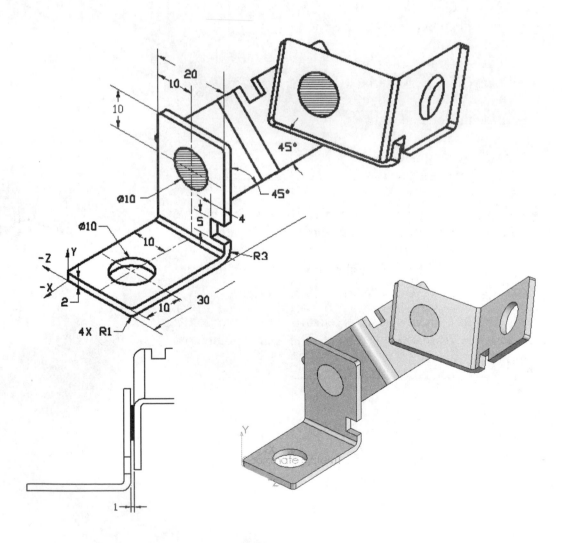

3. Build the assembly. Use the dimensions from the second Check your understanding problem in this chapter. Calculate the overall mass and volume of the assembly. Locate the Center of mass using the illustrated coordinate system. The illustrated assembly contains the following components: three Machined-Bracket components, and two Pin-6 components. Apply the MMGS unit system.

Insert the Base component, float the component, then mate the first component with respect to the assembly reference planes.

- Machined-Bracket, (Item 1): Material 6061 Alloy. The Machine-Bracket component contains two Ø10mm through all holes. Each Machined-Bracket component is mated with two Angle mates. The Angle mate = 45deg. The top edge of the notch is located 20mm from the top edge of the MachinedBracket.
- Pin-6, (Item 2): Material Titanium. The Pin-6 component is 5mms in length and equal in diameter. The Pin-5 component is mated Concentric to the Machined-Bracket, (no clearance). The end faces of the Pin-6 component are Coincident with the outer faces of the Machined-Bracket. There is a 1mm gap between the Machined-Bracket components.

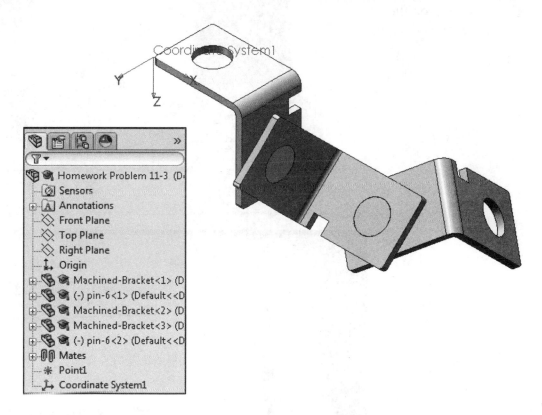

💡 Sample screen shots from an older CSWA exam for an assembly. Click on the additional views to understand the assembly and provided information. Read each question carefully. Understand the dimensions, center of mass and units. Apply needed materials.

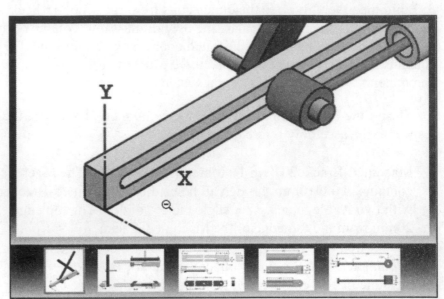

💡 Zoom in on the part if needed.

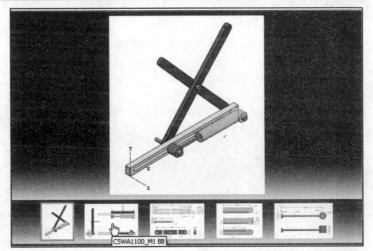

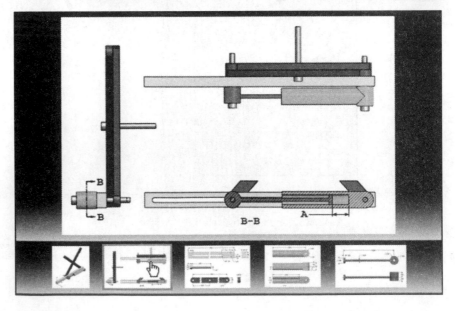

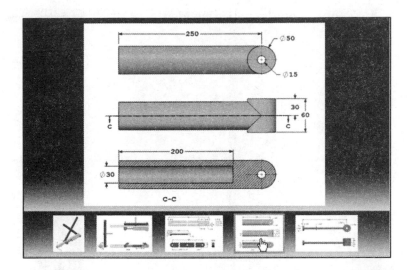

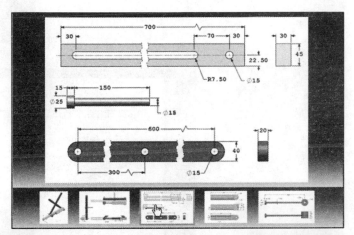

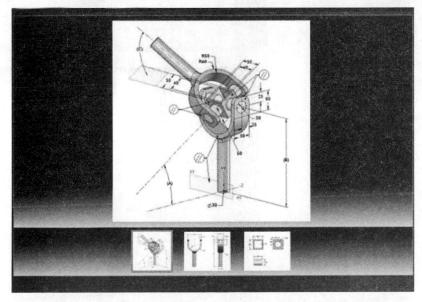

Screen shots from the exam

Zoom in on the part if needed.

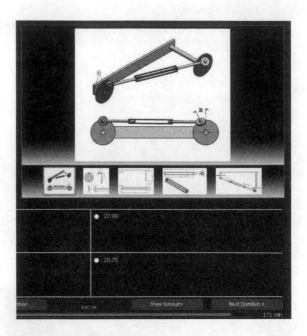

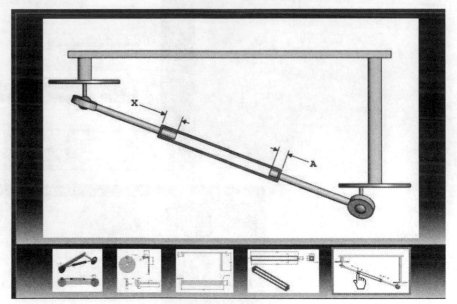

Screen shots from the exam

Appendix

Engineering Changer Order (ECO)

D&M Engineering Change Order		ECO # _____ Page 1 of __

Product Line	☐ Hardware ☐ Software ☐ Quality ☐ Tech Pubs	Author Date Authorized Mgr. Date

Change Tested By

Reason for ECO(Describe the existing problem, symptom and impact on field)

D&M Part No.	Rev From/To	Part Description	Description	Owner

ECO Implementation/Class		Departments	Approvals	Date	
All in Field	☐	Engineering			
All in Test	☐	Manufacturing			
All in Assembly	☐	Technical Support			
All in Stock	☐	Marketing			
All on Order	☐	DOC Control			
All Future	☐				
Material Disposition		ECO Cost			
Rework	☐	DO NOT WRITE BELOW THIS LINE (ECO BOARD ONLY)			
Scrap	☐	Effective Date			
Use as is	☐	Incorporated Date			
None	☐	Board Approval			
See Attached	☐	Board Date			

This text follows the ASME Y14 Engineering Drawing and Related Documentation Practices for drawings. Display of dimensions and tolerances are as follows:

TYPES of DECIMAL DIMENSIONS (ASME Y14.5M)			
Description:	**UNITS: MM**	**Description:**	**UNITS: INCH**
Dimension is less than 1mm. Zero precedes the decimal point.	0.9 0.95	Dimension is less than 1 inch. Zero is not used before the decimal point.	.5 .56
Dimension is a whole number. Display no decimal point. Display no zero after decimal point.	19	Express dimension to the same number of decimal places as its tolerance. Add zeros to the right of the decimal point. If the tolerance is expressed to 3 places, then the dimension contains 3 places to the right of the decimal point.	1.750
Dimension exceeds a whole number by a decimal fraction of a millimeter. Display no zero to the right of the decimal.	11.5 11.51		

TABLE 1 TOLERANCE DISPLAY FOR INCH AND METRIC DIMENSIONS (ASME Y14.5M)		
DISPLAY:	**UNITS: INCH:**	**UNITS: METRIC:**
Dimensions less than 1	.5	0.5
Unilateral Tolerance	$1.417^{+.005}_{-.000}$	$36^{0}_{-0.5}$
Bilateral Tolerance	$1.417^{+.010}_{-.020}$	$36^{+0.25}_{-0.50}$
Limit Tolerance	.571 .463	14.50 11.50

SolidWorks Keyboard Shortcuts

Listed below are some of the pre-defined keyboard shortcuts in SolidWorks:

Action:	Key Combination:
Model Views	
Rotate the model horizontally or vertically:	**Arrow** keys
Rotate the model horizontally or vertically 90 degrees.	**Shift + Arrow** keys
Rotate the model clockwise or counterclockwise	**Alt** + left of right **Arrow** keys
Pan the model	**Ctrl + Arrow** keys
Magnifying glass	**g**
Zoom in	**Shift + z**
Zoom out	**z**
Zoom to fit	**f**
Previous view	**Ctrl + Shift + z**
View Orientation	
View Orientation menu	**Spacebar**
Front view	**Ctrl + 1**
Back view	**Ctrl + 2**
Left view	**Ctrl + 3**
Right view	**Ctrl + 4**
Top view	**Ctrl + 5**
Bottom view	**Ctrl + 6**
Isometric view	**Ctrl + 7**
NormalTo view	**Ctrl + 8**
Selection Filters	
Filter edges	**e**
Filter vertices	**v**
Filter faces	**x**
Toggle Selection Filter toolbar	**F5**
Toggle selection filters on/off	**F6**
File menu items	
New SolidWorks document	**Ctrl + n**
Open document	**Ctrl + o**
Open From Web Folder	**Ctrl + w**
Make Drawing from Part	**Ctrl + d**
Make Assembly from Part	**Ctrl + a**
Save	**Ctrl +s**
Print	**Ctrl + p**
Additional shortcuts	
Access online help inside of PropertyManager or dialog box	**F1**
Rename an item in the FeatureManager design tree	**F2**
Rebuild the model	**Ctrl + b**
Force rebuild – Rebuild the model and all its features	**Ctrl + q**
Redraw the screen	**Ctrl + r**

Cycle between open SolidWorks document	**Ctrl + Tab**
Line to arc/arc to line in the Sketch	**a**
Undo	**Ctrl + z**
Redo	**Ctrl + y**
Cut	**Ctrl + x**
Copy	**Ctrl + c**
Additional shortcuts	
Paste	**Ctrl + v**
Delete	**Delete**
Next window	**Ctrl + F6**
Close window	**Ctrl + F4**
View previous tools	**s**
Selects all text inside an Annotations text box	**Ctrl + a**

In a sketch, the **Esc** key un-selects geometry items currently selected in the Properties box and Add Relations box. In the model, the **Esc** key closes the PropertyManager and cancels the selections.

Use the **g** key to activate the Magnifying glass tool. Use the Magnifying glass tool to inspect a model and make selections without changing the overall view.

Use the **s** key to view/access previous command tools in the Graphics window.

Windows Shortcuts

Listed below are some of the pre-defined keyboard shortcuts in Microsoft Windows:

Action:	Keyboard Combination:
Open the Start menu	Windows Logo key
Open Windows Explorer	Windows Logo key + E
Minimize all open windows	Windows Logo key + M
Open a Search window	Windows Logo key + F
Open Windows Help	Windows Logo key + F1
Select multiple geometry items in a SolidWorks document	Ctrl key (Hold the Ctrl key down. Select items.) Release the Ctrl key.

Helpful On-Line Information

The SolidWorks URL: http://www.solidworks.com contains information on Local Resellers, Solution Partners, Certifications, SolidWorks users groups, and more.

Access 3D ContentCentral using the Task Pane to obtain engineering electronic catalog model and part information.

Use the SolidWorks Resources tab in the Task Pane to obtain access to Customer Portals, Discussion Forums, User Groups, Manufacturers, Solution Partners, Labs, and more.

Helpful on-line SolidWorks information is available from the following URLs:

- http://www.dmeducation.net

    Helpful tips, tricks and what's new in SolidWorks.

- http://www.mechengineer.com/snug/

    News group access and local user group information.

- http://www.nhcad.com

    Configuration information and other tips and tricks.

- http://www.dmeducation.net

    Helpful tips, tricks and what's new in SolidWorks.

- http://www.topica.com/lists/SW

    Independent News Group for SolidWorks discussions, questions and answers.

*On-line tutorials are for educational purposes only. Tutorials are copyrighted by their respective owners.

.

Appendix: Check your understanding Answer key

The Appendix contains the answers to the questions at the end of each chapter in the CSWA Section.

Chapter 8

1. Identify the illustrated Drawing view.

The correct answer is B: Alternative Position View

2. Identify the illustrated Drawing view.

The correct answer is B: Break View.

3. Identify the illustrated Drawing view.

The correct answer is D: Aligned Section View.

4. Identify the view procedure. To create the following view, you need to insert a:

The correct answer is B: Closed Profile: Spline.

5. Identify the view procedure. To create the following view, you need to insert a:

The correct answer is B: Closed Spline .

6. Identify the illustrated view type.

The correct answer is A: Crop View.

7. To create View B from Drawing View A insert which View Type?

The correct answer is Aligned Section View.

8. To create View B it is necessary to sketch a closed spline on View A and insert which View type?

The correct answer is Broken out Section View.

9. To create View B it is necessary to sketch a closed spline on View A and insert which View type?

The correct answer is Horizontal Break View.

Chapter 9

1. Calculate the overall mass of the part, volume, and locate the Center of mass with the provided illustrated information.

    *   Overall mass of the part = 1280.91 grams

- Volume of the part = 474411.54 cubic millimeters
- Center of Mass Location: X = 0.00 millimeters, Y = -29.17 millimeters, Z = 3.18 millimeters

2. Calculate the overall mass of the part, volume, and locate the Center of mass with the provided information.

   - Overall mass of the part = 248.04 grams
   - Volume of the part = 91868.29 cubic millimeters
   - Center of Mass Location: X = -51.88 millimeters, Y = 24.70 millimeters, Z = 29.47 millimeters

3. Calculate the overall mass of the part, volume, and locate the Center of mass with the provided information.

   - Overall mass of the part = 0.45 pounds, Volume of the part = 4.60 cubic inches and the Center of Mass Location: X = 0.17 inches, Y = 0.39 inches, Z = 0.00 inches

4. Calculate the overall mass of the part, volume, and locate the Center of mass with the provided information.

   - Overall mass of the part = 0.28 pounds, Volume of the part = 2.86 cubic inches and the Center of Mass Location: X = 0.70 inches, Y = 0.06 inches, Z = 0.00 inches

Chapter 10

1. Calculate the overall mass of the part, volume, and locate the Center of mass with the provided information.

   - Overall mass of the part = 1.99 pounds
   - Volume of the part = 6.47 cubic inches
   - Center of Mass Location: X = 0.00 inches, Y = 0.00 inches, Z = 1.49 inches

2. Calculate the overall mass of the part, volume, and locate the Center of mass with the provided information.

   - Overall mass of the part = 279.00 grams
   - Volume of the part = 103333.73 cubic millimeters
   - Center of Mass Location: X = 0.00 millimeters, Y = 0.00 millimeters, Z = 21.75 millimeters

3. Calculate the overall mass of the part, volume and locate the Center of mass with the provided information.

   - Overall mass of the part = 2040.57 grams
   - Volume of the part = 755765.04 cubic millimeters

- Center of Mass Location: X = -0.71 millimeters, Y = 16.66 millimeters, Z = -9.31 millimeters

4. Calculate the overall mass of the part, volume and locate the Center of mass with the provided information. Create Coordinate System1 to locate the Center of mass for the model.

- Overall mass of the part = 2040.57 grams

- Volume of the part = 755765.04 cubic millimeters

- Center of Mass Location: X = 49.29 millimeters, Y = 16.66 millimeters, Z = -109.31 millimeters

5. Calculate the overall mass of the part, volume and locate the Center of mass with the provided information.

- Overall mass of the part = 37021.48 grams

- Volume of the part = 13711657.53 cubic millimeters

- Center of Mass Location: X = 0.00 millimeters, Y = 0.11 millimeters, Z = 0.00 millimeters

Chapter 11

1. Calculate the overall mass and volume of the assembly. Locate the Center of mass using the illustrated coordinate system.

- Overall mass of the assembly = 843.22 grams

- Volume of the assembly = 312304.62 cubic millimeters

- Center of Mass Location: X = 30.00 millimeters, Y = 40.16 millimeters, Z = -53.82 millimeters

2. Calculate the overall mass and volume of the assembly. Locate the Center of mass using the illustrated coordinate system.

- Overall mass of the assembly = 19.24 grams

- Volume of the assembly = 6574.76 cubic millimeters

- Center of Mass Location: X = 40.24, Y = 24.33, Z = 20.75

3. Calculate the overall mass and volume of the assembly. Locate the Center of mass using the illustrated coordinate system.

- Overall mass of the assembly = 19.24 grams

- Volume of the assembly = 6574.76 cubic millimeters

- Center of Mass Location: X = 40.24, Y = -20.75, Z = 24.33

Index